Start Your Own Business

EP

Entrepreneur. Press

"If someone had shared these tips with me when I started my company, I could have shaved five years off my learning curve. All true entrepreneurs won't want to put this book down."

—Lillian Vernon
Founder, Lillian Vernon Corp.

THIRD EDITION

Start
Your
Own
Business

RIEVA LESONSKY

and the staff of *ENTREPRENEUR* Magazine

Entrepreneur. Press

Editorial Director: Jere L. Calmes

ISBN 1-932156-65-8

Library of Congress Cataloging-in-Publication Data
Start your own business: the only start-up book you'll ever need /
by Rieva Lesonsky, [editorial director, and the staff of *Entrepreneur*
magazine.—3rd ed.
p. cm.—(Entrepreneur magazine's start up)
Includes index.
ISBN 1-932156-65-8
1. New business enterprises—Management. 2. Small business—
Management. I. Lesonsky, Rieva. II. Entrepreneur Media, Inc. III.
Series.
HD62.5 .E559 2004
658'.041--dc22   2003064245
Printed in Canada

09 08 07 06 05   10 9 8 7 6 5 4 3

Editor: Marla Markman
Proofreader: Karen E. Spaeder
Cover & Book Design: Mark A. Kozak
Production Director: Daryl Hoopes
Production Designer: Andy Markison
Illustrator: John McKinley
Editorial Assistant: Sara Wilson
Indexer: Ted McClellan

Contributing Writers:
Jill Amadio, Leanne Anderson, Jane Easter Bahls, Stephen
Barlas, Stephanie Barlow, Johanna Billings, Bruce Blechman, J. Tol
Broome, Andrew Caffey, Melissa Campanelli, Carolyn Campbell,
Melissa Caresosa, Cassandra Cavanah, Janean Chun, Bob Coleman,
Sandra Eddy, Paul & Sarah Edwards, David Evanson, Iris Lorenz-
Fife, Lorayne Fiorillo, Jerry Fisher, Barbara Frantz, Charles Fuller,
Cheryl Goldberg, Kim Gordon, Cynthia Griffin, Mark Henricks,
Mike Hogan, Frances Huffman, Christopher Keanelly, Danielle
Kennedy, Erika Kotite, Jay Conrad Levinson, David Lindo,
Jacquelyn Lynn, Richard Maturi, Robert McGarvey, Sean Melvin,
Heather Page, Debra Phillips, Marcia Perkins-Reed, Marlene
Piturro, Karen Roy, Edward Rybka, Jill Amadio, Leanne Anderson,
Jane Easter Bahls, Stephen Barlas, Stephanie Barlow, Johanna
Billings, Bruce Blechman, J. Tol Broome, Andrew Caffey, Melissa
Campanelli, Carolyn Campbell, Melissa Caresosa, Cassandra
Cavanah, Janean Chun, Bob Coleman, Sandra Eddy, Paul & Sarah
Edwards, David Evanson, Iris Lorenz-Fife, Lorayne Fiorillo, Jerry
Fisher, Barbara Frantz, Charles Fuller, Cheryl Goldberg, Kim
Gordon, Cynthia Griffin, Mark Henricks, Mike Hogan, Frances
Huffman, Christopher Keanelly, Danielle Kennedy, Erika Kotite,
Jay Conrad Levinson, David Lindo, Jacquelyn Lynn, Richard
Maturi, Robert McGarvey, Sean Melvin, Heather Page, Debra
Phillips, Marcia Perkins-Reed, Marlene Piturro, Karen Roy,
Edward Rybka, David E. Rye, Bev Stehli, Gayle Sato Stodder,
Guen Sublette, Joan Szabo, Conrad Theodore, Bob Weinstein,
Glen Weisman, Geoff Williams, Linda Wroblewski, Barry Zellen

Acknowledgments

Start Your Own Business is the culmination of Entrepreneur's decades of reporting on the world of small business, each year gaining more insight, knowledge and expertise into what makes and breaks successful business ownership. This product is the result of Entrepreneur's 26 years of covering the business of small business.

This book wouldn't have been possible without the hard work and dedication of many people. First and foremost, a heartfelt thank you goes out to Rieva Lesonsky, Entrepreneur's editorial director and this division's mentor and guiding light. It was her vision, leadership and wealth of business knowledge (she is a business guru in her own right) that helped us develop Start Your Own Business into a first-rate product we can all be proud to put the "Entrepreneur" name on.

Thanks also to project editor Karen Axelton, who took an intimidating, sky-high stack of Entrepreneur issues, added her own unique wit and wisdom, and delivered seamless, sparkling prose. A special appreciation goes to Maria Anton, Entrepreneur's senior executive editor, whose amazing memory helped me fulfill my book topic wish list and whose never-ending patience was also amazing as she instructed me in the fine art of navigating our database.

—Marla Markman
Managing Editor
Entrepreneur Magazine

Table Of Contents

ON YOUR MARK. 1

part 1

You Gotta Start Somewhere. 5

part 2

Building Blocks **71**

part 3

Where's The Money? **173**

GET SET 239

part 4

Setting The Stage 243

part 5

You'd Better Shop Around 403

part 7

Net Works **579**

part 8

By The Books **621**

On Your Mark...

W hy did you pick up this book? Perhaps you know you want to be an entrepreneur and take charge of your own life. You've already got a great idea for a business you're sure will be a hit. Or perhaps you think, somewhere in the back of your mind, that maybe you might like to start your own business...but you are not sure what venture to start, what entrepreneurship is really like and whether it's for you.

Whichever of these categories you fall into, you've come to the right place. In Part 1, "You Gotta Start Somewhere," we'll show you what it means to be an entrepreneur. Take our exclusive quiz, and find out if you've got what it takes. Don't have a business idea, or not sure if your idea will fly? You'll learn the secrets to spotting trends before they happen and coming up with dozens of surefire business ideas. We'll also discuss various ways of going into business, including part- and full-time entrepreneurship. Finally, we'll show you the different options for start-up, such as starting from scratch, purchasing an existing business, or buying into a franchise or business opportunity system.

Planning is key to every thriving business, and in Part 2, "Building Blocks," you'll learn just what you need to do to lay the groundwork for success. Find out how to pinpoint your target market, plus dozens of ways to do market research—from hiring experts to money-saving do-it-yourself tips. Since the name you choose can make or break your business, we share plenty of techniques for coming up with the perfect moniker—one that will attract customers to your company in droves. And don't forget the nuts-and-bolts necessities, like getting licenses and permits to operate your business, plus choosing a legal structure—corporation, partnership, sole proprietorship and more. You'll discover all the information you need to guide you through these often confusing steps to start-up.

A business plan is your road map to success, guiding the growth of your business at every stage along the way. We'll show you how to craft a business plan that puts you on the fast track. Finally, find out why you need professional advisors to help you through your start-up, and how to select an accountant and an attorney who can help you make money—without costing you a bundle.

Speaking of money, every entrepreneur knows that adequate start-up capital is essential to success. But just where do you find that crucial cash? In Part 3, "Where's The Money?" we give you the inside scoop on getting the money you need. Discover dozens of sources of capital. We show you secrets to financing your business yourself and how to tap into the most common source of start-up financing (family and friends), plus places you may never have thought of to look for money.

Do you stand a chance of getting venture capital or attracting private investors? You'll find out in this section. And if you're looking for a loan, look no further for the secrets to finding the right bank. We show you what bankers look for when evaluating a loan application— and how to make sure yours makes the grade. Seeking money from Uncle Sam? You'll get all the details about dozens of loan programs from the government, including special assistance for women and minority entrepreneurs. Whatever your needs, you're sure to find a financing source that's right for you.

P A R T

1

You Gotta
Start
Somewhere

Introduction

Buying this book may be the smartest thing you ever did. OK, I may be exaggerating some, but I am serious about the impact that *Start Your Own Business* can have on your life. As the editorial director of *Entrepreneur* magazine, I have been covering the business of entrepreneurship for a long time now, and I can honestly say I have met few entrepreneurs who are sorry they took the leap into business ownership. Most have succeeded (though not necessarily at the business they initially launched); some have returned to life as an employee. But few regret the journey.

Start Your Own Business is designed to help you navigate your own journey to business ownership. We are here to instruct and inspire. To tell you the things you don't know and remind you of the things you do. Some will tell you that the path you are about to embark on is a perilous one, but it's not. However, it is not without its curves, speed bumps and detours. *Start Your Own Business* helps prepare you as you go. You will learn what to expect at each step along the way. A wise person once said, "Forewarned is forearmed." So consider this book part of your arsenal.

I would never presume to tell anyone how to read a book. But the very first thing you might want to do is turn to the following "Pop Quiz" chapter and take our test to determine if you're cut out to be an entrepreneur. My guess is you are, or you wouldn't have bought this book. Some people mistakenly believe you have to be born an entrepreneur to succeed. You don't. You can learn what it takes. That's what this book is all about.

Start Your Own Business takes you step by step through the start-up journey, from how to get an idea for a business to finally opening the doors to your new venture. Along the way, we provide lots of forms, work sheets and checklists you can actually use in your business as well as to make sure you're on the right track. The book is also filled with five different types of helpful tip boxes:

HOT LINK
THIS BOX WILL POINT YOU TO THE TREASURES OF THE INTERNET FOR MORE INFORMATION.

BEWARE!
HEED THE WARNINGS IN THIS BOX TO AVOID COMMON MISTAKES AND PITFALLS.

BRIGHT IDEA
HERE YOU WILL FIND HELPFUL INFORMATION OR IDEAS YOU MAY NOT HAVE KNOWN OR THOUGHT ABOUT BEFORE.

SMART TIP
THIS BOX REVEALS IDEAS ON HOW TO DO SOMETHING BETTER OR MORE EFFICIENTLY OR A METHOD OF WORKING SMARTER.

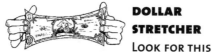

DOLLAR STRETCHER
LOOK FOR THIS BOX TO PROVIDE VALUABLE TIPS ON WAYS YOU CAN SAVE MONEY DURING START-UP.

Finally, at the end of the book, there are three appendices chock full of business resources that list contact addresses and phone numbers:

1. In **"BUSINESS RESOURCES,"** we list business associations, books, and magazines and publications in areas ranging from advertising and marketing to accounting and taxes. We even provide Internet resources and equipment manufacturers.

2. Our **"GOVERNMENT LISTINGS"** appendix provides contact information for Small Business Development Centers, Small Business Administration district offices and state economic development departments across the country.

3. Finally, if you need financing, you will definitely want to check out our listing of **"SMALL-BUSINESS-FRIENDLY BANKS."**

Starting your own business is not as mysterious as some would have you believe (for more on this, see Chapter 3, "What's The Big Idea?") nor as frightening or risky as legend would have it. But it is a journey that is better not taken alone. With *Start Your Own Business* as your companion, you'll be a wiser traveler on the road to business ownership. So what are you waiting for? As an ancient Chinese philosopher once sagely said, "Every journey…must begin with a single step."

—*Rieva Lesonsky*
Editorial Director, Entrepreneur

Pop Quiz

Are you ready to be an entrepreneur?

Do you have what it takes to be an entrepreneur? Only you can answer that question, but this chapter will help you figure it out. You'll learn about the qualities of successful entrepreneurs (as well as the qualities that can hinder your business), plus ways to determine if you're really meant to run your own business. There's even a test you can take to assess your entrepreneurial potential. So what are you waiting for? Read on…and find out if you've got what it takes.

THE ENTREPRENEURIAL PERSONALITY

Every year, hundreds of thousands of people make the transition from employee to entrepreneur. But while some succeed, others fail. Many of those who fail do so because they simply were not ready to make the change.

Quitting a full-time job to start a business isn't something to be taken lightly. Anyone considering striking out on his or her own should carefully assess the proposition before doing so. How do you know if the entrepreneurial life is for you? Self-assessment tests such as the one on page 18 can be used to measure your potential success. But even if a test indicates you've got the right personality for entrepreneurial success, that doesn't necessarily mean you're ready to become one at this point in time. Many questions remain: Do I have enough money? Is my family ready for this? Do people need a product or service like mine? Parts 1, 2 and 3 of this book will help you answer those questions. If the answers are yes, congratulations: You may be on your way to becoming a business owner.

Taking The Plunge

Most successful entrepreneurs recall a sense of urgency

BEWARE!

IF YOU HAVE A FAMILY, MAKE SURE THEY UNDERSTAND THE EMOTIONAL AND FINANCIAL SACRIFICES BUSINESS SUCCESS REQUIRES. WHEN YOUR FAMILY DOESN'T SUPPORT YOUR BUSINESS—IF THEY'RE ALWAYS SAYING, "CAN'T YOU LEAVE THAT ALONE AND COME TO DINNER?"—IT'S GOING TO BE TOUGH TO MAKE YOUR BUSINESS WORK. UNLESS YOUR FAMILY IS READY FOR YOU TO BECOME AN ENTREPRENEUR, CHANCES ARE THIS ISN'T THE RIGHT TIME TO DO IT.

that made starting their own business not just a desire, but a necessity. One entrepreneur says you'll know the time is right when "you can honestly say 'I'll put my house, jewelry and other personal collateral on the line to attain the start-up capital I need for the long-term rewards I deserve.'" Once you're ready to commit your own personal assets, you've probably crossed the line.

But what motivates potential entrepreneurs to stop daydreaming about business ownership and actually do something about it? While many people think one single incident—such as getting fired or being passed over for a promotion—is the impetus for becoming your own boss, most experts agree it's usually a series of frustrations that leads to entrepreneurship.

A fundamental need to control their own destiny ranks very high on most entrepreneurs' list of reasons for starting their own businesses. This need is so strong that entrepreneurs will risk family, future and careers to be their own boss. Unable to feel truly fulfilled working for someone else, these individuals cannot be happy taking orders from a higher-up.

HOT LINK

NEED INSPIRATION? CHECK OUT MYPRIMETIME.COM, WHICH BILLS ITSELF AS YOUR PERSONAL TRAINER FOR LIFE. WHILE THE SUBJECT MATTER COVERS EVERYTHING FROM FITNESS TO RAISING KIDS, THEIR TARGET AUDIENCE IS ANYBODY WITH AN ENTREPRENEURIAL SPIRIT—AND NUMEROUS QUIZZES AND ARTICLES ARE GEARED TO ENTREPRENEURS.

Joe R. Mancuso, president of the Center for Entrepreneurial Management, says, "It's a lot of little incidents, maybe a series of four or five little things coming together at the precise time, that creates the start of a new business." It might be that potential customers start calling you, or perhaps a business in the area goes under and you see an opportunity. Maybe you feel as if you're underemployed (working below your potential salary level or your skill level) or not putting your talents to their best use. Or perhaps you're experiencing all these sentiments at once.

Reality Check

Once you've made the decision to break away, there are a number of things you should do before taking the big step. You need to do thorough market research, make sure you have enough cash and discuss the decision with your family. (You'll find out more about all these steps in Parts 1, 2 and 3 of this book.)

It's important to understand that the rewards of small-business ownership are not instantaneous. You must be ready to defer gratification and make sacrifices to ensure the rewards eventually do come.

You must also make sure you are really ready for the responsibility that comes with being a business owner. When things go wrong, the buck stops with you. You will no longer have the luxury of going home at 5 o'clock while the company president stays all night to fix a chaotic situation. Someone whose only desire is to make a lot of money fast probably won't last long owning his or her own business.

Through surveys and research, experts have found that entrepreneurs share some common personality traits, the most important of which is confidence. They possess confidence not only in themselves, but also in their ability to sell their ideas, set up a business and trust their intuition along the way. Small business is fiercely competitive, and it's the business owners with confidence who will survive. If you can combine this all-important quality with the other characteristics mentioned, then the time is probably right for you.

According to many experts, the final element that determines if you are ready to be an entrepreneur is if you are able to raise significant amounts of money from investors. If you can make people believe in your dream and share your goals so that they are willing to invest hard-earned cash in your venture, chances are you have what it takes.

YOUR STRENGTHS AND WEAKNESSES

It's rare that one person has all the qualities needed to be successful in business. Everyone has strong suits and weak points, and the same is true of business owners. What's important is to understand those strengths and weaknesses. To do this, you need to evaluate the major achievements in your personal and professional life and the skills you used to accomplish them. The following steps will help:

■ **CREATE A PERSONAL RESUME.** Compose a resume that lists your professional and personal experiences as well as your expertise. For each job, describe the duties you were responsible for and the degree of your success. Include professional skills, educational background, hobbies and accomplishments that required expertise or special knowledge.

When complete, this resume will give you a better idea of the kind of business that best suits your interests and experience. It will also serve as a warning flag if you are planning to start a business that falls outside your talents and strengths.

- ■ **ANALYZE YOUR PERSONAL ATTRIBUTES.** Are you friendly and self-motivated? Are you a hard worker? Do you have common sense? Are you well-organized?

Evaluating your personal attributes reveals your likes and dislikes as well as strengths and weaknesses. If you don't feel comfortable around other people, then a business that requires a lot of customer

From The Horse's Mouth

One of the best ways to determine whether you are just daydreaming about becoming an entrepreneur or actually ready for it is to meet with other entrepreneurs and see what they do. Looking at their lifestyles and talking about entrepreneurship can help you figure out whether you are really suited for life as a business owner.

"Usually when you talk to someone who's done it, they'll tell you all the bad things about owning a business, like the time they had to work a 24-hour day or when the power went out. Those are the things you need to learn about beforehand," says one entrepreneur who used this technique. Once you realize that entrepreneurship isn't a 9-to-5 job with a secure income, you may have to re-evaluate your interest.

In addition to meeting with successful entrepreneurs, you might want to talk to a few who weren't so successful. Find out what went wrong with their ventures so you can avoid these problems. Did they fail to conduct market research before forging ahead? Were they unwilling to work long hours? Were they undercapitalized? Did they have misconceptions about what the entrepreneurial lifestyle is really like?

Many potential business owners find it useful to attend seminars or classes in entrepreneurship. You can often find such courses at community colleges or continuing education programs near you. Others seek assistance from consulting firms that specialize in helping small businesses get off the ground. All these methods can give you a taste of reality…and help you decide if you're prepared to take the plunge.

interaction might not be right for you. Or you may want to hire a "people person" to handle customer service, while you concentrate on the tasks you do best.

■ **ANALYZE YOUR PROFESSIONAL ATTRIBUTES.** Small-business owners wear many different hats, but that doesn't mean you have to be a jack-of-all-trades. Just be aware of the areas where you are competent and the areas where you need help, such as sales, marketing, advertising and administration. Next to each function, record your competency level—excellent, good, fair or poor.

GO FOR THE GOAL

In addition to evaluating your strengths and weaknesses, it's important to define your business goals. For some people, the goal is the freedom to do what they want when they want, without anyone telling them otherwise. For others, the goal is financial security.

Setting goals is an integral part of choosing the business that's right for you. After all, if your business doesn't meet your personal goals, you probably won't be happy waking up each morning and trying to make the business a success. Sooner or later, you'll stop putting forth the effort needed to make the concept work. When setting goals, aim for the following qualities:

■ **SPECIFICITY:** You have a better chance of achieving a goal if it is specific. "Raising capital" isn't a specific goal; "raising $10,000 by July 1" is.

■ **OPTIMISM:** Be positive when you set your goals. "Being able to pay the bills" is not exactly an inspirational goal. "Achieving financial security" phrases your goal in a more positive manner, thus firing up your energy to attain it.

■ **REALISM:** If you set a goal to earn $100,000 a month, when you've never earned that much in a year, that goal is unrealistic. Begin with small steps, such as increasing your monthly income by 25 percent. Once your first goal is met, you can reach for larger ones.

■ **SHORT AND LONG TERM:** Short-term goals are attainable in a period of weeks to a year. Long-term goals can be for five, 10 or even 20 years; they should be substantially greater than short-term goals but should still be realistic.

There are several factors to consider when setting goals:

■ **INCOME:** Many entrepreneurs go into business to achieve financial security. Consider how much money you want to make during your first year of operation and each year thereafter, up to five years.

■ **LIFESTYLE:** This includes areas such as travel, hours of work, investment of personal assets and geographic location. Are you willing to travel extensively or to move? How many hours are you willing to work? Which assets are you willing to risk?

■ **TYPE OF WORK:** When setting goals for type of work, you need to determine whether you like working outdoors, in an office, with computers, on the phone, with lots of people, with children and so on.

■ **EGO GRATIFICATION:** Face it: Many people go into business to satisfy their egos. Owning a business can be very ego-gratifying, especially if you're in a business that's considered glamorous or exciting. You need to decide how important ego gratification is to you and what business best fills that need.

BEWARE!

IF YOU HAVE FELT UNFULFILLED AT YOUR JOB FOR A LONG TIME, CHANCES ARE YOU'LL HARBOR RESENTMENT TOWARD YOUR PAST EMPLOYER AFTER YOU START YOUR OWN BUSINESS. BUT IF YOU LEAVE A JOB BECAUSE YOU'RE ANGRY, BE SURE NOT TO TRANSFER THIS ANGER TO YOUR NEW BUSINESS, OR FAILURE IS ALMOST CERTAIN. ONCE YOU START YOUR OWN BUSINESS, YOU MUST LEAVE BEHIND ANY BAD FEELINGS ABOUT YOUR FORMER JOB OR BOSS.

The most important rule of self-evaluation and goal-setting is honesty. Going into business with your eyes wide open about your strengths and weaknesses, your likes and dislikes and your ultimate goals lets you confront the decisions you will face with greater confidence and a greater chance of success.

WHAT'S YOUR EQ?

Common characteristics in areas such as family background, childhood experiences, core values, personalities and more turn up time and time again in studies of entrepreneurs. Find out how you fit the mold by determining your Entrepreneurial Quotient, or EQ.

The following test is no measure of your future success, but it may show you where you excel and where you need to improve to help make your business soar. Answer the following questions with a "yes" or "no," and total your score at the end to find out your EQ.

1. Did your parents immigrate to the United States? ❑ Yes ❑ No
2. Were you a top student in school? ❑ Yes ❑ No
3. Did you enjoy participating in group activities in school, such as clubs, team sports or double dates? ❑ Yes ❑ No
4. Did you prefer to be alone as a youngster? ❑ Yes ❑ No
5. Did you run for office at school or initiate enterprises at an early age, such as lemonade stands, family newspapers or greeting card sales? ❑ Yes ❑ No
6. Were you a stubborn child? ❑ Yes ❑ No
7. Were you cautious as a youngster? ❑ Yes ❑ No
8. Were you daring or adventurous? ❑ Yes ❑ No
9. Do the opinions of others matter a lot to you? ❑ Yes ❑ No
10. Would changing your daily routine be an important motivator for you to start your own enterprise? ❑ Yes ❑ No
11. You might really enjoy work, but are you willing to work overnight? ❑ Yes ❑ No
12. Are you willing to work as long as it takes with little or no sleep to finish a job? ❑ Yes ❑ No
13. When you complete a project successfully, do you immediately start another? ❑ Yes ❑ No
14. Are you willing to commit your savings to start a business? ❑ Yes ❑ No
15. Would you also be willing to borrow from others? ❑ Yes ❑ No
16. If your business should fail, would you immediately work on starting another? ❑ Yes ❑ No
17. Or would you immediately start looking for a job with a regular paycheck? ❑ Yes ❑ No
18. Do you believe being an entrepreneur is risky? ❑ Yes ❑ No
19. Do you put your long- and short-term goals in writing? ❑ Yes ❑ No
20. Do you believe you have the ability to deal with cash flow in a professional manner? ❑ Yes ❑ No
21. Are you easily bored? ❑ Yes ❑ No
22. Are you an optimist? ❑ Yes ❑ No

What's The Score?

1. If yes, score one point; if no, subtract one. Significantly high numbers of entrepreneurs are children of first-generation Americans.
2. If yes, subtract four points; if no, add four. Successful entrepreneurs are not, as a rule, top achievers in school.
3. If yes, subtract one point; if no, add one. Entrepreneurs are not especially enthusiastic about participating in group activities in school.
4. If yes, add one point; if no, subtract one. Studies of entreprenneurs show that, as youngsters, they often preferred to be alone.
5. If yes, add two points; if no, subtract two. Enterprise usually can be traced to an early age.
6. If yes, add one point; if no, subtract one. Stubbornness as a child seems to translate into determination to do things your own way— a hallmark of successful entrepreneurs.
7. If yes, subtract four points; if no, add four. Caution may involve an unwillingness to take risks, a handicap for those embarking on previously uncharted territory.
8. If yes, add four points.
9. If yes, subtract one point; if no, add one. Entrepreneurs often have the faith to pursue different paths despite the opinions of others.
10. If yes, add two points; if not, subtract two. Being tired of a daily routine will often precipitate an entrepreneur's decision to start an enteprise.
11. If yes, add two; if no, subtract six.
12. If yes, add four points.
13. If yes, add two points; if no, subtract two. Entrepreneurs generally enjoy their type of work so much, they move from one project to another—nonstop.
14. If yes, add two points; if no, subtract two. Successful entrepreneurs are willing to use their savings to finance a project.
15. If yes, add two points; if no, subtract two.
16. If yes, add four points; if no, subtract four.
17. If yes, subtract one point.
18. If yes, subtract two points; if no, add two.
19. If yes, add one point; if no, subtract one. Many entrepreneurs make a habit of putting their goals in writing.
20. If yes, add two points; if no, subtract two. Handling cash flow can be critical to entrepreneurial success.

21. If yes, add two points; if no, subtract two. Entrepreneurial personalities seem to be easily bored.

22. If yes, add two points; if no, subtract two. Optimism can fuel the drive to press for success in uncharted waters.

Determining Your EQ

■ **A SCORE OF 35 OR MORE:** You have everything going for you. You have the potential to achieve spectacular entrepreneurial success.

■ **A SCORE OF 15 TO 34:** Your background, skills and talents give you excellent chances for success in your own business. You should go far.

■ **A SCORE OF 0 TO 14:** You have a head start of ability and/or experience in running your own business and should be successful if you apply yourself and learn the necessary skills to make it happen.

■ **A SCORE OF -1 TO -15:** You might be able to make a go of it if you ventured out on your own, but you would have to work extra hard to compensate for a lack of built-in advantages and skills that give other entrepreneurs a leg up in beginning their own businesses.

■ **A SCORE OF -16 TO -43:** Your talents probably lie elsewhere. You should consider whether building your own business is what you really want to do, because you may find yourself swimming against the tide. Working for a company or for someone else, developing a career in a profession, or achieving an area of technical expertise may be far more congenial to you and would allow you to enjoy a lifestyle appropriate to your abilities and interests.

—*Quiz provided by Northwestern Mutual Life Insurance Co.*

> **HOT LINK**
>
> THE ONLINE WOMEN'S BUSINESS CENTER HAS A LOT TO OFFER WOMEN—AND MEN—FROM ANSWERING QUESTIONS ABOUT FINANCING BUSINESSES TO BECOMING AN INTERNATIONAL COMPANY TO FINDING A MENTOR. CHECK IT OUT AT WWW.ONLINEWBC.GOV.

Personal Goals And Objectives Work Sheet

Setting goals not only gives you an ongoing road map for success, but it also shows you the best alternatives should you need or desire a change along the way. You should review your goals on a regular basis. Many do this daily, as it helps them assess their progress and gives them the ability to make faster and more informed decisions. Take a few minutes to fill out the following questionnaire. You will find this very helpful in setting and resetting your goals.

1. The most important reason for being in business for myself is:

_____

_____

2. What I like best about being in business for myself is:

_____

_____

3. Within five years, I would like my business to be:

_____

_____

4. When I look back over the past five years of my career, I feel:

_____

_____

5. My financial condition as of today is:

_____

_____

6. I feel the next thing I must do about my business is:

_____

_____

7. The most important part of my business is (or will be):

_____

_____

8. The area of my business I really excel in is:

_____

_____

What's The Big Idea?

How to get an idea for your business

By Rieva Lesonsky, editorial director of *Entrepreneur*

Many people think it's "oh so mysterious" to start a business. So often I hear, "I can't do it" or "I have no idea what to do." Nonsense! In this chapter, you're going to find out how to get an idea for a business—how you figure out exactly what it is that you want to do and then how to take action on it.

But before we get started, I want you to know that this is a great time to launch a business. When I started with *Entrepreneur* in 1978, it wasn't such a great time to be on your own. People who were entrepreneurs were often thought to be unemployable, people who couldn't get along with their fellow employees or their bosses. Since they couldn't hold a job (or so many people thought), they decided to start their own businesses.

A lot has happened since then: Today, there are about 25 million small businesses in America. Estimates vary, but generally more than 1 million businesses are started every year in the United States. Yet for every American who actually starts a business, there are likely millions more who start each year saying "OK, this is the year I am going to start a business," and then nothing happens.

Everybody has their own roadblock, something that keeps them from taking that first crucial step. Most people are afraid to start; they may fear the unknown or failure or even success. Others are just overwhelmed by the belief they have to start from scratch. They think they have to start with an empty slate and figure out "OK, what product can I invent? What service can I start? What can I do that no one has ever done before?" In other words, they think that they have to reinvent the wheel.

But unless you are a technological genius, trying to reinvent the wheel is a big waste of time. If you are another Bill Gates or Steve Jobs, then this is the way to go. But for most people starting a business, the issue should not be coming up with something so unique that no one has ever heard of it. It's answering the question: "How can I do something better?" or "How can I do it differently than the other guy doing it over there?"

Get The Juices Flowing

How do you start the idea process? First, take out a sheet of paper, and across the top write "Things About Me." List five to seven things about yourself—things you like to do or that you are really good at. Your list might include: I am really good with people, I love kids, I love to read, I love computers, I love numbers, I am good at coming up with marketing concepts. Just write down whatever comes to your mind; it doesn't need to make sense. Once you have your list, number the items down one side of the paper.

On the other side of the paper, list things that you don't think you are good at or you don't like to do. Maybe you are really good at marketing concepts, but you don't like to meet people, or you're really not that fond of kids, or you don't like to do public speaking or you don't want to travel. Don't over-think it; just write down your thoughts. When you are finished, draw a line underneath both lists, then ask yourself: "If there were three to five products or services that would make my personal life better, what would they be?" This is your personal life as a man, woman, father, husband, mother, wife, whatever your situation may be. Determine what products or services would make your life easier or happier, make you more productive or efficient, or simply give you more time.

Next, ask yourself the same question about your business life. Also examine what you like and dislike about your work life as well as what traits people like and dislike about you. Finally, ask yourself why you're seeking to start a business in the first place. Then, when you are done, look for a pattern to emerge (i.e., whether there's a need for a business doing one of the things you like or are good at). To make the process a bit easier, we've provided a "Things About Me" work sheet for you to complete, starting on page 28.

They Delivered

Let me give you an example. I live and work in Irvine, California, a planned community. Most of the fast-food restaurants are located where the neighborhoods are. So in the office areas, there are not many easily accessible places to go on a lunch hour. Several years ago, two young men in Irvine found this lunch situation very frustrating. There weren't many affordable choices. Sure, there were some food courts located in strip centers, but the parking lots were really small and the wait was horrendous.

One day, as they were lamenting their lunch problem, one of

them said "Wouldn't it be great if we could get some good food delivered?" The proverbial light bulb went on—what a concept! Then they did what too many people don't do: They did something about their idea. Coincidentally, they purchased one of *Entrepreneur's* start-up guides and started a restaurant delivery business.

To date, their business has delivered more than 1 million meals! It's neither a complicated business nor an original one. Their competition has gotten stiffer, and yet they are doing phenomenally well. And it all began because they listened to their frustrations and decided to do something about them. Recently, I read that one of the biggest complaints by American workers was the shrinking lunch hour. Some only get 30 minutes, making it nearly impossible to get out, get lunch and get back on time. So while these young entrepreneurs initially thought they were responding to a personal need in our area, they actually struck a universal chord.

That is one way to get ideas, listening to your own (or your coworkers', family's or neighbors') frustrations. The opportunities are all there; you just need to search them out a bit. If your brain is always set in idea mode, then many ideas may come from just looking around or reading. For instance, if you read the article about the shrinking lunch hour, and if you were thinking entrepreneurially, you would say "Wow, maybe there is an opportunity there for me to do something."

Inspiring Moments

Inspiration can be anywhere. Ever get charged a fee for returning a video late? Bet you didn't do anything about it. Well, when Reed Hastings got a whopping $40 late charge, instead of getting mad, he got inspired. Hastings wondered, "How come movie rentals don't work like a health club, where, whether you use it a lot or a little, you get charged the same?" From this thought, Netflix.com, an online DVD rental service, was born. From its start in 1997, Netflix has grown into a big business, offering 15,000-plus titles to more than 1 million subscribers.

Or how about Emily Dalton and Curran Dandurand, who met while working at Mary Kay cosmetics? After spending years work-

BRIGHT IDEA

YOUR HOBBIES MAY LEAD YOU TO BUSINESS IDEAS. IF TENNIS IS YOUR GAME, PERHAPS YOU CAN THINK OF A PRODUCT THAT MAKES SERVING A SNAP. IF THAT SOUNDS TOO TECHNICAL, LOOK AROUND THE COURTS AND SEE IF THERE'S A SERVICE PLAYERS WOULD PAY FOR.

BRIGHT IDEA

IS THERE A HOUSEHOLD CHORE THAT DRIVES YOU UP THE WALL? (ONE SHUDDERS TO THINK OF LIFE BEFORE VACUUM CLEANERS.) COMMON SOURCES OF FRUSTRATION OR IRRITATION ARE GREAT IDEA GENERATORS.

ing in branding and marketing for skin-care and cosmetic giants, the duo decided that the men's personal-care field was underserved and represented lots of opportunity. After doing lots of research (you can't skip this step—for more on how to conduct market research, see Chapter 7), the pair launched Jack Black grooming products in 2000. Today, Jack Black products can be found at Bloomingdales, Nordstrom and Saks Fifth Avenue as well as on the Web. After being in business for only about three years, the company is expecting revenues of $5 million.

And then there's Mary Norton. In 1998, this stay-at-home Mom had a dream about handbags, specifically three of them. The next day she spent $50 for materials and recreated her dream, giving them to her baby-sitter, who was also a retail store manager. It took only 45 minutes for the three bags to sell—and MooRoo Handbags literally went from dream to reality. At her first trade show, Norton took in $65,000 worth of orders. MooRoo is now on track to hit $2 million in sales. Talk about a dream business.

Getting an idea can be as simple as keeping your eyes peeled for the latest hot businesses; they crop up all the time. Many local entrepreneurs made tons of money bringing the Starbucks coffeehouse concept to their hometowns. Or don't overlook the tried and true. Hot businesses often go through cycles. Home improvement and gardening-related businesses are now all the rage, but you wouldn't consider these 21st century businesses.

Another way to make your mark is to find a niche and exploit it. For example, new houses are being built at a record pace in the United States, and many builders are using odd-shaped windows in their designs. Seeing this, Brian Workman and Paul Rodgers launched Blind Corners & Curves in 1999. The company, which specializes in making custom window coverings for oddly shaped windows, boasts sales of more than $1 million a year. Also taking advantage of the new-home-building boom, Donna Quinn started Tall Walls in January 2002, which specializes in decor specially designed for homes with large-sized walls. Today, the company is selling its décor across the United States through its retail store and Web site.

My point: You can take any idea and customize it to the times and

Things About Me Work Sheet

Complete the following self-assessment work sheet as honestly as you can. Just write down whatever comes to mind; don't overthink the exercise. Most likely, your first response will be your best. Once you've finished the exercises, look for patterns (i.e., is there a need for a business doing one of the things you like or are good at?).

1. List at least five things you like to do or are good at.

_____

_____

_____

_____

_____

2. List five things you are not good at or you don't like to do.

_____

_____

_____

_____

_____

3. List three products or services that would make your personal life better.

_____

_____

_____

4. List three products or services that would make your business life better.

_____

_____

_____

5. When people ask what you do, what's your answer (list one occupation or whatever mainly occupies your week)?

_____

_____

_____

Things About Me Work Sheet

6. List three things you enjoy about your work.

    _____

    _____

    _____

7. List three things you dislike about your work.

    _____

    _____

    _____

8. When people tell you what they like most about you, they say:

    _____

    _____

    _____

9. Some people dislike the fact that you:

    _____

    _____

    _____

10. Other than your main occupation, list any other skills you possess, whether you excel at them or not.

    _____

    _____

    _____

11. In addition to becoming more financially independent, you would also like to be more:

    _____

    _____

    _____

12. Write down three things you want to see changed or improved in your community.

    _____

    _____

    _____

your community. Add your own creativity to any concept. In fact, customizing a concept is not a choice; it's something you have to do if you want your business to be successful. You can't just take an idea, plop it down and say "OK, this is it." Outside of a McDonald's or some other major franchise concepts, there are very few businesses that will work with a one-size-fits-all approach.

One of the best ways to determine whether your idea will work in your community is to talk to people you know. If it's a business idea, talk to co-workers and colleagues. Run personal ideas by your family or neighbors. Don't be afraid your friends will steal your idea; it's just not likely. All you have to do is ask.

NEVER SAY DIE

Once you get an idea for a business, what's the most important trait you need as an entrepreneur? Perseverance. When you set out to launch your business, you will be told "no" more times in your life than you have ever been before. And you can't take it personally; you've got to get beyond it and move on to the next person—because eventually, you're going to get to a "yes."

One of my favorite success stories illustrates this point. It happened a while ago, but the moral of the story is as relevant today as it was back then. A magazine reader from Cleveland, Ohio, went to

Thinking It Through

Before you start a business, you have to look at what the potential is, what your product or service is, and whether there is a lot of opportunity to make a good deal of money over the long run. Or is it a "hit-and-run" product, where you're going to get in, make a lot of money, and then get out? That's not necessarily a bad thing; fads have made some entrepreneurs incredibly successful. But remember, once you're in business, one of the hardest things to do is to know when it's time to get out, to let go. And if you guess wrong, if you try to make a classic out of a fad, you are going to start losing all the money you have earned. And no one wants to do that.

Washington, DC, and visited a local bookstore chain called (at the time) Kramer Books. This chain was like Barnes & Noble is today; it sold pastries and coffee alongside the books. This woman loved the concept so much that she returned home to Cleveland vowing to open the same type of bookstore.

There was just one problem: She had neither bookstore nor food experience. But she got an idea. She thought "I live in a big city in the Midwest; what's another city similar to mine?" She went to the library, picked up the Chicago Yellow Pages (today I would recommend you use the Internet to search for information), turned to the bookstore section, and started calling people, looking for a bookstore that was comparable to the one in Washington. She figured in Chicago, there'd be a good chance of finding someone.

And she did. One by one, she called and told the owners that she wanted to start a similar store in Cleveland. She said, "I am no threat to you; can you tell me what to do?" A lot of them said no, but she kept on calling. Eventually, she reached a woman who said, "Pay your own way here, and I will tell you everything I know." So she went to Chicago for two weeks, stayed in a cheap hotel, and actually went in every day as if she worked for this woman. The owner told her how to order books; what kind of food, coffee and cups she needed; how to set it up; and what to look for—everything she would need to know to run this business.

After two weeks, she went home to Cleveland and opened a store. She wrote to us right after she opened. Her point was that you have to just keep trying. She kept going, and finally, she got to the "yes." And that "yes" enabled her to start her business.

JUST DO IT!

Hopefully, by now I have at least somewhat demystified the process of determining what business is right for you. Understand that business start-up is not rocket science. No, I'm not saying it's easy to begin a business; it certainly is not. But it is not as complicated nor as scary as many people think, either. It is a step-by-step, common-

Fit To A "T"

Every December in *Entrepreneur*, we profile the hottest businesses for the coming year. We do a lot of research and a lot of homework, and what we say is absolutely true. But that doesn't mean that it is true for everyone. After all, you may not be good at any of these businesses. Or you could live in an area where the business is already saturated or not viable. Or they simply may not suit you and you'd end up hating your business. Just because you own a business doesn't mean you are going to like doing it, and, if this is true, then chances are you will fail.

Owning a business you hate is the same thing as having a job you hate. It's still hard to get out of bed in the morning, and you are just not going to do it as well. What all this means is that you need to come up with your ideas first, and then assess your traits to see which ideas best suit you.

sense procedure. So take it a step at a time. First step: Figure out what you want to do. Once you have the idea, talk to people to find out what they think. Ask "Would you buy and/or use this, and how much would you pay?"

Understand that many people around you will not encourage you (some will even discourage you) to become an entrepreneur. Some will tell you they have your best interests at heart; they just want you to see the reality of the situation. Some will envy your courage; others will resent you for having the guts to actually do something. You cannot allow these naysayers to dissuade you, to stop your journey before it even begins.

One of the most common warnings you will hear is about the risk. Everyone will tell you it's a risk to start your own business. And, sure, starting a business is risky, but what in life isn't? Plus, there's a difference between foolish risks and calculated ones. If you carefully consider what you're doing, get help when you need it and never stop asking questions, you can mitigate your risk.

You cannot allow the specter of risk to stop you from going forward. Ask yourself "What am I really risking?" And assess the risk. What are you giving up? What will you lose if things don't work out? Don't risk what you can't afford. Don't risk your home, your family

Princeton Checklist For Evaluating Ideas

Princeton Creative Research has developed an excellent criteria checklist for evaluating ideas that is particularly well-suited to the entrepreneur. Ask yourself the following questions when evaluating an idea for a business or a product.

❑ Have you considered all the advantages or benefits of the idea? Is there a real need for it?

❑ Have you pinpointed the exact problems or difficulties your idea is expected to solve?

❑ Is your idea original, a new concept, or is it a new combination or adaptation?

❑ What immediate or short-range gains or results can be anticipated? Are the projected returns adequate? Are the risk factors acceptable?

❑ What long-range benefits can be anticipated?

❑ Have you checked the idea for faults or limitations?

❑ Are there any problems the idea might create? What are the changes involved?

❑ How simple or complex will the idea's execution or implementation be?

❑ Could you work out several variations of the idea? Could you offer alternative ideas?

❑ Does your idea have a natural sales appeal? Is the market ready for it? Can customers afford it? Will they buy it? Is there a timing factor?

❑ What, if anything, is your competition doing in this area? Can your company be competitive?

❑ Have you considered the possibility of user resistance or difficulties?

❑ Does your idea fill a real need, or does the need have to be created through promotional and advertising efforts?

❑ How soon could the idea be put into operation?

As you can see by the examples mentioned above, there are many methods available with which to evaluate your idea. You should pick and choose the criteria that best suit your needs, depending on the type of company and/or the type of product you seek to evaluate.

Source: Princeton Creative Research, Princeton, New Jersey. Reprinted with permission.

or your health. Ask yourself "If this doesn't work, will I be worse off than I am now?" If all you have to lose is some time, energy and money, then the risk is probably worth it.

Determining what you want to do is only the first step. You've still got a lot of homework to do, a lot of research in front of you. Buying this book is a smart first step. Most important: Do something. Don't sit back year after year and say "This is the year I'm going to start my business." Make this the year you really do it!

Business Comparison Work Sheet

This form helps you determine the compatibility of a prospective business with your personal objectives, experience and lifestyle. Assign each business a column number. Answer each question along the left-hand side of the form, assigning a rating of 1 to 4 for each question, with 4 being the strongest. Total each column after you've finished. The opportunities with the highest scores are the most suitable for you.

	Business			
	1	2	3	4
Rate your experience and background in relation to the business.				
Are you familiar with the operations of this type of business?				
Does the business meet your investment goals?				
Does the business meet your income goals?				
Does the business generate sufficient profits?				
Do you feel comfortable with the business?				
Does your family feel comfortable with the business?				
Does the business satisfy your sense of status?				
Is the business compatible with your people skills?				
Is there good growth projected for the overall industry of the business?				
Is the risk factor acceptable?				
Does the business require long hours?				
Is the business location-sensitive?				
Does the business fit your personal goals and objectives?				
Does this business fit your professional skills?				
Totals				

Time Is On Your Side... Or Is It?

*Should you launch your business
part time or full time?*

Should you start your business part time or full time? Even if you ultimately plan to go full time, many entrepreneurs and experts say starting part time can be a good idea.

Starting part time offers several advantages. It reduces your risk because you can rely on income and benefits from your full-time job. Starting part time also allows your business to grow gradually.

"Starting part time is simply the best way," contends Philip Holland, author of *How to Start a Business Without Quitting Your Job*. "You find out what running a business requires, while limiting your liability if it fails."

Yet the part-time path is not without its own dangers and disadvantages. Starting part time leaves you with less time to market your business, strategize and build a clientele. Since you won't be available to answer calls or solve customers' problems for most of the day, clients may become frustrated and feel you're not offering adequate customer service or responding quickly enough to their needs.

Part-time entrepreneurs may also find that prospective customers, suppliers or investors do not take them seriously. Perhaps the biggest problem is the risk of burnout. Holding down a full-time job while running a part-time business leaves you with little, if any, leisure time; as a result, your personal and family life may suffer.

"Working by day and running a business by night creates a host of potential conflicts and can add a tremendous amount of stress," cautions Arnold Sanow, author of *You Can Start Your Own Business*. Sanow says conflicts between a day job and a sideline business are common, as are family problems: "I've seen a lot of divorces as a result of working full time and having a business on the side."

That's not to say a part-time business can't work. It can, Sanow says—if you have excellent time management skills, strong self-discipline, and support from family and friends. Also crucial, he says, is your commitment: "Don't think that, since you already have a job, you don't really have to work hard at your business. You must have a plan of attack."

SMART TIP

WHAT DO YOU DO IF YOU CAN'T AFFORD TO START YOUR BUSINESS FULL TIME BUT NEED TO BE AVAILABLE FULL TIME TO ANSWER CLIENT AND CUSTOMER CALLS? CONSIDER TEAMING UP WITH A PARTNER WHOSE AVAILABLE HOURS COMPLEMENT YOURS.

Market Matters

As with any business, your plan of attack should start with a thorough assessment of your idea's market potential. Often, this step alone will be enough to tell you whether you should start part time or full time.

"You can't become so caught up in your love for what you're doing that you overlook the business realities," cautions homebased-business consultant Sylvia Landman. If you find there is a huge unmet need for your product or service, no major competition and a ready supply of eager customers, then by all means go ahead and start full time. If, on the other hand, you find that the market won't support a full-time business, but might someday with proper marketing and business development, then it is probably best to start part time at first.

To make sure there is a market for your product or service, Landman advises that you investigate factors such as the competition in your industry, the economy in your area, the demographic breakdown of your client base, and the availability of potential customers. If you are thinking of opening an upscale beauty salon, for example, evaluate the number of similar shops in operation, as well as the number of affluent women in the area and the fees they are willing to pay.

Once you have determined there is a need for your business, outline your goals and strategies in a comprehensive business plan. You should always conduct extensive research, make market projections for your business, and set goals for yourself based on these findings, Landman explains. "It gives [you] a tremendous view of the long-range possibilities and keeps the business on the right track," she says. Don't neglect writing a business plan even if you're starting part time: A well-written business plan will help you take your business full time later on.

Certain businesses lend themselves well to part-time operation: Holland cites mail order, food products, direct marketing and service businesses as examples. Doing your market research and business plan will give you a more realistic idea of whether your business can work part time. (For specifics on conducting market research and writing a business plan, see chapters 6, 7 and 10 in Part 2.)

BEWARE!

DON'T BITE THE HAND THAT FEEDS YOU. STARTING A BUSINESS THAT COMPETES WITH YOUR CURRENT EMPLOYER MAY GET YOU IN LEGAL HOT WATER BY VIOLATING NONCOMPETE CLAUSES IN YOUR EMPLOYMENT CONTRACT. IF YOU START A BUSINESS IN THE SAME INDUSTRY, FOCUS ON A SMALL NICHE YOUR EMPLOYER HAS OVERLOOKED.

If you've got your heart set on a business that traditionally requires a full-time commitment, think creatively: There may be ways to make it work on a part-time basis. For instance, instead of a restaurant, consider a catering business. You'll still get to create menus and interact with customers, but your work can all be done during evenings and weekends.

Financial Plan

One major factor in the decision to start part time or full time is your financial situation. Before launching a full-time business, most experts recommend putting aside enough to live on for at least six months to a year. (That amount may vary; completing your business plan will show you in detail how long you can expect to wait before your business begins earning a profit.)

Basic factors to consider include the amount of your existing savings, whether you have assets that could be sold for cash and friends or family members who might offer you financing or loans, and whether your spouse or other family members' salary could be enough to support your family while you launch a business full time.

If, like many people, you lack the financial resources to start full time, beginning part time is often a good alternative. However, even if you do start part time, you'll want to keep some figures in mind: Specifically, how do you know when your business is making enough money that you can say goodbye to your day job?

BRIGHT IDEA

IF KEEPING A FULL-TIME JOB AND A PART-TIME BUSINESS GOING AT THE SAME TIME SOUNDS TOO DIFFICULT, AND TAKING THE FULL-TIME PLUNGE SOUNDS TOO SCARY, CONSIDER TAKING A PART-TIME OR TEMPORARY JOB WHILE YOU START A FULL-TIME BUSINESS. THIS CAN BE A WAY TO ENSURE YOU HAVE SOME SALARY COMING IN, WHILE GIVING YOU TIME TO WORK ON YOUR BUSINESS. PART-TIME JOBS OFTEN OFFER EVENING OR WEEKEND HOURS—A BIG PLUS IF YOU NEED TO BE ACCESSIBLE TO CLIENTS DURING REGULAR BUSINESS HOURS.

A good rule of thumb, according to Sanow, is to wait until your part-time business is bringing in income equivalent to at least 30 percent of your current salary from your full-time job. "With 30 percent of their income, plus all the extra time during the day to promote their business, [entrepreneurs] should be able to make [the transition at that point]," he says. Another good idea: Start putting more money aside while you still have your day job. That way, when you take the full-time plunge, you'll have a financial cushion to supplement the income from your business.

Family Affairs

The emotional and psychological side of starting a business is less cut-and-dried than financial and market aspects, but it's just as important in your decision to start part time or full time.

Begin by discussing the situation with your spouse, significant other or family members. Do they support your decision to start a business? Do they understand the sacrifices both full-time and part-time businesses will require—from you, from them and from the whole family? Make sure your loved ones feel free to bring any objections or worries out in the open. The time to do this is now—not three months after you have committed to your business and it is too late to back out.

Then, work together to come up with practical solutions to the problems you foresee (could your spouse take over some of the household chores you currently handle, for example?). Lay some ground rules for the part-time business—for instance, no work on Sunday afternoons, or no discussing business at the dinner table.

To make your part-time business a success and keep your family happy, "time management is key," says Landman. "Balance the hours

Take It Easy

Does all work and no play make entrepreneurship no fun? Some entrepreneurs who run part-time businesses based on hobbies, such as crafts or cooking, find that going full-time takes all the fun out of the venture. "Going full time turns an adventure into a job," as business expert Arnold Sanow puts it.

"Some entrepreneurs have trouble grasping the fact that their businesses aren't just pastimes anymore," says home-based-business consultant Sylvia Landman. "They can't work at their leisure any longer, and their ventures may require them to develop talents they didn't know they had and perform tasks they'd rather leave to someone else."

Don't get so caught up in the creative aspects of the venture, Landman warns, that you lose sight of the business responsibilities you must assume to make your start-up succeed. Take a realistic look at what going full time will require. Perhaps you can hire people to handle the business aspects you dislike, such as sales or operations.

you have available. Get up early, and don't spend valuable time on frivolous phone calls and other time wasters."

Getting Personal

Besides the effect business ownership will have on your family, equally important to consider is the toll it might take on you. If the idea of taking the full-time business plunge and giving up your comfy salary and cushy benefits keeps you awake at night biting your nails, then perhaps a part-time business is best. On the other hand, if you need to work long hours at your current full-time job, you commute 60 miles round-trip and you have 2-year-old triplets, piling a part-time business on top of all those commitments could be the straw that breaks the camel's back.

Of course, a full-time business does require long, long hours, but a part-time business combined with a full-time job can be even more stressful. If this is the route you're considering, carefully assess the effects on your life. You'll be using evenings, weekends and lunch hours—and, most likely, your holidays, sick days and vacation time—to take care of business. You'll probably have to give up leisure activities such as going to the movies, watching TV, reading or going to the gym. How will you feel the next time you drag yourself home, exhausted after a late night at the office…then have to sit right down and spend four hours working on a project that a client needs the next morning? This is the kind of commitment you will need to make if you expect your part-time business to succeed. Carefully consider whether you have the mental and physical stamina to give your best effort to both your job and your business.

BRIGHT IDEA

IF YOU'RE A PART-TIME ENTREPRE- NEUR SEEKING A FULL-TIME PROFES- SIONAL IMAGE, CHECK OUT BUSINESS INCU- BATORS. FOR A SMALL FEE, BUSINESS INCUBA- TORS PROVIDE OFFICE SPACE, SERVICES SUCH AS ANSWERING PHONES, AND ACCESS TO EQUIPMENT LIKE COPIERS AND FAX MACHINES. THE BIGGEST PLUS: INCUBATORS ALSO PROVIDE START-UP HELP, SUCH AS MARKET- ING AND ACCOUNTING ASSISTANCE.

Decisions, Decisions

Whether to start part time or full time is a decision only you can make. Whichever route you take, the secret to success is an honest assessment of your resources, your commitment level and the support systems you have in place. With those factors firmly in mind, you will be able to make the right choice.

Part-Time Pointers

Balancing a full-time job with a part-time business isn't easy—but it can be done. Arnold Sanow, author of *You Can Start Your Own Business*, suggests these tips to help make your part-time business a success:

- **INVOLVE YOUR FAMILY IN THE BUSINESS WHENEVER POSSIBLE.** Whether it's answering the phone, stuffing envelopes or putting together orders, giving your family the chance to help out is a great way to get more accomplished in less time—while also making your family feel part of your business.
- **BE READY TO GIVE UP PERSONAL TIME.** You won't have much time for television, reading or hobbies you used to enjoy. Be sure the sacrifice is worth it, or both your job and your business will suffer.
- **FOCUS ON THE TASK IN FRONT OF YOU.** When you're at work, focus on work; don't let thoughts of your business distract you.
- **MAKE THE MOST OF EVERY MINUTE.** Use lunch hours or early morning to make phone calls; use commuting time on the train to catch up on paperwork.
- **TAKE ADVANTAGE OF TIME ZONE DIFFERENCES AND TECHNOLOGY.** If you do business with people in other states or countries, make time differences work to your advantage by calling early in the morning or after work. Use faxes and e-mail to communicate with clients at any time of day or night.
- **DON'T OVERSTEP YOUR BOUNDARIES.** Making business calls on company time or using your employer's supplies or equipment for business purposes is a big no-no.
- **BE HONEST.** Only you can assess your situation, but in many cases it's best to be upfront with your boss about your sideline business. As long as it doesn't interfere with your job, many bosses won't mind—and you'll gain by being honest rather than making them feel you have something to hide.

Made From Scratch Or Store-Bought?

Starting a business vs. buying one

When most people think of starting a business, they think of beginning from scratch—developing your own idea and building the company from the ground up. But starting from scratch presents some distinct disadvantages, including the difficulty of building a customer base, marketing the new business, hiring employees and establishing cash flow...all without a track record or reputation to go on.

Some people know they want to own their own businesses but aren't sure exactly what type of business to choose. If you fall into this category, or if you are worried about the difficulties involved in starting a business from the ground up, the good news is that there are other options: buying an existing business, buying a franchise or buying a business opportunity. Depending on your personality, skills and resources, these three methods of getting into business may offer significant advantages over starting from scratch.

BUYING AN EXISTING BUSINESS

In most cases, buying an existing business is less risky than starting from scratch. When you buy a business, you take over an operation that's already generating cash flow and profits. You have an established customer base and reputation as well as employees who are familiar with all aspects of the business. And you do not have to reinvent the wheel—setting up new procedures, systems and policies—since a successful formula for running the business has already been put in place.

On the downside, buying a business is often more costly than starting from scratch. However, it's often easier to get financing to buy an existing business than to start a new one. Bankers and investors generally feel more comfortable dealing with a business that already has a proven track record. In addition, buying a business may give

HOT LINK

IF YOU'RE LOOKING FOR A BUSINESS TO BUY OR A BROKER TO HELP YOU IN YOUR PURCHASE, STOP BY WWW.BIZBUYSELL.COM. IN ADDITION TO SEARCHING 10,000 BUSINESSES FOR SALE AND BROKER LIST- INGS, YOU CAN READ UP ON BUSINESS VALUATION AND FINANCING.

Taxing Matters

You are investigating a business you like, and the seller hands you income tax forms that show a $50,000 profit. "Of course," he says with a wink and a nudge, "I really made $150,000." What do you do?

There may be perfectly legal reasons for the lower reported income. For instance, if the seller gave his nephew a nonessential job for $25,000 a year, you can just eliminate the job and keep the cash. Same goes for a fancy leased car. One-time costs of construction or equipment may have legitimately lowered net profits, too.

What to watch for: a situation where a seller claims he or she made money but just didn't report it to the IRS. If this happens, either walk away from the deal…or make an offer based on the proven income.

you valuable legal rights, such as patents or copyrights, which can prove very profitable.

Of course, there's no such thing as a sure thing—and buying an existing business is no exception. If you're not careful, you could get stuck with obsolete inventory, uncooperative employees or outdated distribution methods. To make sure you get the best deal when buying an existing business, take the following steps.

The Right Choice

Buying the perfect business starts with choosing the right type of business for you. The best place to start is by looking in an industry you are familiar with and understand. Think long and hard about the types of businesses you are interested in and which are the best matches with your skills and experience. Also consider the size of business you are looking for, in terms of employees, number of locations and sales.

Next, pinpoint the geographical area where you want to own a business. Assess the labor pool and costs of doing business in that area, including wages and taxes, to make sure they're acceptable to you. Once you've chosen a region and an industry to focus on, investigate every business in the area that meets your requirements. Start by looking in the local newspaper's classified ad section under "Business Opportunities" or "Businesses for Sale." You can also run your own "Wanted to Buy" ad describing what you are looking for.

Remember, just because a business isn't listed doesn't mean it isn't for sale. Talk to business owners in the industry; many of them might not have their businesses up for sale but would consider selling if you made them an offer. Put your networking abilities and business contacts to use, and you're likely to hear of other businesses that might be good prospects.

Contacting a business broker is another way to find businesses for sale. Most brokers are hired by sellers to find buyers and help negotiate deals. If you hire a broker, he or she will charge you a commission—typically 5 to 10 percent of the purchase price. The assistance brokers can offer, especially for first-time buyers, is often worth the cost. However, if you are really trying to save money, consider hiring a broker only when you are near the final negotiating phase. Brokers can offer assistance in several ways:

- **PRESCREENING BUSINESSES FOR YOU:** Good brokers turn down many of the businesses they are asked to sell, either because the seller won't provide full financial disclosure or because the business is overpriced. Going through a broker helps you avoid these bad risks.
- **HELPING YOU PINPOINT YOUR INTERESTS:** A good broker starts by finding out about your skills and interests, then helps you select the right business for you. With the help of a broker, you may discover that an industry you had never considered is the ideal one for you.
- **NEGOTIATING:** During the negotiating process is when brokers really earn their keep. They help both parties stay focused on the ultimate goal and smooth over problems.
- **ASSISTING WITH PAPERWORK:** Brokers know the latest laws and regulations affecting everything from licenses and permits to financing and escrow. They also know the most efficient ways to cut through red tape, which can slash months off the purchase process. Working with a broker reduces the risk that you'll neglect some crucial form, fee or step in the process.

A Closer Look

Whether you use a broker or go it alone, you will definitely want to put together an "acquisition team"—your banker, accountant and attorney—to help you. (For more on choosing these advisors, see Part 2, Chapter 12.) These advisors are essential to what is called "due diligence," which means reviewing and verifying all the relevant information about the business you are considering. When due diligence is done, you will know just what you are buying and from whom.

The preliminary analysis starts with some basic questions. Why is this business for sale? What is the general perception of the industry and the particular business, and what is the outlook for the future? Does—or can—the business control enough market share to stay profitable? Are the raw materials needed in abundant supply? How have the company's product or service lines changed over time?

You also need to assess the company's reputation and the strength of its business relationships. Talk to existing customers, suppliers and vendors about their relationships with the business. Contact the Better Business Bureau, industry associations and licensing and credit-reporting agencies to make sure there are no complaints against the business.

If the business still looks promising after your preliminary analysis, your acquisition team should start examining the business's potential returns and its asking price. Whatever method you use to determine the fair market price of the business, your assessment of the business's value should take into account such issues as the business's financial health, its earnings history and its growth potential, and its intangible assets (for example, brand name and market position).

To get an idea of the company's anticipated returns and future financial needs, ask the business owner and/or accountant to show you projected financial statements. Balance sheets, income statements, cash flow statements, footnotes and tax returns for the past three years are all key indicators of a business's health. These documents will help you do some financial analyses that will spotlight any underlying problems and also provide a closer look at a wide range of less tangible information.

Among other issues, you should focus on the following:

■ **EXCESSIVE OR INSUFFICIENT INVENTORY:** If the business is based on a product rather than a service, take careful stock of its inventory. First-time business buyers are often seduced by inventory, but it can be a trap. Excessive inventory may be obsolete or may soon become so; it also costs money to store and insure. Excess inventory can mean there are a lot of dissatisfied customers who are experiencing lags between their orders and final delivery or are returning items they aren't happy with.

■ **THE LOWEST LEVEL OF INVENTORY THE BUSINESS CAN CARRY:** Determine this, then have the seller agree to reduce stock to that level by the date you take over the company. Also add a clause to the purchase agreement specifying that you are buying only the inventory that is current and saleable.

Let's Make A Deal

Short on cash? Try these alternatives for financing your purchase of an existing business:

- **USE THE SELLER'S ASSETS.** As soon as you buy the business, you'll own the assets—so why not use them to get financing now? Make a list of all the assets you're buying (along with any attached liabilities), and use it to approach banks, finance companies and factors (companies that buy your accounts receivables).

- **BANK ON PURCHASE ORDERS.** Factors, finance companies and banks will lend money on receivables. Finance companies and banks will lend money on inventory. Equipment can also be sold, then leased back from equipment leasing companies.

- **BUY CO-OP.** If you can't afford the business yourself, try going co-op—buying with someone else, that is. To find a likely co-op buyer, ask the seller for a list of people who were interested in the business but didn't have enough money to buy. (Be sure to have your lawyer write up a partnership agreement, including a buyout clause, before entering into any partnership arrangement.)

- **USE AN EMPLOYEE STOCK OWNERSHIP PLAN (ESOP).** ESOPs offer you a way to get capital immediately by selling stock in the business to employees. If you sell only nonvoting shares of stock, you still retain control. By offering to set up an ESOP plan, you may be able to get a business for as little as 10 percent of the purchase price.

- **LEASE WITH AN OPTION TO BUY.** Some sellers will let you lease a business with an option to buy. You make a down payment, become a minority stockholder and operate the business as if it were your own.

- **ASSUME LIABILITIES OR DECLINE RECEIVABLES.** Reduce the sales price by either assuming the business's liabilities or having the seller keep the receivables.

- **ACCOUNTS RECEIVABLE:** Uncollected receivables stunt a business's growth and could require unanticipated bank loans. Look carefully at indicators such as accounts receivable turnover, credit policies, cash collection schedules and the aging of receivables.

- **NET INCOME:** Use a series of net income ratios to gain a better look at a business's bottom line. For instance, the ratio of gross profit to net sales can be used to determine whether the company's profit margin is in line with that of similar businesses. Likewise, the ratio of net income to net worth, when considered together with projected increases in interest costs, total purchase price and similar factors, can show whether you would earn a reasonable return. Finally, the ratio of net income to total assets is a strong indicator of whether the company is getting a favorable rate of return on assets. Your accountant can help you assess all these ratios. As he or she does so, be sure to determine whether the profit figures have been disclosed before or after taxes and the amount of returns the current owner is getting from the business. Also assess how much of the expenses would stay the same, increase or decrease under your management.

- **WORKING CAPITAL:** Working capital is defined as current assets less current liabilities. Without sufficient working capital, a business can't stay afloat—so one key computation is the ratio of net sales to net working capital. This measures how efficiently the working capital is being used to achieve business objectives.

- **SALES ACTIVITY:** Sales figures may appear more rosy than they really are. When studying the rate of growth in sales and earnings, read between the lines to tell if the growth rate is due to increased sales volume or higher prices. Also examine the overall marketplace. If the market seems to be mature, sales may be static—and that might be why the seller is trying to unload the company.

- **FIXED ASSETS:** If your analysis suggests the business has invested too much money in fixed assets, such as the plant property and equipment, make sure you know why. Unused equipment could indicate that demand is declining or that the business owner miscalculated manufacturing requirements.

- **OPERATING ENVIRONMENT:** Take the time to understand the business's operating environment and corporate culture. If the business depends on overseas clients or suppliers, for example, examine the short- and long-term political environment of the countries involved. Look at the business in light of consumer or economic trends; for example, if you are considering a clothing store that caters to the Generation X lifestyle, will that client base still be intact five or 10 years later? Or if the company relies on just a few major clients, can you be sure they will stay with you after the deal is closed?

Law And Order

While you and your accountant review key financial ratios and performance figures, you and your attorney should investigate the business's legal status. Look for liens against the property, pending lawsuits, guarantees, labor disputes, potential zoning changes, new or proposed industry regulations or restrictions, and new or pending patents; all these factors can seriously affect your business. Be sure to:

- **CONDUCT** a uniform commercial code search to uncover any recorded liens (start with city hall and check with the department of public records).
- **ASK** the business's attorneys for a legal history of the company, and read all old and new contracts.
- **REVIEW** related pending state and federal legislation, local zoning regulations and patent histories.

Legal liabilities in business take many forms and may be hidden so deeply that even the seller honestly doesn't know they exist. How do you protect yourself? First, have your lawyer add a "hold harmless and indemnify" clause to the contract. This assures you're protected from the consequences of the seller's previous actions as owner.

Second, make sure your deal allows you to take over the seller's existing insurance policies on an interim basis. This gives you time to review your insurance needs at greater leisure while still making sure you have basic coverage from the minute you take over. The cost of having a lawyer evaluate a business depends on your relationship with the lawyer, the complexity of the business and the stage at which the lawyer gets involved. Generally, costs range from $1,500 to $10,000 or more.

If you're considering buying a business that has valuable intellectual property, such as a patent, trade secret or brand name, you may want an intellectual property attorney to evaluate it. Generally, this will cost from 0.5 percent to 3 percent of the business's total selling cost.

The Art Of The Deal

If your financial and legal assessments show that the business is a good buy, don't be the first person to bring up the subject of price.

Let the seller name the figure first, and then proceed from there.

Deciding on a price, however, is just the first step in negotiating the sale. More important is how the deal is structured. David H. Troob, chairman of Geneva Companies, a national mergers and acquisitions services firm, suggests you should be ready to pay 30 to 50 percent of the price in cash and finance the remaining amount.

You can finance through a traditional lender, or sellers may agree to "hold a note," which means they accept payments over a period of time, just as a lender would. Many sellers like this method because it assures them of future income. Other sellers may agree to different terms—for example, accepting benefits such as a company car for a period of time after the deal is completed. These methods can cut down the amount of upfront cash you need; Troob advises, however, that you should always have an attorney review any arrangements for legality and liability issues. (For more ideas on financing your purchase, see "Let's Make A Deal" on page 50.)

An individual purchasing a business has two options for structuring the deal (assuming the transaction is not a merger). The first is asset acquisition, in which you purchase only those assets you want. On the plus side, asset acquisition protects you from unwanted legal liabilities since instead of buying the corporation (and all its legal risks), you are buying only its assets.

On the downside, an asset acquisition can be very expensive. The asset-by-asset purchasing process is complicated and also opens the possibility that the seller may raise the price of desirable assets to off-set losses from undesirable ones.

The other option is stock acquisition, in which you purchase stock. Among other things, this means you must be willing to purchase all the business's assets—and assume all its liabilities.

The final purchase contract should be structured with the help of your acquisition team to reflect very precisely your understanding and intentions regarding the purchase from a financial, tax and legal standpoint. The contract must be all-inclusive and should allow you to rescind the deal if you find at any time that the owner intentionally misrepresented the company or failed to report essential information. It's also a good idea to include a noncompete clause in the contract to ensure the seller doesn't open a competing operation down the street.

Remember, you have the option to walk away from a negotiation at any point in the process if you don't like the way things are going. "If you don't like the deal, don't buy," says Troob. "Just because you spent

53

a month looking at something doesn't mean you have to buy it. You have no obligation."

Transition Time

The transition to new ownership is a big change for employees of a small business. To ensure a smooth transition, start the process before the deal is done. Make sure the owner feels good about what is going to happen to the business after he or she leaves. Spend some time talking to the key employees, customers and suppliers before you take over; tell them about your plans and ideas for the business's future. Getting these key players involved and on your side makes running the business a lot easier.

Most sellers will help you in a transition period during which they train you in operating the business. This period can range from a few weeks to six months or longer. After the one-on-one training period, many sellers will agree to be available for phone consultation for another period of time. Make sure you and the seller agree on how this training will be handled, and write it into your contract.

If you buy the business lock, stock and barrel, simply putting your name on the door and running it as before, your transition is likely to be fairly smooth. On the other hand, if you buy only part of the business's assets, such as its client list or employees, then make a lot of changes in how things are done, you'll probably face a more difficult transition period.

Many new business owners have unrealistically high expectations that they can immediately make a business more profitable. Of course, you need a positive attitude to run a successful business, but if your attitude is "I'm better than you," you'll soon face resentment from the employees you've acquired.

Instead, look at the employees as valuable assets. Initially, they'll know far more about the business than you will; use that knowledge to get yourself up to speed, and treat them with respect and appreciation. Employees inevitably feel worried about job security when a new owner takes over. That uncertainty is multiplied if you don't tell them what your plans are. Many new bosses are so eager to start running the show, they slash staff, change prices or make other radical changes without giving employees any warning. Involve the staff in your planning, and keep communication open so they know what is happening at all times. Taking on an existing business isn't always easy, but with a little patience, honesty and hard work, you'll soon be running things like a pro.

BUYING A FRANCHISE

If buying an existing business doesn't sound right for you but starting from scratch sounds a bit intimidating, you could be suited for franchise ownership. What is a franchise—and how do you know if you're right for one? Essentially, a franchisee pays an initial fee and ongoing royalties to a franchisor. In return, the franchisee gains the use of a trademark, ongoing support from the franchisor, and the right to use the franchisor's system of doing business and sell its products or services.

McDonald's, perhaps the most well-known franchise company in the world, illustrates the benefits of franchising: Customers know they will get the same type of food, prepared the same way, whether they visit a McDonald's in Moscow or Minneapolis. Customers feel confident in McDonald's, and as a result, a new McDonald's location has a head start on success compared to an independent hamburger stand.

In addition to a well-known brand name, buying a franchise offers many other advantages that are not available to the entrepreneur starting a business from scratch. Perhaps the most significant is that you get a proven system of operation and training in how to use it. New franchisees can avoid a lot of the mistakes start-up entrepreneurs typically make because the franchisor has already perfected daily routine operations through trial and error.

Reputable franchisors conduct market research before selling a new outlet, so you can feel greater confidence that there is a demand for the product or service. Failing to do adequate market research is one of the biggest mistakes independent entrepreneurs make; as a franchisee, it's done for you. The franchisor also provides you with a clear picture of the competition and how to differentiate yourself from them.

Finally, franchisees enjoy the benefit of strength in numbers. You gain from economies of scale in buying materials, supplies and services, such as advertising, as well as in negoti-

SMART TIP

FOR MORE INFORMATION WHEN INVESTIGATING A FRANCHISE OR BUSINESS OPPORTUNITY, CHECK OUT THIS HELPFUL RESOURCE: FTC PROVIDES A FREE PACKAGE OF INFORMATION ABOUT THE FTC FRANCHISE AND BUSINESS OPPORTUNITY RULE. WRITE TO: FEDERAL TRADE COMMISSION, CRC-240, WASHINGTON, DC 20580, OR VISIT WWW.FTC.GOV.

ating for locations and lease terms. By comparison, independent operators have to negotiate on their own, usually getting less favorable terms. Some suppliers won't deal with new businesses or will reject your business because your account isn't big enough.

Is Franchising Right For You?

An oft-quoted saying about franchising is that it puts you in business "for yourself, but not by yourself." While that support can be helpful, for some entrepreneurs, it can be too restricting. Most franchisors impose strict rules on franchisees, specifying everything from how you should greet customers to how to prepare the product or service.

BEWARE!
IS A FRANCHISE OR BUSINESS OPPORTUNITY SELLER DOING THE HUSTLE? WATCH OUT FOR A SALESPERSON WHO SAYS THINGS LIKE "TERRITORIES ARE GOING FAST," "ACT NOW OR YOU'LL BE SHUT OUT," OR "I'M LEAVING TOWN ON MONDAY, SO MAKE YOUR DECISION NOW." LEGITIMATE SELLERS WILL NOT PRESSURE YOU TO RUSH INTO SUCH A BIG DECISION. IF SOMEONE GIVES YOU THE HUSTLE, GIVE THAT OPPORTUNITY THE THUMBS-DOWN.

That's not to say you will be a mindless drone—many franchisors welcome franchisees' ideas and suggestions on how to improve the way business is done—but, for the most part, you will need to adhere to the basic systems and rules set by the franchisor. If you are fiercely independent, hate interference and want to design every aspect of your new business, you may be better off starting your own company or buying a business opportunity (see the "Buying A Business Opportunity" section on page 63 for more details).

More and more former corporate employees are buying franchises these days. For many of them, a franchise is an excellent way to make the transition to business ownership. As a corporate employee, you were probably used to delegating tasks like ordering supplies, answering phones and handling word processing tasks. The transition to being an entrepreneur and doing everything for yourself can be jarring. Buying a franchise could offer the support you need in making the switch to entrepreneurship.

Do Your Homework

Once you've decided a franchise is the right route for you, how do you choose the right one? With so many franchise systems to choose from, the options can be dizzying. Start by investigating various industries that interest you to find those with growth potential.

Franchise Evaluation Work Sheet

This work sheet will help you determine the attractiveness of each franchise you are considering. Assign each franchise a column number. Answer each question along the left-hand side of the work sheet by assigning a rating of 1 to 3, with 3 being the strongest. Total each column after you've finished. The franchise with the highest score is the most attractive.

	Franchise			
The Franchise Organization	1	2	3	4
Does the franchisor have a good track record?				
Do the principals of the franchise have expertise in the industry?				
Rate the franchisor's financial condition.				
How thoroughly does the franchisor check out its prospective franchises?				
Rate the profitability of the franchisor and its franchisees.				
The Product Or Service				
Is there demand for the product or service?				
Can the product or service be sold year-round?				
Are industry sales strong?				
Rate the product or service in comparison with the competition.				
Is the product or service competitively priced?				
What is the potential for industry growth?				
The Market Area				
Are exclusive territories offered?				
Rate the sales potential of the territory you are considering.				
Is the competition strong in this area?				
How successful are franchises in close proximity to this area?				
The Contract				
Are the fees and royalties associated with the franchise reasonable?				
How attractive are the renewal, termination and transfer conditions?				
If the franchisor requires you to purchase proprietary inventory, how useful is it?				
If the franchisor requires you to meet annual sales quotas, are they reasonable?				
Franchisor Support				
Does the franchisor help with site selection, lease negotiations and store layout?				
Does the franchisor provide ongoing training?				
Does the franchisor provide financing to qualified individuals?				
Are manuals, sales kits, accounting systems and purchasing guides supplied?				
Does the franchisor sponsor an advertising fund to which franchisees contribute?				
How strong are the franchisor's advertising and promotion programs?				
Does the franchisor have favorable national supplier contracts?				
Totals				

Narrow the choices down to a few industries you are most interested in, then analyze your geographic area to see if there is a market for that type of business. If so, contact all the franchise companies in those fields and ask them for information. Any reputable company will be happy to send you information at no cost.

Of course, don't rely solely on these promotional materials to make your decision. You also need to do your own detective work. Start by visiting your library or going online to look up all the magazine and newspaper articles you can find about the companies you are considering. Is the company depicted favorably? Does it seem to be well-managed and growing?

Check with the consumer or franchise regulators in your state to see if there are any serious problems with the company you are considering. If the company or its principals have been involved in lawsuits or bankruptcies, try to determine the nature of the lawsuits: Did they involve fraud or violations of FTC regulatory laws? To find out, call the court that handled the case and request a copy of the petition or judgment.

If you live in one of the 14 states (California, Hawaii, Illinois, Indiana, Maryland, Michigan, Minnesota, North Dakota, New York, Rhode Island, South Dakota, Virginia, Washington and Wisconsin) that regulate the sale of franchises, contact the state franchise authority, which can tell you if the company has complied with state registration requirements. If the company is registered with D&B, request a D&B report, which will give you details on the company's financial standing, payment promptness and other information. And, of course, it never hurts to check with your local office of the Better Business Bureau for complaints against the company.

Does the company still sound good? That means your investigation is just beginning. If you have not already received one, contact the franchisor again and ask for a copy of its Uniform Franchise Offering Circular (UFOC). This disclosure document must, by law, be given to all prospective franchisees within 10 business days before any agreement is signed or money changes hands (whichever is earlier). If a company says it is a franchise but will not give you a UFOC, then contact the FTC—and take your business elsewhere.

The UFOC is a treasure trove of information for those who are serious about franchising. It contains an extensive written description of the company, the investment amount and fees required, any litigation and/or bankruptcy history of the franchisor and its officers, the

It's Show Time

Franchise and business opportunity trade shows can be a great opportunity to explore business investment packages. Attending one is exciting…and overwhelming, so you need to prepare carefully.

BEFORE THE SHOW:

- **CONSIDER WHAT YOU ARE SEEKING FROM A BUSINESS INVESTMENT.** Part time or full time? What type of business do you think you would enjoy? Consider your hobbies and passions.
- **FIGURE OUT YOUR FINANCIAL RESOURCES.** What is liquid, what can you borrow from family and friends, and how much do you need to live on while starting a new business? What are your financial goals for the business?
- **GET SERIOUS.** Dress conservatively, carry a briefcase, leave the kids at home, and take business cards if you have them. Show the representatives you meet that you are a serious prospect.

AT THE SHOW:

- **TAKE A MOMENT TO STUDY THE FLOOR PLAN OF THE EXHIBITORS LISTED.** Circle the businesses you recognize or that look interesting. Make sure you stop by these booths during your visit.
- **DON'T WASTE TIME.** Pass by the sellers who are out of your price range or do not meet your personal goals. Have a short list of questions ready to ask the others:
  1. What is the total investment?
  2. Tell me about a franchisee's typical day.
  3. What arrangements are made for product supply?
  4. Is financing available from the franchisor?
  5. Ask for a copy of the company's UFOC. Not all franchisors will give you one at the show. This is acceptable, but if you are serious about an opportunity, insist on a copy as soon as possible.
- **COLLECT HANDOUT INFORMATION AND BUSINESS CARDS FROM THE COMPANIES THAT INTEREST YOU.**

AFTER THE SHOW:

- **ORGANIZE THE MATERIALS YOU COLLECTED INTO FILE FOLDERS.** Then read through the information more closely.
- **FOLLOW UP.** Call the representatives you met to show them you are interested.

trademark you will be licensed to use, the products you are required to purchase, the advertising program, and the contractual obligations of both franchisor and franchisee. It specifies how much working capital is required, equipment needs and ongoing royalties. It also contains a sample copy of the franchise agreement you will be asked to sign should you buy into the system, as well as three years' worth of the franchisor's audited financial statements.

The UFOC has been revamped to make it less "legalistic" and more readable, so there is no excuse for failing to read yours very carefully. Before you make any decisions about purchasing the franchise, your attorney and accountant should read it as well.

BEWARE!

EXAGGERATED PROFIT CLAIMS ARE COMMON IN FRANCHISE AND BUSINESS OPPORTUNITY SALES. IS A COMPANY PROMISING YOU WILL MAKE $10,000 A MONTH IN YOUR SPARE TIME? IF IT IS A FRANCHISE, ANY STATEMENT ABOUT EARNINGS (REGARDING OTHERS IN THE SYSTEM OR YOUR POTENTIAL EARNINGS) MUST APPEAR IN THE UNIFORM FRANCHISE OFFERING CIRCULAR. READ THE UFOC AND TALK TO FIVE FRANCHISE OWNERS WHO HAVE ATTAINED THE EARNINGS CLAIMED.

CALLING ALL FRANCHISEES

One of the most important parts of the UFOC is a listing of existing franchisees as well as franchisees who've been terminated or have chosen not to renew. Both lists will include addresses and phone numbers. If the list of terminated franchisees seems unusually long, it could be an indication that there's some trouble with the franchisor. Call the former franchisees, and ask them why the agreement was terminated, whether the franchisee wasn't making the grade, or whether he or she had some type of grievance with the franchisor.

Next, choose a random sample of current franchisees to interview in person. This is perhaps the most important step in your research. Don't rely on a few carefully selected names the franchisor gives you; pick your own candidates to talk to.

Visit current franchisees at their location. Talking to existing franchisees is often the best way to find out how much money individual stores actually make. You'll also find out what their typical day is like, whether they enjoy what they do and whether the business is challenging enough. Most will be relatively open about revealing their earnings and their satisfaction with the franchisor; however, the key to getting all the information you need before buying is asking the right questions. Here are some ideas to help you get you started:

- **WAS THE TRAINING** the franchisor offered helpful in getting the business off the ground?
- **IS THE FRANCHISOR** responsive to your needs?
- **TELL ME ABOUT** a typical day for you.
- **HAVE THERE BEEN** problems you did not anticipate?
- **HAS YOUR EXPERIENCE** proved that the investment and cost information in the UFOC was realistic?
- **IS THE BUSINESS SEASONAL?** If so, what do you do to make ends meet in the off-season?
- **HAVE SALES AND PROFITS** met your expectations? Tell me about the numbers in the business.
- **ARE THERE** expansion opportunities for additional franchise ownership in this system?
- **IF YOU KNEW** what you know now, would you make this investment again?

Since running a franchise involves an ongoing relationship with the franchisor, be sure to get the details on the purchasing process—everything that happened from the day the franchisee signed the agreement to the end of the first year in business. Did the parent company follow through on its promises?

Talk to as many franchisees as you can—a broader perspective will give you a more accurate picture of the company. Take careful notes of the conversations so you can refer to them later. Don't hesitate to ask about sensitive topics. One of the most important questions a prospective franchisee should ask, but rarely does, is "What conflicts do you have with the franchisor?" Even established, successful companies have conflicts. What you need to find out is how widespread and common those conflicts are.

Talking to franchisees can also give you something you won't get anywhere else: a feeling for what it's like to run this business day to day. Thinking solely in economic terms is a mistake if you end up with a franchise that doesn't suit your lifestyle or self-image. When you envision running a restaurant franchise, for instance, you may be thinking of all the money you're going to make. Talking to franchisees can bring you back to reality—which is a lot more likely to involve manning a fry station, disciplining employees and working late than cruising around in your Ferrari. Talking to franchisees in a variety of industries can help you make a choice that fits your lifestyle.

Many franchisees and franchising experts say there's no better way to cap off your research than by spending time in a franchisee location to see what your life will be like. Buyers should spend at least one week working in a unit. This is the best way for the franchisor and franchisee to evaluate each other. Offer to work for free. If the franchisor doesn't want you to, you should be skeptical about the investment.

When all your research is completed, the choice between two equally sound franchises often comes down to your gut instinct. That's why talking to franchisees and visiting locations is so important in the selection process.

Proven Purchase

Buying a franchise can be a good way to lessen the risk of business ownership. Some entrepreneurs cut that risk still further by purchasing an existing franchise—one that is already up and running. Not only does an existing franchise have a customer base, but it also has a management system already in place and ongoing revenues. In short, it already has a foundation—something that is very attractive to a lot of entrepreneurs.

Finding existing franchisees who are willing to sell is simply a matter of asking the parent company what's available; you can also check local classified ads to find businesses for sale.

Once you have found some likely candidates, the investigation process combines the same steps used in buying an existing business with those used in buying a franchise. The good news, however, is that you'll get far more detailed financial information than you would when assessing a franchise company. Where other potential franchisees just get vague suggestions of potential earnings, you'll get hard facts.

Of course, there is a price to pay for all the advantages of buying an existing franchise: It is generally much more costly. In fact, the purchase price of an existing location can be two to four times more than what you would pay for a new franchise from the same company. Because you are investing more money, it is even more important to make sure you have audited financial statements and to review them with your CPA.

Once in a while, you'll find a franchise that isn't doing well. Perhaps the current owner isn't good at marketing, isn't putting forth enough effort or isn't following the system correctly. In this case, you may be able to get the existing franchise for what it would cost to buy a new franchise—or even less. It's crucial, however, to make sure the problem is something you can correct and that you'll be able to get the location up to speed fast. After all, you're going to have immediate overhead expenses—for employees, royalties and operating costs—so you need some immediate income as well.

Also be aware that even if a particular franchise location is thriving, it does not necessarily mean the parent company is equally successful. In fact, sometimes franchisees who know the parent company is in trouble will try to unload their franchises before the franchisor goes under. Carefully assess the franchisor's strength, accessibility and the level of assistance they provide. Do not settle for anything less than you would when buying a new franchise.

BUYING A BUSINESS OPPORTUNITY

If a franchise sounds too restrictive for you but the idea of coming up with your own business idea, systems and procedures sounds intimidating, there is a middle ground: business opportunities.

A business opportunity, in the simplest terms, is a packaged business investment that allows the buyer to begin a business. (Technically, all franchises are business opportunities, but not all business opportunities are franchises.)

Unlike a franchise, however, the business opportunity seller typically exercises no control over the buyer's business operations. In fact, in most business opportunity programs, there is no continuing relationship between the seller and the buyer after the sale is made.

Although business opportunities offer less support than franchises, this could be an advantage for you if you thrive on freedom. Typically, you will not be obligated to follow the strict specifications and detailed program that franchisees must follow. With most business opportunities, you would simply buy a set of equipment or materials, and then you can operate the business any way and under any name you want. There are no ongoing royalties in most cases, and no trademark rights are sold.

However, this same lack of long-term commitment is also a business opportunity's chief disadvantage. Because there is no continuing relationship, the world of business opportunities does have its share of con artists who promise buyers instant success, then take their money and run. While increased regulation of business opportunities has dramatically lessened the likelihood of rip-offs, it is still important to investigate an opportunity thoroughly before you invest any money.

Legal Matters

In general, a business opportunity refers to one of a number of ways to get into business. These include the following:

■ **DEALERS/DISTRIBUTORS** are individuals or businesses that purchase the right to sell ABC Corp.'s products but not the right to use ABC's trade name. For example, an authorized dealer of Minolta products might have a Minolta sign in his window, but he can't call his business Minolta. Often, the words "dealers" and "distributors" are used interchangeably, but there is a difference: A distributor may sell to several dealers, while a dealer usually sells direct to retailers or consumers.

On The Level

Network marketing (NM) is a type of business opportunity that is very popular with people looking for part-time, flexible businesses. Some of the best-known companies in America, including Avon, Mary Kay Cosmetics and Tupperware, fall under the NM umbrella.

NM programs feature a low upfront investment—usually only a few hundred dollars for the purchase of a product sample kit—and the opportunity to sell a product line directly to friends, family and other personal contacts. Most NM programs also ask participants to recruit other sales representatives. These recruits constitute a rep's "downline," and their sales generate income for those above them in the program.

Things get sticky when an NM network compensates participants primarily for recruiting others rather than for selling the company's products or services. An NM system in which most of the revenues come from recruitment may be considered an illegal pyramid scheme.

Since network marketing programs are usually exempt from business opportunity regulation and are not defined as franchises under state and federal franchise laws, you will need to do your own investigation before investing any money.

■ **LICENSEES** have the right to use the seller's trade name and certain methods, equipment, technology or product lines. If Business Opportunity XYZ has a special technique for reglazing porcelain, for instance, it will teach you the method and sell you the supplies and machinery needed to open your own business. You can call your business XYZ, but you are an independent licensee.

■ **VENDING MACHINES** are provided by the seller, who may also help you find locations for them. You restock your own machines and collect the money.

■ **COOPERATIVES** allow an existing business to affiliate with a network of similar businesses, usually for advertising and promotional purposes.

■ **NETWORK MARKETING** (see "On The Level" on page 64).

Legal definitions of business opportunities vary, since not all states regulate business opportunities. (The 25 that do are Arizona, California, Connecticut, Florida, Georgia, Illinois, Indiana, Iowa, Kentucky, Louisiana, Maine, Maryland, Michigan, Minnesota, Nebraska, New Hampshire, North Carolina, Ohio, Oklahoma, South Carolina, South Dakota, Texas, Utah, Virginia and Washington.) Even among these, different states have different definitions of what constitutes a business opportunity. Most definitions contain the following:

■ **THE INVESTOR PURCHASES** goods or services that allow him or her to begin a business.

■ **THE PURCHASE INVOLVES** a certain amount of money. In 15 states and under FTC regulations, the minimum investment is $500; in the other 10 states, that figure drops to as little as $100.

■ **THE SELLER MAKES** any one of the following statements during the course of the sale:

1. **THE SELLER WILL ASSIST** in securing locations for display racks or vending devices;

2. **THE SELLER WILL RETURN** the money if the buyer is dissatisfied with the investment;

3. **THE SELLER WILL BUY BACK** the products assembled or produced by the buyer;

4. **THE SELLER GUARANTEES** (or, in some states, implies) that the buyer will be able to generate revenues in excess of the amount of the investment; or

5. **THE SELLER WILL PROVIDE** a marketing plan or a sales plan for the buyer.

If a seller meets the definition of a business opportunity in states that regulate them, it generally means he or she must register the offering with the state authorities and deliver a disclosure document to prospective buyers at least 10 business days before the sale is made. (For more information on states' regulations, check with consumer protection agencies—often a part of the attorney general's office—in your state.)

Checking It Out

Researching a business is a more challenging task than investigating a franchise. Particularly if the business opportunity you are considering does not provide buyers with a disclosure document, you get a lot less information, so you have to do a lot more legwork on your own.

Whenever possible, follow the same steps you would for investigating a franchise. Contact the Better Business Bureau to see if there have been complaints against the company. If the company is registered with D&B, a financial report will give you details on its financial standing and other information.

Also check with the state regulatory agency—either the Commission of Securities or the Commission of Financial Institutions—in the state where the business opportunity has its headquarters. This will tell you if the company is complying with all state regulations. If you discover the company or its principals have been involved in lawsuits or bankruptcies, try to find out more details. Did the suits involve fraud or violations of regulatory laws? A copy of the petition or judgment, which you can get from the court that handled the case, will give you the answers to these questions.

Finally, see if the business opportunity seller will provide you with a list of people who have purchased the opportunity in the past. Don't let the seller give you a few handpicked names; ask for a full list of buyers in your state. Try to track them down, and talk to as many as you can. Were they satisfied with the opportunity? Would they recommend it to friends?

The path to buying a business opportunity is not as clearly defined as the road leading to franchise ownership. The good news, however, is that you have more freedom to make your business opportunity work. More so than with a franchise, the success or failure of your business opportunity depends on you, your commitment and your level of effort. Put that same effort into finding the right business opportunity program, and your chances of success increase exponentially.

Business Evaluation Checklist

If you find a business that you would like to buy, you will need to consider a number of points before you decide whether to purchase it. Take a good, close look at the business, and answer the following questions. They will help you determine whether the business is a sound investment.

❑ **WHY DOES THE CURRENT OWNER** want to sell the business?

❑ **DOES THE BUSINESS** have potential for future growth, or will its sales decline?

❑ **IF THE BUSINESS** is in decline, can you save it and make it successful?

❑ **IS THE BUSINESS** in sound financial condition? Have you seen audited year-end financial statements for the business? Have you reviewed the most recent statements? Have you reviewed the tax returns for the past five years?

❑ **HAVE YOU SEEN COPIES** of all of the business's current contracts?

❑ **IS THE BUSINESS** now, or has it ever been, under investigation by any governmental agency? If so, what is the status of any current investigation? What were the results of any past investigation?

❑ **IS THE BUSINESS** currently involved in a lawsuit, or has it ever been involved in one? If so, what is the status or result?

❑ **DOES THE BUSINESS** have any debts or liens against it? If so, what are they for and in what amounts?

❑ **WHAT PERCENTAGE** of the business's accounts are past due? How much does the business write off each year for bad debts?

❑ **HOW MANY CUSTOMERS** does the business serve on a regular basis?

❑ **WHO MAKES UP THE MARKET** for this business? Where are your customers located? (Do they all come from your community, or are they from across the state or spread across the globe?)

❑ **DOES THE AMOUNT** of business vary from season to season?

❑ **DOES ANY** single customer account for a large portion of the sales volume? If so, would the business be able to survive without this customer? (The larger your customer base is, the more easily you will be able to survive the loss of any customers. If, on the other hand, you exist mainly to serve a single client, the loss of that client could finish your business.)

❑ **HOW DOES THE BUSINESS** market its products or services? Does its competition use the same methods? If not, what methods does the competition use? How successful are they?

Business Evaluation Checklist

- ❑ **DOES THE BUSINESS** have exclusive rights to market any particular products or services? If so, how has it obtained this exclusively? Is it making the best possible use of this exclusivity? Do you have written proof that the current business owner can transfer this exclusivity to you?

- ❑ **DOES THE BUSINESS** hold patents for any of its products? Which ones? What percentage of gross sales do they represent? Would the sale of the business include the sale of any patents?

- ❑ **ARE THE BUSINESS'** supplies, merchandise and other materials available from several suppliers, or are there only a handful who can meet your needs? If you lost the business's current supplier, what impact would that loss have on your business? Would you be able to find substitute goods of the appropriate quality and price?

- ❑ **ARE ANY OF THE BUSINESS'S** products in danger of becoming obsolete or of going out of style? Is this a "fad" business?

- ❑ **WHAT IS THE BUSINESS'S** market share?

- ❑ **WHAT COMPETITION** does the business face? How can the business compete successfully? Have the business's competitors changed recently? Have any of them gone out of business, for instance?

- ❑ **DOES THE BUSINESS** have all the equipment you think is necessary? Will you need to add or update any equipment?

- ❑ **WHAT IS THE BUSINESS'S** current inventory worth? Will you be able to use any of this inventory, or is it inconsistent with your intended product line?

- ❑ **HOW MANY EMPLOYEES** does the business have? What positions do they hold?

- ❑ **DOES THE BUSINESS** pay its employees high wages, or are the wages average or low?

- ❑ **DOES THE BUSINESS** experience high employee turnover? If so, why?

- ❑ **WHAT BENEFITS** does the business offer its employees?

- ❑ **HOW LONG** have the company's top managers been with the company?

- ❑ **WILL THE CHANGE** of ownership cause any changes in personnel?

- ❑ **WHICH EMPLOYEES** are the most important to the company?

- ❑ **DO ANY OF THE BUSINESS'S** employees belong to any unions?

GLOSSARY

ACCOUNTS RECEIVABLE: money due to a business from clients and customers; outstanding invoices

ASSET ACQUISITION: a method of buying a business in which the buyer purchases only those assets of the business he or she wants

BUSINESS BROKER: a person who helps buy and sell businesses, similar to a real estate broker

BUSINESS OPPORTUNITY: legal definitions vary; in its simplest terms, a business opportunity is a packaged business investment that allows the buyer to begin a business

DOWNLINE: the group of sales representatives that a given sales rep has recruited to join a multilevel marketing system; he or she receives a percentage of their sales

DUE DILIGENCE: the process of investigating legal, financial and other aspects of any business deal (such as buying a business) before the deal is completed

EMPLOYEE STOCK OWNERSHIP PLAN (ESOP): a plan that gives employees shares of stock in a company

FACTORS: companies that buy businesses' accounts receivable

FRANCHISEE: the person who buys a system of doing business from a franchisor

FRANCHISOR: a person or company that sells a system of doing business to franchisees and provides them with ongoing training and support

HOLD HARMLESS AND INDEMNIFY: a clause in a contract that protects one party to a business purchase from being held responsible for results of the other party's actions prior to the purchase

INTELLECTUAL PROPERTY: a nontangible property, such as a trade secret, patent or trade name, to which one has legal rights

NETWORK MARKETING (NM): a system of doing business in which participants recruit other sales representatives as part of their "downline" and receive a commission based on sales of their downline as well as on their own sales

PYRAMID SCHEME: an illegal type of network marketing in which participants receive revenues primarily for recruiting others rather than for selling the company's products or services

STOCK ACQUISITION: a method of buying a business in which the buyer purchases the actual stock of the business

UNIFORM FRANCHISE OFFERING CIRCULAR (UFOC): a disclosure document franchisors are legally required to provide for prospective franchisees

PART

2

Building
Blocks

CHAPTER 6

Who Is Your Customer, Anyway?

Defining your market

You've come up with a great idea for a business…but you're not ready to roll yet. Before you go any further, the next step is figuring out who your market is.

There are two basic markets you can sell to: consumer and business. These divisions are fairly obvious. For example, if you are selling women's clothing from a retail store, your target market is consumers; if you are selling office supplies, your target market is businesses (this is referred to as "B2B" sales). In some cases—for example, if you run a printing business—you may be marketing to both businesses and individual consumers.

No business—particularly a small one—can be all things to all people. The more narrowly you can define your target market, the better. This process is known as creating a niche and is key to success for even the biggest companies. Wal-Mart and Tiffany's are both retailers, but they have very different niches: Wal-Mart caters to bargain-minded shoppers, while Tiffany's appeals to upscale jewelry consumers.

"Many people talk about 'finding' a niche as if it were something under a rock or at the end of the rainbow, ready-made. That is nonsense," says Lynda C. Falkenstein, author of *Nichecraft: Using Your Specialness to Focus Your Business, Corner Your Market & Make Customers Seek You Out*. Good niches do not just fall into your lap; they must be very carefully crafted.

Rather than creating a niche, many entrepreneurs make the mistake of falling into the "all-over-the-map" trap, claiming they can do many things and be good at all of them. These people quickly learn a tough lesson, Falkenstein warns: "Smaller is bigger in business, and smaller is not all over the map; it's highly focused."

Practicing Nichecraft

Creating a good niche, advises Falkenstein, involves following a seven-step process:

1. **MAKE A WISH LIST.** With whom do you want to do business? Be as specific as you can: Identify the geographical range and the types of businesses or customers you want your business to target. If you don't know whom you want to do business with, you can't make contact. "You must recognize that you can't do business with everybody," cautions Falkenstein. Otherwise, you risk

exhausting yourself and confusing your customers.

These days, the trend is toward smaller niches (see "Direct Hit," on page 77). Targeting teenagers isn't specific enough; targeting male, African-American teenagers with family incomes of $40,000 and up is. Aiming at companies that sell software is too broad; aiming at Northern California-based companies that provide Internet software sales and training and have sales of $15 million or more is a better goal.

2. **Focus.** Clarify what you want to sell, remembering: a) You can't be all things to all people and b) "smaller is bigger." Your niche is not the same as the field in which you work. For example, a retail clothing business is not a niche but a field. A more specific niche may be "selling maternity clothes to executive women."

To begin this focusing process, Falkenstein suggests using these techniques to help you:

- ■ **MAKE A LIST** of things you do best and the skills implicit in each of them.
- ■ **LIST YOUR ACHIEVEMENTS.**
- ■ **IDENTIFY THE MOST IMPORTANT** lessons you have learned in life.
- ■ **LOOK FOR PATTERNS** that reveal your style or approach to resolving problems.

Your niche should arise naturally from your interests and experience. For example, if you spent 10 years working in a consulting firm, but also spent 10 years working for a small, family-owned business, you may decide to start a consulting business that specializes in small, family-owned companies.

3. **DESCRIBE THE CUSTOMER'S WORLDVIEW.** A successful business uses what Falkenstein calls the Platinum Rule: "Do unto others as they would do unto themselves." When you look at the world from your prospective customers' perspective, you can identify their needs or wants. The best way to do this is to talk to prospective customers and identify their main concerns. (Part 2, Chapter 7 will give you more ideas for ways to get inside customers' heads.)

BEWARE!

EVEN THOUGH MANY BABY BOOMERS ARE NOW OVER 50, DON'T MAKE THE MISTAKE OF MARKETING TO THEM THE SAME WAY YOU WOULD TO SENIORS. BOOMERS DON'T THINK OF THEMSELVES AS "OLD" OR "SENIORS." THE MORAL? THE SAME MARKETING APPROACHES THAT APPEALED TO BOOMERS WHEN THEY WERE 30 WILL APPEAL TO THEM WHEN THEY'RE 50, 60 AND 70.

4. **SYNTHESIZE.** At this stage, your niche should begin to take shape as your ideas and the client's needs and wants coalesce to create something new. A good niche has five qualities:

- **IT TAKES YOU WHERE YOU WANT TO GO**—in other words, it conforms to your long-term vision;
- **SOMEBODY ELSE WANTS IT**—namely, customers;
- **IT'S CAREFULLY PLANNED;**
- **IT'S ONE-OF-A-KIND,** the "only game in town"; and
- **IT EVOLVES,** allowing you to develop different profit centers

and still retain the core business, thus ensuring long-term success.

BEWARE!

MARKETING TO ETHNIC CONSUMERS? DON'T MAKE THESE MISTAKES: STICKING ETHNIC FACES IN THE BACKGROUND OF YOUR MARKETING MATERIALS; "LUMPING" (FOR EXAMPLE, TREATING JAPANESE-, CHINESE- AND KOREAN-AMERICANS AS ONE BIG MASS OF "ASIANS"); OR RELYING ON STEREOTYPES SUCH AS SLANG OR OVERTLY ETHNIC APPROACHES. SUBTLETY AND SENSITIVITY ARE KEYS TO SUCCESS WHEN APPROACHING THESE MARKETS.

5. **EVALUATION.** Now it's time to evaluate your proposed product or service against the five criteria in Step 4. Perhaps you'll find that the niche you had in mind requires more business travel than you're ready for. That means it doesn't fulfill one of the above criteria—it won't take you where you want to go. So scrap it, and move on to the next idea.

6. **TEST.** Once you have a match between niche and product, test-market it. "Give people an opportunity to buy your product or service—not just theoretically but actually putting it out there," suggests Falkenstein. This can be done by offering samples, such as a free miniseminar or a sample copy of your newsletter. The test shouldn't cost you a lot of money: "If you spend huge amounts of money on the initial market test, you are probably doing it wrong."

7. **GO FOR IT!** It's time to implement your idea. For many entrepreneurs, this is the most difficult stage. But fear not: If you did your homework, entering the market will be a calculated risk, not just a gamble.

Keep It Fresh

Once your niche is established and well-received by your market, you may be tempted to rest on your laurels. Not a good idea, says Falkenstein. "[You must] keep growing by re-niching. This doesn't mean totally changing your focus, but rather further adapting it to the environment around you."

Direct Hit

Once upon a time, business owners thought it was enough to market their products or services to "18- to 49-year-olds." Those days are a thing of the past. "The consumer marketplace has become so differentiated, it's a misconception to talk about the marketplace in any kind of general, grand way," says trend consultant Ross E. Goldstein. "You can market to socioeconomic status or to gender or to region or to lifestyle or to technological sophistication. There's no end to the number of different ways you can slice the pie."

Further complicating matters, age no longer means what it used to. Fifty-year-old baby boomers prefer rock 'n' roll to Geritol; 30-year-olds may still be living with their parents. "People now repeat stages and recycle their lives," says Goldstein. "You can have two men who are 64 years old, and one is retired and driving around in a Winnebago, and the other is just remarried with a toddler in his house."

Generational marketing, which defines consumers not just by age, but also by social, economic, demographic and psychological factors, has been used since the early '80s to give a more accurate picture of the target consumer.

A newer twist is cohort marketing, which studies groups of people who underwent the same experiences during their formative years. This leads them to form a bond and behave differently from people in different cohorts, even when they are similar in age. For instance, people who were young adults in the Depression era behave differently from people who came of age during World War II, even though they are close in age.

To get an even narrower reading, some entrepreneurs combine cohort or generational marketing with life stages, or what people are doing at a certain time in life (getting married, having children, retiring), and physiographics, or physical conditions related to age (nearsightedness, arthritis, menopause).

Today's consumers are more marketing-savvy than ever before and don't like to be "lumped" with others—so be sure you understand your niche. While pinpointing your market so narrowly takes a little extra effort, entrepreneurs who aim at a smaller target are far more likely to make a direct hit.

Profiting From Procurement

Looking for a niche? One market many entrepreneurs ignore is the lucrative procurement pie. Although the federal government is by far the biggest customer in this arena, local governments, colleges and universities, school districts, nonprofit organizations, public utilities and corporations also have plenty of procurement opportunities available. The federal government's civilian agencies alone buy products in more than 4,000 categories, ranging from air brakes to zippers.

Contrary to what you might imagine, small businesses often have an edge in competing for procurement dollars. Government rules and regulations are designed to promote fair competition and a level playing field. And government agencies and large contractors are often required by law to give a certain amount of business to small, disadvantaged, women-owned or minority-owned businesses.

How to get started?

- **Check out** the SBA's subcontracting opportunities at http://web.sba.gov/subnet.
- **Agencies like** the U.S. Postal Service, Department of Interior and the Army, as well as many others, send out solicitations to businesses that are on their mailing lists. To find out how to get on the lists, contact the agency you're interested in.
- **Regularly scan** the *Commerce Business Daily*, which lists available contracts; it can be found at many libraries. You can also approach agencies or prime contractors directly and market your services to them.

If you are a woman or a member of a minority group, you will need to be certified as a woman- or minority-owned business to work with government agencies and many large contractors. This can be done several ways. Many cities have their own certification programs or can direct you to the certification programs that they accept. A good general place to start is with the SBA; you can reach them at 6302 Fairview Rd., #300, Charlotte, NC 28210, or call (800) U-ASK-SBA.

Ask yourself the following questions when you think you have found your niche—and ask them again every six months or so to make sure your niche is still on target:

- **WHO ARE** your target clients?
- **WHO AREN'T** your target clients?
- **DO YOU REFUSE** certain kinds of business if it falls outside your niche?
- **WHAT DO CLIENTS** think you stand for?
- **IS YOUR NICHE** in a constant state of evolution?
- **DOES YOUR NICHE** offer what prospective customers want?
- **DO YOU HAVE A PLAN** and delivery system that effectively conveys the need for your niche to the right market?
- **CAN YOU CONFIDENTLY PREDICT** the life cycle of your niche?
- **HOW CAN YOUR NICHE** be expanded into a variety of products or services that act as profit centers?
- **DO YOU HAVE A SENSE** of passion and focused energy with respect to your niche?
- **DOES YOUR NICHE** feel comfortable and natural?
- **HOW WILL PURSUING** your niche contribute to achieving the goals you have set for business?

According to Falkenstein, "Creating a niche is the difference between being in business and not being in business. It's the difference between surviving and thriving, between simply liking what you do and the joy of success."

ON A MISSION

Once you have designed a niche for your business, you're ready to create a mission statement. A key tool that can be as important as your business plan, a mission statement captures, in a few succinct sentences, the essence of your business's goals and the philosophies underlying them. Equally important, the mission statement signals

79

what your business is all about to your customers, employees, suppliers and the community.

The mission statement reflects every facet of your business: the range and nature of the products you offer, pricing, quality, service, marketplace position, growth potential, use of technology, and your relationships with your customers, employees, suppliers, competitors and the community.

"Mission statements help clarify what business you are in, your goals and your objectives," says Rhonda Abrams, author of *The Successful Business Plan: Secrets and Strategies.*

Your mission statement should reflect your business's special niche. However, studying other companies' statements can fuel your creativity. One sample mission statement Abrams developed:

"AAA Inc. is a spunky, imaginative food products and service company aimed at offering high-quality, moderately priced, occasionally unusual foods using only natural ingredients. We view ourselves as partners with our customers, our employees, our community and our environment. We aim to become a regionally recognized brand name, capitalizing on the sustained interest in Southwestern and Mexican food. Our goal is moderate growth, annual profitability and maintaining our sense of humor."

Or consider the statement one entrepreneur developed for her consulting business: "ABC Enterprises is a company devoted to developing human potential. Our mission is to help people create innovative solutions and make informed choices to improve their lives. We motivate and encourage others to achieve personal and professional fulfillment. Our motto is: Together, we believe that the best in each of us enriches all of us."

The Write Words

To come up with a statement that encompasses all the major elements of your business, start with the right questions. Business plan consultant David Tucker says the most important question is, What business are you in? Since you have already gone through the steps of creating your niche, answering this question should be easy for you.

Answering the following questions will help you to create a verbal picture of your business's mission:

1. **WHY ARE YOU IN BUSINESS?** What do you want for yourself, your family and your customers? Think about the spark that ignited your decision to start a business. What will keep it burning?

2. **WHO ARE YOUR CUSTOMERS?** What can you do for them that will enrich their lives and contribute to their success—now and in the future?

3. **WHAT IMAGE OF YOUR BUSINESS DO YOU WANT TO CONVEY?** Customers, suppliers, employees and the public will all have perceptions of your company. How will you create the desired picture?

4. **WHAT IS THE NATURE OF YOUR PRODUCTS AND SERVICES?** What factors determine pricing and quality? Consider how these relate to the reasons for your business's existence. How will all this change over time?

5. **WHAT LEVEL OF SERVICE DO YOU PROVIDE?** Most companies believe they offer "the best service available," but do your customers agree? Don't be vague; define what makes your service so extraordinary.

6. **WHAT ROLES DO YOU AND YOUR EMPLOYEES PLAY?** Wise captains develop a leadership style that organizes, challenges and recognizes employees.

7. **WHAT KIND OF RELATIONSHIPS WILL YOU MAINTAIN WITH SUPPLIERS?** Every business is in partnership with its suppliers. When you succeed, so do they.

8. **HOW DO YOU DIFFER FROM COMPETITORS?** Many entrepreneurs forget they are pursuing the same dollars as their competitors. What do you do better, cheaper or faster than other competitors? How can you use competitors' weaknesses to your advantage?

9. **HOW WILL YOU USE TECHNOLOGY, CAPITAL, PROCESSES, PRODUCTS AND SERVICES TO REACH YOUR GOALS?** A description of your strategy will keep your energies focused on your goals.

10. **WHAT UNDERLYING PHILOSOPHIES OR VALUES GUIDED YOUR RESPONSES TO THE PREVIOUS QUESTIONS?** Some businesses choose to list these separately. Writing them down clarifies the "why" behind your mission.

Putting It All Together

Like anything with lasting value, crafting a mission statement requires time, thought and planning. However, the effort is well worth it. In fact, most start-up entrepreneurs discover that the process of crafting the mission statement is as beneficial as the final statement itself. Going through the process will help you solidify the reasons for what you are doing and clarify the motivations behind your business.

Here are some tips to make your mission statement the best it can be:

Target Market Work Sheet

Use the following exercise to identify where and who your target market is. Once you're done, you'll have an audience to aim for and home in on rather than using a shotgun approach, which is a time and money waster.

Describe the idea:

1. What will the concept be used for? _____

_____

_____

2. Where are similar concepts used and sold? _____

_____

_____

3. What places do my prospects go to for recreation? _____

_____

_____

4. Where do my prospects go for education? _____

_____

_____

5. Where do my prospects do their shopping? _____

_____

_____

6. What types of newspapers, magazines and newsletters do my prospects read? _____

_____

7. What TV and radio stations do my prospects watch and listen to?

_____

_____

■ **INVOLVE THOSE CONNECTED TO YOUR BUSINESS.** Even if you are a sole proprietor, it helps to get at least one other person's ideas for your mission statement. Other people can help you see strengths, weaknesses and voids you might miss. If you have no partners or investors to include, consider knowledgeable family members and close friends, employees or accountants. Be sure, however, to pick only positive, supportive people who truly want you to succeed.

■ **SET ASIDE SEVERAL HOURS—A FULL DAY, IF POSSIBLE—TO WORK ON YOUR STATEMENT.** Mission statements are short—typically more than one sentence but rarely exceeding a page. Still, writing one is not a short process. It takes time to come up with language that simultaneously describes an organization's heart and soul and serves as an inspirational beacon to everyone involved in the business. Large corporations often spend an entire weekend crafting a statement.

■ **PLAN A DATE.** Set aside time to meet with the people who'll be helping you. Write a list of topics to discuss or think about. Find a quiet, comfortable place away from phones and interruptions.

■ **BE PREPARED.** If you have several people involved, be equipped with refreshments, extra lists of topics, paper and pencils. Because not everyone understands what a mission statement is about, explain its meaning and purpose before you begin.

■ **BRAINSTORM.** Consider every idea, no matter how silly it sounds. Stimulate ideas by looking at sample mission statements and thinking about or discussing the 10 questions above. If you're working with a group, use a flip chart to record responses so everyone can see them. Once you've finished brainstorming, ask everyone to write individual mission statements for your business. Read the statements, select the best bits and pieces, and fit them together.

■ **USE "RADIANT WORDS."** Once you have the basic idea in writing, polish the language of your mission statement. "Every word counts," says Abrams. The statement should create dynamic, visual images and inspire action. Use offbeat, colorful verbs and adjectives to spice up your statement. Don't hesitate to drop in words like "kaleidoscope," "sizzle," "cheer," "outrageous" and "marvel" to add zest. If you want customers to "boast" about your goods and services, say so—along with the reasons why. Some businesses include a glossary that defines the terms used in the statement.

Once your mission statement is complete, start spreading the word! You need to convey your mission statement to others inside and outside the business to tell everyone you know where you are going and why. Post it in your office, where you, employees and visitors can see it every day. Print it on company materials, such as your brochures and your business plan or even on the back of your business cards.

When you're launching a new business, you can't afford to lose sight of your objectives. By keeping your mission statement always in front of you, you'll keep your goals in mind—and ensure smooth sailing.

GLOSSARY

B2B SALES: marketing your products and services to other businesses, as opposed to individual consumers

COHORT MARKETING: marketing to people based on the groups or "cohorts" they were part of during their formative years; for example, the World War II cohort, the Depression-era cohort

CONSUMER: an individual who purchases services or products from a business

GENERATIONAL MARKETING: marketing to consumers based on social, economic, demographic and psychological factors

LIFE STAGE MARKETING: marketing to consumers based on what they are doing at a given period in life, such as having children, buying a home or retiring

MISSION STATEMENT: a short written statement of your business goals and philosophies

PHYSIOGRAPHICS: the physical conditions related to aging, such as arthritis or near-sightedness

TARGET MARKET: the specific group of consumers or businesses you want to sell to colleges for a small fee; check with your local community college or Small Business Administration district office for details

If I Build It, Will They Come?

Conducting market research

So you have a great idea for a product—something that's bound to capture the hearts and minds (and wallets) of consumers everywhere. Or perhaps you have stumbled on a service that isn't being offered by anyone else; one that, as far as you can tell, is desperately needed. This is your opportunity! Don't hesitate…don't look back…jump right into it and…

Wait! Before you shift into high gear, you must determine whether there really is a market for your product or service. Not only that, you need to ascertain what—if any—fine-tuning is needed. Quite simply, you must conduct market research.

Many business owners neglect this crucial step in product development for the sole reason that they don't want to hear any negative feedback. They are convinced their product or service is perfect just the way it is, and they don't want to risk tampering with it.

Other entrepreneurs bypass market research because they fear it will be too expensive. With all the other start-up costs you're facing, it's not easy to justify spending money on research that will only prove what you knew all along: Your product is a winner.

Good Question

Whether you hire a professional market research firm or take on the task yourself, your market research should clearly answer the following questions:

- **WHO WILL** buy my product or service?
- **WHY WILL** they buy it?
- **WHERE WILL** they buy it—specialty shops, department stores, mail order?
- **WHAT DO I NEED** to charge to make a healthy profit?
- **WHAT PRODUCTS** or services will mine be competing with?
- **AM I POSITIONING** my product or service correctly? (In other words, if there's a lot of competition, look for a specialized market niche.)
- **WHAT GOVERNMENT REGULATIONS** will my product or service be subject to?

Regardless of the reason, failing to do market research can amount to a death sentence for your product. "A lot of companies skim over the important background information because they're so interested in getting their product to market," says Donna Barson, president and owner of Barson Marketing Inc., a marketing, advertising and public relations consulting firm. "But the companies that do the best are the ones that do their homework."

Consider market research an investment in your future. If you make the necessary adjustments to your product or service now, you'll save money in the long run.

WHAT IT IS, WHAT IT DOES

What exactly is market research? Simply put, it's a way of collecting information you can use to solve or avoid marketing problems. Good market research gives you the data you need to develop a marketing plan that really works for you. It enables you to identify the specific segments within a market that you want to target and to create an identity for your product or service that separates it from your competitors. Market research can also help you choose the best geographic location to launch your new business.

SMART TIP

WHEN DOING ANY TYPE OF SURVEY, WHETHER IT IS A FOCUS GROUP, A QUESTIONNAIRE OR A PHONE SURVEY, PAY ATTENTION TO CUSTOMERS WHO COMPLAIN OR GIVE YOU NEGATIVE FEEDBACK. YOU DON'T NEED TO WORRY ABOUT THE CUSTOMERS WHO LOVE YOUR PRODUCT OR SERVICE, BUT THE ONES WHO TELL YOU WHERE YOU'RE GOING WRONG PROVIDE VALUABLE INFORMATION TO HELP YOU IMPROVE.

Before you start your market research, it's a good idea to meet with a consultant, talk to a business or marketing professor at a local college or university, or contact your local Small Business Administration (SBA) district office. These sources can offer guidance and help you with the first step in market research: deciding exactly what information you need to gather.

As a rule of thumb, market research should provide you with information about three critical areas: the industry, the consumer and the competition.

1. **INDUSTRY INFORMATION:** In researching the industry, look for the latest trends. Compare the statistics and growth in the industry.

What areas of the industry appear to be expanding, and what areas are declining? Is the industry catering to new types of customers? What technological developments are affecting the industry? How can you use them to your advantage? A thriving, stable industry is key; you don't want to start a new business in a field that is on the decline.

2. **CONSUMER CLOSE-UP:** On the consumer side, your market research should begin with a market survey. A thorough market survey will help you make a reasonable sales forecast for your new business. To do a market survey, you first need to determine the market limits or physical boundaries of the location within which your business sells. Next, study the spending characteristics of the population within this location.

Know Thy Enemy

There are two ways to define competitors. One is by strategic groups—competitors who use similar marketing strategies, sell similar products or have similar skills. Under this definition, you might group Toyota and Nissan as competitors within the car industry.

The second, less obvious way to group competitors is by customer—how strongly do they compete for the same customers' dollar? Using this method gives you a wider view of your competitors and the challenges they could pose to your new business.

Suppose you're considering opening a family entertainment center. If there are no other family entertainment centers in the area, you might think you have no competitors. Wrong! Any type of business that competes for customers' leisure time and entertainment dollar is a competitor. That means children's play centers, amusement parks and arcades are all your competitors. So are businesses that, on the surface, don't appear similar, like movie theaters, bookstores and shopping malls. You could even face competition from nonprofit entities, like public parks, libraries and beaches. In short, anything that families might do in their leisure time is your "competition."

Don't limit yourself to the obvious definitions of competition. Start thinking out of the box...and you will be less likely to get sideswiped by an unexpected competitor.

Estimate the location's purchasing power, based on its per-capita income, its median income level, the unemployment rate, population and other demographic factors. Determine the current sales volume in the area for the type of product or service you will sell.

Finally, estimate how much of the total sales volume you can reasonably obtain. (This last step is extremely important. Opening your new business in a given community won't necessarily generate additional business volume; it may simply redistribute the business that's already there.)

3. **KNOW THE COMPETITION:** Based on a combination of industry research and consumer research, a clearer picture of your competition will emerge. Do not underestimate the number of competitors out there. Keep an eye out for potential future competitors as well as current ones.

Examine the number of competitors on a local and, if relevant, national scale. Study their strategies and operations. Your analysis should supply a clear picture of potential threats, opportunities, and the weaknesses and strengths of the competition facing your new business.

When looking at the competition, try to see what trends have been established in the industry and whether there's an opportunity or advantage for your business. Use the library, the Internet and other secondary research sources described below to research competitors. Read as many articles as you can on the companies you will be competing with. If you are researching publicly owned companies, contact them and obtain copies of their annual reports. These often show not only how successful a company is; but also what products or services it plans to emphasize in the future.

You can also gather information on competing businesses first-hand by visiting them in person. Take along a questionnaire, like the "Sample Market Research Competition Questionnaire" on page 92. This one is for a bar/tavern, but you can customize it for your particular business.

MARKET RESEARCH METHODS

In conducting your market research, you will gather two types of data: primary and secondary. *Primary research* is information that comes directly from the source—that is, potential customers. You can compile this information yourself or hire someone else to gather it for you via surveys, focus groups and other methods. *Secondary research* involves gathering statistics, reports, studies and other data from organizations such as government agencies, trade associations and your local chamber of commerce.

SECONDARY RESEARCH

The vast majority of research you can find will be secondary research. While large companies spend huge amounts of money on market research, the good news is that plenty of information is available for free to entrepreneurs on a tight budget. The best place to start? Your local library.

Reference librarians at public and university libraries will be happy to point you in the right direction. Become familiar with the business reference section—you'll be spending a lot of time there. Two good sources to look for: *The Thomas Register of Manufacturers* and the *Harris All-Business Directory*. Both can be found at most libraries and can help you target businesses in a particular industry, read up on competitors or find manufacturers for your product.

To get insights into consumer markets, check out the *U.S. Statistical Abstract*, which you can find at most libraries. It contains a wealth of social, political and economic data. Another source for consumer information is *American Demographics* magazine. Ask reference librarians for other resources targeted at your specific business.

Associations

Your industry trade association can offer a wealth of information such as market statistics, lists of members, and books and reference materials. Talking to others in your association can be one of the most valuable ways of gaining informal data about a region or customer base.

Look in the *Encyclopedia of Associations* (Gale Research), found in most libraries, to find associations relevant to your industry. You may also want to investigate your customers' trade associations for information that can help you market to them. Most trade associations provide information free of charge.

Read your trade associations' publications, as well as those aimed at your target customers, to get an idea of current and future trends and buying patterns. And keep an eye out for more: New magazines and newsletters are launched every year. If you're not following all of them, you could be missing out on valuable information about new products and your competitors.

Government Guidance

Government agencies are an invaluable source of market research, most of it free. Almost every county government publishes population density and distribution figures in widely available census tracts. These publications will show you the number of people living in specific areas, such as precincts, water districts or even 10-block neighborhoods. Some counties publish reports on population trends that show the population 10 years ago, five years ago and today. Watch out for a static, declining or small population; ideally, you want to locate where there is an expanding population that wants your products and services.

The U.S. Census Bureau turns out reams of inexpensive or free business information, most of which is available on the Internet:

HOT LINK

IN THE BUSINESS OF E-COMMERCE? SURVEY SITE (WWW.SURVEYSITE.COM) IS A MARKET RESEARCH COMPANY THAT WILL EVALUATE YOUR E-COMMERCE SITE. THEY OFFER A VARIETY OF SURVEY OPTIONS, FROM WEB-BASED POP-UPS AND E-MAIL SURVEYS TO FOCUS GROUPS. EVEN IF YOU'RE NOT READY FOR PROFESSIONAL ADVICE, EXPLORING THEIR SITE WILL GIVE YOU AN IDEA OF THE QUESTIONS YOU SHOULD BE ASKING IN YOUR OWN RESEARCH.

Sample Market Research Competition Questionnaire

When you visit the competing bars in your area, you want to use the information you gather to develop a competitive strategy for your own establishment. Improve on their strengths and capitalize on their weaknesses. Fill out this questionnaire for each of the bars you visit to help you assess your competition and your customers.

1. What type of bar is it?

2. What is the concept/theme?

4. Does the bar offer a full bar, beer and wine, or just beer?

5. Did you have to wait to be seated? How long?

6. How long did it take to get served?

7. What kind of décor does the bar have?

8. Is the bar clean?

9. Is the layout of the bar and tables efficient?

10. Does the bar serve food?

11. If so, what types of food does it have on the menu?

12. Does the menu offer enough variety?

13. How would you rate the quality of the drinks?

14. How would you rate the quality of the food?

15. Does the cost match the quality/quantity of the food and drinks served?

16. How do you feel about the bar's atmosphere?

17. How is the service?

18. What promotions and sales techniques do you notice?

19. What feedback did you receive from the bartender/wait staff?

20. What information did you get from the customers?

21. List three ways you would improve the bar.

1.

2.

3.

- The Census Bureau's *STATE AND METROPOLITAN AREA DATA BOOK* offers statistics for metropolitan areas, central cities and counties.
- The *MONTHLY PRODUCT ANNOUNCEMENT* lists all Census Bureau products released in the past month. Sign up for a free e-mail subscription at www.census.gov.
- *COUNTY BUSINESS PATTERNS* is an excellent Census product that reports the number of a given type of business in a county by Standard Industrial Classification code (four-digit codes for all industries in the United States).
- For breakdowns by cities, look to the *ECONOMIC CENSUS,* which is published every five years.

Most of these products should be available at your local library. If not, contact your nearest Census office for a list of publications and ordering information, or write to the Bureau of the Census, Attn: Customer Service, Washington, DC 20233, (301) 457-4100. Most Census Bureau reports are also available on CD-ROM or free on the Internet.

The Department of Commerce is another good source of information.

Netting Information

If your market research budget is limited, try CenStats. A free subscription service from the Census Bureau that's available on the Internet, CenStats gives you a lot for a little, letting you access the bureau's most popular databases and information sold via CD-ROM. Search by county under "County Business Patterns" or ZIP code

under "ZIP Business Patterns," and you'll get business profiles for an area that include payroll information and business size by industry. Click on "USA Counties" to get counties' economic and demographic information, including personal income per capita, population size and more.

Test CenStats out by visiting the Census Bureau's Web page (www.census.gov). If you like it, you can sign up online or call (301) 763-4636. The information is free online or is available on CD-ROM for $50.

Survey Says...

"A recent survey shows..." just might be the most over-used, misused and abused phrase in modern life. Try hard enough, and you can find a survey to prove that 4 out of 5 Americans have been aboard a UFO, think they can flap their arms and fly to the moon, or believe Elvis is alive and living in their spare bedroom. With all the half-baked surveys out there, how do you know what to believe?

First, consider the source. Many surveys are conducted by trade associations, which inevitably are biased in favor of good news. This doesn't mean trade association surveys are necessarily inaccurate; just keep in mind that they are likely to play up positive results and downplay negative ones. When looking at any survey, consider what the source has to gain from the information presented. Then you'll have a better idea of whether to take the information with a grain of salt.

In addition, meaningful surveys generally share the following characteristics:

- **SHORT-TERM FOCUS:** In general, respondents are more likely to be accurate when they make predictions about the next three to six months. When it comes to predicting the long term (a year or more ahead), they're usually guessing.

- **ADEQUATE SAMPLE SIZE:** What constitutes adequate size depends on the topic you're surveying. In general, the broader the topic, the larger the number of respondents should be. If the survey talks about broad manufacturing trends, for example, it should survey 1,000 companies or more. Also consider where the respondents come from. If you're starting a small regional business, a large national sample may not be relevant to your needs because the sample size from your area is probably too small to tell you anything about your region.

- **KNOWLEDGEABLE RESPONDENTS:** Asking entrepreneurs in the electronics business to forecast the future of the industry obviously carries more weight than asking the same question of teachers or random people on the street.

- **CONTINUAL REPLICATION:** The best surveys are repeated regularly, using the same methods, so there is a good basis for comparison from survey to survey.

- **SPECIFIC INFORMATION RELEVANT TO YOUR BUSINESS:** In a nutshell, the best surveys are those where respondents answer questions that are narrowly targeted to your region and niche.

For instance, at the Commerce Department's Web site (www.commerce.gov), you'll find the Small Business Advisor, a one-stop electronic link to all the information and services that the federal government provides for the business community. Tax questions? Wondering about how best to deal with all the regulations and red tape? Chances are, you'll find your answers here. Just go to www.business.gov/busadv/index.cfm.

Or you might try the Commerce Department's Economic Indicators Web page (www.economicindicators.gov). Curious if the world is ready to spend money on your exercise equipment for goldfish? Then the Economic Indicators site is for you. Literally, every day, they're releasing key economic indicators from the Bureau of Economic Analysis and the U.S. Census Bureau.

If you're planning to get into exporting, contact the Department of Commerce's International Trade Administration (ITA). The ITA publishes several thousand reports and statistical surveys, not to mention hundreds of books on everything American entrepreneurs need to know about exporting. Most of the reports and books are available on CD-ROM. For information or to order the ITA's 50-page catalog, *Export Programs Guide*, call the Trade Information Center at (800) USA-TRADE or visit www.usatrade.com.

Maps

Maps of trading areas in counties and states are available from chambers of commerce, trade development commissions, industrial development boards and local newspaper offices. These maps show the major areas of commerce and can also help you judge the accessibility of various sites. Access is an important consideration in determining the limits of your market area.

Colleges And Universities

Local colleges and universities are valuable sources of information. Many college business departments have students who are eager to work in the "real world," gathering information and doing research at little or no cost.

Finally, local business schools are a great source of experts. Many business professors do consulting on the side, and some will even be happy to offer you marketing, sales, strategic planning or financial information for free. Call professors who specialize in these areas; if they can't help, they'll be able to put you in touch with someone who can.

Community Organizations

Your local chamber of commerce or business development agency can supply useful information. They are usually free of charge, including assistance with site selection, demographic reports, and directories of local businesses. They may also offer seminars on marketing and related topics that can help you do better research.

D&B

Financial and business services firm D&B offers a range of reference sources that can help start-ups. Some of the information they offer are D&B's *Regional Business Directories*, D&B's family of CD-ROM products and many others.

- **D&B's REGIONAL BUSINESS DIRECTORIES** provide detailed information to help identify new business prospects and assess market potential. Besides basic information (telephone number, address and company description), the directories also tell when the company was started, sales volume, number of employees, parent company (if any) and, if it's a public company, on which exchange it's traded.

- **D&B's MILLION DOLLAR DISC** family, which includes two CD-ROM disks, can help you develop a targeted marketing campaign for B2B sales. The Million Dollar Disc contains a list of 240,000 leading private and public U.S. companies with sales exceeding $5 million or with more than 100 employees. The Million Dollar Disc Plus features 400,000 companies that have sales of more than $3 million or more than 50 employees. This CD-ROM series also includes biographical information on owners and officers, giving insight into their background and business experience. A subscription is available to the Million Dollar Database on the Web at www.dnbmdd.com.

Going Online

These days, entrepreneurs can conduct much of their market research without ever leaving their computers, thanks to the universe of online services and information. Start with the major consumer online services, which offer access to business databases. You can find everything from headline and business news to industry trends and company-specific business information, such as a firm's address, telephone number, field of business and the name of the CEO. This information is critical for identifying prospects, developing mailing lists and planning sales calls.

All the sources mentioned above (trade associations, government agencies) should also have Web sites you can visit to get information quickly. For additional online sources, see "Appendix A."

If you don't have time to investigate online services yourself, consider hiring an information broker to find the information you need. Information brokers are an excellent way to gather information quickly. They can act as a small company's research arm, identifying the most accurate and cost-effective information sources.

To find information brokers, look in the Yellow Pages or ask the research librarian at your local library. Many research librarians deal with information brokers and will be able to give you good recommendations.

PRIMARY RESEARCH

The secondary research you conduct should help you focus your niche and get a better idea of the challenges facing your business. To get a complete picture of your target market, however, you'll need to do some primary research as well.

A market research firm can help you if you feel that primary research is too complicated to do on your own. These firms will charge a few thousand dollars or more, but depending on the complexity of the information you need, you may feel this is money well-spent. Your local chamber of commerce can recommend firms or individuals who can conduct market research for smaller businesses on a budget.

If you need assistance but don't want to spend that kind of cash, you can go to your SBA district office for guidance, and counselors can help you figure out what types of questions you need to ask your target market. As with secondary research, the SBA, SBDCs, colleges and universities are good sources of help with primary research.

20 Questions

Whether you use students, get help from the SBA, use a market research firm or go it alone, there are simple ways you can get the

Cost Analysis Of Primary Research Methods

Before you begin conducting market research, you need to decide what research method will be most effective. One way to do this is to choose the method that will produce the best sample of responses. Another way is to choose the most cost-effective method, and you can use this cost analysis to do so.

Phone Surveys	Cost
Preparation of the questionnaire	
Interviewer's fee	
Phone charges	
Staff time and cost for analysis and presentation of results	
Independent researcher cost, if any	
Other costs—itemize	
Total Phone Survey Costs	

Personal Interviews	Cost
Printing of questionnaires and prompt cards	
Interviewer's fee and expenses	
Incentives for questionnaire response	
Staff time and cost for analysis and presentation of results	
Independent researcher cost, if any	
Other costs—itemize	
Total Personal Interviews Cost	

Mail Surveys	Cost
Printing questionnaires	
Envelopes	
Postage for mailing questionnaire and return postage	
Incentives for questionnaire response	
Staff time and cost for analysis and presentation of results	
Independent researcher cost, if any	
Other costs—itemize	
Total Mail Survey Costs	

Group Discussions	Cost
Interviewer's fee and expenses in recruiting and assembling the groups	
Renting the conference room or other facility and cost of recording media, such as tapes, if used	
Incentives for group participation	
Staff time and cost for analysis and presentation of results	
Independent researcher cost, if any	
Other costs—itemize	
Total Group Discussion Costs	

primary research information you're looking for.

- **FOCUS GROUPS:** A focus group consists of five to 12 potential customers who are asked their opinions in a one-on-one interview. Participants should fit your target market—for example, single men ages 18 to 25, or working mothers. To find participants, just go to your local mall or college campus and ask people fitting your customer profile if they would answer a few questions. Typically, companies pay participants $30 or more.

Although focus group interviews are informal in nature, you should have a list of questions to help you direct the discussion. Start by asking whether your product or service is one the participants would buy or use. If so, what is the highest price they would pay for it? Where would they shop for such a product? Do they like or dislike the product's packaging? Your questions should center on predetermined objectives, such as finding out how high you can price your product or service or what to name your business. The "Sample Focus Group Questionnaire" on page 101 is for a mail order chocolates company, but you can customize for your business.

If you're going the do-it-yourself route, you will probably act as the focus group moderator. Encourage an open-ended flow of conversation; be sure to solicit comments from quieter members, or you may end up getting all your information from only the talkative participants.

BRIGHT IDEA

SMALL FRIES HAVE BIG IDEAS THAT COULD HELP YOUR BUSINESS GROW. IF YOU ARE STARTING A CHILD-RELATED BUSINESS, CONSIDER USING CHILDREN AS MARKETING CONSULTANTS. KIDS THINK CREATIVELY—A BIG ASSET FOR ENTREPRENEURS TRYING TO REACH THIS MARKET. COMPANIES LIKE MICROSOFT AND MTV HIRE KIDS TO LEARN THEIR VIEW. BUT YOU DON'T NEED TO BE SO FORMAL: JUST TRY POLLING THE KIDS YOU KNOW. GET THEIR RESPONSES, ASK THEM FOR SUGGESTIONS AND BRAINSTORM NEW IDEAS.

- **TELEPHONE INTERVIEWS:** This is an inexpensive, fast way to get information from potential customers. Prepare a script before making the calls to ensure you cover all your objectives. Most people don't like to spend a lot of time on the phone, so keep your questions simple, clearly worded and brief. If you don't have time to make the calls yourself, hire college students to do it for you.
- **DIRECT-MAIL INTERVIEWS:** If you want to survey a wider audience, direct mail can be just the ticket. Your survey can be as simple as a postcard or as elaborate as a cover letter, questionnaire and reply

envelope (for an example of the latter type, see pages 102 and 103). Keep questionnaires to a maximum of one page, and ask no more than 20 questions. Ideally, direct-mail surveys should be simple, structured with "yes/no" or "agree/disagree" check-off boxes so respondents can answer quickly and easily. If possible, only ask for one or two write-in answers at most.

Sample Focus Group Questionnaire

1. How many times a year do you purchase fine chocolates for yourself?_____
2. How many times a year do you purchase fine chocolates as gifts:
   for your spouse or significant other?_____
   for your children?_____
   for other relatives?_____ what are their relationships?_____
   for clients or co-workers?_____
3. Do you prefer dark chocolate or milk chocolate?_____
4. Do you prefer to choose your own selection (nuts, chews, creams, etc.) or would you rather purchase a pre-boxed assortment?_____
5. How much do you usually spend for a one-pound box of chocolates?
6. Would you pay more for a box specially wrapped for a gift occasion?
7. For which special occasions do you purchase chocolates?
8. How much would you expect to pay for this half-pound box of gold-foil-wrapped chocolate stars? _____ *(Here you show the product to your group.)*
9. How much would you expect to pay for an 8-ounce solid chocolate Elvis Presley? _____ *(Here you show the product to your group.)*
10. Would you buy an 8-ounce solid chocolate Elvis Presley?_____
11. How many times in the past year have you purchased something by mail order?
    _____
12. Were you pleased with your purchase?_____
13. If so, why?_____
14. If not, why not?_____
15. Would you feel comfortable about the freshness of chocolates you received through the mail?_____
16. What would you expect to pay for shipping and handling?_____
17. Please comment on the name Chocoholic Central (love, like, dislike or hate, and why)_____
18. Please comment on the name For Chocolate Lovers Only (love, like, dislike or hate, and why)_____ _____

Your Own Personal Interior Decorator
OnCall For Pennies!

How would you like to have your very own interior decorator available any time you need her—to redecorate a single room or your entire home, or just to answer all those "little" questions, like what color to repaint the kitchen or how to make the kids' rooms more organized?

Sound wonderful but too expensive? Not so! With *OnCall Designer*, you can get professional interior design services for as little as $50 per room. And we'd like to offer you a charter membership!

But first, we need your help. In order to tailor our service to your needs and desires, we're asking you to fill out the attached questionnaire and send it back. It's a self-mailer, so it's easy! And to show our appreciation for your help, *we'll enroll you as a charter member* of *OnCall Designer*. This entitles you to:

● *Monthly newsletters packed with design tips and ideas*

● *Fantastic discounts on designer books, kits and products*

● *10% off your first decorator request*

Sound exciting? It is! When you receive your first mailing, you'll be thrilled with the quality of our products and services—everything you need to give your home that exclusive designer look. Your friends will want to know how you did it!

Ready to get started? It's as easy as 1, 2, 3:

1. Fill out the attached questionnaire.

2. Fold it and send it back in its own mailer to *OnCall Designer*.

3. Keep the certificate! When you receive your first mailing, you can use the coupon for your 10% discount on the product or service of your choice.

OnCall Designer

This Certificate entitles _____,
a charter member of *OnCall Designer*, to a full 10% off any product
or service offered in Mailing No. 1.

Enjoy!

123 Décor Drive, Dept. 1A, Art Deco, FL 30000   (305) 555-9800   www.oncalldesigner.com

OnCall Designer
Charter Member's Questionnaire

1. What is your favorite decorating style (country, contemporary, traditional, etc.)?
   _____

2. How often do you redecorate?
   ❏ Every year
   ❏ Every two years
   ❏ Every time you can stretch your budget

3. When was the last time you redecorated?_____

4. Which room or rooms did you do and why?_____

5. About how much did you spend on this project?_____

6. What are your biggest decorating problems or concerns? (Go ahead—tell us everything!)_____
   _____
   _____
   _____

7. How many people make up your household?_____

8. If you have kids at home, what are their ages?_____

9. What is the approximate square footage of your home?_____

10. Is it a house, a condo or an apartment?_____

11. How many bedrooms?_____

12. How many baths?_____

13. Do you have a separate family room, office or den? (Please circle all that apply.)

14. Do you have a patio or a deck?_____

15. Would you be interested in tips, tricks and products for outdoor entertaining?
    _____
    _____

16. What is your annual household income?_____

17. Do you have a computer with Internet access?_____

18. Do you own and use a digital camera?_____

19. Do you have a Polaroid camera?_____

We appreciate your answers and comments. They'll help us make *OnCall Designer* perfect for you. Watch for our first mailing—coming soon!

■ **FAX/E-MAIL INTERVIEWS:** Many of the principles used in direct-mail interviews also apply to these surveys. One exception: Never send an unsolicited fax that is more than one page. Give clear instructions on how to respond, and be appreciative in advance for the data you get back.

Making A List...

How do you get the names of potential customers to call or mail questionnaires to? You can get lists from many places, including your suppliers, trade associations or a list-rental company. List-rental companies can let you get access to a mailing list of a specific group of people who fit into your desired market. Refer to your local Yellow Pages for the names of list-rental companies in your area. If none are listed, contact the Direct Marketing Association in New York City. (For more information on mailing lists, see Part 6, Chapter 31.)

A less sophisticated approach to finding potential customer names is picking them at random from the phone book. If you've developed a latex glove for doctors, for example, you can get doctors' names out of the Yellow Pages. Whatever method you use to gather your information, the key to market research is using what you learn. The most sophisticated survey in the world does you no good if you ignore the information and the feedback customers provide.

GLOSSARY

FOCUS GROUP: type of primary market research where a group of potential customers (typically five to 12 of them) come together in an informal environment, under the guidance of a moderator, to discuss a product or service

LIST-RENTAL COMPANY: company that rents mailing lists of consumer or business names and addresses

MARKET RESEARCH: research into the characteristics, spending habits, location and needs of your business's target market, the industry as a whole, and the particular competitors you face

MARKET SURVEY: the study of the spending characteristics and purchasing power of the consumers who are within your business's geographic area of operation

PRIMARY RESEARCH: information you gain directly from the source, such as potential consumers

SECONDARY RESEARCH: information that has already been gathered by other agencies or organizations and compiled into statistics, reports or studies

What's In
A Name?

Naming your business

W hat's in a name? A lot, when it comes to small-business success. The right name can make your company the talk of the town; the wrong one can doom it to obscurity and failure. If you're smart, you'll put just as much effort into naming your business as you did into coming up with your idea, writing your business plan and selecting a market and location. Ideally, your name should convey the expertise, value and uniqueness of the product or service you have developed.

Finding a good business name is more difficult than ever. Many of the best names have already been trademarked. But with advertising costs and competition on the rise, a good name is crucial to creating a memorable business image. In short, the name you choose can make or break your business.

There's a lot of controversy over what makes a good business name. Some experts believe that the best names are abstract, a blank slate upon which to create an image. Others think that names should be informative so customers know immediately what your business is. Some believe that *coined* names (names that come from made-up words) are more memorable than names that use real words. Others think most coined names are forgettable. In reality, any name can be effective if it's backed by the appropriate marketing strategy.

Do It Yourself?

Given all the considerations that go into a good company name, shouldn't you consult an expert, especially if you're in a field in which your company name will be visible and may influence the success of your business? And isn't it easier to enlist the help of a naming professional?

Yes. Just as an accountant will do a better job with your taxes and an ad agency will do a better job with your ad campaign, a naming firm will be more adept at naming your firm than you will. Naming firms have elaborate systems for creating new names, and they know their way around the trademark laws. They have the expertise to advise you against bad name choices and explain why others are good. A name consultant will take this perplexing task off your hands—and do a fabulous job for you in the process.

The downside is cost. A professional naming firm may charge any-where from a few thousand dollars to $35,000 or more to develop a name. The benefit, however, is that spending this money now can save you money in the end. Professional namers may be able to find a better name—one that is so recognizable and memorable, it will cut down your costs in the long run. They have the expertise to help you avoid legal hassles with trademarks and registration—problems that can cost you plenty if you end up choosing a name that already belongs to someone else. And they are familiar with design elements, such as how a potential name might work on a sign or stationery.

If you can spare the money from your start-up budget, professional help could be a solid investment. After all, the name you choose now will affect your marketing plans for the duration of your business. If you're like most business owners, though, the responsibility for thinking up a name will be all your own. The good news: By following the same basic steps professional namers use, you can come up with a meaningful moniker that works without breaking the bank.

What's In Your Name?

Start by deciding what you want your name to communicate. To be most effective, your company name should reinforce the key elements of your business. Your work in developing a niche and a mission statement (see Part 2, Chapter 6) will help you pinpoint the elements you want to emphasize in your name.

Naming consultant Gerald Lewis of Visible Results Group uses retail as an example. "In retailing," Lewis explains, "the market is so segmented that [a name must] convey very quickly what the customer is going after. For example, if it's a warehouse store, it has to convey that impression. If it's an upscale store selling high-quality foods, it has to convey that impression. The name combined with the logo is very important in doing that." So the first and most important step in choosing a name is deciding what your business is.

Should your name be meaningful? Most experts say yes. The more your name communicates to consumers, the less effort you must exert

SMART TIP

WHERE TO GET IDEAS FOR YOUR NEW BUSINESS'S NAME? GET YOUR CREATIVE JUICES FLOWING BY PAYING ATTENTION TO ALL THE BUSINESS NAMES YOU RUN ACROSS IN YOUR DAILY LIFE—WHETHER THE BUSINESSES ARE SIMILAR TO YOURS OR NOT. WHICH NAMES DO YOU LIKE, AND WHY? WHAT MAKES THEM EFFECTIVE? WHICH ONES DON'T YOU LIKE, AND WHY ARE THEY UNAPPEALING? SOON YOU WILL HAVE A CLEARER IDEA OF WHAT MAKES A GOOD (AND BAD) BUSINESS NAME.

to explain it. Alan Siegel, chairman and CEO of Siegelgale, an international communications firm, believes name developers should give priority to real words or combinations of words over fabricated words. He explains that people prefer words they can relate to and understand. That's why professional namers universally condemn strings of numbers or initials as a bad choice.

On the other hand, it is possible for a name to be too meaningful. Naming consultant S.B. Masters cautions that business owners need to beware of names that are too narrowly defined. Common pitfalls are geographic names or generic names. Take the name "San Pablo Disk Drives" as a hypothetical example. What if the company wants to expand beyond the city of San Pablo, California? What meaning will that name have for consumers in Chicago or Pittsburgh? And what if the company diversifies beyond disk drives into software or computer instruction manuals?

Specific names make sense if you intend to stay in a narrow niche forever. If you have any ambitions of growing or expanding, however, you should find a name that is broad enough to accommodate your growth. How can a name be both meaningful and broad? Masters makes a distinction between *descriptive* names (like San Pablo Disk Drives) and *suggestive* names. Descriptive names tell something concrete about a business—what it does, where it's located and so on. Suggestive names are more abstract. They focus on what the business is about. Would you like to convey quality? Convenience? Novelty? These are the kinds of qualities that a suggestive name can express.

For example, we came up with the name "Italiatour" to help promote package tours to Italy, says Masters. Though it's not a real word, the name "Italiatour" is meaningful. Right away, you recognize what's being offered. But even better, the name "Italiatour" evokes the excitement of foreign travel. "It would have been a very different name if we had called it 'Italy-tour,'" says Masters. "But we took a foreign word 'Italia' but one that was very familiar and emotional and exciting to English speakers—and combined it with the English word

BEWARE!

ONE COMMON NAMING ERROR THAT CAN BE FATAL TO A NEW BUSINESS: CHOOSING A NAME THAT'S DIFFICULT TO PRONOUNCE. IF PEOPLE DON'T KNOW HOW TO PRONOUNCE YOUR BUSINESS NAME, THEY WILL BE HESITANT TO SAY IT. THAT MEANS THEY'RE LESS LIKELY TO TELL FRIENDS ABOUT YOUR COMPANY OR TO ASK FOR YOUR PRODUCT BY NAME.

'tour.' It's easy to say, it's unique, and it's unintimidating, but it still has an Italian flavor."

Before you start thinking up names for your new business, try to define the qualities that you want your business to be identified with. If you're starting a hearth-baked bread shop, you might want a name that conveys freshness, warmth and a homespun atmosphere. Immediately, you can see that names like "Kathy's Bread Shop" or "Arlington Breads" would communicate none of these qualities. But consider the name "Open Hearth Breads." The bread sounds home-made, hot and just out of the oven. Moreover, if you diversified your product line, you could alter the name to "Open Hearth Bakery." This change would enable you to hold on to your suggestive name without totally mystifying your established clientele.

Do's And Don'ts

When choosing a business name, keep the following tips in mind:

- **CHOOSE A NAME** that appeals ot only to you, but also to the kind of customers you are trying to attract.
- **TO GET CUSTOMERS TO RESPOND** to your business on an emotional level, choose a comforting or familiar name that conjures up pleasant memories.
- **DON'T PICK A NAME** that is long or confusing.
- **STAY AWAY FROM** cute puns hat only you understand.
- **DON'T USE THE WORD** "Inc." after your name unless your company is actually incorporated.
- **DON'T USE THE WORD** "Enterprises" after your name; this term is often used by amateurs.

Making It Up

At a time when almost every existing word in the language has been trademarked, the option of coining a name is becoming more popular. Perhaps the best names come from professional naming firms. Some examples are Acura, a division of Honda Motor Co. coined by NameLab, and Flixx, a name CDI coined for a chain of video rental stores.

Since the beginnings of NameLab, founder Ira Bachrach has been a particular champion of the coined name. He believes that properly formulated coined names can be more meaningful than existing words. For example, take the name "Acura": Although it has no dictionary definition, it actually suggests precision engineering, just as the company intended. How can that be? Bachrach and his staff created the name "Acura" from "Acu," a word segment that means "precise" in many languages. By working with meaningful word segments (what linguists call morphemes) like "Acu," Bachrach claims to produce new words that are both meaningful and unique.

"One of the reasons a new company is formed is that it has new value; it has a new idea," Bachrach contends. "If you adopt a conventional word, it's hard to express the newness of your idea. But as long as it's comprehensible, a new word will express that newness." Bachrach also admits, however, that new words are not always the best solution. A new word is complex and implies that the service or product you are offering is complex, which may not be what you want to say. Plus, naming beginners might find this type of coining beyond their capabilities.

An easier solution is to use new forms of spellings of existing words. For instance, CDI's creation: "Flixx." "Flixx" draws upon the slang term "flicks," meaning movies. But the unusual spelling makes it interesting, while the double "X" at the end makes it visually appealing. Just as important, "Flixx" is more likely to be available for trademarking than

BEWARE!

MAKE SURE YOUR BUSINESS NAME CLEARLY CONVEYS WHAT YOU DO. A FLOWER SHOP NAMED STARGAZERS, FOR EXAMPLE, PROBABLY WON'T BE THE FIRST PLACE CUSTOMERS THINK OF WHEN BUYING FLOWERS, SINCE THEY'LL PROBABLY EXPECT YOU TO SELL TELESCOPES OR NEW AGE PRODUCTS. YOUR NAME CAN EVEN AFFECT YOUR ABILITY TO RECRUIT EMPLOYEES. SOMEONE INTERESTED IN WORKING AT A FLOWER SHOP WOULDN'T CALL STARGAZERS TO ASK ABOUT JOBS SINCE THEY WOULDN'T EXPECT IT TO BE A FLORIST.

"Flicks," a factor that is important to a chain operation interested in national expansion.

Making A Name

Begin brainstorming, looking in dictionaries, books and magazines to generate ideas. Get friends and relatives to help if you like; the more minds, the merrier. Think of as many workable names as you can during this creative phase. Professional naming firms start out with a raw base of 800 to 1,000 names and work from there. You probably don't have time to think of that many, but try to come up with at least 10 names that you feel good about. By the time you examine them from all angles, you'll eliminate at least half.

The trials you put your names through will vary depending on your concerns. Some considerations are fairly universal. For instance, your name should be easy to pronounce, especially if you plan to rely heavily on print ads or signs. If people can't pronounce your name, they will avoid saying it. It's that simple. And nothing could be more counterproductive to a young company than to strangle its potential for word-of-mouth advertising.

Other considerations depend on more individual factors. For instance, if you're thinking about marketing your business globally or if you are located in a multilingual area, you should make sure that your new name has no negative connotations in other languages. On another note, Master points out, if your primary means of advertising will be in the telephone directory, you might favor names that are closer to the beginning of the alphabet. Finally, make sure that your name is in no way embarrassing. Put on the mind of a child and tinker with the letters a little. If none of your doodlings makes you snicker, it's probably OK.

Chuck Brymer, CEO of naming firm Interbrand, advises name seekers to take a close look at their competition. "The major function of a name is to distinguish your business from others," Brymer observes. "You have to weigh who's out there already, what type of branding approaches they have taken, and how you can use a name to separate yourself."

Testing, Testing

After you've narrowed the field to, say, four or five names that are memorable, expressive and can be read by the average grade-schooler, you are ready to do a trademark search.

Must every name be trademarked? No. Many small businesses don't register their business names. As long as your state government gives you the go-ahead, you may operate under an unregistered business name for as long as you like—assuming, of course, that you aren't infringing on anyone else's trade name.

But what if you are? Imagine either of these two scenarios: You are a brand-new manufacturing business just about to ship your first orders. An obscure little company in Ogunquit, Maine, considers the name of your business an infringement on their trademark and engages you in a legal battle that bankrupts your company. Or, envision your business in five years. It's a thriving, growing concern, and you are contemplating expansion. But just as you are about to launch your franchise program, you learn that a small competitor in Modesto, California, has the same name, rendering your name unusable.

To illustrate the risk you run of treading on an existing trademark with your new name, consider this: When NameLab took on the task of renaming a chain of auto parts stores, they uncovered 87,000 names already in existence for stores of this kind. That's why even the smallest businesses should at least consider having their business names screened. "You never know where your corner store is going to lead," CDI's Lewis notes. "If running a corner store is all a person is going to do, then no, he doesn't need to do a trademark search. But that local business may become a big business someday if that person has any ambition."

Master agrees. "Ensuring that your name is going to be federally registerable is important," she stresses. "And make sure that the individual states that you want to do business in will let you do business under that name."

Enlisting the help of a trademark attorney or at least a trademark search firm before you decide on a name for your business is highly advisable. After all, the extra money you spend now could save you countless hassles and expenses further down the road. Master also warns that business owners should try to contain their excitement about any one name until it has cleared the trademark search: "It can be very demoralizing to lose a name you've been fantasizing about."

Final Analysis

If you're lucky, you'll end up with three to five names that pass all your tests. How do you make your final decision?

Recall all your initial criteria. Which name best fits your objectives? Which name most accurately describes the company you have in mind? Which name do you like the best?

Master says each company arrives at a final decision in its own way. Some entrepreneurs go with their gut or use personal reasons for choosing one name over another. Others are more scientific. Some companies do consumer research or testing with focus groups to see how the names are perceived. Others might decide that their name is going to be most important seen on the back of a truck, so they have a graphic designer turn the various names into logos to see which works best as a design element.

Use any or all of these criteria. You can do it informally: Ask other people's opinions. Doodle an idea of what each name will look like on a sign or on business stationery. Read each name aloud, paying attention to the way it sounds if you foresee radio advertising or telemarketing in your future.

Say It Loud

Professional naming firms devote anywhere from six weeks to six months to the naming process. You probably won't have that much time, but plan to spend at least a few weeks on selecting a name.

Once your decision is made, start building your enthusiasm for the new name immediately. Your name is your first step toward building a strong company identity, one that should last you as long as you're in business.

To Inc. Or Not To Inc.

Choosing a business structure

O f all the decisions you make when starting a business, probably the most important one relating to taxes is the type of legal structure you select for your company.

Not only will this decision have an impact on how much you pay in taxes, but it will affect the amount of paperwork your business is required to do, the personal liability you face and your ability to raise money.

The most common forms of business are sole proprietorship, partnership, corporation and S corporation. A more recent development to these forms of business is the limited liability company (LLC) and the limited liability partnership (LLP). Because each business form comes with different tax consequences, you will want to make your selection wisely and choose the structure that most closely matches your business's needs.

If you decide to start your business as a sole proprietorship but later decide to take on partners, you can reorganize as a partnership or other entity. If you do this, be sure you notify the IRS as well as your state tax agency.

SOLE PROPRIETORSHIP

The simplest structure is the sole proprietorship, which usually involves just one individual who owns and operates the enterprise. If you intend to work alone, this structure may be the way to go.

The tax aspects of a sole proprietorship are appealing because the expenses and your income from the business are included on your personal income tax return, Form 1040. Your profits and losses are recorded on a form called Schedule C, which is filed with your 1040. The "bottom-line amount" from Schedule C is then transferred to your personal tax return. This is especially attractive because business losses you suffer may offset the income you have earned from your other sources.

As a sole proprietor, you must also file a Schedule SE with Form 1040. You use Schedule SE to calculate how much self-employment tax you owe. In addition to paying annual self-employment taxes, you must make estimated tax payments if you expect to owe at least $1,000

in federal taxes for the year and your withholding will be less than the smaller of: 1) 90 percent of your current year tax liability or 2) 100 percent of your previous year's tax liability if your adjusted gross income is $150,000 or less ($75,000 or less if you are married and filing separately). The federal government permits you to pay estimated taxes in four equal amounts throughout the year on the 15th of April, June, September and January. With a sole proprietorship, your business earnings are taxed only once, unlike other business structures. Another big plus is that you will have complete control over your business—you make all the decisions.

There are a few disadvantages to consider, however. Selecting the sole proprietorship business structure means you are personally responsible for your company's liabilities. As a result, you are placing your assets at risk, and they could be seized to satisfy a business debt or a legal claim filed against you.

Raising money for a sole proprietorship can also be difficult. Banks and other financing sources may be reluctant to make business loans to sole proprietorships. In most cases, you will have to depend on your financing sources, such as savings, home equity or family loans.

PARTNERSHIP

If your business will be owned and operated by several individuals, you'll want to take a look at structuring your business as a partnership. Partnerships come in two varieties: general partnerships and limited partnerships. In a general partnership, the partners manage the company and assume responsibility for the partnership's debts and other obligations. A limited partnership has both general and limited partners. The general partners own and operate the business and assume liability for the partnership, while the limited partners serve as investors only; they have no control over the company and are not subject to the same liabilities as the general partners.

Unless you expect to have many passive investors, limited partnerships are generally not the best choice for a new business because of all the required filings and administrative complexities. If you have two or more partners who want to be actively involved, a general partnership would be much easier to form.

One of the major advantages of a partnership is the tax treatment

Howdy, Partner!

If you decide to organize your business as a partnership, be sure you draft a partnership agreement that details how business decisions are made, how disputes are resolved, and how to handle a buyout. You'll be glad you have this agreement if for some reason you run into difficulties with one of the partners or if someone wants out of the arrangement.

The agreement should address the purpose of the business and the authority and responsibility of each partner. It's a good idea to consult an attorney experienced with small businesses for help in drafting the agreement. Here are some other issues you'll want the agreement to address:

● **HOW WILL THE OWNERSHIP INTEREST BE SHARED?** It's not necessary, for example, for two owners to equally share ownership and authority. However, if you decide to do it, make sure the proportion is stated clearly in the agreement.

● **HOW WILL DECISIONS BE MADE?** It's a good idea to establish voting rights in case a major disagreement arises. When just two partners own the business 50-50, there's the possibility of a deadlock. To avoid a deadlock, some businesses provide in advance for a third partner, a trusted associate who may own only 1 percent of the business but whose vote can break a tie.

● **WHEN ONE PARTNER WITHDRAWS, HOW WILL THE PURCHASE PRICE BE DETERMINED?** One possibility is to agree on a neutral third party, such as your banker or accountant, to find an appraiser to determine the price of the partnership interest.

● **IF A PARTNER WITHDRAWS FROM THE PARTNERSHIP, WHEN WILL THE MONEY BE PAID?** Depending on the partnership agreement, you can agree that the money be paid over three, five or 10 years, with interest. You don't want to be hit with a cash-flow crisis if the entire price has to be paid on the spot in one lump sum.

Partnership Agreement

Date _____

Commences _____

Expires _____

Location _____

THIS PARTNERSHIP AGREEMENT is made on this _____ day of _____, 20_____, between the individuals listed below:

_____

_____

_____

The partners listed above hereby agree that they shall be considered partners in business upon the commencement date of this **PARTNERSHIP AGREEMENT** for the following purpose:

_____

_____

The terms and conditions of this partnership are as follows:

1. The **NAME** of the partnership shall be: _____

2. The **PRINCIPAL PLACE OF BUSINESS** of the partnership shall be:

    _____

3. The **CAPITAL CONTRIBUTION** of each partner to the partnership shall consist of the following property, services or cash, which each partner agrees to contribute:

Name Of Partner	Capital Contribution	Agreed-Upon Cash Value	% Share

Furthermore, the **PROFITS AND LOSSES** of the partnership shall be divided by the partners according to a mutually agreeable schedule and at the end of each calendar year according to the proportions listed above.

4. Each partner shall have equal rights to **MANAGE AND CONTROL** the partnership and its business. Should there be differences between the partners concerning ordinary business matters, a decision shall be made by unanimous vote. It is understood that the partners may elect one of the partners to conduct day-to-day business of the partnership; however, no partner shall be able to bind the partnership by act or contract to any liability exceeding $ _____ without the prior written consent of each partner.

5. In the event a partner **WITHDRAWS** from the partnership for any reason, including death, the remaining partners may continue to operate the partnership using the same name. The withdrawing partner shall be obligated to sell his or her interest in the partnership. No partner shall **TRANSFER** interest in the partnership to any other party without the written consent of each partner.

6. Should the partnership be **TERMINATED** by unanimous vote, the assets and cash of the partnership shall be used to pay all creditors with the remaining amounts to be distributed to the partners according to their proportionate share.

7. Any **DISPUTES** arising between the partners as a result of this agreement shall be settled by voluntary mediation. Should mediation fail to resolve the dispute, it shall be settled by binding arbitration.

In witness whereof, this **PARTNERSHIP AGREEMENT** has been signed by the partners on the day and year listed above.

Partner _____

Partner _____

Partner _____

This partnership agreement serves only as a sample. Consult an attorney before you draw up or sign any partnership agreements.

it enjoys. A partnership does not pay tax on its income but "passes through" any profits or losses to the individual partners. At tax time, the partnership must file a tax return (Form 1065) that reports its income and loss to the IRS. In addition, each partner reports his or her share of income and loss on Schedule K-1 of Form 1065.

Personal liability is a major concern if you use a general partnership to structure your business. Like sole proprietors, general partners are personally liable for the partnership's obligations and debt. Each general partner can act on behalf of the partnership, take out loans and make decisions that will affect and be binding on all the partners (if the partnership agreement permits). Keep in mind that partnerships are also more expensive to establish than sole proprietorships because they require more legal and accounting services.

CORPORATION

The corporate structure is more complex and expensive than most other business structures. A corporation is an independent legal entity, separate from its owners, and as such, it requires complying with more regulations and tax requirements.

The biggest benefit for a business owner who decides to incorporate is the liability protection he or she receives. A corporation's debt is not considered that of its owners, so if you organize your business as a corporation, you are not putting your personal assets at risk. A corporation also can retain some of its profits, without the owner paying tax on them.

Another plus is the ability of a corporation to raise money. A corporation can sell stock, either common or preferred, to raise funds. Corporations also continue indefinitely, even if one of the shareholders dies, sells the shares or becomes disabled. The corporate structure, however, comes with a number of downsides as well. A major one is higher costs. Corporations are formed under the laws of each state with its own set of regulations. You will probably need the assistance of an attorney to

BEWARE!

ANY MONEY YOU'VE INVESTED IN A CORPORATION IS AT RISK. DESPITE THE LIABILITY PROTECTION OF A CORPORATION, MOST BANKS AND MANY SUPPLIERS REQUIRE BUSINESS OWNERS TO SIGN A PERSONAL GUARANTEE SO THEY KNOW CORPORATE OWNERS WILL MAKE GOOD ON ANY DEBT IF THE CORPORATION CAN'T.

Preincorporation Agreement

AGREEMENT made this _____ day of _____ , 20_____ , between _____ , _____ , and _____ .

WHEREAS the parties hereto wish to organize a corporation upon the terms and conditions hereinafter set forth; and

WHEREAS the parties wish to establish their mutual rights and responsibilities in relation to their organizational activities;

NOW, THEREFORE, in consideration of the premises and mutual covenants contained herein, it is agreed by and between the parties as follows:

FIRST: The parties will forthwith cause a corporation to be formed and organized under the laws of the state of _____ .

SECOND: The proposed Articles of Incorporation shall be attached hereto as Exhibit A.

THIRD: Within seven days after the issuance of the corporation's certificate of incorporation, the parties agree that the corporation's authorized stock shall be distributed, and consideration paid, as follows:

1.   _____ shares of _____ (insert common preferred) stock shall be issued to _____ in consideration of his/her payment to the corporation of $ _____ cash.

2.   _____ shares of stock shall be issued to _____ in consideration of his/her transfer to the corporation of _____ (list property, real or personal, to be transferred).

3.   _____ shares of stock shall be issued to _____ in consideration of his/her transfer to the corporation of _____ .

4.   ...etc. ...

FOURTH: The corporation shall employ _____ as its manager for a term of _____ years and at a salary of $ _____ per annum, such employment not to be terminated without cause and such salary not to be increased or decreased without the approval of _____ % of the directors.

FIFTH: The parties agree not to transfer, sell, assign, pledge or otherwise dispose of their shares until they have first offered them for sale to the corporation, and then, should the corporation refuse such offer, to the other shareholders, on a pro rata basis. The shares shall be offered at their book value to the corporation, and in the event the corporation refuses, the other shareholders shall have thirty (30) days to purchase the shares. If the corporation or other shareholders do not purchase all the offered shares, the remaining shares may be freely transferred by their owner without price restrictions.

SIXTH: The parties to this agreement promise to use their best efforts to incorporate the organization and to commence its business.

_____

_____

_____

Preincorporation agreements spell out the roles various parties will play in the formation and operation of a corporation.

guide you. In addition, because a corporation must follow more complex rules and regulations than a partnership or sole proprietorship, it requires more accounting and tax preparation services.

Another drawback to forming a corporation: Owners of the corporation pay a double tax on the business's earnings. Not only are corporations subject to corporate income tax at both the federal and state levels, but any earnings distributed to shareholders in the form of dividends are taxed at individual tax rates on their personal income tax returns.

One strategy to help soften the blow of double taxation is to pay the money out as salary to you and any other corporate shareholders who work for the company. A corporation is not required to pay tax on earnings paid as reasonable compensation, and it can deduct the payments as a business expense. However, the IRS has limits on what it believes to be reasonable compensation.

Corporate Checklist

To make sure your corporation stays on the right side of the law, heed the following guidelines:

- **CALL THE SECRETARY OF STATE** each year to check your corporate status.
- **PUT THE ANNUAL MEETINGS** (shareholders' and directors') on tickler cards.
- **CHECK ALL CONTRACTS** to ensure the proper name is used in each. The signature line should read "John Doe, President, XYZ Corp.," never just "John Doe."
- **NEVER USE YOUR NAME** followed by "DBA" (doing business as) on a contract. Renegotiate any old ones that do.
- **BEFORE UNDERTAKING** any activity out of the normal course of business—like purchasing major assets—write a corporate resolution permitting it. Keep all completed forms in the corporate book.
- **NEVER USE CORPORATE CHECKS** for personal debts and vice versa.
- **GET PROFESSIONAL ADVICE** about continued retained earnings not needed for immediate operating expenses.
- **KNOW IN ADVANCE** what franchise fees are due.

S Corporation

The S corporation is more attractive to small-business owners than a regular (or C) corporation. That's because an S corporation has some appealing tax benefits and still provides business owners with the liability protection of a corporation. With an S corporation, income and losses are passed through to shareholders and included on their individual tax returns. As a result, there's just one level of federal tax to pay.

In addition, owners of S corporations who don't have inventory can use the cash method of accounting, which is simpler than the accrual method. Under this method, income is taxable when received and expenses are deductible when paid (see Part 8, Chapter 38).

S corporations can also have up to 75 shareholders. This makes it possible to have more investors and thus attract more capital, tax experts maintain.

S corporations do come with some downsides. For example, S corporations are subject to many of the same requirements corporations must follow, and that means higher legal and tax service costs. They also must file articles of incorporation, hold directors and shareholders meetings, keep corporate minutes, and allow shareholders to vote on major corporate decisions. The legal and accounting costs of setting up an S corporation are also similar to those for a regular corporation.

Another major difference between a regular corporation and an S corporation is that S corporations can only issue one class of stock. Experts say this can hamper the company's ability to raise capital.

In addition, unlike a regular corporation, S corporation stock can only be owned by individuals, estates and certain types of trusts. In 1998, tax-exempt organizations such as qualified pension plans were added to the list. This change provides S corporations with even greater access to capital because a number of pension plans are willing to invest in closely held small-business stock.

Putting Inc. To Paper

To start the process of incorporating, contact the secretary of state or the state office that is responsible for registering corporations in your state. Ask for instructions, forms and fee schedules on incorporating.

It is possible to file for incorporation without the help of an attorney by using books and software to guide you along. Your expense will be the cost of these resources, the filing fees and other costs associated with incorporating in your state.

If you do it yourself, you will save the expense of using a lawyer, which can cost from $500 to $1,000. The disadvantage is that the process may take you some time to accomplish. There is also a chance you could miss some small but important detail in your state's law.

One of the first steps in the incorporation process is to prepare a certificate or articles of incorporation. Some states provide a printed form for this, which either you or your attorney can complete. The information requested includes the proposed name of the corporation, the purpose of the corporation, the names and addresses of those incorporating, and the location of the principal office of the corporation. The corporation will also need a set of bylaws that describe in greater detail than the articles how the corporation will run, including the responsibilities of the company's shareholders, directors and officers; when stockholder meetings will be held; and other details important to running the company. Once your articles of incorporation are accepted, the secretary of state's office will send you a certificate of incorporation.

Rules Of The Road

Once you are incorporated, be sure to follow the rules of incorporation. If you fail to do so, a court can pierce the corporate veil and hold you and the other business owners personally liable for the business's debts.

It is important to follow all the rules required by state law. You should keep accurate financial records for the corporation, showing a separation between the corporation's income and expenses and those of the owners.

The corporation should also issue stock, file annual reports and hold yearly meetings to elect company officers and directors, even if they're the same people as the shareholders. Be sure to keep minutes of shareholders' and directors' meetings. On all references to your business, make certain to identify it as a corporation, using Inc. or

Corp., whichever your state requires. You also want to make sure that whomever you will be dealing with, such as your banker or clients, knows that you are an officer of a corporation. (For more corporate guidelines, see "Corporate Checklist," on page 124.)

LIMITED LIABILITY COMPANY

Limited liability companies, often referred to as "Lacs," have been around since 1977, but their popularity among entrepreneurs is a relatively recent phenomenon. An LLC is a hybrid entity, bringing together some of the best features of partnerships and corporations.

LLCs were created to provide business owners with the liability protection that corporations enjoy without the double taxation. Earnings and losses pass through to the owners and are included on their personal tax returns.

Sound similar to an S corporation? It is, except that an LLC offers business owners even more attractions than an S corporation. For example, there is no limitation on the number of shareholders an LLC can have, unlike an S corporation, which has a limit of 75 shareholders. In addition, any member or owner of the LLC is allowed a full participatory role in the business's operation; in a limited partnership, on the other hand, partners are not permitted any say in the operation.

DOLLAR STRETCHER

IF LIMITED LIABILITY IS NOT A CON-
CERN FOR YOUR BUSINESS, YOU COULD
BEGIN AS A SOLE
PROPRIETORSHIP
OR A PARTNERSHIP
SO THAT MONETARY LOSSES IN THE
EARLY YEARS OF THE COMPANY CAN
SHELTER YOUR OTHER INCOME. THESE
"PASSED THROUGH" LOSSES CAN OFF-
SET OTHER INCOME YOU MAY HAVE.
THEN WHEN THE BUSINESS BECOMES
PROFITABLE, YOU CAN INCORPORATE.

To set up an LLC, you must file articles of organization with the secretary of state in the state where you intend to do business. Some states also require you to file an operating agreement, which is similar to a partnership agreement. Like partnerships, LLCs do not have perpetual life. Some state statutes stipulate that the company must dissolve after 30 or 40 years. Technically, the company dissolves when a member dies, quits or retires.

If you plan to operate in several states, you must determine how a state will treat an LLC formed in another state. If you decide on an LLC structure, be sure to use the services of an experienced accountant who is familiar with the various rules and regulations of LLCs.

Another recent development is the Limited Liability Partnership (LLP). With an LLP, the general partners have limited liability. For example, the partners are liable for their own malpractice and not of that of their partners. This legal form works well for those involved in a professional practice, such as physicians.

THE NONPROFIT OPTION

What about organizing your venture as a nonprofit corporation? Unlike a for-profit business, a nonprofit may be eligible for certain benefits, such as state sales, property and income tax exemptions. The IRS points out that while most federal tax-exempt organizations are nonprofit organizations, organizing as a nonprofit at the state level does not automatically grant you an exemption from federal income tax.

Another major difference between a profit and nonprofit business deals with the treatment of the profits. With a for-profit business,

Laying The Foundation

When making a decision about which business structure to use, answering the following questions should help you narrow down which entity is right for you:

- **HOW MANY OWNERS** will your company have, and what will their roles be?
- **ARE YOU CONCERNED** about the tax consequences of your business structure?
- **DO YOU WANT** to consider having employees become owners in the company?
- **CAN YOU DEAL** with the added costs that come with selecting a complicated business structure?
- **HOW MUCH PAPERWORK** are you prepared to deal with?
- **DO YOU WANT** to make all the decisions in the company?
- **ARE YOU PLANNING** to go public?
- **DO YOU WANT** to protect your personal resources from debts or other claims against your company?
- **ARE FAMILY SUCCESSION** issues a concern?

the owners and shareholders generally receive the profits. With a nonprofit, any money that is left after the organization has paid its bills is put back into the organization. Some types of nonprofits can receive contributions that are tax deductible to the individual who contributes to the organization. Keep in mind that nonprofits are organized to provide some benefit to the public.

Nonprofits are incorporated under the laws of the state in which they are established. To receive federal tax-exempt status, the organization must apply with the IRS. Two applications are required. First, you must request an Employer Identification Number (EIN) and then apply for recognition of exemption by filing Form 1023 (*Charitable Organizations*) or 1024 (*Other Tax-Exempt Organizations*), with the necessary filing fee. (For information on how to apply for an EIN, see Part 8, Chapter 41.)

The IRS identifies the different types of nonprofit organizations by the tax code by which they qualify for exempt status. One of the most common forms is 501(c)(3), which is set up to do charitable, educational, scientific, religious and literary work. This includes a wide range of organizations, from continuing education centers to outpatient clinics and hospitals.

The IRS also mandates that there are certain activities tax-exempt organizations can't engage in if they want to keep their exempt status. For example, a section 50l(c)(3) organization cannot intervene in political campaigns.

Remember, nonprofits still have to pay employment taxes, but in some states they may be exempt from paying sales tax. Check with your state to make sure you understand how nonprofit status is treated in your area. In addition, nonprofits may be hit with unrelated business income tax (UBIT). This is regular income from a trade or business that is not substantially related to the charitable purpose. An exempt organization with $1,000 or more of gross income from an unrelated business must file Form 990-T and pay tax on the income.

If your nonprofit has revenues of more than $25,000 a year, be sure to file an annual report (Form 990) with the IRS. Form 990-EZ

Choosing A Legal Form For Your Business

This chapter provides an overview of the various legal forms under which you might choose to operate your business. This table summarizes the characteristics of six different forms of business: sole proprietorships, general partnerships, limited partnerships, limited liability companies (LLCs), corporations in general, and S corporations. We list four characteristics for each legal form:

- *Control: Who holds authority in a business operating under this form?*
- *Liability: Who is legally liable for any losses the business experiences?*
- *Tax: How will business income and expenses be reported?*
- *Continuity: If a business owner dies or wants to leave the business, does the business continue?*

Sole Proprietorship

Control	Liability	Tax	Continuity
Owner maintains complete control over the business.	Owner is solely liable. His or her personal assets are open to attack in any legal case.	Owner reports all income and expenses on personal tax return.	Business terminates upon the owner's death or withdrawal. Owner can sell but will no longer remain the proprietor.

General Partnership

Control	Liability	Tax	Continuity
Each partner has the authority to enter contracts and make other business decisions unless the partnership agreement stipulates otherwise.	Each partner is liable for all business debts.	Each partner reports partnership income on their individual tax returns. The business does not pay any taxes as its own entity.	Unless the partnership agreement makes other provisions, a partnership dissolves upon the death or withdrawal of a partner.

Limited Partnership

Control	Liability	Tax	Continuity
General partners control the business.	General partners are personally responsible for partnership liabilities. Limited partners are liable for the amount of their investment.	Partnership files annual taxes. Limited and general partners report their share of partnership income or loss on their individual returns.	Death of a limited partner does not dissolve business, but death of general partner might, unless the agreement makes other provisions.

Limited Liability Company

Control	Liability	Tax	Continuity
Owner or partners have authority.	Partners are not liable for business debts.	The partners report income and income tax on their individual tax returns.	Different states have different laws regarding the continuity of LLCs.

Corporation

Control	Liability	Tax	Continuity
Shareholders appoint the board of directors, which appoints officers, who hold the highest authority.	Offers liability protection. A corporation's debt is not considered that of its owners.	Corporation pays its own taxes. Shareholders pay tax on their dividends.	The corporation is its own legal entity and can survive the deaths of owners, partners and shareholders.

S Corporation

Control	Liability	Tax	Continuity
See entry for corporations.	See entry for corporations.	Shareholders report shares of corporate profit or loss on their individual tax returns.	See entry for corporations.

is a shortened version of 990 and is designed for use by small exempt organizations with total assets at the end of the year of less than $25,000.

Form 990 asks you to provide information on the organization's income, expenses and staff salaries that exceed $50,000. You also may have to comply with a similar state requirement. The IRS report must be made available for public review. If you use the calendar year as your accounting period (see Part 8, Chapter 41), file Form 990 by May 15.

For more information on IRS tax-exempt status, download IRS publication 557 (*Types of Tax-Exempt Organizations*) at www.irs.gov.

Even after you settle on a business structure, remember that the circumstances that make one type of business organization favorable are always subject to changes in the laws. It makes sense to reassess your form of business from time to time to make sure you are using the one that provides the most benefits.

GLOSSARY

CORPORATION: a business structure organized under state law and generally treated as a separate tax entity

DEDUCTIONS: business and other expenses that reduce your income

LIMITED LIABILITY COMPANY (LLC): a hybrid business structure that combines tax advantages of a partnership with liability protection of a corporation

PARTNERSHIP: a business that's unincorporated and organized by two or more individuals

S CORPORATION: a type of corporation that provides its owners with tax treatment that is similar to a partnership

SELF-EMPLOYMENT TAX: tax paid by a self-employed person to help finance Social Security and Medicare

SOLE PROPRIETORSHIP: a business entity that usually involves just one individual who owns and operates the enterprise

Get With
The Plan

Creating a winning business plan

Tell friends you're starting a business, and you will get as many different pieces of advice as you have friends. One piece of wisdom, however, that transcends all others is this: Write a business plan.

According to a study conducted for AT&T, only 42 percent of small-business owners bother to develop a formal business plan; of those who do use a plan, 69 percent say it was a major contributor to their success.

Some people think you don't need a business plan unless you're trying to borrow money. Of course, it's true that you do need a good plan if you intend to approach a lender—whether a banker, a venture capitalist or any number of other sources—for start-up capital. But a business plan is more than a pitch for financing; it's a guide to help you define and meet your business goals.

Just as you wouldn't start off on a cross-country drive without a road map, you should not embark on your new business without a business plan to guide you. A business plan won't automatically make you a success, but it will help you avoid some common causes of business failure, such as under-capitalization or lack of an adequate market.

As you research and prepare your business plan, you'll find weak spots in your business idea that you'll be able to repair. You'll also discover areas with potential you may not have thought about before—and ways to profit from them. Only by putting together a business plan can you decide whether your great idea is really worth your time and investment.

What is a business plan, and how do you put one together? Simply stated, a business plan conveys your business goals, the strategies you'll use to meet them, potential problems that may confront your business and ways to solve them, the organizational structure of your business (including titles and responsibilities), and, finally, the amount of capital required to finance your venture and keep it going until it breaks even.

Sound impressive? It can be, if put together properly. A good business plan follows generally accepted guidelines for both form and content. There are three primary parts to a business plan.

The first is the *business concept*, where you discuss the industry, your business structure, your product or service and how you plan to make your business a success.

The second is the *marketplace section*, in which you describe and analyze potential customers: who and where they are, what makes them buy and so on. Here, you also describe the competition and how you will position yourself to beat it.

Finally, the *financial section* contains your income and cash-flow statement, balance sheet and other financial ratios, such as break-even analyses. This part may require help from your accountant and a good spreadsheet software program.

Breaking these three major sections down further, a business plan consists of seven major components:

1. Executive summary
2. Business description
3. Market strategies
4. Competitive analysis
5. Design and development plan
6. Operations and management plan
7. Financial factors

In addition to these sections, a business plan should also have a cover, title page and table of contents.

Executive Summary

Anyone looking at your business plan will first want to know what kind of business you are starting. So the business concept section should start with an executive summary, which outlines and describes the product or service you will sell.

The executive summary is the first thing the reader sees. Therefore, it must make an immediate impact by clearly stating the nature of the business and, if you are seeking capital, the type of financing you want. The executive summary describes the business, its legal form of operation (sole proprietorship, partnership, corporation or limited liability company), the amount and purpose of the loan requested, the repayment schedule, the borrower's equity share, and the debt-to-equity ratio after the loan, security or collateral is offered. Also listed

SMART TIP

ALTHOUGH IT'S THE FIRST PART OF THE PLAN TO BE READ, THE EXECUTIVE SUMMARY IS MOST EFFECTIVE IF IT'S THE LAST PART YOU WRITE. BY WAITING UNTIL YOU HAVE FINISHED THE REST OF YOUR BUSINESS PLAN, YOU ENSURE YOU HAVE ALL THE RELEVANT INFORMATION IN FRONT OF YOU. THIS ALLOWS YOU TO CREATE AN EXECUTIVE SUMMARY THAT HITS ALL THE CRUCIAL POINTS OF YOUR PLAN.

Sample Executive Summary

The business will provide ecology-minded consumers with an environmentally safe disposable diaper that will feature all the elements that are popular among users of disposable diapers but will include the added benefit of biodegradability. The product, which is patent pending, will target current users of disposable diapers who are deeply concerned about the environment as well as those consumers using cloth diapers and diaper services. The product will be distributed to wholesalers who will, in turn, sell to major supermarkets, specialty stores, department stores and major toy stores.

The company was incorporated in 1989 in the state of California under the name of Softie Baby Care. The company's CEO, president and vice president have more than 30 years of combined experience in the diaper industry.

With projected net sales of $871 million in its third year, the business will generate pretax net profits of 8 percent. Given this return, investment in the company is very attractive. Softie Baby Care Inc. will require a total amount of $26 million over three stages to start the business.

1. **THE FIRST STAGE** will require $8 million for product and market development.
2. **THE SECOND STAGE** of financing will demand $12 million for implementation.
3. **THE THIRD STAGE** will require $6 million for working capital until break-even is reached.

First-stage capital will be used to purchase needed equipment and materials to develop the product and market it initially. To obtain its capital requirements, the company is willing to relinquish 25 percent equity to first-stage investors.

The company has applied for a patent on the primary technology that the business is built around, which allows the plastic within a disposable diaper to break down upon extended exposure to sunlight. Lease agreements are also in place for a 20,000-square-foot facility in a light industrial area of Los Angeles, as well as for major equipment needed to begin production. Currently, the company has funding of $3 million from the three principals, with purchase orders for 500,000 units already in hand.

are the market value, estimated value or price quotes for any equipment you plan to purchase with the loan proceeds.

Your executive summary should be short and businesslike—generally between half a page and one page, depending on how complicated the use of funds is.

Business Description

This section expands on the executive summary, describing your business in much greater detail. It usually starts with a description of your industry. Is the business retail, wholesale, food service, manufacturing or service-oriented? How big is the industry? Why has it become so popular? What kind of trends are responsible for the industry's growth? Prove, with statistics and anecdotal information, how much opportunity there is in the industry.

Explain the target market for your product or service, how the product will be distributed, and the business' support systems—that is, its advertising, promotions and customer service strategies.

Next, describe your product or service. Discuss the product's applications and end users. Emphasize any unique features or variations that set your product or service apart from others in your industry.

If you're using your business plan for financing purposes, explain why the money you seek will make your business more profitable. Will you use the money to expand, to create a new product or to buy new equipment?

Market Strategies

Here's where you define your market—its size, structure, growth prospects, trends and sales potential. Based on research, interviews and sales analysis, the marketplace section should focus on your customers and your competition. How much of the market will your product or service be able to capture?

The answer is tricky since so many variables influence it. Think of it as a combination of words and numbers. Write down the who, what, when, where and why of your customers. (You know all this because you researched it in Part 2, Chapter 7.) The answer is critical to determining how you will develop pricing strategies and distribution channels.

Be sure to document how and from what sources you compiled your market information. Describe how your business fits into the overall market picture. Emphasize your unique selling proposition

(USP)—in other words, what makes you different? Explain why your approach is ideal for your market.

Once you've clearly defined your market and established your sales goals, present the strategies you'll use to fulfill those objectives.

■ **PRICE:** Thoroughly explain your pricing strategy and how it will affect the success of your product or service. Describe your projected costs, then determine pricing based on the profit percentage you expect. Costs include materials, distribution, advertising and overhead. Many experts recommend adding 25 to 50 percent to each cost estimate, especially overhead, to ensure you don't underestimate.

■ **DISTRIBUTION:** This includes the entire process of moving the product from the factory to the end user. The type of distribution network you choose depends on your industry and the size of the market. How much will it cost to reach your target market? Does that market consist of upscale customers who will pay extra for a premium product or service, or budget-conscious consumers looking for a good deal? Study your competitors to see what channels they use. Will you use the same channels or a different method that may give you a strategic advantage?

■ **SALES:** Explain how your sales force (if you have one) will meet its goals, including elements such as pricing flexibility, sales presentations, lead generation and compensation policies.

Competitive Analysis

How does your business relate to the competition? The competitive analysis section answers this question. Using what you've learned from your market research, detail the strengths and weaknesses of your competitors, the strategies that give you a distinct advantage, any barriers you can develop to prevent new competition from entering the market and any weaknesses in your competitors' service or product development cycle that you can take advantage of.

HOT LINK

LOOKING FOR INSPIRATION? THE CENTER FOR BUSINESS PLANNING'S LIBRARY OF BUSINESS PLANS INCLUDES FINALISTS IN THE MOOT CORP. COMPETITION AT THE UNIVERSITY OF TEXAS. THE SITE (WWW.BUSINESSPLANS. ORG) ALSO OFFERS RESEARCH RESOURCES AND AN INTER-ACTIVE BUSINESS STRATEGY ANALYSIS. AND THE SBA (WWW.SBAONLINE.SBA.GOV/STARTING/ INDEXBUSPLANS.HTML) OFFERS CLEAR, CONCISE BUSINESS PLAN OUTLINES AND TUTORIALS.

The competitive analysis is an important part of your business plan. Often, start-up entrepreneurs mistakenly believe their product or service is the first of its kind and fail to recognize that competition exists. In reality, every business has competition, whether direct or indirect. Your plan must show that you recognize this and have a strategy to deal with the competition.

Design And Development Plan

This section describes a product's design and charts its development within the context of production, marketing and the company itself. If you have an idea but have not yet developed the product or service, if you plan to improve an existing product or service, or if you own an existing company and plan to introduce a new product or service, this section is extremely important. (If your product is already completely designed and developed, you don't need to complete this section. If you are offering a service, you will need to concentrate only on the development half of the section.)

The design section should thoroughly describe the product's design and the materials used; include any diagrams if applicable. The development plan generally covers these three areas: 1) product development, 2) market development and 3) organizational development. If you're offering a service, cover only the last two.

Create a schedule that shows how the product, marketing strategies and organization will develop over time. The schedule should be tied to a development budget so expenses can be tracked throughout the design and development process.

Operations And Management Plan

Here, you describe how your business will function on a daily basis. This section explains logistics such as the responsibilities of each member of the management team, the tasks assigned to each division of the company (if applicable), and the capital and expense requirements for operating the business.

SMART TIP

YOUR LOCAL SMALL BUSINESS DEVELOPMENT CENTER CAN HELP YOU DEVELOP A BUSINESS PLAN. CALL YOUR LOCAL SBA OFFICE FOR LOCATIONS NEAR YOU.

Describe the business's managers and their qualifications, and specify what type of support staff will be needed for the business to run efficiently. Any potential benefits or pitfalls to the community should also be presented, such as new job creation, economic growth, and possible effects on the environment from manufacturing and how they will be handled to conform with local, state and federal regulations.

Financial Factors

The financial statements are the backbone of your business plan. They show how profitable your business will be in the short and long term, and should include the following: The *income statement* details the business's cash-generating ability. It projects such items as revenue, expenses, capital (in the form of depreciation) and cost of goods. You should generate a monthly income statement for the business's first year, quarterly statements for the second year and annual statements for each year thereafter (usually for three, five or 10 years, with five being the most common).

The *cash-flow statement* details the amount of money coming into and going out of the business—monthly for the first year and quarterly for each year thereafter. The result is a profit or loss at the end of the period represented by each column. Both profits and losses carry over to the last column to show a cumulative amount. If your cash-flow statement shows you consistently operating at a loss, you will probably need additional cash to meet expenses. Most businesses have some seasonal variations in their budgets, so re-examine your cash-flow calculations if they look identical every month.

The *balance sheet* paints a picture of the business's financial strength in terms of assets, liabilities and equity over a set period. You should generate a balance sheet for each year profiled in the development of your business.

After these essential financial documents, include any relevant summary information that's not included elsewhere in the plan but will significantly affect the business. This could include ratios such as return on investment, break-even point or return on assets. Your accountant can help you decide what information is best to include.

Many people consider the financial section of a business plan the most difficult to write. If you haven't started your business yet, how do you know what your income will be? You have a few options. The first is to enlist your accountant's help. An accountant can take your raw data

Finding Funding

One of the primary purposes of a business plan is to help you obtain financing for your business. When writing your plan, however, it's important to remember who those financing sources are likely to be.

Bankers, investors, venture capitalists and investment advisors are sophisticated in business and financial matters. How can you ensure your plan makes the right impression? Three tips are key:

1. **AVOID HYPE.** While many entrepreneurs tend to be gamblers who believe in relying on their gut feelings, financial types are likely to go "by the book." If your business plan praises your idea with superlatives like "one of a kind," "unique" or "unprecedented," your readers are likely to be turned off. Wild, unsubstantiated promises or unfounded conclusions tell financial sources you are inexperienced, naive and reckless.

2. **POLISH THE EXECUTIVE SUMMARY.** Potential investors receive so many business plans, they cannot afford to spend more than a few minutes evaluating each one. If at first glance your proposal looks dull, poorly written or confusing, investors will toss it aside without a second thought. In other words, if your executive summary doesn't grab them, you won't get a second chance.

3. **MAKE SURE YOUR PLAN IS COMPLETE.** Even if your executive summary sparkles, you need to make sure the rest of your plan is just as good and that all the necessary information is included. Some entrepreneurs are in such a hurry to get financing, they submit a condensed or preliminary business plan, promising to provide more information if the recipient is interested. This approach usually backfires for two reasons: First, if you don't provide information upfront, investors will assume the information doesn't exist yet and that you are stalling for time. Second, even if investors are interested in your preliminary plan, their interest may cool in the time it takes you to compile the rest of the information.

When presenting a business plan, you are starting from a position of weakness. And if potential investors find any flaws in your plan, they gain an even greater bargaining advantage. A well-written and complete plan gives you greater negotiating power and boosts your chances of getting financing on your own terms.

and organize it into categories that will satisfy all the requirements of a financial section, including monthly and yearly sales projections. Or, if you are familiar with accounting procedures, you can do it yourself with the help of a good spreadsheet program. (For more information on developing financial statements, see Part 8, Chapter 39.)

A Living Document

You've put a lot of time and effort into your business plan. What happens when it's finished? A good business plan should not gather dust in a drawer. Think of it as a living document, and refer to it often. A well-written plan will help you define activities and responsibilities within your business as well as identify and achieve your goals.

To ensure your business plan continues to serve you well, make it a habit to update yours annually. Set aside a block of time near the beginning of the calendar year, fiscal year or whenever is convenient for you. Meet with your accountant or financial advisor, if necessary, to go over and update financial figures. Is your business heading in the right direction… or has it wandered off course?

Making it a practice to review your business plan annually is a great way to start the year fresh and reinvigorated. It lets you catch any problems before they become too large to solve. It also ensures that if the possibility of getting financing, participating in a joint venture or other such occasion arises, you'll have an updated plan ready to go so you don't miss out on a good opportunity.

Whether you're writing it for the first time or updating it for the fifteenth, creating a good business plan doesn't mean penning a 200-page novel or adding lots of fancy clip art and footnotes. It means proving to yourself and others that you understand your business, and you know what's required to make it grow and prosper.

GLOSSARY

BALANCE SHEET: paints a picture of the business's financial strength in terms of assets, liabilities and equity over a set period

Cash-flow statement: details the money coming into and going out of the business—monthly for the first year and quarterly for each year thereafter

Competitive analysis: section of a business plan that assesses the competition's strengths and weaknesses

Design and development plan: section of a business plan that describes the product's design and charts its development within the context of production, marketing and the company itself

Distribution: means of getting product to the end user; describes entire process of moving product from factory to end user

Executive summary: the opening section of a business plan; describes the business, product or service in brief

Income statement: projects such items as revenue, expenses, capital (in the form of depreciation) and cost of goods

Operations and management plan: section of a business plan that describes how the business will function on a day-to-day basis

Unique selling proposition (USP): what differentiates your product or service from others of a similar type; what makes it unique

Mother, May I?

Don't forget business licenses and permits

When you're embroiled in the excitement of starting a new business, it's easy to ignore the need for licenses and permits. "Oh, that's just bureaucratic mumbo-jumbo," you think. "I'll take care of those little details later, when things settle down."

Sure, getting licenses and permits is about as much fun as visiting the dentist. But failing to do it—and do it right from the beginning—is one of the most common mistakes new entrepreneurs make.

Some licenses or permits are costly and hard to get, and you need to figure them into your start-up budget. Your grand plan for founding a fancy nightclub could grind to a screeching halt if you can't get (or can't afford) the liquor license. It's better to find that out in the beginning than after you've redecorated the building and hired the waitresses.

Or what if your business becomes a success beyond your wildest dreams…then, a few years from now, gets shut down by the county when it's discovered you don't have the proper license or permits? Short of a shutdown, lack of a license could lead to hefty fines, restrictions on your operations, lawsuits from suppliers or employees, problems with the IRS…what a headache! This is one situation where an ounce of prevention really pays off.

Following you'll find some of the most common licenses and permits business owners may need and where you can go for more information.

Fictitious Name (DBA)

If you are starting a sole proprietorship or a partnership, you have the option of choosing a business name or *dba* ("doing business as") for your businesses. This is known as a *fictitious business name*. If you want to operate your business under a name other than your own (for instance, Carol Axelrod doing business as "Darling Donut Shoppe"), you may be required by the county, city or state to register your fictitious name.

Procedures for doing this vary among states. In many states, all you have to do is go to the county offices

SMART TIP

IN MOST CASES, THE NEWSPAPER THAT PRINTS YOUR FICTITIOUS NAME AD WILL ALSO FILE THE NECESSARY PAPERS WITH THE COUNTY FOR A SMALL FEE.

GARY L. GRANVILLE
COUNTY CLERK-RECORDER
12 CIVIC CENTER PLAZA, ROOM 106
POST OFFICE BOX 238
SANTA ANA, CA 92702-0238

FICTITIOUS BUSINESS NAME STATEMENT
Print legibly or type all information and DO NOT ABBREVIATE.

THE FOLLOWING PERSON(S) IS (ARE) DOING BUSINESS AS:

1	Fictitious Business Name(s) Business Phone No. (_____) _____
1A.	☐ New Statement ☐ Refile—List Previous No._____ ☐ Change
2.	Street Address, City & State of Principal place of Business State Zip Code (Do **NOT** use a P.O. Box)
3.	Full name of Registrant (If Corporation, enter corporation name) If Corporation/L.L.C. State of Incorporation or organization Res./Corp. Address (Do **NOT** use a P.O. Box) City State Zip Code
	Full name of Registrant (If Corporation, enter corporation name) If Corporation/L.L.C. State of Incorporation or organization Res./Corp. Address (Do **NOT** use a P.O. Box) City State Zip Code
	Full name of Registrant (If Corporation, enter corporation name) If Corporation/L.L.C. State of Incorporation or organization Res./Corp. Address (Do **NOT** use a P.O. Box) City State Zip Code
4.	(CHECK ONE ONLY) This business is conducted by ( ) an individual ( ) a general partnership ( ) a limited partnership ( ) an unincorporated association other than a partnership ( ) a corporation ( ) a business trust ( ) co-partners ( ) husband and wife ( ) joint venture ( ) Limited Liability Co. ( ) Other-Specify _____
5.	Have you started doing business yet? Yes_____ Insert the date you started: _____ No _____	NOTICE: THIS FICTITIOUS NAME STATEMENT EXPIRES FIVE YEARS FROM THE DATE IT WAS FILED IN THE OFFICE OF THE COUNTY CLERK-RECORDER. A NEW FICTITIOUS BUSINESS NAME STATEMENT MUST BE FILED BEFORE THAT DATE. THE FILING OF THIS STATEMENT DOES NOT OF ITSELF AUTHORIZE THE USE IN THIS STATE OF A FICTITIOUS BUSINESS NAME IN VIOLATION OF THE RIGHTS OF ANOTHER UNDER FEDERAL, STATE, OR COMMON LAW (SEE SECTION 14400 ET SEQ., BUSINESS AND PROFESSIONS CODE).
6.	If Registrant is NOT a corporation, sign below: (See Instructions on the reverse side of this form.) Signature_____ _____ (Type or Print Name)	If Registrant is a corporation, an officer of the corporation signs below: If Registrant is a limited liability company, a manager or an officer signs below. Limited Liability Company Name/Corporation Name Signature and Title of Officer or Manager Print or Type Officer's/Manager's Name and Title

(THIS FEE APPLIES AT THE TIME OF FILING)
FILING FEE $31.00 FOR ONE BUSINESS NAME.
$7.00 FOR EACH ADDITIONAL BUSINESS NAME.
$7.00 FOR EACH ADDITIONAL PARTNER AFTER FIRST TWO.
PROVIDE RETURN STAMPED ENVELOPE IF MAILED.
➡ F059-FictitiousBus.Stmt   (R8/97)   WHITE – CLERK-RECORDER'S COPY, PINK – BANK, NEWSPAPER AND REGISTRANT

and pay a registration fee to the county clerk. In other states, you also have to place a fictitious name ad in a local newspaper for a certain amount of time. The cost of filing a fictitious name notice ranges from $10 to $100. Your local bank may require a fictitious name certificate to open a business account for you; if so, they can tell you where to go to register. In most states, corporations don't have to file fictitious business names unless the corporations do business under names other than their own. Incorporation documents have the same effect for corporate businesses as fictitious name filings do for sole proprietorships and partnerships. (For more on incorporating, see Part 2, Chapter 9.)

147

Business License

Contact your city's business license department to find out about getting a business license, which grants you the right (after you pay a fee, of course) to operate in that city. When you file your license application, the city planning or zoning department will check to make sure your area is zoned for the purpose you want to use it for and that there are enough parking spaces to meet the codes. If you are opening your business in a building that previously housed a similar business, you are not likely to run into any problems.

You can't operate in an area that is not zoned for your type of business unless you first get a variance or conditional-use permit. To get a variance, you'll need to present your case before the planning commission in your city. In many cases, variances are quite easy to get, as long as you can show that your business won't disrupt the character of the neighborhood where you plan to locate.

BEWARE!

INVESTIGATE ZONING ORDINANCES CAREFULLY IF YOU PLAN TO START A BUSINESS AT HOME.
RESIDENTIAL AREAS TEND TO HAVE STRICT ZONING REGULATIONS PREVENTING BUSINESS USE OF THE HOME.

EVEN SO, IT IS POSSIBLE TO GET A VARIANCE OR CONDITIONAL-USE PERMIT. FOR MORE INFORMATION, SEE CHAPTER 18.

Health Department Permit

If you plan to sell food, either directly to customers or as a wholesaler to other retailers, you will need a county health department permit. This costs about $25 and varies depending on the size of the business and the amount and type of equipment you have. The health department will want to inspect your facilities before issuing the permit.

SMART TIP

IT'S GENERALLY MUCH EASIER TO GET A BEER AND WINE LICENSE  THAN A LIQUOR LICENSE. BEER-AND-WINE LICENSES ARE USUALLY ISSUED FOR AN ANNUAL PERIOD AND ARE EASY TO RENEW IF YOU HAVEN'T COMMITTED ANY OFFENSES, SUCH AS SELLING ALCOHOLIC DRINKS TO MINORS.

Liquor, Wine And Beer Licenses

In most states, you'll need to get one type of license to serve wine and beer and another to serve hard liquor. A liquor license is more difficult to obtain than a beer-and-wine license. In some areas, no new liquor licenses are being issued at all; you can only obtain one by buying it from

CITY OF IRVINE
APPLICATION FOR HOME OCCUPATION LICENSE*

License No. _____

BUSINESS NAME: _____

APPLICANT NAME: _____ BUSINESS PHONE: _____

HOME ADDRESS: _____

SPECIFIC TYPE OF BUSINESS/PRODUCT(S): _____

Regulations for Home Occupation Permits are provided so that certain incidental and accessory uses may be established in residential developments under conditions which will ensure their compatibility with the neighborhood. They are intended to protect the rights of the residents to engage in certain home occupations that are harmonious with a residential environment.

Please check with your homeowner's association, or rental property management company for any Conditions, Covenants & Restrictions that may restrict business uses at your property.

In order to be issued a Home Occupation Permit, you must ensure the City of Irvine that the proposed use complies with City requirements as identified in Section V.E-209 of the Zoning Ordinance. By reading and understanding the regulations listed below, as well as signing this application form, you are certifying that your home occupation will conform to all applicable City of Irvine Ordinances:
It is the responsibility of the applicant/licensee to ensure that his/her business complies with all applicable city codes and the city zoning ordinance. In the event it is determined that the business does not comply, the business license may be revoked by the city.

1. My home occupation is an incidental and accessory use and does not change the residential character of my residence;
2. My residence is not the point of customer pick-up or delivery, and my home occupation does not cause an increase in vehicular traffic in the neighborhood;
3. My home occupation is conducted only within an enclosed structure (not in my yard or driveway);
4. There will not at any time be any signs or other exterior evidence relating to my home occupation;
5. My home occupation may be conducted in the garage, but will not, under any circumstances, utilize any space required for off-street parking (as identified in the City of Irvine Zoning Ordinance, Section V.E-400 et. seq.);
6. I understand the only employees who may work at my home-based business are residents of my home;
7. I will not utilize or use any electrical or mechanical equipment which may create visible or audible interference in radio, television or telephone service or may cause fluctuations in line voltage outside the residence; and
8. My home occupation does not now, nor will in the future create noise odors or use Hazardous Materials, in excess of that normally associated with a residential use.

My Home Occupation does not comply with Item _____, above. *Please contact the Development Assistance Center: (714) 724-6308 to discuss you situation, prior to submitting this application.*

I do hereby certify that, under penalty of perjury, to the best of my knowledge and belief, the information contained herein is true and correct:

Signed: _____ Date: _____

If you have any questions, please contact the Development Assistance Center at (714) 724-6308. If we are unable to approve you request for a home-based business you will be invited to attend a hearing pursuant to City Council Ordinance 93-06, Sections II.M-217 and II.M-218, prior to denying your business license. If you are not satisfied with the decision made following your hearing, you may file a Notice of Appeal with the City Clerk within thirty (30) days of receipt of the written decision to deny the license.

* This application must be filed with the completed Business License application.

(For City of Irvine Staff Use Only)

Community Development Department Planning Recommendation:

	APPROVE	DENY

_____ Date _____
(Signature of Community Development Department Representative)
Form #0-27 Rev. 12/96[xxx]

CITY OF IRVINE ● ONE CIVIC CENTER PLAZA ● P.O. BOX 19575, IRVINE, CALIFORNIA 92623-9575 ● (714) 724-6000

an existing license holder. As a result, although the original licenses may have cost less than $100, competition has forced the going price from $2,000 to tens of thousands, depending on the location. One advantage of buying out an existing restaurant is that if it served liquor, you may be able to acquire the license as part of the deal.

If your area is still issuing liquor licenses, in most cases you will have to file an application with the state beverage control board, then post a notice on the premises of your intent to sell liquor. In some states, the beverage control board requires holders of liquor licenses to keep all purchase records for a certain number of years. These records are subject to inspection by the beverage control board or the IRS during that time.

The white pages of your telephone directory will have the number for the nearest beverage control agency, which can give you all the information you need about both types of licenses.

Fire Department Permit

You may need to get a permit from your fire department if your business uses any flammable materials or if your premises will be open to the public. In some cities, you have to get this permit before you open for business. Other areas don't require permits but simply schedule periodic inspections of your business to see if you meet fire safety

License No. _____

BUSINESS LICENSE APPLICATION

Please return to: City of Irvine - Business License
One Civic Center Plaza • P.O. Box 19575
Irvine, California 92623-9575 • (714) 724-6310

Business Name _____

Business Name (other) _____

Street Address _____ Suite _____
(May not be a P.O. Box)

City _____ State _____ Zip _____

Mailing Address _____ City _____ State _____ Zip _____

Business Phone ( ) _____ State Employer ID (SEIN) _____

State Sales Tax No.(RESALE) _____ Federal Employer ID (FEIN) _____

Business Fax ( ) _____

Please describe the exact nature of business activity to be conducted _____

Indicate ownership type ☐Sole proprietorship ☐Partnership ☐Corporation ☐Trust ☐Ltd liability Co.

Indicate type of business ☐Retail ☐Wholesale ☐Manufacturing ☐Service

How many people including owners are working in Irvine for your business?_____

State Professional License No._____ Class _____ Expiration _____

State Contractor License No. _____ Class _____ Expiration _____

I declare under penalty of perjury that I am licensed by the State Contractors License Board _____
(Contractors only) Signature

* THE NAME OF THE FIRST PERSON LISTED WILL BE PRINTED ON THE BUSINESS LICENSE CERTIFICATE
List residence, address, phone, title and driver's license number of Owner, President, Partner, CEO, CFO, etc.

1.

| name | residence address | city | state | zip |

( )

| phone | title | driver's license # | soc. security # |

2.

| name | residence address | city | state | zip |

( )

| phone | title | driver's license # | soc. security # |

On what date will/did your business begin operating in Irvine? _____

ANNUAL GROSS RECEIPTS $ _____

FORM 22-05, REV 05/97[PM]

regulations. If you don't, they will issue a citation. Businesses such as theaters, restaurants, nightclubs, bars, retirement homes, day-care centers and anywhere else where lots of people congregate are subject to especially close and frequent scrutiny by the fire department.

Air And Water Pollution Control Permit

Many cities now have departments that work to control air and water pollution. If you burn any materials, discharge anything into the sewers or waterways, or use products that produce gas (such as paint sprayers), you may have to get a special permit from this

---

Do you sell taxable merchandise or provide a taxable service such as renting merchandise or fabrication labor from you location in Irvine? ❏No ❏Yes

If Yes: What type of goods are sold? _____

Are sales of your product made at the "Business Address" on this application? ❏No ❏Yes
Are sales made at other locations in this city? ❏No ❏Yes

Please list the other sales locations, if applicable. _____

Are you a sales AGENT for another company? ❏No ❏Yes

Please list the name(s) of the person or company. _____

Is this application made to move an existing business from another location? ❏No ❏Yes

If yes, please list the former address _____

Please indicate who the City should contact in the event of an emergency:

1. _____ _____ ( ) _____
    name   title   phone

2. _____ _____ ( ) _____
    name   title   phone

Please list other business locations in Irvine:

1. _____ _____ ( ) _____
    name   address   phone

2. _____ _____ ( ) _____
    name   address   phone

Is this business conducted from your home? ❏No ❏Yes (If yes, complete a Home Occupancy Form)
Did you purchase this business? ❏No ❏Yes If yes, enter the date of purchase? _____

Building Permit is required prior to making any physical modifications to the premises. If you have questions about building modifications, contact the Building & Safety Division at (714) 724-6524.
Does your business create, store, generate, or use hazardous substances or any products that are considered to be corrosive, reactive, ignitable, toxic, and / or ozone depleters? ❏No ❏Yes

It is the responsibility of the applicant / licensee to ensure that his/her business complies with all applicable City Codes and the City Zoning Ordinance. In the event it is determined that the business does not comply, the business license may be revoked by the City. I hereby certify, under penalty of perjury, the information provided on this application is true and correct.

_____ _____ _____
Applicant signature   Print applicant's name and title   Date

Business License Application, cont'd

FORM 22-05, REV 05/97[PM]

START YOUR OWN BUSINESS

department in your city or county.

Environmental protection regulations may also require you to get approval before doing any construction or beginning operation. Check with your state environmental protection agency regarding federal or state regulations that may apply to your business.

Sign Permit

Some cities and suburbs have sign ordinances that restrict the size, location and sometimes the lighting and type of sign you can use outside your business. Landlords may also impose their own restrictions; they are likely to be most stringent in a mall. To avoid costly mistakes, check regulations and secure the written approval of your landlord before you go to the expense of having a sign designed and installed.

County Permits

County governments often require essentially the same types of permits and licenses as cities. If your business is outside of any city or town's jurisdiction, these permits apply to you. The good news: County regulations are usually not as strict as those of adjoining cities.

SMART TIP

YOU CAN FIND OUT WHICH LICENSES AND PERMITS ARE REQUIRED FOR YOUR BUSINESS BY CALLING THE STATE AND LOCAL GOVERNMENT OFFICES IN THE AREA IN WHICH YOU ARE GOING TO OPERATE. ASK THEM TO SEND YOU INFORMATION AND ANY FORMS THAT MAY BE REQUIRED.

State Licenses

In many states, people in certain occupations must have licenses or occupational permits. Often, they have to pass state examinations before they can get these permits and conduct business. States usually require licensing for electricians, auto mechanics, building contractors, plumbers, real estate brokers, collection agents, insurance agents, repossessors and anyone who provides personal services (for example, barbers, cosmetologists, doctors and nurses). Contact your state government offices to get a complete list of occupations that require licensing.

Federal Licenses

In most cases, you won't have to worry about this. However, a few types of businesses do require federal licensing, including meat processors, radio and TV stations, and investment advisory services.

GLOSSARY

AIR AND WATER POLLUTION CONTROL PERMIT: may be required by your city or county if your business burns materials, discharges anything into the sewers or waterways, or uses products that produce gas

BEER AND WINE LICENSES: required by most states to sell beer and wine; does not allow holder to sell hard liquor

COUNTY PERMITS: businesses operating outside a city or town may be required by the county to obtain certain permits

DBA (DOING BUSINESS AS): see fictitious business name

FICTITIOUS BUSINESS NAME: a name other than your own under which you are doing business (for example, Joe Smith doing business as Joe's Auto Body Shop); must typically be registered with the city, county, or state

FIRE DEPARTMENT PERMIT: may be required if your business uses flammable materials or is open to the public

HEALTH DEPARTMENT PERMIT: required by the county health department if you plan to sell food

LIQUOR LICENSE: required by most states to sell hard liquor

SIGN PERMIT: required by some cities and suburbs to erect a sign outside your business

STATE LICENSES: required by many states for people in certain occupations, such as cosmetologists, mechanics, plumbers, electricians and other jobs

CHAPTER 12

You Need Professional Help

Hiring a lawyer and an accountant

Α s you start off on your business journey, there are two professionals you will soon come to rely on to guide you along the path: your lawyer and your accountant. It's hard to navigate the maze of tax and legal issues facing entrepreneurs these days unless these professionals are an integral part of your team.

HIRING A LAWYER

When do you need a lawyer? Although the answer depends on your business and your particular circumstances, it's generally worthwhile to consult one before making any decision that could have legal ramifications. These include setting up a partnership or corporation, checking for compliance with regulations, negotiating loans, obtaining trademarks or patents, preparing buy-sell agreements, assisting with tax planning, drawing up pension plans, reviewing business forms, negotiating and drawing up documents to buy or sell real estate, reviewing employee contracts, exporting or selling products in other states, and collecting bad debts. If something goes wrong, you may need an attorney to stand up for your trademark rights, go to court on an employee dispute or defend you in a product liability lawsuit. Some entrepreneurs wait until something goes wrong to consult an attorney, but in today's litigious society, that isn't the smartest idea. "Almost every business, whatever its size, requires a lawyer's advice," says James Blythe Hodge of the law firm Sheppard, Mullin, Richter & Hampton. "Even the smallest business has tax concerns that need to be addressed as early as the planning stages."

In a crisis situation—such as a lawsuit or trademark wrangle—you may not have time to thoroughly research different legal options. More likely, you'll end up flipping through the Yellow Pages in haste…and getting stuck with a second-rate lawyer. Better to start off on the right foot from

SMART TIP

WHEN A CLIENT REFUSES TO PAY, DO YOU HAND THE CASE TO A LAWYER? SOME ENTREPRENEURS DO, BUT OTHERS HANDLE SMALL LEGAL MATTERS ON THEIR OWN BY USING THEIR ATTORNEY AS A COACH. LAWYERS CAN BE VERY EFFECTIVE IN COACHING YOU TO FILE LAWSUITS IN SMALL-CLAIMS COURT, DRAFT EMPLOYMENT MANUALS AND COMPLETE OTHER LEGAL TASKS.

the beginning by doing the proper research and choosing a good lawyer now. Many entrepreneurs say their relationship with a lawyer is like a marriage—it takes time to develop. That's why it's important to lay the groundwork for a good partnership early.

Choosing An Attorney

How do you find the right attorney? Ask for recommendations from business owners in your industry or from professionals such as bankers or accountants you trust. Don't just get names; ask them for the specific strengths and weaknesses of the attorneys they recommend. Then take the process one step further: Ask your business associates' attorneys whom they recommend and why. (Attorneys are more likely to be helpful if you phrase the request as "If for some reason I couldn't use you, who would you recommend and why?") If you still need more prospects, contact your local Bar Association; many of them have referral services.

Next, set up an interview with the top five attorneys you're considering. Tell them you're interested in building a long-term relationship, and find out which ones are willing to meet with you for an initial consultation without charging a fee.

At this initial conference, be ready to describe your business and its legal needs. Take note of what the attorney says and does, and look for the following qualities:

- **EXPERIENCE:** Although it's not essential to find an expert in your particular field, it makes sense to look for someone who specializes in small-business problems as opposed to, say, maritime law. "Find someone who understands the different business structures and their tax implications," says Hodge. Make sure the lawyer is willing to take on small problems; if you're trying to collect on a small invoice, will the lawyer think it's worth his or her time?

- **UNDERSTANDING:** Be sure the attorney is willing to learn about your business's goals. You're looking for someone who will be a long-term partner in your business's growth. Sure, you're a start-

BRIGHT IDEA

WHEN YOU ARE STARTING A BUSINESS, YOU ARE SHORT OF MONEY FOR JUST ABOUT EVERYTHING—INCLUDING LEGAL SERVICES. REALIZING THIS, MANY LAW FIRMS OFFER A "START-UP PACKAGE" OF LEGAL SERVICES FOR A SET FEE. THIS TYPICALLY INCLUDES DRAWING UP INITIAL DOCUMENTS, ATTENDING CORPORATE BOARD MEETINGS, PREPARING MINUTES, DRAFTING OWNERSHIP AGREEMENTS AND STOCK CERTIFICATES, AND OFFERING ROUTINE LEGAL ADVICE.

up today, but does the lawyer understand where you want to be tomorrow and share your vision for the future?

- **ABILITY TO COMMUNICATE:** If the lawyer speaks in legalese and doesn't bother to explain the terms he or she uses, you should look for someone else.
- **AVAILABILITY:** Will the attorney be available for conferences at your convenience, not his or hers? How quickly can you expect emergency phone calls to be returned?
- **RAPPORT:** Is this someone you can get along with? You'll be discussing matters close to your heart, so make sure you feel comfortable doing so. Good chemistry will ensure a better relationship and more positive results for your business.
- **REASONABLE FEES:** Attorneys charge anywhere from $90 to $300 or more per hour, depending on the location, size and prestige of the firm as well as the lawyer's reputation. Shop around and get quotes from several firms before making your decision. However, beware of comparing one attorney with another on the basis of fees alone. The lowest hourly fees may not indicate the best value in legal work because an inexperienced attorney may take twice as long to complete a project as an experienced one will.
- **REFERENCES:** Don't be afraid to ask for references. Ask what types of businesses or cases the attorney has worked with in the past. Get a list of clients or other attorneys you can contact to discuss competence, service and fees.

Cost Cutters

For many entrepreneurs, the idea of consulting a lawyer conjures up frightening visions of skyrocketing legal bills. While there's no denying that lawyers are expensive, the good news is, there are more ways than ever to keep a lid on costs. Start by learning about the various ways lawyers bill their time:

- **HOURLY OR PER DIEM RATE:** Most attorneys bill by the hour. If travel is involved, they may bill by the day.
- **FLAT FEE:** Some attorneys suggest a flat fee for certain routine matters,

DOLLAR STRETCHER

USING PARALEGALS AS PART OF YOUR LEGAL TEAM CAN BE A GOOD WAY TO CUT COSTS. CERTAIN LEGAL TASKS—PREPAR-  ING A SIMPLE DOCUMENT, FOR INSTANCE—ARE STRAIGHTFORWARD ENOUGH THAT A PARALEGAL MAY BE ABLE TO HANDLE THEM INSTEAD OF A HIGHER-PRICED LAWYER. DON'T ASSUME YOUR LAWYER WILL SUGGEST THIS ROUTE; ASK HIM OR HER ABOUT IT. AND ALWAYS MAKE SURE THE PARALEGAL IS SUPERVISED BY A BUSINESS LAWYER.

such as reviewing a contract or closing a loan.

■ **MONTHLY RETAINER:** If you anticipate a lot of routine questions, one option is a monthly fee that entitles you to all the routine legal advice you need.

Pay Now, Not Later

A new method has arisen to take charge of skyrocketing legal fees. It's called the prepaid legal plan, and more and more small businesses are using it.

Prepaid legal plans have been compared to HMOs because they offer certain basic services for a monthly fee. Prices range from as little as $10 a month to $70 or more; in return, an entrepreneur gets a package of services such as, say, unlimited phone consultation with a lawyer, review of three contracts per month, up to 10 debt collection letters per month and discounts on other legal services.

"Our experience shows 73 percent of all legal problems [members bring] can be resolved with a single telephone call," says Crystal Virtue of Caldwell Legal, U.S.A.

Typically, prepaid legal services contract with one law firm in each state to handle routine matters. Because the service is usually that firm's biggest client, business owners using the service receive a warmer welcome than they might at a big law firm. Specialists are usually available at reduced rates.

When considering a prepaid legal service, here are some factors to consider:

● **WHAT IS INCLUDED?** Check the plan to make sure it has what you need. The number of services offered at a reduced rate may be limited; what are the charges for other services?

● **CONSIDER WHETHER** you'd prefer to build a relationship with one attorney rather than talk to a different lawyer every time you call.

● **ASK OTHER ENTREPRENEURS** who have used such services about the quality of work. Also ask how the company handles conflicts of interest in case you have a dispute against a business that uses the same prepaid firm.

With these caveats in mind, a prepaid legal service firm could be just what a business on a budget needs. For more information, contact the National Resource Center for Consumers of Legal Services at P.O. Box 340, Gloucester, VA 23061 or call (804) 693-9330.

Different Strokes

When you're hit with a lawsuit, the costs can be mind-boggling—even if you win. That's why more and more small businesses are using alternative dispute resolution (ADR), a concept that includes mediation, arbitration and other ways of resolving disputes without resorting to litigation. Both in contracts between businesses or in agreements between employers and employees, people are consenting ahead of time to submit future disputes to ADR. Here are the most common forms of ADR:

- **NEGOTIATION:** In the simplest form of ADR, the two parties (or their lawyers) discuss their differences and agree on a settlement.

- **MEDIATION:** When the two parties need more help in working out a solution, they can hire a neutral third party (a mediator) skilled in asking questions, listening and helping make decisions. The result is a written agreement to settle the dispute; both parties share the mediation costs.

- **ARBITRATION:** An arbitrator hears a case like a judge, then issues a decision. The parties have control over who hears the case—often, an expert in their field. In nonbinding arbitration, the arbitrator makes a recommendation that parties can accept or reject. In binding arbitration, the arbitrator's decision is legally binding.

- **MINI-TRIAL:** Less common, this gives both parties a sense of how their disagreement might resolve in court. They watch their lawyers argue the case as if they were at trial. In most cases, the parties are better able to see the other side and end up settling the case.

- **SUMMARY JURY TRIAL:** Here, a jury of citizens hears a shortened trial and makes a nonbinding decision. Again, this usually helps the parties agree on a settlement.

Any time two parties enter a contract, they can include an agreement to submit any disputes to a specified type of ADR. Your attorney can help you draft a clause specifying how the situation will be handled. If you have employees sign an ADR agreement, make sure they understand that they will lose the option of a jury trial.

Even if you don't have an ADR clause in your contracts, it's still possible to suggest using ADR after a dispute arises. Once they understand how much money, time and aggravation ADR can save, the other side may agree to use it...even if they still don't agree with you.

- **CONTINGENT FEE:** For lawsuits and other complex matters, lawyers often work on a contingency basis. This means that if they succeed, they receive a percentage of the proceeds—usually between 25 and 40 percent. If they fail, they receive only out-of-pocket expenses.
- **VALUE BILLING:** Some law firms bill at a higher rate on business matters if the attorneys obtain a favorable result, such as negotiating a contract that saves the client thousands of dollars. Try to avoid lawyers who use this method, which is also sometimes called "partial contingency."

If you think one method will work better for you than another, don't hesitate to bring it up with the attorney; many will offer flexible arrangements to meet your needs.

When you hire an attorney, draw up an agreement (called an "engagement letter") detailing the billing method. If more than one attorney works on your file, make sure you specify the hourly rate for each individual so you aren't charged $200 an hour for legal work done by an associate who only charges $75 an hour.

This agreement should also specify what expenses you're expected to reimburse. Some attorneys expect to be reimbursed for meals, secretarial overtime, postage and photocopies, which many people consider the costs of doing business. If an unexpected charge comes up, will your attorney call you for authorization? Agree to reimburse only reasonable and necessary out-of-pocket expenses. No matter what methods your attorney uses, here are steps you can take to control legal costs:

- **HAVE THE ATTORNEY ESTIMATE THE COST OF EACH MATTER IN WRITING, SO YOU CAN DECIDE WHETHER IT'S WORTH PURSUING.** If the bill comes in over the estimate, ask why. Some attorneys also offer "caps," guaranteeing in writing the maximum cost of a particular service. This helps you budget and gives you more certainty than just getting an estimate.
- **LEARN WHAT INCREMENTS OF TIME THE FIRM USES TO CALCULATE ITS BILL.** Attorneys keep track of their time in increments as short as six minutes or as long as half an hour. Will a five-minute phone call cost you $50?
- **REQUEST MONTHLY, ITEMIZED BILLS.** Some lawyers wait until a bill gets large before sending an invoice. Ask for monthly invoices and review them. The most obvious red flag is excessive fees; this means that too many people or the wrong people—are working on your file. It's also possible you may be mistakenly billed for

work done for another client, so review your invoices carefully.

■ **SEE IF YOU CAN NEGOTIATE PROMPT-PAYMENT DISCOUNTS.** Request that your bill be discounted if you pay within 30 days of your invoice date. A 5 percent discount can add thousands of dollars to your yearly bottom line.

■ **BE PREPARED.** Before you meet with or call your lawyer, have the necessary documents with you and know exactly what you want to discuss. Fax needed documents ahead of time so your attorney doesn't have to read them during the conference and can instead get right down to business. And refrain from calling your attorney 100 times a day.

■ **MEET WITH YOUR LAWYER REGULARLY.** At first glance, this may not seem like a good way to keep costs down, but you will be amazed at how much it reduces the endless rounds of phone tag that plague busy entrepreneurs and attorneys. More important, a monthly five- or 10-minute meeting (even by phone) can save you substantial sums by nipping small legal problems in the bud before they even get a chance to grow.

Making The Most Of Your Lawyer

Once your relationship with your lawyer is established, keep the lines of communication open. In addition to brief regular meetings, sit down with your attorney once annually to discuss the past year's progress and your goals for the coming year. Meet at your place of business so the attorney can get to know your operation.

How can you tell if your attorney is doing a good job for you? According to attorney Jerry Friedland, the quickest measure is how many legal difficulties you're having. Lawyers should be fending off legal problems. A good attorney identifies potential problems in advance.

Like any competent professional, a good lawyer also returns phone calls promptly, meets deadlines and follows through on promises. A good lawyer is thorough in asking for information

HOT LINK

NEED A QUICK, FREE EXPERT ANSWER? GO TO WWW.SBA.GOV/ANSWERDESK.HTML AND/OR WRITE TO THE ANSWERDESK@SBA.GOV, OR  CALL (800) U-ASK-SBA. THE ANSWER DESK, ACCORDING TO THE SBA, IS THE ONLY NATIONAL TOLL-FREE TELEPHONE SERVICE PROVIDING INFORMATION TO THE PUBLIC ON SMALL-BUSINESS PROBLEMS AND CONCERNS. THEY'RE THERE, READY TO TALK MONDAY THROUGH FRIDAY, FROM 9 A.M. TO 5 P.M. EST.

and discerning your goals. And good lawyers either research what they do not know and explain your options, or refer you to someone who can help.

In evaluating the attorney's work on any matter, consider whether you have been able to meet your goals. If you have met your goals without undue costs, the attorney is probably doing a good job. Once you have found a lawyer who understands your business and does a good job, you have found a valuable asset.

HIRING AN ACCOUNTANT

Don't assume only big companies need the services of an accountant. Accountants help you keep an eye on major costs as early as the start-up stage, a time when you're probably preoccupied with counting every paper clip and postage stamp. Accountants help you look at the big picture.

Even after the start-up stage, many business owners may not have any idea how well they're doing financially until the end of the year,

All The Right Questions

Here are 10 questions to ask when interviewing a potential accountant:

1. **ARE YOU A CPA?** (Don't assume every accountant is.)
2. **ARE YOU LICENSED** to practice in your state?
3. **WHEN AND WHERE** did you receive a license to practice?
4. **WHERE DID YOU GO** to school, and what degrees did you earn?
5. **WHO ARE SOME OF YOUR CLIENTS?** (Call them.)
6. **IN WHAT AREA DO YOU SPECIALIZE?**
7. **HOW BIG OR SMALL ARE YOUR CLIENTS,** and what size were they when you began your relationship with them?
8. **HOW ACCESSIBLE ARE YOU?** (Some accountants are only available during business hours; others will give you their home or pager number.)
9. **TO WHAT PROFESSIONAL ORGANIZATIONS** do you belong? How active are you in those groups?
10. **WHAT ARE YOUR FEES?** (Ask to see some current invoices.)

when they file their tax returns. Meanwhile, they equate their cash flow with profits, which is wrong. Every dollar counts for business owners, so if you don't know where you stand on a monthly basis, you may not be around at the end of the year.

While do-it-yourself accounting software is plentiful and easy to use, it's not the sole answer. Just as having Microsoft Word does not make you a writer, having accounting software doesn't make you an accountant. Software can only do what you tell it to do—and a good accountant's skills go far beyond crunching numbers.

In fact, perhaps no other business relationship has such potential to pay off. Nowadays, accountants are more than just bean counters. A good accountant can be your company's financial partner for life— with intimate knowledge of everything from how you're going to finance your next forklift to how you're going to finance your daughter's college education.

While many people think of accountants strictly as tax preparers, in reality, accountants have a wide knowledge base that can be an invaluable asset to a business. A general accounting practice covers four basic areas of expertise:

1. business advisory services
2. accounting and record-keeping
3. tax advice
4. auditing

These four disciplines often overlap. For instance, if your accountant is helping you prepare the financial statements you need for a loan, and he or she gives you some insights into how certain estimates could be recalculated to get a more favorable review, the accountant is crossing the line from auditing into business advisory services. And perhaps, after preparing your midyear financial statements, he or she might suggest how your performance year-to-date will influence your year-end tax liability. Here's a closer look at the four areas:

1. BUSINESS ADVISORY SERVICES: This is where accountants can really earn their keep. Since the accountant is knowledgeable about your business environment, your tax situation and your finan-

SMART TIP

THE AMERICAN INSTITUTE OF CERTIFIED PUBLIC ACCOUNTANTS HAS A WEB SITE THAT PROVIDES LINKS TO UPDATES, UPCOMING ACTIVITIES, ACCOUNTING-RELATED SOFTWARE AND STATE CPA SOCIETIES—WHOSE WEB SITES PROVIDE LINKS TO MORE SITES AND FREQUENTLY ASKED QUESTIONS. VISIT WWW.AICPA.ORG.

cial statements, it makes sense to ask him or her to pull all the pieces together and help you come up with a business plan and personal financial plan you can really achieve. Accountants can offer advice on everything from insurance (do you really need business interruption insurance, or would it be cheaper to lease a second site?) to expansion (how will additional capacity affect operating costs?). "Accountants can bring a new level of insight to the picture, simply by virtue of their perspective," says CPA David Lifson.

2. ACCOUNTING AND RECORD-KEEPING: Accounting and record-keeping are perhaps the most basic accounting discipline. However, most business owners keep their own books and records instead of having their accountant do it. The reason is simple: If these records are examined by lenders or the IRS, the business owner is responsible for their accuracy; therefore, it makes more sense for the owner to maintain them.

Where accountants can offer help is in initially setting up bookkeeping and accounting systems and showing the business owner how to use them. A good system allows you to evaluate your profitability at any given point in time and modify prices accordingly. It also lets you track expenses to see if any particular areas are getting out of hand. It lets you establish and track a budget, spot trends in sales and expenses, and reduce accounting fees required to produce financial statements and tax returns.

3. **TAX ADVICE:** Tax help from accountants comes in two forms: tax compliance and tax planning. Planning refers to reducing your overall tax burden; compliance refers to obeying the tax laws.

4. **AUDITING:** Auditing services are required for many different purposes, most commonly by banks as a condition of a loan. There are many levels of auditing, ranging from simply preparing financial statements from figures that the entrepreneur supplies, all the way up to an actual audit, where the accountant or other third party gives assurance that a company's financial information is accurate.

Today, more and more accountants are moving into a fifth area: personal financial planning. For many, this is a natural extension of their familiarity with their clients' financial affairs.

Choosing An Accountant

The best way to find a good accountant is to get a referral from your attorney, your banker or a business colleague in the same industry. If you need more possibilities, almost every state has a Society of Certified Public Accountants that will make a referral. Don't underestimate the importance of a CPA (certified public accountant). This title is only awarded to people who have passed a rigorous two-day, nationally standardized test. Most states require CPAs to have at least a college degree or its equivalent, and several of the states also require post-graduate work.

Accountants usually work for large companies; CPAs, on the other hand, work for a variety of large and small businesses. When dealing with an accountant, you can only hope he or she is well-educated and well-versed in your business's needs. Passing the CPA exam, however, is a guarantee of a certain level of ability. Once you have come up with some good candidates, a little preparation is in order before you interview them. The first step in setting the stage for a successful search, says Lifson, is to take an inventory of what you will need. It is important to determine beforehand just how much of the work your company will do and how much of it will be done by the accountant.

Accounting services can be broken down into three broad categories: recording transactions, assembling them, and generating returns and financial statements. Typically, the latter part—that is, the generation of returns and financial statements—requires the highest level of expertise. But though the other activities require a lower skill level, many firms still charge the same hourly rate for them. Given the level of fees you are prepared to pay, you must decide where your responsibility stops and where the accountant's begins.

Once you have compiled your documentation and given some thought to your expectations, you're ready to interview your

SMART TIP

FIND OUT HOW WELL-CONNECTED THE CPA AND HIS/HER FIRM ARE BEFORE MAKING A FINAL DECISION. CPAs ARE OFTEN VALUABLE RESOURCES FOR SMALL BUSINESSES NEEDING TO BORROW MONEY OR TO RAISE CAPITAL FROM OTHER SOURCES. A WELL-CONNECTED CPA MIGHT HELP YOU GET A FOOT IN THE DOOR WITH A BANK OR INVESTOR.

referrals. Five candidates is a good number to start with. For each candidate, plan on two meetings before making your decision. One of these meetings should be at your site; one at theirs. "Both parties need to know the environment the other works in," explains Lifson, who warns you should never hire an accountant without seeing his or her office. During the ensuing interviews, your principal goal is to find out about three

A Little Help From Your Friends

Mentors can be valuable sources of information at any stage of your company's growth.

"It is always in your best interest to reach out to a variety of sources of information when you make decisions," says Ken Yancey, executive director of SCORE (Service Corps of Retired Executives). An SBA partner, SCORE offers 10,500 volunteer members and 389 chapters throughout the United States.

Mentors can often give you a fresh perspective on problems or challenges because they're not personally involved with your business like other advisors, including attorneys, accountants and friends. For this reason, it's important to find not only a mentor who has experience and knowledge, but also someone you can trust and feel at ease with.

Building a relationship takes work on your part, too. "Everyone likes recognition, to get a note, to have someone say thank you. You get goosebumps just thinking about it. That's better than anything for a mentor," says Yancey.

To get matched with a mentor, your first step should be locating your local SCORE chapter. Call (800) 634-0245, or visit www.score.org. If there's not a chapter near you, no problem. SCORE also offers free e-mail counseling provided by 1,200 volunteers with a 48-hour or less turnaround time for quick questions.

Another mentor resource is offered by the Office of Women's Business Ownership. Its Women's Network for Entrepreneurial Training Mentoring Program matches proteges with experienced women mentors. For more information, contact the Office of Women's Business Ownership at (202) 205-6673 or visit www.sba.gov/womeninbusiness/wnet.html.

things: services, personality and fees.

1. **SERVICES:** Most accounting firms offer tax and auditing services. But what about bookkeeping? Management consulting? Pension fund accounting? Estate planning? Will the accountant help you design and implement financial information systems? Other services a CPA may offer include analyzing transactions for loans and financing; preparing, auditing, reviewing and compiling financial statements; managing investments; and representing you before tax authorities.

Although smaller accounting firms are generally a better bet for entrepreneurs (see "The Size of It" on page 169), they may not offer all these services. Make sure the firm has what you need. If it can't offer specialized services, such as estate planning, it may have relationships with other firms to which it can refer you to handle these matters. In addition to services, make sure the firm has experience with small business and with your industry. Someone who is already familiar with the financial issues facing your field of business won't have to waste time getting up to speed.

2. **PERSONALITY:** Is the accountant's style compatible with yours? Be sure the people you are meeting with are the same ones who will be handling your business. At many accounting firms, some partners handle sales and new business, then pass the actual account work on to others.

When evaluating competency and compatibility, ask candidates how they would handle situations relevant to you. For example: How would you handle a change in corporation status from S to C? How would you handle an IRS office audit seeking verification of automobile expenses? Listen to the answers, and decide if that's how you would like your affairs to be handled.

Realize, too, that having an accountant who takes a different approach can be a good thing. "If you are superconservative, it's not a bad thing to have an accountant who exposes you to the aggressive side of life," Lifson says. "Likewise, if you are aggressive, it's often helpful to have someone who can show you the conservative approach." Be sure that the accountant won't pressure you into doing things you aren't comfortable with. It's your money, and you need to be able to sleep at night.

3. **FEES:** Ask about fees up front. Most accounting firms charge by the hour; fees can range from as low as $75 per hour to as much as $275. However, there are some accountants who work on a monthly retainer. Figure out what services you are likely to need and

The Size Of It

Are you dithering over the choice between that large, fancy law or accounting firm with offices in every corner of the globe, or that humble, one-person legal or accounting office down the street? Before you bust your budget to retain Squelch, Withers & Ream, know this: When it comes to professional service firms, bigger isn't always better.

A big law or accounting firm may boast impressive credentials on your first meeting with them. The problem is that they usually boast an impressive price to match. What's more, the hotshot you meet with on your initial conference may not be the person who will actually work on your legal cases or taxes. That task is likely to fall to a less experienced junior partner with limited know-how. This isn't necessarily bad, but make sure you know who will be working on your file and what their experience is. Also be sure you're billed correctly and don't get charged $300 an hour for something a paralegal did.

Only you can decide what is right for you, but make sure you're not being swayed by a big name or a fancy office. While a big law or accounting firm may be right for some small businesses' needs, the reality is that your company will make up a much smaller share of such a firm's client list. As such, you may not get the attention they're devoting to bigger clients. In other words, if Standard Oil has a sudden tax emergency, your file is likely to get put on the back burner. This is one situation where it's better to be a big fish in a small pond.

which option will be more cost-effective for you.

Get a range of quotes from different accountants. Also try to get an estimate of the total annual charges based on the services you have discussed. Don't base your decision solely on cost, however; an accountant who charges more by the hour is likely to be more experienced and thus able to work faster than a novice who charges less.

At the end of the interview, ask for references—particularly from clients in the same industry as you. A good accountant should be happy to provide you with referrals; call and ask how satisfied they were with the accountant's services, fees and availability.

Good Relations

After you have made your choice, spell out the terms of the agreement in an "engagement letter" that details the returns and statements to be prepared and the fees to be charged. This ensures you and your accountant have the same expectations and helps prevent misunderstandings and hard feelings.

Make the most of the accounting relationship by doing your part. Don't hand your accountant a shoe box full of receipts. Write down details of all the checks in your check register—whether they are for utilities, supplies and so on. Likewise, identify sources of income on your bank deposit slips. The better you maintain your records, the less time your accountant has to spend—and the lower your fees will be.

It's a good idea to meet with your accountant every month. Review financial statements and go over any problems so you know where your money is going. This is where your accountant should go beyond number-crunching to suggest alternative ways of cutting costs and act as a sounding board for any ideas or questions you have.

A good accountant can help your business in ways you never dreamed possible. Spending the time to find the right accountant— and taking advantage of the advice he or she has to offer—is one of the best things you can do to help your business soar.

GLOSSARY

ALTERNATIVE DISPUTE RESOLUTION (ADR): a way of resolving disputes without resorting to litigation

BINDING ARBITRATION: form of ADR in which the arbitrator's decision is legally binding

CPA (CERTIFIED PUBLIC ACCOUNTANT): an accountant who has passed a nationally standardized exam in accounting

COMMISSIONED FINANCIAL PLANNER: financial planner who receives commissions on products he or she sells

ENGAGEMENT LETTER: letter of agreement between a lawyer or an accountant and his/her client that spells out the terms

FEE-FOR-SERVICE PLANNER: financial planner who charges a fee for making recommendations on what you should do to achieve your financial goals

NONBINDING ARBITRATION: form of ADR in which the arbitrator makes a recommendation that parties can accept or reject

PREPAID LEGAL PLAN: payment structure in which a client prepays a set monthly fee in return for a fixed amount of legal services per month (differs from monthly retainer in that services are more limited and relationship is not with one law firm, but with a prepaid legal service firm, which has relationships with many law firms)

PART

3

Where's The Money?

Charity
Begins At
Home

*Financing starts with yourself
and friends and relatives*

Once you have decided on the type of venture you want to start, the next step on the road to business success is figuring out where the money will come from to fund it. Where do you start?

The best place to begin is by looking in the mirror. Self-financing is the number-one form of financing used by most business start-ups. In addition, when you approach other financing sources such as bankers, venture capitalists or the government, they will want to know exactly how much of your own money you are putting into the venture. After all, if you don't have enough faith in your business to risk your own money, why should anyone else risk theirs?

DO IT YOURSELF

Begin by doing a thorough inventory of your assets. You are likely to uncover resources you didn't even know you had. Assets could include savings accounts, equity in real estate, retirement accounts, vehicles, recreational equipment and collections. You may decide to sell some assets for cash or to use them as collateral for a loan.

If you have investments, you may be able to use them as a resource. Low-interest-margin loans against stocks and securities can be arranged through your brokerage accounts.

"The downside here is that, if the market should fall and your securities are your loan collateral, you'll get a margin call from your broker, requesting you to supply more collateral," says Vickie Hampton, a certified financial planner and professor of financial planning courses at Texas Tech University in Lubbock, Texas. "If you can't do that within a certain time, you'll be asked to sell some of your securities to shore up the collateral." Also take a look at your personal line of credit. Some businesses have successfully been started on credit cards, although this is one of the most expensive ways to finance yourself (see Part 3, Chapter 15 for more on credit card financing).

If you own a home, consider getting a home equity loan on the part of the mortgage that you have already paid off. The bank will either provide a lump-sum loan payment or extend a line of credit based on the equity in your home. "Depending on the value of your

Personal Balance Sheet

By filling out a personal balance sheet, you will be able to determine your net worth. Finding out your net worth is an important early step in the process of becoming a business owner because you need to find out what assets are available to you for investment in your business.

Assets	Totals
Cash and Checking	
Savings Accounts	
Real Estate/Home	
Automobiles	
Bonds	
Securities	
Insurance Cash Values	
Other	
Total Assets **A**	

Liabilities	Totals
Current Monthly Bills	
Credit Card/Charge Account Bills	
Mortgage	
Auto Loans	
Finance Company Loans	
Personal Debts	
Other	
Total Liabilities **B**	
Net Worth (A-B=C) **C**	

Degree Of Indebtedness

Note: If total liabilities exceed total assets, subtract assets from liabilities to determine degree of indebtedness

(B-A=D)

Total Liabilities	**B**	
Total Assets	**A**	
Degree of Indebtedness	**D**	

home, a home-equity loan could become a substantial line of credit," Hampton says. "If you have $50,000 in equity, you could possibly set up a line of credit of up to $40,000." Home-equity loans carry relatively low interest rates, and all interest paid on a loan of up to $100,000 is tax-deductible. But be sure you can repay the loan—you can lose your home if you do not repay.

Consider borrowing against cash-value life insurance. Hampton says you can use the value built up in a cash-value life-insurance policy as a ready source of cash. The interest rates are reasonable because the insurance companies always get their money back. You don't even have to make payments if you do not want to. Neither the amount you borrow nor the interest that accrues has to be repaid. "The only loss is that if you die and the debt hasn't been repaid," Hampton explains, "that money is deducted from the amount your beneficiary will receive."

If you have a 401(k) retirement plan through your employer and are starting a part-time business while you keep your full-time job, consider borrowing against the plan. "It's very common for such plans to allow you to borrow a percentage of your money that doesn't exceed $50,000," says Hampton. "The interest rate is usually about 6 percent with a specified repayment schedule. The downside of borrowing from your 401(k) is that, if you lose your job, the loan has to be repaid in a short period of time—often 30 days." Consult the plan's documentation to see if this can be an option for you.

Good Benefits

If you have been laid off or lost your job, another source of start-up capital may be available to you. Some states have instituted self-employment programs as part of their unemployment insurance systems.

People who are receiving unemployment benefits and meet certain requirements are recruited into entrepreneurial training programs that show them how to start businesses. This gives them an opportunity to use their unemployment funds for start-up, while boosting their chances of success.

Contact the department in your state that handles unemployment benefits to see if such a program is available to you.

Another option is to use the funds in your individual retirement account (IRA). Within the laws governing IRAs, you can actually withdraw money from an IRA as long as you replace it within 60 days. "This is not a loan, so you don't pay interest," Hampton says. "This is a withdrawal that you're allowed to keep for 60 days." She says it would be possible for a highly organized entrepreneur to juggle funds among several IRAs. "But if you're one day late—for any reason—you'll be hit with a 10 percent premature-withdrawal fee, and the money you haven't returned becomes taxable."

If you are employed, another way to finance your business is by squirreling away money from your current salary until you have enough to launch the business. If you don't want to wait, consider moonlighting or cutting your full-time job back to part-time. This ensures you'll have some steady funds rolling in until your business starts to soar.

One final method may be to apply for a grant. "As cushy as they sound, grants are the hardest kind of money to get," says certified financial planner Alona Sussman. "They're highly competitive, and you have to answer many questions to prove the validity of your business. Also, the application process is long."

People generally have more assets than they realize. Use as much of your own money as possible to get started; remember, the larger your own investment, the easier it will be for you to acquire capital from other sources.

FRIENDS AND FAMILY

Your own resources may not be enough to give you the capital you need. "Most businesses are started with money from four or five different sources," says Mike McKeever, author of *How to Write a Business Plan*. After self-financing, the second most popular source for start-up money is composed of friends, relatives and business associates.

"Family and friends are great sources of financing," says Tonia Papke, owner of small-business consulting firm Management Development International. "These people know you have integrity and will grant you a loan based on the strength of your character."

It makes sense. People with whom you have close relationships know you are reliable and competent, so there should be no problem in asking for a loan, right? Keep in mind, however, that asking for financial help isn't the same as borrowing the car. While squeezing money out of family and friends may seem an easy alternative to dealing with bankers, it can actually be a much more delicate situation. Papke warns that your family members or friends may think lending you money gives them license to meddle. "And if the business fails," she says, "the issue of paying the money back can be a problem, putting the whole relationship in jeopardy."

The bottom line, says McKeever, is that "whenever you put money into a relationship that involves either friendship or love, it gets very complicated." Fortunately, there are ways to work out the details and make the business relationship advantageous for all parties involved. If you handle the situation correctly and tactfully, you may gain more than finances for your business—you may end up strengthening the personal relationship as well.

BEWARE!

WATCH OUT FOR THE RELATIVE OR FRIEND WHO AGREES TO LEND YOU MONEY EVEN THOUGH HE OR SHE CAN'T REALLY AFFORD TO. "THERE WILL ALWAYS BE PEOPLE WHO WANT TO DO ANYTHING THEY CAN TO HELP YOU, WHO WILL GIVE YOU FUNDS THAT ARE CRITICAL TO THEIR FUTURE JUST BECAUSE YOU ASK FOR IT," SAYS MIKE MCKEEVER, AUTHOR OF *HOW TO WRITE A BUSINESS PLAN.* "THESE RELATIVES WILL NOT TELL YOU THEY REALLY CAN'T AFFORD IT, SO YOU MUST BE EXTRA PERCEPTIVE."

The Right Source

The first step in getting financing from friends or family is finding the right person to borrow money from. As you search for potential lenders or investors, don't enlist people with ulterior motives. "It's not a good idea to take money from a person if it's given with emotional strings," says McKeever. "For example, avoid borrowing from relatives or friends who have the attitude of 'I'll give you the money, but I want you to pay extra attention to me.'"

Once you determine whom you'd like to borrow money from, approach the person initially in an informal situation. Let the person know a little about your business, and gauge his or her interest. If the person seems interested and says he or she would like more information about the business, make an appointment to meet with them in a professional atmosphere. "This makes it clear that the subject of discussion will be your business and their interest in it," says McKeever. "You may secure their initial interest in a casual setting, but to go beyond that, you have to make an extra effort. You should do a formal sales presentation and make sure the person has all the facts."

A large part of informing this person is compiling a business plan, which you should bring to your meeting. Explain the plan in detail, and do the presentation just as you would in front of a banker or other investor. Your goal is to get the other person on your side and make him or her as excited as you are about the possibilities of your business.

During your meeting—and, in fact, whenever you discuss a loan—try to separate the personal from the business as much as possible. Difficult as this may sound, it's critical to the health of your relationship. "It's important to treat the lender formally, explaining your business plan in detail rather than casually passing it off with an 'if you love me, you'll give me the money' attitude," says McKeever.

Be prepared to accept rejection gracefully. "Don't pile on the emotional pressure—emphasize that you'd like this to be strictly a business decision for them," says McKeever. "If relatives or friends feel they can turn you down without offending you, they're more likely to invest. Give them an out."

Putting It On Paper

Now it's time to put the loan in motion. First, you must state how much money you need, what you'll use it for and how you'll pay it back. Next, draw up the legal papers—an agreement stating that the person will indeed put money into the business.

Too frequently, business owners fail to take the time to figure out exactly what kind of paperwork should be completed when they borrow from family or friends. "Often small-business owners put more thought into figuring out what type of car to buy than how to structure this type of lending arrangement," says Steven I. Levey, with the accounting firm Gelfond, Hochstadt, Pangburn & Co. Unfortunately, once you've made an error in this area, it's difficult to correct it.

Your loan agreement needs to specify whether the loan is secured (that is, the lender holds title to part of your property) or unsecured,

Start-up Costs Work Sheet

The following two work sheets will help you to compute your initial cash requirements for your business. They list the things you need to consider when determining your start-up costs and include both the one-time initial costs needed to open your doors and the ongoing costs you'll face each month for the first 90 days.

Start-up Capital Requirements
One-time Start-up Expenses

Start-up Expenses	Description	Amount
Advertising	Promotion for opening the business	
Starting inventory	Amount of inventory required to open	
Building construction	Amount per contractor bid and other costs	
Cash	Amount needed for the cash register	
Decorating	Estimate based on bid if appropriate	
Deposits	Check with utility companies	
Fixtures and equipment	Use actual bids	
Insurance	Bid from insurance agent	
Lease payments	Fee to be paid before opening	
Licenses and permit	Check with city or state offices	
Miscellaneous	All other costs	
Professional fees	Include CPA, attorney, etc.	
Remodeling	Use contractor bids	
Rent	Fee to be paid before opening	
Services	Cleaning, accounting, etc.	
Signs	Use contractor bids	
Supplies	Office, cleaning, etc.	
Unanticipated expenses	Include an amount for the unexpected	
Other		
Other		
Other		
Total Start-up Costs		

Start-up Costs Work Sheet

Start-up Capital Requirements
Repeating Monthly Expenses*

Expenses	Description	Amount
Advertising		
Bank service fees		
Credit card charges		
Delivery fees		
Dues and subscriptions		
Health insurance	Exclude amount on preceding page	
Insurance	Exclude amount on preceding page	
Interest		
Inventory	See **, below	
Lease payments	Exclude amount on preceding page	
Loan payments	Principal and interest payments	
Miscellaneous		
Office expenses		
Payroll other than owner		
Payroll taxes		
Professional fees		
Rent	Exclude amount on preceding page	
Repairs and maintenance		
Sales tax		
Supplies		
Telephone		
Utilities		
Your salary	Only if applicable during the first three months	
Other		
Total Repeating Costs		
Total Start-up Costs	Amount from preceding page	
Total Cash Needed		

Include the first three months' cash needs unless otherwise noted.
**Include amount required for inventory expansion. If inventory is to be replaced from cash sales, do not include here. Assume sales will generate enough cash for replacements.*

what the payments will be, when they're due and what the interest is. If the money is in the form of an investment, you have to establish whether the business is a partnership or corporation, and what role, if any, the investor will play. To be sure you and your family and friends have a clear idea of what financial obligations are being created, you have a mutual responsibility to make sure everyone is informed about the process and decide together how best to proceed.

Most important, says McKeever, "Outline the legal responsibilities of both parties and when and how the money should be paid back." If your loan agreement is complex, it's a good idea to consult your accountant about the best ways to structure the loan (see the "Taxing Matters" section below).

Whichever route you take, make sure the agreement is in writing if you expect it to be binding. "Any time you take money into a business, the law is very explicit: You must have all agreements written down and documented," says McKeever. If you don't, emotional and legal difficulties could result that end up in court. And if the loan isn't documented, you may find yourself with no legal recourse.

Taxing Matters

Putting the agreement on paper also protects both you and your lender come tax time. Relying on informal and verbal agreements results in tax quagmires. "In these cases, you have a burden of proof to show the IRS that [the money] was not a gift," says Tom Ochsenschlager, a partner with the accounting firm Grant Thornton LLP. If the IRS views it as a gift, then the lender becomes subject to the federal gift tax rules and will have to pay taxes on the money if it is more than $11,000. Also make sure the person providing the money charges an interest rate that reflects a fair market value.

If your friend or family member wants to give you a no-interest loan, make sure the loan is not more than $100,000. If you borrow more, the IRS will slap on what it considers to be market-rate interest, better known as "imputed interest." That means that, while your friend or relative may not be receiving any interest on the money you borrowed, the IRS will tax them as if they were.

Imputed interest also kicks in if the loan is for more than $10,000 when the business owner has more than $1,000 in annual net investment income, such as interest, dividends and, in some cases, capital gains. To determine the interest rate on these transactions, the IRS uses what it calls the applicable federal rate, which it sets on a regular basis. Keep in mind that if you don't put all the details of the loan in writing, it will be very difficult for you to deduct the interest you pay on it. Additionally, the relative who lent the money won't be able to take a tax deduction on the loss if you find you can't repay.

To be absolutely safe, Ochsenschlager recommends that you make the friend or relative who is providing the money one of the business' shareholders. This effectively makes the transaction an investment in your company and also makes it easier from a tax standpoint for your friend or relative to write off the transaction as an ordinary loss if the business fails. (This applies only if the total amount your company received for its stock, including the relative's investment, does not exceed $1 million.)

In addition, "if your company is wildly successful, your relative will have an equity interest in the business, and his or her original investment will be worth quite a bit more," Ochsenschlager says. In contrast, if a relative gives you a loan and your company goes under, the relative's loss would generally be considered a personal bad debt. This creates more of a tax disadvantage because personal bad debts can be claimed as capital losses only to offset capital gains. If the capital loss exceeds the capital gains, only $3,000 of the loss can be used against ordinary income in any given year. Thus, an individual making a large loan that isn't repaid may have to wait several years to realize the tax benefits from the loss.

If the loan that can't be repaid is a business loan, however, the lender receives a deduction against ordinary income and can take deductions even before the loan becomes totally worthless. (One catch: The IRS takes a very narrow view of what qualifies as a business loan. To qualify as a business loan, the loan would have to be connected to the lender's business.) This will be difficult, so consult an accountant about the best way to structure the loan for maximum tax benefits to both parties.

Making your relative a shareholder doesn't mean you'll have to put up with Mom or Pop in the business. Depending on your company's organizational structure, your friend or relative can be a silent partner if your company is set up as a partnership, or a silent shareholder if you are organized as an S corporation or limited liability company.

Keep 'Em Happy

Even with every detail documented, your responsibilities are far from over. Don't make assumptions or take people for granted just because they are friends or family members. Communication is key.

If your relative or friend is not actively involved in the business, make sure you contact him or her once every month or two to explain how the business is going. "When people invest in small businesses, it often becomes sort of their pet project," says McKeever. "It's important to take the time to keep them informed."

And, of course, there are the payments. Though friends or relatives who invest in your business understand the risks, you must never take the loan for granted. "Don't be cavalier about paying the money back," McKeever says. "That kind of attitude could ruin the relationship."

HOW MUCH IS ENOUGH?

Before you begin planning for the cash needs of your business, you must figure out how much money you will need to live on for the first six to 12 months of your business's operation. The best way to accomplish this is to create a budget that shows where you spent your money in the past 12 months. Make sure you look over the whole 12-month period, because expenses often change a lot from month to month. When creating the schedule, be on the lookout for expenses that could be reduced or eliminated if necessary. Use the form on pages 187 and 188 to create your own budget.

Monthly Budget

Before you begin planning for the cash needs of your business, you must figure out how much money you will need to live on for the first six to 12 months of your business's operation. The best way to accomplish this is to create a budget that shows where you spent your money in the past 12 months. Make sure you look over the whole 12-month period, because expenses often change a lot from month to month. When creating the schedule, be on the lookout for expenses that could be reduced or eliminated if necessary. Use the form on the following page to create your own budget.

	JAN	FEB	MAR	APR	MAY	JUN	JUL	AUG	SEP	OCT	NOV	DEC	TOTAL
Income													
Wages (take-home)—partner 1													
Wages (take-home)—partner 2													
Interest and dividends													
Other													
Total Income													
Expenses													
Auto expenses													
Auto insurance													
Auto payment													
Beauty shop and barber													
Cable TV													
Charity													
Child care													
Clothing													
Credit card payments													

Monthly Budget (cont'd)

	JAN	FEB	MAR	APR	MAY	JUN	JUL	AUG	SEP	OCT	NOV	DEC	TOTAL
Dues and subscriptions													
Entertainment and recreation													
Gifts													
Groceries and dining out													
Health insurance													
Home repairs													
Household													
Income tax (additional)													
Laundry and dry cleaning													
Life insurance													
Medical and dental													
Mortgage payment or rent													
Other debt payments													
Telephone bill													
Tuition													
Utilities													
Vacations													
Other													
Total Expenses													
Cash (Shortfall) Extra													

Nothing Ventured, Nothing Gained

How to find and attract investors

N o matter what type of financing source you approach—
a bank, a venture capitalist or your cousin Lenny—there are two basic
ways to finance a business: equity financing or debt financing. In
equity financing, you receive capital in exchange for part ownership
of the company. In debt financing, you receive capital in the form of
a loan, which must be paid back. This chapter explains various types
of equity financing; the following chapter explains debt financing.

EQUITY BASICS

Equity financing can come from various sources, including venture capital firms and private investors. Whichever source you
choose, there are some basics you should understand before you try
to get equity capital. An investor's "share in your company" comes in
various forms. If your company is incorporated, the investor might
bargain for shares of stock. Or an investor who wants to be involved
in the management of the company could come in as a partner.

Keeping control of your company can be more difficult when you
are working with outside investors who provide equity financing.
Before seeking outside investment, make the most of your own
resources to build the company. "The more value you can add before
you go to the well, the better," says John R. Thorne, a professor of
entrepreneurship. If all you bring to the table is a good idea and some
talent, an investor may not be willing to provide a large chunk of capital without receiving a controlling share of the ownership in return. As
a result, you could end up losing control of the business you started.

Don't assume the first investor to express interest in your business
is a godsend. Even someone who seems to share your vision for the
company may be bad news. "It pays to know your investor," Thorne
says. An investor who doesn't understand your business may pull the
plug at the wrong time—and destroy the company.

How It Works

Because equity financing involves trading partial ownership interest for capital, the more capital a company takes in from equity
investors, the more diluted the founder's control. "The question is,

BRIGHT IDEA

ONE ENTREPRENEUR WHO WANTED TO OPEN A RESTAURANT GOT A LIST OF POTENTIAL INVESTORS BY ATTENDING ALL THE GRAND OPENINGS OF RESTAURANTS IN THE AREA WHERE HE WANTED TO LOCATE. BY ASKING FOR THE NAMES OF PEOPLE WHO INVESTED IN THOSE RESTAURANTS, HE SOON HAD ENOUGH CONTACT NAMES TO FINANCE HIS OWN BUSINESS.

How much management are you're willing to give up?" says attorney Jerry Friedland.

Friedland emphasizes the importance of voting control in the company. Investors may be willing to accept a majority of the *preferred* (nonvoting) stock rather than *common* (voting) stock. Another possibility is to give the investor a majority of the profits by granting dividends to the preferred stockholders first. Or, holders of nonvoting stock can get liquidation preference, meaning they're first in line to recover their investment if the company goes under.

Even if they're willing to accept a minority position, financiers generally insist on contract provisions that permit them to make management changes under certain conditions. These might include covenants permitting the investor to take control of the company if the corporation fails to meet a certain income level or makes changes without the investor's permission.

Investors may ask that their preferred stock be redeemable either for common stock or for cash at a specified number of years later. That gives the entrepreneur a chance to buy the company back if possible but also may allow the investor to convert to common stock and gain control of the company.

Some experts contend that retaining voting control is not important. In a typical high-growth company, the founder only owns 10 percent of the business by the time it goes public. That's not necessarily bad, because 10 percent of $100 million is better than 100 percent of nothing. The key is how valuable the founder is to the success of the company. If you can't easily be replaced, then you have a lot of leverage even though you may not control the business.

"If the entrepreneur is good enough, the investors may find their best alternative is to let the entrepreneur run the company," says Thorne. He advises against getting hung up on the precise percentage of ownership: "If it's a successful business, most people will leave you alone even if they own 80 percent." To protect yourself, however, you should always seek financial and legal advice before involving outside investors in your business.

VENTURE CAPITAL

When most people think of equity financing, they think of venture capital. Once seen as a renegade source of financing for start-up businesses, venture capital—like most kinds of capital—is no longer so easy to come by. The ready to give, give, give venture capitalist is becoming very elusive.

Yes, there are venture capital firms out there. Quite a few, actually. There are Web sites you can go to, like Entrepreneur.com's VC 100 (www.entrepreneur.com/vc100), a directory of venture capital firms that will point you to a slew of them—and you may run into some luck. But at this point in time, luck is exactly what you need to convince venture capitalists to invest in your business. If you think we're trying to discourage you, we are. Money can be found for investing in your company (see Chapter 16), but the era of the venture capitalist happily handing over forklifts of money is over—especially for start-ups.

Venture capital is most likely to be given to an established company with an already proven track record. If you are a start-up, your product or service must be better than the wheel, sliced bread and the PC—with an extremely convincing plan that will make the investor a lot of money. And even that might not be good enough.

EARTH ANGELS

The unpleasant reality is that getting financing from venture capital firms is an extreme long shot. The pleasant reality is that there are plenty of other sources you can tap for equity financing—typically with far fewer strings attached than an institutional venture capital deal. One source of private capital is an investment angel.

Originally a term used to describe investors in Broadway shows, "angel" now refers to anyone who invests his or her money in an entrepreneurial company (unlike institutional venture capitalists, who invest other people's money). Angel investing has soared in recent years as a growing number of individuals seek better returns on their money than they can get from traditional investment vehicles. Contrary to popular belief, most angels are not millionaires. Typically, they earn between $60,000 and $100,000 a year. Which means there are likely to be plenty of them right in your backyard.

Where Angels Fly

Angels can be classified into two groups: affiliated and nonaffiliated. An affiliated angel is someone who has some sort of contact with you or your business but is not necessarily related to or acquainted with you. A nonaffiliated angel has no connection with either you or your business.

It makes sense to start your investor search by seeking an affiliated angel since he or she is already familiar with you or your business and has a vested interest in the relationship. Begin by jotting down names of people who might fit the category of affiliated angel.

■ **PROFESSIONALS:** These include professional providers of services you now use—doctors, dentists, lawyers, accountants and so on. You know these people, so an appointment should be easy to arrange. Professionals usually have discretionary income available

Netting Angels

Looking for angels? Now there's a simple way for them to find you—online. The Angel Capital Electronic Network (ACE-Net), launched by the Small Business Administration, helps accredited angel investors find entrepreneurs in need of capital.

Angels can access ACE-Net's online listings of entrepreneurial companies using a search engine that lets them find out a company's product or service, financing desired and other criteria. Angels can also place search criteria on the network and get e-mailed whenever a company meeting those criteria appears on the network.

Access is limited to accredited investors—those who have a net income in excess of $200,000 and who meet other criteria. Entrepreneurs must also meet certain criteria to be listed. For more information, visit www.sbaonline.sba.gov or http://acenet.csusb.edu, or contact the SBA's Office of Advocacy at (202) 205-6533.

to invest in outside projects, and if they're not interested, they may be able to recommend a colleague who is.

■ **BUSINESS ASSOCIATES:** These are people you come in contact with during the normal course of your business day. They can be divided into four subgroups:

SMART TIP

KEEP THIS IN MIND WHEN CRAFTING YOUR PITCH TO INVESTOR ANGELS: WHEN ANGELS REJECT A POTENTIAL INVESTMENT, IT'S TYPICALLY BECAUSE: 1) THEY DON'T KNOW THE KEY PEOPLE WELL ENOUGH OR 2) THEY DON'T BELIEVE THE OWNER AND MANAGEMENT HAVE THE EXPERIENCE AND TALENT TO SUCCEED.

1. **SUPPLIERS/VENDORS:** The owners of companies who supply your inventory and other needs have a vital interest in your company's success and make excellent angels. A supplier's investment may not come in the form of cash but in the form of better payment terms or cheaper prices. Suppliers might even use their credit to help you get a loan.

2. **CUSTOMERS:** These are especially good contacts if they use your product or service to make or sell their own goods. List all the customers with whom you have this sort of business relationship.

3. **EMPLOYEES:** Some of your key employees might be sitting on unused equity in their homes that would make excellent collateral for a business loan to your business. There is no greater incentive to an employee than to share ownership in the company for which he or she works.

4. **COMPETITORS:** These include owners of similar companies you don't directly compete with. If a competitor is doing business in another part of the country and does not infringe on your territory, he or she may be an empathetic investor and may share not only capital, but information as well.

The nonaffiliated angels category includes:

■ **PROFESSIONALS:** This group can include lawyers, accountants, consultants and brokers whom you don't know personally or do business with.

■ **MIDDLE MANAGERS:** Angels in middle management positions start investing in small businesses for two major reasons—either they're bored with their jobs and are looking for outside interests, or they are nearing retirement or fear they are being phased out.

■ **ENTREPRENEURS:** These angels are (or have been) successful in their own businesses and like investing in other entrepreneurial ventures. Entrepreneurs who are familiar with your industry make excellent investors.

Make The Connection

Approaching affiliated angels is simply a matter of calling to make an appointment. To look for nonaffiliated angels, try these proven methods:

- **ADVERTISING:** The business opportunity section of your local newspaper or The Wall Street Journal is an excellent place to advertise for investors. Classified advertising is an inexpensive, simple, quick and effective way.

- **BUSINESS BROKERS:** Business brokers know hundreds of people with money who are interested in buying businesses. Even though you don't want to sell your business, you might be willing to sell part of it. Since many brokers are not open to the idea of their clients buying just part of a business, you might have to use some persuasion to get the broker to give you contact names. You'll find a list of local business brokers in the Yellow Pages under "Business Brokers."

- **TELEMARKETING:** This approach has been called "dialing for dollars." First you get a list of wealthy individuals in your area. Then you begin calling them. Obviously, you have to be highly motivated to try this approach, and a good list is your most important tool. Look up mailing-list brokers in the Yellow Pages. If you don't feel comfortable making cold calls yourself, you can always hire someone to do it for you.

- **NETWORKING:** Attending local venture capital group meetings and other business associations to make contacts is a time-consuming approach but can be effective. Most newspapers contain an events calendar that lists when and where these types of meetings take place.

- **INTERMEDIARIES:** These are firms that find angels for entrepreneurial companies. They are usually called "boutique investment bankers." This means they are small firms that focus primarily on small financing deals. These firms typically charge a percentage of the amount of money they raise for you. Ask your lawyer or accountant for the name of a reputable firm in your area.

Angels tend to find most of their investment opportunities through friends and business associates, so whatever method you use to search for angels, it is also important to spread the word. Tell your professional advisors and people you meet at networking events, or anyone who could be a good source of referrals, that you are looking for investment capital. You will never know what kind of people they know.

Getting The Money

Once you've found potential angels, how do you win them over? Angels look for many of the same things professional venture capitalists look for:

- **STRONG MANAGEMENT:** Does your management team have a track record of success and experience?
- **PROPRIETARY STRENGTH:** Proprietary does not necessarily mean you must have patents, copyrights or trademarks on all your products. It just means that your product or service should be unusual enough to grab consumers' attention.
- **WINDOW OF OPPORTUNITY:** Investors look for a window of opportunity when your company can be the first in a market and grab the lion's share of business before others.
- **MARKET POTENTIAL:** Investors prefer businesses with strong market potential. That means a restaurateur with plans to franchise stands a better chance than one who simply wants to open one local site.
- **RETURN ON INVESTMENT:** Most angels will expect a return of 20 to 25 percent over five years. However, they may accept a lower rate of return if your business has a lower risk.

If angels consider the same factors as venture capital companies, what is the difference between them? You have an edge with angels because many are not motivated solely by profit. Particularly if your angel is a current or former entrepreneur, he or she may be motivated as much by the enjoyment of helping a young business succeed as by the money he or she stands to gain. Angels are more likely than venture capitalists to be persuaded by an entrepreneur's drive to succeed, persistence and mental discipline.

That is why it is important that your business plan convey a good sense of your background, experience and drive. Your business plan should also address the concerns above and spell out the financing you expect to need from start-up to maturity.

What if your plan is rejected? Ask the angel if he or she knows someone else your business might appeal to. If your plan is accepted, you have some negotiating to do. Be sure to spell out all the terms of the investment in a written agreement; get your lawyer's assistance

BEWARE!

LOOKING FOR AN INVESTOR THROUGH CLASSIFIED ADS? BE AWARE THERE ARE LEGAL IMPLICATIONS WHEN YOU SOLICIT MONEY THROUGH THE NEWSPAPER. ALWAYS GET LEGAL ADVICE BEFORE PLACING AN AD.

here. How long will the investment last? How will return be calculated? How will the investment be cashed out? Detail the amount of involvement each angel will have in the business and how the investment will be legalized.

Examine the deal carefully for the possibility of the investor parlaying current equity or future loans to your business into controlling interest. Such a deal is not made in heaven and could indicate you are working with a devil in angel's garb.

GLOSSARY

ANGEL, ANGEL INVESTOR: describes a private individual who invests money in a business

COMMON STOCK: stock representing equity ownership in a company; it entitles the holder to elect corporate directors and collect dividends

DEBT FINANCING: capital in the form of a loan, which must be paid back

EQUITY FINANCING: capital received in exchange for part ownership of the company

LIQUIDATION PREFERENCE: stockholders with liquidation preference are first in line to recover their investment if the company goes under

NONVOTING STOCK: see preferred stock

PREFERRED STOCK: stock that pays a fixed dividend and is given preference ahead of common stockholders in the event of liquidation

VENTURE: capitalists look for an idea that is well-formulated, well-documented and well protected

VENTURE CAPITAL: generally refers to institutional venture capital firms that invest other people's money and manage it for them; venture capitalists typically seek a high degree of involvement and expect a high rate of return in a short time

VOTING STOCK: see common stock

Can You Bank On It?

The ins and outs of debt financing

Unlike equity financing, where you sell part of your business to an investor, debt financing simply means receiving money in the form of a loan that you will have to repay. There are many sources you can turn to for debt financing, including banks, commercial lenders and even your personal credit cards.

TYPES OF LOANS

You don't need to pinpoint the exact type of loan you need before you approach a lender; he or she will help you decide what type of financing is best for your needs. However, you should have some general idea of the different types of loans available so you will understand what your lender is offering.

There is a mind-boggling variety of loans available, complicated by the fact that the same type of loan may have different terms at different banks. For instance, a commercial loan at one bank might be written with equal installments of principal and interest, while at another bank the loan is written with monthly interest payments and a balloon payment of the principal.

Here is a look at how lenders generally structure loans, with common variations.

■ **LINE-OF-CREDIT LOANS:** The most useful type of loan for the small business is the line-of-credit loan. In fact, it's probably the one permanent loan arrangement every business owner should have with his or her banker since it protects the business from emergencies and stalled cash flow. Line-of-credit loans are intended for purchases of inventory and payment of operating costs for working capital and business cycle needs. They are not intended for purchases of equipment or real estate.

A line-of-credit loan is a short-term loan that extends the cash available in your business's checking account to the upper limit of the loan contract. Every bank has its own method of funding, but, essentially, an amount is transferred to the business's checking account to cover checks. The business pays interest on the actual amount advanced, from the time it is advanced until it is paid back. Line-of-credit loans usually carry the lowest interest rate a bank

SMART TIP

HUD (THE FEDERAL DEPARTMENT OF HOUSING AND URBAN DEVELOPMENT) PROVIDES JOB  AND OTHER GRANTS TO START-UPS AND SMALL BUSINESSES FOR JOB CREATION (FOR EXAMPLE, $10,000 PER JOB CREATED) IN THE FORM OF LOW-INTEREST LOANS, OFTEN IN CONJUNCTION WITH THE SBA. HUD WILL BE ABLE TO PROVIDE THE NAMES AND PHONE NUMBERS OF CITY, COUNTY AND STATE ORGANIZATIONS IN YOUR AREA THAT REPRESENT HUD FOR DEVELOPMENT OF TARGETED GEOGRAPHIC URBAN AREAS.

offers since they are seen as fairly low-risk. Some banks even include a clause that gives them the right to cancel the loan if they think your business is in jeopardy. Interest payments are made monthly, and the principal is paid off at your convenience. It is wise to make payments on the principal often. Bankers may also call this a revolving line of credit, and they see it as an indication that your business is earning enough income.

Most line-of-credit loans are written for periods of one year and may be renewed almost automatically for an annual fee. Some banks require that your credit line be fully paid off for between seven and 30 days each contract year. This period is probably the best time to negotiate.

Even if you don't need a line-of-credit loan now, talk to your banker about how to get one. To negotiate a credit line, your banker will want to see current financial statements, the latest tax returns and a projected cash-flow statement.

■ **INSTALLMENT LOANS:** These loans are paid back with equal monthly payments covering both principal and interest. Installment loans may be written to meet all types of business needs. You receive the full amount when the contract is signed, and interest is calculated from that date to the final day of the loan. If you repay an installment loan before its final date, there will be no penalty and an appropriate adjustment of interest.

The term of an installment loan will always be correlated to its use. A business cycle loan may be written as a four-month installment loan from, say, September 1 until December 31, and would carry the lowest interest rate since the risk to the lender is from one to seven years. Real estate and renovation loans may be written for up to 21 years. An installment loan is occasionally written with quarterly, half-yearly or annual payments when monthly payments are inappropriate.

■ **BALLOON LOANS:** Though these loans are usually written under another name, you can identify them by the fact that the full amount is received when the contract assigned, but only the interest is paid off during the life of the loan, with a "balloon" payment of the principal due on the final day.

Occasionally, a lender will offer a loan in which both interest and principal are paid with a single "balloon" payment. Balloon loans are usually reserved for situations when a business has to wait until a specific date before receiving payment from a client for its product or services. In all other ways, they are the same as installment loans.

- **INTERIM LOANS:** When considering interim loans, bankers are concerned with who will be paying off the loan and whether that commitment is reliable. Interim loans are used to make periodic payments to the contractors building new facilities when a mortgage on the building will be used to pay off the interim loan.

- **SECURED AND UNSECURED LOANS:** Loans can come in one of two forms: secured or unsecured. When your lender knows you well and is convinced that your business is sound and that the loan will be repaid on time, he or she may be willing to write an unsecured loan. Such a loan, in any of the aforementioned forms, has no collateral pledged as a secondary payment source should you default on the loan. The lender provides you with an unsecured loan because it considers you a low risk. As a new business, you are highly unlikely to qualify for an unsecured loan; it generally requires a track record of profitability and success.

A secured loan, on the other hand, requires some kind of collateral but generally has a lower interest rate than an unsecured loan. When a loan is written for more than 12 months, is used to purchase equipment or does not seem risk-free, the lender will ask that the loan be secured by collateral. The collateral used, whether real estate or inventory, is expected to outlast the loan and is usually related to the purpose of the loan.

Since lenders expect to use the collateral to pay off the loan if the borrower defaults, they will value it appropriately. A $20,000 piece of new equipment will probably secure

HOT LINK

WANT TO APPLY FOR A LOAN FROM THE COMFORTS OF HOME? LIVECAPITAL.COM ANALYZES YOUR 20-QUESTION LOAN APPLICATION AGAINST A VARIETY OF LENDERS AND COMES UP WITH OFFERS IN SECONDS. IT MAY ALSO BE A GOOD TRIAL RUN TO HELP YOU DETERMINE WHETHER YOU'RE READY TO GET A LOAN FOR YOUR BUSINESS.

a loan of up to $15,000, receivables are valued for loans up to 75 percent of the amount due, and inventory is usually valued at up to 50 percent of its sale price.

■ **LETTER OF CREDIT:** Typically used in international trade, this document allows entrepreneurs to guarantee payment to suppliers in other countries. The document substitutes the bank's credit for the entrepreneur's up to a set amount for a specified period of time.

■ **OTHER LOANS:** Banks all over the country write loans, especially installment and balloon loans, under a myriad of names. They include:

1. **TERM LOANS,** both short- and long-term, according to the number of years they are written for
2. **SECOND MORTGAGES** where real estate is used to secure a loan; usually long-term, they're also known as equity loans
3. **INVENTORY LOANS** and equipment loans for the purchase of, and secured by, either equipment or inventory
4. **ACCOUNTS RECEIVABLE LOANS** secured by your outstanding accounts
5. **PERSONAL LOANS** where your signature and personal collateral guarantee the loan, which you, in turn, lend to your business
6. **GUARANTEED LOANS** in which a third party—an investor, spouse, or the Small Business Administration—guarantees repayment (for more on SBA-guaranteed loans, see the following chapter)
7. **COMMERCIAL LOANS** in which the bank offers its standard loan for small businesses

Once you have an understanding of the different types of loans available, you are better equipped for the next step: "selling" a lender on your business.

SOURCES OF FINANCING

When seeking debt financing, where do you begin? Carefully choosing the lenders you target can increase your odds of success. Here is a look at various loan sources and what you should know about each.

Bank On It

Traditionally, the paperwork and processing costs involved in making and servicing loans have made the small loans most entrepreneurs seek too costly for big banks to administer. Put plainly, a loan under $25,000—the type many start-ups are looking for—may not be worth a big bank's time.

In recent years, however, the relationship between banks and small business has been improving as more and more banks realize the strength and importance of this growing market. With corporations and real estate developers no longer spurring so much of banks' business, lenders are looking to entrepreneurs to take up the slack.

Many major banks have added special services and programs for small business; others are streamlining their loan paperwork and approval process to get loans to entrepreneurs faster. On the plus side, banks are marketing to small business like never before. On the downside, however, the "streamlining" process often means that, more than ever, loan approval is based solely on numbers and scores on standardized rating systems rather than on an entrepreneur's character or drive.

BRIGHT IDEA

THE FOUNDATION FOR INTERNATIONAL COMMUNITY ASSISTANCE (FINCA) HELPS ENTREPRENEURS FORM THEIR OWN SELF-EMPLOYMENT ASSOCIATIONS. THROUGH A LOAN FROM FINCA, THESE GROUPS OFFER MEMBERS ACCESS TO A SERIES OF SHORT-TERM LOANS THAT PROVIDE WORKING CAPITAL FOR SMALL BUSINESSES. BASED IN WASHINGTON, DC, THE FOUNDATION HAS LOCATIONS IN SEVERAL STATES; CALL (202) 682-1510 FOR MORE INFORMATION.

Given the challenges of working with a big bank, many entrepreneurs are taking a different tack. Instead of wooing the big commercial institutions, they are courting community banks, where "relationship banking" is the rule, not the exception. Even given today's banking climate, it is easier to get a start-up loan from community banks, according to the Independent Community Bankers of America. They can be a little more flexible, don't have a bureaucracy to deal with, and are more apt to make character loans.

Do not get the idea that obtaining a loan from a community bank is a snap, however. You'll still have to meet credit and collateral requirements just as you would at a larger institution. The difference: Smaller banks tend give more weight to personal attributes. If the business is located in town, the banker likely already knows the entrepreneur, and the family has lived in the area for years; these things count more in a community bank.

Whether the bank you target is big or small, perhaps what matters most is developing relationships. If you have done your personal banking at the same place for 20 years and know the people with authority there, it makes sense to target that bank as a potential lender. If you do not have that kind of relationship at your bank, start to get to know bankers now. Visit chamber of commerce meetings; go to networking events; take part in community functions that local bankers or other movers and shakers are part of. A banker with a personal interest in you is more likely to look favorably on your loan application.

Boost your chances of getting a loan by finding a lender whose experience matches your needs. Talk to friends, lawyers or accountants and other entrepreneurs in the same industry for leads on banks that have helped people in your business. Pound the pavement and talk to banks about the type and size of loans they specialize in. Put in the work to find the right lender, and you'll find it pays off.

Commercial Finance Companies

Banks aren't your only option when seeking a loan. Nonbank commercial lenders, or commercial finance companies, have expanded their focus on small business in recent years as more and more small banks, which traditionally made loans to entrepreneurs, have been swallowed up in mergers. The advantage of approaching commercial finance companies is that, like community banks, they may be more willing to look beyond numbers and assets. "Commercial finance companies give opportunities to start-ups and a lot of other companies banks will not lend to," says Bruce A. Jones of the Commercial Finance Association (CFA). Here are some commercial finance companies to get you started:

- Princeton, New Jersey-based **BUSINESS ALLIANCE CAPITAL CORP.**, for instance, offers loans of $150,000 to $1.5 million to entrepreneurs in manufacturing, distribution and service industries who cannot get loans from traditional sources.
- **WACHOVIA** is an SBA lender offering 7(a) and 504 loans with low down payments, fixed and variable interest rates, and longer repayment terms. In most states, Wachovia is a member of the SBA Preferred Lender program. Financing of up to 90 percent is provided on loans from $150,000 to $4.3 million.
- At Hartford, Connecticut-based **BUSINESS LENDERS,** loan evaluators look beyond traditional lending criteria to consider management ability and character. "Somebody who has bad credit could still be a good credit risk," says founder Penn Ritter. "It depends

Franchise Focus

Financing is any start-up entrepreneur's biggest challenge—and it's no different for franchisees. The good news is, franchisors may offer a little extra help in getting the capital you need.

Some franchisors offer direct financing to help franchisees with all or part of the costs of start-up. This may take the form of equipment, real estate or inventory financing. The goal is to free up money so franchisees have more working capital.

Many franchisors are not directly involved in lending but have established preferred relationships with banks and commercial finance companies. Because these lenders have processed loans for other franchisees, they are more familiar with new franchisees' needs.

The franchisor you're interested in can tell you about any direct financing or preferred lender programs available. The Uniform Franchise Offering Circular should also include this information.

If your franchisor doesn't have a preferred lender, you can often find financing by approaching banks that have made loans to other franchisees in the system. Talk to franchisees and see how they financed their businesses.

Once you've found a lender to target, you'll need to provide the same information and follow the same steps as you would with any type of business loan.

on why they had the credit problem."

Commercial lenders require a business plan, personal financial statements and cash-flow projections and will usually expect you to come up with 25 percent of the needed capital yourself. For more information about commercial finance companies, call the CFA at (212) 594-3490.

Give Yourself Credit

One potentially risky way to finance your business is to use your personal credit cards. The obvious drawback is the high interest rate; if you use the card for cash advances rather than to buy equipment, the rates are even higher.

Some entrepreneurs take advantage of low-interest credit card offers they receive in the mail, transferring balances from one card to

BRIGHT IDEA

LOOKING FOR FINANCING? CONSIDER AN UNEXPECTED SOURCE—YOUR VENDORS. VENDORS MAY BE WILLING TO GIVE YOU THE CAPITAL YOU NEED, EITHER THROUGH A DELAYED FINANCING AGREEMENT OR A LEASING PROGRAM. VENDORS HAVE A VESTED INTEREST IN YOUR SUCCESS AND A BELIEF IN YOUR STABILITY, OR THEY WOULDN'T BE DOING BUSINESS WITH YOU. BEFORE ENTERING ANY AGREEMENT, HOWEVER, COMPARE LONG-TERM LEASING COSTS WITH SHORT-TERM LOAN COSTS; LEASING COULD BE MORE COSTLY.

another as soon as interest rates rise (typically after six months). If you use this strategy, keep a close eye on when the rate will increase. Sometimes, you can get the bank to extend the low introductory rate over the phone.

Experts advise using credit card financing as a last resort because interest rates are higher than any other type of financing. However, if you are good at juggling payments, your start-up needs are low, and you are confident you'll be able to pay the money back fairly quickly, this could be the route to take.

APPLYING FOR A LOAN

The next step is applying for the loan. It's important to know what you'll need to provide and what lenders are looking for.

The Loan Application

Think of your loan application as a sales tool, just like your brochures or ads. When you put together the right combination of facts and figures, your application will sell your lender on the short- and long-term profit potential of lending money to your business. To do that, the application must convince your lender that you will pay back the loan as promised and that your managerial ability (and future loans) will result in a profit-making partnership.

"Banks are in the money-lending business," says banker Jon P. Goodman. "To lend money, they need evidence of security and stability. It's that simple."

How can you provide this evidence when your business hasn't even gotten off the ground? Begin by making sure your loan application is both realistic and optimistic. If you predict an increase in sales of between 8 and 12 percent, base your income projections on an increase of 10 percent, and then specify what you intend to do to ensure the additional sales.

Personal Financial Statement

Entrepreneurs in search of start-up financing use personal financial statements as proof of their ability to manage money and be financially responsible.

Statement of financial condition as of_____ , 20_____

INDIVIDUAL INFORMATION	CO-APPLICANT INFORMATION
Name	Name
Home Address	Home Address
City, State & ZIP	City, State & ZIP
Name of Employer	Name of Employer
Title/Position	Title/Position
No. of Years with Employer	No. of Years with Employer
Employer Address	Employer Address
City, State & ZIP	City, State & ZIP
Home Phone Business Phone	Home Phone Business Phone

SOURCE OF INCOME	TOTALS	CONTINGENT LIABILITIES	TOTALS
Salary (applicant)		If guarantor, co-maker or endorser	
Salary (co-applicant)		If you have any legal claims	
Bonuses & commissions (applicant)		If you have liability for a lease or contract	
Bonuses & commissions (co-applicant)		If you have outstanding letters of credit	
Income from rental property		If you have outstanding surety bonds	
Investment income		If you have any contested tax liens	
Other income*		If you listed an amount for any of the above, give details:	
TOTAL INCOME			

*Income from alimony, child support, or separate maintenance income need not be revealed if you do not wish to have it considered as a basis for repaying this obligation.

ASSETS	TOTALS	LIABILITIES	TOTALS
Cash, checking & savings		Secured loans	
Marketable securities		Unsecured loans	
Nonmarketable securities		Charge account bills	
Real estate owned/home		Personal debts	
Partial interest in real estate equities		Monthly bills	
Automobiles		Real estate mortgages	
Personal property		Unpaid income tax	
Personal loans		Other unpaid taxes and interest	
Cash value—life insurance		Other debts—itemize	
Other assets—itemize			
		TOTAL LIABILITIES	
		TOTAL ASSETS	
TOTAL ASSETS		NET WORTH (ASSETS–LIABILITIES)	

Also make sure your application is complete. When a piece of an application is missing, bankers instantly suspect that either something is being hidden or the applicant doesn't know his or her business well enough to pull the information together.

There are 12 separate items that should be included in every loan application. The importance of each one varies with the size of your business, your industry and the amount you are requesting.

1. Cover sheet
2. Cover letter
3. Table of contents
4. Amount and use of the loan
5. History and description of your business
6. Functions and background of your management team
7. Market information on your product or service
8. Financial history and current status
9. Financial projections to demonstrate that the loan will be repaid
10. A list of possible collateral
11. Personal financial statements
12. Additional documents to support the projections

Many of these items are part of your business plan; a few of them will have to be added. Here's a closer look at each section:

1. **COVER SHEET:** This is the title page to your "book." All it needs to say is "Loan application submitted by John Smith, Sunday's Ice Cream Parlor, to Big Bucks Bank, Main Street, Anytown." It should also include the date and your business telephone number.

2. **COVER LETTER:** The cover letter is a personal business letter to your banker requesting consideration of your application for a line of credit or an installment loan. The second paragraph should describe your business. "Our company is a sole proprietorship, partnership or corporation in manufacturing, distributing and retailing X type of goods." The third paragraph is best kept to just one or two sentences that "sell" your application by indicating what your future plans are for your business.

3. **TABLE OF CONTENTS:** This page makes it easy for your banker to see that all the documents are included.

4. **AMOUNT AND USE OF THE LOAN:** This page documents how much you want to borrow and how you will use the loan. If you are buying a new piece of equipment, for instance, it should show the contract price, add the cost of freight and installation,

deduct the amount you will be contributing, and show the balance to be borrowed.

5. **HISTORY AND DESCRIPTION OF THE BUSINESS:** This is often the most difficult to write. The key is to stay with the facts and assume the reader knows nothing about your business. Describe, more fully than in the cover letter, the legal form of your business and its location. Tell why you believe the business is going to succeed. Conclude with a paragraph on your future plans.

6. **MANAGEMENT TEAM:** Bankers know that it's people who make things happen. Your management team might consist of every employee, if they oversee an important part of your operation, or it might be just you and one key person. It also includes any outside consultants you plan to use regularly, such as your accountant or banker. In one or two pages, list each person's name and responsibilities. Where appropriate, describe the background that makes this person the right choice for that job.

7. **MARKET INFORMATION:** You should begin these pages with a complete description of your product line or service, and the market it is directed toward. Next, describe how you have targeted your market niche and how successful you have been. Finally, detail your future plans to add new products or services.

8. **FINANCIAL HISTORY:** Most bankers want to see balance sheets and income (profit and loss) statements. As a start-up, you will need to use projections. Bankers will compare these to norms in your industry.

9. **FINANCIAL PROJECTIONS:** This set of three documents—a projected income statement, balance sheet and cash-flow statement—should show how the business, with the use of the loan, will generate sufficient profits to pay off the loan. Your accountant can help you prepare these documents.

10. **COLLATERAL:** Listing your available collateral—cash reserves, stocks and bonds, equipment, home equity, inventory and receivables—demonstrates your understanding that your banker will normally look for a backup repayment source. Each piece of collateral listed should be described with its cost and current fair market value.

Read The Fine Print

Hallelujah and yippee! You can almost hear the choirs of angels singing as your banker smiles and hands you the loan document. You got the loan!

Not so fast. Before you sign that piece of paper, take a good look at what you're getting into. Many entrepreneurs are so excited about having their loans approved, they fail to read the fine print on their loan agreements. That can lead to trouble later on.

It's a good idea to get the loan documents ahead of time so you have a chance to review them for a couple of days before you sign, according to the American Banker's Association. Bankers won't have a problem sending advance copies of the documents but will generally do so only if they're specifically asked.

Most bankers will be happy to help you understand the fine print, but it's also a good idea to have your accountant and lawyer review the documents, too.

Although it varies slightly from bank to bank, a small-business loan package usually consists of several documents, typically including a loan agreement, a promissory note and some form of guarantee and surety agreement.

- **LOAN AGREEMENT:** This specifies, in essence, the promises you are making to the bank and asks you to affirm that you are authorized to bind your business to the terms of the loan. Most banks require you to verify that all the information on your loan application is still true before they disburse the loan.
- **PROMISSORY NOTE:** This details the principal and interest owed and when payments are due. It outlines the events that would allow the bank to declare your loan in default. Knowing these events ahead of time can help you protect your credit record. Look for "cure" language in the default section. A cure provision allows you a certain amount of time (usually 10 days) to remedy the default after you've been notified by the bank. If such a provision isn't included, ask if it can be added to prevent you from defaulting accidentally (in case a payment is lost in the mail, for example). Also make sure you understand what the bank can and can't do after declaring default.
- **GUARANTEE AND SURETY AGREEMENT:** Because start-ups generally have insufficient operating history or assets on which to base a loan, banks usually require the loan to be guaranteed with your personal assets. The bank may ask you to secure the loan with the equity in your home, for example.

11. **PERSONAL FINANCIAL STATEMENTS:** As a start-up, you will need to add your personal guarantee to any loan the bank makes. The banker will want to see your tax return and balance sheets showing personal net worth. Most banks have pre-printed forms that make pulling these figures together relatively easy.

12. **ADDITIONAL DOCUMENTS:** In this section, you can include whatever documents you feel will enhance your loan package. This might include a copy of the sales contract on a new piece of equipment, a lease and photograph of a new location, blueprints or legal documents. If you are introducing a new product or service, include a product brochure and additional market research information.

This section can help a new business overcome the lack of a track record. While glowing letters won't make a banker overlook weak finances, an assurance from your largest customer that your services are valued can help your banker see your full potential.

What Lenders Look For

Your application is complete, with every "i" dotted and every "t" crossed. But is it enough to get you the cold, hard cash? What are lenders really looking for when they pore over your application? Lenders typically base their decisions on four criteria, often called the "Four C's of Credit":

1. **CREDIT:** The lender will examine your personal credit history to see how well you've managed your past obligations. If you have some black marks on your credit, the banker will want to hear the details and see proof that you repaid what you owed. A couple of late payments are not a big deal, but two or more consecutive missed payments are. Get a copy of your credit history before you turn in your application. This way, you can find out about any problems and explain them before your banker brings them up.

2. **CHARACTER:** Character is hard to measure, but lenders will use your credit history to assess this as well. They take lawsuits, bankruptcies and tax liens particularly seriously in

BRIGHT IDEA

IF YOU ARE A WOMAN OR A MEMBER OF A MINORITY GROUP LOOKING TO PURCHASE A FRANCHISE, YOU MAY BE ELIGIBLE FOR SPECIAL FINANCIAL INCENTIVES OR ASSISTANCE FROM THE FRANCHISOR. ASK FRANCHISORS YOU ARE CONSIDERING WHETHER THEY HAVE SUCH PROGRAMS AND WHAT THE REQUIREMENTS ARE.

evaluating your character. They will also do a background check and evaluate your previous work experience.

3. **CAPACITY:** What happens if your business slumps? Do you have the capacity to convert other assets to cash, either by selling or borrowing against them? Your secondary repayment sources may include real estate, stocks and other savings. The lender will look at your business balance sheet and financial statement to determine your capacity.

4. **COLLATERAL:** As a start-up, you will most likely be seeking a secured loan. This means you must put up collateral—either personal assets, such as stocks or certificates of deposit, or business assets like inventory, equipment or real estate.

A Loan At Last

A good relationship with your banker is just as important after you get that loan as it is in getting one in the first place. The key word is "communication." The bank wants to be told all the good news—and bad news—about your business as soon as it occurs. Most business owners fear telling bankers bad news, but keeping problems hidden would be a mistake. Like any relationship, yours with your banker is built on trust. Keep him or her apprised of your business's progress. Invite your banker to visit your business and see how the proceeds of the loan are being put to good use.

Once you've established a relationship with a banker, it is simple to expand your circle of friends at the bank. Every time you visit, spend some time meeting and talking to people, especially those further up the ladder. Often, the bankers will be the ones to initiate contact Take advantage of this opportunity. The more people you know at the bank, the easier it will be to get the next round of financing.

GLOSSARY

COLLATERAL: anything of value that can be pledged against a loan, including stocks and bonds, equipment, home equity, inventory, and receivables; if you cannot repay the loan, the lender will look to your collateral as a backup source of repayment

CURE PROVISION: part of the default section of a promissory note, the cure provision allows you a certain amount of time (usually 10 days) to remedy a default after you've been notified

GUARANTEE AND SURETY AGREEMENT: for businesses with insufficient operating history or assets on which to base a loan, banks will require the loan to be guaranteed with your personal assets, such as the equity in your home, in a guarantee and surety agreement

LOAN AGREEMENT: written contract specifying terms of a loan

PROMISSORY NOTE: details the principal and interest owed on a loan and when payments are due; it also outlines the events that would allow the bank to declare your loan in default

Ask Your
Favorite
Uncle

*How to get government
loans and grants*

W

here can you go when private financing sources turn you down? For many start-up entrepreneurs, the answer is the U.S. Small Business Administration (SBA). The federal government has a vested interest in encouraging the growth of small business. As a result, some SBA loans have less stringent requirements for owner's equity and collateral than do commercial loans, making the SBA an excellent financing source for start-ups. In addition, many SBA loans are for smaller sums than most banks are willing to lend.

Of course, that doesn't mean the SBA is giving money away. In fact, the SBA does not actually make direct loans; instead, it provides loan guarantees to entrepreneurs, promising the bank to pay back a certain percentage of your loan if you are unable to.

Banks participate in the SBA program as regular, certified or preferred lenders. The SBA can help you prepare your loan package, which you then submit to banks. If the bank approves you, it submits your loan package to the SBA. Applications submitted by regular lenders are reviewed by the SBA in an average of two weeks, certified lender applications are reviewed in three days, and approval through preferred lenders is even faster.

The most basic eligibility requirement for SBA loans is the ability to repay the loan from cash flow, but the SBA also looks at personal credit history, industry experience or other evidence of management ability, collateral and owner's equity contributions. If you own 20 percent or more equity in the business, the SBA asks that you personally guarantee the loan. After all, you can't ask the government to back you if you're not willing to back yourself. The SBA offers a wide variety of loan programs for businesses at various stages of development. Here's a closer look:

7(a) Guaranty Loan Program

The biggest and the most popular SBA loan program is the 7(a) Guaranty Loan Program. The SBA does not lend money itself, but provides loan guarantees of up to $1 million or 75 percent of the total loan amount, whichever is less. For loans that are less than $150,000, the maximum guarantee is 85 percent of the total loan amount.

SBA policy prohibits lenders from charging many of the usual fees associated with commercial loans. Still, you can expect to pay a one-

SMART TIP

WHEN SEEKING AN SBA
LOAN, CHOOSE YOUR BANK
CAREFULLY. NOT ALL BANKERS
ARE VERSED IN SBA LOANS,
SO LOOK FOR ONE WHO
IS EXPERIENCED.

time guarantee fee, which the agency charges the lender and allows the lender to pass on to you.

A 7(a) loan can be used for many business purposes, including real estate, expansion, equipment, working capital and inventory. The money can be paid back over as long as 25 years for real estate and 10 years for equipment and working capital. Interest rates vary with the type of loan you apply for.

LowDoc Program

A general 7(a) loan may suit your business's needs best, but the 7(a) program also offers several specialized loans. One of them, the LowDoc Program, promises quick processing for amounts less than $150,000. "LowDoc" stands for "low documentation," and approval relies heavily on your personal credit rating and your business's cash flow.

"The LowDoc is probably the closest you will get these days to a good, old-fashioned character loan," says Al Stubblefield of the SBA. That fact, combined with the favorable interest rates, fees and maturity terms offered by the SBA, makes the LowDoc program an unusually

Women Only

Women business owners have a friend in Washington: the Office of Women's Business Ownership (OWBO), part of the SBA. The OWBO coordinates federal efforts that support women entrepreneurs and produces publications for women business owners.

The OWBO also manages the Women's Network for Entrepreneurial Training, a mentor program that matches seasoned women entrepreneurs with start-up business owners. In addition, the office directs the Women's Business Centers in 47 states. Women's Business Centers provide assistance, training and business counseling through the SBA. For information about OWBO services, contact the OWBO at 409 Third St. SW, 6th Fl., Washington, DC 20416, (800) U-ASK-SBA or visit www.sba. gov/womeninbusiness.

Business 101

Worried your business acumen isn't as sharp is it could be? Wishing you had taken an accounting class instead of that film history course on John Wayne? Then the Small Business Training Network might be for you.

Also known as the E-Business Institute, the Small Business Training Network is an Internet-based learning environment—functioning like a virtual campus. As their Web site says, they offer online courses, workshops, publications, information resources, learning tools and direct access to electronic counseling and other forms of technical assistance.

The classes run the gamut, from how to start your own business—with titles like "A Primer on Exporting" and "Is Franchising for Me?"—to learning how to develop your own employee handbook, manage cash flow and file for a patent. Most of these workshops are self-paced and usually extremely topical. Some classes were developed within the SBA, while others have been developed by academic institutions, government offices and corporations, such as Bank of America. For more information, log on to www.sba.gov/training.

good deal in today's loan marketplace.

LowDoc loan proceeds can be used for many purposes. Loan applicants seeking less than $50,000 are required to complete only a one-page SBA form. Applicants seeking up to $150,000 submit the same short form, plus supply copies of individual income tax returns for the previous three years and financial statements from all guarantors and co-owners.

The reduced paperwork makes the process easier for banks, too; consequently, banks are more willing to make the small loans. The SBA aims for a two-day turnaround on these loan requests.

SBA Express Program

The SBA Express Program is a close cousin of the LowDoc, also offering loans of up to $250,000. However, SBA Express gets you an answer more quickly because approved SBA Express lenders can use their own documentation and procedures to attach an SBA guarantee to an approved loan without having to wait for SBA approval. The SBA guarantees up to 50 percent of SBA Express loans.

CAPLines

For businesses that need working capital on a short-term or cyclical basis, the SBA has a collection of revolving and nonevolving lines of credit called CAPLines. A revolving loan is similar to a credit card, with which you carry a balance that goes up or down, depending on payments and amounts borrowed. With nonrevolving lines of credit, you borrow a flat amount and pay it off over a set period of time.

CAPLine loans provide business owners short-term credit, with loans that are guaranteed up to $1 million. There are five loan and

---

SBA Loan Document Checklist

Documents To Prepare For A New Business
- ☐ Your SBA loan application form
- ☐ Your personal history statement with your resume and accomplishments
- ☐ Statement of your investment capabilities
- ☐ Current financial statement of all personal liabilities and assets
- ☐ Projection of revenue statement
- ☐ Collateral list

Documents To Prepare For An Existing Business
- ☐ Balance sheet
- ☐ Profit and loss statements
- ☐ Income statement of previous and current year-to-date incomes, including business tax returns
- ☐ Personal financial statement, with each owner itemized, including personal tax returns for each owner
- ☐ Collateral list
- ☐ Your DBA or incorporation paperwork
- ☐ Copy of your business lease
- ☐ Loan request statement, describing business history, loan amount and purpose

line-of-credit programs that operate under CAPLine:

1. **SEASONAL LINE OF CREDIT:** designed to help businesses during peak seasons, when they face increases in inventory, accounts receivable and labor costs
2. **CONTRACT LINE OF CREDIT:** used to finance labor and material costs involved in carrying out contracts
3. **STANDARD ASSET-BASED LINE OF CREDIT (FORMERLY THE GREENLINE LOAN PROGRAM):** helps businesses unable to meet credit qualifications associated with long-term credit; provides financing for cyclical, growth, recurring or short-term needs
4. **SMALL ASSET-BASED REVOLVING LINE OF CREDIT:** provides smaller,

Export Expertise

If exporting is part of your business game plan, the Export-Import Bank of the United States (Ex-Im Bank) can be your biggest ally. Ex-Im Bank is committed to supporting small exporters and provides many financing tools targeted to small businesses, such as working capital guarantees and export credit insurance.

With a working capital guarantee and credit insurance, small businesses can increase sales by entering new markets, expanding their borrowing base, and offering buyers financing while carrying less risk. Often, small exporters do not have adequate cash flow or cannot get a loan to fulfill an export sales order. The Ex-Im Bank working capital guarantee assumes 90 percent of the lender's risk so exporters can access the necessary funds to purchase raw materials or supplies to fulfill an export order.

The export credit insurance protects an exporter from buyer payment default and also allows exporters to extend credit to their international buyers.

To be eligible for the Ex-Im Bank's programs, U.S. exporters must simply meet the Small Business Administration's definition of a small business and have export credit sales of less than $5 million. Business owners can contact Ex-Im Bank directly at (800) 565-3946 or through any commercial lender that works with the agency (see the Lender Locator at www.exim.gov). Based in Washington, DC, the Ex-Im Bank also has regional offices in Chicago, Houston, Miami, New York City, and Long Beach and San Jose, California.

asset-based lines of credit (up to $200,000), with less strict requirements than the standard asset-based program

5. **BUILDER'S LINE OF CREDIT:** used to finance labor and materials costs for small general contractors and builders constructing or renovating commercial or residential buildings

Each of the five credit lines has a five-year maturity but can be tailored to the borrower's needs.

Women And Minority Pre-Qualification Programs

The SBA's Minority and Women's Pre-Qualification Loan Programs help pre-qualify women, veterans and minority entrepreneurs for loans. Under the women's program, entrepreneurs can apply for loans and get up to $250,000; under the minority program, you can get up to $250,000 or more on a case-by-case basis. With the aid of private intermediary organizations chosen by the SBA, eligible entrepreneurs prepare a business plan and complete a loan application. The intermediary submits the application to the SBA.

If the application is approved, the SBA issues you a pre-qualification letter, which you can then take, along with your loan package, to a commercial bank. With the SBA's guarantee attached, the bank is more likely to approve the loan.

BRIGHT IDEA

CHECK OUT THE SBA'S WOMEN'S BUSINESS CENTER, A WEB SITE FOR WOMEN WHO WANT TO START OR EXPAND THEIR BUSINESSES. THERE IS FREE ONLINE COUNSELING AND A WORLD OF INFORMATION ABOUT BUSINESS PRACTICES, MANAGEMENT TECHNIQUES, TECHNOLOGY TRAINING, MARKET RESEARCH AND SBA SERVICES, PLUS SUCCESS STORIES TO INSPIRE YOU. VISIT THE SITE AT WWW.ONLINEWBC.GOV.

MicroLoan Program

SBA financing isn't limited to the 7(a) group of loans. The MicroLoan Program helps entrepreneurs get very small loans, ranging from less than $100 up to $35,000. The loans can be used for machinery and equipment, furniture and fixtures, inventory, supplies and working capital, but not to pay existing debts. This program is unique because it assists borrowers who generally do not meet traditional lenders' credit standards.

MicroLoans are administered through nonprofit intermediaries. These organizations receive loans from the SBA and then turn around and make loans to entrepreneurs. The intermediaries will often walk you through writing your business plan and taking inventory of your business skills.

Maturity terms and interest rates for MicroLoans vary, although terms are usually short; the loans typically take less than a week to process.

504 Loan Program

On the opposite end of the loan size spectrum is the 504 Loan, which provides long-term, fixed-rate loans for financing fixed assets, usually real estate and equipment. Loans are most often used for growth and expansion.

504 Loans are made through Certified Development Companies (CDCs)—nonprofit intermediaries that work with the SBA, banks and businesses looking for financing. There are CDCs throughout the country, each covering an assigned region.

If you are seeking funds up to $1 million to buy or renovate a building or put in some major equipment, consider bringing your business plan and financial statements to a CDC. Typical percentages for this type of package are 50 percent financed by the bank, 40 percent by the CDC and 10 percent by the business.

In exchange for this below-market, fixed-rate financing, the SBA expects the small business to create or retain jobs or to meet certain public policy goals. Businesses that meet these policy goals are those whose expansion will contribute to a business district revitalization, such as an Enterprise Zone; a minority-owned business; an export or manufacturing company; or a company whose expansion will contribute to rural development.

Empowerment/Enterprise Zones

Since 1980, more than 35 states have established programs to designate enterprise zones, offering tax breaks and other incentives to businesses that locate in certain economically disadvantaged areas. States vary widely in the number of zones designated, incentives offered and success of the programs. In some areas, businesses may also qualify for lower utility rates or low-interest financing from eligible government jurisdictions. To be eligible for any of these incentives, businesses must generally meet certain criteria, such as creating new jobs in a community.

> **BRIGHT IDEA**
> LOOKING INTO EXPORTING? LOOK INTO THE U.S. EXPORT ASSISTANCE CENTERS. THESE ONE-STOP SHOPS COMBINE THE TRADE PROMOTION AND EXPORT FINANCE RESOURCES OF THE SBA, THE U.S. DEPARTMENT OF COMMERCE AND THE EXPORT-IMPORT BANK.

In 1993, President Clinton unveiled an Empowerment Zone/ Enterprise Communities initiative, a 10-year plan to provide tax incentives and stimulate community investment and development. Specified urban and rural communities will receive grants and tax breaks for businesses in the area. The federal government's involvement means entrepreneurs in those areas can get federal tax breaks, not just state.

If you choose to locate in an enterprise or empowerment zone, look beyond the tax breaks to consider long-term concerns such as availability of a work force and accessibility of your target market. Make sure the zone offers other support services, such as streamlined licensing and permitting procedures. Most zones that succeed have high development potential to begin with, with good highway access, a solid infrastructure and a trainable labor force.

For more information on enterprise zones, contact your local SBA district office or your state's economic development department, or see Appendix B.

8(a) Program

The SBA's 8(a) program is a small-business set-aside program that gives certified socially and economically disadvantaged companies access to government contracts as well as management and technical assistance to help them develop their businesses. The 8(a) program is envisioned as a starter program for minority businesses, which must leave the program after nine years.

Entrepreneurs who participate in the 8(a) program are eligible for the 7(a) Guaranty Loan and Minority Pre-Qualification programs.

Information, Please

Dealing with the federal government has gotten easier, thanks to the U.S. Business Advisor, an online clearing-house for small business. Instead of contacting dozens of agencies and departments for information on laws and regulations, you can use this one-stop shop to find information on business development, taxes and laws, a variety of workplace concerns as well as government procurement loans. You can find the U.S. Business Advisor at www.business.gov.

Businesses must be owned by a socially and economically disadvantaged individual. Socially disadvented categories include race, ethnicity, gender or physical handicap. To qualify as economically disadvantaged, the person must have a net worth of less than $250,000 as well as two years worth of tax returns.

Export Working Capital Program

If you are planning to export, you should investigate the Export Working Capital Program. This allows a 90 percent guarantee on loans up to $750,000. Loan maturities are typically 12 months, with two 12-month renewal options. Loans can be for single or multiple export sales and can be used for pre-shipment working capital or post-shipment exposure coverage; however, they can't be used to buy fixed assets.

Special Purpose Loans

If you believe you have a special case that requires extra help, you may be in luck. Of course, keep in mind that everybody believes they deserve extra help with financing, but in many situations, the SBA has a loan program tailor-made for your situation. If you're starting a business, for instance, that pollutes the environment, but you plan to spend additional money to reduce the toxins you're putting into the air, soil or water, you may be eligible for a Pollution Control Loan, which are basically 7(a) loans earmarked for businesses that are planning, designing or installing a pollution control facility. The facility must prevent, reduce, abate or control any form of pollution, including recycling.

Or if your business plans to be active in international trade, or your top competition is cheap imports, the International Trade Loan Program is something you should look into. The SBA can guarantee up to $1.25 million for a combination of fixed-asset financing (facilities and equipment), as well as Export Working Capital Program (see above) assistance. The fixed-asset portion of the loan guaranty cannot exceed $1 million, and the nonfixed asset portion cannot exceed $750,000.

As the SBA's Web site says, "Numerous variations of the SBA's basic loan programs are made available to support special needs." So if you believe your business might fall into a category in which the SBA can funnel additional loans to you, it's definitely an avenue worth checking out.

MAKING THE MOST OF THE SBA

The SBA is more than a source of financing. It can help with many aspects of business start-up and growth. The SBA is an excellent place to "get your ducks in a row" before seeking financing. SBA services include free resources to help you with such tasks as writing a business plan and improving your presentation skills—all of which boost your chances of getting a loan.

For more information on other SBA programs, visit the SBA's Web site at www.sbaonline.sba.gov, call the SBA's Answer Desk at (800) U-ASK-SBA or contact your local SBA district office. Your SBA district office can mail you a start-up booklet and a list of lenders and inform you about specialized loans tailored to your industry, and where to go for help with your business plan or putting together financial statements.

GRANTING WISHES

When most people think of grants, they think of money given free to nonprofit organizations. But for-profit companies, and frequently start-ups, can also win grant money. But how do you find these grants? Unfortunately, locating the right grant is a little like looking for your soulmate. The grant is out there, but you're going to have to do a lot of looking to find a good match. A good place to start is at your local bookstore. There are a lot of books about getting grants, with titles like *Grant Writing for Dummies* (John Wiley & Sons) by Beverly A. Browning, *Grantseeker's Toolkit* (John Wiley & Sons) by Cheryl Carter New and James Quick, and *Demystifying Grantseeking* (John Wiley & Sons) by Larissa Golden Brown and Martin John Brown. And then there's the Bible of grant books—the annual *The Grants Register* (Palgrave Macmillan), which lists more than 3,500 grants.

There are other places to

HOT LINK

CHECK OUT WWW.GRANTS.GOV, THE WEB SITE THAT LISTS ALL THE FEDERAL GOVERNMENT'S GRANT PROGRAMS. YOU CAN FIND OPPORTUNITIES IN CATEGORIES RANGING FROM ARTS AND HUMANITIES TO HOUSING AND SCIENCE AND TECHNOLOGY.

look, of course. The most logical place to get an infusion of cash is from Uncle Sam, but you can also win grants from foundations and even some corporations.

Even in the most economically challenged of times, the government is one of the best sources for grants. For instance, the National Institute of Standards and Technology's Advance Technology Program offers grants to co-fund "high-risk, high-payoff projects" that will benefit American industry. Whatever the project is, you can bet it will be scrutinized by a board of qualified experts and academia to the –nth degree.

The Small Business Innovation Research (SBIR) office is another government agency that gives grants. The SBIR specializes in small businesses looking for funding for high-risk technologies. The catch: Unlike the Advance Technology Program, the technology must meet the research and development needs of the federal government. Founded in 1982, the SBIR recently awarded $1.5 billion to start-ups, with grants going to software, biotechnology, health-care and defense companies. So if you're planning on opening a pizzeria, you might have trouble with this one.

But there are federal grants awarded to food and nutrition companies. For instance, a pizzeria that caters to children and specializes in serving nutritious, healthy pizzas may be able to win a grant. You can also check with your state or local government—start with your local or state chamber of commerce.

Of course, finding the grant is the easy part; the hard part is getting the grant. It's a lot like applying to college. You have to jump through the hoops of each organization, which usually involves writing an extensive essay or plan on why you need their money. There are grant-writing businesses out there as well as

BRIGHT IDEA

IF YOU BELIEVE YOUR FUTURE BUSINESS COULD CONTRIBUTE TO COMMUNITY DEVELOPMENT OR EMPOWER A GROUP OF ECONOMICALLY DISADVANTAGED PEOPLE, VISIT YOUR STATE ECONOMIC DEVELOPMENT OFFICE TO FIND OUT WHAT TYPES OF COMMUNITY DEVELOPMENT GRANTS MAY BE AVAILABLE.

BRIGHT IDEA

BUYING A FRANCHISE? MANY MUNICIPALITIES AND STATES HAVE FINANCING PROGRAMS THAT CAN UNDERWRITE THE COST OF A FRANCHISE. BE AWARE, HOWEVER, THAT THE FOCUS OF THESE PROGRAMS IS JOB CREATION. TO FIND PROGRAMS IN YOUR AREA, CALL THE NEAREST SMALL BUSINESS DEVELOPMENT CENTER OR ECONOMIC DEVELOPMENT PROGRAM. IT TAKES A BIT OF INVESTIGATING TO FIND THE PROGRAMS, BUT THE RESULTS COULD BE WELL WORTH THE EFFORT.

grant brokers—people who try to find the right grant for you. You pay them regardless of whether they find you a grant; on the other hand, if they land you a $750,000 grant, you still pay them the flat fee, which is generally from $15 to $100 an hour, depending on their level of success. But if you don't have the funds to pay for a grant-writer or a broker, and you're a decent writer and have a passion for your business, then start researching, and fill out the forms and compose the essay yourself. There's no rule that says you can't try to get a grant on your own. And who knows—you might be successful!

Return Executed Copies 1, 2, and 3 to SBA

OMB APPROVAL NO.3245-0178
Expiration Date:9/30/2006

United States of America

SMALL BUSINESS ADMINISTRATION

STATEMENT OF PERSONAL HISTORY

Please Read Carefully - Print or Type

Each member of the small business or the development company requesting assistance must submit this form in TRIPLICATE for filing with the SBA application. This form must be filled out and submitted by:

1. By the proprietor, if a sole proprietorship.

2. By each partner, if a partnership.

3. By each officer, director, and additionally by each holder of 20% or more of the ownership stock, of a corporation, limited liability company, or a development company.

Name and Address of Applicant (Firm Name)(Street, City, State, and ZIP Code)

SBA District/Disaster Area Office

Amount Applied for (when applicable) | File No. (if known)

1. Personal Statement of: (State name in full, if no middle name, state (NMN), or if initial only, indicate initial.) List all former names used, and dates each name was used. Use separate sheet if necessary.

First   Middle   Last

2. Give the percentage of ownership or stocked owned or to be owned in the small business or the development company

Social Security No.

3. Date of Birth (Month, day, and year)

4. Place of Birth: (City & State or Foreign Country)

Name and Address of participating lender or surety co. (when applicable and known)

5. U.S. Citizen? ☐ YES ☐ NO
If No, are you a Lawful Permanent resident alien: ☐ YES ☐ NO
If non- U.S. citizen provide alien registration number: _____

6. Present residence address:
From:
To:
Address:

Most recent prior address (omit if over 10 years ago):
From:
To:
Address:

Home Telephone No. (Include A/C):
Business Telephone No. (Include A/C):

PLEASE SEE REVERSE SIDE FOR EXPLANATION REGARDING DISCLOSURE OF INFORMATION AND THE USES OF SUCH INFORMATION.

IT IS IMPORTANT THAT THE NEXT THREE QUESTIONS BE ANSWERED COMPLETELY. AN ARREST OR CONVICTION RECORD WILL NOT NECESSARILY DISQUALIFY YOU; HOWEVER, AN UNTRUTHFUL ANSWER WILL CAUSE YOUR APPLICATION TO BE DENIED.

IF YOU ANSWER "YES" TO 7, 8, OR 9, FURNISH DETAILS ON A SEPARATE SHEET. INCLUDE DATES, LOCATION, FINES, SENTENCES, WHETHER MISDEMEANOR OR FELONY, DATES OF PAROLE/PROBATION, UNPAID FINES OR PENALTIES, NAME(S) UNDER WHICH CHARGED, AND ANY OTHER PERTINENT INFORMATION.

7. Are you presently under indictment, on parole or probation?
☐ Yes ☐ No   (If yes, indicate date parole or probation is to expire.)

8. Have you ever been charged with and or arrested for any criminal offense other than a minor motor vehicle violation? Include offenses which have been dismissed, discharged, or not prosecuted (All arrests and charges must be disclosed and explained on an attached sheet.)
☐ Yes ☐ No

9. Have you ever been convicted, placed on pretrial diversion, or placed on any form of probation, including adjudication withheld pending probation, for any criminal offense other than a minor vehicle violation?
☐ Yes ☐ No

10. I authorize the Small Business Administration Office of Inspector General to request criminal record information about me from criminal justice agencies for the purpose of determining my eligibility for programs authorized by the Small Business Act, and the Small Business Investment Act.

CAUTION: Knowingly making a false statement on this form is a violation of Federal law and could result in criminal prosecution, significant civil penalties, and a denial of your loan, surety bond, or other program participation. A false statement is punishable under 18 USC 1001 by imprisonment of not more than five years and/or a fine of not more than $10,000; under 18 USC 645 by imprisonment of not more than two years and/or a fine of not more than $5,000; and, if submitted to a Federally insured institution, under 18 USC 1014 by imprisonment of not more than thirty years and/or a fine of not more than $1,000,000.

Signature | Title | Date

Agency Use Only

11. ☐ Fingerprints Waived
Date   Approving Authority

☐ Fingerprints Required
Date   Approving Authority

Date Sent to OIG

12. ☐ Cleared for Processing
Date   Approving Authority

13. ☐ Request a Character Evaluation
Date   Approving Authority
(Required whenever 7, 8 or 9 are answered "yes" even if cleared for processing.)

PLEASE NOTE: The estimated burden for completing this form is 15 minutes per response. You are not required to respond to any collection of information unless it displays a currently valid OMB approval number. Comments on the burden should be sent to U.S. Small Business Administration, Chief, AIB, 409 3rd St., S.W., Washington D.C. 20416 and Desk Officer for the Small Business Administration, Office of Management and Budget, New Executive Office Building, Room 10202, Washington, D.C. 20503. OMB Approval 3245-0178. PLEASE DO NOT SEND FORMS TO OMB.

SBA 912 (10-03) SOP 5010.4 Previous Edition Obsolete

This form was electronically produced by Elite Federal Forms, Inc.

The Statement of Personal History is an essential document for determining the quality of the person applying for any SBA loan. It's filled out by the sole proprietor, each partner in a partnership, each member of a board of directors, or a manager authorized to act in the best interests of the company.

U.S. SMALL BUSINESS ADMINISTRATION
APPLICATION FOR SBALOWDOC LOAN

OMB Approval No. 3245-0016
Expiration Date: 11/30/2004

A. APPLICANT   Please Print Legibly or Type (ALL BLANKS MUST BE COMPLETED, Use "N/A," If Blank is Not Applicable)

Business Name _____

Trade Name (if different) _____

Type: Proprietorship ☐   Partnership ☐   Corporation ☐   LLC ☐   Other ☐   (Specify)

Address (Physical Location) _____

City _____ State _____ County _____ Zip _____

Mailing Address (if different from above) _____

City _____ State _____ County _____ Zip _____

Phone _____ IRS Tax ID # _____

Business Bank _____ Checking Balance $ _____

Nature of Business _____

Date Business Established _____

Date Current Ownership Established _____

Number of employees _____

Number of affiliate(s) employees _____

Total number of employees after Loan _____

Exporter? Yes ☐ No ☐   Pre-Qual? Yes ☐ No ☐

Franchise? Yes ☐ No ☐   Name _____

B. LOAN REQUEST

AMOUNT $_____ Maturity: _____ Purpose: _____

Have you employed anyone to prepare this application? Yes ☐ No ☐   If Yes, how much was paid? $ _____ How much do you owe? $ _____

Name of Packager _____ Packager's Tax ID No. or Social Security No. _____

C. INDEBTEDNESS: Furnish information on ALL BUSINESS debts. (Attach schedule if needed.) Indicate by an (*) items to be paid by loan proceeds.

To Whom Payable	Purpose	Orig. Date	Cur. Bal.	Int. Rate	Maturity Date	Pmt. Amt.	Pmt Frequency	Collateral	Status

D. PRINCIPALS: Submit a separate Section "D" for each principal of the business (including anyone who was a principal within the last six months).

D1	Full Name _____ Phone _____ Social Security Number _____ Title _____

Address _____ City _____ State _____ Zip _____

Date of Birth _____ Place of Birth (City, ST or Foreign Country) _____ U.S. Citizen? Yes ☐ No ☐ If No, Alien reg. # _____

D2	Percentage Owned _____%	Veteran *: Non-Veteran ☐; Vietnam Era Veteran ☐ Other Veteran ☐	Gender *: Female ☐ Male ☐

Race*: Amer. Indian/Alaska Native ☐ Black/Afr.-Amer. ☐ Asian ☐ Native Hawaiian/Pacific Islander ☐ White ☐ Ethnicity* Hisp./Latino ☐ Not Hisp./Latino ☐

*This data is collected for statistical purposes only. It has no bearing on th credit decision. Disclosure is voluntary. One or more boxes for race may be selected.

D3	PERSONAL FINANCIAL STATEMENT: Complete for all principals with 20% or more ownership. (currently and within the last 6 months).

Liquid Assets $ _____ Ownership in Business $ _____ Real Estate $ _____ Assets Other $ _____ Total Assets $ _____

Liabilities Real Estate $ _____ Liabilities Other $ _____ Total Liabilities $ _____ Net Worth (less value of business) $ _____

Annual Sal. from Bus.$ _____ Other Source of Repayment $ _____ Source _____ Residence: Own ☐ Rent ☐ Other ☐ Mthly Housing $ _____

D4	PAST OR PREVIOUS SBA OR OTHER GOVERNMENT FINANCING: All owners, principals, partners, and affiliates must report these debts.

Borrower Name	Name of Agency	Loan No.	Date	Amount	Balance	Status

D5	ELIGIBILITY AND DISCLOSURES: (THESE QUESTIONS MUST BE COMPLETED. Mark "Yes" box or "No" box as appropriate.):

I.   Are you or your business involved in any pending lawsuits? Yes ☐ No ☐   If Yes, provide the details as Exhibit A.

II.   Do you or your spouse or any member of your household, or anyone who owns, manages, or directs your business or their spouses or members of their households work for the Small Business Administration, Small Business Advisory Council, SCORE or ACE, any Federal Agency, or the participating lender? Yes ☐ No ☐ If Yes, please provide the name and address of the person and the office where employed. Label this Exhibit B.

III.   Affiliates: Do you or the applicant business have any interest in any other business as owner, principal, partner or manager? Yes ☐ No ☐ If Yes, provide details to Lender. (See Applicant Instructions.)

IV.   Are you: (a) presently under indictment, on parole or probation, Yes ☐ No ☐ or (b) have ever been charged with or arrested for any criminal offense other than a minor motor vehicle violation (including offenses which have been dismissed, discharged, or knoll prosequi) Yes ☐ No ☐ or (c) convicted, placed on pretrial diversion, or placed on any form of probation including adjudication withheld pending probation for any criminal offense other than a minor vehicle violation? Yes ☐ No ☐ Cleared for Processing: Date _____ By _____ Fingerprints Waive: Date _____ By _____

V.   I have received and read "STATEMENT REQUIRED BY LAW AND EXECUTIVE ORDER".

If you knowingly make a false statement or overvalue a security to obtain a guaranteed loan from SBA you can be fined up to $10,000 and/or imprisoned for not more than five years under 18 U.S.C.1001; if submitted to a Federally insured istitution, under 18 USC 1014 by Imprisonment of not more than twenty years and/or a fine of not more than $1,000,000. I authorize the SBA's Office of Inspector General to request criminal record information about me from criminal justice agencies for the purpose of determining my eligibility for programs authorized by the Small Business Act, as amended.

VI.   Signature _____ Date _____

E. SIGNATURE

I authorize SBA/Lender to make inquiries as necessary to verify the accuracy of the statements made and to determine my creditworthiness. I agree that if SBA approves this loan application I will not, for at least two years, hire an employee or consultant anyone that was employed by the SBA during the one year period prior to the disbursement of the loan. And, I hereby certify that: (1) as consideration for any Management, Technical, and Business Development Assistance that may be provided, I waive all claims against SBA and its consultants, (2) all information contained in this document and any attachments is true and correct to the best of my knowledge.

Print Name _____ Date _____

Signature _____ Title _____

If Corporation, Attested By: _____
Signature of Corporate Secretary

SBA Form 4-L (8-01) Previous Editions are Obsolete
This form was electronically produced by Elite Federal Forms, Inc.

SUBMIT COMPLETED APPLICATION TO LENDER OF CHOICE

Application for LowDoc Loan

START YOUR OWN BUSINESS

PERSONAL FINANCIAL STATEMENT

U.S. SMALL BUSINESS ADMINISTRATION

As of _____ , _____

Complete this form for: (1) each proprietor, or (2) each limited partner who owns 20% or more interest and each general partner, or (3) each stockholder owning 20% or more of voting stock, or (4) any person or entity providing a guaranty on the loan.

Name	Business Phone
Residence Address	Residence Phone
City, State, & Zip Code	
Business Name of Applicant/Borrower	

ASSETS	(Omit Cents)	LIABILITIES	(Omit Cents)
Cash on hand & in Banks	$	Accounts Payable	$
Savings Accounts	$	Notes Payable to Banks and Others	$
IRA or Other Retirement Account	$	(Describe in Section 2)	
Accounts & Notes Receivable	$	Installment Account (Auto)	$
Life Insurance-Cash Surrender Value Only (Complete Section 8)	$	Mo. Payments $	
		Installment Account (Other)	$
Stocks and Bonds (Describe in Section 3)	$	Mo. Payments $	
		Loan on Life Insurance	$
Real Estate (Describe in Section 4)	$	Mortgages on Real Estate (Describe in Section 4)	$
Automobile-Present Value	$	Unpaid Taxes	$
Other Personal Property (Describe in Section 5)	$	(Describe in Section 6)	
		Other Liabilities	$
Other Assets (Describe in Section 5)	$	(Describe in Section 7)	
		Total Liabilities	$
		Net Worth	$
Total	$	**Total**	$

Section 1. Source of Income		Contingent Liabilities	
Salary	$	As Endorser or Co-Maker	$
Net Investment Income	$	Legal Claims & Judgments	$
Real Estate Income	$	Provision for Federal Income Tax	$
Other Income (Describe below)*	$	Other Special Debt	$

Description of Other Income in Section 1.

*Alimony or child support payments need not be disclosed in "Other Income" unless it is desired to have such payments counted toward total income.

Section 2. Notes Payable to Banks and Others.   (Use attachments if necessary. Each attachment must be identified as a part of this statement and signed.)

Name and Address of Noteholder(s)	Original Balance	Current Balance	Payment Amount	Frequency (monthly,etc.)	How Secured or Endorsed Type of Collateral

SBA Form 413 (3-00) **Previous Editions Obsolete**   (tumble)
This form was electronically produced by Elite Federal Forms, Inc.

The Personal Financial Statement shows a SBA loan officer the assets and liabilities, including source of income, from any business or business owner. It also indicates notes payable to banks and other lending institutions.

Section 3. Stocks and Bonds. (Use attachments if necessary. Each attachment must be identified as a part of this statement and signed).

Number of Shares	Name of Securities	Cost	Market Value Quotation/Exchange	Date of Quotation/Exchange	Total Value

Section 4. Real Estate Owned. (List each parcel separately. Use attachment if necessary. Each attachment must be identified as a part of this statement and signed.)

	Property A	Property B	Property C
Type of Property			
Address			
Date Purchased			
Original Cost			
Present Market Value			
Name & Address of Mortgage Holder			
Mortgage Account Number			
Mortgage Balance			
Amount of Payment per Month/Year			
Status of Mortgage			

Section 5. Other Personal Property and Other Assets. (Describe, and if any is pledged as security, state name and address of lien holder, amount of lien, terms of payment and if delinquent, describe delinquency)

Section 6. Unpaid Taxes. (Describe in detail, as to type, to whom payable, when due, amount, and to what property, if any, a tax lien attaches.)

Section 7. Other Liabilities. (Describe in detail.)

Section 8. Life Insurance Held. (Give face amount and cash surrender value of policies - name of insurance company and beneficiaries)

I authorize SBA/Lender to make inquiries as necessary to verify the accuracy of the statements made and to determine my creditworthiness. I certify the above and the statements contained in the attachments are true and accurate as of the stated date(s). These statements are made for the purpose of either obtaining a loan or guaranteeing a loan. I understand FALSE statements may result in forfeiture of benefits and possible prosecution by the U.S. Attorney General (Reference 18 U.S.C. 1001).

Signature:		Date:	Social Security Number:
Signature:		Date:	Social Security Number:

PLEASE NOTE: The estimated average burden hours for the completion of this form is 1.5 hours per response. If you have questions or comments concerning this estimate or any other aspect of this information, please contact Chief, Administrative Branch, U.S. Small Business Administration, Washington, D.C. 20416, and Clearance Officer, Paper Reduction Project (3245-0188), Office of Management and Budget, Washington, D.C. 20503. PLEASE DO NOT SEND COMPLETED FORMS TO OMB.

Personal Financial Statement, cont'd

OMB Approval No. 3245-0324
Expiration Date: 04/30/2003

Case Number: _____

U.S. Small Business Administration
Request for Counseling

1. Your Name (First, Middle, Last)	2. Telephone Number(s)
	Home _____
	Business _____
3. Email address	Fax _____

| 4. Street Address | 5. City | 6. County | 7. State | 8. Zip |
| | | | | |

9. Race (mark one or more)	10. Ethnicity	12. Do you consider yourself a person with a disability?	13. Veteran Status
a. Native American or Alaskan Native ☐	a. Hispanic Origin ☐		a. Veteran ☐
b. Asian ☐	b. Not of Hispanic Origin ☐	Yes ☐ No ☐	b. Service Connected Disabled Veteran ☐
c. Black or African American ☐	11. Business Owner Gender		c. Disabled Veteran ☐
d. Native Hawaiian or other Pacific Islander ☐	a. Male ☐		d. Non-veteran ☐
e. White ☐	b. Female ☐		
	c. Male/Female ☐		

14. How did you hear of us?			
a. Word of Mouth ☐	d. Chamber of Commerce ☐	g. Television ☐	j. SBA ☐
b. Bank ☐	e. Internet ☐	h. Magazine ☐	
c. Newspapers ☐	f. Radio ☐	i. Other _____	

15. Describe the nature of the counseling you are seeking.

16. Currently in Business? Yes ☐ No ☐ (If no, skip to line 20)   Is this a Home-based Business? Yes ☐ No ☐

17. Type of Business

| 18. Name of Company: | 19. How long in business? |

20. Indicate preferred date & time for appointment:
Date: _____   Time: _____

I request business management counseling service from a Small Business Administration Resource Partner. I agree to cooperate should I be selected to participate in surveys designed to evaluate SBA assistance services. I authorize SBA to furnish relevant information to the assigned management counselor(s). I understand that any information disclosed to be held in strict confidence by him/her.

I further understand that any counselor has agreed not to: (1) recommend goods or services from sources in which he/she has an interest and (2) accept fees or commissions developing from this counseling relationship. In consideration of the counselor(s) furnishing management or technical assistance, I waive all claims against SBA personnel, SCORE and its host organizations, and other SBA Resource Counselors arising from this assistance.

Please note: The estimated burden for completing this form is 15 minutes per response. You are not required to respond to any collection information unless it displays a currently valid OMB approval number. Comments on the burden should be sent to U.S. Small Business Administration, Chief, AIB 409 3rd St., S.W., Washington, D.C 20416 and Desk Officer for the Small Business Administration, Office of Management and Budget, New Executive Office Building, Room 10202, Washington, D.C. 20503. OMB Approval (3245-0091) **PLEASE DO NOT SEND FORMS TO OMB.**

| Signature: | Date: |

SBA Form 641 (6/01) Previous Editions Obsolete   Federal Recycling Program   Printed on Recycled Paper

This form helps the SBA determine what area the applicant needs consulting in. It also serves as feedback for the SBA so it can find out how people heard about its services and how they are used.

SBA PRE-QUALIFICATION LOAN APPLICATION

SBA OFFICE USE ONLY:	DATE RECEIVED:		CID NUMBER:

Legal Name of Business: Tax ID #:

Address of Business:

Business Phone #:   Date Business Established:

Legal Structure: ___ Proprietorship ___ Partnership ___ Corporation

SIC Code#:   Number of Existing Employees:

Describe History of Business: (If NEW business, submit copy of Business Plan)

Describe Business Operation:

Is Business engaged in export trade? Yes ___ No ___   Do you intend to begin exporting as a result of this loan? Yes ___ No ___

* Personal financial statements must be submitted by all owners of 20% or more.

OWNERS/MANAGEMENT (proprietors, partners and shareholders)

Name	SS No.	% Owned	Sex	Military Service Y/N: From: To:	Race
TOTAL					

Submit all information in the section below for each principal of the business. Use separate attachments for each principal.

Date of Birth _____   Place of Birth (City, ST or Foreign Country) _____

Social Security # _____   U.S. Citizen? Yes ___ No ___ If No, Alien reg # _____

I.   Are you or your business involved in any pending lawsuits?   Yes ___ No ___   If Yes, provide the details as Exhibit A.

II.   Do you or your spouse or any member of your household, or anyone who owns, manages or directs your business or their spouses or members of their household work for the Small Business Administration, Small Business Advisory Council, SCORE or ACE, any Federal Agency, or the participating lender?   Yes ___ No ___

     If Yes, please provide the name and address of the person and the office where employed. Label this Exhibit B.

III.   Affiliates: Do you or the applicant business have any interest in any other business as owner, principal, partner or manager?

     Yes ___ No ___ If Yes, please provide details to Lender.

IV.   *Are you: (a) presently under indictment, on parole or probation,   Yes* ___ No ___

     or (b) have ever been charged with or arrested for any criminal offense other than a minor motor vehicle violation (including offenses which have been dismissed, discharged, or nolle prosequi)   Yes* ___ No ___

     or (c) convicted, placed on pretrial diversion, or placed on any form of probation including adjudication withheld pending probation for any criminal offense other than a minor vehicle violation?   Yes* ___ No ___

     (including offenses which have been dismissed, discharge, or nolle prosequi)

V.   *Have any of above individuals, the applicant firm or affiliates (a) been involved in bankruptcy or insolvency proceedings within the last 10 years or (b) have pending personal or business judgments, unsettled lawsuits or major disputes?   Yes* ___ No ___

     *If yes, the loan request must be submitted under the regular 7(a) loan program.

     If you knowingly make a false statement or overvalue a security to obtain a guaranteed loan from SBA you can be fined up to $10,000 and/or imprisoned for not more than five years under 18 U.S.C. 1001; if submitted to a Federally insured institution, under 18 USC 1014 by Imprisonment of not more than twenty years and/or a fine of not more than $1,000,000. I authorize SBA's Office of Inspector General to request criminal record information about me from criminal justice agencies for the purpose of determining my eligibility for programs authorized by the Small Business Act, as amended.

     Signature _____   Date _____

Loan application for the Women and Minority Pre-Qualification Programs

PREVIOUS SBA OR OTHER GOVERNMENT FINANCING
(Requested or obtained by principals, applicant firm or affiliates)

Name of Agency	Declined or Approved	Date of Request	$ Amount	Loan Balance	Current or Past Due

CREDIT HISTORY

Credit Reports Obtained For:	Type of Report	Credit Rating	Comments:		
Applicant					
Principal:					
Principal:					
Principal:					
Other:					

PROPOSED USES AND SOURCES OF FUNDS

USES		SOURCES	
Working Capital		SBA/Bank (requested loan amount)	
Inventory		Equity/Injection (Note 4)	
Machinery & Equipment			
Furniture & Fixtures		Seller Financing	
Real Estate (Note 1) (Purchase, construction, etc.)		Other:	
Purchase of Existing Business (Note 2)		Other:	
Debt Refinance (Note 3)(include in listing below)		Other:	
TOTAL USES:		TOTAL SOURCES:	
Proposed SBA/Bank Maturity		Proposed SBA/Bank Interest Rate	

Note 1.   If financing real estate, who or what entity will hold title?: _____

       If other than the applicant firm, list ownership of real estate:_____

Note 2.   Business Purchase Price _____ Stock or asset purchase: _____ Why is seller selling?_____

Note 3.   If refinancing debts, state benefits to the applicant firm: _____

Note 4.   State the source of injection: _____

BUSINESS INDEBTEDNESS: on all existing business debt, contracts, notes and mortgages payable
(Indicate by an (*) items to be paid w/loan proceeds.)

To Whom Payable	Original Amount	Present Balance	Original Date	Rate of Interest	Maturity Date	Monthly Payment	Current or Past Due	Secured by
	Total				Total			

SBA Temporary Form 2114   7/99   Page 2

Loan application for the Women and Minority Pre-Qualification Program, cont'd

Financial Statements are: ___ Internal ___Acct't Compiled ___Reviewed ___Audited

BALANCE SHEET INFORMATION: (Dollars in Thousands)		Last FYE Date dd/mm/yyyy	Interim Date dd/mm/yyyy	Debit	Credit	Proforma
ASSETS						
	Cash					
	Accounts Rec.					
	Inventory					
	Other					
TOTAL CURRENT ASSETS						
FIXED ASSETS						
OTHER ASSETS						
	Loans to Owners					
TOTAL ASSETS						
LIABILITIES & NET WORTH:						
	Accounts Payable					
	Notes Payable					
	Taxes					
	Other					
	SBA					
TOTAL CURRENT LIABILITIES:						
	Notes Payable					
	SBA					
	Loans From Owners					
	Other					
TOTAL LIABILITIES						
NET WORTH						
TOTAL LIABILITIES & NET WORTH						

PROFORMA RATIO INFORMATION	Applicant	RMA	Ratio	Comments
Proforma Working Capital				
Proforma Current Ratio				
Proforma Quick Ratio				
Accounts Receivable Turnover (in days)				
Inventory Turnover (in days)				
Proforma Debt to Worth Ratio				

HISTORICAL & PROJECTED CASHFLOW FOR REPAYMENT INFORMATION

	(Dollars in Thousands)	Prior Fiscal Yr	Prior Fiscal Yr	Most Recent	Interim	RMA SIC Code	Projection
a	Revenues						
b	Gross Profit						
c	Interest Expense						
d	Owner's Withdrawal, etc.						
e	Net Income (Aftr w/d, dvd, txs)						
f	Depreciation						
g	Cash Flow (c+e+f)						
h	Rent Expense Saved (if applicable)						
I	Other Expense Saved (explain)						
j	Cashflow for Debt Service (g+h+I)						
k	Existing Debt Service (Prin. & Int.)						
I	New Debt Service (Prin. & Int.)						
m	Total Debt Service (k+l)						
n	Debt Coverage Ratio (j/m)						

Combined Household Income: _____ Number in Household: _____

Other Sources of Income: _____ Withdrawals: _____

Loan application for the Women and Minority Pre-Qualification Program, cont'd

235

COLLATERAL SUMMARY	Cost	Market Value	Prior Liens
Land and Buildings			
Machinery & Equipment			
Furniture and Fixtures			
Accounts Receivable			
Inventory			
Other:			
Total			
Evaluation by:		Date:	
Total Cost or Appraised Value			
Less: Prior Liens			
= Net Collateral Value			
COVERAGE RATIO: (net collateral value / loan amount)			

Is firm considered a frequent polluting industry?   Yes   No

* If yes, Phase I must be completed and submitted in the private sector lender's loan package.

OTHER PERTINENT INFORMATION:

MANAGEMENT EXPERIENCE/BACKGROUND
(Describe key management/owner's background & business experience)

CERTIFICATIONS OF APPLICANT AND INTERMEDIARY

I authorize SBA/Lender to make inquiries as necessary to verify the accuracy of the statements made and to determine my creditworthiness. I agree that if SBA approves this loan application I will not, for at least two years, hire as an employee or consultant anyone that was employed by SBA during the one year period prior to the disbursement of the loan. And I hereby certify that: (1) as consideration for any Management, Technical, and Business Development Assistance that may be provided, I waive all claims against SBA and its consultants, and (2) all information contained in this document and any attachments is true and correct to the best of my knowledge.

IF A PROPRIETOR OR GENERAL PARTNER, SIGN HERE:

By: _____ Title: _____   Date: _____
Address: _____

IF A CORPORATION, SIGN HERE:

Corporate Name: _____

By: _____ Title:_____   Date: _____

Attested by: _____
          Signature of Corporate Secretary

INTERMEDIARY:

By: _____ Title: _____   Date: _____

SBA Temporary Form 2114   7/99   Page 4

Loan application for the Women and Minority Pre-Qualification Program, cont'd

GLOSSARY

CERTIFIED DEVELOPMENT COMPANIES (CDCs): nonprofit intermediaries that work with the SBA and banks to make 504 Loans available to entrepreneurs

ENTERPRISE ZONES/EMPOWERMENT ZONES: designated economically disadvantaged zones that offer state and/or federal tax breaks and other incentives to businesses that locate there

MINORITY BUSINESS ENTERPRISE (MBE): a business that is certified owned by a minority entrepreneur; certification can be obtained from a variety of organizations and is generally required for participation in government set-aside programs

Get Set

Y ou have a great idea, a perfect plan and the money to make it all happen. What's the next step? Get set for business with Part 4, "Setting The Stage." Learn how to select a prime location that will get customers to come in…and come back. We'll show you little-known operating options, such as kiosks and carts, plus how to negotiate the lease you want. Or maybe starting your business from home is the solution you seek. If so, you'll learn all the steps to setting up a home office that really works. Whether it's at home or away, once you've found the right site, we share secrets for giving it a professional image with furniture, business cards and stationery that all spell success. Next, stock your shelves with inventory: You'll learn how to choose, track and maintain your product supply and discover the best sources for getting what you need.

Getting paid is the most important part of business ownership; in this section, we'll reveal how to give your customers credit without getting taken, plus tips for accepting credit cards, debit cards and checks and collecting on slow-paying accounts. Since every business needs to use the mail, you won't want to miss our guide to setting up mailing and shipping accounts. Discover how to choose the right carriers, get the best rates and get your packages delivered on time. If employees are part of your game plan, you'll find all the information you need to hire smart. Learn the secrets of a good job interview, low-cost hiring options, and the laws you must know to stay out of hot water. Finally, protect the business you've worked so hard to start by checking out our chapter on insurance. We show you the basic insurance no business owner should be without, plus how to put together the perfect insurance package for your needs.

Now, get geared up for business! Part 5, "You'd Better Shop Around," takes you step by step through setting up your office. In today's high-tech times, there's a dizzying array of equipment options out there. We guide you through the maze of machines to choose just what you need…without breaking the bank. Learn low-cost ways to get equipped, from superstores and mail order to leasing and buying used.

If you're planning to buy a computer for your business—or upgrade the one you already have—we show you how to put together the perfect system. You'll learn the bare-bones hardware and software requirements, plus ways to ensure your computer can be upgraded to meet future needs. We take a look at the latest developments, from notebooks and palmtops to personal information managers and more. Since you'll want the ability to work wherever and whenever you choose, we'll show you all the ways wireless technology can save you time, money and hassles, plus the best tips for putting wireless to work for you.

Calling all entrepreneurs: We share low-cost ways to give your small business all the amenities of a big office: phones, copiers, fax machines and multifunctional devices that let you work faster, smarter and more efficiently. Finally, before you hit the road, be sure to read our chapter on company vehicles. From leasing tips to purchasing plans, we give you all the details on getting the best buy for your business—whether you're looking for one car or a fleet of delivery vehicles.

PART

4

Setting
The
Stage

Location, Location, Location

Choosing a location for your business

Where should you locate your business? One expert will tell you location is absolutely vital to your company's success; another will argue that it really doesn't matter where you are—and they're both right. How important location is for your new company depends on the type of business and the facilities and other resources you need, and where your customers are.

If you're in retailing, or if you manufacture a product and distribution is a critical element of your overall operation, then geographical location is extremely important. If your business is information- or service-related, the actual location takes a back seat to whether the facility itself can meet your needs.

Regardless of the nature of your business, before you start shopping for space, you need to have a clear picture of what you must have, what you'd like to have, what you absolutely won't tolerate and how much you're able to pay. Developing that picture can be a time-consuming process that is both exciting and tedious, but it's essential that you give it the attention it deserves. While many start-up mistakes can be corrected later on, a poor choice of location is difficult—and sometimes impossible—to repair.

TYPES OF LOCATIONS

The type of location you choose depends largely on the type of business you're in, but there are enough mixed-use areas and creative applications of space that you should give some thought to each type before making a final decision. For example, business parks and office buildings typically have retail space so they can attract the restaurants and stores that business tenants want nearby. Shopping centers are often home to an assortment of professional services—accounting, insurance, medical, legal, etc.—as well as retailers. It's entirely possible some version of nontraditional space will work for you, so use your imagination.

■ **HOMEBASED:** This is probably the trendiest location for a business these days, and many entrepreneurs start at home, then move into commercial space as their business grows. Others start at home with no thought or intention of ever moving. You can run a home-based business from an office in a spare bedroom, the basement, the attic—even the kitchen table. On the plus side, you do not need to worry about negotiating leases, coming up with substantial deposits or commuting. On the downside, your room for physical growth is limited, and you may find accommodating employees or meetings with clients a challenge. (For more information about locating a business in your own home, see Part 4, Chapter 18).

- **RETAIL:** Retail space comes in a variety of shapes and sizes and may be located in free-standing buildings, enclosed malls, strip shopping centers, downtown shopping districts, or mixed-use facilities. You will also find retail space in airports and other transportation facilities, hotel lobbies, sports stadiums, and temporary or special event venues.

- **MOBILE:** Whether you're selling to the public or to other businesses, if you have a product or service that you take to your customers, your ideal "location" may be a car, van or truck.

- **COMMERCIAL:** Commercial space includes even more options than retail. Commercial office buildings and business parks offer traditional office space geared to businesses that do not require a significant amount of pedestrian or automobile traffic for sales. You'll find commercial office space in downtown business districts, and business parks, and sometimes interspersed among suburban retail facilities. One office option to consider is an executive suite, where the landlord provides receptionist and secretarial services, faxing, photocopying, conference rooms and other support services as part of the package. Executive suites help you project the image of a professional operation at a more affordable cost and can be found in most commercial office areas. Some executive suites even rent their facilities by the hour to home-based businesses or out-of-towners who need temporary office space.

- **INDUSTRIAL:** If your business involves manufacturing or heavy distribution, you will need a plant or a warehouse facility. Light industrial parks typically attract smaller manufacturers in nonpolluting industries as well as com-

BEWARE!

BE WARY OF INCENTIVES. OFTEN INCENTIVES—SUCH AS FREE RENT OR TAX BREAKS—MAY BE MASKING PROBLEMS. THERE'S USUALLY A GOOD REASON WHY ANY LOCATION OFFERS INCENTIVES, AND YOU NEED TO BE SURE WHAT IT IS BEFORE YOU SIGN UP. YOU SHOULD BE ABLE TO START A PROFITABLE BUSINESS IN THAT LOCATION WITHOUT ANY INCENTIVES—AND THEN LET THE INCENTIVES BE A BONUS.

panies that need showrooms in addition to manufacturing facilities. Heavy industrial areas tend to be older and poorly planned and usually offer rail and/or water port access. Though industrial parks are generally newer and often have better infrastructures, you may want to consider a free-standing commercial building that meets your needs and is adequately zoned.

ISSUES TO CONSIDER

With an overview of what's available, you now need to decide what's most appropriate for your business. Julien J. Studley, president and CEO of Julien J. Studley Inc., a real estate firm that represents commercial tenants nationwide, says the major things tenants are looking for are the best possible deal on the space and an available work force. He says the trend has shifted away from highly visible luxuries to utilitarian, practical buildings. Also, he says, there is much more emphasis on communications and computer support needs today than in the past. Of course, your business may or may not follow the trends. Be systematic and realistic as you consider the following points:

Style Of Operation

Is your operation going to be formal and elegant? Or kicked-back and casual? Your location should be consistent with your particular style and image. If your business is retailing, do you want a traditional store, or would you like to try operating from a kiosk (or booth) in a mall or a cart that you can move to various locations? If you're in a traditional mall or shopping center, will the property permit you to have a sidewalk sale if you want to? Can you decorate your windows the way you want to?

BRIGHT IDEA

CONSIDER STOCKPILING SPACE. IF YOU'RE REASONABLY SURE YOU'RE GOING TO NEED ADDITIONAL SPACE WITHIN A FEW YEARS, IT MIGHT BE WISE TO LEASE A FACILITY OF THAT SIZE NOW AND SUBLEASE THE EXTRA SPACE UNTIL YOU NEED IT. THAT WAY, YOU'LL KNOW THE SPACE WILL BE AVAILABLE LATER ON, AND YOU WON'T BE FACED WITH MOVING.

Demographics

There are two important angles to the issue of demographics. One is your customers; the other is your employees. First, consider who your customers are and how important their proximity to your location is. For a retailer and some service providers,

Demographic Comparison

To see if the community you are considering offers a population with the demographic traits you need to support your business, fill out the following form.

Population	Market A	Market B	Market C
Within 1 mile of your business			
Within 5 miles of your business			
Within 25 miles of your business			

Income	Market A	Market B	Market C
Less than $15,000			
$15,000-$25,000			
$25,000-$35,000			
$35,000-$50,000			
$50,000+			

Age	Market A	Market B	Market C
Preteens			
Teens			
20-29			
30-39			
40-49			
50-59			
60-69			
70+			

Density	Market A	Market B	Market C
Homeowners			
Renters			
Urban			

this is critical; for other types of businesses, it may not be as important. The demographic profile you've developed of your target market will help you make this decision (see Part 2, Chapter 7 for more on developing your target market).

Then, take a look at the community. If your customer base is local, is the population large enough, or does a sufficient percentage of that population match your customer profile to support your business? Does the community have a stable economic base that will provide a healthy environment for your business? Be cautious when considering communities that are largely dependent on a particular industry for their economy; a downturn could be a death knell for your company.

Now think about your work force. What skills do you need, and are people with those talents available? Does the community have the resources to serve their needs? Is there sufficient housing in the appro-

Cart Blanche

Carts and kiosks have become familiar sights in American malls, selling everything from inexpensive gift items to pricey jewelry and artwork. They make mall space affordable for the business owner, and the mall operators benefit from extra rent and a wider variety of merchandise.

Carts and kiosks have contributed to one of the hottest trends in retailing: temporary tenants. Most often these are seasonal businesses that only need to be open for a limited time. For example, a specialty candy shop may open just before Christmas, remain open through Valentine's Day, Easter and Mother's Day, then close for the remainder of the year. Some temporary tenants occupy traditional storefront space, but most opt for carts or kiosks. The most popular site for a temporary operation is a busy mall, but many operators are also finding success in airports and other transportation facilities, at sporting events, and at other creative venues limited only by their imagination and ability to strike a deal with the property manager.

Consider using carts and kiosks to test your product in a retail setting before making the larger investment in a traditional store. Styles range from simple to elaborate; whatever you choose, be sure it's attractive, well-lighted and functional.

priate price range? Will your employees find the schools, recreational opportunities, culture and other aspects of the community satisfactory?

Especially when the economy is strong and unemployment figures are low, you may be concerned about the availability of good workers. Keep in mind that in many areas, few people may be unemployed, but many may be underemployed. If you are offering attractive jobs at competitive wages, you may find staffing your company easier than you thought.

Look beyond the basic employment statistics to find out what the job market is really like. Think about placing a blind test ad (the local economic development agency may do this for you) to see what type of response you will get in the way of applicants before making a final location decision.

Demographic information is available to you through a variety of resources. You could do the research yourself by visiting the library or calling the U.S. Census Bureau and gathering a bunch of statistics, then trying to figure out what they mean, but chances are you probably do not have the time or statistical expertise to do that. So why not let other people do it for you—people who know how to gather the data and translate it into information you can understand and use. Contact your state, regional or local economic development agency (see "To The Rescue" on page 252) or commercial real estate companies and use the data they've already collected, analyzed and processed.

Foot Traffic

For most retail businesses, foot traffic is extremely important. You don't want to be tucked away in a corner where shoppers are likely to bypass you, and even the best retail areas have dead spots. By contrast, if your business requires confidentiality, you may not want to be located in a high-traffic area. Monitor the traffic outside a potential location at different times of the day and on different days of the week to make sure the volume of pedestrian traffic meets your needs.

Accessibility And Parking

Consider how accessible the facility will be for everyone who will be using it—customers, employees and suppliers. If you're on a busy street, how easy is it for cars to get in and out of your parking lot? Is the facility accessible to people with disabilities? What sort of deliveries are you likely to receive, and will your suppliers be able to easily and efficiently get materials to your business? Small package couriers need to get in and out quickly; trucking companies need adequate roads and loading docks if you're going to be receiving freight on pallets.

To The Rescue

One of the best sources of information and assistance for start-up and expanding businesses is state, regional and local economic development agencies. According to Ted M. Levine, chairman of Development Counsellors International, a consulting firm specializing in economic development marketing and analysis, there are nearly 12,000 economic development groups in the United States that charge nothing for their services and assistance.

They are public, private or most often a public/private partnership, and their purpose is to promote economic growth and development in the areas they serve. They accomplish that by encouraging new businesses to locate in their area, and to do that, they've gathered all the statistics and information you'll need to make a decision.

Levine says economic development agencies will help any new business, regardless of size, in four primary ways:

1. Market demographics
2. Real estate costs and availability; zoning and regulatory issues
3. Work-force demographics
4. Referrals to similar companies and other resources

For the best overview, start with your state agency. The state agency can then guide you to regional and local groups for expanded information. (For a complete list of state economic development departments, see Appendix B.)

Find out about the days and hours of service and access to locations you're considering. Are the heating and cooling systems left on or turned off at night and on weekends? If you're inside an office building, are there periods when exterior doors are locked and, if so, can you have keys? A beautiful office building at a great price is a lousy deal if you plan to work weekends but the building is closed on weekends—or they allow you access, but the air conditioning and heat are

Growing Places

Incubators are organizations sponsored by public and private investors that assist start-up and young companies in their critical early days with a variety of well-orchestrated business assistance programs. Incubators provide hands-on management assistance, access to financing, shared office services, access to equipment, flexible leases, expandable space and more—all under one roof.

The time your business can spend in an incubator is limited—typically two years—but it can vary. The idea is to get a fledgling business off the ground, turn it into a sound operation, then let it "leave the nest" to run on its own, making room for another start-up venture in the incubator.

Incubators generally fall into the following categories: technology, industrial, mixed-use, economic empowerment and industry-specific. For more information about incubators and for help finding one appropriate for your business, contact the National Business Incubation Association (NBIA) at (740) 593-4331. For a listing of incubators in your state, send a self-addressed, stamped envelope indicating the information you want to the NBIA at 20 E. Circle Dr., #190, Athens, OH 45701-3751 or visit www.nbia.org.

turned off so you roast in the summer and freeze in the winter.

Be sure, too, that there's ample convenient parking for both customers and employees. As with foot traffic, take the time to monitor the facility at various times and days to see how the demand for parking fluctuates. Also, consider safety issues: The parking lot should be well-maintained and adequately lighted.

Competition

Are competing companies located nearby? Sometimes that's good, such as in industries where comparison shopping is popular. (That's why competing retail businesses, such as fast-food restaurants, antique shops and clothing stores, tend to cluster together.) You may also catch the overflow from existing businesses, particularly if you're located in a restaurant and entertainment area. But if a nearby competitor is only going to make your marketing job tougher, look elsewhere.

Proximity To Other Businesses And Services

Take a look at what other businesses and services are in the vicinity from two key perspectives. First, see if you can benefit from nearby businesses—either by the customer traffic they generate, or because those companies and their employees could become your customers, or because it may be convenient and efficient for you to be their customer.

Second, look at how they will enrich the quality of your company as a workplace. Does the vicinity have an adequate selection of restaurants so your employees have places to go for lunch? Is there a nearby day-care center for employees with children? Are other shops and services you and your employees might want conveniently located?

Image And History Of The Site

What does this address say about your company? Particularly if you're targeting a local market, be sure your location accurately reflects the image you want to project. It's also a good idea to check out the history of the site. Consider how it has changed and evolved over the years.

Ask about previous tenants. If you're opening a restaurant where five

Manufacturer's Site-Planning Checklist

When planning the layout of your manufacturing site, you want to be able to get raw material into the plant and move it through the manufacturing process as efficiently as possible. With this in mind, ask yourself the following questions:

❏ Is your receiving area in a location with easy access to large trucks?

❏ Is there suitable equipment on hand in the receiving area to unload incoming shipments efficiently?

❏ Do you have enough space to adequately warehouse your inventory of raw materials?

❏ Are your raw materials properly labeled in the warehouse area for easy retrieval?

❏ Is your warehouse space for raw material in close proximity to the first station used in the manufacturing process?

❏ Is there enough space on the manufacturing floor for the necessary equipment so the product can be taken through each step without having to backtrack to other stations on the floor?

❏ Have you analyzed each station in the manufacturing process to assure equipment is arranged in the most efficient manner?

❏ Are you maximizing the potential of each station in the manufacturing process by having as many tasks as possible performed in that area without creating a bottleneck?

❏ Is your finished product warehouse area located in close proximity to the last station in the manufacturing process?

❏ Are there proper storage materials and equipment such as floor racks, slip sheets and pallets to handle the finished product?

❏ Is there appropriate materials-handling equipment to move the finished product into storage and out once it is ready to ship?

❏ Is your shipping area in close proximity to the warehouse area for the finished product?

❏ Is your shipping area easily accessible to large trucks?

restaurants have failed, you may be starting off with an insurmountable handicap—either because there's something wrong with the location or because the public will assume that your business will go the way of the previous tenants. If several types of businesses have been there and failed, do some research to find out why—you need to confirm whether the problem was with the businesses or the location. That previous occupants have been wildly successful is certainly a good sign, but temper that with information on what type of businesses they were.

Another historical point you'll want to know is whether a serious crime, tragedy or other notable event occurred on the property. If

Agent Avenues

U nless you have a significant amount of experience in shopping for commercial real estate, it's a good idea to use a qualified real estate agent. Whether you are buying or leasing, an agent can help by pre-screening properties, which saves you time, and by negotiating on your behalf, which can save you money.

Typically the seller or landlord pays the agent's commission, which may raise some questions in your mind about loyalty of the agent. However, keep in mind that the agent doesn't get paid until a deal that satisfies you both is negotiated.

You may opt to use a tenant's or buyer's agent that you pay yourself. In the real estate world, that's called tenant (or buyer) representation, a real estate specialty that is growing in popularity. Especially in tight market situations, it may be to your advantage to invest in an advocate who will negotiate on your behalf. For more information about tenant representation and for help in finding someone to assist you, contact the Society of Industrial and Office Realtors in Washington, DC, at (202) 737-1150 or visit www.sior.com.

Shop for a real estate agent as you would any professional service provider: Ask for referrals from friends and associates; interview several agents; be sure the agent you choose has expertise in the type of property or facility you need; check out the agent's track record, professional history and reputation; clarify how the agent will be compensated and by whom; and draw up a written agreement that outlines your mutual expectations.

so, will the public's memory reflect on your operation, and is that reflection likely to be positive or negative?

Ordinances

Find out if any ordinances or zoning restrictions could affect your business in any way. Check for the specific location you're considering as well as neighboring properties—you probably don't want a nightclub opening up next to your day-care center.

The Building's Infrastructure

Many older buildings do not have the necessary infrastructure to support the high-tech needs of contemporary operations. Make sure the building that you choose has adequate electrical, air conditioning and telecommunications service to meet your present and future needs. It is a good idea to hire an independent engineer to check this out for you, so you are sure to have an objective evaluation.

Utilities And Other Costs

Rent is certainly the major portion of your ongoing facilities expense, but it's not all. Consider extras such as utilities—they're included in some leases but not in others. If they're not included, ask the utility company for a summary of the previous year's usage and billing for the site. Also, find out what kind of security deposits the various utility providers require so you can develop an accurate move-in budget; however, you may not need a deposit if you have an established payment record with the company.

DOLLAR STRETCHER

TO KEEP COSTS DOWN, CONSIDER SHARING SPACE WITH ANOTHER COMPANY THAT DOES NOT COMPETE WITH YOUR BUSINESS, ONE THAT MIGHT EVEN COMPLEMENT YOURS. THIS IS KNOWN AS CO-BRANDING, SUCH AS WHEN A SANDWICH CHAIN PLACES A UNIT IN A CONVENIENCE STORE. PUT YOUR SPACE-SHARING AGREEMENT IN WRITING, DETAILING EACH PARTY'S RIGHTS AND RESPONSIBILITIES, AND GIVE YOURSELF AN OUT IF YOU NEED IT.

If you have to provide your own janitorial service, what will it cost? What are insurance rates for the area? Do you have to pay extra for parking? Consider all your location-related expenses, and factor them into your decision.

Room For Growth

Look at the facility with an eye to the future. It is generally unwise to begin with more space than you need, but if you anticipate growth, be sure the facility

Location Work Sheet

Answer the following questions by indicating whether it is a strength (S) or weakness (W) of the potential site as it relates to your business. Once you have completed a work sheet for each prospective location, compare the relative strengths and weaknesses of each site to determine the value of each to the success of your business.

	S	W
Is the facility large enough for your business?		
Does it meet your layout requirements well?		
Does the building need any repairs?		
Will you have to make any leasehold improvements?		
Do the existing utilities meet your needs, or will you have to do any rewiring or plumbing work? Is ventilation adequate?		
Is the facility easily accessible to your potential clients or customers?		
Can you find a number of qualified employees in the area in which the facility is located?		
Is the facility consistent with the image you would like to maintain?		
Is the facility located in a safe neighborhood with a low crime rate?		
Are neighboring businesses likely to attract customers who will also patronize your business?		
Are there any competitors located close to the facility? If so, can you compete with them successfully?		
Can suppliers make deliveries conveniently at this location?		
If your business expands in the future, will the facility be able to accommodate this growth?		
Are the lease terms and rent favorable?		
Is the facility located in an area zoned for your type of business?		

you choose can accommodate you. Keep your long-range plan in mind, even when short-term advantages make a location look attractive. A great deal on a place you're likely to outgrow in a few years probably is not that great of a deal. Similarly, if there is evidence of pending decline in the vicinity, you should consider whether you want to be located there in five years.

WHAT CAN YOU EXPECT TO PAY?

Real estate costs vary tremendously based on the type of facility, the region, the specific location and the market. A commercial real estate broker will be able to give you an overview of costs in your area. You may want to look at historical data—how has the rate for your type of facility fluctuated over the years? Also ask for forecasts so you know what to expect in the future. Understanding the overall market will be a tremendous help when you begin negotiating your lease.

COMMERCIAL LEASES

If you've never been involved in renting commercial space, your first glimpse of a commercial lease may be overwhelming. They are lengthy, full of jargon and unfamiliar terms, and always written to the landlord's advantage. But they *are* negotiable. Whether you're working on the deal yourself or using an agent, the key to successful lease negotiations is knowing what you want, understanding what the lease document says and being reasonable in your demands.

Especially for retail space, be sure your lease includes a *bail-out clause*, which lets you out of the lease if your sales don't reach an agreed-on amount, and a *co-tenancy clause* so you can break the lease if an anchor store closes or moves. If you have to do a lot of work to get the space ready for occupancy, consider negotiating a *construction allowance*—generally $5 to $25 per square foot—to help offset the costs.

Be sure you clearly understand the difference between *rentable* and *usable* space. Rentable space is what you pay for; usable is what you can use and typically does not include hallways, restrooms, lobbies, elevator shafts, stairwells and so forth. You may be expected to pay a prorated portion of common area maintenance costs. This is not unusual, but be sure the fees are reasonable and that the landlord

Speaking The Language

Following are some of the leases you may come across:

- **FLAT LEASE:** The oldest and simplest type of lease, the flat lease, sets a single price for a definite period of time. It generally is the best deal for the tenant but is becoming increasingly harder to find. (Caution: Avoid a flat lease if the term is too short; a series of short-term flat leases could cost you more in the long run than a longer-term lease with reasonable escalation clauses.)

- **STEP LEASE:** The step lease attempts to cover the landlord's expected increases in expenses by increasing the rent on an annual basis over the life of the agreement. The problem with step leases is that they are based on estimates rather than actual costs, and there's no way for either party to be sure in advance that the proposed increases are fair and equitable.

- **NET LEASE:** Like a step lease, the net lease increases the rent to cover increases in the landlord's costs but does so at the time they occur rather than on estimates. This may be more equitable than a step lease, but it's less predictable.

- **COST OF LIVING LEASE:** Rather than tying rent increases to specific expenses, this type of lease bases increases on the rises in the cost of living. Your rent will go up with general inflation. Of course, the prices for your products and services will also likely rise with inflation, and that should cover your rent increases, so this type of lease can be very appealing.

- **PERCENTAGE LEASE:** This lease lets the landlord benefit from your success. The rent is based on either a minimum amount or a base amount, or a percentage of your business's gross revenue, whichever is higher. Percentages typically range from 3 to 12 percent. With this type of lease, you'll be required to periodically furnish proof of gross sales; to do this, you may allow the landlord to examine your books or sales tax records, or provide a copy of the appropriate section of your tax return. Percentage leases are common for retail space.

is not making a profit on them. Also, check for clauses that allow the landlord the right to remodel at the tenants' expense without approval, and insist on language that limits your financial liability.

Leasehold Improvements

Leasehold improvements are the nonremovable installations—either original or the results of remodeling—that you make to the facility to accommodate your needs. Such improvements are typically more substantial when renting new space, which may consist of only walls and flooring. Often existing space will include at least some fixtures. Get estimates on the improvements you'll need to make before signing the lease so you'll know the total move-in costs and can make a fair construction allowance request.

Negotiating The Lease

The first lease the landlord presents is usually just the starting point. You may be surprised at what you can get in the way of concessions and extras simply by asking. Of course, you need to be reasonable and keep your demands in line with acceptable business practices and current market conditions. A good commercial real estate agent can be invaluable in this area.

Avoid issuing ultimatums; they almost always close doors—and if you fail to follow through, your next "ultimatum" will not mean much. Consider beginning the process with something that is close to your "best and final offer." That way, your negotiations will not be lengthy and protracted, and you can either reach a mutually acceptable deal or move on to a different property. The longer negotiations take, the more potential there is for things to go wrong.

Essentially, everything in the lease is subject to negotiation, including financial terms, the starting rent, rent increases, the tenant's rights and responsibilities, options for renewal, tenant leasehold improvements, and other terms and conditions. You or your agent can negotiate the lease, but then it should be drawn up by an attorney. Typically, the landlord or his attorney will draft the lease, and an attorney you hire who specializes in real estate should review it for you before you sign.

It Still Comes Down To You

Technology and statistics are important elements of your site selection decision, but nothing beats your personal involvement in the process. Real estate brokers and economic development agencies

Business Lease Checklist

After you have chosen a particular site, check the following points before you sign the lease:

❏ Is there sufficient electrical power?

❏ Are there enough electrical outlets?

❏ Are there enough parking spaces for customers and employees?

❏ Is there sufficient lighting? Heating? Air conditioning?

❏ Do you know how large a sign and what type you can erect?

❏ Will your city's building and zoning departments allow your business to operate in the facility?

❏ Will the landlord allow the alterations that you deem necessary?

❏ Must you pay for returning the building to its original condition when you move?

❏ Is there any indication of roof leaks? (A heavy rain could damage goods.)

❏ Is the cost of burglary insurance high in the area? (This varies tremendously.)

❏ Can you secure the building at a low cost against the threat of burglary?

❏ Will the health department approve your business at this location?

❏ Will the fire department approve your business at this location?

❏ Have you included a written description of the property?

❏ Have you attached drawings of the property to the lease document?

❏ Do you have written guidelines for renewal terms?

❏ Do you know when your lease payment begins?

❏ Have you bargained for one to three months of free rent?

❏ Do you know your date of possession?

❏ Have you listed the owner's responsibility for improvements?

❏ Do you pay the taxes?

❏ Do you pay the insurance?

❏ Do you pay the maintenance fees?

❏ Do you pay the utilities?

❏ Do you pay the sewage fees?

❏ Have you asked your landlord for a cap of 5 percent on your rent increase?

❏ Have you included penalty clauses in case the project is late and you are denied occupancy?

❏ Have you retained the right to obtain your own bids for signage?

❏ Can you leave if the center is never more than 70 percent leased?

❏ Has a real estate attorney reviewed your contract?

can give you plenty of numbers, but remember their job is to get you to choose their location. To get a balanced picture, take the time to visit the sites yourself, talk to people who own or work in nearby businesses, and verify the facts and what they really mean to the potential success of your business.

GLOSSARY

ABSOLUTE NET LEASE: a lease in which the tenant agrees to pay a basic rent and be responsible and separately pay for all maintenance, operating and other expenses of the building or office

AMENITIES: any material goods, services or intangible items that increase the comfort, attractiveness, desirability and value of an office suite or building

ASSEMBLAGE: the combining of two or more contiguous properties into one large property; an assemblage will often make the one large property more valuable than the separate parts

ASSESSMENT: the determination or setting of a tax or other charge based on a building's estimated value

ATTORNMENT: a lease provision that the tenant agrees, in advance, to accept and pay rent or other required payments to a new landlord or legal owner of the property

BINDING LETTER OF INTENT: a letter of intent would be upheld in a court of law as the actual leasing of space by the tenant from the landlord and by the landlord to the tenant regardless of whether an actual lease document was agreed to or signed

BUILDING STANDARD WORKLETTER: a list and/or detailed specifications of the construction items (both quantity and quality) that will be provided by the developer to be used in building out a tenant's office space

CONTIGUOUS OFFICE SPACE: office suites adjacent to each other or having a common demising wall

EASEMENT: the right of an individual or entity to use the land of another individual or entity, usually for a specific purpose

ESCALATOR(S): term used to describe how a tenant's payment for rent or service shall increase

HOLDOVER RENT: an extremely high rent intended as a penalty to a tenant who continues to use or remain in possession of a leased premises beyond the lease term

LEASEHOLD IMPROVEMENTS: the construction, fixtures, attachments, and any and all the physical changes and additions made to lease premises where made by the tenant (with or without the landlord's permission), or on the tenant's behalf by the landlord or a representative (e.g., subcontractor) of the tenant

Leasing agent: an individual who specializes in leasing commercial real estate, including office, retail and industrial space; a leasing agent must work for a principal broker and be licensed

Letter of intent: a signed agreement by both tenant and landlord prior to the lease setting forth primary terms, conditions and considerations that are to form the basis of the lease

Liability of landlord provision: a lease clause severely limiting the landlord's liability for use of the building and office space by tenants, guests, employees, visitors, etc.

Market rent: the current rental rates paid by tenants for like use (office space) in buildings of comparable size with similar qualities of construction and building amenities, and comparable surrounding neighborhood characteristics and environment; term is often used in renewal clauses as the rent that will be paid if lease renewal occurs

Rent abatement: a concession offered by a landlord as an inducement to tenants to lease office space; provides for a reduction of monthly rent by omitting a required payment for a specific number of months

Tenant construction workletter: an addendum or attachment to the lease document that details the responsibilities of both the tenant and the landlord as they relate to the construction of the tenant's office space

Tenant improvements: the construction, fixtures, physical changes and additions made to an office space, for the benefit of the tenant, by the tenant (usually with the landlord's permission), or on the tenant's behalf by the landlord or a representative (subcontractor)

No Place Like Home

Starting a homebased business

By Paul & Sarah Edwards, authors, *Working From Home*

Whether your ambition is to run a homebased business or to grow your enterprise beyond your home as soon as cash flow allows it, starting at home is a good choice for you. Two out of three companies (of all sizes) begin in a spare bedroom, garage, basement or sometimes even a bathroom. That's how companies as diverse as Apple Computer, Baskin-Robbins ice cream, Electronic Data Systems, Hallmark cards, the *Lillian Vernon* catalog, and Purex began. Of course, the Internet makes operating a virtual company from home more feasible and popular than ever.

If you want to hang your shingle at home, either permanently or temporarily, here are some things you must consider:

■ **FIRST, IS IT LEGAL TO HANG YOUR SHINGLE OR SIGN THERE?** This is one of the many possible restrictions on your being permitted to make your home a working castle. Whether and how flexibly you can operate a business from your home is covered in local zoning ordinances and also by the covenants, codes and restrictions (CC&Rs) of homeowner and condo associations.

■ **HOW ARE YOU GOING TO SEPARATE YOUR HOME AND WORKPLACE?** While the demanding hours required to start any business affects an entrepreneur's family, when you bring the workplace into the home, your family's needs must be taken into account even more.

■ **HOW ARE YOU GOING TO ESTABLISH AND MAINTAIN A PROFESSIONAL IMAGE?** This is especially important if your address is on Cow Path Lane or your dog loves to bark or your teenager's playing the drums in the next room.

CAN YOU WORK FROM HOME LEGALLY?

Most cities and many counties have zoning ordinances that limit, to one degree or another, whether you can operate a business from home. While many communities have modernized their zoning ordinances to recognize that a computer-based business isn't like a noisy auto body repair shop, an odorous hair salon, or a 6 a.m. gathering point for a construction or cleaning crew, many communities ban certain kinds of businesses and prescribe limitations which may handicap some businesses. Here are some common activities communities don't like and may restrict with their zoning code:

- **INCREASED VEHICULAR TRAFFIC,** both moving and parked on the street
- **PROMINENT SIGNS**
- **EMPLOYEES NOT RELATED TO YOU** who are working in your home
- **USE OF THE HOME MORE FOR BUSINESS** than as a residence (determined by percentage of space used for the business)
- **SELLING RETAIL GOODS** to the public—sometimes communities limit this to specific hours
- **STORING DANGEROUS AMOUNTS OR KINDS OF MATERIALS** inside or outside your home

So if you're planning to launch your business from home, the first thing to do is to check out what commercial activity your city or county allows in your neighborhood. This is becoming easier to do, as many communities are making their codes available on their Web sites. You just need to know what the zoning classification is for your home (that is, R-1, R-2, R-3, etc.), which is easily found at your city or county zoning office.

While many people blithely ignore zoning, a complaining neighbor

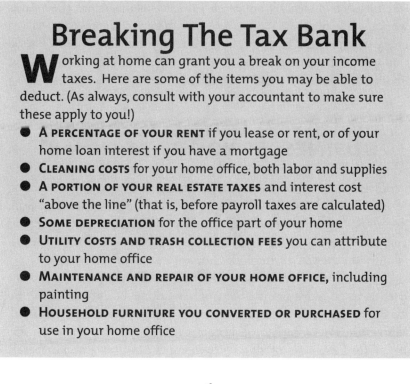

Breaking The Tax Bank

Working at home can grant you a break on your income taxes. Here are some of the items you may be able to deduct. (As always, consult with your accountant to make sure these apply to you!)

- **A PERCENTAGE OF YOUR RENT** if you lease or rent, or of your home loan interest if you have a mortgage
- **CLEANING COSTS** for your home office, both labor and supplies
- **A PORTION OF YOUR REAL ESTATE TAXES** and interest cost "above the line" (that is, before payroll taxes are calculated)
- **SOME DEPRECIATION** for the office part of your home
- **UTILITY COSTS AND TRASH COLLECTION FEES** you can attribute to your home office
- **MAINTENANCE AND REPAIR OF YOUR HOME OFFICE,** including painting
- **HOUSEHOLD FURNITURE YOU CONVERTED OR PURCHASED** for use in your home office

can throw a real kink in your business plan, as you may find yourself with a cease and desist order and have to suddenly move or close down. So find out what you're allowed to do, and get along with your neighbors. With their support, you may be able to get a waiver of restrictions, called a variance or conditional-use permit.

Also, some people choose to rent a private mailing box with a street address to use as their official business address. If you do that, be sure that your city does not make a physical inspection of the business premises before granting a city business license.

SMART TIP

KNOWING WHEN TO MOVE FROM YOUR HOME OFFICE CAN BE VITAL TO YOUR BUSINESS. HERE ARE SOME SIGNS TO WATCH FOR: 1) BEING IN A COMMERCIAL LOCATION OR OUTSIDE OFFICE WILL HELP YOUR BUSINESS GROW, 2) YOUR CURRENT REVENUE OR ANTICIPATED NEW REVENUE WILL PAY FOR THE ADDITIONAL COSTS, OR 3) YOUR FAMILY SITUATION DETRACTS FROM YOUR ABILITY TO DO BUSINESS.

While you may not have a zoning problem, if you rent or belong to a homeowners or property owners association (which all condominium and co-op owners do), you may find even harsher restrictions on operating a homebased business. Homeowner agreements are often harder to change, but often so many members are themselves working at home these days, the restrictions are not enforced. Still, an angry neighbor can cause problems for your homebased business. So find out where you stand, and if you are moving somewhere new, check out the restrictions before signing a lease or contract.

WILL YOU LOOK LIKE A REAL BUSINESS IF YOU'RE AT HOME?

That's up to you. The negative connotation implied by referring to homebased business as "cottage industry" is disappearing. Still, presenting a professional image can be a challenge if your 4-year-old answers your phone or if your clients are confronted with piles of laundry on the way through the house to your office.

The best standard for how a homebased business should present itself is to be indistinguishable from any other business. There's no need for your business image to convey where your office is located. Web sites, for example, are becoming the most important "storefront" for businesses of all sizes, and yours can be as good or better than any. In fact, chances are good that many, if not most, of the Web sites you encounter were designed by homebased Web site designers.

What's important is that your Web site address, like your e-mail address, be one that is easy to enter and preferably memorable. (Think of the value Amazon.com and Monster.com have created with simple names that don't even relate to what they do.) Even if you house your Web site on one of the services that offers inexpensive or free Web sites like Bigstep.com and Homestead.com, you can still get a personalized Web address (URL) without the "thisisafreewebsite.com" added on to the end of your Web site name. It will cost you something extra, but it's well worth the price in terms of your image and convenience for those you may be doing business with. Think about what your URL will look like if you paint it on the side of your vehicle. For more tips on crafting your business Web site, turn to Part 7, Chapter 36.

Other ways to present a professional image while operating your business from home include:

■ **HAVE A SEPARATE TELEPHONE LINE FOR YOUR BUSINESS.** While your second line can be a residential line, opting for a business line will enable you to have one and sometimes two Yellow Pages listings and will enable people to call directory assistance or use Internet-based Yellow Pages to find your business by name. These benefits can easily justify the additional cost of a business line. Also, locate your business phone away from household noise.

■ **ANSWER YOUR PHONE IN A FORMAL AND PROFESSIONAL MANNER.** If other family members answer your business line, make sure they do the same, including using your company name. While you can use voice mail, like nearly every corporation does today, one way of gaining a competitive edge is to actually answer your phone or have someone answer it for you. Customers and prospective customers almost always prefer to talk with a live human being rather than deal with voice mail.

> **BEWARE!**
>
> TO PROTECT YOURSELF FROM UNEXPECTED FINANCIAL PAIN AND STRESS, GET A HOME OFFICE ENDORSEMENT OR RIDER TO YOUR HOMEOWNERS OR RENTERS INSURANCE POLICY TO COVER LIABILITY TO CLIENTS COMING TO YOUR HOME. ALSO CONSIDER A SEPARATE POLICY OR ENDORSEMENT TO COVER LOSSES OF BUSINESS PROPERTY AND COMPUTER DATA AND SOFTWARE.

■ **USE VOICE MAIL TO CAPTURE CALLS WHEN YOU'RE AWAY.** Better yet, to give your callers a sense of more personal service, consider going a step beyond, and use one of the personal communications assistant technologies like Oryx (www.prioritycall.com), Personal Assistant (www.lucent.com), Solo Call (www.solopoint.com) or Wildfire (www.wildfire.com). These services provide callers with more choices and can help them locate you quickly if needed.

■ **TAKE CARE THAT YOUR PAPER COLLATERALS HAVE A CONSISTENT, QUALITY LOOK.** While you can certainly design your own letter-head, envelopes, business cards, brochures and invoice statements, if you don't have a visual sense—and not everyone does—consider using a professional to do your design work. You can either have the final product professionally printed or print items as you need them on your own printer. Try coordinating your materials with your Web site for an even snazzier look. (To read all about creating your business image, turn to Chapter 19).

■ **MAKE SURE YOUR BUSINESS ADDRESS IS PROFESSIONAL.** If your home's street address is something like Cow Path Lane or Lazy Daisy Road, it's a good idea to not use it as the address where business mail and packages are delivered. We recommend using street addresses from a business district: You can rent from a mail-receiving service or an office suite complex. P.O. box addresses tend to make clients distrustful; you also can't receive FedEx or UPS deliveries at a P.O. box.

HEADING OFF HOMEBASED HASSLES

Since almost 9 out of 10 people who operate a home business have a family, keeping personal and work spaces separate is critical to peaceful domestic relations. So location, location, location is the first thing to think about. If you can have your office in a separate struc-ture, like a garage or a guest house in the backyard, you probably need to think no further.

But since the typical homebased business is located inside a home, you need to consider noise and family traffic patterns when deciding where to put your office. Of course, if you're locating your business at home so you can care for your children, you may choose to com-promise privacy for a vantage point that will enable you to see or hear what your children are doing while you work.

DOLLAR STRETCHER

CONSIDER CONVERTING EXISTING FUR-
NITURE AND EQUIPMENT, SUCH AS

 DESKS AND COM-
PUTERS, IN YOUR
HOUSEHOLD TO USE

FOR BUSINESS PURPOSES. YOU CAN
THEN DEPRECIATE THEM AT THEIR CUR-
RENT VALUE, SAVING YOU TAX DOLLARS.

If occupying a separate room is not possible, use furniture, screens, and room dividers to physically divide a larger room, such as the living room or den, to create a sense of physical separateness. This can also be significant in passing the exclusive-use test needed to qualify for a home office tax deduction. This test requires that the part of your home you deduct, which can be a portion of a room, must be used only for business. Two exceptions are if you're storing inventory or using a room to provide day care; then you can also deduct the use of the space as part of your residence.

If you have customers coming to your home, locating your office where it can have a separate entrance or be close to an entrance to your home can save you time and trouble. If business visitors must walk through your home to get to your office, it's important to keep personal areas of your home neat and uncluttered by personal items, such as laundry and children's toys. About half of home offices are located in a spare bedroom, which hopefully has a relatively soundproof door.

By having a separate telephone line for your business, you can avoid family squabbles over using the telephone and avoid tying up your only line with personal calls during business hours. Also, consider locating your fax machine away from family sleeping areas so late-night faxes won't wake you or your family.

While many parents do care for their children while working, you can't expect to work at 100 percent efficiency with children underfoot, so consider other options. The most common ones are getting help from relatives, using outside day-care services, or hiring a nanny to care for children while you're working.

Another less used but creative solution is setting up a cooperative day-care arrangement with four or five other parents who work from home and alternatively taking turns caring for the children. You may only be able to work four days a week, but in those four days you can be more productive than you would be in five days with your children competing for your attention.

If, like many people, you live in an inconvenient location or simply don't have enough space to meet with customers or clients in your home office, consider meeting at their location or a neutral spot

Hit The Books

For tips, tricks and helpful hints, here's some recommended reading:

- *BEST HOME BUSINESSES FOR THE 21ST CENTURY* (Tarcher/Putnam) by Paul & Sarah Edwards
- *HOME-BASED BUSINESS FOR DUMMIES* (IDG) by Paul & Sarah Edwards with Peter Economy
- *HOME BUSINESSES YOU CAN BUY* (Tarcher/Putnam) by Paul & Sarah Edwards
- *MAKING MONEY IN CYBERSPACE* (Tarcher/Putnam) by Paul & Sarah Edwards
- *MAKING MONEY WITH YOUR COMPUTER AT HOME* (Tarcher/Putnam) by Paul & Sarah Edwards
- *OUTFITTING YOUR SMALL OFFICE FOR MUCH LESS* (AMACOM) by Walter Zooi and Paul & Sarah Edwards
- *WORKING FROM HOME*, 5th edition (Tarcher/Putnam) by Paul & Sarah Edwards

like a restaurant, offer pickup and delivery services, and use video-conferencing for meetings.

How you dress while you work at home affects how you feel about your work and the image you project. While most people working in traditional offices dress informally on the job, you may find it helpful not to dress too casually. One recent survey found most people who work at home take daily showers or baths, so while it may be fine to work in PJs, chances are they're not the best choice for all-day wear.

Whether you only use your home as a launching pad for a larger business or home is your final destination, once you have gotten your home office set up, your home can be a satisfying base of operations. You're ready to work like any business.

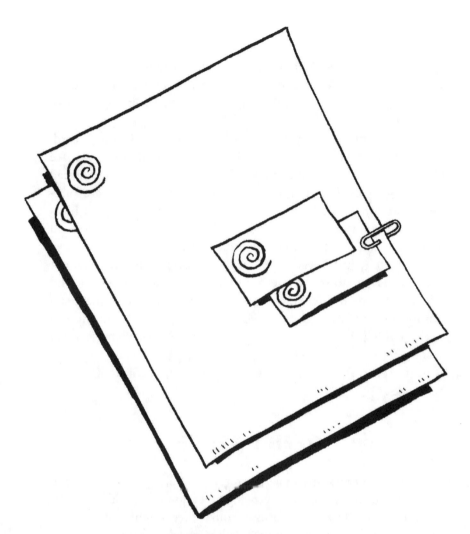

First
Impressions

Creating a professional image

T hese days, it is just not enough to create a terrific product, offer super service and have a solid business plan to back you up. Your company image is equally important to the overall success of your business.

Think about it. Every time you hand out your business card, send a letter or welcome a client into your office or store, you are selling someone on your company. Your business card, letterhead and signage—just like traditional print, radio or TV ads—are valuable selling tools. The look of your office also helps "sell" your business by conveying an image, whether it is that of a funky, creative ad agency or a staid, respectable accounting firm.

Fortunately, just because you are a start-up company does not mean you have to look like one. Your logo, business card, signage and style are all part of a cohesive image program known as corporate identity. And with the right corporate identity, your company can appear highly professional and give the impression of having been in business for years.

In this chapter, we will discuss how to create a corporate image that works.

OFFICE SPACE

When you are a start-up with limited capital, it may be tempting to put all your money into advertising and equipment and skimp on office furniture. How you furnish your office might not seem to matter, especially if your customers will not see it. And if your office is located at home, the dining room table might look like the most logical choice.

But a nicely furnished office is not just a matter of aesthetics. Grabbing whatever furniture is at hand and plunking it down without a thought to organization can put you at a major disadvantage in terms of productivity.

Everything In Its Place

Improving your own and your employees' performance involves a lot more than finding comfortable chairs. It involves placement of offices or cubicles within the building, proximity to equipment, lighting, desk space, meeting areas, privacy and more. People spend most of their waking hours at the office, so its design has a tremendous effect on morale.

How can you create a high-performance office? The first step is addressing organizational issues...of who sits where. The days of big "power desks" and hierarchical corner offices are over. More businesses are turning to flexible environments ideal for small companies where the business owner probably doubles as salesperson.

With today's emphasis on team-building, office design is moving away from compartmentalized offices and moving toward large spaces where teams of employees can work. When setting up your space, think about who needs to work with whom and which employees share what resources. If you group those people together, you enhance their productivity.

In addition to maximizing your own and your employees' productivity, your office may also function as a marketing tool if clients or customers visit. Think about what visitors will see when they come by. Will they be bombarded with noise from one department near the entrance? Or will they see a series of closed doors with seemingly no

On The Outside

The inside of your office may look great, but don't stop there. What about the outside? If the first impression a potential customer has of your business is a shabby door or an unkempt parking lot, you're not sending the right message...and all your hard work in designing an attractive, efficient office could be going to waste.

Step outside your place of business and take a long, hard look at the parking lot, sidewalks, windows, outside lighting, landscaping and the outside of the building itself. A well-maintained building projects an industrious, professional image. Weeds, trash, broken sidewalks, tattered awnings, dirty windows, dead plants and overflowing trash containers send the message "We don't care."

Whether you're in a retail location or an office building, take the time to check the property from the outside, and make sure it's inviting and appealing every day.

activity taking place? Visitors should not be overwhelmed by chaos as they walk through your building, but they should see signs of life and get glimpses of the daily activities going on at your company.

Putting It All Together

Once considered some trendy European way to make business owners spend a lot of money, ergonomics has gained respect in recent years. Simply put, this term refers to designing and arranging furnishings and space to fit the natural movements of the human body. Ergonomics can help you and your employees avoid repetitive stress injuries from typing or bending and can prevent common problems, like back pain, which often sideline entrepreneurs and their employees.

Noise pollution is one of the biggest problems in many offices. One good way to decrease noise is to cover computer printers with sound shields. Covering a printer can cut noise by more than 90 percent...and increase concentration accordingly.

Buy adjustable chairs. A good chair allows the user to adjust the

What's In Store?

Got a retail location? Ask yourself these questions to make sure your store has the "eye appeal" it needs to keep customers coming back:

- **ARE YOUR SHELVES CLEAN** and neat? Is merchandise displayed so people can see it easily?
- **IS THE AREA** around your cash registers or terminals clean and orderly?
- **CAN YOU FIND FORMS,** packaging and related materials quickly and easily?
- **ARE LIGHT FIXTURES CLEAN,** bright and working properly?
- **IS THERE PLENTY OF ROOM** between counters and shelves so that aisles are wide and free of barriers?
- **ARE GLASS SURFACES CLEAN** and floors vacuumed or swept and scrubbed regularly?

seat height and the tension of the backrest. The seat should angle forward slightly to keep from cutting off your circulation. Boost the benefits of a good chair by providing footrests. Elevating the feet slightly while typing or sitting at a desk reduces lower back strain and improves circulation, keeping you more alert.

Make sure the desk and chair arrangement you choose allows you to keep the tops of your knuckles, the tops of your wrists and your forearms all in a straight line as you work on your computer. Your computer monitor should be at or below your eye level. Use an under-desk keyboard tray and monitor stand, if necessary, to get everything in line.

Another often-ignored problem in offices is lighting. Too much or too little lighting causes eye strain and tiredness, decreasing productivity. To cut down on the glare, put filters on computer screens. Use individual lamps to illuminate desk work and help eyes adjust from overlit computer screens to underlit paper. Install mini-blinds to let each employee control the amount of light to match the task at hand and the time of day.

You can find office furniture touted as ergonomic at a variety of sources, from office supply superstores to traditional office furniture retailers. Just because something claims to be ergonomic, however, does not mean it is right for you. Always test furnishings before you buy them. Sit in the chair and make sure it is comfortable; sit at the desk and make sure it is the right height. Make sure your desk and chair work together and that there is plenty of legroom under the desk.

When you buy furniture, look for solid construction, particularly in desks. The "ready-to-assemble" desks available at home or office superstores are often poor quality. Most are made of particleboard, which won't stand up to heavy use. A better option for those on a budget is to buy used office furniture.

SMART TIP

IF YOU DO A LOT OF COMPUTER WORK, CONSIDER INVESTING IN AN "L"-SHAPED DESK, WITH YOUR COMPUTER AND KEYBOARD TRAY ON THE SMALL SIDE OF THE "L." THIS GETS YOUR COMPUTER OUT OF THE WAY AND ENSURES YOU HAVE PLENTY OF WORK SPACE WHEN YOU NEED IT.

More and more furniture dealers nowadays sell used (also called "reconditioned") office furniture. You can find everything from a single desk and chair to a full fleet of cubicles for your whole staff. Typically, furniture has been repaired and repainted where necessary.

In some cases, you will be able to save up to 70 percent over the cost of the same items new. You can find used furniture sources in the Yellow Pages, or look in your local newspaper's classified ad section for individuals selling used pieces. Flea markets, auctions and estate sales can be other sources of used items.

HOT LINK

NOT SURE WHERE IT'S ALL GOING TO GO? ROSS FURNITURE (HTTP://ROSSFURNITURE.COM/DESIGN.HTML) OFFERS FREE SHAREWARE FOR MAC AND WINDOWS SO YOU CAN FIGURE OUT WHERE TO PUT YOUR DESK AND YOUR WORKTABLE WITHOUT DRAGGING THEM ALL OVER THE ROOM.

DESIGNING A LOGO

Before you start designing a business card or picking colors for your letterhead, you need a logo. Featuring your company name, embellished with a little color and perhaps a few graphic touches here and there, your logo is the most important design element because it is the basis for all your other materials: stationery, packaging, promotional materials and signage.

"Through the use of color and graphics, your logo should reflect the overall image you want your company to convey," says Richard Gerstman of Interbrand, a brand identity and marketing consulting firm. "It should give people a feel for what your company is all about."

For example, say your product is an organic facial cream you will be marketing to health-conscious consumers. Your logo should represent your product's best benefits—being all-natural and environmentally sound. Creating a simple, no-nonsense logo using earth tones and a plain typeface will give the impression of a product that is "back-to-basics," which is exactly what you want to achieve. Take that same product and give it a slick, high-tech look with neon colors, however, and people won't associate your logo with the down-to-earth product you're selling.

Logos come in two basic forms: abstract symbols (like the apple in Apple Computer) or logotypes, a stylized rendition of your company's name. You can also use a combination of both. Alan Siegel, chairman and CEO of Siegelgale, a design firm specializing in corporate identity, warns that promoting an abstract symbol can prove very costly for a small business on a budget. In addition, he says, such logos are harder to remember. "A logotype or word mark is much easier to recall," Siegel says. If you do use an abstract symbol, Siegel advises, always use it in connection with your business name.

Trying to create a logo on your own may seem like the best way to avoid the high costs of going to a professional design firm, which will charge anywhere from $4,000 to $15,000 for a logo alone. However, be aware that there are thousands of independent designers around who charge much less. According to Stan Evenson, founder of Evenson Design Group, entrepreneurs on a tight budget should shop around for a designer. "There are a lot of [freelance] designers who charge rates ranging from $15 to $150 per hour, based on their experience," he says. But don't hire someone because of their bargain price. Find a designer who's familiar with your field…and your competition. If the cost still seems exorbitant, Evenson says, "Remember that a good logo should last at least 10 years. If you look at the amortization of that cost over a 10-year period, it doesn't seem so bad."

Even if you have a good eye for color and a sense of what you want your logo to look like, you should still consult a professional designer. Why? They know whether or not a logo design will transfer easily into print or onto a sign, while you might come up with a beautiful design that can't be transferred or would cost too much to be printed. Your logo is the foundation for all your promotional materials, so this is one area where spending a little more now really pays off later.

BUSINESS CARDS

Once you have your logo, it's time to apply it to the marketing items you will use most, such as business cards. A good business card should convey the overall image of your business—not easy, considering the card measures only 2 inches by 3 inches. How can you possibly get a message across in such a small amount of space?

You can't expect your business card to tell the whole story about your company. What you should expect it to do is present a professional image people will remember. "A business card can make or break a client's first impression of your

BRIGHT IDEA

ASK OWNERS OF NON COMPETING BUT RELATED BUSINESSES IF YOU CAN DISPLAY SOME OF YOUR BUSINESS CARDS ON THEIR COUNTERS. A PET-SITTER, FOR EXAMPLE, COULD LEAVE HER BUSINESS CARDS ON THE COUNTER AT A PET STORE. OFFER TO DO THE SAME FOR THEM.

In The Cards

Business cards don't have to be boring. If your industry allows for a little creative flair, here are some ideas to try.

- **USE 4-INCH-BY-7-INCH CARDS** that fold over (like a mini-brochure), cards made of plastic or cards with photos on them. If your business relies on a lot of phone contact, consider cards that are pre-punched to fit in a Rolodex.

- **ALTHOUGH THEY ARE MORE EXPENSIVE** than standard business cards, cards in nontraditional shapes get attention. Try a teddy bear shape for a day-care service, for example, or a birthday cake for a party planner.

- **TEXTURED PAPER** can add to a card's interest (make sure it does not detract from readability, though), as can colored paper. In general, stay with lighter shades that enhance readability.

- **THERMOGRAPHY,** a process that creates raised, shiny print, adds interest to a card. Embossing and foil stamping are two other imprinting processes that can give your card visual appeal.

company," Evenson says. That little card makes as much of an impression as your personal appearance—the suit you wear or the briefcase you carry.

The color, wording and texture of your business card have a lot to do with its appeal and its ability to convey your company image. Use common sense when you are designing your business card. If your business markets children's toys and games, you might try using bright, primary colors and words written in a child's script. On the other hand, if you run a financial consulting service, then you would want your business card to convey professionalism and reliability, so stick to traditional looks such as black printing on a gray, beige or white background.

Of course, professional designers claim entrepreneurs should not try to attempt designing a business card on their own, but

BEWARE!

EVALUATE BUSINESS CARD DESIGNS WITH THESE CRITERIA IN MIND:

- IS THE CARD EASY TO READ?
- DOES THE DESIGN CATCH YOUR EYE? (A GOOD DESIGNER CAN MAKE EVEN AN ALL-TYPE CARD APPEALING.)

- IS YOUR NAME OR THE BUSINESS'S NAME IMMEDIATELY IDENTIFIABLE?

many cash-strapped business owners have no other choice. The best course of action: Look at all the business cards you receive, and emulate the cards that you like. You have more leeway if you are in a creative business, such as party planning or retailing, but in general, keep the following tips in mind:

- **USE YOUR LOGO AS THE BASIS.** Make it the largest element on the card.
- **DON'T MAKE THE CARD** an unusual shape.
- **KEEP IT SIMPLE.** Do not cram too much information on the card.
- **DO INCLUDE THE ESSENTIALS**—your name, title, company name, address, phone and fax numbers and e-mail address.
- **MAKE SURE THE TYPEFACE** is easily readable.
- **STICK TO ONE OR TWO COLORS.**

    Once you've got business cards, make the most of them:

- **ALWAYS GIVE PEOPLE** more than one card (so they can give it to others).
- **INCLUDE YOUR CARD** in all correspondence.
- **CARRY CARDS WITH YOU** at all times, in a card case so they're clean and neat.

SELECTING STATIONERY

Every time you mail a letter to a prospective client or to an existing customer, the missive leaves a long-lasting impression of your company. In a service business, your written materials are among your company's most important marketing items. And if you run a homebased business that doesn't have a commercial location or sign, introducing your company to clients through the mail can be one of your most effective marketing techniques. The paper stock you choose, as well as the colors and graphics embellishing it, plays an important role in the image your stationery presents to your customers. A hot, neon-pink stock may work well for a new suntan cream manufacturer, but not for a more conservative accounting service. Your stationery should tie in with your business cards, featuring

SMART TIP

KEEP YOUR BUSINESS CARDS, LETTER-HEAD AND OTHER MATERIALS CURRENT. IF THE PHONE COMPANY CHANGES YOUR AREA CODE, TOSS YOUR OLD STATIONERY AND CARDS AND HAVE NEW ONES PRINTED. USE IT AS AN EXCUSE TO CALL EVERYONE ON YOUR CLIENT AND PROSPECT LIST AND REMIND THEM OF WHAT YOU CAN DO FOR THEM.

the same color scheme and overall look.

Do not get so caught up in the design elements of your business stationery that you forget the obvious. Every piece of business stationery should include the basics: company name or logo, address, e-mail and Web site addresses, and phone and fax numbers. You want to make it as easy as possible for your clients to respond to your offer by making all the information they need readily available. Attach your business card to each letter as well, so clients can put it in their Rolodexes for future reference.

DESIGNING YOUR SIGN

Retailers and restaurateurs alike realize the power of a good sign. Some companies rely on drive-by or "walk-by" traffic for customers, and if that's the case with your company, your sign may be the most important element of your entire corporate identity.

A good sign must do more than just attract attention; it also has to be readable from a good distance. That's why your original logo is so important—one that looks great on a tiny business card may not transfer well to a huge sign above your store. Clearly, going to a professional in the first stages of developing your image is essential. If you find out your great logo can't be reproduced on a sign, you'll have to go back to square one and rethink your logo, which will end up costing you more in the long run.

In recent years, a whole host of new signage materials has emerged to provide more variety and individuality. This also means it's harder to choose among all the possibilities, which include neon, plastic, metal, wood and more. Do some investigating before making your final decision; there is a wide range of prices for various materials. Depending on your location, sign placement can make a big difference, too. Options include a free-standing sign, a wall sign, a projecting sign or a roof sign.

Since you probably don't have the know-how or the equipment

DOLLAR STRETCHER

CHECK OUT INSTANT SIGN STORES, WHICH CREATE SIGNS FOR A FRACTION OF THE COST. YOU MAY BE LIMITED IN SELECTION AND WON'T GET THE  HANDHOLDING YOU WOULD FROM A DESIGNER. HOWEVER, IF YOU ARE ON A BUDGET AND YOUR SIGN IS NOT THE KEY ELEMENT OF YOUR MARKETING STRATEGY, THIS COULD BE YOUR BEST BET.

DOLLAR STRETCHER

CREATING YOUR IMAGE CAN BE COSTLY, BUT YOU DON'T HAVE TO SPLURGE ON THE WHOLE WORKS AT ONCE. TO SAVE MONEY, START WITH THE KEY ITEMS THE PUBLIC WILL SEE IMMEDIATELY. IF YOU EXPECT TO ATTRACT MOST OF YOUR CLIENTS THROUGH SALES CALLS, FOR INSTANCE, PUT MORE MONEY INTO YOUR BUSINESS CARDS; IF YOU EXPECT TO LURE PEOPLE WITH YOUR SIGN, PUT THE MONEY THERE.

necessary to make a sign yourself, you will have to go to an outside manufacturer. Do not expect manufacturers to offer suggestions or point out any problems with your design if you have come up with one on your own. That's not their job.

Before you head to the manufacturer with your design specifications, check your local zoning laws. You may find that the design you've come up with for your fried chicken restaurant—a 30-foot neon number in the shape of a chicken—isn't allowed in your area. If you are moving into a shopping center, the developer may have additional regulations governing signage that can be used in the facility.

Most entrepreneurs need professional assistance with signage since they do not have experience in this area. You probably will not know how big the letters should be to be visible from down the block, and you may not know which materials fare best in inclement weather. For this reason, you should visit a professional—either a designer or a sign fabricator. A good designer knows when fabricators are cutting corners and not using the material requested or doing a shoddy job. A designer will also be present at the time of installation to make sure the sign is properly installed.

The cost of a sign varies greatly depending on the materials and type of sign. Buying directly from a fabricator can cost as little as $500, but you run the risk of not meeting zoning requirements. If you hire a designer, you'll pay a design fee in addition to fabrication costs, but you have a better guarantee that the finished product will work for you.

Taking Stock

The lowdown on inventory

Where would an apparel company be without clothing? An auto supply store without auto parts? A computer company without computers? Nowhere, of course. Understanding and managing your inventory is one of the most critical factors in business success.

Yet many entrepreneurs fail to answer such basic questions as "What items are the winners and losers?" and "How often does inventory turn over?" Don't make this mistake.

"Companies can increase their profitability 20 to 50 percent through prudent inventory management," says John Newman, a professor of entrepreneurship. "Some companies have more than doubled their profitability."

INVENTORY CONTROL

There is more to inventory control than simply buying new products. You have to know what to buy, when to buy it and how much to buy. You also need to track your inventory—whether manually or by computer—and use that knowledge to hone your purchasing process.

Start-up entrepreneurs are at a disadvantage when it comes to inventory control. "Many of them don't know how to set realistic inventory levels," says Newman, "so they wind up buying too much or too little."

Maintaining Enough Inventory

Your business's basic stock should provide a reasonable assortment of products and should be big enough to cover the normal sales demands of your business. Since you won't have actual sales and stocking figures from previous years to guide you during start-up, you must project your first year's sales based on your business plan.

When calculating basic stock, you must also factor in lead time—the length of time between reordering and receiving a product. For instance, if your lead time is four

BEWARE!

INVENTORY CONTROL DOESN'T JUST MEAN COUNTING. TAKE PHYSICAL CONTROL OF YOUR INVENTORY, TOO. LOCK IT UP OR RESTRICT ACCESS. REMEMBER THAT INVENTORY IS MONEY.

weeks and a particular product line sells 10 units a week, then you must reorder before the basic inventory level falls below 40 units. If you do not reorder until you actually need the stock, you'll have to wait four weeks without the product.

Insufficient inventory means lost sales and costly, time-consuming back orders. Running out of raw materials or parts that are crucial to your production process means increased operating costs, too. Your employees will be getting paid to sit around because there's no work for them to do; when the inventory does come in, they'll be paid for working overtime to make up for lost production time. In some situations, you could even end up buying emergency inventory at high prices.

One way to protect yourself from such shortfalls is by building a safety margin into basic inventory figures. To figure out the right safety margin for your business, try to think of all the outside factors that could contribute to delays, such as suppliers who tend to be late or goods being shipped in from overseas. Once you have been in business a while, you'll have a better feel for delivery times and will find it fairly easy to calculate your safety margin.

Avoiding Excess Inventory

Avoiding excess inventory is especially important for owners of companies with seasonal product lines, such as clothing, home accessories, and holiday and gift items. These products have a short "shelf life" and are hard to sell once they are no longer in fashion. Entrepreneurs who sell more timeless products, such as plumbing equipment, office supplies or auto products, have more leeway because it takes longer for these items to become obsolete.

No matter what your business, however, excess inventory should be avoided. It costs money in extra overhead, debt service on loans to purchase the excess inventory, additional personal property tax on unsold inventory and increased insurance costs. One merchandise consultant estimates that it costs the average retailer from 20 to 30 percent of the original inventory investment just to maintain it. Buying excess inventory also reduces your liquidity—something to be avoided. Consider the example of an auto supply retailer who finds himself with the opportunity to buy 1,000 gallons of antifreeze at a huge discount. If he buys the antifreeze and it turns out to be a mild winter, he'll be sitting on 1,000 gallons of antifreeze. Even though he knows he can sell the antifreeze during the next cold winter, it's still taking up space in his warehouse for an entire year—space that could be devoted to more profitable products.

When you find yourself with excess inventory, your natural reaction will probably be to reduce the price and sell it quickly. Although this solves the overstocking problem, it also reduces your return on investment. All your financial projections assume that you will receive the full price for your goods. If you slash your prices by 15 to 25 percent just to get rid of the excess inventory, you're los-

On With The Show

Trade shows are the primary way for new businesses to find suppliers. All major suppliers in an industry display their products at seasonal trade shows, where retailers go to buy and look at new items.

Although retailers buy from various sources year-round, trade shows are an important event in every store owner's buying cycle. Most retailers attend at least one trade show per year. Smart buyers come prepared with a shopping list and a seasonal budget calculated either in dollar amounts or in quantities of various merchandise.

Practically every major city hosts one or more trade shows relevant to specific retailers. You can contact your local chamber of commerce or convention and visitor's bureau for upcoming shows in your city or state. Your industry's trade publications should also list relevant trade shows. *Tradeshow Week* magazine offers a directory of trade shows at their Web site (www.tradeshowweek.com).

ing money you had counted on in your business plan.

Other novice entrepreneurs react to excess inventory by being overly cautious the next time they order stock. However, this puts you at risk of having an inventory shortage. To avoid accumulating excess inventory, set a realistic safety margin and order only what you're sure you can sell.

Inventory And Cash Flow

Cash-flow problems are some of the most common difficulties small businesses encounter, and they are usually the first signs of serious financial trouble ahead. According to Resource Evaluation Inc., a management consulting firm, tying money up in inventory can severely damage a small company's cash flow.

To control inventory effectively, prioritize your inventory needs. It might seem at first glance that the most expensive items in your inventory should receive the most attention. But in reality, less expensive items with higher turnover ratios have a greater effect on your business than more costly items. If you focus only on the high dollar-value items, you run the risk of running out of the lower-priced products that contribute more to your bottom line.

Divide materials into groups A, B and C, depending on the dollar impact they have on the company (not their actual price). You can then stock more of the vital A items while keeping the B and C items at more manageable levels. This is known as the ABC approach.

Oftentimes, as much as 80 percent of a company's revenues come from only 20 percent of the products. Companies that respect this "80-20 rule" concentrate their efforts on that key 20 percent of items. "It's a major mistake to try to manage all products the same way," says K. Roscoe Davis, a professor of production management.

Once you understand which items are most important, you'll be able to balance needs with costs, carrying only as much as you need of a given item. It's also a good idea to lower your inventory holding levels, keeping smaller quantities of an item in inventory for a short time rather than keeping large amounts for a long time. Consider ordering fewer items but doing so more often.

Tracking Inventory

A good inventory-tracking system will tell you what merchandise is in stock, what is on order, when it will arrive and what you've sold. With such a system, you can plan purchases intelligently and quickly recognize the fast-moving items you need to reorder and the slow-moving items you should mark down or specially promote.

You can create your own inventory tracking system or ask your accountant to set one up for you. Systems vary according to the amount of inventory displayed, the amount of backup stock required, the diversity of merchandise and the number of items that are routinely reordered compared to new items or one-time purchases.

Some retailers track inventory using a *manual tag system*, which can be updated daily, weekly or even monthly. In a manual tag system, you remove price tags from the product at the point of purchase. You then cross-check the tags against physical inventory to figure out what you have sold.

For example, a shoe-store retailer could use the tag system to produce a monthly chart showing sales according to product line, brand name and style. At the top of the chart, he would list the various product lines (pumps, sneakers, loafers), and down the left margin, the various brand names and different styles. At the intersecting spaces down the column, he would mark how many of each brand were sold, in what style and color, whether the shoes were on sale or discounted, and any other relevant information.

Dollar-control systems show the cost and gross profit margin on individual inventory items. A basic method of dollar control begins at the cash register, with sales receipts listing the product, quantity sold and price. You can compare sales receipts with delivery receipts to determine your gross profit margin on a given item. You can also use software programs to track inventory by type, cost, volume and profit. (For more on computerized inventory tracking, see the section on "Computerized Inventory Control," on page 291).

Unit-control systems use methods ranging from eyeballing shelves to using sophisticated bin tickets—tiny cards kept with each type of product that list a stock number, a description, maximum and minimum quantities stocked, cost (in code), selling price and any other information you want to include. Bin tickets correspond to office file cards that list a stock number, selling price, cost, number of items to a case, supply source and alternative source, order dates, quantities and delivery time.

Retailers make physical inventory checks daily, weekly or as often as is practical—once a year at the minimum. Sometimes an owner will assign each employee responsibility for keeping track of a group of items or, if the store is large enough, hire stock personnel to organize and count stock.

Computerized Inventory Control

While manual methods may have their place, most entrepreneurs these days find that computerizing gives them a far wider range of information with far less effort. Inventory software programs now on the market let you track usage, monitor changes in unit dollar costs, calculate when you need to reorder, and analyze inventory levels on an item-by-item basis. You can even expand your earlier ABC analysis to include the profit margin per item.

In fact, many experts say that current computer programs are changing the rules of the ABC analysis. By speeding up the process of inventory control, computers give you more time so you can devote as much attention to the B and C items as to the A's. You can even control inventory right at the cash register with point-of-sale (POS) software systems. POS software records each sale when it happens, so your inventory records are always up-to-date. Better still, you get much more information about the sale than you could gather with a manual system. By running reports based on this information, you can make better decisions about ordering and merchandising.

With a POS system:

■ **YOU CAN ANALYZE SALES DATA,** figure out how well all the items on

BRIGHT IDEA

APICS CAN PROVIDE EXPERT ADVICE ON INVENTORY MANAGEMENT AND SUGGEST SOFTWARE PROGRAMS TO USE; YOU CAN CONTACT THEM AT (800) 444-2742 OR WWW.APICS.ORG IN ADDITION, MANY COMPUTER AND SOFTWARE VENDORS SPONSOR FREE SEMINARS TO INTRODUCE NEW LINES OF INVENTORY CONTROL PRODUCTS TO PROSPECTIVE BUYERS.

your shelves sell, and adjust purchasing levels accordingly.

- **YOU CAN MAINTAIN A SALES HISTORY** to help adjust your buying decisions for seasonal purchasing trends.
- **YOU CAN IMPROVE PRICING ACCURACY** by integrating bar-code scanners and credit card authorization ability with the POS system.

There are plenty of popular POS software systems that enable you to use add-on devices at your checkout stations, including electronic cash drawers, bar-code scanners, credit card readers, and receipt or invoice printers. POS packages frequently come with integrated accounting modules, including general ledger, accounts receivable, accounts payable, purchasing and inventory control systems. In essence, a POS system is an all-in-one way to keep track of your business's cash flow.

Features to consider in a POS system include the following:

- **EASE OF USE:** Look for software with a user-friendly graphical interface.
- **ENTRY OF SALES INFORMATION:** Most systems allow you to enter inventory codes either manually or automatically via a bar-code scanner. Once the inventory code is entered, the systems call up the standard or sales price, compute the price at multiple quantities and provide a running total. Many systems make it easy to enter sales manually when needed by letting you search for inventory codes based on a partial merchandise number, description, manufacturing code or vendor.
- **PRICING:** POS systems generally offer a variety of ways to keep track of pricing, including add-on amounts, percentage of cost, margin percentage and custom formulas. For example, if you provide volume discounts, you can set up multiple prices for each item.
- **UPDATING PRODUCT INFORMATION:** Once a sale is entered, these systems automatically update inventory and accounts receivable records.
- **SALES TRACKING OPTIONS:** Different businesses get paid in different ways. For example, repair or service shops often keep invoices open until the work is completed, so they need a system that allows them to put sales on hold. If you sell expensive goods and allow installment purchases, you might appreciate a loan calculator that tabulates monthly payments. And if you offer rent-to-own items, you'll want a system that can handle rentals as well as sales.
- **SECURITY:** In retail, it's important to keep tight control over cash receipts to prevent theft. Most of these systems provide audit trails so you can trace any problems.
- **TAXES:** Many POS systems can support numerous tax rates—useful

if you run a mail order business and need to deal with taxes for more than one state.

Perhaps the most valuable way POS systems help you gain better control of your business is through their reporting features. You can slice and dice sales data in a variety of ways to determine what products are selling best at what time, and to figure out everything from the optimal ways to arrange shelves and displays to what promotions are working best and when to change seasonal promotions.

Reporting capabilities available in POS programs include sales,

Phone Phonies

Watch out! As an entrepreneur, you're a potential target for one of the most common—and potentially most costly—business scams: telemarketing con artists selling overpriced, poor-quality office supplies. Here are some tips to protect your business:

- **THE FTC** requires telemarketers to disclose that it's a sales call, who they are and the total cost of what they are selling—so don't be afraid to ask.
- **MAKE SURE YOUR EMPLOYEES ARE SCAM-AWARE,** and establish a procedure for handling such calls.
- **KEEP TRACK OF ALL ORDERS,** and limit the number of staff who are allowed to order.
- **IF YOU RECEIVE MERCHANDISE** you didn't order—and the seller cannot prove you did—you can keep the materials and are not obligated to pay.

costs, and profits by individual inventory items, by salesperson, or by category for the day, month and year to date. Special reports can include sales for each hour of the day for any time period. You can also create multiple formats for invoices, accounting statements and price tags. Additional reports include day-end cash reconciliation work sheets and inventory management. Examine a variety of POS packages to see which comes closest to meeting your needs.

Every business is unique; you may find that none of the off-the-shelf systems meets your requirements. Industry-specific POS packages are available—for auto repair shops, beauty and nail salons, video rental stores, dry cleaners and more. In addition, some POS system manufacturers will tailor their software to your needs.

Inventory Turnover

When you have replaced 100 percent of your original inventory, you have "turned over" your inventory. If you have, on the average, a 12-week supply of inventory and turn it over four times a year, the count cycle plus the order cycle plus the delivery cycle add up to your needs period. Expressed as an equation, it would read:

Count Cycle + Order Cycle + Delivery Cycle = Needs Period

For instance, suppose you decided to count inventory once every four weeks (the count cycle). Processing paperwork and placing orders with your vendors take two weeks (the order cycle). The order takes six weeks to get to you (delivery cycle). Therefore, you need 12 weeks' worth of inventory from the first day of the count cycle to stay in operation until your merchandise arrives.

You can improve your inventory turnover if you count inventory more often—every two weeks instead of every four—and work with your suppliers to improve delivery efficiency. Alternate ways of distributing goods to the store could cut the delivery cycle down to three weeks, which would cut inventory needs to six weeks. As a result, inventory turnover could increase from four times a year to eight times.

Another way to look at turnover is by measuring sales per square foot. Taking the average retail value of inventory and dividing it by the number of square feet devoted to a particular product will give you your average sales per square foot.

You should know how many sales per square foot per year you need to survive. Calculate your sales per square foot once a month to make sure they are in line with your expectations.

INVENTORY ACCOUNTING

If you spend a few minutes considering inventory, how you account for that inventory, and the taxes you must pay on it, you'll never again question the need for an accountant. However, it's important for every entrepreneur to have a basic understanding of inventory accounting, even if you rely on your accountant to do the actual numbers. There are two methods used for inventory valuation:

The *last in, first out* (LIFO) method assumes that you will sell the most recently purchased inventory first. For instance, suppose you bought 10 ceiling fans a year ago at $30 each. A week ago, you purchased a second lot of 10 ceiling fans, but now the price has gone up to $50 each. By using the LIFO method, you sell your customers the $50 ceiling fans first, which allows you to keep the less expensive units (in terms of your inventory cost) in inventory. Then, when you have to calculate inventory value for tax purposes, LIFO allows you to value your remaining inventory (the $30 fans) at substantially less than the $50 fans, so you pay less in taxes.

BRIGHT IDEA

A LETTER OF CREDIT FROM A MAJOR CUSTOMER CAN BE USED AS A FORM OF SECURITY IN ESTAB- LISHING RELATIONSHIPS WITH SUP- PLIERS. FOR INSTANCE, IF YOU'RE STARTING A BUSINESS MANUFAC- TURING GARDEN HOSES, YOU COULD GET A LETTER OF CREDIT FROM YOUR BIGGEST CUSTOMER WHEN THE ORDER IS PLACED, SHOWING THAT THE CUS- TOMER HAS CONTRACTED TO BUY THE FINISHED HOSES. THE MATERIAL TO MAKE THE HOSES IS THEN PURCHASED USING THE LETTER OF CREDIT AS SECURITY... AND YOU DON'T HAVE TO PUT UP A PENNY TO BUY THE MATERIAL.

First in, first out (FIFO) was the traditional method used by most businesses before inflation became common. Under FIFO, the goods you receive first are the goods you sell first. Under this method, you value inventory at its most recent price. FIFO is usually used during periods of relatively low inflation since high inflation and increasing replacement costs tend to skew inventory accounting figures.

LIFO establishes the value of your inventory based on the most recent quantity received, while FIFO establishes the value of your inventory based on the oldest item in it. You can use either dollar control or unit control with these methods. Match your system to your needs, based on your accountant's recommendations.

The One And Only

For decades, conventional wisdom warned that depending on a sole supplier could sink your business. After all, such a situation could spell doom if there were any interruption in your supply of products.

However, there are some situations where relying on a sole supplier makes sense. For example, if you're a specialty clothing retailer and most of your sales come from a certain product line, you may find yourself with a sole supplier. In some cases, there is only one supplier who can deliver the raw materials you need to make a product. In other cases, a company strikes an agreement with a sole supplier in return for special pricing deals.

The key to making a sole supplier relationship work is to make sure all the right safeguards are in place. Protect yourself by asking suppliers about backup product sources. Find out how many manufacturing plants and distribution centers exist in their product pipeline. Ask what contingency plans they have to supply you in case of emergency. What are their obligations to you in the event of a shortage? Will their top one or two customers get all the products they need, while your business has to wait in line?

Keep up-to-date on alternative supply sources that could help your business survive temporary shutdowns from your sole supplier. Use your trade association directory and industry networking contacts to help expand your supplier pipeline. Above all, make sure you feel comfortable entering into a sole supplier relationship before you sign on the dotted line.

Buying Inventory

Your inventory control system will tell you when to buy replacement inventory, what to buy (and what not to buy), and how much to buy.

The *open-to-buy* is the amount budgeted for inventory purchases for a given period, usually one, three or four months. Since you are a start-up without past performance to guide you, you must calculate the open-to-buy by determining the gross sales you need to pay store overhead and cover your other costs.

Your business plan should give you an idea of the basic stock levels and monthly or seasonal sales volume you need to have during start-up. After your business has been up and running for several months to a year, your inventory control system will provide this information.

Figure out your open-to-buy using the following formula:

planned inventory	$25,000
plus planned sales	+$25,000
equals	**$50,000**
less actual inventory	-$27,000
less stock on order	-$13,000
equals open-to-buy	**$10,000**

Most seasonal retailers calculate their open-to-buy seasonally to accommodate variations in the type of merchandise they sell and seasonal sales fluctuations. Instead of figuring open-to-buy in dollars, some retailers approach trade shows and other merchandise sources with a list of what they need to fill out their inventories and meet sales projections. But whether they work with dollars or by unit, experienced retailers recommend that the owner of a seasonal business should feel free to go beyond the budget or use less than the entire open-to-buy amount. In fact, you should leave room for unanticipated items.

SUPPLIERS

Suppliers are essential to any retail business. Depending on your inventory selection, you may need a few or dozens of suppliers. Sometimes suppliers will contact you through their sales representatives, but more often, particularly when you are starting out, you will need to locate them yourself—either at trade shows, wholesale showrooms and conventions, or through buyers directories, industry contacts, the Business-to-Business Yellow Pages and trade journals.

Suppliers can be divided into four general categories.

1. **MANUFACTURERS:** Most retailers will buy through independent representatives or company salespeople who handle the wares of different companies. Prices from these sources are usually lowest, unless the retailer's location makes shipping freight expensive.

2. **DISTRIBUTORS:** Also known as wholesalers, brokers or jobbers, distributors buy in quantity from several manufacturers and warehouse the goods for sale to retailers. Although their prices are higher than a manufacturer's, they can supply retailers with small orders from a

variety of manufacturers. (Some manufacturers refuse to fill small orders.) A lower freight bill and quick delivery time from a nearby distributor often compensate for the higher per-item cost.

3. **INDEPENDENT CRAFTSPEOPLE:** Exclusive distribution of unique creations is frequently offered by independent craftspeople, who sell through reps or at trade shows.

4. **IMPORT SOURCES:** Many retailers buy foreign goods from a domestic importer, who operates much like a domestic wholesaler. Or, depending on your familiarity with overseas sources, you may want to travel abroad to buy goods.

HOT LINK

TRADE SHOWS ARE A GREAT PLACE TO SHOW OFF YOUR PRODUCTS TO THE PUBLIC AS WELL AS POTENTIAL SUPPLIERS. AT THE SAME TIME, YOU CAN CHECK OUT THE COMPETITION. THEY'RE ALSO A GREAT RESOURCE FOR NETWORKING. TO FIND A TRADE SHOW IN YOUR AREA, VISIT THE ULTIMATE TRADE SHOW RESOURCE (WWW.TSNN.COM), AN ONLINE DIRECTORY OF MORE THAN 15,000 TRADE SHOWS AND CONFERENCES.

Dealing With Suppliers

Reliability is the key factor to look for in suppliers. Good suppliers will steer you toward hot-selling items, increasing your sales. If you build a good relationship and your business is profitable for them, suppliers may be willing to bail you out when your customers make difficult demands. Remember, though, that suppliers are in business to make money. If you go to the mat with them on every bill, ask them to shave prices on everything they sell to you, or fail to pay your bills promptly, don't be surprised when they stop calling.

As a new business owner, you can't expect to receive the same kind of attention a long-standing customer gets right off the bat. Over time, however, you can develop excellent working relationships that will be profitable for both you and your suppliers. Once you have compiled a list of possible suppliers, ask for quotes or proposals, complete with prices, available discounts, delivery terms and other important factors. Do not just consider the terms; investigate the potential of your supplier's financial condition, too. And ask them for customer references; call these customers and find out how well the supplier has performed. If there have been any problems, ask for details about how they were reconciled. Every relationship hits bumps now and then; the key is to know how the rough spots were handled. Was the supplier prompt and helpful in resolving the problem, or defensive and uncooperative?

Be open, courteous and firm with your suppliers, and they will respond in kind. Tell them what you need and when you need it. Have a specific understanding about the total cost, and expect delivery on schedule. Keep in constant communication with your suppliers about possible delays, potential substitutions for materials or product lines, production quality, product improvements or new product introductions and potential savings.

Suppliers often establish a minimum order for merchandise, and this minimum may be higher for first orders to cover the cost of setting up a new store account. Some suppliers also demand a minimum number of items per order.

Payment Plans

While most service providers bill you automatically without requiring credit references, equipment and merchandise suppliers are more cautious. Since you are just getting started, you will not be able to give them trade references, and your bank probably will not give you a credit rating if your account has just opened.

If your supplier is small, the manner in which you present yourself is important in establishing credit. You may find the going tougher when dealing with a large supplier. A personal visit will accelerate your acceptance.

Present your financial statements and a description of your prospects for success in your new business. Don't even think of inflating your financial statements to cover a lack of references. This is a felony and is easily detected by most credit managers.

Some suppliers will put you on a c.o.d. basis for a few months, knowing that if you are underfinanced, you will soon have problems with this payment method. Once you pass that test, they will issue you a line of credit. This creates a valid credit reference you can present to new suppliers until credit agencies accumulate enough data on your business

SMART TIP

WHILE IT IS ALMOST IMPOSSIBLE TO GET EXCLUSIVE RIGHTS TO A MANUFACTURER'S GOODS, YOU CAN ASK THAT A SALES REPRESENTATIVE NOT SELL IDENTICAL MERCHANDISE TO ANOTHER STORE IN THE IMMEDIATE AREA. HOWEVER, YOU MAY BE EXPECTED TO BUY LARGE AMOUNTS OF THE PRODUCT TO MAKE UP FOR LOST SALES TO OTHER STORES.

to approve you for suppliers. Most suppliers operate on a trade credit basis when dealing with other businesses. This basically means that when you're billed for a product or service, you have a certain grace period before the payment is due (typically 30 days). During this time, the supplier will not charge interest.

Carefully consider all costs, discounts and allowances before deciding whether to buy an item. Always take into account what the final shelf cost of any item will be. The most common discounts are given for prompt payment; many suppliers also give discounts for payment in cash. When you can, make sure you specify on all orders how the goods are to be shipped so they will be sent in the least expensive way.

Occasionally, suppliers grant customers discounts for buying in quantity, usually as a freight allowance for a specific amount of merchandise purchased. Some suppliers pay an increasing percentage of the freight bill as the retailer's orders increase; others simply cover the entire freight cost for purchases over a minimum amount.

If you order merchandise from distant suppliers, freight charges can equal as much as 10 percent of your merchandise cost. Ask what a manufacturer's or supplier's freight policy is before ordering, and make sure the order is large enough to warrant the delivery charges. If the manufacturer does not pay freight on back orders, you might consider canceling a back order and adding it to the next regular shipment.

Become familiar with each of your suppliers' order-filling priorities. Some suppliers fill orders on a first-in, first-out basis; others give priority to the larger orders while customers with smaller orders wait.

Consequently, most retailers specify a cancellation date on their orders. In other words, any goods shipped after that date will be returned to the suppliers. By specifying a cutoff date, you increase the chances that your orders will be shipped promptly and arrive in time.

Give careful attention to shipments when they arrive. Check to make sure you've received the correct amount and type of merchandise, and make sure the quality matches the samples you were shown.

HOT LINK

BEFORE YOU GO TO A TRADE SHOW IN SEARCH OF INVENTORY SUPPLIERS, DO YOUR HOMEWORK. THE TRADE SHOW LEARNING CENTER (WWW.FASTSIGNS.COM/LEARNING CENTERS/LEARNINGCENTERS.HTML—CLICK ON "TRADE SHOW LEARNING CENTER") PROVIDES A WEALTH OF INFORMATION, BUDGETS AND PLANNING WORK SHEETS TO HELP YOU PREPARE.

GLOSSARY

80-20 RULE: principle of inventory control that says 80 percent of a business's sales typically come from 20 percent of its inventory; as a result, most attention should be focused on that 20 percent that generates the most profit

ABC METHOD: method of inventory control that divides items into A, B and C groups based on their importance to the business; most attention is then devoted to the A, or essential, items

COUNT CYCLE: the period at which you count your inventory; a four-week count cycle means you count inventory every four weeks

DELIVERY CYCLE: the time it takes for inventory to be delivered; a 10-week delivery cycle means inventory takes 10 weeks to arrive

DOLLAR-CONTROL SYSTEM: system of inventory tracking where sales receipts are compared with delivery receipts to determine the cost and gross profit margin on individual inventory items

FIRST IN, FIRST OUT (FIFO): method of inventory accounting that assumes items purchased first are sold first; typically used during times of low inflation

LAST IN, FIRST OUT (LIFO): method of inventory accounting that assumes most recently purchased items are sold first; allows business owner to value inventory at the less expensive cost of the older inventory; typically used during times of high inflation

LETTER OF CREDIT: a letter from a major customer showing that the customer has contracted to buy from you; can be used as a form of security in establishing relationships with suppliers

MANUAL TAG SYSTEM: system of inventory tracking in which tags are removed from products at the time of the sale and then cross-checked against physical inventory later to figure out what was sold

NEEDS PERIOD: the sum of the count cycle, delivery cycle and order cycle

OPEN-TO-BUY: the amount budgeted for inventory purchases for a given period, usually one, three or four months

ORDER CYCLE: the time it takes to process paperwork and place orders with your vendors for inventory

POINT-OF-SALE (POS) SOFTWARE: software that records information about inventory, sales and profits at the point of sale

TRADE CREDIT: practice of billing a business for products or services with a grace period (typically 30 days) before payment is due

TURNOVER: turning over your inventory means that 100 percent of original inventory has been sold

UNIT-CONTROL SYSTEM: system of inventory tracking in which bin tickets are kept with each product type, listing stock number, description, maximum and minimum quantities stocked, cost (in code) and selling price; these tickets correspond to office file cards that list a stock number, selling price, cost, number of items to a case, supply source, order dates, quantities and delivery time

To Your
Credit

Offering your customers credit

Getting paid for your products or services is what business is all about. These days, there are more options than ever for accepting payment. Whether you are in a B2B or consumer-oriented industry, your choices can include extending credit, taking checks, and accepting credit or debit cards.

With so many options, it's easy for a new business owner to get caught up in the excitement of making sales and to forget the necessity for a well-thought-out credit policy. Deciding what forms of payment you will accept, how you will handle them and what collection methods you'll use to ensure debts are paid is essential to any small business' success.

ESTABLISHING A CREDIT POLICY

Credit can make or break a small business. A too-lenient credit policy can set the stage for collection and cash-flow problems later, while a creatively and carefully designed policy can attract customers and boost your business's cash flow.

Many small businesses are reluctant to establish a firm credit policy for fear of losing their customers. What they do not realize is that a consistent credit policy not only strengthens your company, but also creates a more professional image in your customers' eyes.

A well-thought-out credit policy accomplishes four things:

1. **AVOIDS BOTH** bad debts and hard feelings
2. **STANDARDIZES CREDIT PROCEDURES,** providing employees with clear and consistent directions
3. **DEMONSTRATES TO EMPLOYEES** and customers that the company is serious about managing credit
4. **HELPS THE BUSINESS OWNER** define how credit fits into the overall sales and marketing plan

To establish a smart credit policy, start by investigating the way your competition handles credit. Your goal is to make it easy to buy your products. If your competition offers better terms, they have an advantage. You must meet your competitors' credit terms to attract customers.

At the same time, be cautious not to go too far with your credit policy. Novice entrepreneurs are often tempted to offer lower prices

and longer payment terms to take business away from competitors. Credit is a double-edged sword. You want to attract customers with your credit policy, but you do not want to attract customers who are not creditworthy. Be aware that some troubled companies routinely switch from supplier to supplier whenever they reach their credit limit with one. Others are outright con artists that take advantage of new and naive entrepreneurs.

How to protect yourself? One good way to start is to write a short, simple statement that sums up the intent and spirit of your company's credit policy. For example, a liberal policy might read: "Our credit policy is to make every reasonable effort to extend credit to all customers recommended by sales management, provided a suitable credit basis can be developed."

A conservative policy might say: "Our company has a strict credit policy, and credit lines will be extended only to the most creditworthy accounts. New customers who fail to meet our credit criteria will need to purchase using cash-on-delivery terms until they establish their ability and willingness to pay on our terms."

Base your policy selection—conservative or liberal—on your industry, the size and experience of your staff, the dollar amount of your transactions, your profit margins and your appetite for risk. Also consider the industry to which you're selling. If your customers are in "soft" industries such as construction or computers, for example, you would do well to use a conservative policy.

If you do adopt a liberal credit policy for your business, make sure you are prepared to handle the collection calls. Liberal policies will require you to be aggressive when customers do not pay on time.

Give 'Em Credit

The simplest customer credit policy has two basic points: 1) limiting credit risk and 2) diligently investigating each company's creditworthiness.

No matter how credit-worthy a customer is, never extend credit beyond your profit margin. This policy ensures that if you aren't paid, at least your expenses will be paid. For example, if you mark up your product or service 100 percent of costs, you can then safely risk that amount without jeopardizing your company's cash flow. To gauge a company's credit-worthiness, draft a comprehensive credit application that contains the following:

- Name of business, address, phone and fax number
- Names, addresses, Social Security numbers of principals
- Type of business (corporation, partnership, sole proprietorship)
- Industry
- Number of employees
- Bank references
- Trade payment references
- Business/personal bankruptcy history
- Any other names under which the company does business
- A personal guarantee that the business owners promise to pay you if their corporation is unable to

Your credit application should also specify what your credit terms are and the consequences of failing to meet them. Indicate what late fees you'll charge, if any; that the customer is responsible for any attorney fees or collection costs incurred at any time, either during or prior to a lawsuit; and the venue where such a suit would be filed. Have your credit application form reviewed by an attorney specializing in creditors' rights to make sure it is in line with your state's regulations.

Once a potential customer has completed the application, how do you investigate the information? One way to verify the facts and assess the company's credit history is to call credit-reporting agencies. Some companies' payment history will also be available through D&B. Because credit agencies' reporting can be unreliable, however, it's also a good idea to call others in the industry and try to determine that company's payment record and reputation. Most industries have associations that trade credit information.

Also ask customers how much

SMART TIP

WHEN DEALING WITH A NEW CLIENT, IT'S A GOOD IDEA TO PROTECT YOURSELF BY ASKING FOR PART OF YOUR PAYMENT UP FRONT. THIS IS AN ESPECIALLY GOOD POLICY IF THE CLIENT IS A NEW OR FLEDGLING BUSINESS. NO MATTER HOW CREDIT-WORTHY A CUSTOMER IS, NEVER EXTEND CREDIT BEYOND YOUR PROFIT MARGIN.

credit they think they will need. This will help you estimate the volume of credit and the potential risk to your business. Finally, as one entrepreneur says, "Use your intuition. If someone doesn't look you straight in the eye, chances are they won't let you see what's in their wallet, either."

Payment Due

Once you've set your credit policy, it's important to stick to it and do your part to ensure prompt payment. The cornerstone of collecting accounts receivable on time is making sure invoices go out promptly and accurately. If you sell a product, get the invoice out to the customer at the same time the shipment goes out. If you're in a service industry, track your billable hours daily or weekly, and bill as often as your contract or agreement with the client permits. The sooner the invoice is in the mail, the sooner you get paid.

To eliminate any possibility of confusion, your invoice should contain several key pieces of information. First, make sure you date it accurately and clearly state when payment is due, as well as any penalties for late payment. Also specify any discounts, such as discounts for payment in 15 days or for payment in cash.

Each invoice should give a clear and accurate description of the

Collect Call

Having trouble collecting on a bill? Your Better Business Bureau (BBB) may be able to help. Many BBBs now assist with B2B disputes regarding payment as part of their dispute resolution service. BBBs do not operate as collection agencies, and there is no charge beyond standard membership dues.

When the BBB gets involved, there can be three possible outcomes. First, the account may be paid; second, the BBB can serve as a forum for arbitration; third, if the company refuses to pay or arbitrate, the complaint is logged in the BBB's files for three years.

Most businesses find a call from the BBB a powerful motivator to pay up. If the debtor belongs to the BBB and refuses to pay, its membership could be revoked.

To find out if the BBB in your area offers this service, call the membership services department.

Sample Collection Reminders

Remember to keep reminders friendly but firm.

REMINDER!

Invoice #: _____

You are past due on your payment.

Amount now due: $ _____

Date: _____

Thank you for your prompt attention.

SECOND REMINDER!

Invoice #: _____

In reviewing your account, we have determined
that the above invoice has not been paid
and is now seriously past due.

Amount now due: $ _____

Date: _____

Thank you for your prompt attention.

FINAL REMINDER!

Invoice #: _____

We have not yet received payment for
the above mentioned invoice. Unless payment
is received within 10 days, we will be forced to
initiate legal collection proceedings. If you have
made payment, please contact us immediately.

Amount now due: $ _____

Date: _____

goods or services the customer received. Inventory code numbers may make sense to your computer system, but they don't mean much to the customer unless they are accompanied by an item description.

It's also important to use sequentially numbered invoices. This helps make things easier when you need to discuss a particular invoice with a customer and also makes it easier for your employees to keep track of invoices.

Before sending out an invoice, call the customer to ensure the price is correct, and check to make sure prices on invoices match those on purchase orders and/or contracts.

Know the industry norms when setting your payment schedules. While 30 days is the norm in most industries, in others, 45- or 60-day payment cycles are typical. Learn your customers' payment practices, too. If they pay only once a month, for instance, make sure your invoice gets to them in plenty of time to hit that payment cycle. Also keep on top of industry trends and economic ups and downs that could affect customers' ability to pay.

Promptness is key not only in sending out invoices, but also in following up. If payment is due in 30 days, don't wait until the 60th day to call the customer. By the same token, however, don't be overeager and call on the 31st day. Being too demanding can annoy customers, possibly losing you a valuable client. Knowledge of industry norms plus your customers' payment cycles will guide you in striking a middle ground.

Constant communication trains customers to pay bills promptly and leads to an efficient, professional relationship between you and them. Usually, a polite telephone call to ask about a late payment will get the ball rolling, or at least tell you when you can expect payment. If any problems exist that need to be resolved before payment can be issued, your phone call will let you know what they are so you can start clearing them up. It could be something as simple as a missing packing slip or as major as a damaged shipment.

The first 15 to 20 seconds of the call are crucial. Make sure to project good body language over the phone. Be professional and firm, not wimpy. Use a pleasant

SMART TIP

TRY THIS PROACTIVE APPROACH TO PROMPT A CUSTOMER TO PAY FASTER: ABOUT 10 DAYS BEFORE PAYMENT IS DUE, CALL TO ASK IF THE CUSTOMER RECEIVED THE BILL. MAKE SURE THEY ARE SATISFIED WITH THE PRODUCT; THEN POLITELY ASK "DO YOU ANTICIPATE ANY PROBLEMS PAYING YOUR BILL ON TIME?"

voice that conveys authority, and respect the other person's dignity. Remember the old saying: You catch more flies with honey than with vinegar.

What if payment still is not made after an initial phone call? Don't let things slide. Statistics show that the longer a debt goes unpaid, the more difficult it will be to collect and the greater chance that it will remain unpaid forever. Most experts recommend making additional phone calls rather than sending a series of past-due notices or collection letters. Letters are easier to ignore, while phone calls tend to get better results.

If several phone calls fail to generate any response, a personal visit may be in order. Try to set up an appointment in advance. If this isn't possible, leave a message stating what date and time you will visit. Make sure to bring all the proper documentation with you so you can prove exactly what is owed. At this point, you are unlikely to get full payment, so see if you can get the customer to commit to a payment plan. Make sure, however, that you put it in writing.

If the customer refuses to meet with you to discuss the issue or won't commit to a payment plan, you may be facing a bad debt situation and need to take further action. There are two options: using the services of an attorney or employing a collection agency. Your lawyer can advise you on what is best to do.

If you decide to go with a collection agency, ask friends or business owners for referrals, or look in the Yellow Pages to find collectors who handle your type of claim. To make sure the agencies are reputable, contact the Better Business Bureau or the Securities Division of your secretary of state's office. Since all collection companies must be bonded with the state, this office should have them on file.

For more information on collection agencies, you can also contact the Association of Credit and Collection Professionals (www.collector.com). Most reputable collection firms are members of this international organization.

Many collection agencies take their fee as a cut of the collected money, so there is no upfront cost to you. Shop around to find an agency with a reasonable rate. Also compare the cost of using a collection agency to the cost of using your lawyer. You may be able to recover more of the money using one option or the other, depending on the total amount of the debt and the hourly rate or percentage the lawyer or agency charges.

ACCEPTING CHECKS

Bounced checks can cut heavily into a small business's profits. Yet a business that doesn't accept personal checks can't expect to stay competitive. How can you keep bad checks out of your cash register? Here are some steps to establishing a check-acceptance policy that works.

Start with the basics. Since laws regarding the information needed to cash checks vary greatly among states (and even within states), begin by contacting your local police department. They can familiarize you with the laws and regulations that govern checks in your state. Some police departments have seminars instructing businesses on how to set up proper check-cashing policies.

While rules vary among states, there are some good general rules of thumb to follow. When accepting a check, always ask to see the customer's driver's license or similar identification card, preferably one that has a photograph. Check the customer's physical characteristics against his identification. If you have reason to question his identity, ask the customer to write his signature on a separate piece of paper. Many people who pass bad checks have numerous false identifications and may forget which one they are using. Ask for the customer's home and work telephone numbers so you can contact him in case the check bounces. Don't cash payroll checks, checks for more than the amount of purchase or third-party checks.

Be observant. Desktop-publishing software, laser printers and scanners have made it easier for people to alter, forge or duplicate checks. To avoid accepting a forged or counterfeit check, evaluate the document very carefully. Smudge marks on the check could indicate the check was rubbed with moist fingers when it was illegally made. Smooth edges on checks are another sign of a possibly counterfeit document; authentic checks are perforated either on the top or left side of the check.

SMART TIP

FOR MORE INFORMATION ON PREVENTING BAD CHECKS, CONSULT THIS HELPFUL RESOURCE: *CHECK FRAUD PREVENTION MANUAL* PROVIDES INFORMATION ON HOW TO DETECT FRAUDULENT CHECKS, HOW TO ADOPT PROCEDURES TO REDUCE YOUR BUSINESS'S EXPOSURE TO BAD CHECKS AND WHERE TO TURN FOR HELP. IT IS FREE TO ABA MEMBERS. CONTACT THE AMERICAN BANKERS ASSOCIATION, 1120 CONNECTICUT AVE. NW, WASHINGTON, DC 20036, OR ORDER THROUGH THE ASSOCIATION'S CUSTOMER SERVICE DEPARTMENT AT (800) 338-0626.

Smudged handwriting or signs that the handwriting has been erased are other warning signs that you might be dealing with an illegal check.

Be especially cautious with new checks. A large majority of bad checks are written on new accounts. Many businesses will not accept checks that don't have a customer's name preprinted on them. If the check is written on a brand-new account (one with check number, say, below 300), protect yourself by asking to see two forms of ID.

Establish a waiting period for refunds. Merchants can easily be stiffed when a customer makes a purchase by check and returns the merchandise the next day for a cash refund. When the check bounces, the merchant is out the cash paid for the refund. To avoid this scenario, many entrepreneurs require a five- to seven-business-day grace period to allow checks to clear the bank before cash refunds are paid.

Consider getting electronic help. If you process a large volume of checks, you might benefit from the services of a check-verification company. By paying a monthly fee, ranging from $25 to $100 (depending on your company's size and volume of checks), you can tap into a company's database of individuals who write bad, stolen or forged checks. This is done by passing a customer's check through an electronic "check reader" at your checkout stand. If the check matches a name in the company's database, the check is refused.

> **BRIGHT IDEA**
> REQUIRE EMPLOYEES TO SIGN THEIR INITIALS ON CHECKS THEY ACCEPT. NO ONE WANTS TO HAVE THEIR INITIALS ON A CHECK THAT MIGHT BOUNCE, SO EMPLOYEES WILL BE EXTRA CAREFUL ABOUT FOLLOWING YOUR CHECK ACCEPTANCE POLICY.

Using a "check reader" from companies like TeleCheck, a check-verification and check guarantee company, is quick and efficient. They can approve a check within seconds, which is generally as fast as, or faster than, a merchant getting acceptance for a credit card purchase.

Check-verification companies also offer a check-guarantee service. If a check is approved by a check-verification company, and it later turns out to be a bad check, the merchant gets reimbursed for the value of the check. This guarantee service reduces the risk of accepting bad checks. Getting a handle on the bad checks that might pass through your business certainly has its benefits. For small merchants, one bad check can wipe out an entire day's profits.

Whatever check-acceptance policy you develop, make sure your employees clearly understand the procedure to follow. Also be sure to post your check-acceptance policy prominently where customers can see it. Specify any charges for bounced checks, what forms of ID are required, and what types of checks you will and will not accept. Posting signs helps prevent disgruntlement when customers wait in line, only to find at the register that you can't accept their check. What if you do receive a bad check? In most cases, after a check bounces, the bank allows you another attempt to deposit it. After that, the responsibility for collecting the money falls on you.

Contact the customer, either by phone or mail. (Again, consult your local police on the proper procedure; some states require that a registered letter be sent and a specific amount of time elapse before other action can be taken.) Keep your cool; there's nothing gained by being angry or hostile about the situation. Most people bounce checks by accident. Explain the situation, and request immediate payment plus reimbursement for any bank charges you have incurred.

If the person still refuses to pay, or you cannot get ahold of them, you have several options. The first, and probably the easiest, is to hold the check for a short time (up to six months) from the date it was written. Although banks will not allow the check to be deposited a third time, they will cash the check if there are sufficient funds. Call the debtor's bank periodically to see if the funds are there. When they are, cash the check immediately.

Another option is going to the police. Since, through your check-acceptance procedure, you collected all the information needed to prosecute, you should be able to complete the proper paperwork. However, the hassle of hiring a lawyer, identifying suspects and going to court may be more effort than you want to expend for a $200 check. In that case, your best bet is to use a collection agency. (For more details on this, see the "Payment Due" section on page 307).

ACCEPTING CREDIT CARDS

Why should a small-business owner accept credit cards? There are dozens of reasons. First and foremost, research shows that credit cards increase the probability, speed and size of customer purchases. Many people prefer not to carry cash, especially when traveling. Others prefer to pay with credit cards because they know that it will be easier to return or exchange the merchandise.

Accepting credit cards has several advantages for business owners as well. It gives you the chance to increase sales by enabling customers to make impulse buys even when they do not have enough cash in their wallets or sufficient funds in their checking accounts. Accepting credit cards can improve your cash flow, because in most cases you receive the money within a few days instead of waiting for a check to clear or an invoice to come due. Finally, credit cards provide a guarantee that you will be paid, without the risks involved in accepting personal checks.

Merchant Status

To accept major credit cards from customers, your business must establish merchant status with each of the credit card companies

A Private Affair

MasterCard, Visa and American Express all have their place. But there's another option you may not have considered: issuing a private-label credit card with your company's name on it.

In addition to all the usual advantages of credit cards, a private-label credit card program allows businesses to focus on who their customers are. For example, your program can gather data about customer purchases, buying patterns, income and demographics.

Small businesses can save money and eliminate hassles by using an outside administrator that specializes in private-label credit cards. A number of banks have entered this arena; ask your banker if he or she administers such programs. If not, the banker may be able to recommend a private-label credit card administration company.

Administration companies can do everything from setting up the operation to developing specialized marketing programs, designing the credit cards, training employees and developing lists of potential customers. Fees vary depending on the number of services provided and the size of your customer base.

Before choosing an administration company, talk to other business owners who use private-label credit card programs to see if they're happy with the service and if the administration company does a good job handling customer applications, payments and the like. Weigh the cost of any program against the benefits you expect to get from it.

whose cards you want to accept. You'll probably want to start by applying for merchant status with American Express or Discover. For these cards, all you need to do is contact American Express or Discover directly and fill out an application.

However, chances are you'll want to accept Visa and MasterCard, too, since these are used more frequently. You cannot apply directly to Visa or MasterCard; because they are simply bank associations, you have to establish a merchant account through one of several thousand banks that set up such accounts, called "acquiring banks."

The first thing you need to understand about accepting credit cards, explains Debra Rossi of Wells Fargo Bank, is that the bank views this as an extension of credit. "When we give you the ability to accept credit cards, we're giving you the use of the funds before we get them. By the time the money arrives in the cardholder's account, it could be another 30 days," Rossi says. There's also the real concern that if your company goes out of business before merchandise is shipped to customers, the bank will have to absorb losses.

While the requirements vary among banks, in general a business does not have to be a minimum size in terms of sales. However, some banks do have minimum requirements for how long you should have been in business. This doesn't mean a start-up can't get merchant status; it simply means you may have to look a little harder to find a bank that will work with you.

While being considered a "risky business"—typically a start-up, mail order or homebased business—is one reason a bank may deny your merchant status request, the most common reason for denial is simply poor credit. Approaching a bank for a merchant account is like applying for a loan. You must be prepared with a solid presentation that will persuade the bank to open an account for you.

You will need to provide bank and trade references, estimate what kind of credit card volume you expect to have and what you think the average transaction size will be. Bring your business plan

BEWARE!

TO PROTECT AGAINST CREDIT CARD FRAUD, FOLLOW THESE STEPS EVERY TIME A CREDIT PURCHASE IS MADE:

- CHECK THE SIGNATURE ON THE CHARGE SLIP AGAINST THE ONE ON THE BACK OF THE CARD. THIS MAY SEEM BASIC, BUT YOU'D BE SURPRISED AT HOW OFTEN IT IS NEGLECTED.
- VERIFY THE CARD'S EXPIRATION DATE.
- CHECK THE FREQUENTLY UPDATED BULLETIN LISTING CANCELED CARD NUMBERS.

and financial statements, along with copies of advertisements, marketing pieces and your catalog if you have one. If possible, invite your banker to visit your store or operation. Banks will evaluate your product or service to see if there might be potential for a lot of returns or customer disputes. Called "charge-backs," these refunds are very expensive for banks to process. They are more common among mail order companies and are one reason why these businesses typically have a hard time securing merchant status.

In your initial presentation, provide a reasonable estimate of how many charge-backs you will receive, then show your bank why you do not expect them to exceed your estimates. Testimonials from satisfied customers or product samples can help convince the bank your customers will be satisfied with their purchases. Another way to reduce the bank's fear is to demonstrate that your product is priced at a fair market value.

Mail Order Madness

It's ironic: While mail order businesses perhaps more than any other venture rely on credit cards as a means of payment, mail order companies also typically find it more difficult to get merchant status. Why? The credit card industry has been burned by mail order "con artists." Even in legitimate mail order businesses, the percentage of charge-backs is much higher than in other types of businesses.

If you have a phone-intensive or mail order business and are having difficulty securing merchant status, try one of these tactics:

- **SET A LIMIT ON THE VOLUME** of transactions you will process each month until the account is established.
- **OFFER TO PAY A HIGHER DISCOUNT FEE** for the first six months as a "loss reserve."
- **OFFER TO LET THE BANK** hold on to your share of deposits for a few extra days to give it time to screen any unusual transactions.
- **CONSIDER PUTTING UP A CASH DEPOSIT** to protect the bank against large numbers of charge-backs.

If you make special arrangements like these, be sure to get a written agreement specifying how long they will be in effect.

BEWARE!

DON'T ASK ANOTHER MERCHANT TO DEPOSIT YOUR SALES SLIPS FOR YOU, AND NEVER LET ANOTHER BUSINESS DEPOSIT SLIPS THROUGH YOUR ACCOUNT. THIS PRACTICE IS CALLED "LAUNDER-ING" SALES SLIPS, AND NOT ONLY IS IT PROHIBITED BY VISA AND MASTERCARD, BUT IT IS ALSO ILLEGAL IN SOME STATES. HONEST BUSINESS OWNERS HAVE BEEN WIPED OUT BY SCAM ARTISTS WHO ASK THEM TO DEPOSIT THEIR SALES SLIPS, THEN RACK UP THOUSANDS OF DOL-LARS IN PHONY SALES, WHICH LATER TURN INTO CHARGE-BACKS.

Rossi at Wells Fargo says the bank's goal is to find out if your business is profitable and if it will be around for a long time to come. "We approve a lot of start-up businesses, and in those cases, we rely on the personal financial picture of the business principals," she says. "We look at [their personal] tax returns and at where they got the money to start the business. We also look to see if you're a customer at Wells Fargo and at your relationship with Wells."

As Rossi's comment suggests, the best place to begin when try-ing to get merchant status is by approaching the bank that already holds your business accounts. If your bank turns you down, ask around for recommendations from other business owners who accept plastic. You could look in the Yellow Pages for other businesses in the same category as yours (homebased, retail, mail order). Call them to ask where they have their merchant accounts and whether they are satisfied with the way their accounts are handled. When approaching a bank with which you have no relationship, you may be able to sweeten the deal by offering to switch your other accounts to that bank as well.

If banks turn you down for merchant status, another option is to consider independent credit card processing companies, which can be found in the Yellow Pages. While independents often give the best rates because they have lower overhead, their application process tends to be more time-consuming, and start-up fees are sometimes higher.

You can also go through an independent sales organization (ISO). These are field representatives from out-of-town banks who, for a commission, help businesses find banks willing to grant them mer-chant status. Your bank may be able to recommend an ISO, or you can look in the Yellow Pages under "Credit Cards." An ISO can match your needs with those of the banks he or she represents, without requiring you to go through the application process with all of them.

Money Matters

Enticing your bank with promising sales figures can also boost your case since the bank makes money when you do. Every time you accept a credit card for payment, the bank or card company deducts a percentage of the sale—called a "merchant discount fee"—and then credits your account with the rest of the sale amount.

Here are some other fees you can expect to pay. All of them are negotiable except for the discount fee:

- **START-UP FEES** of around $100
- **EQUIPMENT COSTS** of $250 to $1,000, depending on whether you lease or buy a handheld terminal or go electronic
- **MONTHLY STATEMENT FEES** of $4 to $20
- **TRANSACTION FEES** of 5 to 50 cents per purchase
- **THE DISCOUNT RATE**—the actual percentage you are charged per transaction based on projected card sales volume, the degree of risk and a few other factors (the percentage ranges from 1.5 to 3 percent; the higher your sales, the lower your rate)
- **CHARGE-BACK FEES** of up to $15 per return transaction
- **MISCELLANEOUS FEES,** including a per-transaction communication cost of 5 to 12 cents for connection to the processor, a postage fee for sending statements, and a supply fee for charge slips

There may also be some charges from the telephone company to set up a phone line for the authorization and processing equipment. Before you sign on with any bank, consider the costs carefully to make sure the anticipated sales are worth the costs.

Getting Equipped

Once your business has been approved for credit, you will receive a start-up kit and personal instructions in how to use the system. You don't need fancy equipment to process credit card sales. You can start with a phone and a simple imprinter that costs under $30. However, you'll get a better discount rate (and get your money credited to your account faster) if you process credit card sales electronically.

Although it's a little more expensive initially, purchasing or leasing a terminal that allows you to swipe the customer's card through for an instant authorization of the sale (and immediate crediting of your merchant account) can save you money in the long run. Cash registers can also be adapted to process credit cards. Also, using your personal computer as opposed to a terminal to get authorization can cut costs per transaction even more.

Once you obtain merchant account status, make the most of it. The credit card and bank industries hold seminars and users' conferences covering innovations in the industry, fraud detection techniques and other helpful subjects. You can ask a credit card company's representatives for details... and keep on top of ways to get more from your customers' credit cards.

ACCEPTING DEBIT CARDS

In addition to credit cards and checks, there's a new form of payment that more and more small businesses are accepting these days: ATM or debit cards. Consumers like the cards because they eliminate the hassle of writing checks, offset the need to carry wads of cash and ensure security, thanks to a customer-activated secret personal identification number (PIN).

Many merchants, too, prefer accepting debit cards over credit cards or checks. Debit cards can even be better than cash. Debit is less expensive than a credit card or check and is not vulnerable to employee theft like cash is. Debit is also a guaranteed transaction: Money is immediately debited from the customer's account and deposited into yours—giving you instant access to funds. Finally, debit gives you access to consumers who don't have credit cards.

Getting Online

Installing a debit system in your business can be as easy as walking into your bank, filling out an application requesting debit acceptance capabilities, and clearing some counter space next to your cash register for a debit terminal and printer (some banks can interface directly with your cash register).

You can purchase equipment for as little as $200 to $500, or check out monthly leasing options. You may find that you already have most of the necessary equipment. Some merchants' existing credit terminals can simply be reprogrammed to accept debit cards as well. If your terminals don't already have printers, however, you'll need to install them, since federal regulations require merchants to provide receipts for debit card transactions.

Electronic devices that accept both credit and debit cards are available on the market. Some are even integrated with the cash register. Because the debit PIN-pad terminal needs to be within easy reach of the customer and clerk, however, smaller businesses may opt for a stand-alone POS debit system. When you buy the service from a bank or other payment service provider, look for a system that accepts both credit and debit cards. A joint system takes up less counter space and is usually less confusing for clerks and customers to handle.

Another consideration is where your POS takes place. Restaurant merchants, for example, may choose to collect the bill from patrons while they are still seated at their tables. In this case, you'll need the capability to take the PIN pad to each table for customers to key in their PIN. Such technology is available through most major financial institutions that provide debit equipment.

Beware, however, that not all banks are experienced in debit card services. Although sticking with your current financial institution when setting up a debit card system may have its advantages, make sure your bank understands debit before signing on with them.

Once you find a bank to service your debit needs, you will most likely be required to fill out a simple one-page application. Applying for debit is not like requesting merchant credit card status, which is an extension of credit, and thus is a risk for the bank. Since debit cards are a guaranteed transaction, the credit of the applicant merchant is not evaluated as stringently.

Once you've set up your POS terminal, the fee you pay for its use depends on which debit network you're connected to. Banks typically don't charge merchants a percentage of each debit card sale. Instead, the bank might charge merchants somewhere between 10 and 25 cents for each transaction.

While there's no doubt the cost per debit transaction adds up, it's still significantly less than some other options. For example, check processing typically runs from 18 to 50 cents per check, not taking into account the costs of bounced checks. Cash handling can also be expensive. Entrepreneurs who accept debit cards say they like the safety and security of this method. The bottom line: Debit offers your customers another way to pay…and the easier you make it for customers to buy, the more sales your business will ring up.

GLOSSARY

CHARGE-BACK: when a customer purchases an item using a credit card, then returns it, this is called a charge-back

DEBIT CARD: a card (often the customer's ATM card) that can be used to debit money directly from the customer's checking account

DISCOUNT RATE: the actual percentage the merchant is charged per credit card transaction by the credit card company or bank; the discount rate is based on sales volume, risk and other factors

INDEPENDENT SALES ORGANIZATION: representatives from out-of-town banks that, for a commission, match businesses with banks that will grant them merchant status

LAUNDERING: the practice of depositing one merchant's sales slips through another merchant's account; it is illegal in many states and prohibited by both Visa and MasterCard

MERCHANT ACCOUNT: an account that allows a merchant to accept payment from customers via credit card; may be granted through banks or directly from a credit card company

PRIVATE-LABEL CREDIT CARD: a credit card a merchant issues with his or her business's name on it

It's In
The Mail

*Setting up mailing and
shipping accounts*

M

ail is one of the lifelines of your business and, depending on your industry, it can also be one of your biggest costs. That's why it's so important to figure out the most efficient, convenient and economical ways to send mail. This chapter covers everything you need to know—from postage metering and sorting to letter-opening machines and overnight services—to deliver that letter, the sooner the better.

MAILING EQUIPMENT

There is a variety of mailing machines available on the market that can help you save time—so you can spend it on more important things, like growing your business.

Postage Meters

Buying your own postage meter saves a small business time and money. No more licking and sticking envelopes and stamps. With today's electronic mailing machines, you don't even have to stand in line at the post office to get your meter reset.

Electronic postage meters consist of a base through which envelopes are guided for stamping, which can be rented, leased or bought from a mailing equipment manufacturer; and a meter, which must be leased from a mailing equipment manufacturer. The faster and more automated the machine, and the more features it incorporates, the more it costs to rent, lease or own.

The primary difference between bases is how letters are fed through the machines. The least costly models require you to feed letters, one at a time, through a roller. More expensive models offer semiautomatic or fully automated letter feeding. Options for the base include stackers, which stack your mail, and sealers, which automatically wet and seal each envelope as it passes through the base.

Even the smallest office can benefit from a meter to determine exact postage and print out a stamp, and a scale to weigh mail. The U.S. Post Office estimates accurate weighing can save customers up to 20 percent on mailings.

An efficient, automated mailing machine can also save hours of time if you handle direct mail or large mailings. Mail that's presorted and bar-coded bypasses many of the post office handling steps and is delivered 24 hours sooner than mail lacking automated preparation, according to the USPS. (And if you don't think a day makes a difference, consider the results of a study by market research firm The Gallup Organization and mailing equipment manufacturer Pitney Bowes. Their study found that 11 percent of executives surveyed at large and midsize companies said the net income of their businesses would jump 5 percent if they received payments one day sooner!)

The latest mailing systems are multifunctional, handling everything from printing, folding, stapling, inserting, sealing, labeling, weighing and stamping to sorting, stacking and putting on a wrapper or binder. Many interact with a computer so you can track exactly how, when and to whom orders are sent out. Some PC-based systems can be programmed to simultaneously handle different sized paper—checks, invoices, brochures—without stopping the machine to reset the equipment.

The most popular mailing equipment combines meters with electronic scales; other machines have additional capabilities such as automatic feed and envelope-sealing functions. Speeds can vary from 25 to 200 envelopes a minute.

Besides faster delivery time and the ease of resetting by telephone or computer, metered mail machines offer other benefits:

■ **POSTAL ACCOUNTING:** Tracking and controlling money spent on direct mail, letters, parcel post, priority and express mail is easier. Because there is one dispenser with precise postage, accounting is streamlined, and you know exactly how much postage remains in the meter.

■ **PARCEL POST DATING:** If your third-class letters and packages are metered, the stamp date requires the post office to expedite those items on the date received, thereby providing better service on less expensive classes of mail.

■ **POSTMARK ADS:** Postage meters not only print stamps on your mail, but they can print an advertising message, too. Postmark ads can include your company logo and name, giving your company extra advertising exposure.

Postal Scales

Besides postage meters, the second crucial piece of mailing equipment most businesses need is a postal scale. Scales are sold in 5-, 10-,

30-, 100- and 200-pound capacities and can be purchased as stand-alone units or combined with a postage meter. A postal scale ensures that you're not paying more than you need to for your outgoing mail. What to look for when buying? Both electronic and manual versions are available. Because manual scales require you to read the postage amount, they increase the chance of human error. Electronic scales are more expensive, but their digital readouts reduce errors and ensure you get the most value from your scale.

DOLLAR STRETCHER

IF RISING POSTAGE COSTS ARE PUTTING THE SQUEEZE ON YOUR NEW BUSINESS, TRY SHRINKING YOUR MAILINGS. MANY DIRECT-MAIL AND CATALOG COMPANIES ARE SAVING BY REDUCING THEIR MAILINGS' DIMENSIONS. KEEP YOUR MAILINGS WITHIN THE SIZE OF THE USPS' LETTER CLASSIFICATION OF 6-BY-11 INCHES, WITH THICKNESS NO MORE THAN ONE-QUARTER INCH.

Depending on the type, size and weight of letters and packages you will be mailing, you may wish to look for a machine that lets you compare rates between various carriers, such as the USPS and FedEx. You may also want a feature that automatically converts a ZIP code to the proper zone for calculating zone-dependent rates for carriers such as United Parcel Service (UPS).

Consider ease of use, especially if a number of people will be using the scale. Some models have easy-to-read keypads and user prompts. Consider the size of the weighing platform and maximum weight the machine can handle to make sure it can accommodate the types of packages you'll be sending. For shipments that exceed the scale's weighing capacity, look for a scale that will allow you to manually enter the weight for rate calculation.

If you need your scale to interface with a postage meter, you'll want to be sure the model you choose is compatible with your metering equipment.

Questions to ask the dealer:

■ **WHAT ADJUSTMENTS** will need to be made to the scale if postage rates change? What charges are involved?

■ **DOES THE SCALE OFFER** alternative pricing options based on various postal classifications?

■ **DOES THE SCALE HAVE** a password feature to help guard against unauthorized uses?

■ **WHAT ARE ITS SIZE** and weight limitations?

■ **HOW SHOULD THE MACHINE** be maintained?

■ **WHAT TYPE OF MAINTENANCE** agreement is offered?
■ **DOES THE SCALE** offer rates for foreign mailings?
■ **DOES THE SCALE** offer rates for FedEx and UPS?

Letter-Folding Machines

When you are preparing for a promotional mailing, you may find yourself dealing with hundreds or thousands of letters or brochures. Folding letters yourself can be very time-consuming; it's also unnecessary, thanks to today's letter-folding machines.

When buying a letter-folding machine, consider the volume the machine is capable of processing. Low-end equipment processes a few hundred pieces per hour; high-end equipment is capable of operating at speeds from 1,500 to 7,000 sheets per hour. Also, consider the types of fold the equipment can provide. Some of the possibilities are c-fold (standard letter), z-fold (accordion fold), double fold, single fold, right-angle fold and brochure fold.

Sheets are fed either through a friction feeder or a vacuum feeder. Friction feeders have a rubber wheel that pulls the sheets through; frequent use can cause this kind of feeder to wear out. Friction feeders can also smudge a newly printed document. Vacuum feeders, while sturdier and more effective for handling coated papers, can be substantially more expensive and are only available on high-volume letter-folding machines.

You may also want to buy a model that includes a batch counter or a total counter. Batch counters keep the machine from folding too many sheets together. Total counters tell you how many sheets have already been folded. You'll find a memory setting useful if you typically produce the same types of jobs on a regular basis. The memory setting allows you to enter the instructions for processing a particular type of job once, then call up that job whenever you need to apply the same parameters.

You should also check to see how the equipment handles paper jams. Better-designed machines can release rollers, giving you easier access to the problematic areas. Finally, you may want to consider a model with an inserter, which

BRIGHT IDEA

PRESORTING BULK MAIL SAVES MONEY BUT TAKES TIME. SPEED UP THE PROCESS BY USING MAIL CONSOLIDATION COMPANIES—FIRMS THAT PRESORT MAIL AND DELIVER IT TO BULK-MAIL CENTERS AROUND THE COUNTRY. TO FIND SUCH COMPANIES, LOOK IN THE YELLOW PAGES UNDER "MAILING SERVICES."

automatically inserts your documents into envelopes.

Questions to ask the dealer:

- **HOW MANY PIECES** can it process per hour?
- **DOES THE MACHINE** offer friction or vacuum feed?
- **WHAT TYPES OF FOLDS** is the machine capable of?
- **HOW MANY SHEETS** can it fold at once?
- **HOW EFFECTIVE IS IT** at handling stapled sheets? (Many cannot

Pushing The Envelope

Looking for ways to prune postal bloat? The Direct Marketing Association offers this checklist of cost-cutting ideas:

1. **FINE-TUNE YOUR MAILING LIST.**
   - Stop mailing to duplicate names.
   - Eliminate nonresponders and marginal prospects. There are many mailing list software programs that can help you keep your mailing lists current.

2. **BE SURE YOU'RE USING ACCURATE ADDRESSES.**
   - Check for correct ZIP codes, especially when using addresses supplied by customers.
   - Watch for mail shipped to wrong suite or apartment numbers.
   - Check for missing directionals, such as "N." for "North."

3. **TAKE ADVANTAGE OF POSTAL DISCOUNTS AND SERVICES.**
   - Use the USPS' National Change of Address list to keep your mailing list current.
   - Print "Address Correction Requested" on the face of your mail. The Postal Service will tell you if the recipient files a change of address.
   - Investigate commingling your mail with that of other small mailers to take advantage of discounts available mainly to large mailers. Contact your local mailing service for more information.
   - Print your bar-coded ZIP+4 on business reply mail. The Postal Service charges much less for cards using the nine-digit zips.
   - Stockpile mail to build up larger volumes.

handle this automatically and will require hand feeding.)

- **WHAT COUNTER FEATURES** are available?
- **WHAT TYPES AND SIZES** of paper can it handle?
- **HOW SHOULD THE MACHINE** be maintained?
- **WHAT TYPE OF MAINTENANCE** agreement is offered?
- **DOES IT HAVE** an automatic feeder?
- **DOES IT HAVE** a memory setting?
- **HOW ARE** paper jams handled?

Letter-Opening Machines

Letter-opening machines can greatly speed up the opening of mail. Some can process up to 600 envelopes per minute.

What to look for when buying? There are two types of letter openers: chadders and slitters. Chadders open envelopes by cutting one-eighth of an inch from the end. Slitters, while quite a bit more expensive ($1,000 or more), cut through the top seam of the envelope and reduce the risk of damaging the contents of the envelope.

Most models can handle standard #10 envelopes. More expensive models will accommodate different sizes and thicknesses of incoming mail. An automated feeder will send your mail through the machine; joggers will help settle the contents of the envelope so they don't get cut; counters let you count the number of pieces being processed.

Another feature you may find helpful is an automatic date-and-time stamp to help you keep track of when mail arrives. Because letter-openers are usually quite reliable, maintenance contracts are usually not required.

Questions to ask the dealer:

- **DOES THE OPENER** use a chadder or a slitter?
- **WHAT SIZES OF ENVELOPES** can the machine handle?
- **DOES IT HAVE** an automatic feeder? A jogger? A counter?
- **CAN INCOMING MAIL** be time- and date-stamped?

Lease Or Buy?

Mailing equipment can be rented, leased or purchased outright. You may prefer to lease to conserve working capital, then upgrade equipment as your business grows. Renting is the easiest method, because if you need to cut costs at any time, you simply hand the equipment back and walk away. If you are leasing, you are obligated to make all the payments specified in the lease. However, leasing offers advantages, including lower rates than renting and the ability to roll the lease over for upgraded equipment.

If a mailing equipment salesperson sells you on leased equipment that ends up being too sophisticated for your needs, some suppliers will purchase the competitor's lease and give you their own equipment. When shopping around for equipment, ask if there are any special promotions available before you sign.

Basic machines lease from about $25 to $35 per month, more sophisticated machines for $60 and up. Anything more expensive than that is usually best suited to large corporations. The average lease is for five years and can include maintenance and free postage refills; the average rental agreement is for one year.

Carefully read the contracts you are offered, and, if renting, make sure there is no mention of the word "lease." Also, always ask what options you have if you need to get out of a lease.

Make sure the company is postal-certified with the USPS. Salespeople should be knowledgeable about their industry and about the latest USPS regulations and rates, and they should ask you questions about your mailing process—how many boxes, how frequently you ship—so the equipment they recommend fits both your business and budget.

When shopping for mailing equipment, allow the salespeople enough time to make their pitch. The right mailing equipment can save you money, but only if you give the salesperson enough time to analyze your needs.

SENDING MAIL

Sending your mail under the appropriate classification can save your business hundreds—or even thousands—of dollars each year, depending on how much and how frequently you mail. The post office divides mail into six classifications:

1. Express mail
2. Priority mail
3. First class mail
4. Periodicals
5. Standard mail (A)
6. Standard mail (B)

Express mail offers next-day service 365 days a year. (For more on this, see the next section on "overnight mail.") Priority mail can be used when the speed and expense of express mail is not necessary but preferential handling is still desired. Priority mail offers two-day delivery to most U.S. addresses. The maximum weight for priority mail is 70 pounds.

Your local post office can supply you with priority mail labels, stickers, envelopes and boxes at no extra charge. The 2-pound flat-rate envelope is typically convenient to use. The rate of postage is the same as that charged for a 2-pound piece of priority mail, regardless of weight. A presort discount is available for large mailings. Priority mail can be insured, registered, certified or sent c.o.d. for additional charges.

First-class mail is used for sending letters, postcards, greeting cards, checks and money orders. If your first-class item weighs more

Change Of Address

Sick of standing in line at the post office? Try going online to the post office instead. At the USPS' Web site (www.usps.gov), you'll find dozens of time- and money-saving services.

Click on the ZIP codes icon from the home page, and you can look up ZIP codes for addresses nationwide. Or keep tabs on packages by using the site's Express Mail tracking feature.

There's also a "rate calculator" that helps you find the most cost-effective method of mailing letters and packages. Just enter the article's weight plus ZIP codes of the origin and destination, and up pops the price for shipping it by various methods.

Want shipping supplies sent to your door? Click on "Business Center," then "Shipping Supplies" to order express or priority mail envelopes, labels, boxes and tags after registering your business information.

You can even order stamps at www.stampsonline.com with your credit card (a small shipping charge applies).

than 11 ounces, use priority mail. Additional services such as certificates of mailing, certified, registered and c.o.d. can also be purchased for first-class mail. All first-class mail receives prompt handling and transportation.

The periodicals rate is available to publishers or registered news agents approved for periodicals mailing privileges. Other rates must be paid for magazines and newspapers mailed by the general public.

Standard mail (A) is used primarily by retailers, catalogers and other advertisers to promote their products and services. This is the type of mail you'd be using if, for example, you were sending out a direct-mail piece to 1,000 potential customers. To qualify for standard mail (A) rates, you buy a standard rate permit from the post office. There is an annual fee for this (about $150), and other fees may be charged depending on the degree to which you are automating your mail. Standard mail (A) is available in two subclasses: regular (also called "bulk rate") and nonprofit. Standard rate (B) is for parcels weighing 1 pound or more.

For a mailing to get standard mail (A) rates, you must be mailing a minimum 200 pieces or 50 pounds per mailing; the pieces must each weigh less than 16 ounces. There are a variety of discounts available. Essentially, the more work you do in advance in terms of sorting, bundling and labeling, the lower postal rate you'll pay. At the minimum, nonautomated level, you'll need to presort your mail by ZIP code, mark it with "Bulk Rate" and pack it in trays. The more automated you get, the lower your per-piece mailing cost gets. The post office has specific guidelines for automation, including bar-coding, standards for address accuracy and requirements for automation compatibility.

To find out more about mail classifications and how to prepare your mail the least expensive way, visit the USPS' Web site at http://ribbs.usps.gov or go to one of the USPS' Postal Service Business Centers. These centers can advise you on preparing and designing mailings, discounts for presorting and saturation mailings, bar coding, ZIP+4 strategies and other ways to cut your mailing costs. Some also sponsor educational seminars for business owners.

The USPS will also bring your mailing list up to its standards and add the ZIP+4 extension to all complete addresses once at no cost. To find out where the closest Business Center is, contact your local post office.

Mailing equipment manufacturers or distributors (look in the

Business-to-Business Yellow Pages under "Mailing Equipment") often sponsor educational seminars on mailing as well.

OVERNIGHT MAIL

When your California company's proposal has to be in your New York client's hands, pronto, how do you get it there? Well, there are a variety of ways to send overnight mail.

The biggest players in the field are DHL Worldwide Express, FedEx, UPS and the USPS. Each will come right to the doorsteps of even the smallest homebased businesses.

When deciding on an express mail carrier, first think about the services you need. Will you be sending one package per week or 15 per day? Domestically or internationally? Do you want delivery the same day, the next day, or in two or three days? Will you be shipping by air or ground?

BEWARE!

LIABILITY IS AN IMPORTANT CONSIDERATION WHEN CHOOSING AN AIR COURIER. EACH COURIER SETS A PREDETERMINED MAXIMUM DOLLAR AMOUNT THAT YOU WILL BE PAID IF A PACKAGE IS LOST. IF YOU REGULARLY SEND PACKAGES WORTH MORE THAN THE COURIER'S LIMIT, LOOK INTO ACQUIRING ADDITIONAL INSURANCE.

When you are choosing an international courier, first ask the company for a list of countries it delivers to. Also remember that courier services overseas differ from domestic services in two ways. First, your package may be turned over to a foreign delivery service once it reaches the country to which it's being sent. Second, customs regulations require documentation for clearance of your export shipments.

Whether domestic or international, ask about a courier's hours and days of service and if there are extra charges for deliveries on Saturdays. Companies may allow you to set up daily pickup times or may provide pickup on an as-needed basis. Typically, you get volume dis-

HOT LINK

NOT SURE WHERE TO START WHEN YOU'VE GOT TO SEND A PACKAGE OR AN OVERNIGHT LETTER? SMARTSHIP.COM WILL SHOW YOU THE WAY. YOU CAN COMPARE RATES, FIND OUT THE CLOSEST DROP-OFF CENTER FOR THE CARRIER OF YOUR CHOICE, AND EVEN ORDER PICK-UP WITH OUT SO MUCH AS USING THE TELEPHONE.

counts based on how much mail you send.

Most companies also offer a range of delivery times—for example, "next business day, a.m." or "next business day, p.m." Some may even offer same-day delivery for an extra fee. Other services offered may include management reports and acknowledgement cards.

Courier services are highly competitive and are eager to acquire new business. As a business owner, you have clout with courier services, so don't hesitate to ask questions and negotiate for special rates and services. Once you know what your express mail needs are likely to be, compare them against what the different courier services offer.

GLOSSARY

BATCH COUNTER: feature on a letter-folding machine that prevents the machine from folding too many sheets together

CHADDER: type of letter-opening machine that cuts one-eighth of an inch from the end of the envelope

FRICTION FEEDER: feeder on a letter-folding machine that pulls sheets through using a rubber wheel

JOGGER: mechanism on a letter-opening machine that helps settle contents of envelopes so they don't get cut

SEALER: part of a postage meter's base that seals mail

SLITTER: type of letter-opening machine that slits the seam of the envelope

STACKER: part of a postage meter's base that stacks mail

TOTAL COUNTER: feature on a letter-folding machine that tells you how many sheets have been folded

VACUUM FEEDER: feature feeder on a letter-folding machine that pulls sheets through using vacuum technology

People Who Need People

Hiring your first employee

T o hire or not to hire, that is the question in the mind of the new entrepreneur. You see, hiring even one employee changes everything. Suddenly, you need payroll procedures, rules regarding hours, and a policy for vacation pay. You're hit with a multitude of legal requirements and management duties you'd never have to deal with if you worked solo.

To decide whether you need employees, take a closer look at your ultimate goals. Do you want to create the next Starbucks, or do you simply want to work on your own terms without a boss looking over your shoulder? If your goals are modest, then adding a staff may not be the best solution for you.

If you do need employees, there are plenty of ways to meet your staffing needs—without driving yourself nuts. From temporaries and independent contractors to employee leasing, the following chapter takes a closer look at the do's and don'ts of staffing your business. Read it over, and you will have a better idea whether to hire—or not to hire—is the right solution for you.

HOW TO HIRE

The employees you hire can make or break your business. While you may be tempted to hire the first person who walks in the door, "just to get it over with," doing so can be a fatal error. A small company can not afford to carry dead wood on staff, so start smart by taking time to figure out your staffing needs before you even begin looking for job candidates.

Job Analysis

Begin by understanding the requirements of the job being filled. What kind of personality, experience and education are needed? To determine these attributes, sit down and do a job analysis covering the following areas:

- **THE PHYSICAL/MENTAL TASKS** involved (ranging from judging, planning and managing to cleaning, lifting and welding)
- **HOW THE JOB WILL BE DONE** (the methods and equipment used)
- **THE REASON THE JOB EXISTS** (including an explanation of job goals

Job Analysis

Date:_____ Prepared By:_____

Title:_____ Department:_____

Job Title:_____

Reporting To:_____

Major Responsibilities:_____

_____

_____

Minor Responsibilities:_____

_____

_____

Education/Experience Required:_____

_____

_____

Goals/Objectives of Position:_____

_____

_____

Knowledge/Skills Required:_____

_____

_____

Physical Requirements:_____

_____

_____

Special Problems/Hazards:_____

_____

_____

Number of People Supervised:_____

Reporting To:_____

and how they relate to other positions in the company)

■ **THE QUALIFICATIONS NEEDED** (training, knowledge, skills and personality traits)

If you are having trouble, one good way to get information for a job analysis is to talk to employees and supervisors at other companies that have similar positions.

Job Description

Use the job analysis to write a job description and a job specification. Drawing from these concepts, you can then create your recruitment materials, such as a classified ad.

The job description is basically an outline of how the job fits into the company. It should point out in broad terms the job's goals, responsibilities and duties. First, write down the job title and whom that person will report to. Next, develop a job statement or summary describing the position's major and minor duties. Finally, define how the job relates to other positions in the company. Which are subordinate and which are of equal responsibility and authority?

For a one-person business hiring its first employee, these steps may seem unnecessary, but remember, you are laying the foundations for your personnel policy, which will be essential as your company grows. Keeping detailed records from the time you hire your first employee will make things a lot easier when you hire your 50th.

The job specification describes the personal requirements you expect from the employee. Like the job description, it includes the job title, whom the person reports to, and a summary of the position. However, it also lists any educational requirements, desired experience, and specialized skills or knowledge required. Include salary range and benefits. Finish by listing any physical or other special requirements associated with the job, as well as any occupational hazards.

Writing the job description and job specifications will also help you determine whether you need a part- or full-time employee, whether the person should be permanent or temporary, and whether

SMART TIP

IT'S EASY TO HIRE EMPLOYEES WHO ARE JUST LIKE YOU, BUT IT'S OFTEN A BIG MISTAKE. ESPECIALLY WITH YOUR FIRST EMPLOYEE, TRY TO FIND SOMEONE WHO COMPENSATES FOR YOUR STRENGTHS AND WEAKNESSES. WHILE PERSONAL COMPATIBILITY IS IMPORTANT, HIRING A CARBON COPY OF YOURSELF COULD LEAVE YOUR FIRM ILL-PREPARED FOR FUTURE CHALLENGES.

Job Description

Date:_____ Prepared By:_____

Title:_____ Department:_____

Job Description

Job Title:_____ Reporting To:_____

Job Statement:_____

_____

_____

_____

Major Duties

1._____

2._____

3._____

4._____

5._____

6._____

7._____

Minor Duties

1._____

2._____

3._____

4._____

5._____

6._____

7._____

Relationships:

Number of People Supervised:_____

Person Giving Work Assignments:_____

you could use an independent contractor to fill the position (more on all these options later).

Writing The Ad

Use the job specification and description to write an ad that will attract candidates to your company. The best way to avoid wasting time on interviews with people who do not meet your needs is to write an ad that will lure qualified candidates and discourage others. Consider this example:

Interior designer seeks inside/outside salesperson. Flooring, drapes (extensive measuring), furniture, etc. In-home consultations. Excellent salary and commission. PREVIOUS EXPERIENCE A NECESSITY. San Francisco Bay Area. Send resume to G. Green at P.O. Box 5409, San Francisco, CA 90842.

This job description is designed to attract a flexible salesperson and eliminate those who lack the confidence to work on commission. The advertiser asks for expertise in "extensive measuring," the skill he has had the most difficulty finding. The job location should be included to weed out applicants who don't live in the area or aren't willing to commute or relocate. Finally, the capitalized "PREVIOUS EXPERIENCE A NECESSITY" underscores that he will hire only candidates with previous experience.

To write a similarly targeted ad for your business, look at your job specifications and pull out the top four or five skills that are most essential to the job. Don't, however, list requirements other than educational or experience-related ones in the ad. Nor should you request specific personality traits (such as outgoing, detail-oriented) since people are likely to come in and imitate those characteristics when they don't really possess them. Instead, you should focus on telling the applicants about the excitement and challenge of the job, the salary, what they will get out of it and what it will be like working for you.

Finally, specify how applicants should contact you. Depending on the type of job (professional or nonskilled) you are trying to fill, you may want to have the person send a cover letter and a resume, or simply call to set up an appointment to come in and fill out an application.

Recruiting Employees

The obvious first choice for recruiting employees is the classified ad section of your local newspaper. Place your ad in the Sunday or weekend edition of the largest-circulation local papers.

Beyond this, however, there are plenty of other places to recruit good employees. Here are some ideas:

- **TAP INTO YOUR PERSONAL AND PROFESSIONAL NETWORK.** Tell everyone you know—friends, neighbors, professional associates, customers, vendors, colleagues from associations—that you have a job opening. Someone might know of the perfect candidate.

- **CONTACT SCHOOL PLACEMENT OFFICES.** List your openings with trade and vocational schools, colleges and universities. Check with your local school board to see if high schools in your area have job training and placement programs.

- **POST NOTICES AT SENIOR CITIZEN CENTERS.** Retirees who need extra income or a productive way to fill their time can make excellent employees.

- **USE AN EMPLOYMENT AGENCY.** Private and government-sponsored agencies can help with locating and screening applicants. Often their fees are more than justified by the amount of time and money you save.

- **LIST YOUR OPENING WITH AN APPROPRIATE JOB BANK.** Many professional associations have job banks for their members. Contact groups related to your industry, even if they are outside your local area, and ask them to alert their members to your staffing needs.

- **USE INDUSTRY PUBLICATIONS.** Trade association newsletters or industry publications often have classified ad sections where members can advertise job openings. This is a very effective way to attract skilled people in your industry.

- **GO ONLINE.** There are a variety of online job banks and databases that allow employers to list openings. These databases can be searched by potential employees from all over the country. Often, you can even receive resumes online. This is an especially good way to search for tech-savvy employees.

Pre-Screening Candidates

Two important tools in pre-screening job candidates are the resume and the employment application. If you ask applicants to send in a resume, that will be the first tool you use to screen them. You will then have qualified candidates fill out an application when they come in for an interview. If you don't ask for a resume, you will probably want to have prospective employees come in to fill out applications, then review the applications and call qualified candidates to set up an interview.

In either case, it is important to have an application form ready before you begin the interview process. You can buy generic application forms at most office-supply stores, or you can develop your own application form to meet your specific needs. Make sure any application form you use conforms to Equal Employment Opportunity Commission (EEOC) guidelines regarding questions you can and cannot ask (see "Off Limits" on page 347 for more on this).

Your application should ask for specific information such as name, address and phone number; educational background; work experience, including salary levels; awards or honors; whether the applicant can work full or part time as well as available hours; and any special skills relevant to the job (foreign languages, familiarity with software programs, etc.). Be sure to ask for names and phone numbers of for-

Willing And Able

The Americans With Disabilities Act (ADA) of 1990 makes it illegal for employers with 15 or more employees to refuse to hire qualified people with disabilities if making "reasonable accommodations" would enable the person to carry out the duties of the job. That could mean making physical changes to the workplace or reallocating certain responsibilities.

While the law is unclear on exactly how far an employer must go to accommodate a person with disabilities, what is clear is that it's the applicant's responsibility to tell the employer about the disability. Employers are not allowed to ask whether an applicant has a disability or a history of health problems. However, after the applicant has been given a written or verbal explanation of the job duties, you may then ask whether he or she can adequately perform those duties or would need some type of accommodation.

For further clarification, read the *Enforcement Guidance: Pre-employment Disability-Related Questions and Medical Examinations* document, which is available online from the Equal Employment Opportunity Commission at www.eeoc.gov/docs/preemp.html.

mer supervisors to check as references; if the candidate is currently employed, ask whether it is OK to contact his or her current place of employment. You may also want to ask for personal references. Because many employers these days hesitate to give out information about an employee, you may want to have the applicant sign a waiver that states the employee authorizes former and/or current employers to disclose information about him or her.

When screening resumes, it helps to have your job description and specifications in front of you so you can keep the qualities and skills you are looking for clearly in mind. Since there is no standard form for resumes, evaluating them can be very subjective. However, there are certain components that you should expect to find in a resume. It should contain the prospect's name, address and telephone number at the top, and a brief summary of employment and educational experience, including dates. Many resumes include a "career objective" that describes what kind of job the prospect is pursuing; other applicants state their objectives in their cover letters. Additional information you may find on a resume or in a cover letter includes references, achievements and career-related affiliations.

Look for neatness and professionalism in the applicant's resume and cover letter. A resume riddled with typos raises some serious red flags. If a person can't be bothered to put his or her best foot forward during this crucial stage of the game, how can you expect him or her to do a good job if hired?

There are two basic types of resumes: the "chronological" resume and the "functional" resume. The chronological resume, which is what most of us are used to seeing, lists employment history in reverse chronological order, from most recent position to earliest. The functional resume does not list dates of employment; instead, it lists different skills or "functions" that the employee has performed.

Functional resumes have become more popular in recent years. In some cases, they are used by downsized executives who may be quite well-qualified and are simply trying

BRIGHT IDEA

IF RELEVANT, ASK EMPLOYEES TO SEND SAMPLES OF THEIR WORK WITH THEIR RESUMES OR TO BRING THEM TO THE INTERVIEW. ANOTHER TECHNIQUE: ASK THEM TO COMPLETE A PROJECT SIMILAR TO THE ACTUAL WORK THEY'D BE DOING (AND PAY THEM FOR IT). THIS GIVES YOU A STRONG INDICATION OF HOW THEY WOULD PERFORM ON THE JOB...AND GIVES THEM A CLEAR PICTURE OF WHAT YOU EXPECT FROM THEM.

Job Application

NAME/ADDRESS

Last:	First:	Middle Initial:	Social Security Number
Address:			
City:	State:	ZIP:	Telephone:

DESIRED EMPLOYMENT

Position:	Date You Can Start:	Desired Salary:
Are You Currently Employed?	If Employed, May We Contact Your Current Employer?	
Have You Applied to This Company Before?	If So, Where & When?	

EDUCATION

	Name & Location of School		
High School			
	Years Attended (Diploma/Degree)	Date Graduated	Grade Completed
University/College Undergraduate	Name & Location of School		
	Years Attended (Diploma/Degree)	Date Graduated	Grade Completed
University/College Graduate	Name & Location of School		
	Years Attended (Diploma/Degree)	Date Graduated	Grade Completed
Trade, Business or Correspondence School	Name & Location of School		
	Years Attended (Diploma/Degree)	Date Graduated	Grade Completed

EMPLOYMENT HISTORY

Employer:	Job Title:
Address:	Duties:
Phone:	Salary:
Date From: Date To:	Reason for Leaving:
Employer:	Job Title:
Address:	Duties:
Phone:	Salary:
Date From: Date To:	Reason for Leaving:
Employer:	Job Title:
Address:	Duties:
Phone:	Salary:
Date From: Date To:	Reason for Leaving:

344

Job Application

REFERENCES

Name:	Occupation:
Address:	Relationship:
Phone Number:	Years Known:
Name:	Occupation:
Address:	Relationship:
Phone Number:	Years Known:
Name:	Occupation:
Address:	Relationship:
Phone Number:	Years Known:

PHYSICAL RECORD

Do you have any physical disabilities that would prevent you from performing the work for which you are applying? If so, describe:

Have you ever been injured?   Provide Details:

In case of emergency notify: Name: Address: Phone:

ADDITIONAL AREAS OF EXPERTISE

Areas of specialized study, research or additional experience:

List the foreign languages you speak fluently: Read: Write:

U.S. Military Service: Rank: Present member in National Guard or Reserves:

_____   _____
Signature   *Date*

FOR EXTERNAL USE ONLY

Interviewer:	Date:
Comments:	

to downplay long periods of unemployment or make a career change. In other cases, however, they signal the applicant is a job-hopper or has something to hide.

Because it's easy for people to embellish resumes, it's a good idea to have candidates fill out a job application, by mail or in person, and then compare it to the resume. Because the application requires information to be completed in chronological order, it gives you a more accurate picture of an applicant's real history.

Beyond functional and chronological resumes, there is another type of resume that's more important to be on the lookout for. That's what one consultant calls an "accomplishment" vs. a "responsibility" resume.

The responsibility resume is just that. It emphasizes the job description, saying things like "Managed three account executives; established budgets; developed departmental contests." An accomplishment resume, on the other hand, emphasizes accomplishments and results, such as "Cut costs by 50 percent" or "Met quota every month." Such a resume tells you that the person is an achiever and has the bottom line firmly in mind.

When reading the resume, try to determine the person's career patterns. Look for steady progress and promotions in past jobs. Also look for stability in terms of length of employment. A person who changes jobs every year is probably not someone you want on your team. Look for people with three- to four-year job stints.

At the same time, be aware of how economic conditions can affect a person's resume. During a climate of frequent corporate downsizing, for example, a series of lateral career moves may signal that a person is a survivor. This also shows that the person is interested in growing and willing to take on new responsibilities, even if there was no corresponding increase in pay or status.

By the same token, just because a resume or a job application has a few gaps in it doesn't mean you should overlook it entirely. You could be making a big mistake. Stay focused on the skills or value the job applicant could bring to your company.

Off Limits

Equal Employment Opportunity Commission (EEOC) guide-lines, as well as federal and state laws, prohibit asking certain questions of a job applicant, either on the application form or during the interview. What questions to sidestep? Basically, you can't ask about anything not directly related to the job, including:

- **AGE OR DATE OF BIRTH** (except when necessary to satisfy applicable age laws)
- **SEX, RACE, CREED,** color, religion or national origin
- **DISABILITIES** of any kind
- **DATE AND TYPE** of military discharge
- **MARITAL STATUS**
- **MAIDEN NAME** (for female applicants)
- **IF A PERSON IS A CITIZEN;** however, you can ask if he or she, after employment, can submit proof of the legal right to work in the United States

OTHER QUESTIONS TO AVOID:

- **HOW MANY CHILDREN** do you have? How old are they? Who will care for them while you are at work?
- **HAVE YOU EVER** been treated by a psychologist or a psychiatrist?
- **HAVE YOU EVER** been treated for drug addiction or alcoholism?
- **HAVE YOU EVER** been arrested? (You may, however, ask if the person has been convicted if it is accompanied by a statement saying that a conviction will not necessarily disqualify an applicant for employment.)
- **HOW MANY DAYS** were you sick last year?
- **HAVE YOU EVER** filed for workers' compensation? Have you ever been injured on the job?

In doubt whether a question (or comment) is offensive or not? Play it safe and zip your lip. In today's lawsuit-happy environment, an offhanded remark could cost you plenty.

Interviewing Applicants

Once you've narrowed your stack of resumes down to 10 or so top candidates, it's time to start setting up interviews. If you dread this portion of the process, you're not alone. Fortunately, there are some

Family Affair

Want to get good employees and tax savings, too? Consider putting your family members to work for you.

Hiring family, especially children, enables you to move family income out of a higher tax bracket into a lower one. It also enables you to transfer wealth to your kids without incurring federal gift or estate taxes.

Even preteen children can be put to work stuffing envelopes, filing or sorting mail. If their salary is reasonable, it is considered earned income and not subject to the "kiddie tax" rules that apply to kids under 14. And if your business is unincorporated, wages paid to a child under 18 are not subject to Social Security or FICA taxes. That means neither you nor your child has to pay these taxes. Finally, employed youngsters can make tax-deductible contributions to an individual retirement account.

Be sure to document the type of work the family member is doing and pay them a comparable amount to what you'd pay another employee, or the IRS will think you're putting your family on the payroll just for the tax breaks. Keep careful records of time worked, and make sure the work is necessary to the business.

Your accountant can suggest other ways to take advantage of this tax situation without getting in hot water.

ways to put both yourself and the candidates at ease—and make sure you get all the information you need to make a smart decision. Start by preparing a list of basic interview questions in advance. While you won't read off this list like a robot, having it in front of you will ensure you cover all the bases and also make sure you ask all the candidates the same questions.

The initial few moments of an interview are the most crucial. As you meet the candidate and shake his or her hand, you will gain a strong impression of his or her poise, confidence and enthusiasm (or lack thereof). Qualities to look for include good communication skills, a neat and clean appearance, and a friendly and enthusiastic manner.

Put the interviewee at ease with a bit of small talk on neutral topics. A good way to break the ice is by explaining the job and describing the company—its business, history and future plans.

Then move on to the heart of the interview. You will want to ask about several general areas, such as related experience, skills, educational training or background, and unrelated jobs. Open each area with a general, open-ended question, such as "Tell me about your last job." Avoid questions that can be answered with a "yes" or "no" or that prompt obvious responses, such as "Are you detail-oriented?" Instead ask questions that force the candidate to go into detail. The best questions are follow-up questions such as "How did that situation come about?" or "Why did you do that?" These queries force applicants to abandon pre-planned responses and dig deeper.

Here are some suggestions to get you started:

- **IF YOU COULD DESIGN** the perfect job for yourself, what would you do? Why?
- **WHAT KIND OF SUPERVISOR** gets the best work out of you?
- **HOW WOULD YOU DESCRIBE** your current supervisor?
- **HOW DO YOU** structure your time?
- **WHAT ARE THREE THINGS** you like about your current job?
- **WHAT WERE YOUR THREE** biggest accomplishments in your last job? In your career?
- **WHAT CAN YOU DO** for our company that no one else can?
- **WHAT ARE YOUR** strengths/weaknesses?
- **HOW FAR DO YOU THINK** you can go in this company? Why?
- **WHAT DO YOU EXPECT** to be doing in five years?
- **WHAT INTERESTS YOU MOST** about this company? This position?
- **DESCRIBE THREE SITUATIONS** where your work was criticized.
- **HAVE YOU HIRED PEOPLE BEFORE?** If so, what did you look for?

Your candidate's responses will give you a window into his or her knowledge, attitude and sense of humor. Watch for signs of "sour grapes" about former employers. Also be alert for areas people seem reluctant to talk about. Probe a little deeper without sounding judgmental.

Pay attention to the candidate's nonverbal cues, too. Does she seem alert and interested, or does she slouch and yawn? Are his clothes wrinkled and stained, or clean and neat? A person who can't make an effort for the interview certainly won't make one on the job if hired.

Finally, leave time at the end of the interview for the applicant to ask questions—and pay attention to what he or she asks. This is the time when applicants can really show they have done their homework and researched your company...or, conversely, that all they care about is what they can get out of the job. Obviously, there is a big difference between the one who says, "I notice that your biggest competitor's sales have doubled since launching their Web site in January.

Do you have any plans to develop a Web site of your own?" and the person who asks, "How long is the lunch break?" Similarly, candidates who can't come up with even one question may be demonstrating that they can't think on their feet.

End the interview by letting the candidate know what to expect next. How much longer will you be interviewing? When can they expect to hear from you? You are dealing with other people's livelihoods, so the week that you take to finish your interviews can seem like an eternity to them. Show some consideration by keeping them informed.

During the interview, jot down notes (without being obvious about it). After the interview, allow five or 10 minutes to write down the applicant's outstanding qualities and evaluate his or her personality and skills against your job description and specifications.

Checking References

After preliminary interviews, you should be able to narrow the field to three or four top candidates. Now's the time to do a little detective work.

It's estimated that up to one-third of job applicants lie about their experiences and educational achievements on their resumes or job applications. No matter how sterling the person seems in the interview process, a few phone calls up front to check out their claims could save you a lot of hassle—and even legal battles—later on. Today, courts are increasingly holding employers liable for crimes employees commit on the job, such as drunk driving, when it is determined that the employer could have been expected to know about prior convictions for similar offenses.

Unfortunately, getting that information has become harder and harder to do. Fearful of reprisals from former employees, many firms have adopted policies that forbid releasing detailed information. Generally, the investigating party is referred to a personnel department, which supplies dates of employment, title and salary—period.

There are ways to dig deeper, however. Try to avoid the human resources department if at all possible. Instead, try calling the person's former supervisor directly. While the supervisor may be required to send you to personnel, sometimes you'll get lucky and get the person on a day he or she feels like talking.

Sometimes, too, a supervisor can tip you off without saying anything that will get him or her in trouble. Consider the supervisor who, when contacted by one potential employer, said, "I only give good references." When the employer asked, "What can you tell me about X?" the supervisor repeated, "I only give good references." Without saying anything, he said it all.

Depending on the position, you may also want to do education checks. You can call any college or university's admissions department to verify degrees and dates of attendance. Some universities will require a written request or a signed waiver from the applicant before releasing any kind of information to you.

If the person is going to be driving a company vehicle, you may want to do a motor vehicle check with the motor vehicle department. In fact, you may want to do this even if he or she will not be driving for you. Vehicle checks can uncover patterns of negligence or drug and alcohol problems that he or she might have.

If your company deals with property management, such as maintenance or cleaning, you may want to consider a criminal background check as well. Unfortunately, national criminal records and even state records are not coordinated. The only way to obtain criminal records is to go to individual courthouses in each county. Although you can't run all over the state to check into a person's record, it's generally sufficient to investigate records in three counties—birthplace, current residence and residence preceding the current residence.

For certain positions, such as those that will give an employee access to your company's cash (a cashier or an accounting clerk, for instance), a credit check may be a good idea as well. You can find credit reporting bureaus in any Yellow Pages. They will be able to provide you with a limited credit and payment history. While you should not rely on this as the sole reason not to hire someone (credit reports are noto-

DOLLAR STRETCHER

WHENEVER POSSIBLE, LOOK FOR EMPLOYEES YOU CAN CROSS-TRAIN  INTO DIFFERENT JOB RESPONSIBILITIES. A WELDER WITH COLLEGE COURSES IN ENGINEERING AND A SECRETARY WITH HUMAN RESOURCES EXPERIENCE ARE WORKERS ONE BUSINESS OWNER HAS SUCCESSFULLY CROSS-TRAINED. CROSS-TRAINED EMPLOYEES CAN FILL IN WHEN OTHERS ARE ABSENT, HELPING KEEP COSTS DOWN.

rious for containing errors), a credit report can contribute to a total picture of irresponsible behavior. And if the person will have access to large sums of money at your company, hiring someone who is in serious debt is probably not a very good idea.

Be aware, however, that if a credit check plays any role in your decision not to hire someone, you must inform them that they were turned down in part because of their credit report.

If all this seems too time-consuming to handle yourself, you can contract the job out to a third-party investigator. Look in the Yellow Pages for firms in your area that handle this task. The cost averages about $100—a small price to pay when you consider the damages it might save you.

After The Hire

Congratulations! You have hired your first employee. Now what?

As soon as you hire, call or write the applicants who didn't make the cut and tell them you'll keep their applications on file. That way, if the person you hired isn't the best—or is so good that business doubles—you won't have to start from scratch in hiring your second employee.

For each applicant you interviewed, create a file including your interview notes, the resume and the employment application. For the person you hire, that file will become the basis for his or her personnel file. Federal law requires that a job application be kept at least three years after a person is hired.

Even if you don't hire the applicant, make sure you keep the file. Under federal law, all recruitment materials, such as applications and resumes, must be kept for at least one year after the employment decision has been made. In today's climate, where applicants sometimes sue an employer who decides not to hire them, it's a good idea to maintain all records related to a hire (or nonhire). Especially for higher-level positions where you narrow the field to two or three candidates, put a brief note or memo in each applicant's file explaining why he or she was or wasn't hired.

The hiring process doesn't end with making the selection. Your new employee's first day is critical. People are most motivated on their first day. Build on the momentum of that motivation by having a place set up for them to work, making them comfortable and making them feel welcome. Don't just dump them in an office and shut your door. Be prepared to spend some time with them, explaining job duties, introducing them to their office mates, getting them started on tasks or even taking them out to lunch. By doing so, you are building rapport and setting the stage for a long and happy working relationship.

ALTERNATIVES TO FULL-TIME EMPLOYEES

The traditional full-time employee is not your only hiring option. More employers are turning to alternative arrangements, including leased employees, temporary employees, part-timers and interns. All these strategies can save you money and headaches, too.

Leased Employees

If payroll paperwork, personnel hassles and employee manuals sound like too much work to deal with, consider an option that's growing in popularity: employee leasing.

Employee leasing—a means of managing your human resources without all the administrative hassles—first became popular in California in the early '80s, driven by the excessive cost of health-care benefits in the state. By combining the employees of several companies into one larger pool, employee leasing companies (also known as professional employer organizations, or PEOs) could offer business owners better rates on health care and workers' compensation coverage.

Today, there are more than more than 2 million leased employees in the United States, and the employee leasing industry is projected to continue growing at an annual rate of more than 20 percent each year, according to the National Association of Professional Employer Organizations (NAPEO).

But today, employee leasing firms do a lot more than just offer better health-care rates. They manage everything from compliance with state and federal regulations to payroll, unemployment insurance, W-2 forms and claims processing—saving clients time and money. Some firms have even branched out to offer "extras" such as pension and employee assistance programs.

SMART TIP

MOTIVATING INDEPENDENT CONTRACTORS CAN BE TOUGH. HOW DO YOU MAKE THEM FEEL LIKE PART OF YOUR BUSINESS? COMMUNICATION IS KEY. SEND REGULAR MEMOS OR HOLD IN-PERSON MEETINGS WITH INDEPENDENT CONTRACTORS TO LET THEM KNOW WHAT'S GOING ON IN THE COMPANY. ALSO INCLUDE THEM IN COMPANY SOCIAL EVENTS, SUCH AS HOLIDAY PARTIES OR COMPANY PICNICS.

Look Before You Lease

How do you decide if an employee leasing company is for you? The National Association of Professional Employer Organizations (NAPEO) suggests you look for the following:

- **SERVICES THAT FIT** your human resources needs. Is the company flexible enough to work with you?
- **BANKING AND CREDIT** references. Evidence that the company's payroll taxes and insurance premiums are up-to-date. Request to see a certificate of insurance.
- **INVESTIGATE THE COMPANY'S** administrative competence. What experience does it have?
- **UNDERSTAND HOW EMPLOYEES'** benefits are funded. Do they fit your workers' needs? Find out who the third-party administrator or carrier is and whether it is licensed if your state requires this.
- **MAKE SURE THE LEASING** company is licensed or registered if required by your state.
- **ASK FOR CLIENT** and professional references, and call them.
- **REVIEW THE AGREEMENT** carefully and try to get a provision that permits you to cancel at short notice—say, 30 days.

For a list of NAPEO member organizations in your area, contact the NAPEO at (703) 836-0466 or write to 901 N. Pitt St., #150, Alexandria, VA 22314, or search their directory online at www.napeo.org/index-j.html.

While many business owners confuse employee leasing companies with temporary help businesses, the two organizations are quite different. Generally speaking, temporary help companies recruit employees and assign them to client businesses to help with short-term work overload or special projects on an as-needed basis, according to a spokesperson with the American Staffing Association. With leasing companies, on the other hand, a client business generally turns over all its personnel functions to an outside company, which will administer these operations and lease the employees back to the client.

According to the NAPEO, leasing services are contractual arrangements in which the leasing company is the employer of record for all or part of the client's work force. Employment responsibilities are typically shared between the PEO and the client, allowing the client to retain essential management control over the work performed by the employees.

Meanwhile, the PEO assumes responsibility for a wide range of employer obligations and risks, among them paying and reporting wages and employment taxes out of its own accounts as well as retaining some rights to the direction and control of the leased employees. The client, on the other hand, has one primary responsibility: writing one check to the PEO to cover the payroll, taxes, benefits and administrative fees. The PEO does the rest.

Who uses PEOs? According to the NAPEO, small businesses make up the primary market for leasing companies since—due to economies of scale—they typically pay higher premiums for employee benefits. If an employee hurts his or her back and files a workers' compensation claim, it could literally threaten the small business's existence. With another entity as the employer of record, however, these claims are no longer the small-business owner's problem. PEOs have also been known to help business owners avoid wrongful termination suits and negligent acts in the workplace, according to a NAPEO spokesperson.

Having to comply with a multitude of employment-related statutes, which is often beyond the means of smaller businesses, is another reason PEOs are so popular with entrepreneurs. According to the NAPEO, with a leasing company, you basically get the same type of human resources department you would get if you were a Fortune 500 firm.

BEWARE!

BE SURE YOU UNDERSTAND THE PRECISE LEGAL RELATIONSHIP BETWEEN YOUR BUSINESS AND A LEASING COMPANY. SOME PEOPLE CONSIDER THE LEASING COMPANY THE SOLE EMPLOYER, EFFECTIVELY INSULATING THE CLIENT FROM LEGAL RESPONSIBILITY. OTHERS CONSIDER THE CLIENT AND THE LEASING COMPANY JOINT EMPLOYERS, SHARING LEGAL RESPONSIBILITY. HAVE AN ATTORNEY REVIEW YOUR AGREEMENT TO CLARIFY ANY RISKS.

Before hiring a professional employer organization, be sure to shop around since not all offer the same pricing structures and services. Fees may be based on a modest percentage of payroll (3 to 5 percent) or on a per-employee basis. When comparing fees, consider what you would pay a full-time employee to handle the administrative chores the PEO will take off your hands. (For more information on what to look for, see "Look Before You Lease," on page 354).

355

Temporary Employees

If your business's staffing needs are seasonal—for example, you need extra workers during the holidays or during busy production periods—then temporary employees could be the answer to your problem. If the thought of a temp brings to mind a secretary, think again. The services and skills temporary help companies offer small businesses have expanded.

Today, some companies specialize in medical services; others find their niche in professional or technical fields, supplying everything from temporary engineers, editors and accountants to computer programmers, bankers, lab support staff and even attorneys.

With many temporary help companies now offering specialized employees, many business owners have learned that they don't have to settle for low skill levels or imperfect matches. Because most tem-

Temporary Treatment

How do you make the most of your temporary workers once they've come on board? For one, "don't treat them any differently from your other employees," says a spokesman for the American Staffing Association. "Introduce them to your full-time workers as people who are there to help you complete a project, to relieve some overtime stress, or to bring in some skills you might not have in house."

And don't expect temporary workers to be so well-trained that they know how to do all the little (but important) things, such as operating the copier or answering the phone. "Spend some time giving them a brief overview of these things, just as you would any new employee," advises Steinberg.

One strategy for building a better relationship with your temporary workers is to plan ahead as much as possible so you can use the same temporaries for an extended period of time—say, six months. Or try to get the same temporaries back when you need help again. This way, they'll be more productive, and you won't have to spend time retraining them.

porary help companies screen—and often train—their employees, entrepreneurs who choose this option stand a better chance of obtaining the quality employees they need for their business.

In addition to pre-screened, pre-trained individuals, temporary help companies offer entrepreneurs a slew of other benefits. For one, they help keep your overhead low. For another, they save you time and money on recruiting efforts. You don't have to find, interview or relocate workers. Also, the cost of health and unemployment benefits, workers' compensation insurance, profit-sharing, vacation time and other benefits doesn't come out of your budget since many temporary help companies provide these resources to their employees. (According to Tim Brogan of the American Staffing Association, "Virtually any employee who wants benefits can find a company that offers them.")

How do you find the temporary help company that best suits your needs—from light secretarial to specialized technical support? First, look in the Yellow Pages under "Employment Contractors—Temporary Help." Call a few and ask some questions, including:

- **DO YOU HAVE INSURANCE?** Look for adequate liability and workers' compensation coverage to protect your company from a temporary worker's claim.
- **DO YOU CHECK** on the progress of your temporaries?
- **HOW DO YOU RECRUIT** their temporaries?
- **HOW MUCH TRAINING** do you give temporaries? (According to the American Staffing Association, nearly 90 percent of the temporary work force receives free skills training of some kind.)
- **WHAT BENEFITS** do you offer your temporaries?
- **SHOULD A TEMPORARY FAIL** to work out, does the firm offer any guarantees? Look for a firm that can provide a qualified temp right away.
- **HOW QUICKLY** can you provide temporaries? (When you need one, you'll usually need one right away.)

Also ask the company to provide references. Contact references and ask their opinions of the temporary help company's quality level, reliability, reputation, service and training.

Before securing the services of a temporary help company, also consider your staffing needs. Do you need a part- or full-time temporary employee? What are your expectations? Clearly defining your needs helps the company understand and provide what you are looking for.

Defining the expected duration of your needs is also very important.

While many entrepreneurs bring on a temporary worker for just that—temporary work—some may eventually find they would like to hire the worker full time. Be aware that, at this point, some temporary help firms require a negotiated fee for "stealing" the employee away from them. Defining your needs upfront can help you avoid such penalties.

Because a growing number of entrepreneurs purposely use temporary workers part time to get a feel for whether they should hire them full time, many temporary help companies have begun offering an option: temporary-to-full-time programs, which allow the prospective employer and employee to evaluate each other. Temporary-to-full-time programs match a temporary worker who has expressed an interest in full-time work with an employer who has like interests. The client is encouraged to make a job offer to the employee within a predetermined time period, should the match seem like a good one. According to the American Staffing Association, 74 percent of temporary workers decide to become temporary employees because it's a way to get a full-time job.

Last, but not least, before contracting with a temporary help company, make sure it is a member of a trade association such as the American Staffing Association. This means: 1) The company has agreed to abide by a code of ethics and good practices, 2) it is in the business for the long haul—meaning it has invested in its industry by becoming a member of its trade association, and 3) it has access to up-to-date information on trends that impact its business.

Part-Time Personnel

Another way to cut overhead cost and benefits costs while gaining flexibility is by hiring part-time workers. Under current law, you are not required to provide part-timers with medical benefits.

What are the other benefits to you? By using permanent part-timers, you can get more commitment than you'd get from a temp but more flexibility than you can expect from a nine-to-fiver. In some industries, such as fast food, retail and other businesses that are open long hours, part-timers are essential to fill the odd hours during which workers are needed.

A traditional source of part-time employees is students. They typically are flexible, willing to work odd hours and do not require high wages. High school and college kids like employers who let them fit their work schedule to the changing demands of school.

Although students are ideal for many situations, there are potential drawbacks to be aware of. For one thing, a student's academic or social demands may impinge on your scheduling needs. Some students feel that a manicure or a tennis game is reason enough to change their work schedules. You'll need to be firm and set some standards for what is and is not acceptable.

Students are not the only part-timers in town, however. One often overlooked source of employees is retired people. Often, seniors are looking for a way to earn some extra money or fill their days. Many

The Intern Alternative

Some colleges encourage students to work, for a small stipend or even free, through internship programs. Student interns trade their time and talents in exchange for learning marketable job skills. Every year, colleges match thousands of students with businesses of all sizes and types. Since they have an eye on future career prospects, the students are usually highly motivated.

Does your tiny one-person office have anything to offer an intern? Actually, small companies offer better learning experiences for interns since they typically involve a greater variety of job tasks and offer a chance to work more closely with senior employees.

Routine secretarial or "gofer" work won't get you an intern in most cases. Colleges expect their interns to learn specialized professional skills. Hold up your end of the bargain by providing meaningful work. Can you delegate a direct-mail campaign? Have an intern help on photo shoots? Ask her to put together a client presentation?

Check with your local college or university to find out about internship programs. Usually, the school will send you an application, asking you to describe the job's responsibilities and your needs in terms of major, skill level and other qualifications. Then the school will send you resumes of students it thinks could work for you.

The best part of hiring interns? If you're lucky, you'll find a gem who'll stay with your company after the internship is over.

of these people have years of valuable business experience that could be a boon to your company.

Seniors offer many of the advantages of other part-time employees without the flakiness that sometimes characterizes younger workers. They typically have an excellent work ethic and can add a note of stability to your organization. If a lot of your customers are seniors, they may prefer dealing with employees their own age.

Parents of young children, too, offer a qualified pool of potential part-time workers. Many stay-at-home moms or dads would welcome the chance to get out of the house for a few hours a day. Often, these workers are highly skilled and experienced.

Finally, one employee pool many employers swear by is people with disabilities. Workers from a local shelter or nonprofit organization can excel at assembling products or packaging goods. In most cases, the charity group will work with you to oversee and provide a job coach for the employees. To find disabled workers in your area, contact the local Association of Retarded Citizens office or the Easter Seals Society.

BRIGHT IDEA

LIKE THE IDEA OF PART-TIME WORKERS BUT GOT A FULL-TIME SLOT TO FILL? TRY JOB SHARING—A STRATEGY IN WHICH TWO PART-TIMERS SHARE THE SAME JOB. SUSAN WORKS MONDAYS, TUESDAYS AND HALF OF WEDNESDAYS; PAM TAKES OVER WEDNESDAY AFTERNOONS, THURSDAYS AND FRIDAYS. TO MAKE IT WORK, HIRE PEOPLE WHO ARE COMPATIBLE IN SKILLS AND ABILITIES, AND KEEP LINES OF COMMUNICATION OPEN.

Outsourcing Options

One buzzword you are increasingly likely to hear is "outsourcing." Simply put, this refers to sending certain job functions outside a company instead of handling them in-house. For instance, instead of hiring an in-house bookkeeper, you might outsource the job to an independent accountant who comes in once a month or does all the work off-site.

More and more companies large and small are turning to outsourcing as a way to cut payroll and overhead costs. Done right, outsourcing can mean you never need to hire an employee at all!

How to make it work? Make sure the company or individual you use can do the job. That means getting (and checking) references. Ask former or current clients about their satisfaction. Find out what industries and what type of workload the firm or individual is used to handling. Can you expect your deadlines to be met, or will your small business's projects get pushed aside if a bigger client has an emergency?

Make sure you feel comfortable with who will be doing the work and that you can discuss your concerns and needs openly. Ask to see samples of work if appropriate (for example, if you're using a graphic design firm).

If your outsourcing needs are handled by an individual, you're dealing with an independent contractor. The IRS has stringent rules regulating exactly who is and is not considered an independent contractor. The risk: If you consider a person an independent contractor and the IRS later reclassifies him or her as an employee, you could be liable for that person's Social Security taxes and a wide range of other costs and penalties.

For more on independent contractors, see Part 8, Chapter 41. If you're still in doubt, it always pays to consult your accountant. Making a mistake in this area could cost you big.

GLOSSARY

CROSS-TRAINING: training employees to fill more than one position

EMPLOYEE LEASING COMPANY: company that administers personnel functions for clients and "leases" the client's employees back to them; also known as a professional employer organization (PEO)

EXECUTIVE SEARCH FIRM: company that recruits executive, technical or professional job candidates for client companies; also called recruitment firm or headhunter

JOB DESCRIPTION: an outline of how a job fits into the company, listing broad goals and basic responsibilities

JOB SPECIFICATION: more detailed than a job description, this describes the job but also lists specific education, experience, skills, knowledge, or physical requirements for performing the job

OUTSOURCING: practice of sending certain job functions outside a company instead of having an in-house department or employee handle them; functions can be outsourced to a company or an individual

TEMPORARY HELP COMPANY: company that recruits employees to work for client companies on a temporary basis

WAIVER: form that typically accompanies or is part of an employment application; when signed by applicant, it authorizes former employers or schools to release information about the applicant

Treat Your "Children" Well

Developing an employee benefits plan

Once you have great employees on board, how do you keep them from jumping ship? One way is by offering a good benefits package.

Many small-business owners mistakenly believe they cannot afford to offer benefits. But while going without benefits may boost your bottom line in the short run, that penny-wise philosophy could strangle your business's chance for long-term prosperity. "There are certain benefits good employees feel they must have," says Ray Silverstein, founder of PRO, President's Resource Organization, a small-business advisory network.

Heading the list of must-have benefits is medical insurance, but many job applicants also demand a retirement plan, disability insurance and more. Tell these applicants no benefits are offered, and often top-flight candidates will head for the door.

The positive side to this coin: Offer the right benefits, and your business may just jump-start its growth. "Give employees the benefits they value, and they'll be more satisfied, miss fewer workdays, be less likely to quit, and have a higher commitment to meeting the company's goals," says Joe Lineberry, a senior vice president at Aon Consulting, a human resources consulting firm. "The research shows that when employees feel their benefits needs are satisfied, they're more productive."

BENEFIT BASICS

The law requires employers to provide employees with certain benefits. You must:

- **GIVE EMPLOYEES TIME OFF TO VOTE,** serve on a jury and perform military service.
- **COMPLY WITH ALL WORKERS' COMPENSATION REQUIREMENTS** (see Part 5, Chapter 25).
- **WITHHOLD FICA TAXES** from employees' paychecks and pay your own portion of FICA taxes, providing employees with retirement and disability benefits.
- **PAY STATE AND FEDERAL UNEMPLOYMENT TAXES,** thus providing benefits for unemployed workers.

- **CONTRIBUTE TO STATE SHORT-TERM DISABILITY** programs in states where such programs exist.
- **COMPLY WITH THE FEDERAL FAMILY AND MEDICAL LEAVE** Act (see "Family Matters," below).

You are not required to provide:

- **RETIREMENT PLANS**
- **HEALTH PLANS** (except in Hawaii)
- **DENTAL OR VISION PLANS**
- **LIFE INSURANCE PLANS**
- **PAID VACATIONS,** holidays or sick leave

In reality, however, most companies offer some or all of these benefits to stay competitive.

Most employers provide paid holidays for Christmas Day, New Year's, Memorial Day, Independence Day, Labor Day and Thanksgiving Day. Many employers also either allow their employees to take time off without pay or let them use vacation days for religious holidays.

Most full-time employees will expect one to two weeks' paid vacation time per year. In explaining your vacation policy to employees, specify how far in advance requests for vacation time should be made, and whether in writing or verbally.

There are no laws that require employers to provide funeral leave, but most do allow two to four days' leave for deaths of close family

Family Matters

The federal Family and Medical Leave Act (FMLA) requires employers to give workers up to 12 weeks off to attend to the birth or adoption of a baby, or the serious health condition of the employee or an immediate family member.

After 12 weeks of unpaid leave, you must reinstate the employee in the same job or an equivalent one. The 12 weeks of leave does not have to be taken all at once; in some cases, employees can take it a day at a time.

In most states, only employers with 50 or more employees are subject to the Family and Medical Leave Act. However, some states have family leave laws that place family leave requirements on businesses with as few as five employees. To find out your state's requirements, contact your state labor department members. Companies that don't do this generally allow employees to use some other form of paid leave, such as sick days or vacation.

Legal Matters

Complications quickly arise as soon as a business begins offering benefits, however. That's because key benefits such as health insurance and retirement plans fall under government scrutiny, and "it is very easy to make mistakes in setting up a benefits plan," says Kathleen Meagher, an attorney specializing in benefits at Kirkpatrick Lockhart LLP.

And don't think nobody will notice. The IRS can discover in an audit that what you are doing does not comply with regulations. So can the U.S. Department of Labor, which has been beefing up its audit activities of late. Either way, a goof can be very expensive. "You can lose any tax benefits you have enjoyed, retroactively, and penalties can also be imposed," Meagher says.

The biggest mistake? Leaving employees out of the plan. Examples range from exclusions of part-timers to failing to extend benefits to clerical and custodial staff. A rule of thumb is that if one employee gets a tax-advantaged benefit—meaning one paid for with pretax dollars—the same benefit must be extended to everyone. There are loopholes that may allow you to exclude some workers, but don't even think about trying this without expert advice.

Such complexities mean it's good advice never to go this route alone. You can cut costs by doing preliminary research yourself, but before setting up any benefits plan, consult a lawyer or a benefits consultant. An upfront investment of perhaps $1,000 could save you far more money down the road by helping you sidestep expensive potholes.

Expensive Errors

Providing benefits that meet employee needs and mesh with all the laws isn't cheap—benefits probably add 30 to 40 percent to base pay for most employees—and that makes it crucial to get the most from these dollars. But this is exactly where many small businesses fall short, because often their approach to benefits is riddled with costly errors that can get them in financial trouble with their insurers or even with their own employees. The most common mistakes:

■ **ABSORBING THE ENTIRE COST OF EMPLOYEE BENEFITS:** Fewer companies are footing the whole benefits bill these days. According to a survey of California companies by human resources management consulting firm William M. Mercer, 91 percent of employers require employee contributions toward health insurance, while 92 percent require employees to contribute toward the cost of insuring dependents. The size of employee contributions varies from a few dollars per pay period to several hundred dollars monthly, but one plus of any co-payment plan is that it eliminates employees who don't need coverage. Many employees are covered under other policies—a parent's or spouse's, for instance—and if you offer insurance for free, they'll take it. But even small co-pay requirements will persuade many to skip it, saving you money.

■ **COVERING NONEMPLOYEES:** Who would do this? Lots of business owners want to buy group-rate coverage for their relatives or friends. The trouble: If there is a large claim, the insurer may

Above And Beyond

What does COBRA mean to you? No, it's not a poisonous snake coming back to bite you in the butt. The Consolidated Omnibus Budget Reconciliation Act (COBRA) extends health-insurance coverage to employees and dependents beyond the point at which such coverage traditionally ceases.

COBRA allows a former employee after he or she has quit or been terminated (except for gross misconduct) the right to con-tinued coverage under your group health plan for up to 18 months. Employees' spouses can obtain COBRA coverage for up to 36 months after divorce or the death of the employee, and children can receive up to 36 months of coverage when they reach the age at which they are no longer classified as depend-ents under the group health plan.

The good news: Giving COBRA benefits shouldn't cost your company a penny. Employers are permitted by law to charge recipients 102 percent of the cost of extending the benefits (the extra 2 percent covers administrative costs).

The federal COBRA plan applies to all companies with more than 20 employees. However, many states have similar laws that pertain to much smaller companies, so even if your company is exempt from federal insurance laws, you may still have to extend benefits under certain circumstances. Contact the U.S. Department of Labor to determine whether your company must offer COBRA or similar benefits, and the rules for doing so.

want to investigate. And that investigation could result in disallowance of the claims, even cancellation of the whole policy. Whenever you want to cover somebody who might not qualify for the plan, tell the insurer or your benefits consultant the truth.

■ **SLOPPY PAPERWORK:** In small businesses, administering benefits is often assigned to an employee who wears 12 other hats. This employee really isn't familiar with the technicalities and misses a lot of important details. A common goof: Not enrolling new employees in plans during the open enrollment period. Most plans provide a fixed time period for open enrollment. Bringing an employee in later requires proof of insurability. Expensive litigation is sometimes the result. Make sure the employee overseeing this task stays current with the paperwork and knows that doing so is a top priority.

■ **NOT TELLING EMPLOYEES WHAT THEIR BENEFITS COST:** "Most employees don't appreciate their benefits, but that's because nobody ever tells them what the costs are," says PRO's Silverstein. Many experts suggest you annually provide employees with a benefits statement that spells out what they are getting and at what cost. A simple rundown of the employee's individual benefits and what they cost the business is very powerful.

■ **GIVING UNWANTED BENEFITS:** A work force composed largely of young, single people doesn't need life insurance. How to know what benefits employees value? You can survey employees and have them rank benefits in terms of desirability. Typically, medical and financial benefits, such as retirement plans, appeal to the broadest cross-section of workers.

If workers' needs vary widely, consider the increasingly popular "cafeteria plans," which give workers lengthy lists of possible benefits plus a fixed amount to spend.

HEALTH INSURANCE

Health insurance is one of the most desirable benefits you can offer employees. There are several basic options for setting up a plan:

■ **A TRADITIONAL INDEMNITY PLAN, OR FEE FOR SERVICE:** Employees choose their medical care provider; the insurance company either pays the provider directly or reimburses employees for covered amounts.

- **MANAGED CARE:** The two most common forms of managed care are the Health Maintenance Organization (HMO) and the Preferred Provider Organization (PPO). An HMO is essentially a prepaid health-care arrangement, where employees must use doctors employed by or under contract to the HMO and hospitals approved by the HMO. Under a PPO, the insurance company negotiates discounts with the physicians and the hospitals. Employees choose doctors from an approved list, then usually pay a set amount per office visit (typically $10 to $25); the insurance company pays the rest.

HOT LINK

YOU CAN CHECK OUT STANDARD & POOR'S INSURANCE RATINGS AT WWW.FUNDS-SP.COM.

- **SELF-INSURANCE:** When you absorb all or a significant portion of a risk, you are essentially self-insuring. An outside company usually handles the paperwork, you pay the claims, and sometimes employees help pay premiums. The benefits include greater control of the plan design, customized reporting procedures and cash-flow advantages. The drawback is that you are liable for claims, but you can limit liability with "stop loss" insurance—if a claim exceeds a certain dollar amount, the insurance company pays it.

- **ARCHER MEDICAL SAVINGS ACCOUNTS:** Under this program, an employee of a small employer (50 or fewer employees) or a self-employed person can set up an Archer MSA to help pay health-care expenses. The accounts are set up with a U.S. financial institution and allow you to save money exclusively for medical expenses. When used in conjunction with a high deductible insurance policy, accounts are funded with employees' pretax dollars. Under the Archer MSA program, disbursements are tax-free if used for approved medical expenses. Unused funds in the account can accumulate indefinitely and earn tax-free interest. Health-savings accounts (HSAs), available as of January 2004, are similar to MSAs but are not restricted to small employers.

HOT LINK

SMALL-BUSINESS OWNERS CAN EVALUATE THEIR OPTIONS AND CONSULT WITH INSURANCE BROKERS FREE AND ONLINE AT BENEFITMALL.COM (WWW.BENEFIT MALL.COM). THIS SITE ALSO OFFERS A CRASH COURSE ON INSURANCE ITSELF, SO YOU CAN KNOW WHAT YOU'RE LOOKING AT WHEN YOU COMPARE PLANS FOR YOUR BUSINESS.

Cost Containment

The rising costs of health insurance have forced some small businesses to cut back on the benefits they offer. Carriers that write policies for small businesses tend to charge very high premiums. Often, they demand extensive medical information about each employee. If anyone in the group has a pre-existing condition, the carrier may refuse to write a policy. Or, if someone in the company becomes seriously ill, the carrier may cancel the policy the next time it comes up for renewal.

Further complicating matters, some states are mandating certain health-care benefits so that if an employer offers a plan at all, it has to include certain types of coverage. Employers who can't afford to comply often have to cut out insurance altogether.

The good news: Many states are trying to ease the burden by passing laws that make it easier for small businesses to get health insurance and that prohibit insurance carriers from discriminating against small firms. (MSAs, described above, are in part a response to the problems small businesses face.) The following states make some special provision concerning small employers and health insurance: California, Connecticut, Illinois, Iowa, Kansas, Maine, Massachusetts, New Jersey, North Carolina, Oregon, South Carolina, Tennessee, Wisconsin and Wyoming.

Until more laws are passed, what can a small business do? There are ways to cut costs without cutting into your employees' insurance plan. A growing number of small businesses band together with other entrepreneurs to enjoy economies of scale and gain more clout with insurance carriers.

Many trade associations offer health insurance plans for small-business owners and their employees at lower rates. Your business may have only five employees, but united with the other, say, 9,000 association members and their 65,000 employees, you have substantial clout. The carrier issues a policy to the whole association; your business's coverage cannot be terminated unless the carrier cancels the entire association.

Associations are able to negotiate lower rates and improved coverage because the carrier doesn't want to lose such a big chunk of business. This way, even the smallest one-person company can choose from the same menu of health-care options that big companies enjoy.

Associations aren't the only route to take. In some states, business owners or groups have set up health-insurance networks among

businesses that have nothing in common but their size and their location. Check with your local chamber of commerce to find out about such programs in your area.

Some people have been ripped off by unscrupulous organizations supposedly peddling "group" insurance plans at prices 20 to 40 percent below the going rate. The problem: These plans don't pay all policyholders' claims because they're not backed by sufficient cash reserves. Such plans often have lofty-sounding names that suggest a larger association of small employers.

How to protect yourself from a scam? Here are some tips:

- **COMPARE PRICES.** If it sounds too good to be true, it probably is. Ask for references from other companies that have bought from the plan. How quick was the insurer in paying claims? How long has the reference dealt with the insurer? If it's less than a few months, that's not a good sign.

- **CHECK THE PLAN'S UNDERWRITER.** The underwriter is the actual insurer. Many scam plans claim to be administrators for underwriters that really have nothing to do with them. Call the underwriter's headquarters and the insurance department of the state in which it's registered to see if it is really affiliated with the plan. To check the underwriter's integrity, ask your state's insurance department for its "A.M. Best" rating, which grades companies according to their ability to pay claims. Also ask for its "claims-paying ability rating," which is monitored by services like Standard & Poor's. If the company is too new to be rated, be wary.

- **MAKE SURE THE COMPANY FOLLOWS STATE REGULATIONS.** Does the company claim it's exempt? Check with your state's insurance department.

- **ASK THE AGENT OR ADMINISTRATOR TO SHOW YOU WHAT HIS OR HER COMMISSION, ADVANCE OR ADMINISTRATIVE COST STRUCTURE IS.** Overly generous commissions can be a tip-off; some scam operations pay agents up to 500 percent commission.

■ **GET HELP.** Ask other business owners if they have dealt with the company. Contact the Better Business Bureau to see if there are any outstanding complaints. If you think you're dealing with a questionable company, contact your state insurance department or your nearest Labor Department Office of Investigations.

RETIREMENT PLANS

A big mistake some business owners make is thinking they cannot afford to fund a retirement plan in lieu of putting profits back into the business. But less than half of the employees at small companies participate in retirement plans. And companies that do offer this benefit report increased employee retention and happier, more efficient workers. Also, don't forget about yourself: Many business owners are at risk of having insufficient funds saved for retirement.

To encourage more businesses to launch retirement plans, the Economic Growth and Tax Relief Reconciliation Act of 2001 provides a tax credit for costs associated with starting a retirement plan, including a 401(k) plan, SIMPLE plan or Simplified Employee Pension (SEP). The credit equals 50 percent of the first $1,000 of qualified start-up costs, including expenses to set up and administer the plan and educate employees about it. For more information, see IRS Form 8881, *Credit for Small Employer Pension Plan Start-up Costs.*

Don't ignore the value of investing early. If, starting at age 35, you invested $3,000 each year with a 14 percent annual return, you would have an annual retirement income of nearly $60,000 at age 65. But $5,000 invested at the same rate of return beginning at age 45 only results in $30,700 in annual retirement income. The benefit of retirement plans is that savings grow tax-free until you withdraw the funds—typically age 59. If you withdraw funds before that age, the withdrawn amount is fully taxable and also subject to a 10 percent penalty. The value of tax-free investing over time means it's best to start right away, even if you start with small increments.

Besides the long-term benefit of providing for your future, setting up a retirement plan also has the immediate gratification of cutting taxes.

BRIGHT IDEA

IRS PUBLICATION 560, *RETIREMENT PLANS FOR SMALL BUSINESS*, DESCRIBES RULES FOR SEP, SIMPLE AND OTHER QUALIFIED PLANS. IT'S FREE; VISIT WWW.IRS.GOV OR CALL (800) TAX-FORM.

Here is a closer look at a range of retirement plans for yourself and your employees.

Individual Retirement Account (IRA)

An IRA is a tax-qualified retirement savings plan available to anyone who works and/or their spouse, whether the individual is an employee or a self-employed person. One of the biggest advantages of these plans is that the earnings on your IRA grow on a tax-deferred basis until you start withdrawing the funds. Whether your contribution to an IRA is deductible will depend on your income level and whether you are covered by another retirement plan at work.

You also may want to consider a Roth IRA. While contributions are not tax deductible, withdrawals you make at retirement will not be taxed. The maximum annual contribution individuals can put in either a Roth or a traditional IRA is $3,000 for 2004, assuming they meet the eligibility requirements.

To qualify for Roth IRA contributions, a single person's adjusted gross income (AGI) must be less than $95,000, with benefits phasing out completely at $110,000. For married couples filing jointly, the AGI must be less than $150,000. The contribution amount is decreased by 30 percent (35 percent if 50 or older) until it is eliminated completely at $160,000 for joint filers. For 2005 to 2007, the contribution limit for both single and joint filers climbs to $4,000 per person and to $5,000 per person in 2008. After that, contributions are indexed to inflation.

Regardless of income level, you can qualify for a deductible IRA as long as you do not participate in an employer sponsored retirement plan, such as a 401(k). If you are in an employer plan, you can qualify for a deductible IRA if you meet the income requirements. Keep in mind that it's possible to set up or make annual contributions to an IRA any time you want up to the date your federal income tax return is due for that year, not including extensions. The contribution amounts for deductible IRAs are the same as for Roth IRAs.

For joint filers, even if one spouse is covered by a retirement plan, the spouse who is not covered by a plan may make a deductible IRA contribution if the couple's adjusted gross income is $150,000 or less. Like the Roth IRA, the amount you can deduct is decreased in stages above that income level and is eliminated entirely for couples with incomes over $160,000. Nonworking spouses and their working partners can contribute up to $6,000 to IRAs ($3,000 each), provided the working spouse earns at least $6,000. It's possible to contribute an additional $500 for each spouse who is at least 50 years old at the end of the year, as long as there is the necessary earned income. For example, two spouses over 50 could contribute a total of $7,000 if there is at least $7,000 of earned income.

Savings Incentive Match Plan For Employees (SIMPLE)

SIMPLE plans are one of the most attractive options available for small-business owners. With these plans, you can choose to use a 401(k) or an IRA as your retirement plan.

Manual Labor

Sooner or later, every entrepreneur needs to write a manual. An employee policy manual, a procedures manual or a safety manual are just a few of the more important ones.

Even if you only have one employee, it's not too soon to start putting policies in writing. Doing so now—before your staff grows—can prevent bickering, confusion and lawsuits later when Steve finds out you gave Joe five sick days and he only got four.

How to start? As with everything, begin by planning. Write a detailed outline of what you want to include.

As you write, focus on making sure the manual is easy to read and understand. Think of the simplest, shortest way to convey information. Use bullet points and numbered lists, where possible, for easier reading.

A lawyer or a human resources consultant can be invaluable throughout the process. At the very least, you'll want your attorney to review the finished product for loopholes.

Finally, ensure all new employees receive a copy of the manual and read it. Include a page that employees must sign, date and return to you stating they have read and understood all the information in the manual and agree to abide by your company's policies. Maintain this in their personnel file.

A SIMPLE plan is just that—simple to administer. This type of retirement plan doesn't come with a lot of paperwork and reporting requirements.

You can set up a SIMPLE IRA only if you have 100 or fewer employees who have received $5,000 or more in compensation from you in the preceding year. The employer must make contributions to the plan by either matching each participating employee's contribution, dollar for dollar, up to 3 percent of each employee's pay, or by making an across-the-board 2 percent contribution for all employees, even if they don't participate in the plan, which can be expensive.

The maximum amount each employee can contribute to the plan can't be more than $9,000 for 2004; the amount increases to $10,000 in 2005. After that, the amount will be indexed for inflation. Participants in a SIMPLE IRA who are age 50 or over at the end of the calendar year can also make a catch-up contribution of an additional $1,500 in 2004, $2,000 in 2005 and $2,500 in 2006.

Simplified Employee Pension (SEP) Plan

As its name implies, this is the simplest type of retirement plan available. Essentially, a SEP is a glorified IRA that allows you to contribute a set percentage up to a maximum amount each year. Paperwork is minimal, and you don't have to contribute every year. And regardless of the name, you don't need employees to set one up.

If you do have employees—well, that's the catch. Employees do not make any contributions to SEPs. Employers must pay the full cost of the plan, and whatever percentage you contribute for yourself must be applied to all eligible employees. The maximum contribution is 25 percent of an employee's compensation (up to a maximum of $200,000) or $40,000, whichever is less.

As your company grows, you may want to consider other types of retirement plans, such as Keogh or 401(k) plans. For more information on these retirement plans, see *Entrepreneur's* start-up guide No. 1812, *Growing Your Business*.

Where To Go

With so many choices available, it's a good idea to talk to your accountant about which type of plan is best for you. Once you know what you want, where do you go to set up a retirement plan?

Banks, investment companies, full-service or discount brokers, and independent financial advisors can all help you set up a plan that meets your needs. Many of these institutions also offer self-managed brokerage accounts that let you combine investments in mutual funds, stocks, bonds and certificates of deposit (CDs).

LOW-COST BENEFITS

In addition to the standard benefits discussed above, there are plenty of benefits that cost your company little or nothing but reap huge rewards in terms of employee satisfaction and loyalty. Consider these ideas:

- **NEGOTIATE DISCOUNTS** with local merchants for your employees. Hotels, restaurants and amusement parks may offer discounts on their various attractions, including lodging and food through corporate customer programs. Warehouse stores, such as Sam's Club, allow discounted membership to employees of their corporate members. Movie theaters provide reduced-rate tickets for companies' employees. Don't forget to offer employees free or discounted prices on your own company products and services.
- **ASK A LOCAL DRY CLEANER** for free pickup and delivery of your employees' clothes. Or ask a garage for free transportation to and from work for employees having their cars serviced there. Many businesses are willing to provide this service to capture—and keep—new customers.
- **OFFER FREE LUNCH-TIME SEMINARS** to employees. Health-care workers, financial planners, safety experts, attorneys and other professionals will often offer their speaking services at no charge. Education is beneficial for both your employees and your business.
- **OFFER SUPPLEMENTAL INSURANCE** plans that are administered through payroll but are paid for by the employee. Carriers of health, life, auto and accident insurance typically offer these plans at a lower rate to employers, so everybody benefits.
- **OFFER A PREPAID LEGAL-SERVICES PLAN** administered through payroll but paid for by the employee. Like insurance, the purpose of the prepaid legal service is to provide protection against the emotional and financial stress of an employee's legal problems. Such services include phone consultations regarding personal or business-related legal matters, contract and document review, preparation of wills, legal representation in cases involving motor vehicle

SMART TIP

TAKING TIME TO THANK YOUR EMPLOYEES PAYS OFF IN PERFORMANCE. SOME WAYS TO  SHOW APPRECIATION: SEND BIRTHDAY CARDS TO WORKERS' HOMES. WRITE CONGRATULATORY NOTES FOR A JOB WELL DONE. USE FOOD TO BOOST MORALE—POPSICLES ON A HOT DAY OR HOT CHOCOLATE IN THE WINTER. SMALL THINGS MAKE A BIG DIFFERENCE IN MAKING EMPLOYEES FEEL VALUED.

violations, trial defense services and IRS-audit legal services.

The employer deducts the monthly service fee from the paychecks of those employees who want to take advantage of the service. Typical fees range from $15 to $25 per month per employee and cover most routine and preventive legal services at no additional cost. More extensive legal services are provided at a lower rate when offered in this manner, saving employees money.

■ **HOW ABOUT AN INTEREST-FREE COMPUTER-LOAN PROGRAM?** Making it easier for employees to purchase computers for their personal use increases the technical productivity of employees on the job. The employee chooses the computer and peripherals based on the employer's parameters. (For example, the computer must be a Macintosh, and the entire package may not exceed $3,000.) The company purchases the system, allows the employee to take it home, and deducts the payments from his or her paycheck. Although there's some initial capital outlay, it is recouped quickly. Any computer experience an employee can gain at home will most likely help enhance his or her proficiency in the workplace.

■ **LET EMPLOYEES PURCHASE EXCESS INVENTORY** from your business at a significant discount via sample sales or employee auctions. Arrange these purchases in conjunction with regularly scheduled companywide "yard sales" for employees to buy and sell their personal belongings.

One of the most appreciated, but most overlooked, benefits is membership in a credit union. There are some 6,000 well-established, state-chartered credit unions throughout the United States and Canada that accept start-up businesses as members—at no charge.

The benefits to your employees are threefold: Most likely they'll increase their savings rates (especially if you offer automatic payroll deduction), have access to lower loan rates, and pay lower fees—if any—for services. Services credit unions frequently offer include:

■ Automatic payroll deductions
■ Individual retirement accounts

- Savings certificates (often at higher yields than at banks or savings and loans)
- Personal and auto loans
- Lines of credit
- Checking accounts
- Christmas club accounts

Only state-chartered credit unions are allowed to add new companies to their membership rosters. To find a credit union that will accept your company, call your state's league of credit unions. You can also write to the National Credit Union Association, P.O. Box 431, Madison, WI 53701, or call (800) 356-9655, to receive a list of state leagues, or print the list off their Web site at www.creditunion.org.

When comparing credit unions, get references and check them. Find out how communicative and flexible the credit union is. Examine the accessibility. Are there ATMs? Is there a location near your business? Consider the end users—your employees.

Once your company is approved, designate one person to be the primary liaison with the credit union. That person will maintain information about memberships as well as enrollment forms and loan applications. Kick things off by asking a credit union representative to conduct on-site enrollment and perhaps return periodically for follow-up or new sign-ups.

EMPLOYEE POLICIES

Now that you have employees, you'll need to set policies on everything from pay rates to safety procedures. Many of these policies are regulated by federal and state laws. Here's what you need to know.

Paying Employees

There are many state and federal laws that regulate the paying of employees, including the calculation of overtime, minimum wage, frequency of payment, and rules for payment upon termination. Because your business may be subject to both state and federal laws (the primary federal law being the Fair Labor Standards Act, or FLSA), which are often quite different and conflicting, you should check with the applicable government agencies, your local chamber of commerce, and appropriate financial and legal experts to determine which laws apply and how to correctly apply them.

Nonexempt And Exempt Employees

Under the FLSA, all employees are classified as either exempt or nonexempt. A nonexempt employee is entitled to a minimum wage and overtime pay as well as other protections set forth in the FLSA.

Exempt employees are not protected under these rules. However, if you wish to classify an employee as exempt, you must pay him or her a salary. Anyone paid on an hourly basis is automatically considered nonexempt; however, there can be nonexempt employees who are paid a salary.

BRIGHT IDEA

WANT TO GET AN IDEA WHAT OTHERS IN YOUR INDUSTRY ARE PAYING WORKERS? THE BUREAU OF LABOR STATISTICS OFFERS THE *NATIONAL COMPENSATION SURVEY* FOR MOST REGIONS OF THE COUNTRY. THE INFORMATION IS BROKEN DOWN BY OCCUPATION AND BY VARIOUS LEVELS OF EXPERIENCE WITHIN THAT OCCUPATION. THE BUREAU ALSO HAS INFORMATION ABOUT BENEFITS. TO ACCESS THE REPORTS, VISIT HTTP://STATS.BLS.GOV/NCS, OR CALL THE BUREAU OF LABOR STATISTICS' REGIONAL OFFICES.

If salary is not the determining factor, what factors determine whether an employee is exempt? Under FLSA and most state laws, an exempt employee is one whose job responsibilities, more than 50 percent of the time, involve the regular exercise of discretionary powers and can be characterized as:

- **EXECUTIVE:** usually a manager who directs the work of other employees and has the authority to make recommendations affecting the status of those employees (e.g., hiring, firing, promotions, etc.)
- **ADMINISTRATIVE:** a person who performs office or nonmanual work under general supervision and which primarily involves special assignments or requires specialized training, experience or education
- **PROFESSIONAL:** a person who is engaged in a recognized profession such as medicine or law or in a field of learning that is specialized and predominantly intellectual or creative

There are additional exempt categories for more specialized employees, such as professional artist, computer professional or outside salesperson. In addition, your business may be subject to both federal and often more restrictive state laws governing the exempt status of employees. In those instances, an employee must meet the requirements for exemption under both federal and state law.

Tip Credits

States sometimes set minimum wage laws above or below the federal minimum wage standard. If your business is subject to both state and federal wage laws, you'll have to pay the higher of the two.

Under federal law (the Small Business Job Protection Act of 1996), you may apply tips received by an employee against the employee's minimum hourly wage, provided that: 1) The employee makes at least $30 in tips, 2) the employer pays at least 50 percent of the federal minimum wage, 3) the employee has been informed of the applicable law governing minimum wage and tip credits, and 4) the employee retains all the tips received by him or her (no tip pooling with other employees). However, if the hourly wage paid by the employer when added to the tip credit is less than the minimum wage, the employee must make up the difference.

Once again, you will need to make sure there are no contrary state laws governing if and when you can use tip credits to meet your minimum wage obligations. For example, California law requires a higher minimum wage than federal law and thus applies to California employers and employees. Because California law prohibits crediting tips against minimum wage payments, tip credits are unavailable in California.

Overtime Requirements

Excluding certain industry-specific exceptions, federal and state law requires that nonexempt employees be paid overtime. Under the FLSA, nonexempt employees must be paid one-and-a-half times their normal rate of pay for hours worked in excess of 40 hours during a workweek. A workweek is defined as seven consecutive 24-hour periods. Although a workweek can begin on any day, it must be fixed for that employee and cannot be changed so as to evade applicable overtime laws. Most states also have their own overtime laws, and if they are more favorable to employees, those are the ones you must

BEWARE!

As a boss, are you a saint...or a Scrooge? Read Jim Miller's *Best Boss, Worst Boss* (Fireside Books) to get an idea how you rate. Miller collected real-life stories (like the tightwad boss who charges employees 30 cents per personal call). Good bosses, by contrast, are generous, compassionate and empowering. Result? Happier, more productive and loyal employees.

follow. For example, under California law, employees who work more than eight hours during a single day are entitled to overtime, even if they do not work more than 40 hours during a given work-week (the federal requirement).

Remember, nonexempt employees can be salaried as well as hourly. So don't make the mistake of assuming that, just because an employee is salaried, he or she is exempt from overtime.

WORKPLACE SAFETY

Why worry about safety? Because failing to do so could literally destroy your business. Besides the human loss, workplace accidents cost money and time. You could be liable for substantial penalties that could wipe out your business's cash flow. The Occupational Safety and Health Administration's (OSHA) penalty for willful violations of safety rules that could result in death or serious physical harm is $5,000 to $70,000. So paying attention to safety is definitely worth your while.

OSHA Regulations

All employers, whether they have one employee or 1,000, are subject to federal OSHA requirements. However, in states where a federally certified plan has been adopted, the state plan governs. State standards must be at least as strict as the federal standards.

Businesses that use nonemployee workers, such as independent contractors or volunteers, are not subject to OSHA. Workers are considered employees under OSHA if you:

■ **CONTROL THE ACTIONS** of the employee
■ **HAVE THE POWER** to control the employee's actions
■ **ARE ABLE TO FIRE THE EMPLOYEE** or modify employment conditions

Small employers (with 10 or fewer employees) don't have to report injuries and illnesses. However, that doesn't mean they are exempt from OSHA regulations.

Compliance With OSHA

The first step in complying with OSHA is to learn the published safety standards. The standards you must adhere to depend on the industry you're in.

Every business has to comply with general industry standards, which cover things like safety exits, ventilation, hazardous materials, personal protective equipment like goggles and gloves, sanitation, first aid and fire safety.

Under OSHA, you also have a general duty to maintain a safe workplace, which covers all situations for which there are published standards. In other words, just because you complied with the standards that specifically apply to your industry doesn't mean you're off the hook. You also need to keep abreast of possible hazards from new technology or rare situations the government may have thought of and published standards for.

Sound exhausting? Help is available. Start with your insurance carrier. Ask if an insurance company safety specialist can visit your business and make recommendations. Insurers are typically more than happy to do this since the safer your business is, the fewer accident claims you'll file. The government can also help you set up a safety program. Both OSHA and state safety organizations conduct safety consultation programs. Check to see what programs your state safety department offers, too. You'll find local offices of government agencies as well as state organizations listed in the government pages of your phone book, usually under "Labor Department," "Department of Commerce" or a similar name.

Don't forget to tap into the resources of your chamber of commerce, industry trade association and other business groups. Many offer safety seminars and provide safety training literature free or for a nominal charge. In addition, there are private consultants who can help small businesses set up safety programs that meet OSHA regulatory standards. Your lawyer may be able to recommend a good one in your area.

Put It In Writing

When you have a safety program in place, put it in writing with a safety manual (see "Manual Labor" on page 374). Your safety manual should explain what to do in the event of a fire, explosion, natural disaster or any other catastrophe your business may face. Make sure you keep well-stocked fire extinguishers and first-aid kits at convenient locations throughout your building. Also make sure employees know where these are located and how to use them. In addition to emergency procedures, your safety manual should explain proper procedures for performing any routine tasks that could be hazardous. Ask employees for input here; they are closest to the jobs and may know about dangerous situations that aren't obvious to you.

Finally, have an insurance professional, a government representative and an attorney review the finished manual. You're putting your company's commitment to safety on the line, so make sure you get it right.

Emphasize the importance of safety with meetings, inspections and incentive programs. These don't have to cost a lot (or anything). Try establishing a "Safe Employee of the Month" award or giving a certificate for a free dinner for winning suggestions on improving safety.

DISCRIMINATORY TREATMENT?

Although sexual harassment is one of the biggest issues facing employers these days, it's not the only type of discrimination you need to be concerned about. Under the Civil Rights Act of 1991, employees who believe they were victims of job discrimination due to race, religion, sex or disability are entitled to a trial by jury.

While companies with fewer than 15 employees are generally exempt from federal discrimination laws, most states have their own laws prohibiting discrimination, which, in addition to protecting a wider range of categories of employees, include smaller businesses within their scope and procedural and evidentiary standards more favorable to claimants. Apart from the tendency of some juries to award plaintiffs disproportionately high monetary damages, litigation in this area of the law can be extremely costly, even if you prevail. One attorney estimates the average legal fees for defense in a sexual harassment suit, regardless of the verdict, are upwards of $75,000.

Concerns over discrimination are more important than ever in today's increasingly diverse business world. If you run a small business, chances are you will be dealing with employees from many cultures, races and age groups. How can you keep things running harmoniously and protect your business from legal risk? The best policy is to make sure that everyone in your workplace understands what constitutes harassment and discrimination—and also understands the benefits of a diverse workplace.

BEWARE!

LEARN TO SPOT SOME OF THE SIGNS THAT SEXUAL HARASSMENT MAY BE OCCURRING IN YOUR COMPANY. INCREASED ABSENTEEISM, DROP-OFFS IN PRODUCTIVITY AND LACKLUSTER PERFORMANCE ARE ALL SIGNS THAT SOMETHING MAY BE WRONG.

Big companies may spend thousands on diversity training, but there are plenty of low-cost options available:

■ **LEARN AS MUCH AS YOU CAN** from books on the subject and from exposure to people who are different from you.

■ **INVESTIGATE VIDEO SERIES** on managing diversity. Many are available for rental or purchase.

■ **CONSIDER PUBLIC PROGRAMS.** A growing number of Urban League, chamber of commerce, Small Business Administration and community college seminars and courses are bringing business owners together to learn about diversity issues.

As the business owner, it's important to set a good example. Some ground rules to help keep you out of trouble:

■ **DON'T TOUCH EMPLOYEES** inappropriately.

■ **NEVER DATE SOMEONE** who works for you.

■ **DON'T DEMEAN OTHERS** or make suggestive comments. Watch your mouth; what seems humorous to some may offend others.

■ **BE SENSITIVE TO DIVERSITY** of all kinds. Are employees in their 50s making condescending remarks about the "young upstarts" in their 20s? Two white women in their 40s might face a cultural conflict if one is from the Midwest and the other is from the West Coast, or if one has children and the other doesn't.

■ **IF YOU DECORATE YOUR OFFICE** for the holiday season, don't include some religious symbols and leave out others. Many employers opt for a seasonal approach and use décor such as snowflakes and candles.

Put policies regarding discrimination and harassment in writing as part of your employee manual (see "Manual Labor" on page 374). Outline the disciplinary action that will be taken and the process by which employees can make their complaints known.

Hold a brief orientation meeting to introduce employees to your new policy or reacquaint them with the one already in place. Spell out very plainly what is and isn't acceptable. Many employees are especially confused about what constitutes sexual harassment. You don't want your staff walking around scared to say hello to one another.

BRIGHT IDEA

PEEVED AT PAYROLL PAPERWORK? COMPANIES WITH AS FEW AS FIVE EMPLOYEES CAN BENEFIT FROM USING A PAYROLL SERVICE. WHEN COMPARISON SHOPPING, GET REFERENCES, ASK ABOUT SERVICES, AND INQUIRE IF THE PAYROLL SERVICE KEEPS ABREAST OF FEDERAL AND STATE PAYROLL REGULATIONS. RATES DEPEND ON EMPLOYEES AND FREQUENCY OF PAYROLL.

Even if an incident does arise, the good news for business owners: Most complaints can be solved at the company level, before the issue comes close to a courtroom. To make this work, however, time is of the essence. Don't put off dealing with complaints, or the victim is likely to stew.

Give both parties a chance to tell their side of the story. Often, the cause is a simple misunderstanding. To cover all your bases, you may want to have a neutral consultant or human resources professional from outside the company investigate the matter.

GLOSSARY

AMERICANS WITH DISABILITIES ACT (ADA): law passed in 1990 that prohibits employers with 15 or more employees to refuse to hire people with disabilities if making "reasonable accommodations" would enable the person to perform the job

CONSOLIDATED OMNIBUS BUDGET RECONCILIATION ACT (COBRA): law requiring employers to extend health insurance coverage to employees and dependents beyond the point at which such coverage traditionally ceases (such as the termination or death of the covered employee)

FAMILY AND MEDICAL LEAVE ACT (FMLA): law requiring certain employers to give employees 12 weeks of unpaid leave for the birth or adoption of a baby or the serious illness of the employee or a close family member

OCCUPATIONAL SAFETY AND HEALTH ADMINISTRATION (OSHA). federal agency that regulates workplace safety

Cover
Your
Assets

Getting business insurance

One of the most common mistakes start-up business owners face is failing to buy adequate insurance for their businesses. It's an easy error to make: Money is tight, and with so many things on your mind, protecting yourself against the possibility of some faraway disaster just doesn't seem that important. "Oh, I will get insurance," you promise yourself, "one of these days." Soon, "one of these days" comes and goes, and you're still uninsured. Only now, your business has gotten much bigger…you've put a lot more into it…and you have a lot more to lose. Everything, to be exact.

It doesn't take much. A fire, a burglary, the illness of a key employee—any one of these could destroy everything you've worked so hard to build. When you think of all the time, effort and money you're investing in your business, doesn't it make sense to invest a little extra to protect it?

Following is a closer look at the types of business insurance available and what most entrepreneurs need, plus tips for keeping costs under control. (Health insurance is covered in the previous chapter.)

BASIC INSURANCE NEEDS

The basic business insurance package consists of four fundamental coverages—workers' compensation, general liability, auto and property/casualty—plus an added layer of protection over those, often called an umbrella policy. In addition to these basic needs, you should also consider purchasing business interruption coverage and life and disability insurance.

Workers' Compensation

Workers' compensation, which covers medical and rehabilitation costs and lost wages for employees injured on the job, is required by law in all 50 states.

Workers' comp insurance consists of two components, with a third optional element. The first part covers medical bills and lost wages for the injured employee; the second encompasses the employer's liability, which covers the business owner should the spouse or children of a worker who's permanently disabled or killed

decide to sue. The third and optional element of workers' compensation insurance is employment practices liability, which insures against lawsuits arising from claims of sexual harassment, discrimination and the like.

"Employment practices liability protects the unknowing corporation from the acts of the individual," according to a spokesperson at the Independent Insurance Agents of America (IIAA), an industry association. "Whether you need it depends on the size of your business and how much control you have over the daily work of employees." This is something you may need to worry about as your company grows.

According to the IIAA, it is often hard for small companies to get workers' compensation insurance for reasonable rates. Consequently, some states have a risk-sharing pool for firms that can't buy from the private market. Typically state-run and similar to assigned risk pools for car insurance, these pools generally don't provide the types of discounts offered in the voluntary market and thus are an "insurance of last resort."

Because insurance agents aren't always up-to-date on the latest requirements and laws regarding workers' comp, you should check with your state, as well as your agent, to find out exactly what coverage you need. Start at your state's department of insurance or insurance commissioner's office.

Generally, rates for workers' comp insurance are set by the state, and you purchase insurance from a private insurer. The minimum amount you need is also governed by state law. When you buy workers' comp, be sure to choose a company licensed to write insurance in your state and approved by the insurance department or commissioner.

If you are purchasing insurance for the first time, the rate will be based on your payroll and the average cost of insurance in your industry. You'll pay that rate for a number of years, after which an experience rating will kick in, allowing you to renegotiate premiums.

Depending on the state you are located in, the business owner will be either automatically included or excluded from coverage; if you want something different, you'll need to make special arrangements. While excluding yourself can save you several hundred dollars, this can be penny-wise and pound-foolish. Review your policy before choosing this option, because in most states, if you opt out, no health benefits will be paid for any job-related injury or illness by your health insurance provider.

A better way to reduce premiums is by maintaining a good safety record. This could include following all the Occupational Health and Safety Administration guidelines related to your business, creating an employee safety manual and instituting a safety training program.

Another way to cut costs is to ensure that all jobs in your company are properly classified. Insurance agencies give jobs different classification ratings depending on the degree of risk of injury.

General Liability

Comprehensive general liability coverage insures a business against accidents and injury that might happen on its premises as well as exposures related to its products.

For example, suppose a visiting salesperson slips on a banana peel while taking a tour of your office and breaks her ankle. General lia-

The Name's Bond

Sometimes confused with insurance, bonding is a guarantee of performance required for any business, either by law or by consumer demand. The most common businesses that bond employees are general contractors, temporary personnel agencies, janitorial companies and companies with government contracts. Bonding helps ensure that the job is performed and that the customer is protected against losses from theft or damage done by your employees.

Although you still have to pay on claims if your employees are bonded, bonding has the side benefit of making your business more desirable to customers. They know that if they suffer a loss as the result of your work, they can recover the damages from the bonding company. The difference between a bond and insurance is that a bonding company ensures your payment by requiring security or collateral if a claim is made against you.

bility covers her claim against you. But let's say your company is a window-sash manufacturer, with hundreds of thousands of its window sashes installed in people's homes and businesses. If something goes wrong with them, general liability covers any claims related to the damage that results.

The catch is that the damage cannot be due to poor workmanship. This points to one difficulty with general liability insurance: It tends to have a lot of exclusions. Make sure you understand exactly what your policy covers…and what it doesn't.

You may want to purchase additional liability policies to cover specific concerns. For example, many consultants purchase "errors and omissions liability," which protects them in case they are sued for damages resulting from a mistake in their work. A computer consultant who accidentally deletes a firm's customer list could be protected by this insurance, for example.

Companies with a board of directors may want to consider "directors and officers' liability" (D&O), which protects top executives against personal financial responsibility due to actions taken by the company.

How much liability coverage do you need? Experts say, $2 million to $3 million of liability insurance should be plenty. The good news is that liability insurance isn't priced on a dollar-for-dollar basis, so twice the coverage won't be twice the price.

The price you'll have to pay for comprehensive general liability insurance depends on the size of your business (measured either by square footage or by payroll) and the specific risks involved.

Auto Insurance

If your business provides employees with company cars, or if you have a delivery van, you need to think about auto insurance. The good news here is that auto insurance offers more of an opportunity to save money than most other types of business insurance. The primary strategy is to increase your deductible; then your premiums will decrease accordingly. Make sure, however, that you can afford to pay the deductibles should an accident happen. For additional savings, remove the collision and comprehensive coverage from older vehicles in your fleet.

Pay attention to policy limits when purchasing auto coverage. Many states set minimum liability coverages, which may be well below what you need. "If you don't have enough coverage, the courts can take everything you have, then attach your future corporate income, thus possibly causing the company severe financial hardship or even bankruptcy," says Mike Fox, an account executive with Wausau Insurance Companies. "I recommend carrying at least $1 million in liability coverage."

Property/Casualty Coverage

Most property insurance is written on an all-risks basis, as opposed to a named-peril basis. The latter offers coverage for specific perils spelled out in the policy. If your loss comes from a peril not named, then it isn't covered.

Make sure you get all-risks coverage. Then go the extra step and carefully review the policy's exclusions. All policies cover loss by fire, but what about such crises as hailstorms and explosions? Depending on your geographic location and the nature of your business, you may want to buy coverage for all these risks.

Whenever possible, you should buy *replacement cost insurance*, which will pay you enough to replace your property at today's prices, regardless of the cost when you bought the items. It's protection from inflation. (Be sure your total replacements do not exceed the policy cap.)

For example, if you have a 30,000-square-foot building that costs $50 per square foot to replace, the total tab will be $1.5 million. But if your policy has a maximum replacement of $1 million, you're going to come up short. To protect yourself, experts recommend buying replacement insurance with inflation guard. This adjusts the cap on the policy to allow for inflation. If that's not possible, then be sure to review the limits of your policy from time to time to ensure you're still adequately covered.

> **BRIGHT IDEA**
> KEEP DETAILED RECORDS OF THE VALUE OF YOUR OFFICE OR STORE'S CONTENTS OFF-PREMISES. INCLUDE PHOTOS OF EQUIPMENT PLUS COPIES OF SALES RECEIPTS, OPERATING MANUALS AND ANYTHING ELSE THAT PROVES WHAT YOU PURCHASED AND HOW MUCH WAS PAID. THAT WAY, IN CASE OF A FIRE, A FLOOD OR OTHER DISASTER, YOU CAN PROVE WHAT WAS LOST. IT'S ALSO IMPORTANT TO BE ABLE TO PROVE YOUR MONTHLY INCOME SO YOU ARE PROPERLY REIMBURSED IF YOU HAVE TO CLOSE DOWN TEMPORARILY.

Umbrella Coverage

In addition to these four basic "food groups," many insurance agents recommend an additional layer of protection, called an *umbrella policy.* This protects you for payments in excess of your existing coverage or for liabilities not covered any of your other insurance policies.

Business Interruption Coverage

When a hurricane or earthquake puts your business out of commission for days—or months—your property insurance has it covered. But while property insurance pays for the cost of repairs or rebuilding, who pays for all the income you're losing while your business is unable to function?

For that, you'll need business interruption coverage. Many entrepreneurs neglect to consider this important type of coverage, which can provide enough to meet your overhead and other expenses during the time your business is out of commission. Premiums for these policies are based on your company's income.

Package Deal

If figuring out what insurance you need makes your head spin, calm down; chances are, you won't have to consider the whole menu. Most property and casualty companies now offer special small-business insurance policies.

A standard package policy combines liability; fire, wind and vehicle damage; burglary; and other common coverages. That's enough for most small stores and offices, such as an accounting firm or a gift store. Some common qualifiers for a package policy are that your business occupy less than 15,000 square feet and that the combined value of your office building, operation and inventory be less than $3 million.

Basic package policies typically cover buildings, machinery, equipment and furnishings. That should protect computers, phones, desks, inventory and the like against loss due to robbery and employee theft, in addition to the usual risks such as fire. A good policy pays full replacement cost on lost items.

A package policy also covers business interruption, and some even offer you liability shelter. You may also be covered against personal liability. To find out more about package policies, ask your insurance agent; then shop around and compare.

Read All About It

Want to know more about insurance? Check out these books and publications:

- *INSURING YOUR HOME BUSINESS AND INSURING YOUR BUSINESS AGAINST A CATASTROPHE:* These brochures are available free from the Insurance Information Institute (III), 110 William St., New York, NY 10038. Send a self-addressed, stamped envelope; indicate on the envelope which brochures you want.

- *INSURING YOUR BUSINESS:* Written by Sean Mooney, this book is published by III Press and is available through its publications department. Call (800) 331-9146, fax (212) 732-1916, or e-mail publications@iii.org. Cost: $10 plus $3.50 shipping and handling.

- *EMPLOYER'S WORKERS' COMPENSATION COST CONTROL HANDBOOK:* This book is published by the National Foundation for Unemployment Compensation & Workers' Compensation, 1331 Pennsylvania Ave., #600, Washington, DC 20005-6143, (202)637-3434. Cost: $20 (includes shipping and handling).

- *THE SELF-INSURER:* This magazine is published by the Self-Insurance Institute of America Inc. Request a complimentary copy online at www.siia.org.

Life Insurance

Many banks require a life insurance policy on the business owner before lending any money. Such policies typically take the form of term life insurance, purchased yearly, which covers the cost of the loan in the event of the borrower's death; the bank is the beneficiary.

Term insurance is less costly than permanent insurance at first, although the payments increase each year. Permanent insurance builds equity and should be considered once the business has more cash to spend. The life insurance policy should provide for the families of the owners and key management. If the owner dies, the creditors are likely to take everything, and the owner's family will be left without the income or assets of the business to rely on.

Another type of life insurance that can be beneficial for a small business is "key person" insurance. If the business is a limited partnership or has a few key stockholders, the buy-sell agreement should specifically authorize this type of insurance to fund a buyback by the surviving leadership. Without a provision for insurance to buy capital, the buy-sell agreement may be rendered meaningless.

The company is the beneficiary of the key-person policy. When the key person dies, creating the obligation to pay, say, $100,000 for his or her stock, the cash with which to make that purchase is created at the same time. If you don't have the cash to buy the stock back from the surviving family, you could find yourself with new "business partners" you never bargained for—and wind up losing control of your business.

In addition to the owners or key stockholders, any member of the company who is vital to operations should also be insured.

Disability Insurance

It's every businessperson's worst nightmare—a serious accident or a long-term illness that can lay you up for months, or even longer. Disability insurance, sometimes called "income insurance," can guarantee a fixed amount of income—usually 60 percent of your average earned income—while you're receiving treatment or are recuperating and unable to work. Because you are your business's most vital asset, many experts recommend buying disability insurance for yourself and key employees from day one.

HOT LINK

CHECK OUT TRAVELERS PROPERTY CASUALTY'S ONLINE INSURANCE CENTER (WWW.TRAVELER SPC.COM—CLICK ON "SMALL BUSINESS CENTER"). DESIGNED FOR SMALL BUSINESSES, IT'S FILLED WITH CALCU- LATORS TO HELP YOU DETERMINE HOW MUCH INSURANCE YOU NEED AND THE WORTH OF YOUR BUSINESS PROPERTY. DON'T MISS THEIR MONEY-SAVING TIPS AND SAFETY CHECKLIST.

There are two basic types of disability coverage: short term (anywhere from 12 weeks to a year) and long term (more than a year). An important element of disability coverage is the waiting period before benefits are paid. For short-term disability, the waiting period is generally seven to 14 days. For long-term disability, it can be anywhere from 30 days to a year. If being unable to work for a limited period of time would not seriously jeopardize your business, you can decrease your premiums by choosing a longer waiting period.

Another optional add-on is "business overhead" insurance, which pays for ongoing business expenses, such as office rental, loan payments and employee salaries, if the business owner is disabled and unable to generate income.

CHOOSING AN INSURANCE AGENT

Given all the factors that go into business insurance, deciding what kind of coverage you need typically requires the assistance of a qualified insurance agent.

Type Of Agent

Selecting the right agent is almost as important, and sometimes as difficult, as choosing the types of coverage you need. The most fundamental question regarding agents is whether to select a direct writer—that is, someone who represents just one insurance company—or a broker, who represents many companies.

Some entrepreneurs feel they are more likely to get their money's worth with a broker because he or she shops all kinds of insurance companies for them. Others feel brokers are more efficient because they compare the different policies and give their opinions, instead of the entrepreneur having to talk to several direct writers to evaluate each of their policies. Another drawback to direct writers: If the insurance company drops your coverage, you lose your agent, too, and all his or her accumulated knowledge about your business.

Still, some people prefer direct writers. Why? An agent who writes insurance for just one company has more clout there than an agent who writes for many. So when something goes wrong, an agent who works for the company has a better chance of getting you what you need. Finally, direct writers often specialize in certain kinds of business and can bring a lot of industry expertise to the table.

Finding An Agent

To find an insurance agent, begin by asking a few of your peers whom they recommend. If you want more names, a trade association in your state may have a list of recommended agencies or offer some forms of group coverage with attractive rates (see the "Cost Containment" section in Chapter 24 for more).

Once you have a short list of agencies to consider, start looking for one you can develop a long-term relationship with. As your business grows and becomes more complicated, you'll want to work with someone who understands your problems. You don't want to spend a lot of time teaching the agent the ins and outs of your business or industry.

Find out how long the agency has been in business. An agency with a track record will likely be around to help you in the future. If the agency is new, ask about the principals; have they been in the industry long enough that you feel comfortable with their knowledge and stability?

One important area to investigate is loss-control service (which includes everything from fire-safety programs to reducing employees' exposures to injuries). The best way to reduce your premiums over the long haul is to minimize claims, and the best way to do that is through loss-control services. Look for a broker who will review and analyze which of the carriers offer the best loss-control services.

Another consideration is the size of the agency. The trend in insurance is consolidation. If you're looking for a long-term relationship, you want to avoid an agency that is going to get bought out. One way to get a handle on whether the agency you are considering is a likely acquirer (or acquiree) is by looking at the agency's owner. If he or she is older and is not grooming a successor, there's more chance

Policy Pointers

Looking for some of the best small-business insurance resources on the Web? Check these out:

- **SAFEWARE (WWW.SAFEWARE.COM) AND SOUTH COAST METRO INSURANCE BROKERS (WWW.COVERAGELINK.COM):** These companies cover computers against damage, theft, power surges and other high-tech disasters.
- **INSURANCE INFORMATION INSTITUTE (WWW.III.ORG):** This site puts business insurance news, facts and figures at your fingertips. Click on "Business" to start. From there, "News" gives you recent developments, sorted by topic.
- **CIGNA (WWW.CIGNA.COM):** Despite its bent toward larger companies, this user-friendly site contains a slew of informative and entertaining insurance-related resources.
- **CNA (WWW.CNA.COM):** While its technical language requires you to be well-versed in insurance lingo to fully comprehend it, this site has a "Commercial Insurance for Small and Medium-Sized Businesses" section that breaks down insurance coverage by industry. Click on "Products & Services" to find information on Commercial Insurance.

the agency will get bought out than that it will be doing the buying.

Verify the level of claims service each agency provides. When a claim arises, you don't want the agent telling you to call some toll-free number. If that's his or her idea of claims service, keep looking. An agency that gets involved in the claims process and works with the adjustor can have a positive impact on your settlement, while an agency that doesn't get involved tends to minimize your settlement.

You want an insurance agency that will stay on top of your coverage and be on the spot to adjust it as your business changes. Of course, it's always difficult to separate promises from what happens after the sale is closed. However, you might ask would-be agents how often they will be in touch. Even for the most basic business situation, the agent should still meet with you at least twice a year. For more complex situations, the agent should call you monthly.

Staking Your Claim

Though you hope it never happens, you may someday have to file an insurance claim. These tips should make it easier:

- **REPORT INCIDENTS IMMEDIATELY.** Notify your agent and carrier right away when anything happens—such as a fire, an accident or theft—that could result in a claim.

- **TAKE STEPS TO PROTECT YOUR PROPERTY FROM FURTHER DAMAGE.** Most policies cover the cost of temporary repairs to protect against further damage, such as fixing a window to prevent looting.

- **IF POSSIBLE, SAVE DAMAGED PARTS.** A claims adjustor may want to examine them after equipment repairs have been made.

- **GET AT LEAST TWO REPAIR ESTIMATES.** Your claims adjuster can tell you what kind of documentation the insurance company wants for bids on repairs.

- **PROVIDE COMPLETE DOCUMENTATION.** The insurance company needs proof of loss. Certain claims require additional evidence. For example, a claim for business interruption will need financial data showing income before and after.

- **COMMUNICATE WITH YOUR AGENT AND CLAIMS ADJUSTER.** Though your claim is against the insurance company, your agent should be kept informed so he or she can help if needed.

You also want to make sure the company your agent selects or represents is highly rated. While there are numerous rating agencies, the most prolific is A.M. Best, which rates the financial strength of insurance companies from A++ to F, according to their ability to pay claims and their size. You can find their rating book, *Best Rating Guide*, at your local library or you can search Best's ratings online at www.ambest.com. You will have to register with the site for access, but searching is free. Look for a carrier rated no lower than B+.

Also make sure the agent you choose is licensed by the state. The best way to find out is by calling your state insurance department, listed in the telephone book. If you can't find a number there, call the National Insurance Consumer helpline at (800) 942-4242.

Ask for references, and check them. This is the best way to predict how an agent will work with you.

Last but not least, trust your gut. Does the agent listen to you and incorporate your concerns into the insurance plan? Does he or she act as a partner or just a vendor? A vendor simply sells you insurance. Your goal is to find an agent who functions as a partner, helping you analyze risks and decide the best course of action. Of course, partnership is a two-way street. The more information you provide your agent, the more he or she can do for you.

INSURANCE COSTS

As with most other things, when it comes to insurance, you get what you pay for. Don't pay to insure against minor losses, but don't ignore real perils just because coverage carries hefty premiums.

You can lower your premiums with a higher deductible. Many agents recommend higher deductibles on property insurance and putting the money you save toward additional liability coverage.

How much can you afford for a deductible or uninsured risk? Look at your cash flow. If you can pay for a loss out of cash on hand, consider not insuring it.

Business Insurance Planning Work Sheet

Types Of Insurance	Required (Yes/No)	Yearly Cost	Cost Per Payment
1. General liability insurance			
2. Product liability insurance			
3. Errors and omissions liability insurance			
4. Malpractice liability insurance			
5. Automotive liability insurance			
6. Fire and theft insurance			
7. Business interruption insurance			
8. Overhead expense insurance			
9. Personal disability			
10. Key person insurance			
11. Shareholders' or partners' insurance			
12. Credit extension insurance			
13. Term life insurance			
14. Health insurance			
15. Group insurance			
16. Workers' compensation insurance			
17. Survivor-income life insurance			
18. Care, custody and control insurance			
19. Consequential losses insurance			
20. Boiler and machinery insurance			
21. Profit insurance			
22. Money and securities insurance			
23. Glass insurance			
24. Electronic equipment insurance			
25. Power interruption insurance			
26. Rain insurance			
27. Temperature damage insurance			
28. Transportation insurance			
29. Fidelity bonds			
30. Surety bonds			
31. Title insurance			
32. Water damage insurance			
Total Annual Cost		$	$

You can also save money on insurance by obtaining it through a trade group or an association. Many associations offer insurance tailored to your industry needs—everything from disability and health to liability and property coverage. You can also help keep insurance costs down by practicing these good insurance habits:

- **REVIEW YOUR NEEDS AND COVERAGE ONCE A YEAR.** If your circumstances or assets have changed, you may need to adjust your insurance coverage.
- **ASK YOUR INSURANCE AGENT FOR RISK-REDUCTION ASSISTANCE.** He or she should be able to visit your premises and identify improvements that would create a safer facility.
- **CHECK OUT NEW INSURANCE PRODUCTS.** Ask your agent to keep you up-to-date on new types of coverage you may want to consider.
- **TAKE TIME TO SHOP FOR THE BEST, MOST APPROPRIATE COVERAGE.** A few hours invested upfront can save thousands of dollars in premiums or claims down the road.

GLOSSARY

BONDING: a guarantee of performance required, either by law or consumer demand, for many businesses, most typically general contractors, temporary personnel agencies, janitorial companies and businesses with government contracts

BROKER: an insurance agent who represents many different insurance companies

BUSINESS INTERRUPTION INSURANCE: pays for the cost of repairing or rebuilding business as well as income lost while business is out of commission

DIRECT WRITER: an insurance agent who represents one insurance company; see also Broker

DISABILITY INSURANCE: pays a fixed percentage of average earnings should the insured be unable to continue working due to disability

EMPLOYMENT PRACTICES LIABILITY INSURANCE: an optional part of workers' compensation coverage, this protects the corporation from being sued for acts of individual employees (such as in a sexual harassment case)

ERRORS AND OMISSIONS LIABILITY COVERAGE: protects professionals, such as consultants or accountants, from damages resulting from an error or omission in their work

GENERAL LIABILITY COVERAGE: insures the business against accidents and injuries that happen on its premises as well as exposure to risk related to its products

KEY PERSON INSURANCE: life insurance policy taken out on "key people" in the company, where the beneficiary is the company; proceeds are used to buy out the deceased's shares or ownership interest in the company

PACKAGE POLICY: insurance policy that combines several standard coverages, such as liability, burglary and vehicle, in one package

PROPERTY/CASUALTY COVERAGE: protects physical property and equipment of the business against loss from theft, fire or other perils; all-risk coverage covers against all risks; named-peril coverage covers only against specific perils named in the policy

REPLACEMENT COST INSURANCE: covers cost of replacing property at current prices

UMBRELLA COVERAGE: protects you for payments in excess of your existing coverage or for liabilities not covered in your other policies

WORKERS' COMPENSATION INSURANCE: covers medical and rehabilitation costs and lost wages for employees injured at work; required by law in all states

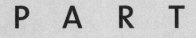

5

You'd Better
Shop
Around

Stuff

Business equipment basics

S tuff. Comedian George Carlin once built an entire routine around America's continuing fascination with, well, stuff. While some may fantasize about cars, jewelry and the like, business owners entertain visions of an entirely different sort. Their stuff of choice? Any and all pieces of equipment that promise to keep their businesses humming—from computers to fax machines and copiers.

What types of equipment do you actually need? It will vary depending on the demands of your business. In general, however, there are several basic pieces of equipment most new business owners need. (These are discussed in more detail throughout Part 5.)

- Computer
- Software
- Modem
- Fax machine
- Copier
- Phone
- Answering machine/Voice mail
- Cellular phone
- Pager
- Postage meter
- Calculator

Look over the list and consider which items you can't live without, which would be nice to have, and which (if any) you don't need. When equipping a start-up business, you must tread a fine line. On one end of the spectrum are the entrepreneurs who rush out and buy every big-ticket, bells-and-whistles item they see, convinced that they need it for their business. Feeling a compulsion to buy the latest technological tools simply because they're cutting edge, these entrepreneurs often end up spending way beyond their budget, only to find that the items they bought sit idle or aren't compatible.

At the other end of the spectrum is the entrepreneur who tries to make do with the bare bones. In an effort to save a few dollars, these business owners sacrifice efficiency and productivity, chugging along with a prehistoric computer, a one-line phone or a modem that crawls at a snail's pace. In short, they're penny-wise and pound-foolish.

Today's business climate is so fast-paced, clients won't do business with you if you can't keep up. Assess each item, and determine how it could benefit your business. Would you use a copier often enough to make it worth the cost? Will a fax machine pay for itself in a matter of weeks? A critical purchase may justify spending some extra money.

COST CUTTERS

Equipping your business can be a costly proposition. Fortunately, there are several different avenues you can take to keep the expenses to a minimum.

Financing Plan

If you're buying expensive equipment, consider having the manufacturers "lend" you money by selling the equipment to you over a period of time.

There are two types of credit contracts commonly used to finance equipment purchases: the *conditional sales contract*, in which the purchaser does not receive title to the equipment until it is paid for; and the *chattel-mortgage contract*, in which the equipment becomes the property of the purchaser on delivery, but the seller holds a mortgage claim against it until the contract amount is fully paid.

There are also lenders who will finance 60 to 80 percent of a new equipment purchase, while you pay down the balance as a down payment. The loan is repaid in monthly installments, usually over one to five years or the usable life of the equipment. (Make sure the financing period does not extend past the usable life of the equipment; you don't want to be paying for something you can no longer use.)

DOLLAR STRETCHER

WANT TO KEEP EQUIPMENT COSTS WAY DOWN? CONSIDER LAUNCHING FROM A BUSINESS INCUBA-TOR, WHERE SERVIC  ES, FACILITIES AND EQUIPMENT ARE SHARED AMONG SEVER-AL BUSINESSES. (FOR MORE ON INCUBA-TORS, SEE PART 4, CHAPTER 17).

By using your equipment suppliers to finance the purchase, you reduce the amount of money you need upfront.

When Lease Is More

Another way to keep equipment costs down is to lease instead of buy. These days, just about anything can be leased—from computers and heavy machinery to complete offices. The kind of business you're in and the type of equipment you're considering are major factors in determining whether to lease or buy. If you are starting a one-person business and only need one computer, for instance, it probably makes more sense to buy. On the other hand, if you are opening an office that will have several employees and require a dozen computers, you may want to look into leasing.

Package Deal

As you put together an equipment leasing package, consider these issues:

- **WHAT EQUIPMENT** do you need and for how long?
- **DO YOU WANT** to bundle service, supplies, training and the equipment lease itself into one contract?
- **HAVE YOU ANTICIPATED** your company's future needs so you can acquire adequate equipment?
- **WHAT IS THE TOTAL** payment cost?

Also ask the following questions about each leasing source you investigate:

- **WHO WILL YOU BE DEALING WITH**—is there a separate company financing the lease? This is not desirable.
- **HOW LONG HAS THE COMPANY BEEN IN BUSINESS?** As a general rule, deal only with financing sources that have been operating at least as many years as the term of your proposed lease.

- **DO YOU UNDERSTAND THE TERMS** and conditions during and at the end of the lease.
- **IS CASUALTY INSURANCE** (required to cover damage to the equipment) included?
- **WHO PAYS** the personal property tax?
- **WHAT ARE THE OPTIONS** regarding upgrading and trading in equipment?
- **WHO IS RESPONSIBLE** for repairs?

According to the Equipment Leasing Association of America (ELA), approximately 80 percent of U.S. companies lease some or all of their equipment, and there are some thousands of equipment-leasing firms nationwide catering to that demand. "[Leasing is] an excellent hedge against obsolescence," explains a spokesperson at the ELA, "especially if you're leasing something like computer equipment and want to update it constantly."

Other leasing advantages include: making lower monthly payments than you would have with a loan, getting a fixed financing rate instead of a floating rate, benefiting from tax advantages, conserving working capital and avoiding cash-devouring down payments, and gaining immediate access to the most up-to-date business tools. The equipment also shows up on your income statement as a lease expense rather than a purchase. If you purchase it, your balance sheet becomes less liquid.

Leasing also has its downside, however: You may pay a higher price over the long term. Another drawback is that leasing commits you to retaining a piece of equipment for a certain time period, which can be problematic if your business is in flux.

Every lease decision is unique, so it's important to study the lease agreement carefully. Compare the costs of leasing to the current interest rate, examining the terms to see if they're favorable. What is the lease costing you? What are your savings? Compare those numbers to the cost of purchasing the same piece of equipment, and you'll quickly see which is the more profitable route.

Because they tend to have little or no credit history, start-ups often find it difficult or even impossible to lease equipment. However, some companies will consider your personal rather than business credit history during the approval process.

If you decide to lease, make sure you get a closed-end lease without a balloon payment at the end. With a closed-end lease, nothing is owed when the lease period ends. When the lease period terminates, you just turn the equipment in and walk away. With an open-end lease, it's not that simple. If you turn in the equipment at the end of the lease and it's worth less than the value established in the contract, then you are responsible for paying the difference. If you do consider an open-end lease, make sure you're not open to additional charges such as wear and tear.

Finally, balloon payments require you to make small monthly payments with a large payment (the balloon) at the end. While this allows you to conserve your cash flow as you're making those monthly payments, the bad news is, the final balloon payment may be more than the equipment is worth.

There are many different avenues through which you can secure an equipment lease:

- **BANKS AND BANK-AFFILIATED FIRMS** that will finance an equipment lease may be difficult to locate, but once found, banks may offer some distinct advantages, including lower costs and better customer service. Find out whether the bank will keep and service the lease transaction after it's set up.
- **EQUIPMENT DEALERS AND DISTRIBUTORS** can help you arrange financing using an independent leasing company.
- **INDEPENDENT LEASING COMPANIES** can vary in size and scope, offering many financing options.
- **CAPTIVE LEASING COMPANIES** are subsidiaries of equipment manufacturers or other firms.
- **BROKER/PACKAGERS** represent a small percentage of the leasing market. Much like mortgage or real estate brokers, these people charge a fee to act as an intermediary between financial resources and lessees.

For more information on leasing, the ELA in Arlington, Virginia, and the Business Technology Association (BTA) in Kansas City, Missouri, offer member directories. The ELA allows you to personalize your directory and pay for only the information you need, which could result in paying well under $100 or well over. The BTA offers a directory on CD-ROM for $650 for the general public, while BTA members receive a free copy but pay $425 for additional CD-ROMs. *The Leasing Sourcebook*, published by Bibliotechnology Systems and Publishing Co., is a directory of companies leasing equipment. You can also check your local Yellow Pages for listings of leasing companies.

WISE BUYS

If your calculations show that buying makes more sense for you, you've still got some decisions to make. First and foremost, where to buy?

Buying New Equipment

The same piece of new equipment that costs $400 at one store can cost $1,000 at another. It all depends on where you go. Here are some of the most common sources for buying new equipment, with a look at the pros and cons of each.

■ **SUPERSTORES:** Office or electronics superstores usually offer rock-bottom prices because they buy from manufacturers in volume. On the downside, remember that you won't get delivery or installation from a superstore. For service, you will probably have to call the manufacturer. Nor can you expect a lot of qualified help choosing the right equipment since superstores are unlikely to be staffed by expert employees. If you know exactly what you need, however, or you have a knowledgeable friend or associate who can help you, a superstore could be an option for you.

■ **SPECIALTY STORES:** Small electronics stores or office equipment retailers are likely to offer more assistance in putting together a package of products. Salespeople will be more knowledgeable than at superstores, and service will be more personal. Some even offer service plans. On the downside, prices go up accordingly.

■ **DEALER DIRECT SALES:** Check your Yellow Pages for companies that sell direct to consumers. Many manufacturers choose this option as a way of maintaining their service-oriented reputation. On the plus side, you will get assistance from highly knowledgeable salespeople who can help you put together the right system of products. You may also get delivery, installation and training at no extra cost. Many entrepreneurs swear by this method of buying. The downside: Since you're deal-

DOLLAR STRETCHER

IF YOU PURCHASE ALL YOUR EQUIPMENT FROM A SINGLE SUPPLIER, YOU MAY BE ABLE TO NEGOTIATE VOLUME DISCOUNTS, FREE SHIPPING AND OTHER EXTRAS. BE AWARE, THOUGH, THAT PURCHASING FROM A SINGLE VENDOR ALSO LIMITS YOUR OPTIONS; FOR EXAMPLE, THE MERCHANT YOU CHOOSE FOR YOUR COMPUTER SYSTEM MAY NOT OFFER THE BRAND OF PRINTER YOU WANT.

ing with one manufacturer, you won't get to compare brands.

No matter what source you buy your equipment from, however, be sure to investigate the type of service and support you'll get before you whip out your wallet. A tempting price may seem like a compelling reason to forgo solid service when you buy, but it won't seem like such a good deal when the equipment grinds to a halt in the middle of an urgent project... and the vendor is nowhere to be found.

HOT LINK

THE ACTIVE SALES ASSISTANT (WWW.ACTIVE BUYERSGUIDE.COM) ALLOWS YOU TO SET YOUR PERSONAL PREFERENCES FOR OFFICE MACHINES, COMPUTERS, SOFTWARE AND MORE BEFORE IT DISPLAYS PRODUCT REVIEWS TO HELP YOU FIND EXACTLY WHAT YOU'RE LOOKING FOR— EVEN IF YOU DON'T KNOW WHAT THAT IS YET.

To get the most from your equipment vendors, it's important to lay the proper groundwork and let them know you are a valuable customer. One way to do that is to make sure you send in the service registration card that comes with the product. Contact the vendor before problems arise to ask for all the relevant telephone and fax numbers so you know what to do if disaster strikes. Maintain contact with the vendor by asking questions as they come up and giving the vendor any comments or ideas that might improve the product. This identifies you as an active user and builds your relationship with the vendor.

Before you buy, prioritize what's important to your company; then get the answers to these questions:

- **HOW LONG DOES THE WARRANTY LAST?**
- **DOES THE VENDOR OFFER A MONEY-BACK GUARANTEE?** Many computer peripherals, for instance, come with 30-day money-back guarantees. Use this time to make sure the item works with the rest of your system.
- **DOES THE VENDOR CHARGE A RESTOCKING FEE?** Even when a company offers a money-back guarantee, the company may charge a restocking fee of up to 15 percent of the product's cost on returns.
- **WHAT FEES, IF ANY, DOES THE VENDOR CHARGE FOR TECHNICAL SUPPORT?**
- **HOW EASY IS IT TO REACH TECHNICAL SUPPORT?** Try calling before you buy the product to see how long you're put on hold and whether the company returns calls.
- **WHAT HOURS IS TECHNICAL SUPPORT AVAILABLE?** Be aware of time zones. If you're in California and your East Coast vendor shuts

down at 5 p.m., you could be out an afternoon's work if your computer breaks down after 2 p.m. California time.

■ **HOW QUICKLY CAN THE VENDOR FIX PROBLEMS?** What are the repair costs and time frames (on-site repair, 24-hour turnaround, etc.)?

■ **DOES THE VENDOR OFFER ANY VALUE-ADDED SERVICES?**

Buying Used Equipment

If new equipment is out of your price range, buying used equipment can be an excellent cost cutter. There are several sources for buying used; one little-known avenue is an asset remarketing company.

Asset remarketers work with equipment leasing companies to resell repossessed office equipment through a network of dealers and wholesalers—and sometimes directly to business owners. The prices are a fraction of the cost of buying or leasing brand-new equipment.

It is also simpler buying repossessed equipment through an asset remarketer than going to a bankruptcy auction. As in most auctions,

Lemon Alert

Whether you are buying used equipment from an individual or a business, take these steps to make sure you don't get stuck with a lemon.

● **KNOW THE MARKET.** Do some research before you make an offer. Read the classifieds to learn the going rates for the items you want. Notice how quickly items move: Is it a seller's market, or do you see the same ads run again and again?

● **TRY BEFORE YOU BUY.** Just as you would with new equipment, it's essential to "test drive" used equipment. Run diagnostic tests; make sure all the parts are working; ask about any problems. (Often, the item is still worth buying even with the cost of repairs.)

● **BRING A BUDDY.** If you're a novice, it helps to take a more experienced friend or colleague with you when you test the equipment. He or she can ask questions you may not think of and pinpoint problems you might miss.

● **DON'T FEEL COMFORTABLE?** Don't buy. Never let anyone talk you into a purchase or make you feel guilty. If you don't feel good about it, walk away.

Leasing Vs. Purchasing Equipment Work Sheet

Answer the following questions to help determine whether it is better to lease or purchase equipment for your business in terms of cost, cash availability, tax benefits and obsolescence.

Cost	Lease	Purchase
What is the required down payment for the lease or loan?		
What is the length of the lease or loan?		
What is the monthly payment of the lease or loan?		
Are there balloon payments associated with the lease or loan?		
What is the amount of the balloon payment?		
What is the cost of an extended warranty if purchasing one?		
What is the total cost of the lease or loan (including maintenance and warranties) over its lifetime?		

Cash Availability	Lease	Purchase
Is there sufficient cash flow to handle the monthly lease or loan payments? (Answer yes or no.)		
Are maintenance costs included in the lease or loan (Answer yes or no.)		
What are the maintenance costs associated with the item?		
What are the insurance costs included in the lease or loan, if any?		
What are the estimated insurance costs associated with the item?		
If business is seasonal, does the lease or the loan fit periods of sufficient cash flow better?		

Tax Benefits	Lease	Purchase
Can the item be depreciated for tax purposes in a lease or loan?		
What is the depreciable life of the item?		
What is the estimated depreciable expense of the item over its depreciable life?		
What is the amount of other tax benefits associated with this item?		

Obsolescence	Lease	Purchase
What is the operable lifetime of the item?		
What is the total cost of the item spread over this lifetime (divide cost by lifetime)?		
What is the technological lifetime of the item?		
Will the item need to be replaced due to technological advancement?		
What is the total cost of the item spread over the technological lifetime (divide cost by lifetime)?		

the asset remarketing company accepts bids—but that is where the similarities end. Asset remarketers keep equipment in warehouses, which buyers visit at their convenience as they would a discount office equipment retailer. Often, the remarketer has a price sheet showing the equipment's original price and its approximate resale value. Use this price sheet as a guideline in making your offer.

Leasing companies and asset remarketers must resell equipment at a fair market price, so three bids are usually required. There is no set deadline, but these companies are eager to move their equipment out of storage and into the highest bidder's hands, so if you see something you want, move fast. If you want to buy, make an offer to the asset remarketing firm, which then sends it to the leasing company's asset recovery manager. Some asset remarketers may require a $100 deposit when the leasing company accepts the bid; you will then need to pay with cash, certified funds or cashier's check within a few days.

While finding asset remarketing companies is as easy as calling a local repossession company in the Yellow Pages, be careful to find a reputable company. While some states regulate asset remarketing or repossession firms, there are unscrupulous remarketers in many states who hang out their shingle, pocket consumers' deposits, then disappear. The safest way to find an honest asset remarketer is to call a leasing company's asset recovery manager and ask for the name of a local firm. Some leasing companies prefer to sell to end users directly, and they may ask for a description of the equipment you want to purchase.

In addition to asset remarketers or leasing companies, you can also buy used equipment from individuals (look in the local classifieds) or check your Yellow Pages for used equipment retailers, such as the Aaron Rents & Sells chain nationwide. The resale of used equipment is becoming more common, so in most cities, you will have several sources to choose from.

GLOSSARY

ASSET REMARKETERS, ASSET REMARKETING COMPANIES: firms that work with equipment leasing companies to resell repossessed office equipment through a network of dealers and wholesalers as well as directly to business owners

BALLOON PAYMENTS: lease arrangement that requires small

monthly payments with a large payment (the balloon) at the end of the lease

CHATTEL-MORTGAGE CONTRACT: type of credit contract used for equipment purchase in which the equipment becomes the property of the purchaser on delivery, but the seller holds a mortgage claim against it until the contract amount is fully paid

CLOSED-END LEASE: type of equipment lease in which no money is owed when the lease period ends; the lessee simply turns in the equipment and walks away

CONDITIONAL SALES CONTRACT: type of credit contract used for equipment purchase in which the purchaser does not receive title to the equipment until it is paid for

OPEN-END LEASE: type of equipment lease in which, if the value of the equipment at the end of the lease is less than the value established in the lease contract, the lessee must pay the difference

Get Wired!

Shopping for your computer system

By Mike Hogan, *Entrepreneur's* technology editor and author of
Entrepreneur's start-up guide *How to Start an e-Learning Business*

Y ou may be starting your first business. But you've probably already had experience with a desktop computer and the other productivity equipment you'll need to get your business off the ground. If you've had a job before, your boss no doubt provided you with a PC and a phone and, at least, access to a copier, a fax machine, a printer and so forth.

But now it's your turn to lay down the cash, so you'll need to know these devices at a slightly deeper level. No, that doesn't mean being able to disassemble and reassemble a PC against a stopwatch like a Marine does his M-16. But you'll want to know a little more than simply how to turn on your computer and then launch your favorite programs.

Computers and peripherals are constantly evolving, but knowing a few general specifications in each product category will help you find the best deal on the right equipment for your business—and that's not the same for everyone. There's no one "right" PC brand or printer type, one right phone system or fax solution any more than everyone needs the same model Chevy or Ford.

You're unique, and your business idea probably is, too; and, either way, your business will have its own unique set of equipment needs that probably differ from those of the company next door. And, of course, we all have different amounts of money to spend. We assume that you want to spread your precious start-up dollars as far as you can.

The good news on that front is that prices for office equipment have gone down every year for the past three decades, while features have continued to improve with every new version of hardware and software. That's been true in every product category every year, so you can expect to get a better price and a more capable bundle of equipment that you could have found this time last year.

Also, you can expect your computer and telecommunications equipment to be one of your best business allies. As we've evolved from an industrial to an information-based economy, small businesses have used their office tools to be more competitive against larger businesses, which, let's face it, have a lot of built-in market advantages.

But your size has its advantages, too; and your office equipment can help you level the playing field. It's been small, nimble businesses responding to opportunity that have made the past 30 years one of the most productive and profitable periods in American history. In the process, many have become large businesses.

So how do you go about outfitting your future Fortune 500 company?

BEING WELL-CONNECTED

Let's start by behaving as if you're already a Fortune 500 company—in miniature. Over the decades, large businesses have learned quite a bit about getting the most out of their office equipment. The first lesson

Sidekicks

The Filofax, Daytimer, Day Planner—businesspeople have relied on them for years to keep contacts and to-do lists, notes and sundry other bits of information always at hand. But these organizers can bulge to binder size, and they don't connect to anything but your pen.

A better solution is a PDA (personal digital assistant) that fits in a shirt pocket or a purse. At a minimum, your PDA includes a PIM (personal information manager) duplicating the functionality of older organizers. Some also include extras like special business calculators and accept a wide range of custom-built programs. Pocket PC handhelds even have versions of popular programs you use on your Windows desktop. Unlike paper-based alternatives, once you enter information into one of these devices using their pens, touchscreens or small keypads, it's available to other programs written for that platform.

PDAs come in many shapes, sizes and feature combinations. At one end of the scale are $100 to $150 Palm or Sharp Zaurus models focused on size and simplicity. But marrying a cell phone or other advanced features and connectivity options can boost your PDA's price tag to $700 to $900.

The many models from Palm Computing, Handspring and Sony using the Palm operating system have the most third-party software options. But Windows CE-based Pocket PCs like the Hewlett-Packard iPAQ, Casio Cassiopeia and Toshiba "e series" are fast attracting supporters. Pocket PCs also typically include the most upscale features.

is: You don't buy equipment; you buy systems.

As you shop for PCs, faxes and phones, keep in mind that the overriding goal is to make all this stuff work well together; and, to the extent possible, talk to one another—that is, share data. If your personal digital assistant (PDA) can't easily transfer data to your desktop or your fax machine can't accept computer files or you're building contact lists/address books in a lot of different and incompatible applications, you're duplicating effort. You're losing time. Efficiency today means being well-connected—both inside and outside the walls of your company.

Even if you start off as a solo operator working from a home office, you're still going to need connections to clients and suppliers in the wider world. That not only means phone, fax and Internet connections, but also some level of connectivity in the applications that make them work—e-mail, instant messaging, Web protocols and more.

At some point, you may want to share proposals, spreadsheet and other files—not only among co-workers, but possibly, customers and suppliers as well. That suggests you'll want to stick with the most popular operating systems and applications to improve your chances of collaboration with others. Certainly, you'll want to do that within your own company.

IT Takes Two

Incidentally, even if you are starting as a solo operator, you'll need at least two connected computers. And if you're like many businesspeople today, you probably already own three or four "computing devices"—PC, laptop, PDA, cell phone—with a lot of wired and/or wireless connections among them and other office equipment.

But why two desktop computers? Actually, one of those could be a laptop for travel. But even if you're a shut-in, you still need two

Take Note

Portables can be broken into three classes. Thin-and-lights are the most popular size and the one usually identified as a laptop. They generally weigh 6 to 8 pounds, have 14- to 15-inch displays (mostly 14 inches) and near-equivalent functionality to a desktop PC.

For the frequent traveler, ultralights range between 3 and 5 pounds with 12-inch displays and require some functionality compromises in the interest of portability and battery life.

Another category is desktop replacement notebooks that start around 8 pounds and can weigh 12 pounds or more. They almost always have at least 15-inch displays and have the option for a docking station or port replicator that gives them all the functionality of a desktop computer.

It's best to pick a notebook with Intel's Pentium 4M or AMD Athlon XP mobile processor. The exception are ultralight systems using the older Pentium III M processor—in all likelihood at very attractive prices. The III M is past its prime in terms of thin-and-light or heavier portables, but acceptable in the short term when your primary focus is to get as much battery life as possible from an ultralight.

While you can save money on the front end, any other portable with last-generation chips is likely to be obsolete before its time and lose any resale value. Also, there's an opportunity cost as far as your productivity is concerned.

Generally, portables have an $800 to $1,000 price premium over an equivalent desktop PC, ranging from $1,200 to $3,000 or more, depending on features. Look for at least 256MB of DDR SDRAM, a 20GB hard drive, an active-matrix color display, a built-in pointing device, and a multipurpose bay that can house removable hard, optical or floppy drives or a spare battery. Your notebook is likely to have a multitude of ports for expansion and an 802.11 wireless networking radio—either through Intel's Centrino chip suite or through another provider.

because of that inevitable day when your hard drive crashes or you get a virus or there is some inscrutable problem with your PC's on/off button—whatever. Your PC is likely to become the heart and soul of your operation; and, while computer equipment is very durable, all equipment fails.

Also, a PC is unique because you're constantly changing its software configuration and your critical data all day long, every day. After months or years of electrical signals zipping back and forth, there's bound to be a crossed signal sometime.

When your toaster breaks, it's no big deal. But what will you do when that machine that holds your critical business information fails? Even if you're among that small fraction of people who back up their data religiously and have it available somewhere on tape or CD-ROM, how long will it take you to run out and buy a new PC and add all the software you regularly use configured just the way you like it so you can start loading that data? How many hours or days can your business go before you get back online with your customers?

Realistically, you don't want even one hour of lost productivity. At a minimum, you need at least one duplicate of your main PC's entire setup that you can immediately turn to without losing a step. As mentioned, that duplicate image could be a laptop used for travel. Ideally, it will be another desktop just as capable or nearly so as your first.

That second computer doesn't have to sit idle until an emergency. It can be working in the meantime to help carry the computing load on your local area network (LAN)—and, for that matter, your wide area network, which includes your connection to the Internet and your Web site, another must-have for a modern business.

So you need to start shopping, not for computers, but for a network for your computers. That's not as complicated as it sounds, especially since Windows and other popular operating systems have networking capabilities built in these days. At the LAN level, that will be over an Ethernet connection. You'll also want to connect smaller devices to your network via various wired or

SMART TIP

BEFORE YOU BUY IT, TOUCH AND FEEL IT. CHECK OUT COMPUTER EQUIPMENT THAT YOU MIGHT BE CONSIDERING BUYING ONLINE AT RETAIL STORES. YOU MAY BE ABLE TO FIND THESE SYSTEMS AT OFFICE DEPOT, STAPLES, CIRCUIT CITY, COMPUSA OR FRY'S, AND YOU MAY EVEN END UP BUYING RETAIL BECAUSE YOU LIKE THE PRICE OR FINANCING ARRANGEMENTS. ONE ADVANTAGE OF LOCAL RETAIL STORES: LOCAL REPAIR SERVICES.

wireless protocols that will be built into your different devices.

But the goal is always the same: to share data as effortlessly as you can so as to reduce repetitive data handling tasks.

SERVING IT UP

So instead of going shopping for a bunch of hardware, lets go shopping with your network in mind.

Ultimately, it will extend to a virtual network that will include all those places and devices you use to do work. That includes your PDA, your laptop and your cell phone, with their various operating systems and application software. It might even include the back deck of your house or your kitchen table, if they happen to be locations where you like to work. Computer/phone connections are still far from automatic and so diverse that we'll have to save discussion of wireless connectivity for Chapter 28 on page 439.

But the most logical place to start on our goal of connectivity across your entire working universe is by connecting those two computers we already decided you need. Despite the fast uptake in 802.11-based networking products, the most common approach is still to create a wired Ethernet LAN.

One of those computers is likely to be your primary workstation where you usually generate your spreadsheets, do accounting, create sales presentations and write customer letters. If you run a one-person operation, that's usually where the "master copy" of all your stuff is kept.

But it doesn't have to be. Remember, we said we don't want the money for that second computer to be wasted, and one of the ways to make it pull its weight is to network it to the first and assign it certain computing tasks. Networking lets you share computing power and divvy up your workload among different systems.

For example, as companies grow, they often find it cheaper and more convenient to keep master copies of software and even data on a central PC and give each employee's workstation access to more or less of it, depending on the employee's access privileges.

In small offices, that central PC may well be your workstation. At the same time, it's often convenient to get your printer, fax and scanner off your desk by attaching them to a second PC that can accept jobs from all the other PCs on the network. Another increasingly common use of a second PC is as a communications server to your e-commerce Web site and to house the several e-mail boxes and instant messaging archives you and co-workers will collect.

As mentioned, if you travel or work at home and the office or different spots around your home, you may prefer that your second computer be a laptop. Portables come in all shapes and sizes today, and you can easily find one powerful enough to perform any or all of the desktop duties described above.

Any PC that delivers data and other services to multiple devices is called a "server." The word "server" is also used to refer to the operating system—software like Windows 2000 or its successor Windows XP. These operating systems include all the features you'll need to connect your server to other computers, sometimes called "clients."

Connections

The traditional way to create your LAN is to string very inexpensive Category 5 cable (it looks a lot like the typical phone line on steroids) between the Ethernet adapters of two or more PCs. You may need to buy a small and inexpensive Ethernet card to plug in to one or more of your PCs if any of them is either old or cheap. But the easier approach is to make built-in Ethernet a must-have on your PC shopping list.

As a matter of fact, Ethernet has become such a common feature of today's business-class PCs that it may not even cost you extra for the ability to transfer data at 10 or 100 megabits per second (Mbps). Vendors like Dell are beginning to include Ethernet adapters in their business PCs that are capable of transferring data at 1 gigabit per second, although any 10/100Mbps adapter will do just fine.

Easier still is to network your PCs wirelessly using 802.11 or Wi-Fi network adapters. These come in a variety of adapter types and connect to your PC in different ways. Similarly, unable to accept an Ethernet card, some small devices like PDAs and cell phones rely on the wireless Bluetooth or Infrared communication methodologies. Again, we'll get into wireless connectivity in Chapter 28 on page 439.

Flying Business Class

What's a business-class PC? In brief, one that includes various connectivity components like built-in Ethernet and the software utilities to manage networking, as well as the slots, bays and ports needed to expand memory, storage and business peripherals.

A business-class PC isn't necessarily more expensive than today's well-equipped home computers, but it's not the cheapest PC you can buy either. In its standard configuration, it's priced in the midrange. But you don't necessarily want to buy the standard configuration.

While high-end consumer systems focus on multimedia entertainment, gaming and other recreational activities, a business user's money is better spent getting just a little more of all the standard stuff. You want more memory, storage, a higher-resolution or larger display because all these things not only make computing more pleasant, but also enhance your productivity.

They can help you do more in less time; and, if you're in business, time is money. Waiting for databases to update, insufficient memory errors, waiting for Web pages to download—these things waste your time. You want to have the best business productivity enhancer you can afford.

That's not going to be one brand, model or configuration. No one PC is right for every user. On the other hand, a computer is a general-purpose tool, and, at any given time, there will be several different models that will suit your business—or can be configured to.

Often, though, there is some product that captures the sweet spot in a category—the ideal confluence of price and features—and it becomes a bestseller. Sometimes, but not always, that product is recognized in computer magazine reviews, which generally give good product advice. You also might hear about it from business associates or in computer-related chat rooms.

Common Pieces And Parts

PC components change pretty quickly—always for the better. It's hard to take a snapshot of PC functionality that won't go out of date pretty quickly. But we can give you a few guidelines:

- **CPU:** Starting with the brains of the computer or the central processing unit, you'll want your systems powered by nothing less than

Go Retro!

Budget tight? What about a late-model PC that's only been driven around the block a few times? Much like a low-mileage automobile, you can find "refurbished" PCs from the outlet stores of major PC makers like Dell, IBM and Hewlett-Packard that are new in every respect but price tag.

As with autos, you avoid that first-year depreciation hit; and even with new-PC prices at record lows, you can save 20 to 50 percent or more this way, or get more PC for your buck.

Because of their no-questions-asked return policies, direct sales vendors wind up with a lot of PCs custom-built for buyers who, for one reason or another, change their minds. Many times, these "used" PCs have never left the packing carton, but consumer protection laws prevent vendors from selling them as new.

Vendors routinely refurbish, retest, re-warranty and deeply discount these returns. Refurbished PCs get new warranties, although they may be limited. So? Renegotiate.

Aim for a three-year on-site parts and labor warranty. Remember, these discounted computers are taking up space and other resources that manufacturers would rather devote to full-priced systems. They want to get rid of them, so make an offer.

an Intel Pentium 4 or equivalent Athlon XP class processor from Advanced Micro Devices as opposed to, say, Celrons, Durons, Pentium IIIs or earlier generations. System clock speeds have been soaring higher pretty quickly in recent years, so you shouldn't invest in anything less than a 2.4GHz Pentium 4 or Athlon XP 2100+ machine with 512KB of on-chip cache memory and 400MHz frontside bus for processor-to-memory transfers. On-chip cache is critically important to your processor's performance.

- **RAM:** Random Access Memory is also critically important. Considerably slower and cheaper than cache, RAM is the bucket your computer's processor uses to hold vast amounts of data and program instructions while it works. The standard amount of RAM is always climbing as the programs we use become ever more ambitious. Consider 512MB to be the minimum for a business-class PC, and you really should have 1GB. Here's where the price of your PC jumps the most. But adding memory is the single-most beneficial thing you can to enhance your PC's performance.

- **HARD DRIVE:** One or more physical hard drives, each of which can be divided into multiple logical drives are, the warehouses where you store multi-megabyte programs and gigabytes worth of data. This is the permanent storage location of your programs and files, and, if only because they are so inexpensive, there's no reason to have a PC with less than 80GB of storage. The real price differential comes with the speed at which the platters in your hard drive spin. Another productivity enhancer: Make sure you don't buy anything slower than a 7200RPM drive.

- **OPTICAL DRIVE:** It's pretty hard to find a computer without a CD-ROM drive these days. In fact, it's hard to find one without a rewritable CD. But time marches on, and, today, it's preferable to have a rewritable DVD in your PC. For starters, DVD platters hold 4.3GB instead of the 650MB of CD-ROMs. That's enough to hold a first-run movie, although the principal business application is to copy all your hard drive data onto one or more rewritable DVD discs and then store them off-site. Of all your backup alternatives, none is so reliable, so durable and so cheap as simply copying the contents of your hard drives to an optical drive. Any of the popular DVD rewriting methods will be able to read your CD-ROM discs as well.

- **DISPLAY:** To put it bluntly, monitors are dead. Long live liquid crystal displays (LCDs). These thin-line, low-power alternatives to the hot, bulky monitor are still a good deal more expensive to buy. But prices are falling fast, and they not only save a huge amount of desktop space, but also enough in power and cooling costs over a traditional monitor that they are actually cheaper in the long run. A 15-inch LCD is the viewing equivalent of a 17-inch monitor but has a higher resolution and is easier on the eyes. Depending on features, it should cost $300 to $400. Spend a couple hundred dollars more, and a 17-inch LCD will provide higher resolution and contrast, and a wider viewing angle for, say, group presentations. Either is cheapest when purchased from a dis-

SMART TIP

GOOD COMPUTING PRACTICE DICTATES THAT YOU TRY TO MAINTAIN THE SAME BRAND AND MODEL AND, TO THE EXTENT POSSIBLE, THE SAME COMPONENTS ACROSS ALL YOUR COMPUTERS TO REDUCE SUPPORT COSTS. BUT RAPID COMPONENT TURNOVER MAKES THIS DIFFICULT. YOUR BEST CHANCE OF "CLONING" SYSTEMS YOU ALREADY HAVE IS BUYING FROM RESELLERS OF REFURBISHED OR USED PCS SUCH AS REFURBDEPOT (WWW.REFURBDEPOT.COM), MICROSECONDS (WWW.MICROSECONDS.NET) OR USED-PCS.COM (WWW.USED-PCS.COM).

count warehouse store separate from your PC.

- **MODEMS:** One of your best business investments today is broadband Internet access. Depending on your location, that could be via a phone company's T1, ATM fiber relay or DSL, or the same cable that brings content to your TV. Each requires its own. At the very least, your PC is likely to include a 56K modem for connections over a phone line, at least as an available option. Not much to think about there except, even if you have a broadband connection, the $30 to $50 you'll need to spend to get a 56K modem is well worth it in the event your broadband connection fails.

Getting A Better Grade

While nothing prevents you from buying parts at CompUSA and building your own PC from the motherboard up, you'll find that the economics argue against that. Likewise, upgrades of your PC's CPU seldom makes good economic sense anymore with new PC prices so low.

But it's still relatively easy and economically feasible to add memory, storage and peripherals. Make sure your new PC has free memory sockets, drive bays, PCI peripheral slots and ports. Usually, all these become more bountiful as you move from a desktop to minitower to full tower case. But there are some upgrade possibilities you should demand in even the smallest computer.

- **MEMORY:** Always insist that all the initial memory on a new PC be included on a single DIMM (dual inline memory module). Insist on at least one open memory slot.

- **STORAGE:** It's hard to say which is happening faster—the growth in hard-drive capacity or the fall in hard-drive prices. We measure storage in gigabytes these days, and you should be able to add another 80GB of storage for less than $100. While more is always better, at the very least, insist that your new PC have one free internal 3½-inch storage bay that can accept another hard drive. Also insist on at least one externally available 5¼-inch drive bay into

SMART TIP

NEED IT FIXED? MOST COMPUTER RETAIL STORES HAVE A REPAIR DEPARTMENT TO FIX OR INSTALL NEW HARDWARE, EVEN IF YOU PURCHASED THE PC ELSEWHERE. THE PRICE TO HAVE A PROFESSION-AL DEBUG YOUR PC OR INSTALL AN UPGRADE—$50 TO $75 AN HOUR—MAY SOUND STEEP. BUT ASK YOUR-SELF: HOW MUCH IS YOUR TIME WORTH, AND IS TINKERING WITH A PC THE BEST USE OF IT?

which you may want to add another kind of optical drive than the one that will ship with your PC.

■ **PERIPHERALS:** Or to be more precise, boards for peripherals. You never know whether you may choose to add a different graphics adapter, a wireless networking card, a board for an external stor-

The Well-Dressed PC

A business-class PC should include the following specifications. Minimum configurations should have enough headroom to run the latest software for three years. Better-configured systems from brand-name manufacturers might still have resale value for up to five years.

CPU	2.4GHz Pentium 4 or Athlon XP 2100+ with at least 512KB of on-chip cache
Display	15-inch LCD capable of 1024x768 dpi or 17-inch LCD capable of 1280x1024 dpi
Free Bays	one or two free internal 3.5-inch bays; one or two free 5¹/₄-inch external bays
Free Slots	at least two full-sized PCI slots
Graphics	1280x1024 dpi-capable graphics adapter either built in or as a PCI card compatible with a 4X or 8X Advanced Graphics Port (AGP) and 32MB video memory
Hard Drive	80GB serial ATA with 7200RPM
Memory	minimum 512MB of 266GHz or faster DDR (double data rate) SDRAM
Modem	56K board or software modem
Optical Drive	32X Combo DVD-ROM/CD-RW rewritable, 4X DVD-R/CD-RW or 48X CD-R/CD-RW
Ports	at least 6 USB 2.0 ports distributed in front and back
Price	between $1,000 and $1,500, depending on feature combination
System Bus	400MHz or 533MHz frontside bus

age device or scanner, or who knows. Insist on two open PCI slots on even the smallest desktops.

- **PORTS:** Increasingly, the things that hang off your PC—mice, trackballs, keyboards, still and video cameras, external drives, printers and scanners—are relying on the new high-bandwidth FireWire and USB 2.0 ports, especially the latter. They often replace legacy serial, parallel and PS/2 ports—sometimes even PCI slots. No need to give up legacy connections yet, but make sure your PC still has a half dozen USB 2.0 ports both front and back. If you're lucky, you may also find a Windows PC with a built-in FireWire port for multimedia connections. Add-on FireWire or USB 2.0 hubs cost $50 to $100.

OFFICE PRODUCTIVITY SOFTWARE

A computer is useless without the right software to support your business activities. The following sections describe several types of software almost every business computer needs.

Security Software

First and foremost, you need to protect your individual PC and your whole network against various viruses, worms, Trojans and other harmful code that is literally scattered across the Internet, as well as the bad guys who prowl around your virtual neighborhood, looking for an unguarded point of entry. Look for all-encompassing security suites like those from Symantec, McAfee and Zone Alarm that include a firewall to prevent unwanted intrusions, regularly updated antivirus definitions, e-mail scanning and various other components to help you differentiate between friendly and unfriendly Internet callers. These suites may be software or Web services. *Cost: $50 to $100.*

Accounting

After security, you need accounting or financial software to manage your checkbooks, bank accounts, invoices, bills and even taxes. You may start with personal financial software and convert to an accounting program as your business grows. Either type does the checkbook and other math for you and provides a kind of template to help you arrange your accounts. Many programs let you pay bills and download bank account information electronically, use your printer to create checks, and link to tax preparation software so you can manage your taxes without a CPA. One of these programs is an absolute must for keeping track of bills, sending invoices and tracking cash flow. See Part 8, Chapter 38 for a list of popular programs.

Word Processing

Word processing software is an absolute must for your documents, proposals, customer letters and so forth. Today's word processors offer innumerable capabilities—spell-checking, document formatting, typeface and font controls, graphics support, and mail merge for addressing letters. Most have direct links to the Internet and other applications—for example, a Microsoft Word

How Suite It Is

The most convenient and cheapest way to buy the standard group of office productivity applications is in a suite, such as Microsoft Office, Lotus SmartSuite, Corel WordPerfect Suite and Sun StarOffice. By far, the most popular of these is Microsoft Office, which contains different combinations of Word, Excel, Access, PowerPoint, and possibly FrontPage and Publisher.

Typically, the cost of a productivity suite is much less than purchasing each of these products separately, a big reason why these products are so often purchased in a bundle.

Furthermore, since just about every business needs these basic programs, computer manufacturers often include an office suite on the hard drive of a system or will offer a discount price on a suite as a system upgrade to get your business.

If the system you're considering doesn't already include a productivity software bundle, ask about special pricing if one is purchased with a system or if the software can be included in the cost of the sale. Buying one of these suites alone could cost $250 to $550, depending on the components included, and then you have to install them all yourself.

If you do buy an office productivity suite with your computer, check to make sure that it is a full-fledged version of the leading suites mentioned above and that it includes all the components you need. You don't want a less-capable suite for consumers like Microsoft Works. At the same time, you may not need every single option in a productivity suite--presentation software, for example.

table can accept data from an Excel spreadsheet and get automatically updated when the spreadsheet changes. The longest-running contenders in the word processing category are Microsoft Word, Lotus Word Pro, Corel's WordPerfect and Sun's StarOffice Writer. *Cost: $75 to $350.*

Spreadsheets/Databases

A spreadsheet or database program can be used for simple data management, chart/graph creation, and mathematical calculations of all kinds. With a little experience, it's even possible to create customized applications, such as a dynamic customer directory, a workflow tool, and a report generator. Leading general-purpose, programmable databases include Microsoft Access, Lotus Approach and StarOffice Base. Popular spreadsheets include Microsoft Excel, Corel Quattro Pro, Lotus 1-2-3 and StarOffice Calc. *Cost: $100 to $400.*

Presentation

Presentation software lets you create graphical slide shows for display on a notebook or desktop computer with greater ease and more impact than slides or transparencies. These packages can provide full-color text and chart creation, animation and other special effects. Contenders in this category are Microsoft PowerPoint, Lotus Freelance Graphics, Corel Presentations and StarOffice Impress. *Cost: around $350.*

Contact Management

Contact management software is a combination of electronic calendar, date book, address book, contact-tracking database, and electronic personal assistant or to-do list. These tools help you keep track of all the little bits of information that are so important to business life and are also so easy to misplace. Contact management software can remind you of appointments, track attempts to reach customers, log your work hours, dial the telephone and more. Minimal versions are usually bundled with a Smartphone or a PDA. More powerful desktop versions include Microsoft's Outlook, Interact's ACT and FrontRange Solutions' GoldMine. *Cost: $100 to $300.*

File Backup

Backup software enables you to make copies of an entire file system or just important data files to restore on the inevitable day you have a drive failure or a virus infection. Backup software requires a storage device to save or copy data to. Traditionally, this has been a tape drive, DAT drive or removable hard drive using file compression/backup software like Seagate's Backup Exec or Dantz Retrospect. Now that optical drives are so cheap and plentiful, a better alternative is to back up to a rewritable CD-ROM or DVD-ROM disc using something like DVD X copy from 321 Studios. Roxio Easy CD Creator and Pinnacle Systems Instant CD-DVD let you burn your own CD or DVD discs. Either way, backup software *costs under $100*.

PERIPHERALS

You can't get along with a PC alone. Every PC needs access to a lot of supporting equipment—printers, for example.

Printers

You have two choices in office printers: a laserjet for high-volume documents, or an inkjet printer that prints documents more slowly and expensively, but which also can print full-color graphics and even high-resolution photos.

Actually, there is really no reason to choose just one. You're networked, remember? There is a wide range of both laser and inkjet printers with a variety of capabilities available from long-standing manufacturers at a wide range of price points—all of them low. You should be able to find a laserjet and inkjet that both fit comfortably within your budget.

Printing is a simple matter of directing a file over your network backbone to the right device, depending on what the job requires. But even if you buy both types of printers, you don't have to buy both right off the bat. Likewise, you probably won't invest equal amounts on both. It depends on which type of printing your operation needs the most.

Laser Printers

The overwhelming majority of printing in offices involves simple

SMART TIP
ONE KEY DIFFERENCE AMONG PRINTERS IS DEPENDABILITY AT HIGHER USE LEVELS. ALL PRINTING DRUMS HAVE A SPECIFIC DUTY CYCLE RATING IN PAGES PER MONTH. PRINTERS FOR SMALL WORK GROUPS SHOULD BE ABLE TO PRINT 50,000 TO 100,000 PPM MONTHLY. A ONE-YEAR WARRANTY IS TYPICAL OF MOST PRINTERS.

black-and-white text documents. If your business is like most, you'll probably have the greatest need for a workhorse laser printer that can print large volumes of proposals and memos, newsletters and client letters. Much of the printing is draft mode not intended for external consumption.

Laser printers typically deliver copies at speeds of 4 to 25 pages per minute (ppm) or more, with a quality range between 600 and 2400 dpi. Basic business-use laser printers range from $300 to $1,000 and should be sufficient for both low- and high-end applications.

An entry-level printer from Hewlett-Packard, Epson, Lexmark, Brother or Canon that prints text at 4 to 6 pages per minute with 600 x 600 dpi resolution will cost $300 to $500, depending on additional features like double-sided printing, multiple paper trays or trays for special media. Any of those features can add quite a few dollars.

If you require high-quality output or if you need a laser that can serve two to five people, $650 to $1,000 will buy you a real workhorse printer that will print 25ppm at 1200 x 1200 dpi and include other premium features like full duplex printing and special media handling. Printers like this typically have 350-sheet trays that will hold transparencies, envelopes, labels, cards and bond paper.

Inkjet Printers

Of course, it's a full-color world, so sooner or later, you're going to want to add color to your charts, graphs, letterhead and product photos. High-resolution graphics and true color are becoming an increasingly important element of hard copy output, and that's where a color inkjet comes in handy.

An inkjet printer creates images by squirting microscopic beads of ink onto the paper, so it's more flexible in mixing together different colored dots to achieve photo-quality representations. Most inkjets offer monochrome resolutions of 600 x 600 dpi at print speeds of 4 to 20 ppm, and color resolutions up to 4,800 x 1,200 dpi at vastly slower speeds that depend on the complexity of the image. Typically, the higher

BEWARE!

THERE ARE A COUPLE OF DRAWBACKS TO DOING VOLUME PRINTING ON INKJET PRINTERS. FIRST, IT'S OFTEN EASY TO SMEAR AND SMUDGE NEWLY PRINTED PAGES IF THEY AREN'T CAREFULLY HANDLED. ALSO, IT GENERALLY COSTS A BIT MORE TO TURN OUT A BLACK-AND-WHITE INKJET PAGE THAN ONE FROM A LASER PRINTER. IT MAY ONLY BE A PENNY PER PAGE, BUT THE AMOUNT CAN ADD UP OVER TIME.

DOLLAR STRETCHER

REPLACING TONER CARTRIDGES IS EXPENSIVE, SO BEFORE YOU CHOOSE A PRINTER, CHECK OUT THE AMOUNT OF PAGES PRINTABLE WITH ITS INK CARTRIDGE ON A REVIEW WEB SITE LIKE CNET'S NEWS.COM. ALSO BUY A PRINTER THAT HAS WIDELY AVAILABLE CARTRIDGES AND ARE DISCOUNTED ON WEB SITES SPECIALIZING IN PRINTING CONSUMABLES. RAPID TURNOVER IN PRINTER GENERATIONS CAN MAKE CARTRIDGES HARD TO FIND FOR OLDER MODELS, SO STICK WITH POPULAR BRANDS.

the output rate and print quality, the higher the cost will be.

Inkjet prices typically range between $100 and $500, but there are many much more expensive inkjets; and, in any case, price depends on a great variety in feature combinations. One Hewlett-Packard Deskjet very appropriate for a small office offers 20 ppm text printing, 4,800 x 1,200 dpi color resolution, two-sided printing, and an Ethernet connection for $250.

There are color laser printers using various technologies available, but, in general, a color inkjet is going to be a better purchase value for a new business.

Scanners

An increasing number of companies need to capture color images to, say, use in a newsletter or brochure or on a Web page. Here is where an inexpensive scanner can help. Scanners are also useful for capturing text documents that can then be manipulated, edited, added to and stored in a PC.

A scanner takes a picture of a page, a book or a photo laid on its screen. Scanners are very often bundled with optical character recognition (OCR) software for translating the scanner's "photograph" into characters a computer can edit. Sometimes they include drawing or photo editing software for manipulating images.

You may require one or both applications in your office. OCR can save countless hours of retyping. Grabbing images using a scanner creates a graphics file without requiring you to recreate a picture using a graphics program.

Scanners range in price as widely as printers do. A quality scanner costs between $100 and $500 with the overwhelming number of alternatives at the low end of the price spectrum. Oftentimes, it is the particular software or paper-handling features that affects scanner prices.

However, for general office use, an entry-level scanner in the $100 to $150 price range will support a direct-capture capability of 2400 x 4800 dpi—remember, 300 dpi is generally very pleasing to the human eye. That more than suffices for everyday uses.

If, however, you are looking for the highest quality scanning when, say, creating artwork for offset printing or publication, you can find scanners with a resolution of 1600 x 3200 dpi and 48-bit color input and output—that is, the capacity to differentiate among 281 trillion color shades and 65,500 shades of gray.

The best scanner manufacturers are often the best printer vendors—Canon, Epson and Hewlett-Packard—since the optical technologies for printing and scanning are related.

A Multifunction Alternative

Copying and faxing use similar processes. That creates the possibility that, in some cases, you may want to mix a few of these peripherals in what's known as a multifuction device (MFD). You often can find different combinations in one space-saving box at prices far below what it would cost to buy them separately. In fact, MFDs were created specifically with small businesses in mind.

The idea sounds great, and in space-constrained situations, an MFD can be a lifesaver. But it's not without trade-offs.

Remember office equipment is constantly improving—bringing you more for less in every generation. The rub is that evolution proceeds at a different pace among different device types. If you buy an MFD, you might find that you outgrow the laser printer or copier (in terms of volume of copies needed) faster than your needs for a new scanner and fax. Likewise, you may like the scan features but not be crazy about the way your MFD prints.

The saving grace here is that most such devices are so inexpensive—from $150 to $800—that you are not heavily invested. No one says you can't buy the high-volume version of any one of the devices to augment the MFD and still have a bargain. Price very much depends on the combination of features and quality each component brings to the party.

The real expense is in consumables, which get used up more

BEWARE!

DON'T FALL PREY TO SOME OF THE BARGAINS BEING OFFERED USING DESKTOP VERSIONS OF INTEL'S PENTIUM 4.

THESE "DESKNOTES" GENERALLY RUN HOT, DON'T RUN THE PROCESSOR AT FULL SPEED, AND HAVE A TERRIBLE BATTERY LIFE.

YOU CAN IDENTIFY THEM BY THEIR VERY LOW PRICES AND LARGE SIZES NEEDED TO HOUSE ADDITIONAL COOLING DEVICES, AND THE GREAT DIFFICULTY YOU'LL HAVE FINDING OUT WHAT MODEL OF PENTIUM 4 THEY CONTAIN.

Computer Shopping List

Use this handy shopping list to price and computerize your office.

Expense	Low End	High End
2.4GHz Pentium 4 or AMD Athlon XP 100+ PC or better		
15-inch or better liquid crystal display		
Windows laptop		
PDA (Palm or Pocket PC)		
Printer		
Scanner		
Copier		
Fax machine		
MFD		
Uninterruptible power supply		
Office productivity suite		
Security software		
Accounting software		
Desktop or Web publishing software		
High-speed Internet access		
Total Expenses	$	$

quickly than individual devices and could require multiple cartridges. Hewlett-Packard virtually owns this category, although Samsung, Brother and Epson also have offerings.

CAN'T LOSE

There are a lot of choices to make when purchasing a computer. Fortunately, there is ample information both online and in books and magazines that you can use to educate yourself about every component and software product you might consider.

If you take the time to research and even test-drive your choices, you can greatly improve the odds that your final decision will result in long-term satisfaction with your computer purchase.

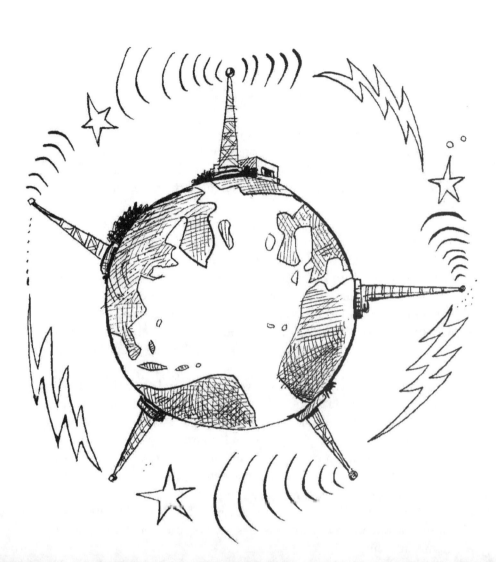

Air Time

Working without wires

By Mike Hogan, *Entrepreneur's* technology editor and author of
Entrepreneur's start-up guide *How to Start an e-Learning Business*

T he last time America relied on a wireless communications system, it was called the Pony Express. Information traveled rather slowly.

Then the landscape became dotted with telegraph poles. The increased speed of communications revolutionized the economy, closing the distance between individuals and America's far-flung communities. Telecommunications increased the pace and possibilities of business.

But the telephone network that evolved is no longer a comfortable fit for the fast-moving, information-based economy that America has become. The current telephone network just doesn't have the flexibility to keep up with the pace of business anymore—at least not working alone. For one thing, the Public Switched Telephone Network (PSTN) requires us to be tethered by telephone wire to a desk or a wall jack. We're in an analogous relationship with the Category 5 cable that transports most business data between our computers.

Being stationary, being tied down, that's simply not the way we work anymore—at least, not most of us. Analysts estimate that up to 65 percent of the American work force is away from "the office" on the average workday—perhaps telecommuting from home or touching down temporarily at retail job sites or satellite offices, maybe on a factory floor or a construction site. Most executives, managers and, especially, America's huge army of salespeople simply have jobs that keep them "on the road." If you think about it, those who spend all day in meetings are "on the road," too, for all intents and purposes.

And as anyone who travels on business can tell you, the demands of the job—the deadlines, the action items, the reports, record-keeping, myriad decisions and messages—are in no way diminished by your absence. The demands on your time just keep on coming, especially the messages.

A large portion of them are literally trash that needs to be shoveled out of your inbox. But hiding amid the spam and other unsolicited drek are a handful of messages that contain very important demands or opportunities from very important people. They can't wait for your return.

AND THIS IS NOW

That's the problem, and increasingly, wirelessness is the solution. We've already embarked on another communications revolution, and it's generating a prairie fire of interest.

It's defined by a rather small difference from the last major change in communications—wires, or rather, the lack of them. But that delivers a tremendous benefit—the freedom to be productive and/or communicate away from a wall whenever and wherever the mood or necessity moves us.

As the pace of deadlines accelerates, the product of our labor—increasingly information contained in data files—can no longer wait until we get back to the office. And, of course, nowadays we need to be reachable anywhere, any time.

That kind of "connectivity" is a tall order, and it will take awhile for us to get there. Like most societal changes of this proportion, the sizzle arrives excruciatingly long before the steak; and so far, we've only had a taste of what is a much broader vision.

SMART TIP

BUDGET IS ALWAYS AN ISSUE, BUT DON'T HESITATE TO REPLACE YOUR WIRELESS DEVICES WITH NEWER MODELS THAT LET YOU WORK FASTER, EASIER, BETTER. WIRELESS COMMUNICATIONS WILL CONTINUE TO BE CAUGHT IN THE SAME CYCLE OF PLUMMETING PRICES AND IMPROVING CAPABILITIES THAT CHARACTERIZES THE COMPUTER INDUSTRY. EARLY TECHNOLOGY ADOPTERS ALWAYS PAY MORE, BUT OFTEN REALIZE HIGHER OVERALL RETURNS ON THE INVESTMENT (AND CAPITAL EQUIPMENT TAX BREAKS).

Ironically, the ability to work without wires won't be achieved by replacing—but rather, by augmenting—the ubiquitous PSTN. It's there, it works, the telephone is easy to use, and it's familiar to every American and will continue to fulfill its mission of landline voice communications for years to come—at least, among consumers.

With the rapid build-out of the Internet, it's no longer the only game in town for business calls. But which of these nationwide backbones your voice and data travel over isn't something you have to worry about.

THE WIRELESS LINEUP

The real productivity issue has to do with how you receive voice and data transmissions over the last mile from the network and you.

That's where wires will be replaced by transmission over several different radio bands—as appropriate. There will still be times when PSTN or TV cable or Category 5 networking cable is the most convenient and cost-effective transmission medium. But, increasingly, you'll use radio waves over one or more of these different radio bands to carry your communication packets.

Each has its unique benefits and shortcomings, so no single wireless technology answers every need. Some, like Bluetooth or infrared, are rather narrowband, but cheap and with low-power requirements. They're useful for short-range data transfers, but not the best choice for, say, sending voice over great distances. Other radio types, like fixed wireless or satellite or even microwave, are primarily backbone technologies today used mostly by communication service providers or companies large enough to underwrite their own communications networks. They aren't something you need to worry about at this stage of their evolution.

The real action, the keenest area of interest, for wireless communications is in midrange solutions—perhaps, by virtue of the combination of relatively low capital costs and flexible transmission characteristics. You're probably most familiar with the wide array of cellular radio types, which are rather narrowband, but capable of sending voice and data over great distances while expending only a moderate amount of battery power.

Then there are the much newer and growing number of 802.11x or Wi-Fi flavors. These were originally designed for wideband, short-range data transfers—an alternative or adjunct to your office LAN cable. While some argue that the 802.11 band is the single answer to all wireless communications problems, it's not in the short term.

Wi-Fi radios are relatively power-hungry, which isn't an insurmountable technical problem. But it is a problem that has to be solved at a cost comparable to other perfectly acceptable solutions;

and there are other business problems that have to be dealt with before Wi-Fi can move out of your office.

An important advantage all wireless communication types have over the phone network is that they don't require a single constantly open circuit over which an analog wavestream is transmitted. Instead, analog data types, like voice or even video, are converted to digital packets that can be intermingled with data packets and sent through the air with different priorities attached. This creates an invisible network that's more efficient than traditional PSTN transmissions, and with plenty of headroom for future growth.

Having everything digital also makes the management of our many different communication types easier at the receiving end. We aren't there yet, but another promise of wireless technology is a universal inbox where you can receive voice, data, faxes, e-mail, instant messages, all digital data packets in one place using one familiar interface to move, forward, delete and even combine them all.

CELL PHONES EVERYWHERE

Unless you were a trucker in a former life, plying the interstates armed with a ham radio handle, your experience with wirelessness is probably less than a decade old. For most of us, it began with a short-range cordless phone at home and a car phone at work.

This was a high-end device that cost a lot to install and could operate only in the relatively few areas where service was provided—and you were still tethered to your automobile.

Today, cell phones have replaced car phones and now compete with office phones and PCs as the average businessperson's most important productivity tool. Phones still ride in cars, but they are vastly cheaper, smaller, more fully featured and cover much wider areas.

Hitting The Wall

Between 2001 and 2002, the meteoric rise in the purchase of new cell phones and subscriptions ground to a halt. Recent attempts to jump-start sales with expensive new data services such as Internet browsing and file downloading have met a cool reception in America and mixed success overseas. Less bandwidth-intensive, consumer-oriented data services, like downloading music, games and ring tones, have been better received.

But it isn't clear whether consumers can buy enough entertainment services to justify the billions providers need to spend to upgrade today's second-generation cells to new, broadband third-generation (3G) networks. Cell companies had hoped to partially underwrite the huge capital outlays needed to build out 3G cells by providing business data services. But it's not clear how many Americans will ever find a cell phone's small screen and lack of memory and keyboard attractive for Internet browsing, e-mailing and file downloading.

You may experience 3G some day. But true 2.4Mbps 3G bandwidth seems far off—even though some carriers already advertise their networks as "3G." That's likely to impact your voice calls in two ways: coverage and quality of service.

In the United States, cell phone coverage has been spreading out from high-population areas and along the interstates to more rural areas a lot more slowly than we would like. If you own a cell phone, you know that service is spotty and disconnections frequent even in supposedly well-covered areas.

Small wonder that about a third of cell phone customers change carriers every year—a phenomenon known as churn. This, even though you lose your phone number—particularly onerous for business customers—and pay early withdrawl penalties to get out of phone contracts.

Those 3G networks also will be needed to improve the quality of voice calls as the number of subscribers inevitably picks up again and so does the load on the network. But again, since the recession, providers can no longer rely on new customers to replace dissatisfied ones; and more moderate growth projections make the possibility of large capital projects iffy. The interim plan is to ease into 3G through intermediate 2.5G networks, relying on a variety of overlays, software tuneups and cross-carrier agreements.

The question is, Will carriers do something before unheard of—improve service? Maybe, after they've responded to market softness by cutting prices and trying every marketing gimmick conceivable—from bundling service types to offering a billion minutes' worth of weekend calling.

Plan Ahead

Cell phone service plans hardly need another complication. They're already very difficult to compare. The complexity is likely to increase as competition heats up and providers fight for market share. Most wireless carriers have corporate associations with landline providers and can be expected to mix new options from their nonwireless divisions with their already-complex wireless service plans.

The best way to get a fix on what kind of a cell phone user you are is to examine your own usage patterns on past cell phone bills. That includes the number of prime-time minutes a month, of course; but also whether your calls are mostly local or long distance, during weekdays or weekends? Which special services, like caller ID or answering service, you use?

In many cases, you can save money by using a cell phone rather than a landline for long-distance and toll calls—but not always. You'll also need to check your landline and broadband service bills to understand how you really use all your different communications services. After voice, you'll have to decide which provider offers your best option for data downloads.

The good news is, increased competition by landline providers in wireless markets and long-distance providers in local markets and all combinations thereof should help both prices and service bundling, so you eventually will have less minutiae to consider.

It's not guaranteed, but at the very least, increased competition from more providers has the price pendulum swinging in your favor.

WI-FI SMORGASBORD

Wi-Fi has brought business-class networking to people's homes. Despite all the marketing blather about ease of use, that's not an endeavor just anyone has the patience to attempt. There must be something truly compelling about being able to wirelessly connect different computers in different rooms and share Internet access and files.

It's not difficult to see the appeal in the office. Private companies that are compelled to deliver ever-higher levels of productivity every quarter long ago came to understand the benefits of having all your computing devices working in unison and able to share workloads and data (see Chapter 27 on page 417).

In a small office, Wi-Fi is unquestionably the easiest way to have all your desktops, printers, laptops, whatever connected.

Ch-ch-changes

Wired networks are cheap and fast—until you have to make a change. Many working environments are very fluid today, with new employees being added and work-groups being formed for temporary projects and then disbanded. No one wants to pull Category 5 cable and, maybe, install and configure one or more Ethernet switches or routers every time a new workstation or office is added or the company grows into a new building.

Wi-Fi networks have proved to be an easy way to add connections out on "the edge" of established office networks. They conform to the standard Ethernet protocol and deliver comparable data transfer capability—up to 54Mbps for 802.11a and 802.11g networks. That's their primary appeal to businesses today—that and being able to bring broadband Internet access quickly to a new workplace—even if that workplace is a kitchen table or a back porch at home or a hotel or a cafe on the road.

SMART TIP

NOTE: INCREASINGLY, BEING OUT ON "THE EDGE" OF A COMPANY'S NETWORK MEANS COMMUNICATING WITH AN ENTERPRISE NETWORK FROM A WI-FI-EQUIPPED PORTABLE AT HOME, OR AT A HOTEL, AN AIRPORT OR A COFFEE SHOP. ALL YOU NEED IS A WI-FI PC CARD ADDED TO YOUR LAPTOP AND TO BE WITHIN RANGE OF A WI-FI ACCESS POINT.

SMART TIP

WI-FI'S BENEFITS COME AT THE EXPENSE OF BATTERY LIFE IN A LAPTOP OR A PDA.

SAVE POWER BY TURNING OFF YOUR WIRELESS ADAPTER WHEN NOT IN USE. IF ITS SOFTWARE SCANS FOR ACCESS POINTS IN THE BACKGROUND, TURN THAT OFF, TOO. WHILE YOU'RE AT IT, IF YOU'RE JUST WRITING MEMOS OR E-MAIL, TURNING DOWN THE BRIGHTNESS OF YOUR PORTABLE'S DISPLAY AND YOUR CPU'S SPEED CAN BE BIG POWER-SAVERS, TOO.

Even on a bad day or in the most difficult office setting, the slowest Wi-Fi network flavor, 802.11b, can deliver data at 2.4Mbps to 5.5Mbps, 100 to 300 feet through the air. With the right access point layout, you'll get 11Mbps from a 802.11b network, 54Mbps from 802.11a and 802.11g; and, while bandwidth is one of those things we can never get enough of, that's plenty fast for most situations.

To give you a real sense of just how fast Wi-Fi is, data downloads from today's cellular networks proceed at the pace of the still widely used PC modem—about 56Kbps. A Wi-Fi-equipped computer with an Internet connection can download and transfer data hundreds of times faster.

Plummeting Prices

Setting up a wireless LAN isn't that different from setting up a wired one—you just don't have to pull cable through office walls and behind desks. It can open up networked computing and Internet access sharing to places that just wouldn't have been connected otherwise—your back porch, a seat in an airport waiting area or a table at a coffee shop.

There are literally several hundred different manufacturers of Wi-Fi access points, routers and PC cards—so many that the price of the average, bare-bones Wi-Fi adapter has plummeted in a couple of years from near $1,000 to under $100. An 802.11b Wi-Fi receiver for your laptop may sell for as little as $40.

But there still are a range of prices you can pay, depending on the speed of the Wi-Fi protocol being used and special features the access point may have, such as various kinds of security or customization for special situations. While in-office Wi-Fi adapters are generally set to operate over a maximum range of under 300 feet, vendors are already finding various ways to push the limits, especially outdoors or over open spaces like factories.

There are several different hardware options for connecting your PCs, offering you maximum flexibility in configuring your network. You start with a drive-sized standalone router connected to the broadband modem of your Internet gateway and its headwater PC. The connection might be a Cat 5 cable, a USB wire or even wireless. Each of the other PCs on your network also needs an access point, which might be free-standing and connected in the ways above or with a Wi-Fi card installed in one of its PCI slots.

The Wi-Fi Alliance has exerted a strong influence over vendors to ensure the interoperability among different brands of like-standard Wi-Fi adapters. You shouldn't have any more problems mixing different brands on your office network than you do PC brands.

BEWARE!

WHEN RESEARCHING WI-FI HARDWARE PROVIDERS, FIND OUT IF THEY OFFER TOLL-FREE TECH SUPPORT. YOU MAY NEED IT FOR INSTALLATION. WHILE WI-FI HARDWARE IS FAIRLY STANDARD, WI-FI CONFIGURATION SOFTWARE IS STILL A WORK IN PROGRESS. ALSO, THE NUMBER OF DIFFERENT OPERATING SYSTEMS YOU HAVE AND THE IP ADDRESS HANDLING AND OTHER PECULIARITIES OF SOME PC BRANDS ADD SMALL COMPLICATIONS THAT CAN STYMIE YOU. ONCE UP AND RUNNING, YOUR NETWORK WILL LIKELY BE TROUBLE-FREE.

However, again, vendors often add special features to certain adapter models that only work when your network consists entirely of that model. A common example is the addition of virtual private network (VPN) tunnels to keep Wi-Fi data packets from being snatched from midair.

Wi-Fi Security

The weakness of 802.11's WEP (Wireless Enterprise Protocol) security is legendary. Hackers amuse themselves by flying over or driving through neighborhoods and office parks with Wi-Fi-equipped portables, "sniffing" out networks they can crash for fun or profit. Some traveling businesspeople also have learned they can park and "borrow" an Internet connection from a neighboring business that may not have WEP turned on.

The IEEE electrical engineers standards-setting body is working on a new 802.11i standard that will ensure better build-in security for 802.11b, 802.11a and 802.11g networks, but its ratification could be a year or more away. In the meantime, the Wi-Fi Alliance has introduced an interim Wi-Fi Protected Access (WPA) that should make it tougher for crackers of any kind to crash your networks. WPA has a better process for screening network users and employs a tougher encryption lock to make it more difficult for hackers to crack messages even if they can intercept them.

By this writing, WPA encryption should be shipping with all flavors of new Wi-Fi adapters, although you may have to download the WPA software from vendor sites to retrofit your older adapters. And, of course, these security measures don't work unless you turn them on. Companies are reluctant to do that because it slows down network traffic a bit.

Getting Hot

Their low prices, ease of use and big productivity returns have Wi-Fi networks popping up in airports, bookstores, coffee shops, hotels, even convenience stores. These wireless communication zones or hot spots are not only a convenience for you if you're a business traveler, but they could also represent a way to build traffic or merchandise your own retail operation.

It doesn't cost much to turn any high-traffic location into a paying Wi-Fi hot spot—a few hundred dollars for hardware. The major expense is the monthly fee for an Internet connection that will vary by the bandwidth you need. Revenue-sharing with a hotspot aggregator like Wayport (www.wayport.com) or Boingo Wireless (www.boingo.com) can get you turnkey expertise for user authentication, security and network maintenance as well as worldwide marketing.

Wi-Fi radios are becoming standard issue for laptops and, one day, will be in most PDAs and phones. They're even finding their way into clip-on badges and other portable devices.

If Wi-Fi hotspots keep proliferating at their current rapid rate, they may even become adjuncts to the world's several cellular networks for data download and even better voice-call coverage, as they already are in many offices and industrial plants.

SMART TIP

IN THE OFFICE, WI-FI'S RANGE TOPS OUT AT 300 FEET. BUT IT ALL DEPENDS ON THE OBSTACLES BETWEEN USERS AND THE PLACEMENT OF ACCESS POINTS. TAKE AWAY THE OBSTACLES OR ADD A MORE POWERFUL ANTENNA TO A WI-FI ROUTER/ACCESS POINT, AND IT'S CAPABLE OF MUCH GREATER RANGE—GOOD FOR, SAY, TRANSMITTING DATA BETWEEN DIFFERENT LANs IN DIFFERENT BUILDINGS.

Wi-Fi already provides several times the bandwidth that cellular carriers hope to deliver through 3G networks, and Wi-Fi hotspots are growing organically, with a much smaller capital investment spread out over many buyers.

Chipset manufacturers are already busy creating Wi-Fi radios that combine several different protocols etc. devices with different combinations of cell, Wi-Fi, Bluetooth, are on their roadmaps.

Whatever the scenario or situation, there is a wireless solution. Wireless networking of our computers and ourselves is an idea whose time has obviously come.

GLOSSARY

S2G: second-generation digital cellular networks that send voice as packets rather than as the continuous waves used in analog networks

2.5G: intermediate improvements to digital cellular networks that improve voice-call quality and permit data transfers to cell phones at speeds up to 144Kbps

3G: third-generation cellular networks being architected for better voice calls, Web browsing and data downloads at speeds up to 2.4Mbps

802.11x: any of several wireless local area networking standards—aka, Wi-Fi—that transfers data packets over the 2.4GHz or 5GHz radio bands up to 300 feet at speeds up to 54Mbps

BAND: a radio frequency or contiguous range of frequencies that comprise a channel used by a particular wireless protocol

BANDWIDTH: the amount of data that can be sent through a channel as if through a pipe measured in bits per second, a "wider" channel permitting faster transfer rates

BLUETOOTH: a short-range (30 feet) wireless protocol for transferring voice and data among cell phones and computing devices over the 2.4GHz radio band

BROADBAND: wireless frequencies, such as Wi-Fi, that offer many times the bandwidth of narrowband frequencies, such as cellular, that in turn usually have far greater range

CELL: the area covered by a radio signal from a transmitter/receiver, usually overlapping other cells to create a seamless transmission network

CDMA: Code Division Multiple Access is the dominant second-generation wireless protocol used in North America by Sprint PCS, Verizon Wireless and others who are building 3G networks to be called CDMA2000 1X

FREQUENCY: the rate at which an electrical current alternates, usually measured in Hertz (Hz) and often used to denote a band on the radio spectrum, such as 800MHz or 2.4GHz

GSM/GPRS: Global System for Mobile Communications is used for voice calls, while General Packet Radio Service is a companion data channel used by AT&T Wireless, T-Mobile and Cingular Wireless, among others

Wise Buys

*Shopping for phone systems,
fax machines and copiers*

B etter, faster, cheaper. These are the buzzwords of technology change, and they apply to such basic office devices as telephones, fax machines and copiers. With so many new and cheaper devices coming onto the market all the time, we face a dizzying array of choices when it comes to selecting our office communications equipment, making our selection harder than ever. But that's only because the choices we now have are so good, and the prices more attractive than ever before.

WHAT'S MY LINE?

Selecting a telephone system is a big decision for most companies, since it will be your primary means of communicating with clients, vendors and employees, even in the Internet age! If you don't ask the right questions, you could end up with a system that doesn't meet your needs or one that will become obsolete in no time at all. There are many issues to consider when choosing your phone system, including your business, staff, logistical and budgetary requirements.

There are many different phone systems to choose from. The simplest phones, with minimal features, are very inexpensive—under $10 for the simplest, up to several hundred dollars for the most advanced—but as your business grows, so will your needs. That's why it is important to plan for the future—otherwise, cheaper can end up being more expensive.

If your business is a homebased or small business with only one or two employees, you may find you can work with two plain-old residential lines, with one dedicated to voice calls and the other suitable for both voice as well as fax and data use. But if your business is growing rapidly, you may have to start that long journey into the realm of corporate telephone systems—and learn some new lingo such as PBX (Private Branch Exchange) systems, KSU (Key System Units) and KSU-less systems. There are three types of phone systems to consider:

■ **RESIDENTIAL PHONES:** Most homes are equipped to handle up to two residential lines, ideal for the smallest businesses—just ask your phone company to activate, or (if necessary) install, the second line.

You can add many features to your home telephone service from your local phone company, such as voice mail, call-waiting, caller ID, call forwarding and three-way calling. These features make it possible for a home business to enjoy telephone features long available only to business customers.

■ **SMALL-BUSINESS MULTIPLE-LINE PHONES:** The next step up is to small-business multiple-line phones. A business that has more than two employees who spend much of their day on the phone needs a phone system that can handle all calls efficiently. A popular small-business phone is the Key System Unit-less (KSU-less), which is ideal for a business with up to a dozen or so staff members. The typical business using a KSU-less phone system has two to four incoming lines that serve up to a dozen stations, each needing only light to medium phone usage.

It's called "KSU-less" because it does not need a computerized central control system called a "key system unit." These are relatively inexpensive and easy to install, requiring minimal or no rewiring. If you find your small or homebased business needs to manage many voice and data lines, a KSU-less system might be just the answer. KSU-less Systems are priced around $150 to $400 per line, which—believe it or not—is considered cheap for a business telephone system, though quite a lot more than what you're used to for your residential line. A KSU-less phone system may include features like call transfer, intercom, speaker, three-way conferencing, hold, flash for call-waiting, redial, and memory for programming speed-dial numbers.

■ **LARGE BUSINESS MULTIPLE-LINE PHONES:** A business that has more than a dozen employees making a large number of phone calls needs a bigger phone system that can handle many outside lines and extensions. With this phone system, one or more high-bandwidth T1 lines are necessary to effectively handle the load, and the voice-mail system will need a large number of

SMART TIP

WITH BOTH KSU OR PBX SYSTEMS, YOU CAN ADD FEATURES INCLUDING VOICE MAIL, CALLER ID, INTRA-OFFICE PAGING, AUTOMATIC REDIAL, PROGRAMMABLE MEMORY, CALL-CONFERENCING AND VIDEO TELECONFERENCING, CALL-WAITING, AND A COMPUTER TELEPHONY ADAPTOR (CTA) SO YOU CAN DO "DATABASE DIALING" DIRECT FROM YOUR COMPUTER AS WELL AS "DESKTOP MESSAGING," WHICH ENABLES THE RETRIEVAL OF VOICE, FAX AND E-MAIL MESSAGES DIRECTLY FROM YOUR COMPUTER SCREEN.

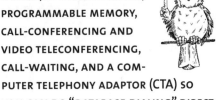

ports. One popular large business system is the Private Branch Exchange or PBX system, which creates a miniature phone network inside the office and is scalable up to virtually any size. A less expensive large business system is a Key System, which can be used for a business with up to around 60 employees.

These systems differ mainly in how much phone traffic they can handle and how much they cost. Key Systems run slightly higher than KSU-less, starting at $200 or more per line and up, but in addition they require professional—and expensive—installation, configuration and maintenance, which is not required for the less complex KSU-less systems. PBX Systems can cost upward of $800 per line, plus substantial installation, configuration and maintenance costs. The reason why KSU and PBX systems are more expensive is the complexity of their control unit, which is the brains of the phone system, containing all the circuitry to connect your phones to the incoming lines from the phone company and to accessories like intercom, paging, music-on-hold and voice mail. The central control unit can cost from $500 to $2,000.

Facing The Vendor

Choosing the right vendor can mean the life or death of your communications system. When selecting features for your telephone system, stay focused on your most important needs. Many of the new and more advanced features will never be fully used by your employees, so don't let your sales rep drive your decision. Properly setting up your phone system and maintaining it is vital to reliable and professional communications, so odds are you will work with a vendor or a dealer when you make your purchase, and they will help you with the wiring, configuration and ongoing maintenance of your system. Keep the following points in mind when selecting a vendor:

■ **PICK A VENDOR THAT IS FAMILIAR WITH YOUR COMPANY SIZE,** and make sure the dealer is selling you a product they know and trust.

Phone System Checklist

Before you select your phone service, there are some important questions you should ask that will better prepare you.

Business Requirements

❑ How many incoming lines do you have/need?

❑ How many incoming and outgoing calls per day do you (or will you) average?

❑ Do you need direct inward dialing (DID), and if so, for how many staff?

❑ How many modem and fax lines do you need?

❑ Do you need an automated attendant, or will you have a receptionist who will answer and route calls?

❑ Do you need voice mail, and if so, what features do you want?

❑ Do you need to be able to switch phones on and off?

❑ Do you need power-fail back-up?

❑ What is your expected growth over the next five years?

Staff Requirements

❑ How many staff members will need a telephone?

❑ How many staff members will need voice mail?

❑ How many staff members will need caller ID?

❑ How many staff members will need speakerphone capabilities?

❑ Do you need phones in public areas or just in offices and cubicles?

Additional Questions

❑ Will you be using your telephone system for both voice and data?

❑ Will you need 11 lines for large call volume as well as fast Internet connections?

❑ Do you need dial-in capabilities for mobile users?

❑ Do you need a paging system?

❑ Do you have a tech person on staff, or will you need outside support?

❑ Do you already have wire and phone jacks in the desired locations?

Once you can answer these questions, you are ready to contact telephone system vendors, your local phone company and/or contractors for quotes on your new or upgraded telephone system. But if any of these questions baffle you, it means you need to do more homework and become better versed in telecommunications lingo. That will better prepare you for when you sit down with vendors and sales reps, so you can assess their solutions with minimal risk of being oversold a system that surpasses your needs.

Avoid either a brand-new and unknown commodity, or an older and potentially obsolete product.

■ **ASK FOR REFERENCES FROM OTHER CUSTOMERS** so you can benefit from the experience of your peers.

■ **ASK THE VENDOR ABOUT THE WARRANTY,** support capabilities, the total price tag including installation and maintenance, whether they provide training, and if they are manufacturer-trained and authorized.

Keeping Costs Down

Before you buy your system, make sure you comparison shop. Take advantage of the Internet. There are many telephone system vendors with online stores and search engines waiting to find you attractive prices. If you work in a one-vendor town, fear not: The Internet can help you find alternative vendors in other cities and towns that might offer you more competitive pricing. When choosing a phone system, remember, while a KSU-less System is attractive financially, it will not be able to grow with you, so if you plan on adding more than a dozen employees, consider your growth plans before you make your final decision. As you conduct your research and prepare for purchasing your phone system, consider some common money-saving methods:

■ **CONSIDER SECOND-HAND.** Used phone systems might be cheaper, but be careful with second-hand higher-end systems like KSU and PBX, which require computerized central control systems that are fragile and may be obsolete (just like a used computer quickly becomes behind the times). Also, the more expensive systems are often proprietary, so make sure the system you're considering can work with other manufacturers' accessories and services. Your vendor may have used systems available from customers who have recently upgraded, but the most common place to find second-hand systems is on the Internet. For instance, you can find a variety of used and refurbished telephone systems at UsedPhonesForLess (www.store.yahoo.com/usedphonesforless/index.html), which carries second-hand systems from most manufacturers.

■ **WIRE FOR FUTURE GROWTH.** When wiring your network, install extra capacity to handle your growth—and avoid bringing the technicians back in to rewire your office.

■ **LOOK FOR SEASONAL DISCOUNTS.** Plan ahead and ask your dealer/ vendor if there are price breaks at the end of the year or quarter.

■ **CHECK LOCAL PHONE RATES.** Local phone rates may vary a great deal depending on your system—Key System, KSU-less or PBX systems will be subject to different monthly service fees—so don't forget to factor this into your budget. Also, check long-distance rates, and shop for a long-distance package that meets your needs.

■ **REMEMBER TO BUDGET FOR INSTALLATION AND SERVICE.** If you select a PBX or Key System, you'll probably need it installed and serviced by a technician. The price tag for your phone system's wiring, setup and configuration, as well as its ongoing mainte- nance will rival the cost of the system itself, so brace yourself!

Get The Message

The popularity of voice-mail systems has greatly surpassed old- fashioned answering machines, but many smaller businesses continue to use them. The cost is right—a one-time payment for the machine frees you from the recurring monthly fees for voice-mail service. But answering machines have their disadvantages—namely, they don't work if there is a power failure (unless you have backup electricity), and answering machines wear out and sometimes fail.

Most small businesses prefer using a voice-mail service, since there are many obvious benefits, including availability of service even in the event of a power failure and no mechanical worries such as a jammed tape or a power-surge that wipes out a digital answering machine's messages. Plus, a voice-mail system can grow with your business. Voice mail will cost you about $12 to $18 per line, depending on the number of lines.

Going The Distance

Long-distance service can be a business's most expensive telecom- munications expense—luckily, rates have dramatically fallen in recent years, and there are plenty of choices out there, including new flat- rate unlimited calling plans for around $60 per line, per month. And with the Internet available to make comparison shopping easier, long distance has never been more affordable.

While price is an important consideration, bear in mind that serv- ice plans vary, and the smaller carriers may not be able to provide your company with the level of support you require. For instance, not all long-distance carriers provide operator support, so if you require an operator—for either collect or overseas calls—operator service could be essential to you. Or if there is a service disruption during off-peak hours, without support, you'll be left helpless until the next business

It's Free!

Voice over Internet Protocol (VoIP) is a new technology that offers the promise of nearly free long-distance and international calling by using the Internet to bypass telephone networks, so even international calls are priced as if local. But the reality is still imperfect, resulting in a number of common complaints arising from disappointing audio quality, interoperability issues, new and unproven vendors, and evolving standards.

In time, the growth of the VoIP market will result in improved quality; in fact, some users have already found notable improvements in call quality. With increased support for industry-standard protocols, gradually, VoIP technology is finding its place in corporate networks. For new businesses, especially tech-savvy ones, VoIP can dramatically reduce long-distance phone costs. However, for VoIP to really make a difference, you need to have significant long-distance costs.

But the long-distance toll is just one factor to consider. Experts say one big problem with IP telephony is that the cost of system ownership and handsets can mount. Remember, VoIP is an emerging technology, and like all emerging technologies, it comes with a higher "total cost of ownership." Though the call might be free, the IT support and infrastructure costs behind that "free call" might prove to be surprisingly pricey. There are several new VoIP appliances on the market that are comparable in price to a conventional phone—in the range of $200 to $1,000—but they lock you into one vendor's standard, and there is no way to know if that standard will be in use a year from now. For more information on VoIP technology, Ohio State University has published a guide online at www.cis.ohio-state.edu/~jain/refs/ref_voip.htm#books.

day, which could mean lost business—and money.

Take a close look at your long-distance calling needs. If you are primarily a local or regional company, national or international long distance may not be all that critical to your operations. And get a feel for the times of days you make calls, as well as your call volumes, before selecting your plan. Some carriers will offer you a long-term contract in exchange for a lower rate, and while the savings might be attractive, a long-term contract will limit your choices. And some plans require you to meet a certain number of monthly minutes called

a *waive minimum*, and if you don't reach this threshold, you have to pay the monthly service charge. So be careful, and don't commit to unrealistic minimums.

Cheaper Choices

For businesses with a dozen employees or less, prepaid calling cards have become popular, offering cheap long distance from the office or on the road. They are basically debit cards you purchase for a certain amount of money—usually $5, $10, $20 or $30—and each is good for a specific number of minutes. The major benefit of using a debit card is the price, which can be as low as a penny per minute for domestic long-distance calls. However, some cards have lots of hidden fees, such as an activation fee, a monthly maintenance fee, a per-call service fee, and a payphone surcharge that can substantially increase the cost per minute, so it ends up being more expensive than advertised. All require calling a local or toll-free number, and then inputting a long PIN, which takes additional time. Be careful—several prepaid card providers have gone out of business, leaving customers with useless prepaid cards.

There are also long-distance service providers who use "dial arounds," those 10-10-ABC numbers frequently advertised on TV, such as 1010-220 or 1010-ATT. They also provide inexpensive long distance, but like prepaid cards, these require dialing additional numbers and have hidden costs such as a minimum price per call, which can result in higher costs than advertised.

JUST THE FAX!

Fax machines seemed like magic when they first appeared in the 1980s. The benefit of a fax is that you can get a hard copy of a document to someone located miles away in just a few moments. Now, in the age of e-mail, a fax seems somewhat less magical, and may be heading toward extinction. But there are still times when faxing a hard copy, such as a signed sales order or contract, is still necessary.

Faxes sport many different features and functions:

- **MEMORY** lets you store documents in electronic form.
- **AUTOMATIC FAX/PHONE SWITCHES** detect incoming faxes and activate the fax without manual intervention.
- **SPEED-DIAL** saves time for frequent-faxers.
- **OUT-OF-PAPER RECEPTION** saves incoming faxes in memory if the machine runs out of paper.
- **QUICK SCAN** lets you scan a page into memory before beginning a transmission. That means you don't have to wait at the machine until it finishes sending the original.
- **DUAL SCAN** lets you send and receive faxes at the same time. For example, you can scan an outgoing fax into memory while a fax is being received. The scanned fax is then sent directly from memory when the phone line becomes free.

Fax machines with higher sending speeds are usually more expensive, but they'll pay for themselves over time with reduced long-distance bills. Faxes range in price from around $100 for plain-paper inkjets, to more than $400 for laser faxes, and upward of $1,000 for a multifunction fax-plus combo with laser output.

DOLLAR STRETCHER

FAXES HAVE PROVED RELIABLE DURING THEIR THREE- TO FIVE-YEAR LIFE EXPECTANCY, SO IF YOU RECEIVE LESS THAN 60 FAXED PAGES PER MONTH, IT'S PROBABLY CHEAPER TO SKIP A SERVICE PLAN AND JUST REPLACE YOUR FAX IF IT DIES. IF YOU DO ELECT A SERVICE CONTRACT, EXPECT TO PAY ABOUT $50 A YEAR FOR A MACHINE THAT MIGHT ONLY BE WORTH $100.

HOT LINK

YOU DON'T NEED YOUR OWN MACHINE TO SEND A FAX. COMPANIES LIKE JFAX.COM AND FAXBACK.COM  PROVIDE FAX SERVICES OVER THE INTERNET, SO YOU CAN DO AWAY WITH THOSE EXTRA PHONE LINES AND MAINTENANCE HASSLES. FAXBACK.COM PROVIDES THE SOFTWARE, FAX-ON-DEMAND, BROADCASTING AND WEB-TO-FAX SOLUTIONS. PRICES TYPICALLY INCLUDE A $4.95 MONTHLY FEE, PLUS A 10-CENT FEE PER PAGE FAXED AND A ONE-TIME SETUP FEE OF $10.

DO YOU COPY?

Even though the photocopier was invented by Xerox half a century ago, it remains an essential business tool, and recent price drops now make it possible for even the smallest business to afford one. With ink-jet printing technology instead of the pricier laser output, copiers are available for under $100. Some issues to consider as you begin your search for a photocopier are your copy volume, your budget, and if you need color or black and white will do.

Generally speaking, there are three basic grades or classes of photocopy machines, in three different price categories, and with different copy speeds (measured in cpm, or copies per minute.)

■ **PC-GRADE COPIER:** These are designed to produce 500 to 1,500 copies monthly and can cost from as little as $100 to about $500. However, the low cost may be outweighed by the lack of features, capacity, high cost per copy, and lack of available support service. Copy speeds are also slow, at about 6 to 9 cpm.

■ **BUSINESS-GRADE COPIER:** This is the most common grade of

Read The Fine Print!

Before you buy a copier for your business, make sure you investigate the following:

● **THE WARRANTY:** Be sure to read the fine print.

● **SUPPORT:** Does the vendor offer 24/7 phone and e-mail support? Will they make onsite visits 24/7/365? How fast do they react to emergency calls?

● **THE PRICE TAG:** Don't forget to factor in the equipment as well as the setup and maintenance costs.

● **TRAINING:** Is training included? If not, turn and run.

● **EXPANSION:** If you require a small but reliable system, be sure the vendor can provide the necessary expansion support and products, or you may find yourself with an obsolete system when your company grows.

● **MANUFACTURER-TRAINED:** Technicians should always be manufacturer-trained, certified and well-versed in the latest cabling and installation solutions. Many are not "manufacturer-trained," even if the vendor offers what they call "manufacturer support."

● **AUTHORIZED DEALERS:** Make sure you get the right support from your vendor by ensuring that the product you select comes with adequate product support, something only an "authorized dealer" can provide. There are plenty of "gray market" resellers that do not have the authority or resources to offer ongoing system support.

machine; available features and machine size vary. Sizes range from a simple desktop model to a large stand-alone machine. Business-grade machines have a low cost per copy and are designed to produce up to 50,000 copies monthly. Prices range from $2,000 to $15,000. Copy speeds are faster in this category, in the 10 to 49 cpm range.

- **COMMERCIAL-GRADE COPIER:** These offer the fullest range of features and produce 50-plus cpm. Key differences from a business-grade machine are higher monthly copy volume, higher maintenance costs and lower cost per copy. Prices range from $25,000 up to six figures.
- **PRE-OWNED COPIERS:** With thousands of well-maintained copiers ending their leases and being repossessed monthly, purchasing a pre-owned copier maybe your best choice, and you won't suffer the 40 percent depreciation that happens the minute you receive your brand-new copier.

As we said above, copier speed is measured in cpm or ppm.

Budget Basics

Many businesses have learned the hard way that photocopiers can be money pits. Before getting yours, prepare a budget so you don't experience any unpleasant—and costly—surprises. When determining your copier budget, consider:

- **STARTING POINT:** Factor in the price of the machine and the terms of a lease if you don't purchase outright.
- **CONSUMABLES:** Don't forget costs such as paper, toner, and, in the case of color machines, developer and fuser oil.
- **MAINTENANCE:** Figure in your service requirements and the cost for a service plan to meet those needs.
- **COLOR COSTS:** If you're considering a color copier, have a seat. Your machine will require much more service than a black-and-white one. Color copying is more complex, requiring more steps, different inks and more precision movements.
- **THE KINKO'S ALTERNATIVE:** For a small business, with just one or two employees and only occasional copying needs, Kinko's may still make a lot of sense. If you use less than one ream (500 pages) of copy paper each month, you'll find it cheaper to outsource your copying to the nearest photocopy center.

Copiers can generate from 6 cpm to more than 100 cpm, with prices starting at under $100 up to several hundred thousand dollars for the most robust, feature-rich and speedy systems. Copiers come in analog and digital versions, but most vendors are making digital copiers. As with faxes, you can get varying print qualities—with the cheaper inkjet copiers offering both color and black-and-white copying for under $100 and higher-resolution laser copiers in the thousands of dollars. If your copier is going to set you back thousands of dollars, you might consider leasing it. Typical leases run from three to five years. As with your phone system, you should select a copier that meets your current as well as your future copying needs. If you already have a machine, check out its page counter, and you can get a feel for your volume. If you currently go to Kinko's, you can keep track of your copy volume by carefully keeping your receipts. Just starting out? Then it's best to go with a small PC-grade copier rather than one of the pricier higher-end machines. The price is right, and you won't have to devote your limited resources to such a large capital expenditure.

There are many different copier features available—the more features, the more you have to pay. Some common features include:

- **SORTERS FOR COLLATING**
- **BUILT-IN STAPLERS**
- **MULTIPLE PAPER TRAYS,** most commonly letter, legal and tabloid sizes
- **ENLARGING AND REDUCING**
- **DOCUMENT FEEDERS,** which include automatic document feeders, and recirculating automatic document feeders, also known as "duplexers" for two-sided copying

If you don't need a top-of-the-line copier, check out your nearest office supply or computer store, where frequent discounts, promotions and rebates can get you great deals and frequent sales. You can also get a store warranty to augment the manufacturer's warranty for a low price.

For a heavy-duty machine, consult an experienced dealer or vendor who can help you make the right choice. When shopping around for a dealer or a vendor, remember to ask some tough questions: How long have they been around? Do they have customers similar in size and budget to your company? Do they sell several different brands or just one manufacturer's copier? (A one-manufacturer dealer doesn't provide the same variety. But if you're a lifelong Xerox customer, your loyalty should translate into better service.) Do they provide

24/7/365 service calls and emergency maintenance? Will they provide customer references?

At Your Service

No matter what copier you select, it won't be worth much when it breaks down—and a breakdown at some point is inevitable. So be sure to minimize disruption and frustration by finding a good dealer to service your machine—and that should begin at the time of purchase.

You can get a service contract through your dealer or separately. There are different service plans, such as "minimum monthly volume plans," but if you don't make all the copies you planned, you still pay the same amount. There are also "all-inclusive service contracts," where you pay a fixed price per copy, and the service provider includes all the consumables, including toner. This makes it a lot easier for you to manage, especially if you are a small business.

Be sure to find out what is covered in your service plan. Dealers differ widely on what "parts" are included when they say they cover "parts and labor." Some parts commonly wear out, but those can be

---

Photocopier Checklist

Before you select your photocopier, there are some important questions you should ask that will better prepare you to make the right choice:

❑ How many copiers do you want to purchase?

❑ What is your budget for this purchase?

❑ When do you need the copier(s) by?

❑ Approximately how many copies of an original do you generally make at one time?

❑ Approximately how many copies will you be making per month?

❑ How many copies do you want to be able to make per minute?

❑ What size copies will you be making? Letter-size, legal, ledger, tabloid

❑ What kind of paper stock will you be copying onto? Card, coated, cover, labels, standard copy, transparencies

❑ What features do you want? Account codes, automatic document feeder, duplex copying, editing features, full-bleed printing of 11 x 17 paper, sorter/stapler, transparency cassette, etc.

❑ Do you want to connect the copier to a computer network so it can serve as a printer and/or scanner?

included in what is called a "preventive maintenance service," which covers those components not routinely included in a traditional service plan. And while this costs more, it saves you from replacing expensive components, like the copier-drum, that are known to wear out. Your distance from the dealer can also affect service pricing since they incorporate their travel time when determining the cost of your service contract. So local service providers can be less expensive.

A service plan will typically set you back between 1 and 2 cents per page copied. But remember, not all copiers need a service plan. If you buy a low-end copier for under $1,000 that is not equipped with a feeder or a sorter, it may be cheaper to pay for service as you require it.

Bye, Bye Paper

For businesses being consumed by those endless piles of paper, electronic document management systems (EDMS)—or digital document management systems (DDMS) as they are also called—enable you to store and retrieve digital copies of your papers on a corporate network or the Internet. After 9/11, with increased attention to security and protecting documents, off-site EDMS became an attractive solution for preserving corporate data in an increasingly uncertain world.

When making your selection, be aware that EDMS systems offer a wide range of file retrieval options—from simple index-based searches to supporting ones that include all your documents' content. Be sure to select a system that best matches the way your company organizes and retrieves files. A starter EDMS includes a scanner with a document feeder for high-volume scanning, a computer system with a large hard-drive for storing the documents, and the EDMS software itself. Once you get a system, the first step is to scan all your hard copy into it, which are then indexed. EDMS prices have dropped a lot recently: You can now buy a system for as little as $2,400 for a very small business of one or two employees, though the price rises steeply as your staff size increases and can quickly get as high as five and six figures, due to high storage costs as well as software licensing fees.

EDMS can save you money in the long run, since you'll need a lot less office space for storing your computer files. And your staff will save time retrieving information from the files. But the bigger your company, the higher the price since EDMS licensing is done on a per-user basis. So as your company grows, your EDMS budget will have to increase accordingly.

In the years ahead, we might finally see the arrival of the long-imagined "paperless office," but until then, the photocopiers and fax machines that we need to manage all our paper will remain a fact of life.

GLOSSARY

AGGREGATORS: long-distance providers that offer low rates by recruiting 50 to 100 clients, then negotiating a group discount with a long-distance carrier based on the projected calling volume; they allow smaller companies to obtain rates typically reserved for larger companies, but add an extra level of bureaucracy when resolving service problems

AUTOMATED ATTENDANT (OR AUTO-ATTENDANT): a phone system accessory that answers the phone electronically, allowing callers to route themselves through a series of menu prompts (i.e., press 1 for sales) to the appropriate department or extension; many come equipped with a basic automated attendant system

AUTOMATED CALL DISTRIBUTOR (ACD): a phone system accessory that routes incoming calls among a set of extensions to ensure they are handled efficiently; generally used in call centers that process many incoming calls

BANDED RATES: programs that charge different rates depending on how far the call is traveling; using banded rates may be more cost-efficient for firms that make many calls to nearby area codes

BATCH PROCESSING: lets you program a fax machine to send multiple faxes to a single phone number or to multiple numbers

BILLING INCREMENTS: specifies the minimum amount of time charged for a call and how calls are rounded once this minimum is met; carriers traditionally round calls to the next full minute; newer programs often set a minimum billing period of 30 seconds and round subsequent calls to six-second increments; this type of billing will typically save you 10 percent compared to full-minute billing

DEDICATED SERVICE: a type of program designed for firms with large monthly long-distance bills; dedicated service means that your firm leases a line (typically a T1 line) between your PBX and the local office of your long-distance carrier; you pay more for the leased line but save money on each call made using the leased line; it costs less on a per-minute basis since the long-distance company doesn't have to pay the local service provider an access fee for each call; a T1 and dedicated service should be less expensive than regular switched service if you spend more than $5,000 on long distance per month

DUPLEX COPYING: the ability to automatically copy on both sides of a page; can be a useful feature, but it tends to be prone to paper jams; if you want duplex copying, equip the copier with a document feeder called a recirculating automatic document feeder (RADF), which can handle two-sided originals

GROUP 4: an international standard for fax machines that operate over digital (such as ISDN) phone lines; can transfer a page in as little as two seconds, but you can't use them over ordinary phone lines; most often used to send faxes between two offices that are already connected by digital lines; most fax machines today operate over the national Group 3 standard

REMOTE DIAGNOSTICS: a system that connects to your phone line and automatically calls the dealer if a problem arises; can speed repair time and help ensure that maintenance schedules are accurately followed

SWITCHED SERVICE: most small companies sign up for switched service plans, which use the local telephone company to connect your calls to your long-distance carrier; a bit more expensive on a per-minute basis than dedicated service but requires no additional installation or monthly payments

V.17, V.34: new sending standards that enable faxes to be sent quickly; V.17-compatible fax machines send faxes to other V.17 machines at 14,400 bits per second (bps), while the newer V.34 standards send faxes at 33,600 bps to other such enabled machines

WAIVE MINIMUM: the minimum calling volume needed to waive the monthly service charge; many small-business programs have a waive minimum of $25 or $100

Hit
The
Road

Should you lease or buy a car?

D oes your business need a company vehicle for making deliveries, traveling to clients' offices, carrying equipment and more? Whether buying or leasing a vehicle is more advantageous for you depends on a variety of factors. And if you need several cars or vans for salespeople or delivery drivers, you may be eligible for fleet leasing programs that can save you big money. Here's a closer look at the different ways to get your business on the road.

THE LEASING OPTION

Vehicle leasing is a contract between a lessor (the dealer) and a lessee (the customer) for a new vehicle to be used for a specified time period and a specified payment. The title of the vehicle remains in the lessor's name as owner, but insurance, registration and other fees are paid by the lessee.

There are two types of leases: open-end and closed-end (see "Learning the Lingo" on page 474). The former can last up to five years and offers lower monthly payments. However, if the assessed value of the car when you turn it in is less than the car's book value, you have to pay the difference (called a residual).

Although your monthly payments will probably be higher, the closed-end lease allows you to walk away clean. Provided the car has normal wear and tear and you're within the mileage limits imposed by the lease, you simply hand the car back to the dealer when the lease is up, with no residual payment. (Of course, you must pay for any damage the car may have incurred.)

You can also roll the closed-end lease over and drive off in another brand-new car. Dealers are partial to this type of lease because it keeps customers coming back, so they're more likely to sweeten the deal if they think you'll be a lessee for the long term.

BRIGHT IDEA

EVEN IF YOU DECIDE LEASING ISN'T FOR YOU, YOU CAN STILL BENEFIT FROM LEASING PROGRAMS. WHEN CARS COME OFF A LEASE, THEY ARE OFTEN SOLD AT DEALERSHIPS AS USED CARS. THEY'RE IN BETTER SHAPE THAN A CAR THAT'S TRADED IN. THEY'VE GOT LOW MILEAGE, THEY'RE WELL-MAINTAINED, AND THE DEALERS KNOW THEIR HISTORY SINCE THEY'RE THE ONES WHO LEASED THEM ORIGINALLY.

BEWARE!

DON'T SIGN A LEASE THAT IS LONGER THAN TWO YEARS. THE INTEREST ON A FOUR- OR FIVE-YEAR LEASE CAN MAKE PAYMENTS SKYROCKET.

How does leasing compare to buying? Leasing payments are generally lower than financing payments because you pay only for part of the depreciation of the vehicle during the time you lease it rather than for the price of the entire vehicle. However, at the end of, say, a two-year lease, the car could still be worth several thousand dollars, which means the dealer ends up with both your payments and a highly resaleable vehicle. You'll also have no vehicle to trade in should you decide to purchase rather than lease the next time around.

In addition to lower monthly payments, some dealers are attracting lessees with smaller or no down payments. At the same time, many leases now offer higher mileage caps, meaning you can drive more free miles.

It's usually easier to qualify for financing to lease a car than to buy one. And unlike buying, your leasing arrangement is not considered a loan and therefore is not a liability when seeking financing for your business.

Of course, paying cash for a car will net you a better price than either leasing or financing a purchase, but is that the best way to use your available capital? When you consider that the greatest benefit of leasing for the self-employed is the tax deduction for leasing payment interest, you may think twice about using your savings or stretching your credit line to buy a vehicle.

Leasing is a good option for you if:

- **YOU LIKE TO DRIVE BRAND-NEW MODELS EVERY TWO YEARS.** It's easy to roll over a lease from one new car to another.
- **YOU'D RATHER KEEP YOUR CAPITAL IN THE BANK.**
- **YOU CAN LIVE WITHIN THE LEASE'S MILEAGE RESTRICTION.** Calculate the average mileage you will drive on business each year, and negotiate a cap. Make sure you read the fine print for the exact figure.
- **YOU WANT TO DRIVE A LUXURY CAR BUT HAVE AN ECONOMY BUDGET.** High-end vans, light trucks, sports cars and exotic imports can be within your grasp with no-down-payment leases. Plus, the net deductions when you lease luxury cars are generally greater than the deductions when you buy.
- **YOU NEED TO MAKE A STATEMENT FOR IMAGE PURPOSES.** Like it or

Learning The Lingo

To help novices understand what's involved in leasing a vehicle; here is a glossary of terms you may encounter when negotiating a lease:

- **ADDITIONAL INSURED:** In a lease transaction, the vehicle belongs to the lessor, but the insurance is the responsibility of the lessee. As owner, the lessor must be named as "additional insured" on your insurance policy.
- **BUSINESS LEASE:** This is a lease agreement in which at least 50 percent of the vehicle's use is business-related (excluding commuting) to qualify for special tax treatment.
- **CAPITALIZED COST:** This is the selling price of the vehicle plus any lessee costs, fees or taxes. It is used as a basis for calculating your monthly lease payments.
- **CAPITALIZED COST REDUCTION:** You can reduce the capitalized cost by paying a lump sum of money, receiving a rebate from the dealer or the manufacturer, or getting a trade-in allowance for a vehicle. A capitalized cost reduction is often incorrectly called a down payment.
- **CLOSED-END LEASE:** Recommended for most people, this type of lease specifies the lessee is not accountable for the value of the vehicle at the end of the lease but is responsible for excess mileage and wear and tear. This lease generally gives the lessee an option to buy the car when the lease runs out.
- **LESSEE:** This is the lease client or party paying for the use of the vehicle.
- **LESSOR:** This is the party funding the lease of the vehicle, such as the car dealer, the bank or the leasing company.
- **MILEAGE ALLOWANCE:** This is the lessee's estimate of the mileage expected to be driven during the term of the vehicle's lease. Some leases impose penalties if you drive an average of more than 15,000 miles a year.
- **OPEN-END LEASE:** Sometimes called a finance or equity lease, the open-end lease requires that the lessee guarantee the value of the leased vehicle at the end of the term, regardless of the mileage and the condition of the car. This means you must pay the difference between the estimated value and the market price of the car when the lease runs out.
- **RESIDUAL VALUE:** This is the estimated value of the leased vehicle at the end of the lease term.
- **SECURITY DEPOSIT:** This is an amount generally collected by the lessor at the start of the lease. This deposit is usually refundable at the end of the lease.

not, we are judged by the cars we drive; the more expensive-looking the car, the more success we are perceived to have achieved. Arguments against leasing? Here are a few points to consider:

- **DON'T LEASE IF YOU WANT TO OWN THE CAR AT THE END OF THE TERM.** In addition to the payments you've already made, you'll be charged the residual value before you can take possession of the vehicle.

- **DON'T LEASE IF VEHICLES TAKE A BEATING IN YOUR LINE OF BUSINESS.** Wear-and-tear charges can cripple your budget when you turn the car in.

- **DON'T LEASE IF YOU PLAN TO KEEP THE CAR FOR MORE THAN FOUR YEARS;** otherwise, you'll be paying for the same vehicle twice.

- **DON'T LEASE IF YOU ARE NOT SURE YOU CAN MAKE THE MONTHLY PAYMENTS.** Terminating a lease early usually means being liable for the difference between the value of the car and the amount you've already paid. Ask what the penalties are before you sign.

- **DON'T SIGN A LEASE UNTIL YOU'VE TALKED TO A FINANCE COMPANY ABOUT INSURANCE.** If you damage the car, your own insurer may only pay its current cash value, and the lessor may expect you to pay the penalty for early termination. It's typical for the finance company to provide "gap protection" for free and pay the dealer the difference you owe. In addition, the dealer may require you to carry higher insurance.

- **DON'T LEASE IF YOU PLAN TO KEEP THE CAR LONGER THAN THE LIFE OF ITS WARRANTY.** You'll be responsible for repairs after the warranty runs out.

Sit down with your accountant and compare the tax benefits of leasing and buying. Leasing allows you to deduct some or all of your lease payments and interest, depending on how much you use the car for business. Keep in mind, however, that these deductions are subject to "inclusion amounts"—specific amounts added back to your taxable income according to IRS tables.

Still, if you're interested in a luxury car, you're probably better off leasing. The net deductions for leasing luxury cars are generally greater than the deductions when you buy.

Purchasing allows you to deduct the depreciation of the vehicle up to certain limits. You can save all your receipts—for gas, insurance and so on—and deduct those costs; or, if you own your business car, you can also use the simpler "standard mileage method"—which simply means deducting a standard amount per mile. You don't have this option with leased cars; however, in many cases, you get a bigger deduction by saving receipts, so you would not want to use the standard mileage method anyway.

From a tax standpoint, the lease or buy decision generally comes down to the cost of the vehicle—the more expensive it is, the greater the tax advantages of leasing.

FLEET LEASING

Need more than one company vehicle? Good news: Leasing a small fleet of cars, minivans or pickups is easier and more advantageous than ever.

Retail leases are for consumers who want personal-use vehicles; commercial leases are generally for companies that need more than one car. Businesses that buy or lease 10 or more vehicles qualify as commercial fleet buyers and are given a fleet registration number (obtained through the dealer), entitling them to all available manufacturers' and dealers' fleet incentive programs.

While manufacturers have always offered attractive discount programs to commercial fleet buyers, there have rarely been such programs for the small fleet lessee requiring fewer than 10 cars. Nowadays, however, many dealers are beginning to offer their own programs to business owners and will work with you to get your business. In fact, some dealers can get you a fleet registration number even if you lease only a few cars.

"There are far fewer restrictions on what constitutes a commercial fleet these days, both at the manufacturing end and in dealerships, so the small-business person can get into fleet leasing much more easily," says Ed Bobit, publisher of *Automotive Fleet*, a car and truck leasing management magazine. Manufacturers are also making it easier for small businesses to finance the leasing of their fleets, with flexible programs and special financing plans.

To decide whether fleet leasing is

DOLLAR STRETCHER

THERE'S A GROWING MARKET FOR LEASING USED VEHICLES, WITH WARRANTIES THAT COVER THE FULL TERM OF THE LEASE. MANY OF THESE CARS ARE 2-YEAR-  OLD LUXURY VEHICLES STILL IN THEIR PRIME AND COMING OFF FIRST-TIME LEASES—SOME WITH FEWER THAN 25,000 MILES ON THE ODOMETER. BECAUSE LEASED VEHICLES ARE GENERALLY WELL-MAINTAINED AND UNDER THREE-YEAR WARRANTIES, THESE CARS AND TRUCKS ARE OFTEN A VERY GOOD DEAL.

for you, sit down with your accountant and estimate what it will cost, taking into account monthly lease payments, insurance, gas, oil, maintenance and license fees. Will you need to hire someone to manage the fleet? If not, how will you keep tabs on regular tune-ups and administrative matters?

You may decide it is more economical to give your employees an allowance and have them lease their own cars. These and other questions should be put to your accountant before making a decision on fleet leasing. Always check to see what the penalties are for terminating a lease early, especially if your cash flow tends to fluctuate from month to month.

Fleet Factors

The typical considerations of leasing are multiplied when you lease several vehicles, so consider these possible pitfalls before you sign on the dotted line:

- **HIGHER INSURANCE COVERAGE:** Some dealers require you to increase your insurance coverage since they, not you, own the leased vehicles. Shop around for prices before you order your fleet because insurance can amount to a lot of money. As a business owner, you can probably get a blanket policy to cover both your business and your fleet.
- **OVEREXTENDING YOUR HARD-EARNED BUCKS:** Six shiny new vehicles in your company parking lot may boost your ego, but do you really need them? It's easy to get carried away when ordering a fleet, so make sure you have analyzed your needs thoroughly before signing on the dotted line.
- **NEGLECTING TO ASK ABOUT MILEAGE LIMITS:** These can vary radically and can cost you as much as 15 to 20 cents for each mile you drive the car over the limit. If you cover 50,000 miles a year, it pays to buy rather than lease.
- **FAILING TO COMPARE BUYING PRICE WITH LEASE PRICE:** Dealers may have vehicles on the lot they are anxious to get rid of and will give you a special deal if you buy rather than lease. Ask the fleet manager to work out the figures for buying vs. leasing so you can see the difference, and always get it in writing.
- **PUTTING DOWN TOO MUCH MONEY:** Don't be talked into a down payment that's bigger than normal—first month's payment, a small deposit and license fees.
- **FORGETTING STATE TAXES:** Although some states, such as Nevada

477

and Texas, have no state taxes, others, such as California, have high registration fees and taxes, which must be paid up front when you lease a car.

- **GETTING BURIED UNDER THE PAPERWORK:** Operating a fleet of vehicles, however small, requires at the very least keeping track of mileage and expenses with a running report on each vehicle so you can budget your cash outlay.

Know Your Options

Once you've decided fleet leasing is for you, here are some additional questions to ask:

- **DO YOU NEED MINIVANS, PICKUPS OR PASSENGER CARS?** Determine what each vehicle will be used for.
- **DO YOU NEED TO SPECIALLY EQUIP** the vans and pickups?
- **WHAT OPTIONS DO YOU NEED** on each vehicle? Air conditioning and radios are probably needed, but leave the fancy options off the price tag.
- **HOW MUCH TRUNK OR CARGO SPACE** is needed to accommodate your product?
- **HOW MANY MILES A YEAR** will you clock? Most leases allow you 12,000 to 15,000 miles annually before charging you by the mile.
- **CAN YOU LEASE DIFFERENT TYPES OF VEHICLES** from a single manufacturer? Leasing your fleet from a single dealer is more efficient and economical, so shop around for a dealer that sells each of the types of vehicles you require rather than having to buy your compact pickup from one dealer and your full-sized van from another.

When visiting dealerships, ask to meet with the fleet manager. He or she will be much more knowledgeable about programs and special deals than regular floor salespeople.

Don't just shop around for vehicles; shop different lenders as well. Get a lease quote from the dealer first, then run it through your bank to check for lower interest rates.

There are several fleet financing companies that will discuss

SMART TIP

THE PAPERWORK INVOLVED IN FLEET MANAGEMENT CAN OVERWHELM FIRST-TIME FLEET OWNERS. TO HELP, MANY AUTOMOTIVE GAS COMPANIES HAVE COMMERCIAL PROGRAMS THAT NOT ONLY GIVE YOU A DISCOUNT ON FUEL FOR YOUR FLEET, BUT ALSO PROVIDE ITEMIZED REPORTS AND BILLING SYSTEMS, ORGANIZED BY VEHICLE OR CREDIT CARD, THAT TRACK MILEAGE AND EXPENSES. MANUFACTURERS MAY ALSO OFFER SUCH PROGRAMS. SOME COMPANIES CHARGE FOR THIS SERVICE; OTHERS OFFER IT FREE.

incentive programs, modified payments and your buying needs. To find them, ask your dealer to provide a business line of credit or to recommend a leasing company with whom the dealer already does business. Check out other lenders under "Leasing" in your Business-to-Business Yellow Pages. Ask your bank about its fleet leasing programs. Or use a buying service, which negotiates the deal and sets up the financing. You can find these in the Yellow Pages under "Automobile Brokers" or through auto clubs.

ROAD TEST

Whether they lease or buy, many people skip one crucial step in obtaining a business vehicle: taking the car out for a comprehensive test drive. Unless you get out in traffic with the car, you could be making a serious mistake. Performance and handling can only be judged on the road. Also check the following items:

■ **CAN YOU REACH** all the controls without stretching?

■ **ARE THE SEATS** comfortable?

■ **IS THE SEAT ADJUSTABLE** to your preferred driving position?

■ **IS VISIBILITY GOOD** on all four sides?

■ **ARE THE SEAT BELTS** comfortable?

■ **DO THE POSITIONS** of the break and gas pedals cause you fatigue?

The test drive is an opportunity to check the car's handling and response. Use this nine-point checklist:

1. **IS THE ACCELERATION** responsive?
2. **HOW QUICKLY** do the brakes respond?
3. **IS THERE VIBRATION** at highway speeds?
4. **DOES THE SUSPENSION** provide a smooth ride?
5. **DO THE GEARS** shift easily?
6. **IS THERE LOSS** of power when accelerating?
7. **IS THERE A LOT** of cabin noise?
8. **HOW IS THE STEERING** control on curves?
9. **DOES THE CAR** have straight-line ability at highway speeds?

Don't play the car stereo or talk to the salesperson unnecessarily while taking your test drive. You need to be able to "listen" to the car and concentrate on its performance.

Most salespeople have a route already mapped out for test drives, but you should insist on driving in road conditions similar to those you encounter in your normal driving. Your route should include left and right turns, stops at traffic signals, merging traffic, hills and bumps. See if you can take a test drive alone; you'll pay more attention to the car's performance without the salesperson breathing down your neck.

Make sure the model you test drive is the same as the one you want to buy. If you want to test drive a sedan and only a hatchback is available, come back when they have a sedan on the premises, or go somewhere else. If you can't decide what size engine you want, try them all and compare their power. If optional equipment you're considering, such as a moon roof, isn't on the test vehicle, have the salesperson show you another vehicle with the equipment so you can check out its operation. Try out various features, such as tailgates, van doors and convertible tops, for convenience and ease of handling. If the convertible top is difficult to operate, you may be paying for a high-priced option you won't use. A van door or a tailgate that's awkward or too small for easy loading and unloading will waste time while you're making deliveries.

Pull down the sun visor to make sure it doesn't block your view,

Full Disclosure

Confused by all the fine print on the leasing contract? You're not alone. The good news: Regulations issued by the Federal Reserve Board should simplify and clarify auto leases.

The rules require leasing companies to use a revised disclosure format, which includes segregating certain disclosures that were previously scattered throughout the contract. To make comparisons easier, contracts must also disclose the total amount of payments. In addition, leasing companies must:

- **MAKE THE DISCLOSURE** of costs paid at the lease signing easier to understand
- **INCLUDE STRONG WARNINGS** about possible penalties for excessive wear and tear or early lease termination
- **INCLUDE A DISCLOSURE** with any percentage rate indicating the limitations of the rate information
- **INCLUDE A MATHEMATICAL PROGRESSION** that shows how the monthly payment is calculated and the relationship of terms such as "residual value" and "gross capitalized cost" (see "Learning The Lingo" on page 474)

and practice parallel parking—is the car easy to maneuver? When backing up, do you have good rear-view visibility? Do you have enough legroom? Check out the air conditioning and heater—are they too noisy? Don't hurry through your test drive. You're spending a lot of money, so take as much time as you need to really get a feel for the vehicle, and insist on both highway and local street driving.

During your test drive, ask as many questions as you feel are necessary to make an informed decision. Don't be intimidated by salespeople. If they're rude, walk out of the dealership.

Last but not least, remember that you can haggle over prices whether you are buying or leasing, so don't accept the dealer's first offer. Keep working until you get the deal you want.

Go!

All systems are go and you're ready to launch your new business. To make sure the launch is successful, Part 6, "Strut Your Stuff," shows you how to spread the word about your company. Find out how to create a marketing and advertising campaign that works…without spending a fortune. From direct mail and print ads to radio and catalogs, we share smart strategies to make your business the talk of the town. You'll also learn about the single best way to promote your business: public relations. From special events to community projects to media coverage, we show you dozens of ways to get your business noticed—most of them virtually free!

If the idea of selling scares you, you're not alone. That's why we provide everything you need to know to sell like a pro. Learn how to get over your fear of cold calls, techniques for overcoming objections, how to spot hot prospects and how to close the sale. Once you've made the sale, the game isn't over: You've got to keep the customer coming back. Our secrets to great customer service will give you the edge you need to win repeat business…over and over again.

These days, using the Internet is an essential part of every successful business start-up. In Part 7, "Net Works," you'll learn the latest ways to get the most from the Net. First, we'll show you how the Net can help you handle key start-up tasks such as market research and competitive intelligence, hiring your first employees and even finding financing. Next, we'll reveal the steps to setting up your business's Web site, including finding the best Internet service provider, choosing a Web designer or doing it yourself and more. Finally, you'll discover why the Net has become one of the best ways to promote and market your business, and how to navigate the tricky waters of online advertising and marketing. From web sites and newsgroups to affiliate programs and more, we share the smartest strategies to attract customers online—and keep them coming back for more.

If you're doing everything right, you'll be dealing with a bundle of money. In Part 8, "By The Books," we show you the strategies to make the most of your money. Whether or not you're a math whiz, you'll want to read our bookkeeping basics, which contain everything you need to know to keep track of your finances. You'll learn the accounting methods that can make a difference come tax time, what records to keep and why, and whether to computerize or do it by hand.

Check out our step-by-step look at creating financial statements, income statements, cash-flow statements and other important indicators that help you measure your money. Then learn ways to manage your finances, including secrets to pricing your product or service; how to get short-term capital infusions when you're low on cash; how to determine your overhead, profit margin and more. We also show you how to stay out of trouble when the tax man comes calling. Get the inside scoop on payroll taxes, personal vs. corporate tax returns, and what to file when. Learn what you can deduct . . . and what you can't.

To keep you on the path to success, our final chapter takes a closer look at success and failure factors. Find out what causes businesses to succeed or fail and how you can learn from mistakes along the way to make your business better than ever!

PART

6

Strut Your Stuff

CHAPTER 31

To Market, To Market

*Advertising and marketing
your business*

Y ou may know how to build the perfect product or provide excellent service, but do you know how to market and advertise your business? If not, all your expertise won't help keep your business afloat. Without marketing, no one will know your business exists— and if customers don't know you're there, you won't make any sales.

Advertising does not have to mean multimillion-dollar TV commercials. There are plenty of ways to market your business that are affordable or even free. All it takes is a little marketing savvy...which you will have plenty of after reading this chapter.

CREATING A MARKETING PLAN

Every start-up venture needs a business plan, yet many entrepreneurs do not realize a marketing plan is equally vital.

Unlike a business plan, the marketing plan focuses on the customers. A marketing plan includes numbers, facts and objectives, but it is not primarily numerical; it is strategic. It is your plan of action— what you will sell, to whom you will sell it and how often, at what price, and how you will get the product to the buyer. Here's a closer look at putting together a marketing plan that works.

STEP ONE: DEFINE YOUR PRODUCT. The first part of the marketing plan defines your product or service and its features and benefits in detail, then shows how it is different from the competition's. The more clearly and succinctly you describe your product in your marketing plan, the better you will communicate with your target customer.

Markets and products have become extremely fragmented. There are hundreds of special-interest magazines, for example, each targeted to a very specific market segment. It's the same with restaurants, cars and retail clothing stores, just to name a few industries. Positioning your product competitively requires an understanding of this fragmented market. Not only must you be able to describe your product, but you must also be able to describe your competitor's product and show why yours is better.

Positioning your product involves two steps. First, you need to analyze your product's features, and then decide how they differentiate your product from its competitors. Second, you need to decide what type of buyer is most likely to purchase your product.

Pricing and placement are critical to competitive positioning. In today's marketing culture, pricing cannot be separated from the product.

Take grocery stores, for example. The full-service supermarket is still the most popular form of grocery distribution. But today, busy families want faster service and more convenience, even if it means higher prices. As a result, convenience stores, home delivery services, personal shoppers and takeout restaurants have proliferated. At the same time, warehouse grocery retailing has also increased. Warehouse stores cater to customers who prefer low prices to convenience.

Service, distribution and price are the essential elements of the product offered by supermarket, convenience and warehouse stores. To develop a successful marketing plan, you need to analyze how these same elements fit into your business. What are you selling—convenience? Quality? Discount pricing? You can't offer it all. Knowing what your customers want helps you decide what to offer.

STEP TWO: DESCRIBE YOUR TARGET CUSTOMER. Developing a profile of your target customer is the second step in an effective marketing plan. You can describe customers in terms of demographics—age,

Position Powers

The right image packs a powerful marketing punch. To make it work for you, follow these steps:

- **CREATE A POSITIONING STATEMENT** for your company. In one or two sentences, describe what distinguishes you from your competition.
- **TEST YOUR POSITIONING STATEMENT.** Does it appeal to your target audience? Refine it until it speaks directly to their wants and needs.
- **USE THE POSITIONING STATEMENT** in every written communication to customers.
- **CREATE IMAGE MARKETING MATERIALS** that communicate your positioning. Don't skimp.
- **INCLUDE YOUR TEAM IN THE IMAGE** marketing plan. Help employees understand how to communicate your positioning to customers.

sex, family composition, earnings and geographical location—as well as lifestyle. Ask the following: Are my customers conservative or innovative? Leaders or followers? Timid or aggressive? Traditional or modern? Introverted or extroverted? How often do they purchase what I offer? How much of it at a time? Are there peak buying periods or times of the year when people won't buy my product or service? (Part 2, Chapters 6 and 7 explain in detail how to define your target customer.)

STEP THREE: CREATE A COMMUNICATION STRATEGY. Your target customer must not only know your product exists, but also have a favorable impression of its benefits. Communication includes everything from logo design and advertising to public relations and promotions.

Market Planning Checklist

Before you launch a marketing campaign, answer the following questions about your business and your product or service:

❏ Have you analyzed the total market for your product or service? Do you know which features of your product or service will appeal to different market segments?

❏ In forming your marketing message, have you described how your product or service will benefit your clients?

❏ Have you prepared a pricing schedule? What kinds of discounts do you offer, and to whom do you offer them?

❏ Have you prepared a sales forecast?

❏ Which media will you use in your marketing campaign?

❏ Do your marketing materials mention any optional accessories or added services that consumers might want to purchase?

❏ If you offer a product, have you prepared clear operating and assembly instructions if required? What kind of warranty do you provide? What type of customer service or support do you offer after the sale?

❏ Do you have product liability insurance?

❏ Is your packaging likely to appeal to your target market?

❏ If your product is one you can patent, have you done so?

❏ How will you distribute your product?

Find out what your target customers read and listen to. You need to know this to get their attention. In addition to where to place your message, consider how frequently customers will need to receive it.

This part of the marketing plan should spell out your promotional objectives. What do you want to achieve? Do you want people to recognize your company name? Know where you're located? How much money can you spend to get your message across? What media are available, and which will work best? Finally, how will you evaluate the results?

Ask yourself the right questions and analyze your answers, and you'll come up with a marketing plan that will help you achieve your goals.

Setting An Advertising Budget

You'll need to devote a percentage of projected gross sales to your annual advertising budget. A good rule of thumb is to devote 2 to 5 percent of anticipated gross sales to this need.

There are two primary methods of determining your business's advertising budget more specifically. First is the *cost method*, which theorizes that an advertiser can't afford to spend more than he or she has. For instance, using the cost method to determine the advertising budget, and devoting 5 percent of gross sales, a business projecting $300,000 in gross sales in a given year would have $15,000 for that year, or about $1,250 per month, to spend on advertising. (Since businesses typically advertise more heavily when they first open, the same business could allocate more—about $2,500—for its grand opening.)

This may not seem like much money, and for some companies it will not be enough. These companies base their advertising budgets on the amount of money they need to attract the customer or sell the product. This is called the *task method*. A company using the task method typically determines how much money is needed based on past experience. Of course, as a start-up you won't have experience to go on. In this case, you will have to base the figures on your business plan and market survey, which should estimate the costs you'll incur.

BEWARE!

DON'T MESS WITH SUCCESS. ONCE YOU FIND AN ADVERTISING IDEA THAT WORKS FOR YOU, STICK WITH IT. REPETITION IS KEY TO GETTING YOUR MESSAGE ACROSS.

WHERE TO ADVERTISE

Once you know your target customers, it'll be easier to determine which media will work well for you. Much of this is just common sense, based on your product, method of sales and audience.

Sure, it would be great if you could afford to buy a full-page color ad in *Time* magazine or a 60-second commercial during the Super Bowl. But in addition to being beyond your budget, such ads aren't even the most effective way to go for a small company.

Small companies succeed by finding a niche, not by targeting every Tom, Dick and Harry. (Remember the "Who Is Your Customer, Anyway?" chapter in Part 2?) Similarly, you need to target your advertising focus as narrowly as possible to the media that will reach your customers. Your customers' location, age, income, interests and other information will guide you to the right media.

For example, if you run a business selling model train supplies nationwide by mail order, it makes sense to advertise in one of the many national magazines, newsletters or circulars catering to this hobby rather than advertising in, say, *The New York Times*. On the other hand, if you sell model trains from a hobby shop rather than via mail order, the vast majority of your customers will be drawn from the area. Therefore, advertising in national hobbyist magazines would net you only a few customers. In this case, it makes more sense to advertise in newspapers or magazines or do commercials on cable TV or radio shows targeting the local area.

Like any aspect of running a business, marketing involves a measure of trial and error. As your business grows, however, you will quickly learn which advertising media are most cost-effective and which draw the most customers to your company. Here is a closer look at the different types of advertising methods and tips for succeeding with each.

PRINT ADVERTISING

The print ad is the basic unit of advertising, the fountainhead from which all other forms of advertising spring. Knowing the principles of creating print ads will help you get results in any other advertising media you use. Print ads have helped launch some of the most successful products and services we know. And there's no reason they can't work for you, too—if you observe a few hard-and-fast rules.

Most print ads out there are poorly conceived and, as a result, perform badly. If an ad lacks a strong motivating message, especially in the crowded marketplace of a newspaper or magazine, it becomes a costly

Go For The Pros

Can you create your own advertising copywriting and design? If you have a background in marketing and advertising, the answer is yes. If not, however, you're better off hiring a professional. No matter how creative you are, a commercial artist or a graphic designer can vastly improve almost any ad created by an entrepreneur.

However, since no one knows your business better than you, it's a good idea to develop your own rough draft first. Think about the key benefits you want to get across, what makes your company different from and better than the rest, and the major advantages of doing business with you. Then put pencil to paper and draw a rough sketch.

If you're reluctant to spend the money on a copywriter and a graphic designer, don't be. Printing, distributing and placing your advertising and marketing materials is going to be costly in itself. If the materials you're paying to have printed aren't well-written, eye-catching and effective, you're wasting your money.

Graphic design and copywriting is one area of business where it's possible to get good work at substantial savings. Plenty of freelance, one-person graphic design and copywriting businesses exist, many of them quite reasonably priced. Ask friends, other business owners or your chamber of commerce for referrals. Many copywriters and designers will cut you a price break on the first project in hopes of winning your business in the future.

Or consider approaching a college or an art school. Many talented students will work for reduced rates (or even for free) for the chance to add your ad to their portfolios.

lesson—one your business will be lucky to survive. The good news? With so many bad ads out there, if you can put together a good one, you're way ahead of the game.

Whether you are developing an ad yourself or having someone else craft it for you, make sure it follows the five fundamentals of successful ads.

1. **IT SHOULD ATTRACT ATTENTION.** That sounds obvious, but nothing else matters unless you can do this. And that means having a truly arresting headline and visual element.

2. **IT SHOULD APPEAL TO THE READER'S SELF-INTEREST OR ANNOUNCE NEWS.** An ad that takes the "you" point of view and tells readers how they will benefit from your product or service piques and keeps their interest. And if, in addition, it has news value ("Announcing a bold new breakthrough in moisturizers that can make your skin look years younger"), your ad has a better than fighting chance.

3. **IT SHOULD COMMUNICATE YOUR COMPANY'S UNIQUE ADVANTAGE.** In other words, why should the prospect pick your firm over a competitor's?

4. **IT SHOULD PROVE YOUR ADVANTAGE.** The most convincing way to do that is through testimonials and statistics.

5. **IT SHOULD MOTIVATE READERS TO TAKE ACTION.** This is usually accomplished by making a special offer that "piggybacks" your main sales thrust. Such offers include a free trial, a discount or a bonus.

SMART TIP

CAN'T COME UP WITH IDEAS FOR YOUR AD? TRY A BRAINSTORMING SESSION. JOT DOWN WORDS OR PHRASES RELATED TO YOUR PRODUCT OR SERVICE AND ITS BENEFITS. THEN SEE WHAT ASSOCIATIONS THEY TRIGGER. WRITE DOWN ALL THE IDEAS YOU CAN THINK OF WITHOUT CENSORING ANYTHING. FROM THOSE ASSOCIATIONS—WHETHER WORDS, PHRASES OR VISUAL IMAGES— COME IDEAS THAT MAKE GOOD ADS.

SMART TIP

SOMETIMES THE STORY OF YOUR BUSINESS CAN MAKE AN INTERESTING "HOOK" FOR A PRINT AD OR A BROCHURE. THE SOCIAL WORKER WHO STARTED A MAID SERVICE COULD USE A HEADLINE LIKE "WHY I GAVE UP SOCIAL WORK TO RID THE WORLD OF DUST BALLS." IF YOUR STORY'S INTRIGUING ENOUGH, IT COULD GET READERS HOOKED.

An ad does not have to do a "hard sell," as long as it is an all-out attempt to attract, communicate with and motivate the reader. That process starts with the single most important element of any ad: the headline.

Headlines That Work

Some of the biggest flops in advertising contained convincing copy that never got read because the ads lacked a great headline or visual element to hook the passing reader.

David Ogilvy, founding partner of legendary ad agency Ogilvy & Mather, said that on the average, five times as many people read the headlines of ads as read the body copy. Headlines that work best, according to Ogilvy, are those that promise the reader a benefit—more miles per gallon, freedom from pimples or fewer cavities.

Flip through a magazine or a newspaper and see what you notice about the ads. Typically, it is the headlines that your eyes go to first. Then notice how many of those headlines promise a benefit of some kind.

However, expressing a benefit is not enough if the way you communicate it is dull and hackneyed. Your headline should be unusual or arresting enough to get interest. Here are some examples of headlines that got noticed:

- ■ "WHEN DOCTORS FEEL ROTTEN, THIS IS WHAT THEY DO."
- ■ "WHY SOME FOODS EXPLODE IN YOUR STOMACH."
- ■ "HOW A FOOL STUNT MADE ME A STAR SALESMAN."

John Caples, author of *Tested Advertising Methods*, recommends beginning headlines with such words or phrases as "New," "Now," "At last," "Warning" or "Advice" to pique interest. He also suggests using one- or two-word headlines and giving readers a test in the headline to get them involved (such as "Do you have an iron deficiency? Take this simple test to find out").

Whatever you do, don't use your company name as the headline for your ad. This is one of the most common mistakes small companies make. Would you read an ad whose most eye-catching element was "Brockman Financial Services"? We thought not.

Ads That Stand Out

Imagine scanning a convention half full of people dressed in formal attire and suddenly noticing that one brazen attendee is wearing overalls and a red flannel shirt. Is it safe to say your eyes would be riveted to that individual? Your first reaction might be "How dare he?" but you'd also probably be curious enough to walk over and find out what this audacious character is all about.

Such nonconformity can have the same riveting effect in advertising. Imagine scanning a newspaper page full of well-groomed little ads and then noticing that one of

SMART TIP

MAKE SURE ALL YOUR ADS ANSWER EVERY CUSTOMER'S NUMBER-ONE QUESTION: "WHAT'S IN IT FOR ME?"

497

Golden Opportunity

It's a publication absolutely everyone gets, refers to and saves on their bookshelves for a year or more. It's the Yellow Pages—but, for too many entrepreneurs, it's an opportunity they fail to fully take advantage of.

Look at most Yellow Pages ads and what do you see? A sea of sameness. Most businesses still use their name as the major focus of the ad. They rely on rubber-stamped cliches like "prompt, courteous service" and "friendly staff." Even when they do identify specific product or service benefits, the descriptions are virtually identical to neighboring ads.

Like any ad, your Yellow Pages ad should have a strong benefit headline, a call to action, and compelling supporting copy highlighting the elements that make your product or service different and special. Here are ways some typical small businesses could improve their ads. The ideas could be adapted to many businesses.

- **TV REPAIR:** Try a headline that leads in with "Check these possible fix-it-yourself solutions before you call us." Besides intriguing the reader with information that might save them money, the company ingratiates itself by unselfishly suggesting ways to avoid a service call. If the problem is more serious (as it usually is), this shop is likely to get the nod.
- **TIRE STORE:** How about a headline like: "Do your tires show any of these warning signs?" Here the ad lists some of the characteristics of a worn tire, with the implication that it might be time to buy new ones.
- **PLUMBER:** One thing you almost never see in the Yellow Pages is a strong testimonial as an ad headline. Imagine a headline for a plumber that reads "Your company really came to the rescue when I needed you." This would be followed by the customer's name in small print, then a list of reasons why the prospect should choose your service over others.

If your Yellow Pages ad is too small to accommodate a major headline plus all the details of your product or service, get rid of some details. Use terms like "full-service dealer" or "wide name-brand selection" instead of a full list of your wares.

them—drawn in pencil, let's say—stands out from the crowd. All of a sudden, the other little ads become invisible, and the scribbled one grabs all the attention. That ad has accomplished the single most difficult task small-business advertising faces—simply getting noticed.

Ideally, your advertising should reflect your company in both look and message. An ad represents you and what you have to offer. If it's generic, it won't have the power to grab attention or persuade prospects to take action.

A small ad that exhibits something a little unexpected often steals the thunder of much larger, more traditional ads that surround it. But what can you say in a small space that gets noticed and makes an impression? Here are a few ideas that could work with a variety of products or services.

- **FOR A RESTAURANT:** Use a large but short headline that can't help but arouse curiosity, such as "Oh, my God!" This would then be followed by an explanation that this is usually the reaction when one of Francisco's Super-Subs (or whatever large-serving entrée) is placed in front of a customer.
- **FOR A BED AND BREAKFAST INN:** Try a cut-out with the big headline "Tape to your mirror tonight!" Below the headline is a box of copy that reads: "Just a reminder that you should call and make reservations this morning if the two of you want to spend an unforgettable weekend at Martha's Inn in Nantucket."
- **FOR A BEAUTY SALON:** Use a small ad with the headline "Can we have your autograph?" in quotes. Follow with copy that reads: "Be ready to draw the attention of admirers when you leave Noreen's Cut 'n' Curl—for people are sure to recognize you as the goddess you are."
- **FOR A CARPET CLEANER:** Try a small ad that shows a blowup of a dust mite with the headline "They're hiding in your carpet." The body copy then explains that these bugs are invisible to the naked eye but are accumulating by the thousands in your uncleaned carpet.

Ad Placement

There are two principal publication categories to consider for print advertising. The first, newspapers, has a positive and a negative side. On

The Good Word

Third-party praise—whether from a customer, an industry organization or a publication—is one of the most effective tools you can use to give your ad, commercial or direct-mail package added credibility. This can take a variety of forms:

- **IF YOUR BUSINESS HAS RECEIVED SOME KIND OF PRIZE,** mention in the press or other honor, don't hesitate to put it in your advertising. "Rated #1 By *Dog Groomers Monthly*" or "Voted 'Best Value' By *The Chagrin Falls Gazette*" are good ways to establish your product or service's benefit in customers' eyes.

- **TESTIMONIALS FROM INDIVIDUAL CUSTOMERS** carry weight, too. "Wanda's Party Planners Gave My Son The Best Birthday Ever!—Jane Smith, Wichita, Kansas," attracts customers' attention. How to get testimonials? If a customer says something nice about your business, don't let the compliment slide—ask, then and there, if you can use the testimonial in your sales materials. (You may want to get this in writing, just to be on the safe side.) Most customers will be happy to comply.

- **EVEN IF YOUR COMPANY HASN'T GOTTEN RECOGNITION,** perhaps you can use a part, a process or an ingredient from one of your suppliers that has received praise. For example, you could say "Made With The Flame Retardant Rated #1 By The American Fire Safety Council." This tells your customers you think highly enough of them to provide them with such a great product or ingredient.

- **IF YOU'RE A MEMBER OF THE BETTER BUSINESS BUREAU,** that's an implied endorsement, too. Be sure to post your BBB plaque prominently on your store or office wall or use the logo on your letterhead.

the plus side, you can get your ad in very quickly. That enables you to run an ad that, for example, capitalizing on some market turn of events that saves your prospects money if they act fast and buy from you. This could be very exciting news for them, and that's perfect because they are in a "newsy" frame of mind when they read the newspaper.

On the downside, newspapers usually have a shelf life of just 24 hours. Therefore, if you run your ad on Monday, you can't depend on anyone discovering that ad on Tuesday. As the saying goes, "Nobody wants to read yesterday's news."

If your budget allows for multiple insertions—that is, running your ad more than once—do so. Regular exposure of the ad builds recognition and credibility. If some of your prospects see your ad but do not respond to your first insertion, they may well respond to your second or third. If you have confidence in your ad's message, do not panic if the initial response is less than you wanted. More insertions may bring a better response.

The second type of publication is magazines, for which there are specialty categories of every kind. This allows you to target any of hundreds of special-interest groups. Another advantage of magazines, especially monthlies, is that they have a longer shelf life; they're often browsed through for months after publication. So your ad might have an audience for up to six months after its initial insertion. Moreover, readers spend more time per sitting with a magazine than a newspaper, so there is more chance they will run across your ad.

One researcher found the following about magazine ads:

- **A TWO-PAGE SPREAD** attracts about one-quarter more readers than a one-page ad.
- **A FULL-PAGE AD** attracts about one-third more readers than a half-page ad.
- **POSITIONING IN THE FRONT OR BACK** of the magazine doesn't matter in terms of noticeability.
- **PEOPLE RESPOND BETTER TO ILLUSTRATIONS** or photos showing the product in use than to those that show it just sitting there.
- **ADS THAT HAVE PEOPLE IN THEM** attract more attention than those without people.

When advertising in any print medium, contact the publication first and ask for a media kit. This contains rate information for various sizes of ads as well as demographic information about the publication's readership—age, income and other details to help you decide if this is where your buyers are. The media kit also indicates specifications for the format in which you'll have to deliver your ad to the publication.

RADIO AND TV ADVERTISING

Many entrepreneurs believe that TV and radio advertising is beyond their means. But while national TV advertising is out of the entrepreneur's price range, advertising on local stations and, especially, on cable TV can be surprisingly affordable. Armed with the right information, the small-business owner may find that TV and radio advertising delivers more customers than any other type of ad campaign. The key is to have a clear understanding of the market so the money spent on broadcast advertising isn't wasted.

"A lot of advertising decisions are made more from the heart than from the head," says William Witcher, author of *You Can Spend Less and Sell More*, a guide to low-cost advertising. Witcher warns entrepreneurs not to get so swept up in the idea of advertising on TV or radio that they neglect to do the necessary research.

Sitting down and coming up with a well-thought-out advertising plan is crucial, Witcher says. "Don't feel that you can simply throw a bunch of dollars into the advertising mill and create miracles."

Planning is especially essential if you are approaching broadcast advertising for the first time. When you are first starting out, it's important to educate yourself about the media, and the only way to do that is to talk to a lot of people. This includes advertising representatives from TV and radio stations, other business owners, and your customers.

Experts suggest entrepreneurs take the following steps before diving into broadcast advertising:

- **ESTABLISH YOUR TARGET MARKET BY ASKING YOURSELF WHO YOUR CUSTOMERS ARE AND, THEREFORE, WHOM YOU WANT TO REACH WITH YOUR ADVERTISING.** This may seem obvious, but many advertisers don't have any idea whom they're selling to.
- **SET A ROUGH BUDGET FOR BROADCAST ADVERTISING.** Come up with an amount that won't strain your business but will allow you to give broadcast advertising a good try. Many stations suggest running ads for at least three months. This can easily cost several thousand dollars for a TV campaign. Radio generally costs a little less, although rates vary depending on the size of the market, the station's penetration, and the audience of the show on which you want to advertise.
- **CONTACT SALES MANAGERS AT TV AND RADIO STATIONS IN YOUR AREA AND ARRANGE TO HAVE A SALESPERSON VISIT YOU.** Ask salespeople for a list of available spots on shows during hours that reach your target audience.

- **TALK TO OTHER BUSINESSPEOPLE IN YOUR AREA ABOUT THEIR EXPERIENCES WITH BROADCAST ADVERTISING.** While salespeople from TV and radio stations can be helpful, they are, after all, trying to sell you something. It is your responsibility to be a smart consumer.
- **ASK ABOUT THE "AUDIENCE DELIVERY" OF THE AVAILABLE SPOTS.** Using published guides (Arbitron or Nielsen), ask the salesperson to help you calculate the CPM (cost per thousand) of reaching your target audience. Remember, you are buying an audience, not just time on a show, and you can calculate pretty exactly how much it's going to cost you to reach every single member of that audience.
- **INQUIRE ABOUT THE PRODUCTION OF YOUR COMMERCIAL.** As a general rule, TV stations charge you to produce your commercial (prices range from about $200 to $1,500), while radio stations will put your ad together for free. However, some independent TV stations will include production for free if you enter into an agreement to advertise for at least three months. And with a similar contract, some radio stations will provide a well-known personality to be the "voice" of your business at no extra cost.

Compare the various proposals. Look at the CPMs, and negotiate the most attractive deal based on which outlet offers the most cost-effective way of reaching your audience. Buying time well in advance can help lower the cost. For TV ads, stick with 30-second spots, which are standard in the industry. And keep in mind that the published rates

The Small Stuff

Should you use your limited advertising budget to create larger, more visible ads that restrict you to advertising less frequently, or smaller, less visible ads that you can then afford to run more frequently?

The answer: smaller ads more frequently. The reason is that most people—even those who are likely candidates for your product—typically don't respond to ads the first time they see them. Prospects may have to notice an ad a number of times and develop a level of comfort with it (especially if the product or service is new to them) before they take action. The more often prospects see your ad, the more comfortable they will become and the better the chance they will respond to it.

Lights, Camera, Action

Advertising on cable TV is one thing—but have you ever thought about hosting your own show on cable TV? It's easier than you think—and could make you and your business a household name!

You could never afford to run a 30-minute commercial for your business. But on public access, you can put on a 30-minute show promoting you and your business. For instance, the owner of an antique shop could host a weekly show on restoring, finding and pricing antiques. A car-repair specialist could host a weekly car-care show. The possibilities are endless.

The Federal Communications Commission requires cable systems in the 100 largest markets to provide free public access channels. Call your local cable station, and request their public access guidelines. They'll require a commitment for a specific number of shows and will want to know your format.

There are three basic show formats that work for different businesses:

1. **INTERVIEW SHOWS** work well for any industry that can draw on a large number of experts.
2. **DEMONSTRATION SHOWS** work for labor-intensive businesses such as plumbing or car repair.
3. **LIVE CALL-IN SHOWS** are effective for professional advisors such as consultants or accountants.

Be creative. Even if your business doesn't lend itself to a show, you can benefit from public access by providing your products or services as prizes on someone else's show.

Rehearse before you go on the air, and be sure to promote your show. Put a sign in your window; sponsor store specials on items featured on the show; mention the show in your print ads or fliers. Offer to send free information or coupons to any viewer who writes or calls. This way, you build a mailing list of interested customers.

offered by TV and radio stations are often negotiable. Generally, rates vary widely during the first quarter of the year, and sometimes during the third quarter or late in the fourth quarter, traditionally slow seasons for many businesses. But expect to pay full rates during the rest of the year or during popular shows or prime time.

Getting Help

Once you've gone through all these steps, you should have a good idea of what is involved in broadcast advertising. But learning to be a smart consumer in the TV and radio market isn't always easy. If you're worried about making the right choice on your own, consider hiring a consultant or an advertising agency to guide you.

Advertising agency owner Gene Murray says that for most small businesses, radio is probably the best solution. TV is more expensive and often reaches a broader audience than a small company needs.

When approaching radio stations, learn their demographics, and look at how closely they match your target market. Murray says sorting out demographics is one area where hiring an ad agency or consultant can really help. "If the businessperson tries to do it on their own, they may get confused because every radio station in the country says they are number one in a certain time spot or with a certain audience," says Murray.

DOLLAR STRETCHER

GET YOUR AD ON THE RADIO—FOR FREE—BY BARTERING YOUR PRODUCTS OR SERVICES FOR AIR TIME. CALLED "TRADE-OUT," THIS PRACTICE IS COMMON. RADIO STATIONS NEED EVERYTHING FROM JANITORIAL SERVICES AND GRAPHIC DESIGNERS TO PRODUCTS THEY CAN GIVE AWAY AS ON-AIR PRIZES, SO WHATEVER YOU SELL, YOU'RE LIKELY TO FIND A READY MARKET.

Many business owners find that even local TV stations cover such a broad geographical area that they reach a lot of people who will probably never visit their stores. Unless you offer an unusual product or service that will draw people from far away, advertising on a TV with a 250-mile radius may mean paying for 240 worthless miles. That's why radio can be the best option if you only need to reach a small geographical area.

Another option that can help an advertiser pinpoint a small geographic area is cable TV. With stations featuring all-news, sports, music, weather and other specialized topics, cable lets you microtarget the groups that fit your customer profile.

For example, a business owner looking to reach upscale members of the community might try advertising on CNN. A sporting goods store might make a big splash by advertising locally during the national broadcast of Monday Night Football, often carried by ESPN.

Cable allows an advertiser to target specific towns, without wasting money covering viewers who are too far away to use the company's product or service. And cable is very inexpensive as well. A prime 30-second spot on cable that only reaches viewers in a city of about 36,000 households costs less than $50.

DIRECT MAIL

Direct mail encompasses a wide variety of marketing materials, including brochures, catalogs, postcards, newsletters and sales letters. Major corporations know that direct-mail advertising is one of the most effective and profitable ways to reach out to new and existing clients.

What's the advantage? Unlike other forms of advertising, in which you're never sure just who is getting your message, direct mail lets you communicate one-on-one with your target audience. That allows you to control who receives your message, when it is delivered, what is in the envelope and how many people you reach.

To create an effective direct-mail campaign, start by getting your name on as many mailing lists as possible. Junk mail isn't junk when you're trying to learn about direct mail. Obtain free information every chance you get, especially from companies that offer products or services similar to yours. Take note of your reaction to each piece of mail, and save the ones that communicate most effectively, whether they come from large or small companies.

The most effective direct-mail inserts often use key words, colors and types of inserts that can be adapted into your own mailer. Make sure the colors you use promote the appropriate image. Neon colors, for example, can attract attention for party-planner or gift basket businesses. On the other hand, ivory and gray are usually the colors of choice for lawyers, financial planners and other business services.

To involve the reader in the ordering process, many mailers enclose stickers that say "Yes" or "No" to be pasted on

HOT LINK

GET YOUR BUSINESS TARGET WITH THESE TWO DIRECT-MAIL WEB SITES:

● MEDIAFINDER.COM OFFERS A COMPREHENSIVE SEARCHABLE DATABASE OF PRINT MEDIA AND LOTS OF USEFUL LINKS FOR ADVERTISING AND DIRECT MAIL.

● DIRECT MARKETING ONLINE (WWW.DMNEWS.COM) OFFERS BUSINESS UPDATES AND THREE FREE E-MAIL NEWSLETTERS—*THE CRM WEEKLY, E-MAIL MARKETING WEEKLY* AND *IMARKETING NEWS DAILY.*

the order form. Companies such as Publisher's Clearing House take this technique farther by asking recipients to find hidden stickers throughout the mailing and paste them on the sweepstakes entry. It also asks customers to choose their prizes, which gets them even more involved.

Next, read up on the subject. A wealth of printed information is available to help educate yourself about direct mail. *Do-It-Yourself Direct Marketing: Secrets for Small Business* by Mark S. Bacon, is a comprehensive manual that touches on all aspects of direct mail. Two of the better-known publications are *DM News*, a weekly trade paper, and *Direct Magazine*, a monthly.

The Direct Marketing Association (DMA), in New York City, is a national trade organization for direct marketers. For a catalog that highlights many of the direct marketing industry's books, a free brochure that lists a variety of direct marketing institutes and seminars across the country, or more information about joining, call the DMA at (212)768-7277. You can also visit the group's Web site at www.the-dma.org.

Mailing Lists

No matter what type of direct mail you send out, you'll need a mailing list. The basic way to build a mailing list is by capturing name and address information for everyone who buys or shows interest in your product. If you sell by mail, you'll already have this information. If not, you can get it off customers' checks. Hold a drawing and ask customers to fill out an entry card or drop their business cards in a bowl. Or simply put a mailing list book next to your cash registers where customers can sign up to receive mailers and advance notices of sales. You can also gather names by placing a classified or display ad in print, then compiling the names of people who respond to your ad.

The list you develop using your own customers' names is called your "house list." Of course, when you're first starting out, your house list is likely to be skimpy. To augment it, one way to go is to rent a mailing list. There are two ways to rent a mailing list: approaching the company you want to rent from directly or using a list broker.

Any company that mails merchandise or information to its customers—catalog companies, magazine publishers, manufacturers, etc.—usually has a list manager, who handles inquiries and orders for the mailing list. If, for example, you know that subscribers to *Modern Photography* magazine are likely to be good prospects for your product, then you can rent their subscriber list directly. Another good source is local newsletters or group membership lists. Many organizations will let you use their member lists; these can be very cost-effective.

If you are not sure whose list you want, then call a mailing list broker. List brokers know all the lists available and can advise you on what type of list would work best for your business. Many can also custom-create lists based on your requirements. You can find brokers in the Yellow Pages under "Mailing Lists" and "Mailing Services," and in the classified sections of mail-order trade magazines. The DMA can also refer you to brokers. Another source is the bimonthly directory *Standard Rate and Data Service Direct Marketing List Source*, available in most libraries.

Some list companies let you sample a list before making a purchase. Rental costs typically range from $50 to $80 per thousand names. This is for a one-time use only. (List owners typically "seed" their lists with their own names and addresses so they can tell if you use the list more than once.) Lists will typically be shipped on computer disks so you can easily use them with your computer; others send preprinted names on mailing labels.

Most experts agree renting fewer than 5,000 names isn't worthwhile, primarily because a large mailing doesn't cost much more per piece than a small mailing, and the returns are higher. Start with about 5,000 names for your first mailing, and consider it a test.

BRIGHT IDEA

A GROWING NUMBER OF LIST PUBLISHERS SELL LISTS ON CD-ROM. SINCE THESE LISTS MAY NOT BE UPDATED AS REGULARLY AS OTHER LIST SOURCES, BE SURE TO ASK HOW CURRENT THE LIST IS BEFORE YOU BUY. THE FLIER FORMAT, WHILE IMPARTING THE BASIC MESSAGE, IS A BIT "DOWNSCALE" FOR A SOMEWHAT SOPHISTICATED SERVICE.

If your response is less than 1 or 2 percent, something is wrong. Either the market isn't right for your product, your mailer isn't attention-grabbing enough, or your prices are too high. If you get a response of 2 percent or higher, then you are on the right track.

Once you develop a complete mailer, continue to test your enclosures by adding or eliminating one important element at a time and keeping track of any upward or downward changes in response.

Brochures

For many businesses, especially service companies, a brochure is the building block of all marketing materials. A brochure is an information piece that doubles as an image maker. The look and feel of the brochure can not only describe the benefits of your product or service, but also convey your legitimacy and professionalism. A brochure can make your small company look just as substantial as a more established rival, making it a great equalizer.

The good news is that a brochure does not have to be expensive. It can be almost as cheap to produce as a flier, as long as it's well-written and well-designed. A brochure can be as uncomplicated as a piece of folded paper—the same piece of letter-sized paper that would otherwise be a flier. By folding it twice, as you would a letter, then turning it upright so it opens like a book, you have the basis for a brochure.

The magic of the brochure format is that it allows for a more dramatic presentation of the material than does a flier. Think of your brochure cover as the stage curtain, creating anticipation of the excitement that lies inside. An eye-catching headline on the cover is like the master of ceremonies, piquing the prospect's interest about what's behind the "curtain." Inside, you first need to pay off the promise, or claim, in the cover headline with another headline, then use the remaining space for elaboration.

The principles of writing successful brochures are basically the same as those for writing print ads (see the "Print Advertising" section on page 494). However, brochures offer more room than ads, so there is a tendency to get long-winded and wordy. Keep your brochure brief, with enough information to interest readers but not so much repetition that they get bored.

The sample on page 511 shows a "before and after" makeover of a brochure for a company called My Right Hand that provides business support services. The first step in boosting this brochure's appeal was coming up with a tempting headline for the cover. The goal is to arouse the interest of potential clients—the harried sole proprietor who needs help with the detailed paperwork involved in running a business alone. The revised headline "How To Free Your Business From Paperwork Purgatory" accomplishes that goal.

In this or any other headline, it's important to go beyond the ordinary. Give your headline an unexpected word or phrase that

DOLLAR STRETCHER

KEEP YOUR HOUSE MAILING LIST UP TO DATE BY CLEANING IT REGULARLY. TO DO THIS, SEND OUT MAILERS WITH THE NOTATION "ADDRESS CORRECTION REQUESTED." THE POST OFFICE WON'T CHARGE YOU FOR SENDING YOU THE NEW ADDRESSES OF YOUR CUSTOMERS WHEN THE CARDS ARE RETURNED.

expresses the idea in a memorable fashion. Adding the word "purgatory" gives this headline extra drama and emotion and puts the worst face on paperwork.

When the prospect flips the page, he or she finds a short-story-length headline that builds on the cover: "PAPERWORK. It ties you up. It slows you down. It ticks you off. All good reasons to delegate it to us...a service you'll feel confident calling MY RIGHT HAND."

This headline pushes the prospect's buttons (i.e., sensitivities) by emphasizing that paperwork is a grind, a bore and a frustration. The buzzword "delegate" is used because delegation is recognized as essential to entrepreneurial success when a business has grown too big for one person to handle. And, since confidence and trust are key in giving your business papers to an unknown company, the headline also emphasizes the company's trustworthiness by using the word "confident."

The overall look of a brochure is key to making a good impression on prospective customers. Here are some tips to make sure yours is inviting to the eye:

- **HAVE THE DESCRIPTIVE COPY TYPESET IN A FAIRLY LARGE SIZE.** There's no bigger turnoff for a prospect than squinting at fly-speck-sized printing.
- **USE LIGHT-COLORED PAPER.** This, too, makes the brochure easier to read.
- **BREAK UP THE COPY WITH SUBHEADS.** This makes the overall brochure less formidable to read.
- **ADD SOMETHING UNEXPECTED VISUALLY.** One idea is to have an illustrator create a cartoon to use on the cover.
- **USE THE BACK OF YOUR BROCHURE** for a "business biography." This is a good place to talk about how your company got started, how it has succeeded and where it is today.
- **ALWAYS USE ENDORSEMENTS,** testimonials or other credibility-raising elements.

Spend a little extra money. It's worth it to have your brochure printed on card stock or quality heavyweight paper. A key part of the impression it makes is the way it feels in the customer's hand.

Before:

The flier format, while imparting the basic message, is a bit "downscale" for a somewhat sophisticated service.

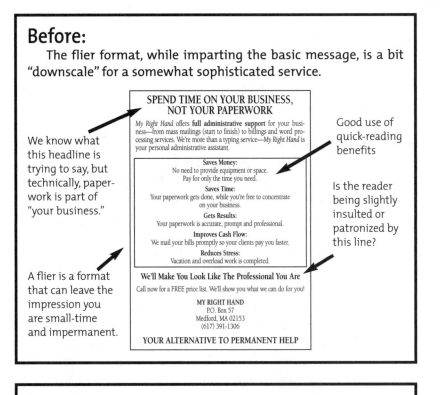

We know what this headline is trying to say, but technically, paper-work is part of "your business."

A flier is a format that can leave the impression you are small-time and impermanent.

Good use of quick-reading benefits

Is the reader being slightly insulted or patronized by this line?

The flier content:

SPEND TIME ON YOUR BUSINESS, NOT YOUR PAPERWORK

My Right Hand offers **full administrative support** for your business—from mass mailings (start to finish) to billings and word processing services. We're more than a typing service—*My Right Hand* is your personal administrative assistant.

Saves Money:
No need to provide equipment or space.
Pay for only the time you need.

Saves Time:
Your paperwork gets done, while you're free to concentrate on your business.

Gets Results:
Your paperwork is accurate, prompt and professional.

Improves Cash Flow:
We mail your bills promptly so your clients pay you faster.

Reduces Stress:
Vacation and overload work is completed.

We'll Make You Look Like The Professional You Are

Call now for a FREE price list. We'll show you what we can do for you!

MY RIGHT HAND
P.O. Box 57
Medford, MA 02153
(617) 391-1306

YOUR ALTERNATIVE TO PERMANENT HELP

After:

A brochure gives you a more polished image. It says you are seasoned, sophisticated and professional.

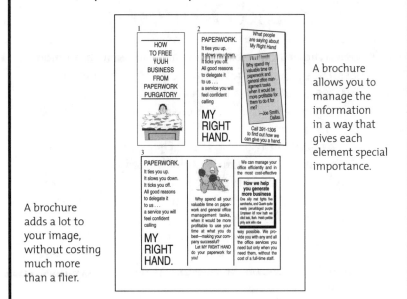

A brochure adds a lot to your image, without costing much more than a flier.

A brochure allows you to manage the information in a way that gives each element special importance.

Sales Letters

Whether you send it out solo or as part of a direct-mail package (see "Package Deal" on page 524), a sales letter can be one of your most effective marketing tools, allowing you to speak one-on-one to prospects and customers. What makes a good sales letter? There are three key rules:

1. **START WITH A HOOK.** Begin your letter with a provocative thought or idea that "hooks" readers and makes them want to keep reading.
2. **GIVE THEM THE FACTS FAST.** Quickly list the top two or three benefits of doing business with your company.
3. **END PERSUASIVELY.** Close the letter with a strong argument that compels readers to respond.

How long should a sales letter be? The standard answer is "long enough to do the job." And yes, it takes longer to persuade a prospective customer to buy than to merely get him to inquire further. But in today's high-tech age, people become impatient with anything that takes much longer than an eyeblink to read.

Does this mean the sales letter is dying out? No; people will still read sales letters. However, they don't like it when you make them work at it—so keep it lean and mean.

Equal in importance to your message (some would say more

Added Dimension

Add dimension to your sales letters—literally—by attaching some type of small item to the letter. Make it something that ties in to the letter's headline or subject. For example:

- **A PLUMBER** could stick a minipacket of aspirin to a letter with a headline reading "Pipes giving you a headache? Take two of these, and call us in the morning."
- **CHILD'S PLASTIC PLAY SCISSORS** attached to the letter could be combined with a "Cut your costs..." message.
- **OR TRY A PACKET OF COFFEE** with a headline like "Sit down, have a cup of coffee on us, and learn how you can profit from stocking Steve's Safety Bolts."

A 3-D item inside gives your direct-mail package bulk. Recipients are curious and more likely to open the letter. Once they see what's inside, they'll read on to find out the connection between the item and the words.

important) is the look of your letter. It should be visually inviting. As soon as prospective customers pull your letter out of the envelope, before they read one word of your sales message, they instantly have a positive or negative reaction based on the overall look of the letter. If it's crammed with words, readers will get a negative impression right away.

To have the best chance of being read, your letter should be open and airy-looking with short paragraphs—including some that are one sentence or even one word long. (A one-word paragraph? Here's how: Write something like "I have one word for suppliers who say they can't offer you a one-year guarantee." Follow that with a one-word paragraph such as "Baloney!" or any similar word you want to use. It is a real attention-getter.

Strip your sales message down to the essentials so readers can breeze through it. This may mean hacking out words and phrases you have slaved over. But each extra bit you take out increases your chances of actually getting a response.

Last but not least, be sure to use "you." This is a good rule of thumb in any form of advertising, but especially in a sales letter, where you are, in a sense, talking to the prospect face-to-face. Always talk about your product or service in terms of its benefit to the reader, such as "You'll save more than 50 percent." Sounds obvious, but it's easy to lapse into the impersonal "We" mode, as in "We offer our customers discounts of more than 50 percent."

Postcards

The humble postcard has the power to beat all other direct marketing formats when it comes to generating sales leads. Why is the postcard so effective? It's much less costly to prepare and mail than other direct-mail efforts, but that's not its greatest strength. It can be mailed out practically overnight, but that's not its greatest strength, either.

The real power of a postcard is that it takes only a flip of the wrist for recipients to get your message. They read their name on it, then flip it over to see what's on the other side. Simple, but incredibly powerful. Why? Because a huge percentage of direct mail never even gets opened. That's the key word—"opened." A postcard never has to overcome that obstacle. Even a folded flier has to be opened and

A Little Surgery Can...

This company's old letter is a good first start. It's persuasive and has immediacy. All it needs is some additional structure and a little nipping and tucking to make it work even harder.

Before

It's not too late to lower your property tax.

1. **Dec. 26 Deadline:** The town of Plainville just mailed the Fiscal 1991 Real Estate Tax Bills. You still have until December 26 to contest your assessed valuation and get an abatement that would lower your taxes.

2. **Get an expert:** Property owners can obtain abatements on their own; however, the adjustment is usually nominal. For substantial reduction of property taxes, the services of a professional CPA and real estate tax expert is advised to substantiate your case.

3. **No-risk contingent fee:** My firm, Property Tax Associates, only gets paid if I successfully reduce your property tax. I know what method is currently being used in Plainville to assess your property. I know how similar properties are assessed. And I can evaluate whether your assessment is taking advantage of the full depreciation deductions to which you are entitled and apply declining value multipliers. In short, I am a property tax abatement expert and have successfully lowered the property taxes of my clients by thousands of dollars.

4. **Free evaluation:** I know the Plainville real estate market and can quickly evaluate your current assessment and tax situation, at no obligation to you. I will not take your case if I do not believe I can substantially reduce your real estate taxes. My fee is based on a percentage of your actual tax reduction. So it is in my interest as well to make sure your taxes are lowered to the full limit of the law.

5. **You must act quickly:** State law limits the number of days an abatement application can be filed. Call me at (508) 429-2527 for an appointment now so there will be enough time to properly and legally substantiate your tax reduction request.

Property Tax Associates
Rocco Beatrice, CPA, MST, MBA
156 Mitchell Road
Holliston, MA 01746
(508) 429-2527

Suggested Operations:

A. Headline transplant: The old headline telegraphs a strong benefit— but may work better as a sub-head, beneath the new head-line.

B. Personalization implant: Who are you talking to? With no salutation, this letter doesn't draw readers in.

C. Pace lift: The old letter opens a little slowly and dully. That can be a turnoff to the impatient, indifferent reader.

D. Paragraph liposuction: The old letter has a few oversize paragraphs that look formidable to read. That immediately disinvites the reader.

A letter with potential . . .

...Make A Letter Better

After

Will you OVERPAY Your Property Tax Again This Year?

It's not too late to lower it if you act by the <u>December 26 deadline</u>.

Mr. George Wagner
R-B Electronics
1313 Azure Blvd.
Plainview, MA 01746

Dear Mr. Wagner,

Will you be "nailed" again this year?

Amazingly, six out of every 10 property owners overpay on their property taxes . . . and you could be one of them.

But if you act by December 26—the deadline for contesting your assessed valuation—you can get an abatement that will lower your taxes.

Why you should call Property Tax Associates:

1. **Get a larger abatement.** You can expect a much larger cut than you could obtain on your own because of our special understanding and knowledge of the abatement process.

2. **Pay only if you get a reduction.** You don't pay us unless we successfully reduce your tax. And our fee is based on a percentage, so it is in our interest to get your taxes reduced as low as possible.

3. **Get a free evaluation.** It costs you nothing to learn if you have a chance for an abatement. We know the Plainview real estate market and can quickly evaluate your assessment and tax situation, without obligation.

We've helped many owners like you save thousands on their property taxes. And we can do the same for you.

MAKE NO MISTAKE: The city will not reduce your tax automatically. You must apply by December 26 for a reduction—or overpay again. Call me at (508) 429-2527 today so there is enough time to evaluate and prepare your request.

Sincerely,

Rocco Beatrice
Certified Public Accountant

Suggested Operations:

A. Headline transplant:
The new headline pushes an emotional "hot button" that gets prospects riled up—and ready to act.

B. Personalization implant:
A letter with opening personalization enables you to bond one-to-one with the reader. That connection is the same that any sales rep hopes to achieve. And a letter is a sales rep.

C. Pace lift:
The new letter opens with a provocative, one-sentence "hook," then quickly hops from point to point.

D. Paragraph liposuction:
The new letter keeps paragraphs lean, mean and easy to read.

Potential released

unfolded, while all a postcard requires is a flick of the wrist.

More than letters, postcards convey a sense of urgency, making them an ideal way to notify customers of a limited-time offer or special sale. Don't restrict yourself to the standard 4-by-6-inch postcard format, either. Postcards can be as big as a letter-sized piece of paper, and many really benefit from that extra size. This costs more (although still not as much as a full direct-mail package), but it gives you more room to dramatize your offer. If you do use a larger size, you can make it a picture postcard, with just a large visual on the front and words on the back next to the recipient's name and address.

Consider the "before and after" makeover (on page 517) on a postcard for SWD Truck Repair. Like many service businesses, SWD's services aren't an impulse purchase—meaning buyers usually don't leap for the phone right after getting the promotional mailer.

What's a great way to get more attention in the nanosecond of time it takes the recipient to turn the postcard over? First, the company needs a catchier nickname to use for the purposes of advertising. In this case, "The Truck Doctor" fits the bill perfectly. Nicknames can work for many types of service businesses. Some examples:

■ **FOR A WEDDING PLANNER:** The Marriage Maestro
■ **FOR AN AUTO MECHANIC:** The Car Medic
■ **FOR A FAX MACHINE REPAIR SERVICE:** The Fax Fixer
■ **FOR A PARTY PLANNING SERVICE:** The Party Smarty
■ **FOR A CARPENTER:** The Wood Wizard

You get the idea. Next, add an eye-catching graphic on the front of the postcard, along with a provocative headline or teaser that conveys the company's benefit. In this example, the illustration shows a struggling truck, and the headline urges "Call for a free checkup at the Truck Doctor." It's a nice play on words that offers a benefit few can resist—a free service. Cartoons with copy balloons, as shown here, are an excellent way to cut through the advertising clutter and grab the reader's attention.

Fliers

A hybrid of the postcard and brochure, fliers give you more room to get your message across than a postcard but are cheaper (and easier to design) than a brochure.

Fliers are ideal for certain situations, such as for posting on a bulletin board, sticking under car windshield wipers in a parking lot or stuffing in mailboxes. They are also a good tool to enclose in a sales

Before:

This postcard has the basics—for a business card. But it's supposed to grab attention as an advertisement, and it doesn't.

What makes this company special? What makes it worth remembering? There's no telling from this card.

After:

This approach catches your eye with the cartoon, the contrasting panels and the proposition.

This headline makes an attractive offer from a memorably named mechanic.

The relevant cartoon makes your message interesting and more palatable.

letter if, for example, you want to notify recipients about a short-term sale or upcoming special event.

Because fliers' primary benefit is that they convey information quickly, make sure yours is easy to read and stands out. Try bright colors to grab the viewer's eye, and use large type so information can be seen from a distance. Keep type brief and to the point. A crowded flier won't get anyone's attention.

While fliers are a useful addition to a marketing campaign, don't use them as your only direct-mail tool, or you could come off looking amateurish.

Catalogs

For mail order entrepreneurs, a catalog is the backbone of their businesses. But even if selling by mail is only a small part of what your business is about, you would be surprised to find out how much you can benefit from a catalog.

If you're picturing the hefty Spiegel catalog or a glossy magazine like those sent by Pottery Barn, don't despair. A catalog can be as basic as a four-page, black-and-white fold-over and still be successful. Here are six tips to ensure yours is, too:

Direct Hits

Try these attention-getting direct-mail ideas to power up your business:

- **REACTIVATION VOUCHER:** Mail a $20 no-strings-attached voucher to any customer you haven't seen in six months or longer. Few can turn it down…and even fewer will spend only $20.
- **MAGALOG:** If you have a catalog, give it more value by enhancing it with problem-solving editorial content. This creates a combination magazine and catalog.
- **$2 BILL:** Send a $2 bill with a questionnaire asking about product/service preferences.
- **WE'VE MISSED YOU:** Send a card to clients you haven't seen in a year telling them they're missed. Include a discount coupon.
- **BIRTHDAY CALL:** Record all customers' birth dates, and make sure that they get a special call or card from you.

1. **Keep it simple.** Don't try to reinvent the wheel. Catalogs look the way they do for a reason. Almost every format you can imagine has been tested numerous times, and the formulas you see most often are the overall winners. Choose a size from one of the most common catalog sizes.

2. **Borrow from the best.** The surest way to plot your catalog layout is to study other catalogs—at least 50 or 60, black and white as well as color. You'll then have a collection of the best ideas from the best designers and copywriters money can buy. Study the catalogs, and note any useful ideas.

3. **Start a clip file.** Collect useful layout ideas, and divide your clippings into categories with a folder for each of them. Make folders for front covers, back covers and order forms. Then

Gifts That Keep On Giving

Do you offer customers gift certificates? Many entrepreneurs don't, not realizing how this can boost sales. Here are some suggestions to make the most of this sales tool and also prevent fraud:

- **Don't buy generic gift certificates** from stationery or office supply stores. These can easily be duplicated. Invest in custom-designed certificates.

- **Avoid cash refunds.** State on the certificate that if more than $5 in change is due, it will be issued in the form of another gift certificate.

- **Keep a log.** Record the number, date of sale and dollar amount of each gift certificate sold. Be sure to note when the certificate is redeemed.

- **Use security features** like an embossed logo or watermark to prevent photocopying.

    Properly used, certificates are like money in the bank for your business since customers often don't redeem them till months later.

make folders to suit any special interests you may have.

4. **SKETCH A BASIC LAYOUT.** Once you gather ideas, you will probably notice the layouts follow a few general patterns. Some use lots of words and only a few illustrations; others use lots of illustrations and few words. Choose one or two basic layouts, and substitute your products for theirs. Examine your clip files for ideas, and adjust those ideas to fit your products.

BEWARE!

DON'T LAUNCH A DIRECT-MAIL CAMPAIGN (ESPECIALLY A CATALOG) UNTIL YOU'RE SURE YOU CAN HANDLE THE ORDERS YOU MIGHT RECEIVE. IF FULFILLMENT SYSTEMS AREN'T IN PLACE AND ORDERS DON'T GET SENT OUT, YOU'LL LOSE CREDIBILITY—AND FUTURE BUSINESS.

For a handmade craft product, handwritten copy and illustrations may work; for something high-tech, a slicker look works best. Sketch your ideas, and jot down copy. Next, weed out the bad ideas, and improve on the good ones.

5. **FIND THE PERFECT PRINTER.** Shop around—you'll be amazed at the range of prices printers quote you for the same job. If you live in a small town, call large printers in nearby metropolitan areas since they often offer substantial savings and give quotes over the phone. Get at least four bids on any print job you plan to run, and get up to 20 on a big one.

The printers will want to know the physical dimensions of your catalog, the number of pages to be printed, the kind of paper you want (stay with the cheapest newsprint to start with), and the number of catalogs you want.

The more catalogs you print, the cheaper your cost per unit. In addition to the catalogs you mail out, you need to include a fresh catalog with each order shipped, give away catalogs as a form of advertising, and have extras to send when someone expresses interest. If you plan to, say, mail 10,000 catalogs, print 20,000.

6. **PUT IT ALL TOGETHER.** You can spend tens of thousands of dollars on a mail order catalog—but why should you, when you can produce an attention-getting book so cheaply? Do as much as you can yourself—product drawings, photos, copy. Today's technology, from "idiot-proof" cameras to simple desktop publishing programs, makes catalog production and layout simpler than ever.

But the key to catalog success isn't the technology—it's understanding your customers. Show them why they should buy from you

and no one else. Target them with the right mailing lists. And remember, the more you do yourself, the more you save.

Need more help? The Direct Marketing Association can refer you to catalog consultants in your area.

Newsletters

Publishing a company newsletter is a great way to get the word out about your business…and keep past customers coming back.

Most people actually look at newsletters rather than pitch them into the trash with the rest of the ads.

"The primary benefit of a customer newsletter is keeping your existing customers informed about what you're doing," says Elaine Floyd, author of *Marketing With Newsletters*. Newsletters are also a good way to reach new customers because, if done correctly, they come off as more informative and with less sales hype than most items consumers receive in the mail. In addition to telling readers about your product or service, newsletters inform them about developments in your industry or theirs and share information that affects them. "People might not think they need your product or service," says Floyd. "Reading an informative newsletter helps convince them they do."

The businesses that benefit most from newsletters are those that have to educate customers about the advantages of using their product or service. If you own a candy shop, for example, you might not have enough pertinent information for customers to justify a newsletter. On the other hand, a computer consultant could do a real service by publishing a newsletter about the latest software and hardware.

Your newsletter does not have to be all information. Including a coupon, a special offer or other call to action helps get people to buy. Also, always give upcoming sales or promotions a prominent place in your newsletter. "The promotional aspects of your newsletter should be woven in with the informational," advises Floyd. If you're reporting on your industry, talk about your company's place within the industry. If you're talking about a trend in the economy—the rise of dual-income households, let's say—then tie in the fact that using your company's service helps free up valuable time.

Floyd recommends using the following formula, which she calls RISE, to be sure your newsletter covers all the bases:

- **RECOGNITION:** Your newsletter should tell people who you are, what you do and where they can find you. If consumers have to read through two pages of text to find the name of your company, you're not increasing your name recognition. Use your company logo on the newsletter.
- **IMAGE:** Your newsletter is an extension of your company's image. If it's interesting and professional-looking, customers will think well of your business. If it's not, they may doubt your credibility. With desktop publishing programs, Floyd says most people can create their own professional-looking newsletter or have it done fairly cheaply by a freelancer.

■ **SPECIFICS:** Give your readers specific reasons why they should choose your product or service. Vague assertions like "We're the best" don't work nearly as well as matter-of-fact details about exactly what you can do for them.

Premium Prospects

Whether you call them premiums, advertising specialties or flat-out bribes, gifts are a marketing gimmick that works with all demographic groups. Studies show 40 percent of people remember an advertiser's name up to six months after receiving a gift. Thirty-one percent still use the item up to a year later.

Premiums can be used to generate leads, build name awareness, thank customers, increase store traffic, introduce new products, motivate customers and create an unconscious obligation to buy. Premiums can be used at trade shows, open houses, special events and grand openings.

Classic premiums include T-shirts, baseball caps, jackets, headbands, writing instruments, desk and office accessories, scratch pads and mugs. Mouse pads and screen savers are some of the more recent premiums gaining in popularity.

How to make a premium work for you? Research it first. Make sure the item is matched with your target audience. Also make sure the item is good quality. A cheap premium that breaks or doesn't work in the first place makes a negative impression—just the opposite of what you want.

When choosing a premium, ask five questions:
1. **HOW MANY PEOPLE** do I want to reach?
2. **HOW MUCH MONEY** do I have to spend?
3. **WHAT MESSAGE** do I want to print?
4. **WHAT GIFT** will be most useful to my prospects?
5. **IS THIS GIFT UNIQUE** and desirable? Would I want it?

You can find specialty advertising firms listed in the Yellow Pages. Ask to see their catalogs; compare sample quality and prices.

While the gift is being offered, focus your marketing and advertising efforts on it. There's no more powerful word in advertising than "free," so put the power of freebies to work for you.

■ **ENACTMENT:** Make the reader take action—whether by picking up the phone, mailing in a reply card or coming down to your store.

Strapped for things to write about—or don't have time to write it yourself? Try asking your industry trade association for news services that provide copy in return for a monthly subscription fee. This also ensures the articles are professionally written.

If you can't find a news service, use a clippings service to get story

Package Deal

While direct mail can mean everything from a postcard to a catalog, many business owners get the best response from sending out a direct-mail "package." In addition to the sales letter and brochure (see the "Sales Letters" and "Brochures" sections earlier in this chapter), this typically includes three other elements:

1. **THE OUTSIDE ENVELOPE:** There are two schools of thought on this. One school swears that "teaser" copy on the envelope can get recipients to open it. On the other hand, some people throw away anything that looks like junk mail. The opposite strategy is to trick readers into opening your mail by sending direct mail that looks like personal letters. Software programs can print addresses so they look like handwriting. Put only your address, not your company name, on the return address to arouse the recipient's curiosity.

2. **A RESPONSE FORM:** The form should be easy to fill out. Be sure to include your phone number in case the prospect wants to ask a question or order by phone.

3. **A REPLY ENVELOPE:** Enclosing postage-paid reply envelopes helps get orders. Even if you can't afford postage-paid envelopes, include a pre-addressed reply envelope. If the prospect has to put the mailing down and search for an envelope, they may have time to have second thoughts.

ideas. Though clippings from other publications can't be reprinted without the writer's permission, they can give you ideas for articles of your own and keep you updated on hot industry topics.

Tap clients for copy by featuring a "Client of the Month," showing how your product or service solved a problem they were facing. Or you can team with related businesses; for example, an interior designer could have guest columns written by florists or furniture store owners.

Easy ways to get clients to contribute? Conduct a survey—and print the results. Start a "Letters to the Editor" column. Add a "Q&A" column, where customers can pose their problems and other customers can write in with solutions.

Keep your writing style simple, and make sure you get help proofreading if your spelling skills are not up to snuff. A newsletter full of typos or grammatical errors shows clients you're a careless amateur.

Newsletters can be monthly, semimonthly or quarterly, depending on what your budget is, how much available time you have and how fast-paced your industry is. Quarterly publications are generally sufficient to get your name in front of customers; then increase frequency if needed. The key is to be consistent, so do not take on more than you can handle.

Renting a mailing list isn't generally a good idea for newsletters, says Floyd. "Your newsletter will be better received if the reader knows about you or needs your product," she says. Floyd recommends sending newsletters only to current customers, qualified leads and referrals. When someone gives you a business card, send him or her a newsletter. Then you or a salesperson can call the person later, using the newsletter as a starting point to ask about products or services they might need.

CLASSIFIED ADS

Classified ads don't draw the huge response of a display ad, but they still provide the most economical way to get your business into the public eye. And since they demand neither the eye-catching design of a display ad nor the clever wording of a direct-mail campaign, almost anyone can write them.

What should your ad say? The Newspaper Association of America (NAA) recommends listing your product or service's main benefit. Does it make people money? Improve their self-image? Use a catchy statement, such as "Feel Good Now!" to create an impact. Not every reader is looking for the same benefit, so list as many as you can afford. The more readers know about your business, the more they will trust you.

Experts also recommend using white space to make your classified ad stands out from the competition. White space works especially well in newspapers, which sell ads for pennies a word or by the line. If you place just a few words in each line—the first line listing a benefit, the second the name of your company, the third your address, for example—you have a striking, centered ad surrounded by white space.

HOT LINK

SOME THINGS NEVER CHANGE—AND YOUR DIRECT MAIL CAN BENEFIT FROM LESSONS OF THE PAST. AT THE NATIONAL MAIL ORDER ASSOCIATION'S SITE (WWW.NMOA.ORG), YOU'LL FIND ALL SORTS OF INFORMATION, BUT DON'T MISS THE EXHIBITS IN THE SITE'S "MUSEUM" SECTION, INCLUDING THE WINNERS OF PRENTICE-HALL'S 1942 BETTER-LETTER CONTEST.

These brief ads work best when they offer a commonly sold product or service such as tax preparation or catering. Listing the benefits of each isn't essential because the public knows what to expect. White space in classifieds is also effective when you offer a catalog or another form of literature describing your product. In this case, you might place the main benefit in an opening line that is designed to grab the reader's attention, and below the benefit list how to send for the information, noting its price if any. For example, "Play Backgammon Like a Pro" would be a good benefit line in an ad offering free information about a booklet that shows backgammon players how to improve their game.

Ads that use white space are less common in magazines since these ads are often twice as costly as a typical newspaper classified. However, they are often more effective as well—even more so than in a newspaper because few other white space ads will be competing for the attention of the readers.

Before placing a classified ad, write or call the publications that interest you and ask for an advertising kit (also called a media or press kit). Ad kits include guidelines in the form of pamphlets, booklets, or newsletters, which will help you construct your ad and give you tips on choosing the main benefit, consolidating words or determining whether the tone should be boldly stated or instead employ a conservative description and a list of benefits. Most ad kits also list demographic information about the readers.

Finally, repeat your ad as often as possible, so long as it brings in enough money to justify its expense. Repeating ads helps customers gain familiarity with your product or service and helps break down sales resistance. Once the ad stops pulling in new accounts, it's time to develop a new ad. A classified that uses fewer words will cost less to run, so it doesn't have to pull as well to justify itself. But sometimes adding more words can help your sales, too. It doesn't hurt to experiment.

How much profit do you need to make on classifieds? Unless you're running a one-product, one-sale business, you can build a profitable operation through classifieds just by breaking even, or even by coming in a little under the money since many of those buyers will become your repeat customers.

CO-OP ADVERTISING

How can small retailers or distributors maintain a high profile without spending lots of money? One answer is co-op advertising.

Co-op advertising is a cooperative advertising effort between suppliers and retailers—such as between a soda company and a convenience store that advertises the company's products.

Both retailers and suppliers benefit: retailers because co-op advertising increases the amount of money they can spend on ads, and suppliers through increased local exposure and better sales.

Although each manufacturer or supplier that uses co-op advertising sets up its own individual program, all co-op programs run on the same basic premise. The retailer or distributor builds a fund (called accrual) based on the amount of purchases made from the supplier. Then, when the retailer or distributor places ads featuring that supplier's products, the supplier reimburses all or part of the cost of the ad, up to the amount accrued.

To start using co-op advertising, begin by asking your suppliers what co-op programs they offer. Follow their rules to be sure you get reimbursed. Some suppliers require that ads feature only their products, not any other supplier's. Others ask that no competing products be included.

Though procedures may vary, there are three basic steps to filing a claim for reimbursement. First, show "proof of performance." For print ads, this is just a copy of the ad exactly as it was printed. If you buy TV or radio ads, you will need a copy of the script with station affidavits of the dates and times aired.

Next, document the cost of the advertising—usually with copies of applicable invoices from the publication or station where you ran

Coupon Cutters

I f you want to attract and keep customers, you need to offer an incentive. A coupon for a free sample or service or a discount on your normal prices can be just the nudge a customer needs to try your new business. Coupons help you reach many goals: introducing a new product or service, increasing repeat business, beating the competition and more.

One of the most powerful ways to use coupons is through direct mail. This method is especially good for occasions such as grand openings or new product/service introductions. How to make the most of your direct-mail coupon campaign? Keep these tips in mind:

- **COUPONS CAN BE OFFERED** as a "Thank you for buying from us" or a "Stop by and try us" message.
- **A COUPON CAN BE A SINGLE ITEM** for a one-shot promotion or used in combination with other offers.
- **THE VALUE MUST BE SUBSTANTIAL** enough to make it worthwhile. Better to err on the side of giving too big a discount than to seem cheap.
- **USE COUPON PROMOTIONS SPARINGLY.** They wear themselves out if overused.
- **BE CLEAR.** State exactly what the offer is, how long it lasts and the terms of redemption.
- **COLOR-CODE YOUR COUPONS** if a variety of groups will receive them. For example, if you're mailing to six ZIP codes, color-code them differently so you know how many were redeemed from each area.

The newest way to distribute coupons: on the Internet. Design your Web page so people can e-mail you to receive coupons. This way, you can add them to your mailing list even before the coupons are redeemed. Or consider using a Web coupon service, which offers coupons in booklets by mail or online for consumers to download and print out themselves.

the ad. Third, fill out and submit a claim form, which you can get from the supplier.

Other steps to make the most of co-op advertising:

- **KEEP CAREFUL RECORDS** of how much you have purchased from each supplier.
- **IF YOU TRY SOMETHING UNUSUAL,** such as a sales video or a catalog, get prior approval from each vendor before proceeding.
- **IF YOU'RE PREPARING YOUR OWN ADS,** work with an advertising professional to prepare an ad you think will appeal to the manufacturer. Keep in mind the image the manufacturer presents in its own ads.
- **MAKE SURE YOUR COMPANY'S NAME STANDS OUT** in the ad. Your goal is not so much to sell the supplier's product but to get customers into your store.
- **IF THERE'S NO ESTABLISHED CO-OP PROGRAM,** pitch your ad campaign to the vendor anyway.
- **EXPECT VENDORS TO HELP OUT;** after all, you're bringing them business. If your vendor doesn't offer advertising co-op money, you should look for another vendor who does.
- **BE SURE TO FOLLOW UP.** Money goes only to those who submit claims.

MEASURING ADVERTISING EFFECTIVENESS

Just as important as creating a strong marketing plan is following through on the results. How will you know which ads are working if you do not analyze the results? Check the effectiveness of your advertising programs regularly by conducting one or more of the following tests:

- **RUN THE SAME AD IN TWO DIFFERENT PUBLICATIONS WITH A DIFFERENT IDENTIFYING MARK ON EACH ONE.** Ask customers to clip the ad and bring it in for a discount or a free sample. Or, if you are running an ad that asks customers to order by mail, put a code in your company address such as "Dept. SI." By looking at the marks on the clipped ads or the addresses on the mail-in orders, you will be able to tell which ad pulled better.
- **OFFER A PRODUCT AT DIFFERENT PRICES IN DIFFERENT MAGAZINES.** This has the added benefit of showing whether consumers will buy your product at a higher price.
- **ADVERTISE AN ITEM IN ONE AD ONLY.** Don't have any signs or other-

wise promote the item in your store or business. Then count the calls, sales or special requests for that item. If you get calls, you'll know the ad is working.

■ **STOP RUNNING AN AD THAT YOU REGULARLY RUN.** See if dropping the ad affects sales.

■ **CHECK SALES RESULTS WHENEVER YOU PLACE AN AD FOR THE FIRST TIME.**

Checks like these will give you some idea of how your advertising and marketing program is working. Be aware, however, that you can't expect immediate results from an ad. Especially with small ads—the type most entrepreneurs are likely to be running—you need to give the reader a "getting to know you" period during which he or she gets to feel comfortable with your business.

One study showed that an ad from a new company has to be noticed by a prospect a total of nine times before that prospect becomes a customer. The bad news: Two out of every three times you expose a prospect to your marketing message, it's ignored. That means you have to expose a customer to your message an average of 27 times before he or she will buy.

Evaluate an ad's cost-effectiveness, too. Consider the CPM. A cheaper ad is no bargain if it does not reach many of your prospects.

GLOSSARY

CPM (COST PER THOUSAND): figure that tells you how much it costs to reach 1,000 potential customers with a given form of advertising

DIRECT MAIL: any form of advertising material that is mailed directly to potential customers, including catalogs, brochures, letters, fliers, postcards and newsletters

HOUSE LIST: the mailing list a business develops in-house, comprising of names and addresses collected from current or potential customers

LIST BROKER: company that rents mailing lists of potential customers to other businesses

POSITIONING STATEMENT: one- or two-sentence statement summarizing what differentiates your business from the competition

PREMIUM: any free giveaway to customers (also called ad specialties); common premiums include key chains, caps, T-shirts, pens and desk accessories

TRADE-OUT: term used in radio industry to refer to bartering products or services for air time

Advertising Checklist

Overview

❑ Have you defined your advertising objectives and written them down?

❑ What exactly do you want to communicate to your potential customers?

❑ How will you measure the effectiveness of your ad?

❑ Are you communicating buyer benefits?

❑ Have you strategized an advertising campaign?

❑ Is the timing right?

❑ Do you have a planned advertising budget?

❑ Are you prepared for a successful response?

❑ Have you asked suppliers about cooperative programs?

❑ Have you made sure that employees (if any) are informed of your goals?

❑ Have all appropriate employees reviewed your advertising and approved of it?

❑ What is your lead time for ad placement? Some newspapers require only a few days; some magazines require two months or longer.

Specifics

❑ Does your ad present a central idea or theme?

❑ Does your message require a response?

❑ Have you told customers where and how to reach you?

❑ Is your ad clear and concise?

❑ Is your ad consistent with your desired business image?

Files

❑ Are you keeping files on all aspects of each ad?

❑ Where did the ad run? What were the results? (Number of sales? Sales increases?)

❑ Have you reflected/brainstormed/evaluated?

❑ What variables (weather, competition, etc.) have you targeted for further study?

Competitors And Customers

❑ Are you watching competitors? (If advertisers repeat ads, try to determine why.)

❑ Are you listening to your customers? What do they want? What's important to them?

❑ What media are most cost-effective to reach your customers?

Spread
The Word

How to promote your business

Paid advertising isn't the only way to spread the word about your business. In fact, one of the best ways to get your business noticed does not have to cost you a dime. We are talking about public relations.

Public relations is a broad category, spanning everything from press releases and networking at chamber of commerce meetings to sponsoring contests or holding gala special events. This chapter will show you the basics of public relations and give you plenty of ideas to get started. And ideas are what it's all about, because when it comes to public relations, you are limited only by your own imagination.

GETTING PUBLICITY

Just what is public relations? And how does it differ from advertising? Public relations is the opposite of advertising. In advertising, you pay to have your message placed in a newspaper, TV or radio spot. In public relations, the article that features your company is not paid for. The reporter, whether broadcast or print, writes about or films your company as a result of information he or she received and researched.

Publicity is more effective than advertising, for several reasons. First, publicity is far more cost-effective than advertising. Even if it is not free, your only expenses are generally phone calls and mailings to the media.

Second, publicity has greater longevity than advertising. An article about your business will be remembered far longer than an ad.

Publicity also reaches a far wider audience than advertising generally does. Sometimes, your story might even be picked up by the national media, spreading the word about your business all over the country.

Finally, and most important, publicity has greater credibility with the public than does advertising. Readers feel that if an objective third party—the magazine, newspaper or radio reporter—is featuring your company, you must be doing something worthwhile.

Why do some companies succeed in generating publicity while others don't? It's been proved time and time again that no matter how large or small your business is, the key to securing publicity is identifying your target market and developing a well-thought-out public relations campaign. To get your company noticed, follow these seven steps. You'll notice that many are similar or identical to steps you went through when developing your marketing plan in the last chapter.

1. **WRITE YOUR POSITIONING STATEMENT.** This sums up in a few sentences what makes your business different from the competition.

2. **LIST YOUR OBJECTIVES.** What do you hope to achieve for your company through the publicity plan you put into action? List your top five goals in order of priority. Be specific, and always set deadlines.

   Using a clothing boutique as an example, some goals may be to:

   - **INCREASE YOUR STORE TRAFFIC,** which will translate into increased sales.

   - **CREATE A HIGH PROFILE** for your store within the community.

3. **IDENTIFY YOUR TARGET CUSTOMERS.** Are they male or female? What age range? What are their lifestyles, incomes and buying habits? Where do they live?

4. **IDENTIFY YOUR TARGET MEDIA.** List the newspapers and TV and radio programs in your area that would be appropriate outlets. Make a complete list of the media you want to target, then call them and ask whom you should contact regarding your area of business. Identify the specific reporter or producer who covers your area so you can contact them directly. Your local library will have media reference books that list contact names and numbers. Make your own media directory, listing names, addresses, and telephone and fax numbers. Separate TV, radio and print sources. Know the "beats" covered by different reporters so you can be sure you are pitching your ideas to the appropriate person.

5. **DEVELOP STORY ANGLES.** Keeping in mind the media you're approaching, make a list of story ideas you can pitch to them. Develop story angles you would want to read about or see on TV. Plan a 45-minute brainstorming session with your spouse, a business associate or your employees to come up with fresh ideas.

If you own a toy store, for example, one angle could be to donate toys to the local hospital's pediatric wing. If you own a clothing store, you could alert the local media to a fashion trend in your area. What's flying out of your store so fast you can't keep it in stock? If it's

SMART TIP

FIND OUT THE TIME FRAME IN WHICH THE MEDIA YOU ARE INTERESTED IN WORK. MAGAZINES, FOR INSTANCE, TYPICALLY WORK SEVERAL MONTHS IN ADVANCE, SO IF YOU WANT TO GET A STORY ABOUT YOUR BUSINESS IN THE DECEMBER ISSUE, YOU MAY NEED TO SEND IN YOUR IDEA IN JUNE.

Meet The Press

Think of a press release as your ticket to publicity—one that can get your company coverage in all kinds of publications or on TV and radio stations. Editors and reporters get hundreds of press releases a day. How to make yours stand out?

First, be sure you have a good reason for sending a press release. A grand opening, a new product, a record-setting sales year, a new location or a special event are all good reasons.

Second, make sure your press release is appropriately targeted for the publication or broadcast you're sending it to. The editor of *Road & Track* is not going to be interested in the new baby pacifier you've invented. It sounds obvious, but many entrepreneurs make the mistake of sending press releases at random without considering a publication's audience.

To ensure readability, your press release should follow the standard format: typed, double-spaced, on white letterhead with a contact person's name, title, company, address and phone number in the upper right-hand corner. Below this information, put a brief, eye-catching headline in bold type. A dateline—for example, "Los Angeles, California, April 10, 2004—" follows, leading into the first sentence of the release.

Limit your press releases to one or two pages at most. It should be just long enough to cover the six basic elements: who, what, when, where, why and how. The answers to these six questions should be mentioned in order of their importance to the story to save the editor time and space.

Don't embellish or hype the information. Remember, you are not writing the article; you are merely presenting the information and showing why it is relevant to that publication in hopes that they will write about it. Pay close attention to grammar and spelling. Competition for publicity is intense, and a press release full of typos or errors is more likely to get tossed aside.

Some business owners use attention-getting gimmicks to get their press releases noticed. In most cases, this is a waste of money. If your release is well-written and relevant, you don't need singing telegrams or a bouquet of flowers to get your message across.

If you have the money to invest, you may want to try sending out a press kit. This consists of a folder containing a cover letter, a press release, your business card, and photos of your product or location. You can also include any other information that will convince reporters your business is newsworthy: reprints of articles other publications have written about your business, product reviews, or background information on the company and its principals. If you do send out a press kit, make sure it is sharp and professional-looking and that all graphic elements tie in with your company's logo and image.

shirts featuring the American flag, you could talk to the media about the return of patriotism. Then arrange for a reporter to speak with some of your customers about why they purchased that particular shirt. Suggest the newspaper send a photographer to take pictures of your customers wearing the shirts.

6. MAKE THE PITCH. Put your thoughts on paper, and send them to the reporter in a "pitch letter." Start with a question or an interesting fact that relates your business to the target medium's audience. For instance, if you were writing for a magazine aimed at older people, you could start off "Did you know over half of women age 50 and older have not begun saving for retirement?" Then lead into your pitch: "As a Certified Financial Planner, I can offer your readers 10 tips to start them on the road to a financially comfortable retirement..." Make your letter no longer than one page; include your telephone number so the reporter can contact you.

If appropriate, include a press release with your letter (see "Meet The Press" on page 536). Be sure to include your positioning statement in any correspondence or press releases you send.

7. FOLLOW UP. Following up is the key to securing coverage. Wait four to six days after you've sent the information, then follow up your pitch letter with a telephone call. If you leave a message on voice mail and the reporter does not call you back, call again until you get him or her on the phone. Do not leave a second message within five days of the first. If the reporter requests additional information, send it immediately and follow up to confirm receipt.

Talking To The Media

Once you reach the reporter on the telephone, remember that he or she is extremely busy and probably on deadline. Be courteous, and ask if he or she has time to talk. If not, offer to call back at a more convenient time. If the reporter can talk to you, keep your initial pitch to 20 seconds; afterward, offer to send written information to support your story ideas.

The following tips will boost your chances of success:

- **IF A REPORTER REJECTS YOUR IDEA,** ask if he or she can recommend someone else who might be interested.

- **KNOW EXACTLY WHAT YOU'RE GOING TO SAY** before you telephone the reporter. Have it written down in front of you— it's easier, and you'll feel more confident.

- **EVERYONE LIKES A COMPLIMENT.** If you've read a story you particularly enjoyed by the reporter you're contacting, let him or her know. This will also show that you're familiar with the reporter's work.

- **BE PERSISTENT.** Remember, not everyone will be interested. If your story idea is turned down, try to find out why and use that information to improve your next pitch. Just keep going, and don't give up. You will succeed eventually.

- **DON'T BE A PEST.** You can easily be persistent without being annoying. Use your instincts; if the reporter sounds rushed, offer to call back.

- **BE HELPFUL AND BECOME A RESOURCE** by providing reporters with information. Remember, they need your story ideas. There are only so many they can come up with on their own.

- **ALWAYS REMEMBER THAT ASSISTANTS GET PROMOTED.** Be nice to everyone you speak with, no matter how low they are on the totem pole. After you establish a connection, keep in touch; you never know where people will end up.

- **SAY THANK YOU.** When you succeed in getting publicity for your business, always write a thank-you note to the reporter who worked on it with you. You'd be surprised how much a note means.

Plan your publicity efforts just as carefully as you plan the rest of your business. You'll be glad you made the effort when you see your company featured in the news—and when you see the results in your bottom line.

BRIGHT IDEA

CAPITALIZE ON OLD-FASHIONED PUBLICITY STUNTS. NO, YOU DON'T HAVE TO SWALLOW GOLDFISH OR SIT ATOP A TELE-PHONE POLE, BUT CON-SIDER THE LANDSCAP-ING COMPANY WHOSE PRECISION LAWN-MOWING TEAM SHOWS OFF ITS FANCY FOOTWORK WHILE MARCHING IN LOCAL PARADES.

Social Graces

Does your business use recycled paper products or donate to a homeless shelter? A growing number of consumers consider such factors when deciding whether to patronize your business. A business's "social responsibility" quotient can make a difference to its bottom line.

If you think getting involved in social causes would work for your business, here are some things to consider. First and foremost, customers can smell "phony" social responsibility a mile away, so unless you're really committed to a cause, don't try to exploit customers' concerns to make a profit.

Business consultant David Calabria suggests these steps to making social responsibility work for you—and your community:

- **SET GOALS.** What do you want to achieve? What do you want your company to achieve? Do you want to enter a new market? Introduce a new product? Enhance your business's image?

- **DECIDE WHAT CAUSE YOU WANT TO ALIGN YOURSELF WITH.** This may be your toughest decision, considering all the options out there: children, the environment, senior citizens, homeless people, people with disabilities— the list goes on. Calabria suggests considering a cause that fits in with your products or services; for example, a manufacturer of women's clothing could get involved in funding breast cancer research. Another way to narrow the field is by considering not only causes you feel strongly about, but also those that your customers consider significant.

- **CHOOSE A NONPROFIT OR OTHER ORGANIZATION TO PARTNER WITH.** Get to know the group, and make sure it's sound, upstanding, geographically convenient and willing to cooperate with you in developing a partnership.

- **DESIGN A PROGRAM, AND PROPOSE IT TO THE NONPROFIT GROUP.** Besides laying out what you plan to accomplish, also include indicators that will measure the program's success in tangible terms.

- **NEGOTIATE AN AGREEMENT WITH THE ORGANIZATION.** Know what they want before you sit down, and try to address their concerns upfront.

- **INVOLVE EMPLOYEES.** Unless you get employees involved from the beginning, they won't be able to communicate the real caring involved in the campaign to customers.

- **INVOLVE CUSTOMERS.** Don't just do something good and tell your customers about it later. Get customers involved, too. A sporting goods store could have customers bring in used equipment for a children's shelter, then give them a 15 percent discount on new purchases. Make it easy for customers to do good; then reward them for doing it.

You're The Expert

As an entrepreneur, it's your responsibility to get your business noticed—which means you've got to toot your own horn. You need to do whatever it takes to let others know you exist and that you are an expert source of information or advice about your industry.

Being regarded as an industry expert can do wonders for your business. How can you get your expertise known?

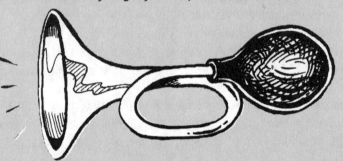

- **START BY MAKING SURE** you know everything you can about your business, product and industry.
- **CONTACT EXPERTS** in the field and ask them how they became experts.
- **TALK TO AS MANY GROUPS** as possible. (If public speaking strikes fear in your heart, you'd better get over it. This is one skill you're going to need as an entrepreneur.) Volunteer to talk to key organizations, service clubs, business groups... whomever might be interested in what you have to say. Do it free of charge, of course, and keep it fun, interesting and timely.
- **CONTACT INDUSTRY TRADE PUBLICATIONS** and volunteer to write articles, opinion pieces or columns. (If you can't do that, write a letter to the editor.)
- **OFFER SEMINARS OR DEMONSTRATIONS** related to your business (a caterer could explain how to cook Thai food, for instance).
- **HOST (OR GUEST ON) A LOCAL RADIO** or TV talk show.

Do all this, and, by the time you contact media people and present yourself as an expert, you'll have plenty of credentials.

SPECIAL EVENTS

Ever since the first Wild West Show was staged to sell "Doctor Winthrop's Miracle Elixir," businesspeople have understood the value of promotional events. Even the most obscure product or service takes on new cachet when accompanied by a dash of showmanship. From "fun runs" to fashion shows, contests to concerts, businesses have learned it pays to be associated with special events.

In fact, special events are one of the fastest-growing areas of marketing today. And while large corporations shell out billions each year to host events, small companies, too, can use promotions to reach their market in a way no conventional method could.

No matter how spectacular an event is, however, it can't stand alone. You can use advertising or public relations without doing a special event, but you need both advertising and public relations to make your event work. How do you put together the right mix to make your event successful?

First, you must know what you want to accomplish. The desired outcome of event marketing is no different from that of any other marketing effort: You want to draw attention to your product or service, create greater awareness of it and increase sales.

While the number of special event ideas is infinite, some general categories exist. Following are some of the most popular:

- **GRAND OPENINGS:** You're excited about opening your new business. Everyone else will be, too…right? Wrong. You have to create the excitement, and a knockout grand opening celebration is the way to do it. From start to finish, your event has to scream "We're here. We're open. We're ready to go. We're better than, different from and more eager to serve you than our competitors. We want to get to know you and have you do business with us."

A grand opening is one of the best reasons to stage a special event. No one thinks twice about why you're blowing your own horn. What you do want people to think about is what

BEWARE!

BEFORE SPONSORING A CONTEST OR GIVING AWAY A PRIZE, MAKE SURE YOU CON-TACT THE FTC, A LAWYER SPE-CIALIZING IN GAMES AND PROMOTIONS, OR YOUR SECRETARY OF STATE'S OFFICE TO CHECK OUT THE FTC GUIDELINES GOVERNING DIFFERENT TYPES OF PROMOTIONS.

a great time they had at your event.

That means no run-of-the-mill, garden-variety ribbon-cutting. Be original. If you own an electronics store, open your doors via remote control. If you are opening a yarn store, unravel a huge knitted ribbon. If you sell sporting goods, reel in both ends of an enormous bow until the ribbon is untied. Whatever your specialty, do something unusual, entertaining and memorable.

Also give thought to what other activities go along with your grand opening. Design a terrific invitation, do plenty of publicizing, provide quality refreshments and entertainment, select a giveaway that promotes your business (and draws people into the store to get it), and incorporate some way of tracking who attended your event (contest entry forms, coupons, free newsletter subscriptions, birthday club sign-ups and so on).

BRIGHT IDEA

WHENEVER POSSIBLE, TIE YOUR BUSINESS TO A CURRENT EVENT OR TREND. DOES YOUR PRODUCT OR SERVICE SOMEHOW RELATE TO THE OLYMPICS, THE PRESIDENTIAL ELECTION, THE ENVIRONMENT, THE HOT MOVIE OF THE MOMENT? WHETHER YOU'RE PLANNING A SPECIAL EVENT OR JUST SENDING OUT A PRESS RELEASE, YOU CAN GAIN PUBLICITY BY ASSOCIATION.

■ **ENTERTAINMENT AND NOVELTY ATTRACTIONS:** Time, space and popular appeal are three things to consider if and when you host or sponsor a one-time special attraction. If space permits and a beach motif fits your business, having a huge sand castle built in your parking lot might draw attention and business for the entire time it takes to construct it.

Just keep in mind that the novelties and entertainment shouldn't last so long or be so distracting that no one finds the time or inclination to do business with you. Think of these events as the appetizer, with your product or service as the main course.

■ **HOLIDAYS AND SEASONS:** Some of the most common and easily developed special events are based on holidays or times of year. For example, during the Christmas season, Santa's Workshop can be found in thousands of communities, not just the North Pole. Or kick off the summer season with a Beach Boys music marathon.

Again, when planning an event tied to a holiday or season, make originality your motto. If the average December temperature in your city is a balmy 76 degrees, then don't dredge up icicles and fake snow for the store. Take a cue from your locale: Put antlers on pink flamingos and dress Santa in shorts and sunglasses.

■ **CELEBRITY APPEARANCES:** Working with celebrities is like buying a volatile stock—high risk but high return. If you are willing to go out on a limb, you may harvest the sweetest fruit. Many celebrities are affable, cooperative and generous if they are treated professionally and supplied with all the necessary details in advance.

The key to using a celebrity to promote your business is knowing what kind of "personality" is appropriate for your company and marketing goals. Think about whom you want to attract, what kind of media coverage you want to generate, and what kind of lasting impression you want to create.

Whether you are seeking soap stars, sports stars or movie stars, it's usually best to contact their agents first. If you don't know who a star's agent is, contact a talent agency or the organization the celebrity works for.

Unless you know celebrities personally, you must consider the arrangement a commercial venture for them. There are literally hundreds of details to work out and opportunities at every turn for something to go wrong unless you are experienced in dealing with celebrities or you have contacted a reputable talent or public relations agency to help you.

Celebrities don't have to be nationally known names, either. Think about local celebrities in your community who might be willing to be part of your special event. A politician, well-known businessperson or community leader can be an excellent addition to your big day.

■ **CO-SPONSORING:** You can partner with complementary businesses to host an event, or you can take part as a sponsor of an established charity or public cause. Sporting events, fairs and festivals have proved to be popular choices with good track records for achieving marketing goals. Keep in mind, not every event is right for every business. As with any marketing strategy, your event must be suited to your customers' needs.

Think about how your company can benefit any event. If you are a florist, for instance, you could provide flowers for a wide range of charity luncheons or galas. A health-food

BRIGHT IDEA

GET PUBLICITY BY GIVING AN AWARD TO A MEMBER OF YOUR COMMUNITY. AN ENVIRONMENTAL CONSULTANT COULD PRESENT AN AWARD FOR THE MOST ENVIRONMENTALLY SOUND BUSINESS; A HOUSE-PAINTING SERVICE COULD HONOR THE MOST COLORFUL OR PRETTIEST HOUSE IN TOWN.

retailer could provide free energy bars to participants in a local 10K race. Whatever you do, be sure to promote it with press releases, a sign in your window or a mention in the event's program.

- **ANNIVERSARY CELEBRATIONS:** This is one special event most people can relate to. Staying in business for a number of years is something to be proud of, so why not share the achievement with others? Throw a party and invite current, past and prospective customers to enjoy your anniversary, too.

- **GAMES AND CONTESTS:** From naming a mascot to guessing the number of jelly beans in a jar, contests are a proven means of attracting attention. But they pay off big only when they're properly promoted and ethically managed. Be sure your prizes are first-rate and that you get the word out in a timely and professional manner. Let people know how and when they can participate. Think through all the ramifications of judging, selecting and awarding a prize. Check out the need for special permits or licenses well before staging any contest (it never hurts to get a legal opinion just to be on the safe side). Above all, deliver on your promises.

NETWORKING

The ability to network is one of the most crucial skills any start-up entrepreneur can have. How else will you meet the clients and contacts necessary to grow your business?

But many people are put off by the idea of networking, thinking it requires a phony, glad-handing personality that oozes insincerity. Nothing could be farther from the truth.

Think a moment. What does a good networker do? How does he or she act? What is his or her basic attitude? You'll probably be surprised at how much you instinctively know about the subject.

You may decide, for example, that a good networker should be outgoing, sincere, friendly, supportive, a good listener or someone who follows up and stays in touch. To determine other skills an effective networker

BRIGHT IDEA

ALWAYS BE ALERT TO NETWORKING OPPORTUNITIES. DON'T RULE OUT TRAFFIC SCHOOL, LITTLE LEAGUE GAMES, AEROBICS CLASS AND OTHER NONBUSINESS EVENTS AS CHANCES TO SHARE YOUR STORY. LEISURE ACTIVITIES PROVIDE A NATURAL SETTING FOR NETWORKING AND ENCOURAGE RELATIONSHIP-BUILDING.

needs, simply ask yourself "How do I like to be treated? What kinds of people do I trust and consider good friends?"

Now that you have an idea of what attributes a good networker must have, take an objective look at your own interactive abilities. Do you consider yourself shy and regard networking groups as threatening? Do you tend to do all the talking in a conversation? Do you give other people referrals and ideas without a thought to your own personal gain? Can people count on your word?

Image Power

Throughout this book, we've touched on various aspects of developing a corporate image. Your business cards, logo, signage and letterhead all tie into that image. So do your marketing materials and ads. It's equally important to keep your image in mind when planning a publicity campaign.

Any events or causes you participate in should be in keeping with your business image. If your company is in a fun, creative industry, like a toy store, you can get zany and silly with special events like a balloon-popping race or pot-bellied pig races. On the other hand, if you're in a serious industry like medical transcription or accounting, it makes more sense to take part in more serious events like a 10K walk or a blood drive.

The publications and broadcast stations you target with your publicity must fit your image, too. A company that makes clothes targeted at teenage skateboarders would prefer publicity in a cutting-edge lifestyle magazine rather than in a mainstream publication aimed at middle-aged moms. Think about how the publication or broadcast will affect your image, and make sure the results will be positive.

Don't forget the most important parts of your public image: yourself and your employees. Your marketing materials and corporate sponsorships can tout your socially responsible, kindhearted company…but if your employees are rude and uncaring toward customers, all your efforts to promote that image will be in vain.

Make sure your employees understand the image you are trying to convey to customers and how they contribute to creating that image. Show them by example how you want them to behave whenever they're in the public eye.

STARR YOUR OWN BUSINESS

Many people go to networking events, but very few know how to network effectively. Networking is more than just getting out and meeting people. Networking is a structured plan to get to know people who will do business with you or introduce you to those who will.

The best way to succeed at networking is to make a plan, commit to it, learn networking skills and execute your plan. To make the best plan, ask yourself: What do I want to achieve? How many leads (prospects) do I want per month? Where do my customers and prospects go to network? What business organizations would benefit my business? How can I build my image and my business's image? What would I like to volunteer to do in the community?

The Meet Market

To make the most of any networking situation, heed the following do's and don'ts:

- **DON'T SPEND TOO MUCH TIME WITH ONE PERSON, OR YOU DEFEAT THE PURPOSE OF NETWORKING.** Your objective is to take advantage of the entire room. If you spend three minutes with a prospect, that gives you a possibility of 20 contacts per hour. Spending five minutes with each person reduces that to 12 contacts and so on.

- **DO GIVE OTHERS THE CHANCE TO SELL, TOO.** At a networking event, everyone wants to sell. You may have to play buyer to get a chance to be a seller. You must be able to wear both hats.

- **DO KNOW THE KINDS OF PROBLEMS YOU CAN SOLVE RATHER THAN A BUNCH OF BORING FACTS ABOUT YOUR PRODUCT OR SERVICE.** Talk in terms of how you benefit customers rather than the product or service you offer.

- **DON'T BE NEGATIVE.** Never complain about or bad-mouth a person or business. You never know whether the prospect you're talking to has some connection, interest or affiliation with the people, company or product you're slamming.

- **DON'T FORGET YOUR MANNERS.** "Please" and "thank you" go a long way toward creating a good impression.

- **DO BE PREPARED.** When people ask you what you do, be ready to describe your business in one short, interesting sentence that intrigues and enlightens.

Make a five-year networking plan listing your five best customers, five targeted prime prospects and five targeted organizations. Next, set goals for involvement in each organization, determine how much time you will need to commit to each organization and prospect, and decide what kinds of results you expect.

Now that you have a plan, get committed. Tell yourself that you will devote enough time and effort to make it work. Half the battle of networking is getting out there and in the swim.

The other half of the battle is learning to network effectively. Typically, ineffective networkers attend several networking groups but visit with the same friends each time. Obviously, this behavior defeats the entire purpose of networking. If you stick with familiar faces, you never meet anyone new. And since most people stay within their circle of friends, newcomers view the organization as a group of cliques. This is one reason people fear going to new organizations by themselves—they're afraid no one will notice them.

The trick with networking is to become proactive. This means taking control of the situation instead of just reacting to it. Networking requires going beyond your comfort zone and challenging yourself. Try these tips:

- **SET A GOAL TO MEET FIVE OR MORE NEW PEOPLE AT EACH EVENT.** Whenever you attend a group, whether a party, a mixer or an industry luncheon, make a point of heading straight for people you don't know. Greet the newcomers (they will love you for it!). If you don't make this goal a habit, you'll naturally gravitate toward the same old acquaintances.

- **TRY ONE OR TWO NEW GROUPS PER MONTH.** You can attend almost any organization's meetings a few times before you must join. This is anoth-

er way to stretch yourself and make a new set of contacts. Determine what business organizations and activities you would best fit into. It may be the chamber of commerce, the arts council, a museum society, a civic organization, a baseball league, a computer club or the PTA. Attend every function you can that synergizes your goals and customer/prospect interaction.

- **CARRY YOUR BUSINESS CARDS WITH YOU EVERYWHERE.** After all, you never know when you might meet a key contact, and if you don't have your cards with you, you lose out. Take your cards to church, the gym, parties, the grocery store, even on walks with the dog.

- **DON'T MAKE A BEELINE FOR YOUR SEAT.** Frequently, you'll see people at networking groups sitting at the dinner table staring into space—half an hour before the meal is due to start. Why are they sitting alone? Take full advantage of the valuable networking time before you have to sit down. Once the meeting starts, you won't be able to mingle.

- **DON'T SIT BY PEOPLE YOU KNOW.** Mealtime is a prime time for meeting new people. You may be in that seat for several hours, so don't limit your opportunities by sitting with your friends. This is a wonderful chance to get to know new people on either side of you. Sure, it's more comfortable to hobnob with familiar faces. But remember, you are spending precious time and money to attend this event. Get your money's worth; you can talk to your friends some other time.

- **GET ACTIVE.** People remember and do business with leaders. Don't just warm a chair—get involved and join a committee or become a board member. If you don't have time, volunteer to help with hospitality at the door or checking people in. This gives you a reason to talk to others, gets you involved in the inner workings of the group, and provides more visibility.

- **BE FRIENDLY AND APPROACHABLE.** Pretend you are hosting the event. Make people feel welcome. Find out what brought them there, and see if there's any way you can help them. Introduce them to others, make business suggestions or give them a referral. Not only will you probably make a friend, but putting others at ease eliminates self-consciousness. A side benefit: What goes around comes around. If you make the effort to help others, you'll soon find people helping you.

■ **SET A GOAL FOR WHAT YOU EXPECT FROM EACH MEETING.** Your goals can vary from meeting to meeting. Some examples might be: learning from the speaker's topic, discovering industry trends, looking for new prospects or connecting with peers. If you work out of your home, you may find your purpose is simply to get out and talk to people face to face. Focusing your mind on your goal before you even walk into the event keeps you on target.

■ **BE WILLING TO GIVE TO RECEIVE.** Networking is a two-way street. Don't expect new contacts to shower you with referrals and business unless you are equally generous. Follow up on your contacts; keep in touch; always share information or leads that might benefit them. You'll be paid back tenfold for your thoughtfulness.

GLOSSARY

PITCH LETTER: an introductory letter sent to members of the media in an effort to get publicity for a business; sometimes this is a cover letter accompanying a press release

POSITIONING STATEMENT: statement that sums up, in one or two sentences, what differentiates your business from others

PRESS KIT: packet (typically a folder) containing a cover letter, a press release, photos and additional information about a business; sent to members of the media to get publicity for the business

PRESS RELEASE: standard written notice sent to the media in an effort to get publicity for your business

Show & Sell

Effective selling techniques

N o matter what business you're in, if you're an entrepreneur, you're in sales. "But I hate to sell," you groan. You're not alone. Many people are intimidated by selling—either because they're not sure how to proceed or they think they don't have the "right" personality to sell.

Well, guess what? Anyone can sell—anyone, that is, who can learn to connect with the customer, listen to his or her needs and offer the right solutions. In fact, as your business's founder, you're better positioned than anyone else to sell your products and services. Even if you have a team of crack salespeople, there's no one else who has the same passion for, understanding of and enthusiasm about your product as you do. And, once you finish reading this chapter, you'll have plenty of sales skills as well.

UNDERSTANDING YOUR UNIQUE SELLING PROPOSITION

Before you can begin to sell your product or service to anyone else, you have to sell yourself on it. This is especially important when your product or service is similar to those around you. Very few businesses are one-of-a-kind. Just look around you: How many clothing retailers, hardware stores, air conditioning installers or electricians are truly unique?

The key to effective selling in this situation is what advertising and marketing professionals call a "unique selling proposition" (USP). Unless you can pinpoint what makes your business unique in a world of homogeneous competitors, you cannot target your sales efforts successfully.

Pinpointing your USP requires some hard soul-searching and creativity. One way to start is to analyze how other companies use their USPs to their advantage. This requires careful analysis of other companies' ads and marketing messages. If you analyze what they *say* they sell, not just their product or service characteristics, you can learn a great deal about how companies distinguish themselves from competitors.

For example, Charles Revson, founder of Revlon, always used to

BEWARE!

say he sold *hope*, not makeup. Some airlines sell friendly service, while others sell on-time service. Neiman Marcus sells luxury, while Wal-Mart sells bargains.

Each of these is an example of a company that has found a USP "peg" on which to hang its marketing strategy. A business can peg its USP around *product* characteristics, *price* structure, *placement* strategy (location and distribution) or *promotional* strategy. These are what marketers call the "four P's" of marketing. They are manipulated to give a business a market position that sets it apart from the competition.

Sometimes a company focuses on one particular "peg," which also drives the strategy in other areas. A classic example is Hanes L'Eggs hosiery. Back in an era when hosiery was sold primarily in department stores, Hanes opened a new distribution channel for hosiery sales. The idea: Since hosiery was a consumer staple, why not sell it where other staples were sold—in grocery stores?

That placement strategy then drove the company's selection of product packaging (a plastic egg) so the pantyhose did not seem incongruent in the supermarket. And because the product did not have to be pressed and wrapped in tissue and boxes, it could be priced lower than other brands.

Here's how to uncover your USP and use it to power up your sales:

■ **PUT YOURSELF IN YOUR CUSTOMER'S SHOES.** Too often, entrepreneurs fall in love with their product or service and forget that it is the customer's needs, not their own, that they must satisfy. Step back from your daily operations, and carefully scrutinize what your customers really want. Suppose you own a pizza parlor. Sure, customers come into your pizza place for food. But is food all they want? What could make them come back again and again and ignore your competition? The answer might be quality, convenience, reliability, friendliness, cleanliness, courtesy or customer service.

Remember, price is never the only reason people buy. If your competition is beating you on pricing because they are larger, you have to find another sales feature that addresses the customer's

Making Time

Many new business owners fall into a common cycle: They have so much work to do, there is no time for marketing and sales. A few months go by, and work slows down—so you begin marketing heavily, doing everything you can think of until work rolls in again. Then you stop marketing, focus on work…and repeat the whole cycle all over again.

No matter how busy you are, you must always make time for marketing and sales, or you'll find yourself trapped on this economic roller-coaster. Consider this: In the fastest-growing small companies in the United States, the company presidents spend an average of 40 percent of their time each week on advertising and marketing. As the owner of a start-up, you should expect marketing to consume 60 percent of your time or more.

Kim T. Gordon, president of marketing consulting firm National Marketing Federation Inc., says a well-rounded sales and marketing program reaches out to prospects in three stages of readiness: cold, warm and hot. Cold prospects are companies or people you've targeted but that have little or no information about you. Warm prospects are those you've familiarized with your products and services. With a little legwork, they'll eventually turn into hot prospects—a category that also includes current customers and referrals.

To get off the economic roller coaster, focus on all prospects in all three stages. Don't neglect the warm prospects, or they'll soon cool off again. Adopt an overall marketing strategy that combines sales tactics with the marketing strategies discussed throughout Part 6.

---

needs and then build your sales and promotional efforts around that feature.

■ **KNOW WHAT MOTIVATES YOUR CUSTOMERS' BEHAVIOR AND BUYING DECISIONS.** Effective marketing requires you to be an amateur psychologist. You need to know what drives and motivates customers. Go beyond the traditional customer demographics, such as age, gender, race, income and geographic location, that most businesses collect to analyze their sales trends. For our pizza shop example, it is not enough to know that 75 percent of your customers are in the 18-to-25 age range. You need to look at their motives for buying pizza—taste, peer pressure, convenience and so on.

Perhaps one of the best marketing tips I ever heard was from an entrepreneur who sold training products. He told me cosmetics and liquor companies are great examples of businesses that know the value of psychologically oriented promotion. People buy these products based on their desires (for pretty women, luxury, glamour and so on), not on their needs.

■ **UNCOVER THE REAL REASONS CUSTOMERS BUY YOUR PRODUCT INSTEAD OF A COMPETITOR'S.** As your business grows, you'll be able to ask your best source of information: your customers. For example, the pizza entrepreneur could ask them why they like his pizza over others, plus ask them to rate the importance of the features he offers, such as taste, size, ingredients, atmosphere and service. You will be surprised how honest people are when you ask how you can improve your service.

Since your business is just starting out, you won't have a lot of customers to ask yet, so "shop" your competition instead. Many retailers will routinely drop into their competitors' stores to see what and how they are selling. If you are really brave, try cornering a few of the customers after they leave the premises and ask what they like and dislike about the competitors' products and services.

Once you have gone through this three-step market intelligence process, you need to take the next—and hardest—step: clearing your mind of any preconceived ideas about your product or service and being brutally honest. What features of your business jump out at you as something that sets you apart? What can you promote that will make customers want to patronize your business? How can you position your business to highlight your USP?

Do not get discouraged. Successful business ownership is not about having a unique product or service; it's about making your product stand out—even in a market filled with similar items.

COLD-CALLING

The aspect of selling that strikes the greatest fear in people's hearts is usually cold calls. A good way to make cold calls more appealing is to stop thinking of them as "cold" calls. Try thinking of them as "introductory" calls instead. All you are trying to do is introduce yourself and your business to the prospect.

It's important to understand the purpose of introductory calls so you have a realistic attitude about this type of business development activity. Phone prospecting takes longer to pay off than other types of marketing efforts, so go into it knowing you're exploring a new frontier, and it's going to take some time to get results.

Just as with any marketing method, you should never make introductory calls without a predetermined plan. First, always use a targeted list of prospects when making your calls. If your product is household cleaning services, why call a random neighborhood if you have no knowledge of income levels, number of household wage earners, or number of children? If you sell nutritional products to hospitals, why call nurses or doctors if a third-party pharmacy makes all the buying decisions? Get the right list of prospects.

You can obtain information about prospects from the list broker who provides you with the list; if you are working from your house list, you should already have the information. If for some reason you don't, try an introductory call like the following: "We provide mobile pet grooming for dogs and cats. Would that be a service your customers would want to know about, Mr./Ms. Veterinarian?"

Next, determine the best time frames for calling. If you are selling financial services to upper-income CEOs or entrepreneurs, wouldn't it be nice to know when their corporate fiscal years end? Perhaps most of their investment purchases are made two to four weeks prior to that year-end close-out. That's when they know how much extra income needs to be sheltered in a pension plan.

Sometimes timing is your ace in the hole. Granted, follow-up calls throughout the year may make that one important sale possible, but knowing when to instigate the first call is a priceless piece of information.

Third, plan by preparing a "sales script" ahead of time. Write down what you are going to say, what responses the prospect is likely to have and how you will reply to them. No, you're not going to follow this word for word, but if you're nervous about making calls, it helps to have something in front of you. Chances are, after you get beyond the opening sentences, you'll be able to "wing it" just fine.

If preparation for cold-calling is easy but actually making calls is painful for you, here are seven easy steps to get you on the phone fast.

1. **PERSONALIZE EACH CALL BY PREPARING MENTALLY.** Your mind-set needs to be aligned with your language, or the conversation will not ring true. You need to work on developing a warm, but not sugar-coated, telephone voice that has that "Don't I know you?"

Voice-Mail Victories

When making cold calls, always leave voice-mail messages if possible instead of leaving messages with a secretary. No one can transmit your enthusiasm for your products or services the way you can. Here are some tips to make the most of voice mail.

- **STATE YOUR BUSINESS.** Clearly tell prospects who you are and why they should be interested in talking to you. "Hello, my name is Jane Smith, and I'm with the Smith Co. We're the people who conduct one-day Sales Power seminars all over the country. Our seminar is coming to your area, and I'd like to tell you about it."
- **OFFER GOOD NEWS.** After identifying yourself and your business, say, "I have some really good news I'd like to share with you."
- **BE COURTEOUS.** Use the phrase "I'd appreciate the courtesy of a return call at (number)." Be careful of your tone of voice so that you don't sound condescending.
- **FOLLOW UP WITH A FAX.** Send a fax that says "Mr. Wilson, please check your voice mail for an important message." Or leave a voice-mail message saying "I'm faxing you the information; if it is of interest to you, please give me a call."
- **ALWAYS LEAVE YOUR PHONE NUMBER—TWICE.** Repeat your number near the end of the message. Practice writing it down as you talk so you don't go too quickly.

or "Gee, you sound familiar" ring to it.

2. **PERFECT YOUR PHONE STYLE ALONE BEFORE MAKING ANY CALLS.** If you are self-conscious about calling, you need to feel safe to act uninhibited. Try this: Gather a tape recorder, a mirror, a sales journal of incoming and outgoing phone scripts, a pen and a legal-sized pad. Either write or select a favorite phone dialogue, then talk to yourself in the mirror. Do you look relaxed, or are your facial expressions rigid? Our exteriors reflect our inner selves. If you look like you're in knots, your voice will sound strained as well.

Push the "record" button on your tape recorder, and pretend you're talking to a new prospect. Play back the tape, and listen to your conversation. Ask yourself how you could improve your delivery. If your voice seems unnatural and the dialogue contrived, do not despair. As you practice and participate in real phone experiences, you will improve. Mastering the art of cold-calling is no different than improving your golf swing or skiing techniques.

3. **CREATE FAMILIARITY ALL AROUND YOU.** Use family photos, framed testimonial letters, motivational quotes, or whatever gets you in a positive, enthusiastic mood. If you like, play some music that inspires you.

4. **USE YOUR IMAGINATION.** Pretend you are a prospective customer calling a bookstore to see if they have a book in stock. If it helps, record how you sound to get the feel of your inquiring phone voice. It's always easier to imagine you're a customer in need of information than a salesperson trying to force your way into the customer's time. The inquiry call is good practice because the tone of the conversation is "Can you help me?" or "I need some information." Try to convey that same attitude when you use the phone to contact future customers.

5. **WATCH YOUR TONE OF VOICE.** You do not want to sound sheepish and embarrassed, nor do you want to be arrogant. The ideal tone is warm, businesslike, curious and straight to the point. A good option is a cut-to-the-chase statement or a question such as: "I've got a problem. We are offering a two-for-one special during

BEWARE!

NEVER, EVER WASTE A BUYER'S TIME. WHENEVER YOU CALL ON A PROSPECT, WHETHER IN PERSON OR BY PHONE, BE ORGANIZED AND PREPARED WITH FACTS, FIGURES, DEMONSTRATIONS AND ANSWERS.

Team Work

The right sales team—whether they are in-house employees or outside sales representatives—make a big difference in how quickly your company grows. How to make sure you're hiring the right people? Try these tips:

- **DON'T RELY SOLELY ON RESUMES.** Good salespeople sell themselves so well, they don't even need resumes.

- **TRY PLACING A CLASSIFIED AD** that says "Send resume to (address) or call (number)." Don't even look at the resumes; just interview the people who call. These are the people who won't be afraid to pick up the phone and make cold calls.

- **IN THE FIRST PHONE CONTACT,** if the applicant doesn't ask for an appointment, stop right there. If the person doesn't ask for an interview now, he or she won't ask for orders later.

- **DOES THE PERSON SOUND LIKE SOMEONE** you want to spend time with? If you don't want to, neither will your customers.

- **WHEN THEY FIRST CALL,** tell them you're busy and will call them back. Then don't. If they don't call back, they lack the persistence you need in a salesperson.

- **DOES THE APPLICANT LISTEN?** If they're too busy talking, they'll be too busy to listen to your customers.

- **AT THE END OF THE CALL,** say you plan to talk to several candidates and will get back to them. Wait until one says "You don't need to talk to more people. I'm the one you want." That's the kind of person you need.

the next 30 days on all our coffee drinks, just to get people into the store. I need to know if you have ever stopped in while shopping at the mall, and, if not, why not? We have got the greatest ice-blended mochas in town."

6. **MAKE YOUR GOAL A FAST "50 IN 150"—THAT IS, 50 CALLS IN 150 MINUTES.** Three minutes per call is all you need. With so many voice-mail systems intercepting calls today, this should be easy. Never give people the impression you have time to chat. Chatting is not prospecting. You're on a mission. Get to the point, then move to the next prospect.

7. **TAKE FIVE AFTER 15.** After 15 calls, take a five-minute break—stretch,

eat, sip a soda, turn on some tunes, and pat yourself on the back because you're making it happen. Then grab the phone for 15 more calls.

FOLLOWING UP

Your initial cold call typically will not result in a sale, or even in an appointment to make a sales presentation. One study shows it takes an average of seven contacts, impressions or follow-ups to make a sale.

Think of each follow-up contact as a chance to get closer to the prospect and change his or her mind about meeting with you. Plan your follow-up contacts carefully, and be flexible and creative.

How do you start the follow-up call? Here are some lead-in lines:

■ **"I THOUGHT OF A FEW THINGS THAT MIGHT HELP YOU DECIDE..."**
■ **"SOMETHING NEW RECENTLY HAPPENED THAT I THOUGHT YOU MIGHT WANT TO KNOW ABOUT..."**
■ **"THERE HAS BEEN A CHANGE IN THE STATUS OF..."**
■ **"I WAS THINKING ABOUT YOU AND WANTED TO TELL YOU ABOUT..."**

Here are other sales tools you can use in follow-up situations:

■ **A PERSONAL NOTE:** A handwritten note on your company note

Get Organized

No matter how dedicated you are, your follow-up won't get results unless you track your efforts. A good follow-up tracking system includes these components:

● **COMPUTER:** Check out the many contact management and sales follow-up programs available. There's sure to be one that fits your work style. When you've got all the information on computer, your mind is free for more important things...like thinking of new, creative ways to follow up.

● **BUSINESS CARD FILE:** When you meet new prospects, write personal and business information about them on the back of their business cards. Transfer this information to your computer ASAP.

● **DAILY PLANNER:** Use whatever organizer or calendar system you prefer to keep your appointments and notes in when you're on the move.

cards is far more effective than a typed business letter.

■ **AN ENDORSEMENT FROM A MUTUAL FRIEND:** A friend is far more influential than you are.

■ **AN ARTICLE ABOUT YOUR COMPANY:** Something in print can work wonders. You can even send articles about the prospect's company or, better yet, about a personal interest of the prospect's. "Thought you might be interested in…"

■ **AN INVITATION TO VISIT YOUR FACILITY:** Bring the prospect to your home turf.

■ **A MEAL:** Meetings in a nonbusiness environment are powerful and help you build personal relationships that lead to sales.

MAKING SALES PRESENTATIONS

Your cold calls and follow-up efforts have paid off, and you have made an appointment to visit a prospect in person and make a sales presentation. How can you make sure it's a success? Four elements determine whether a sale will be made or not:

1. **RAPPORT:** putting yourself on the same side of the fence as the prospect
2. **NEED:** determining what factors will motivate the prospect to listen with the intent to purchase
3. **IMPORTANCE:** the weight the prospect assigns to a product, feature, benefit, price or time frame
4. **CONFIDENCE:** your ability to project credibility, to remove doubt, and to gain the prospect's belief that the risk of purchase will be less than the reward of ownership

Here is a closer look at the steps you can take to make your sales presentation a success.

Before The Presentation

■ **KNOW YOUR CUSTOMER'S BUSINESS.** Potential clients expect you to know their business, customers and competition as well as you know your own product or service. Study your customer's industry. Know its problems and trends. Find out who the company's biggest competitors are. Some research tools include the company's annual report, brochures, catalogs, and newsletters; trade publications; chamber of commerce directories; and the Internet.

■ **WRITE OUT YOUR SALES PRESENTATION.** Making a sales presentation isn't something you do on the fly. Always use a written presentation. The basic structure of any sales presentation includes five key points: Build rapport with your prospect, introduce the business topic, ask questions to better understand your prospect's needs, summarize your key selling points,

> **BRIGHT IDEA**
> CONDITION PROSPECTS TO SAY YES BY ASKING QUESTIONS THEY WILL AGREE WITH. "IT'S A GREAT DAY, ISN'T IT?" OR "YOU GOT AN EARLY START TODAY, DIDN'T YOU?" LITTLE QUESTIONS LIKE THESE HELP START CUSTOMERS ON A MOMENTUM THAT BUILDS TRUST. SUBCONSCIOUSLY, BECAUSE THEY ARE AGREEING WITH YOU, THEY BEGIN TO TRUST YOU.

and close the sale. Think about the three major selling points of your product or service. Develop leading questions to probe your customer's reactions and needs.

■ **MAKE SURE YOU ARE TALKING TO THE RIGHT PERSON.** This seems elementary, but many salespeople neglect to do it. Then, at the last minute, the buyer wriggles off the hook by saying he or she needs a boss's, spouse's or partner's approval. When you are setting the appointment, always ask "Are you the one I should be talking to, or are there others who will be making the buying decision?"

In The Customer's Office

■ **BUILD RAPPORT.** Before you start discussing business, build rapport with your prospect. To accomplish this, do some homework. Find out if you have a colleague in common. Has the prospect's company been in the news lately? Is he or she interested in sports? Get a little insight into the company and the individual so you can make the rapport genuine.

■ **ASK QUESTIONS.** Don't jump into a canned sales spiel. The most effective way to sell is to ask the prospect questions and see where he or she leads you. (Of course, your questions are carefully structured to elicit the prospect's needs—ones which your product just happens to be able to fill.)

Ask questions that require more than a yes or no response, and that deal with more than just costs, price, procedures and the technical aspects of the prospect's business. Most important, ask questions that will reveal the prospect's motivation to purchase, his or her problems and needs, and the prospect's decision-making processes. Don't be afraid to ask a client why he or she feels a certain way. That's how you'll get to understand your customers.

■ **TAKE NOTES.** Don't rely on your memory to remind you of what's important to your prospect. Ask up front if it's all right for you to take notes during your sales presentation. (Prospects will be flattered.)

Presentation Perfect

Want to improve your sales presentation skills? Use these strategies to hone your speaking abilities:

● **TAG-TEAM-SELL FOR EVALUATION PURPOSES.** Have a colleague go on sales calls with you once a week to listen to your presentation. Create a review form for them to fill out immediately after your performance. (Include your strengths as well as your weaknesses.) Read it right away, and talk about what you can do to improve.

● **RECORD YOUR TELEPHONE SALES CONVERSATIONS.** Use them as a self-monitor of your ability to present a clear and confident message. Play them back. If you can't stand your voice, change your pitch.

● **READ A CHAPTER FROM A SALES BOOK ALOUD, RECORDING IT ON AUDIOTAPE.** Play it in your car. You'll learn about sales and about how you present your pitch. Would you buy from yourself? If not, record another version with style and emotion.

● **VIDEOTAPE THE FIRST FIVE MINUTES OF YOUR SALES PRESENTATION.** Ask a friend or colleague to be the prospect. Watch the video together, and rate your performance. Repeat the process once a week for two months. Work to eliminate your two worst habits; at the same time, work to enhance your two best strengths.

Above all, be yourself. Don't put on an act. Your personality will shine if you believe in what you are saying. Being genuine will win the prospect's confidence...and the sale.

Write down key points you can refer to later during your presentation.

Be sure to write down objections. This shows your prospect you are truly listening to what he or she is saying. In this way, you can specifically answer objections by showing how the customer will benefit from your product or service. It could be, for instance, by saving money, raising productivity, increasing employee motivation, or increasing his or her company's name recognition.

■ **LEARN TO LISTEN.** Salespeople who do all the talking during a presentation not only bore the prospect, but also generally lose the sale. A good rule of thumb is to listen 70 percent of the time and talk 30 percent of the time. Don't interrupt. It's tempting to step in and tell the prospect something you think is vitally important. Before you speak, ask yourself if what you're about to say is really necessary.

When you do speak, focus on asking questions. Pretend you are Barbara Walters interviewing a movie star: Ask questions, then shut up. You can improve your listening skills by taking notes, observing your prospect's body language, not jumping to conclusions and concentrating on what your prospect is saying.

■ **ANSWER OBJECTIONS WITH "FEEL," "FELT" AND "FOUND."** Don't argue when a prospect says "I'm not interested," "I just bought one," or "I don't have time right now." Simply say "I understand how you feel. A lot of my present customers felt the same way. But when they found out how much time they saved by using our product, they were amazed." Then ask for an appointment. Prospects like to hear about other people who have been in a similar situation.

■ **PROBE DEEPER.** If a prospect tells you "We're looking for cost-savings and efficiency," will you immediately tell him how your product meets his need for cost-savings and efficiency? A really smart salesperson won't—he or she will ask more questions and probe deeper: "I understand why that is important. Can you give me a specific example?" Asking for more information—and listening to the answers—enables you to better position your product and show you understand the client's needs.

BRIGHT IDEA

OFFER A FIRST-TIME INCENTIVE TO HELP CLINCH THE SALE. IF PROSPECTS LIKE YOUR PRODUCT OR SERVICE, THEY'LL BE INCLINED TO MAKE A DECISION NOW RATHER THAN WAIT A FEW DAYS OR PUT OFF THE DECISION INDEFINITELY. FIRST-TIME INCENTIVES MIGHT INCLUDE: "10 PERCENT OFF WITH YOUR PURCHASE TODAY" OR "WITH TODAY'S PURCHASE, YOU'LL RECEIVE ONE FREE HOUR OF CONSULTATION."

- **FIND THE "HOT BUTTON."** A customer may have a long list of needs, but there is usually one "hot button" that will get the person to buy. The key to the hot button is that it is an emotional, not practical, need—a need for recognition, love or reinforcement. Suppose you are selling health-club memberships. For a prospect who is planning a trip to Hawaii in two months, the hot button is likely to be losing a few pounds and looking good in a bikini. For a prospect who just found out he has high blood pressure, the hot button could be the health benefits of exercise. For a busy young mother, the hot button may be the chance to get away from the kids for a few hours a week and reduce stress.

- **ELIMINATE OBJECTIONS.** When a prospect raises an objection, don't immediately jump in with a response. Instead, show empathy by saying "Let's explore your concerns." Ask for more details about the objection. You need to isolate the true objection so you can handle it. Here are some ways to do that:

  1. OFFER A CHOICE. "Is it the delivery time or the financing you are concerned about?"

  2. GET TO THE HEART OF THE MATTER. "When you say you want to

---

The Price Isn't Right

How do you overcome that most common objection, "Your price is too high"? Lawrence L. Steinmetz, author of *How to Sell at Prices Higher Than Your Competitors*, says you need to learn how to acknowledge that your price is higher than competitors'—then use that as a selling tool.

Showing that customers get more services, better warranties or higher-quality products for the extra cost makes the higher price seem less imposing. Telling them why the competition's services or products don't measure up differentiates you from the competition and convinces customers you're worth the extra money.

Whatever you do, don't be too willing to negotiate or slash prices. "When you ask a customer 'Is that too much?' you are encouraging him or her to beat you up," says Steinmetz.

With the right ammunition, you can turn price problems into selling points.

think about it, what specifically did you want to think about?"

3. WORK TOWARD A SOLUTION. Every sale should be a win-win deal, so you may need to compromise to close the deal: "I'll waive the delivery charge if you agree to the purchase."

As you get more experience making sales calls, you'll become familiar with different objections. Maintain a list of common objections and ways you have successfully dealt with them.

■ **CLOSE THE SALE.** There is no magic to closing the sale. If you have followed all the previous steps, all you should have to do is ask for the customer's order. However, some salespeople make the mistake of simply not asking for the final decision. It's as if they forget what their goal is!

For some, "closing" sounds too negative. If you're one of them, try changing your thinking to something more positive, such as "deciding." As you talk with the customer, build in the close by having fun with it. Say something like "So how many do you want? We have it in a rainbow of colors; do you want them all?" Make sure to ask them several times in a fun, nonthreatening way; you're leading them to make the decision.

SMART TIP

SELL BENEFITS, NOT FEATURES. THE BIGGEST MISTAKE ENTREPRENEURS MAKE IS IN FOCUSING ON WHAT THEIR PRODUCT OR SERVICE IS (ITS FEATURES). RATHER, IT'S WHAT IT DOES (ITS BENEFITS) THAT'S IMPORTANT. A HEALTH-FOOD PRODUCT CONTAINS NUTRIENTS THAT ARE GOOD FOR THE BODY. THAT'S WHAT IT IS. WHAT THE PRODUCT DOES IS MAKE THE CUSTOMER THINNER, MORE ENERGETIC, AND ABLE TO ACCOMPLISH MORE WITH LESS SLEEP. ALWAYS CONCENTRATE ON HOW YOUR PRODUCT WILL BENEFIT YOUR CUSTOMER.

SMART TIP

TRYING TO SCARE UP BUSINESS? IF YOUR PRODUCT IS NECESSARY BUT NOT VERY APPEALING OR EXCITING, ONE WAY TO MOTIVATE CUSTOMERS IS BY DESCRIBING THE CONSEQUENCES OF NOT USING YOUR PRODUCT. FOR PRODUCTS THAT INCREASE SECURITY, SAFETY OR HEALTH, FEAR CAN BE AN EFFECTIVE BUSINESS-BOOSTING TOOL.

After The Sale

■ **FOLLOW UP.** What you do after the sale is as crucial as what you do to get it. "Nearly 85 percent of all sales are produced by word-of-mouth referrals," says sales guru Brian Tracy. "In other words, they're the result of someone telling a friend or associate to buy a product or service because the customer was satisfied." Concentrate on developing future and referral business with each satisfied customer. Write thank-you notes, call the customer after the sale to make sure he or she is satisfied, and maintain a schedule of future communications. Be in front of that client, and always show attention and responsiveness. (For more on retaining customers, see Part 6, Chapter 34.)

■ **ASK FOR FEEDBACK.** Ask customers what you need to do to maintain and increase their business. Many customers have minor complaints but will never say anything. They just won't buy from you again. If you ask their opinions, on the other hand, they'll be glad to tell you—and, in most cases, will give you a chance to solve the problem.

Pass It On

Referrals are among a salesperson's best weapons. Yet many salespeople fail to take advantage of this powerful marketing tool. Here are secrets to getting and making the most of referrals:

● **ASK FOR SPECIFIC REFERRALS.** Many salespeople ask for referrals by saying "Do you know anyone else who might be interested in my product?" The prospect replies "Not off the top of my head, but I'll let you know if I think of anyone." And that's where it ends.

● **MORE EFFECTIVE IS TO ASK** for a specific referral that deals with a need your business addresses. For instance, ask "Steve, at your last Rotary Club meeting, did you talk to anyone who was thinking about moving or selling a home?"

● **GATHER AS MUCH INFORMATION** about the referral as possible. Use this to prepare for the cold call.

● **ASK YOUR CUSTOMER FOR PERMISSION** to use his or her name when contacting the referral.

● **ASK YOUR CUSTOMER TO HELP YOU** get an appointment with the referral.

● **CONTACT THE REFERRAL** as soon as possible.

● **INFORM YOUR CUSTOMER** about the outcome of the referral. People like to know when they have been of help.

● **PROSPECT FOR REFERRALS** just as you would for sales leads.

Speaking Effectively

The difference between good and great salespeople is the way they deliver their messages. You can have the greatest sales pitch in the world, but if you deliver it with no enthusiasm, sincerity or belief, you will lose the sale.

Here are some suggestions to improve your speaking skills and power up your presentations:

- **SPEAK CLEARLY.** If the prospect doesn't understand you, you won't get the sale.
- **LEAN FORWARD.** Leaning into the presentation gives the prospect a sense of urgency.
- **DON'T FIDGET.** Knuckle-cracking, hair-twirling and similar nervous habits detract from your presentation.
- **DON'T "UM," "AH" OR "ER."** These vocal tics are so irritating, they make the prospect focus on the flaws rather than the message. Best cure? Practice, practice, practice.
- **BE ANIMATED.** Act as if the best thing in the world just happened to you.
- **VARY YOUR VOICE.** Don't drone on in a monotone. Punch the critical words. Go from high to low tones. Whisper some of the key information as if it's a secret. Get the prospect to lean into your words. Make him or her feel special for receiving this message.
- **LOOK PROSPECTS IN THE EYE.** Eye contact signals credibility and trustworthiness.
- **FOLLOW THE PROSPECT'S LEAD.** Keep your tone similar to his or her tone. If the prospect is stuffy and conservative, do not get too wild.
- **RELAX.** High anxiety makes prospects nervous. Why do salespeople get nervous? Either they are unprepared or they need the money from the sale. Calm down. Never let them see you sweat.

SMART TIP

WHAT'S THE BEST WAY TO GET THROUGH TO A PROSPECT? SEND A LETTER, THEN FOLLOW IT UP WITH A PHONE CALL. NEXT BEST IS A REFERRAL. THEN COMES A COLD CALL, THEN A PERSONAL VISIT. LEAST EFFECTIVE IS A SINGLE DIRECT-MAIL PIECE.

BRIGHT IDEA

WANT TO BOOST SALES? OFFER A 100 PERCENT GUARANTEE. THIS MINIMIZES CUSTOMER OBJECTIONS AND SHOWS YOU BELIEVE IN YOUR PRODUCT OR SERVICE. PRODUCT GUARANTEES SHOULD BE UNCONDITIONAL, WITH NO HIDDEN CLAUSES LIKE "GUARANTEED FOR 30 DAYS." USE GUARANTEES FOR SERVICES, TOO: "SATISFACTION GUARANTEED. YOU'LL BE THRILLED WITH OUR SERVICE, OR WE'LL REDO IT AT OUR EXPENSE."

Keep 'Em Coming Back

Offering superior customer service

To the ordinary entrepreneur, closing and finalizing the sale is the completion of serving the customer's needs. But for the pro, this is only the beginning. Closing the sale sets the stage for a relationship which, if properly managed by you, the entrepreneur, can be mutually profitable for years to come.

Remember the "80-20 rule" discussed in an earlier chapter? The rule states that 80 percent of your business comes from 20 percent of your customers. Repeat customers are the backbone of every successful business. So now that you know how to land customers, it is time to learn how to keep them.

BUILDING CUSTOMER RELATIONSHIPS

It's tempting to concentrate on making new sales or pursuing bigger accounts. But attention to your existing customers, no matter how small they are, is equally essential to keeping your business thriving. The secret to repeat business is following up in a way that has a positive effect on the customer.

Effective follow-up begins immediately after the sale, when you call the customer to say "thank you" and find out if he or she is pleased with your product or service. Beyond this, there are several effective ways to follow up that ensure your business is always in the customer's mind.

■ **LET CUSTOMERS KNOW WHAT YOU ARE DOING FOR THEM.** This can be in the form of a newsletter mailed to existing customers (see Part 6, Chapter 31), or it can be more informal, such as a phone call. Whichever method you use, the key is to dramatically point out to customers what excellent service you are giving them. If you never mention all the things you're doing for them, customers may not notice. You are not being cocky when you talk to customers about all the work you have done to please them. Just make a phone call and let them know they don't have to worry because you handled the paperwork, called the attorney or double-checked on the shipment—one less thing they have to do.

■ **WRITE OLD CUSTOMERS PERSONAL, HAND-WRITTEN NOTES FREQUENTLY.**

"I was just sitting at my desk, and your name popped into my head. Are you still having a great time flying all over the country? Let me know if you need another set of luggage. I can stop by with our latest models anytime." Or, if you run into an old customer at an event, follow up with a note: "It was great seeing you at the CDC Christmas party. I will call you early in the new year to schedule a lunch."

■ **KEEP IT PERSONAL.** Voice mail and e-mail make it easy to communicate, but the personal touch is lost. Don't count these as a legitimate follow-up. If you're having trouble getting through, leave a voice-mail message that you want to talk to the person directly or will stop by his or her office at a designated time.

■ **REMEMBER SPECIAL OCCASIONS.** Send the regular customers birthday cards, anniversary cards, holiday cards…you name it. Gifts are excellent follow-up tools, too. You don't have to spend a fortune to show you care; use your creativity to come up with interesting gift ideas that tie into your business, the customer's business or his or her recent purchase.

■ **PASS ON INFORMATION.** If you read an article, see a new book, or hear about an organization that a customer might be interested in, drop a note or make a quick call to let them know.

■ **CONSIDER FOLLOW-UP CALLS AS BUSINESS DEVELOPMENT CALLS.** When you talk to or visit old clients or customers, you'll often find they have referrals to give you, which can lead to new business.

With all that your existing customers can do for you, there's simply no reason not to stay in regular contact with them. Use your imagination, and you'll think of plenty of other ideas that can help you develop a lasting relationship.

CUSTOMER SERVICE

There are plenty of things you, the entrepreneur, can do to ensure good customer service. And when you're a one-person business, it's easy to stay on top of what your customers want. But as you add employees, whether it's one person or 100, you are adding more links to the customer service chain—and creating more potential for poor service along the way.

That's why creating a customer service policy and adhering to it is so important. Here are some steps you can take to ensure that your clients receive excellent service, every step of the way.

HOT LINK

FEELING ALONE? WISH YOU HAD SOME PLACE TO ADVISE YOU ON BETTER CUSTOMER SERVICE? TRY THE INTERNATIONAL CUSTOMER SERVICE ASSOCIATION'S WEB SITE (WWW.ICSA.ORG). YOU'RE REQUIRED TO JOIN THE ORGANIZATION TO REALLY REAP THE BENEFITS, BUT THERE ARE PLENTY OF THEM, FROM NETWORKING OPPORTUNITIES TO CUSTOMER SERVICE TRAINING PROGRAMS.

- **PUT YOUR CUSTOMER SERVICE POLICY IN WRITING.** These principles should come from you, but every employee should know what the rules are and be ready to live up to them.
- **ESTABLISH SUPPORT SYSTEMS THAT GIVE THE EMPLOYEES CLEAR INSTRUCTIONS FOR GAINING AND MAINTAINING SERVICE SUPERIORITY.** These systems will help you out-service any competitor by giving more to customers and anticipating problems before they arise.
- **DEVELOP A MEASUREMENT OF SUPERB CUSTOMER SERVICE.** Then reward employees who practice it consistently.
- **BE CERTAIN THAT YOUR PASSION FOR CUSTOMER SERVICE RUNS RAMPANT THROUGHOUT YOUR COMPANY.** Your employees should see how good service relates to your profits and to their future with the company.
- **BE GENUINELY COMMITTED TO PROVIDING MORE CUSTOMER SERVICE EXCELLENCE THAN ANYONE ELSE IN YOUR INDUSTRY.** This commitment must be so powerful that every one of your customers can sense it.
- **SHARE INFORMATION WITH PEOPLE ON THE FRONT LINES.** Meet regularly to talk about improving service. Solicit ideas from employees—they are the ones who are dealing with the customers most often.
- **ACT ON THE KNOWLEDGE THAT CUSTOMERS VALUE ATTENTION, COMPETENCE, PROMPTNESS AND DEPENDABILITY.** They love being treated as individuals and being referred to by name. (Don't you?)

Interacting With Customers

Principles of customer service are all very well, but you need to put those principles into action with everything you do and say.

There are certain "magic words" that customers want to hear from you and your staff. Make sure all your employees understand the importance of these key words:

■ **"HOW CAN I HELP?"** Customers want the opportunity to explain in detail what they want and need. Too often, business owners feel the desire or the obligation to guess what customers need rather than carefully listening first. By asking how you can help, you begin the dialogue on a positive note (you are "helping," not "selling"). And by using an open-ended question, you invite discussion.

■ **"I CAN SOLVE THAT PROBLEM."** Most customers, especially B2B customers, are looking to buy solutions. They appreciate direct answers in a language they can understand.

Go To The Source

Excellent customer service is more than what you say or do for the customer; it also means giving customers a chance to make their feelings known. Here are some suggestions for finding out what your customers want, need and care about:

● **ATTEND TRADE SHOWS AND INDUSTRY EVENTS THAT ARE IMPORTANT TO YOUR CUSTOMERS.** You'll find out what the competition is doing and what kinds of products and services customers are looking for.

● **NURTURE A HUMAN BOND, AS WELL AS A BUSINESS ONE, WITH CUSTOMERS AND PROSPECTS.** Take them out to lunch, dinner, the ballgame or the opera. In the relaxed atmosphere of socializing, you'll learn the secrets that will allow you to go above and beyond your competition.

● **KEEP ALERT FOR TRENDS; THEN RESPOND TO THEM.** Read industry trade publications; be active in trade organizations; pay attention to what your customers are doing.

● **ASK FOR FEEDBACK.** Survey your customers regularly to find out how you're doing. Send postage-paid questionnaire cards or letters; call them by phone; set up focus groups. Ask for suggestions, then fix the trouble areas revealed.

Whatever you do, don't rest on your laurels. Regularly evaluate your product or service to be sure it is still priced, packaged and delivered right.

■ **"I DON'T KNOW, BUT I'LL FIND OUT."** When confronted with a truly difficult question that requires research on your part, admit it. Few things ruin your credibility faster than trying to answer a question when you are unsure of all the facts. Savvy buyers may test you with a question they know you can't answer, and then just sit quietly while you struggle to fake an answer. An honest reply enhances your integrity.

■ **"I WILL TAKE RESPONSIBILITY."** Tell your customer you realize it's

Complaint Department

Studies show that the vast majority of unsatisfied customers will never tell you they're unsatisfied. They simply leave quietly, then tell everyone they know not to do business with you. So when a customer does complain, don't think of it as a nuisance—think of it as a golden opportunity to change that customer's mind and retain his or her business.

Even the best product or service meets with complaints or problems now and then. Here's how to handle them for positive results:

● **LET CUSTOMERS VENT THEIR FEELINGS.** Encourage them to get their frustrations out in the open.

● **NEVER ARGUE** with a customer.

● **NEVER TELL A CUSTOMER** "You do not have a problem." Those are fighting words.

● **SHARE YOUR POINT OF VIEW** as politely as you can.

● **TAKE RESPONSIBILITY FOR THE PROBLEM.** Don't make excuses. If an employee was sick or a third-party supplier let you down, that's not the customer's concern.

● **IMMEDIATELY TAKE ACTION** to remedy the situation. Promising a solution, then delaying it only makes matters worse.

● **EMPOWER YOUR FRONT-LINE EMPLOYEES** to be flexible in resolving complaints. Give employees some leeway in deciding when to bend the rules. If you don't feel comfortable doing this, make sure they have you or another manager handle the situation.

● **IMAGINE YOU'RE THE ONE WITH THE COMPLAINT.** How would you want the situation to be handled?

your responsibility to ensure a satisfactory outcome to the transaction. Assure the customer you know what she expects and will deliver the product or service at the agreed-upon price. There will be no unexpected expenses or changes required to solve the problem.

■ **"I WILL KEEP YOU UPDATED."** Even if your business is a cash-and-carry operation, it probably requires coordinating and scheduling numerous events. Assure your customers they will be advised of the status of these events. The longer your lead time, the more important this is. The vendors customers trust the most are those who keep them apprised of the situation, whether the news is good or bad.

■ **"I WILL DELIVER ON TIME."** A due date that has been agreed upon is a promise that must be kept. "Close" does not count.

■ **"MONDAY MEANS MONDAY."** The first week in July means the first week in July, even though it contains a national holiday. Your clients are waiting to hear you say "I deliver on time." The supplier who consistently does so is a rarity and well-remembered.

■ **"IT WILL BE JUST WHAT YOU ORDERED."** It will not be "similar to," and it will not be "better than" what was ordered. It will be exactly what was ordered. Even if you believe a substitute would be in the client's best interests, that's a topic for discussion, not something you decide on your own. Your customer may not know (or be at liberty to explain) all the ramifications of the purchase.

■ **"THE JOB WILL BE COMPLETE."** Assure the customer there will be no waiting for a final piece or a last document. Never say you will be finished "except for…"

■ **"I APPRECIATE YOUR BUSINESS."** This means more than a simple "Thanks for the order." Genuine appreciation involves follow-up calls, offering to answer questions, making sure everything is performing satisfactorily, and ascertaining that the original problem has been solved.

Neglecting any of these steps conveys the impression that you were interested in the person only until the sale was made. This leaves the buyer feeling deceived and used, and creates ill will and negative advertising for your company. Sincerely proving you care about your customers leads to recommendations…and repeat sales.

Going Above And Beyond

These days, simply providing adequate customer service is not enough. You need to go above and beyond the call of duty to provide customer service that truly stands out. How to do this?

Begin by thinking about your own experiences as a customer—what you have liked and disliked in certain situations. Recall the times you were delighted by extra efforts taken to accommodate your needs or outraged by rudeness or negligence. This will give you greater insight into what makes for extraordinary customer service.

To put yourself in the customer's shoes, try visiting a wide range of businesses your customers are likely to frequent. This could include your direct competitors, as well as companies that sell related products and services. Observe how customers are treated, in addition to the kinds of services that seem to be important to them. Then adapt your business accordingly.

Going above and beyond is especially important when a customer has complained or if there is a problem with a purchase. Suppose an order is delayed. What can you do?

- **CALL THE CUSTOMER PERSONALLY** with updates on the status of the order and expected arrival time.
- **HAND-DELIVER THE MERCHANDISE** when it arrives.
- **TAKE 20 OR 30 PERCENT** off the cost.
- **SEND A NOTE APOLOGIZING** for the delay…tucked inside a gift basket full of goodies. These are all ways of showing the customer you're on his side.

Going above and beyond doesn't always mean offering deep discounts or giving away products. With a little ingenuity and effort, you can show customers they are important at any time. Suppose you've just received the newest samples and colors for your home furnishings line. Why not invite your best customers to a private showing, complete

CREATE EXTERNAL INCENTIVES TO
KEEP CUSTOMERS COMING BACK.

OFFER CUSTOMERS
FREE MERCHANDISE
OR SERVICES AFTER
THEY BUY A CERTAIN
AMOUNT. THIS GETS
THEM IN THE HABIT OF BUYING
AGAIN AND AGAIN.

with music, appetizers and a coupon good for one free hour of consultation?

Emergency orders and last-minute changes should be accommodated when possible, especially for important occasions such as a wedding or a big trade show. Customers remember these events…and they will remember your flexibility and prompt response to their needs, too.

Being accessible also wins loyalty. One entrepreneur who runs a computer chip company has installed a customer service line on every employee's telephone, from the mail room clerk on up. This means every caller gets through to a real person who can help him or her, instead of getting lost in a voice-mail maze.

Customer loyalty is hard to win and easy to lose. But by going above and beyond with your customer service, you'll soon see your sales going above and beyond those of your competitors.

PART

7

Net Works

Net
Rewards

Using the Net for success

Even if your business is not Internet-related, make sure to check out the Internet. You'd be surprised: The Internet has myriad ways to assist you as you begin your journey, from helping you do market research and competitive intelligence inexpensively and easily, to finding available financing and legal forms, and even the right employees.

And remember: Once your business is up and running and you are achieving some success, the Internet can also help you run your business more efficiently. For example, by allowing you to do your banking online, make travel arrangements online and ship products online, you can save time and money.

MARKET RESEARCH

Market research is an important tool to use when starting a business. Simply put, it's a process used to define the size, location, and/or makeup of the market for a product or service. Market research can help you find out in-depth information about your particular industry or business environment, expansion possibilities for your company in the United States and abroad, and customer spending habits for cross-selling and up-selling opportunities.

The Internet has become an important tool for gathering marketing information. The best place to start for basic demographic information is the U.S. Census Bureau's Web site (www.cenus.gov). Besides free demographic data such as population estimates by country, median household income by state, and home ownership data, its Web site details the type of information you can glean from the Census, and links to other federal government statistical resources. One of the best features is the American Factfinder Web site at (http://factfinder.census.gov/servlet/BasicFactsServlet), which provides excellent access to census information, including a "Search Your Street" feature that displays a map.

The Statistical Abstract of the United States (www.census.gov/statab/www) has statistical information from government and private sources complied by the Census Bureau. It can be downloaded for free at the Web site. Another good resource is the Census Bureau's International Database (www.census.gov/ipc/www.idbnew.html), which furnishes data on foreign countries.

Also, don't miss KnowThis.com's (www.knowthis.com) marketing virtual library. There is a section on the site called "Market Research" that contains links to a wide variety of market research Web resources. Another good site is BizMiner.com (www.bizminer.com), which lets you choose from more than 900,000 industry reports, 30,000 financial analysis profiles, and 3,000 area-vitality profiles, all online.

Also check out MarketResearch.com (www.marketresearch.com), which has more than 50,000 research reports from hundreds of sources consolidated into one accessible collection that's updated daily. No subscription fee is required, and you pay for only the report sections you need with its "Buy by the Slice" feature. You can also save on shipping charges by opting for "Instant Online Delivery."

You may want to conduct your own online or offline market research, and the Web can help here as well. Information about both techniques can be found at the Web sites for the American Marketing Association at www.marketingpower.com and the Marketing Research Association at www.mra-net.org.

For more market research help, see Part 1, Chapter 7.

COMPETITIVE INTELLIGENCE

Competitive intelligence is essentially understanding and learning what is happening in the world outside your business so you can be as competitive as possible. It means learning as much as possible—as soon as possible—about your industry in general, your competitors, or even your county's particular zoning rules. In short, it empowers organizations to anticipate and face challenges head on.

"The key to competitive intelligence is early warning," says Bonnie Hohhof, editor of the Society of Competitive Intelligence Professionals' *Competitive Intelligence* magazine. "Getting a hint that something is coming down the pike that will affect your ability to be competitive. While getting this information doesn't mean you can change what's going on, at least

SMART TIP

NEED IN-DEPTH INFORMATION ON A PARTICULAR INDUSTRY? CHECK OUT TRADE ASSOCIATION WEB SITES OR THE WEB SITES OF MAJOR CONSULTING FIRMS. THEY OFTEN HAVE FREE WHITE PAPERS OR STUDIES THAT CAN GIVE A LOT OF INSIGHT—WITHOUT HAVING TO PAY HIGH CONSULTING FEES.

you can figure out a way of dealing with it before it causes significant heartburn."

Hohhof says the Web is a great place to do competitive intelligence. "The Web is a time-saving device when it comes to competitive intelligence," she says. "Without the Web, you would have to access [this information] over the phone or in person. With the Web, you can get information anytime, and it's often as up-to-date as possible."

One of best sites for competitive intelligence is Hoover's Online (www.hoovers.com), which, for a fee, provides in-depth profiles of more than 18,000 public and private companies. However, there is also free content available. You can research competitors, track stock market performance, and keep tabs on IPOs.

Don't Do That!

Here are some online competitive intelligence don'ts from Bonnie Hohhof, editor of the Society of Competitive Intelligence Professionals' *Competitive Intelligence* magazine:

- **DON'T GET LOST IN CYBERSPACE.** The Internet is vast, and if you're not careful, you could spend so much time researching or hunting down little pieces of information that you get lost— or worse, no results. If you can't find what you are looking for, consider calling someone else to track down the answers.

- **DON'T JUST RELY ON GOOGLE.** When searching for information online, keep in mind that there is life beyond Google. The Web sites of university libraries, for example, offer tutorials about the best way to search the Web, and these can be helpful if you're looking for something very specific, like a tutorial or a white paper.

- **DON'T BELIEVE EVERYTHING YOU READ.** There are a lot of Web sites that may offer erroneous or invalid information. Before using research or information on a Web site at face value, make sure it has a date, is attributed to someone, and has contact and background information on that person. Anytime any of these pieces are missing, it's a red flag. Also, when looking at competitive sites, remember that a lot of the information on the site is marketing-related, which is not always 100 percent true, so keep this in mind as well.

Other good sites include:

- **D&B's WEB SITE** (www.dnb.com) provides information on companies relevant to your business through a searchable database of companies in the United States and around the world for a fee.
- **DIALOG'S WEB SITE** (www.dialog.com) has a pay-as-you go option, called DialogSelect, which allows you to search through 50,000 objective and respected publications and documents online and pay for each article or report on a case-by-case basis.
- **FULD & CO.'S INTERNET INTELLIGENCE INDEX** (www.fuld.com/Tindex/I3.html) allows users to gather information from a wide variety of public services for free. It contains links to more than 600 intelligence-related Internet sites, covering everything from macroeconomic data to individual patent and stock quote information.
- **KNOWX.COM** (www.knowx.com) reports on bankruptcies, liens, judgments and such against individuals and businesses. Some reports are free; others require a fee.
- **REUTER'S MULTEX INVESTOR SITE** (www.multexinvestor.com) offers access to research reports produced by financial research firms. Some reports are free, but most others require a fee.
- **THOMAS REGISTER'S WEB SITE** (www.thomasregister.com) provides listings of thousands of companies in a variety of industries for free.
- **YAHOO! FINANCE** (http://finance.yahoo.com) has everything from up-to-the minute market summaries to stock research to financial news, and much of it is free.

Usenet groups for a particular industry can also be a great source of information. To find these groups, check out http://groups.google.com.

Also, don't forget to regularly check the national newswires and the press release newswires—PRNewswire.com and Businesswire.com. Also, regularly check the Web sites of your local chamber of commerce, Better Business Bureau and newspapers, as well as federal and state government's Web sites and the Web sites of your trade association, and trade magazines and newspapers.

Finally, make sure to consistently check the Web sites of your major competitors, suppliers and clients.

FINDING FINANCING

The Internet can also be a good place to find financing to help launch your business. A great place to start is the Small Business

Administration (SBA) and its financing page at www.sba.gov/financing, which offers a full library to introduce you to the world of financing, especially the SBA's own loan products.

Many states also offer financing information and applications online through their economic development department Web sites. A quick search on a site like Google will direct you to these types of sites, or see Appendix B for a state-by-state listing.

Also be sure to check out BusinessFinance.com (www.business finance.com), where for free you can search for business funding by category. If you have a complete business plan and you're ready to show it to VC firms and private angel investors, Vfinance.com (www.vfinance.com) is for you. This site is a leading connection point for entrepreneurs and investors seeking early-stage deals.

For more financing tips, see Part 3, "Where's the Money," on page 173.

LEGAL AND BUSINESS FORMS

Determining what legal and business forms you need to start a business can be challenging enough. But once you have figured this out, getting the forms can be even more daunting, and time-consuming and expensive.

There are many resources on the Web to help you find the legal and business forms you need, as well as easily download forms, eliminating the need to call your lawyer, accountant or consultant each time you have to obtain a document. This way, you save on their expensive hourly rates.

A quick Internet search will direct you to sites where you can find the business letters, legal forms, business agreements, contracts, notices, sales and marketing documents, checklists, handbooks, manuals, business guides, policies or spreadsheets you need to efficiently run your business. Many sites provide free business forms, while some require a nominal fee to download more specialized forms.

BEWARE!

THERE ARE MANY BUSINESS FORMS, CONTRACTS AND LETTERS AVAILABLE FOR FREE OR FOR A NOMINAL FEE ON THE INTERNET. WHILE THEY CAN BE GREAT RESOURCES, CAUTION MUST BE USED AS TO THE LEGALITY OF THE BUSINESS FORM FOR YOUR PARTICULAR SITUATION. IF IN DOUBT, IT'S ALWAYS BEST TO CONTACT A PROFESSIONAL TO DISCUSS YOUR SITUATION.

A good place to start is FindLaw for Business (http://biz.findlaw.com), the business site of FindLaw.com, an all-encompassing Web site with legal resources for lawyers, businesses and consumers. You can click on links to download free general legal forms as well as legal and business forms by state. For example, you can download a variety of forms from the office of the Alabama Secretary of State, includ-ing forms for LLCs, LLPs, limited partnerships, for-profit corporations, nonprofit corporations and more.

Another popular site is USlegal forms.com, which offers thousands of business forms online—some more specialized to an industry than others—for a fee. Another good site for forms is Office Depot's Web site (www.officedepot.com). A section of the site contains a handy page of free downloadable forms that can be customized for your own professional use.

Also, log onto www.geocities.com/capitolHill/1802/buslegal.html, and you'll find links to Web sites that are indices or compilations of links to sources of legal and business forms, or to Web sites that actually contain legal and business forms.

Finally, you can search Yahool's directory for the most popular sites for legal forms at http://dir.yahoo.com/Business_and_Economy/Shopping_and_Services/Publishers/Law/Forms.

TAX SITES

In general, online tax sites allow you to download tax forms easily, receive tax information, and e-file, or file your taxes online.

E-filing offers a quicker and cheaper alternative to working with traditional accountants, and is increasingly intuitive and easy. You'll also make less filing mistakes, because when filing online, there are usually verification steps along the way, enabling you to check and review your information before it is sent. It also speeds up the return of refunds. In fact, some studies say that electronic filers typically get their refunds in as few as 10 to 16 days, while by mail, it can take 10 to 16 weeks.

If you usually do your taxes yourself, another plus of filing online is that "you don't have to go to the post office to get your forms, and you don't have to worry about mailing it in on time, because you'll probably end up [doing your taxes] on April 13," says Ray Boggs, vice president, small/medium business and home office research at research firm IDC.

The most popular online tax site is the IRS' site at www.irs.gov. A section of the site, accessible at www.irs.gov/businesses/small/index.html, is dedicated to small businesses. Here, you can order a suite of free products developed especially for small-business owners, view a streaming video of an IRS Small Business Workshop, and many other resources. You can also download multiple small-business forms. If you are unsure which tax publications may be relevant to you, consult the site's "Starting a Business" section, which provides an overview of your federal tax responsibilities.

To file taxes online, the IRS site directs you to the Electronic Tax Payment System's (EFTPS) Web site at www.eftps.gov, where you can enroll to file taxes online. The EFTPS was developed by the IRS and Financial Management Service to enable taxpayers to pay their federal taxes electronically. Once enrolled, EFTPS-OnLine lets you use the Internet, PC software or phone to initiate tax payments to EFTPS directly, 24/7, for free. EFTPS payments may also be initiated through your financial institution (to do this, you may incur a fee from your financial institution). Business taxpayers can pay all types of federal taxes through EFTPS-OnLine, including business taxes, estimated payments, penalties and interest.

Two leading online tax Web sites are TurboTax.com and HRBlock.com. For a fee, these sites offer online filing of federal and state income taxes, plus loads of tax information, such as articles and tips specifically for small businesses. Also be sure to check out Unclefed.com, which is a site that offers forms, bulletins and data on IRS regulations.

For more information on taxes, see Part 8, Chapter 41.

ONLINE BANKING

Once your company is up and running, you'll probably want to start banking online. Online banking enables you to perform all routine banking activities, such as keeping track of accounts and balances, account transfers, online deposits, check reconciliation, payroll functions, stop-payment requests, online bill payment and more—without ever having to leave your computer.

In general, online banking saves time and can be more efficient than doing your banking offline. You can access real-time information and perform transactions anytime, day or night, from anywhere, enabling you to have more control over your finances.

"Online banking is a much lower cost method for small businesses to use to manage their money, as opposed to going to a branch or dealing with paper," says Avivah Litan, vice president and research director, financial services at research firm Gartner Inc. "It allows them to automate their check reconciliation, it's much quicker to make payments electronically than it is with checks, they can control their payments—scheduling much more tightly—and they can run payroll for their employees for a pretty low cost, and in general save

CyberBanking

Some small businesses use online-only banks, which have no physical presence. Beyond convenience, online banks say their branchless model enables them to pass their cost savings on to customers in the form of lower fees. There are not many pure-play online banks anymore, but one that is still successful is NetBank Inc. (www.netbank.com). The company also has a platform for small businesses. It's features include:

- **DEDICATED RELATIONSHIP MANAGERS:** All small-business customers have their own banking relationship manager, reachable by phone or e-mail.
- **DEDICATED CUSTOMER CARE UNIT:** NetBank's small-business customer service team acts as a "one-stop" contact for transactional needs.
- **ENHANCED ACCOUNT ADMINISTRATION FEATURES:** Customers can set up multiple account users and define authority levels for each user.
- **ONLINE BILL PAYMENT:** Small-business customers can make 10 free payments per month and receive e-mail notification when new electronic bills are posted to their accounts.

themselves lot of time."

More and more small businesses are using online banking, according to Christine Barry, a banking analyst at Celent Communications, a researcher for financial services. She says that 21 percent of small businesses will be banking online by 2005, up from 3 percent in 2001 and 12 percent in 2003.

Most major banks offer Internet banking and online bill payment. Your bank probably does, too. A very popular site for small businesses is Wells Fargo.com (www.wellsfargo.com), which has 340,000 active online small-business customers, according to Litan. FleetBank.com (www.fleetbank.com) also has a high number of small-business users.

You can also use accounting software programs such as Intuit's QuickBooks (www.quickbooks.com) or Microsoft Business Solutions—Great Plains (www.microsoft.com), or personal finance software like Intuit's Quicken (www.quicken.com) or Microsoft Money (www.microsoft.com) to do online banking and online bill payment. These programs let you manage all your checking accounts in one place as well as view an unlimited history of your accounts, depending on how you set up the software. And many banks allow file transfers between their programs and these software packages.

BEWARE!

IF YOU PAY YOUR BILLS ONLINE, YOU WILL SAVE ON POSTAGE, OF COURSE. BUT KEEP IN MIND: SOME BANKS THAT OFFER ONLINE BILL PAYMENT DO SO FOR A FEE. AND THE FEE COULD BE HIGHER IF YOU USE YOUR PERSONAL FINANCE OR ACCOUNTING SOFTWARE TO PAY BILLS ONLINE THROUGH YOUR BANK. SO CHECK AHEAD OF TIME, AND MAKE SURE THE SAVINGS MAKE SENSE TO YOU.

SMART TIP

THE U.S. POSTAL SERVICE (USPS) NOW OFFERS USPS ONLINE PAYMENT  SERVICES BUSINESS EDITION, AN ONLINE BILL PAYING SERVICE THAT LETS BUSINESS CUSTOMERS MAKE BILL PAYMENTS ELECTRONICALLY. TO SUBSCRIBE TO THE SERVICE—FOR THE MONTHLY FEE OF $9.95 FOR THE FIRST 12 PAYMENTS, $2.95 FOR EACH ADDITIONAL FIVE PAYMENTS, AND THE FIRST MONTH FREE—VISIT WWW.USPS.COM/PAYBILLS.

ONLINE SHIPPING

Once your company is up and running, the Web sites of the major carriers—the U.S. Postal Service (www.usps.com), FedEx (www.fedex.com) and UPS (www.ups.com)—can help you ship your merchandise quickly and easily.

These sites allow you to do things like prepare and print domestic and international shipping labels, request carrier pickups, get maps and directions to the nearest drop-off locations as well as the latest drop-off times, determine the cost of sending a shipment from anywhere, view a recipient's signature online, order supplies online, and track package status online. Features and services vary; check each site for details.

USPS' Web site, for example, offers Click-N-Ship, an online shipping service that lets you print and pay for labels with postage using your credit card, PC and printer. You can also calculate rates, find ZIP Codes, validate and save addresses, and print labels without postage—all in one convenient location. The Web site also offers Net Post Mailing Online, which allows you to prepare and send hard-copy mail from your computer.

BRIGHT IDEA

WHAT COULD BE MORE CONVENIENT THAN PRINTING YOUR OWN POSTAGE RIGHT FROM YOUR COMPUTER? JUST SET UP AN ACCOUNT WITH AN AUTHORIZED PROVIDER, AND YOU CAN USE PC POSTAGE FROM THE U.S. POSTAL SERVICE. YOU CAN SET UP A PC POSTAGE ACCOUNT WITH YOUR CREDIT CARD OR AUTOMATIC DEDUCTION FROM YOUR BANK ACCOUNT WITH ACH DEBIT. PC POSTAGE SERVICE PROVIDERS ARE PITNEY BOWES (WWW.PITNEYBOWES.COM), ENDICIA (WWW.ENDICIA.COM) AND STAMPS.COM.

STOCKING UP

The Internet is also helpful because it allows you to buy your office supplies—from pens to furniture to laptops—online. Shopping online saves you time—you don't have to go to a crowded mall or store to buy your supplies—and in some cases money, because you may not be charged sales tax, and many sites offer free shipping.

In addition, shopping for office supplies online "allows you to easily comparison shop, which makes you a better buyer, especially for commodity-type items," says IDC's Boggs.

Oftentimes, Web sites also have special areas on their sites targeted specifically to small businesses, where you can sign up to receive product information, price drops and special offers via e-mail.

The leading office supply sites for small businesses are OfficeDepot.com, OfficeMax.com and Staples.com. These sites offer special features for small businesses. At Staples.com, for example, you can sign up for "e-mail Reminders," where Staples will e-mail you a reminder to re-order new supplies before you run out. OfficeDepot.com has a section called "Your Business Center," which offers a "Small Business Handbook" and a complete online directory of Web resources that inform, educate and help.

Auction sites are also good places to buy office supplies. EBay has a section on its site called eBay Business (http://pages.ebay.com/business marketplace/index.html) that brings together all eBay's business and industry listings under one easy-to-browse Web destination. It focuses heavily on office technology products, such as computers and networking devices, as well as wholesale lots of consumer goods and services, such as insurance and shipping.

SMART TIP

THE INTERNET IS ALSO HELPFUL IF YOUR COMPUTER OR PRINTER BREAKS. VISIT THE MANUFACTURER'S WEB SITE AND READ THE INSTRUCTION MANUAL TO TRY TO FIX IT YOUR-SELF. IF THAT DOESN'T WORK, TRY THE FAQS, OR SEE IF THERE'S A SERVICE SUPPORT NUMBER LISTED. GETTING A PROBLEM SOLVED OVER THE PHONE IS A LOT LESS TIME-CONSUMING THAN CALLING A SERVICE PER-SON AND SCHEDULING A TIME TO FIX IT.

Other auction sites to check out are Bid4Assets.com (www.bid4assets.com), Liquidation.com (www.liquidation.com), and DellAuctions.com (www.dellauctions.com), which allows you to buy used and refurbished computers, peripherals and software of any brand.

HIRING EMPLOYEES

Hiring the best possible candidate for a position is extremely important to your success. But where do you find quality applicants, especially since you most likely don't have a human resources department you can turn to? The Internet may have the answers. After all, there are many Web sites that allow you to post a job online—and find the right candidate—quickly and easily.

Most newspapers have Web sites that allow you to post a classified ad online. You'll also want to check out the leading online job sites. There are thousands of Web sites where employers can post job vacancies, but the most popular sites are Careerbuilder.com, Monster.com, and Yahoo!'s HotJobs.com (http://yahoo.hotjobs.com). These sites regularly have millions of resumes in their databases.

There are lesser-known sites to explore, such as BrilliantPeople.com, FlipDog.com, JobBankUSA.com, and NationJob.com. You can also check out niche sites such as Accounting.com for accounting positions or Dice.com for technology professionals.

In general, local newspaper sites allow you to reach a smaller,

Help Wanted

Looking for someone to help you out with a particular project? The Internet can help as well. Consider Elance Inc. and its Web site (www.elanceonline.com), an online marketplace that allows you to post descriptions of your projects free of charge in categories such as graphic design, Web design, software development, engineering and business strategy—and to receive proposals from a global pool of professional service providers. With Elance, you post a project on the marketplace, and qualified service providers in relevant categories bid on the project. You then determine which bidder is the best service provider for you by reviewing feedback from previous customers, bid amounts, and service provider portfolios and experience.

Although Elance is the market leader, there are other companies offering a similar business model, including FreelancersDirect.com, 123Lance.com, Contractedwork.com and Freelance Seek (www.freelanceseek.com).

local audience of candidates, while an online job site allows you to reach a wider, national audience. However, posting a job opportunity on either type of site offers you advantages like 24-hour access to job postings, unlimited text for postings, quick turnaround for postings, and the ability to link to networks of other job sites. Online sites also allow you to screen candidates, search resume databases, and keep your ad online for a long period of time—usually 30 to 60 days—vs. a newspaper ad, which runs for only one weekend.

"Online sites are great because you'll undoubtedly receive many responses and e-mails, which you can put into a folder and open them when you want to," says John Dooney, HR manager, employment and strategy at the Society for Human Resource Management. "You'll get a real perspective that helps you see what kinds of candidates are out there."

BOOKING TRAVEL ONLINE

Once your company is up and running, you'll most likely have to travel, and the Internet is a great way to order low-cost airplane tickets and book low-cost hotel rooms and rental cars. In fact, small firms often turn to online travel Web sites in search of rock-bottom air fares because they do not have kind of bargaining power that large companies wield to win airline discounts.

The leading online travel sites are Expedia.com, Orbitz.com, Priceline.com and Travelocity.com. Also check out Hotels.com, the largest provider of discount lodging worldwide.

SMART TIP

NEED TO FIND AN EMPLOYEE FOR YOUR SPECIFIC INDUSTRY? TRY A TRADE ASSOCIATION'S WEB SITE, MANY OF WHICH HAVE CLASSIFIED SECTIONS OR JOB BOARDS. THESE SITES ALLOW YOU TO POST JOB LISTINGS AT A LOW COST AND RECEIVE RESPONSES FROM A VERY TARGETED POOL OF CANDIDATES.

Site In Shining Armor

Setting up your company Web site

W hy put your business online? Because the Net enlarges your business's realm of possibilities. It allows you to communicate with anyone anywhere (or thousands of people at once) with e-mail. You can search for information from millions of sources covering every subject under the sun. Advertising your product or service, showing potential customers your wares and allowing them to purchase immediately, doing test marketing, joining discussion groups with like-minded individuals, sourcing products, sending a monthly newsletter to customers, and linking with affiliated vendors are all part of what you can do with the Web. So the question isn't "if" you should embrace it but "how."

SOUNDS LIKE A PLAN

Having an e-commerce plan is as important as your original business plan. Because you're exploring new territory, making decisions about technology, marketing, and establishing a new set of vendor relationships, a well-thought-out plan will guide you.

As Kevin Hakman explains in Webmonkey's online tutorial to writing an e-business plan (http://hotwired.lycos.com/webmonkey), the first step is deciding what kind of experience you want your online customers to have. Think not only about today, but also two and five years down the road. "If you set up your solution correctly now," says Hakman, "when your company grows and expands, you can add on to the original foundation without tossing out your prior efforts."

Your e-commerce plan starts with Web site goals. Who are your target customers? What do they need? Are they getting information only, or can they buy products at your site? These key questions, asked and answered early, will determine how much time and money you'll need to develop and maintain an online presence.

Second, decide what products or services you will offer. How will you position and display them? Will you offer both online and offline purchasing? How will you handle shipping and returns? Additionally, don't overlook the customer's need to reach a live person.

As you explore the Web for vendors to support your e-business, have a clear idea of how you want to handle the "back end" of the business. If you decide to sell online, you will need a shopping cart program, a means of handling credit card information, and a fulfillment process. However, you may decide that your site is informational only and that you will continue to process transactions offline. These are all important business decisions.

Last and most important, is your promotional strategy, which gets even more important when you think about the millions of Web sites out there, and wonder how you will get anyone to visit yours And remember: The promotional strategy for your Web site is no less or no more important than the promotional strategy for your business as a whole.

"The Web site should be viewed as an integral part of the marketing effort; as another 'front door,' if you will, into the business," says Frank Catalano, an Auburn, Washington, marketing strategy consultant and co-author of *Internet Marketing for Dummies*. "After all, the site is a way to distribute information, gather customer feedback and even sell a product or service. Just promoting a Web site without regard to overall business goals and other marketing efforts is pointless."

THE NAME GAME

Once you've decided to have a Web site, your first to-do item is to make a list of possible Web site names. Then run, do not walk, to the nearest computer, log on to the Internet, go to your favorite search engine and type in "domain registration." you will find a list of companies such as www.namesecure.com, www.siteleader.com, www.nomonthly.com, www.register.com and the original www.networksolutions.com that will guide you through domain registration. For a modest fee ($15 to $70), you can register a domain for two years. Register.com is particularly helpful because, like similar services, it tells you if the name you've chosen is taken, but it goes a step further by offering a list of alternative names that are

DOLLAR STRETCHER

MANY DOMAIN REGISTRATION SERVICES OFFER ADDITIONAL FREE OR LOW-COST OPTIONS. DOMAIN PARKING, WHICH IS HOLDING YOUR NAME  AT NO CHARGE UNTIL YOU'RE READY TO LAUNCH, IS ONE FEATURE. E-MAIL FORWARDING ALLOWS YOU TO USE YOUR NEW DOMAIN NAME TO RECEIVE E-MAIL, WHILE DOMAIN FORWARDING DIRECTS TRAFFIC TO AN EXISTING SITE OR WEB PAGE.

still available. Let's say that you sell flowers and you would like to register your online name as www.flowers.com. A search shows that www.flowers.com is taken. Your next choice is www.buyflowers.com, but that's already spoken for as well. Register.com offers several alternatives, such as: www.bulbousplants.com, www.flowersplant.com, www.flowerspath.com, and digflowers.com. From the available names, choose one that is the easiest to spell and remember.

Once you've chosen a name, prompts on the domain registration site will guide you through a simple registration procedure. You will generally be offered one-, two- or three-year registration packages; choose based on whether you are completely happy with the name or think you'll want to switch in a year or so.

Why is domain name registration imperative? Because more than 13 million new Web sites were registered in 2002, and your potential competitors are snatching up more than 35,000 domain names every day. Everyone wants a catchy name, so registering yours ensures that no one else can use it as long as you maintain your registration. For a small investment, you can hold your place on the Internet until you launch.

With your e-commerce name established, evaluate your initial advertising and office supplies budget, which should be part of your business plan. For example, make sure you've done everything you can do offline to tell people about your site before you go online, such as printing your Web address on your business cards, brochures, letterhead, invoices, press releases and advertisements. Stick it on other items, too—mouse pads, T-shirts, promotional key chains and even the company van.

WEB SITE BASICS

Now that you've done some important preliminary work, you're ready for the big challenge—designing and building your company's Web site. A Web page is a text document that usually includes formatting and links to other pages. This special formatting is called tags, which are part of hypertext markup language (HTML) and are used to link one

Success By Design

For a successful Web site, follow these general do's and don'ts of site design.

Do:

- Make your site easy to navigate.
- Use a consistent look and feel throughout your site.
- Make sure your Web site works on more than one browser.

Don't:

- Use text and color combinations that are too busy or distracting visuals that make the site head to read.
- Let the content, especially the links, on your Web site become outdated; update regularly.

page, section or image to another.

What makes a good Web site? Before getting enmeshed in design details, get the big picture by writing a site outline. A well-thought-out site outline includes:

- Content
- Structure
- Design
- Navigation
- Credibility

An outline helps you get the most out of your e-commerce budget. You will know whether you or someone in your company can do each piece yourselves or if you need outside help. That way, when you hire someone, it will be for only the parts of the job that you will need to have outsourced. Lillian Vernon, founder of the $250 million-a-year catalog firm, designed her original Web site for a fraction of what her competitors spent. How? "It's a total misconception that you have to throw [big] dollars at an e-commerce solution. You have to be a very careful shopper among vendors," she says. Bringing a detailed outline to prospective Web designers makes the process more efficient.

- **CONTENT:** The key to a successful site is content. Give site visitors lots of interesting information, incentives to visit and buy, and ways to contact you. Once your site is up and running, continually update and add fresh content to keep people coming back for more.
- **STRUCTURE:** Next, structure your site. Decide how many pages to

have and how they will be linked to each other. Choose graphics and icons that enhance the content. Pictures of adorable kids of different ages, for example, might work well if you're selling children's clothes, with pictures of toys and books that site visitors can click on to jump to other pages within your site where they can buy these items.

At this point, organize the content into a script. Your script is the numbered pages that outline the site's content and how pages flow from one to the next. Page one is your home page, the very first page that site visitors will see when they click on your URL. Arrange all the icons depicting major content areas in the order you want them. Pages two through whatever correspond to each icon on your home page. Following our example of selling kids clothes, perhaps you'd start with the icon labeled "birth through 1 year" of an infant as page two. Pages three through 12 might be all products and services pertaining to that age range. Page 13, then, would start with the icon from your home page labeled "kids ages 1 to 3 years."

Writing a script ensures your Web site is chock-full of great content that is well-organized. Write well, give site visitors something worthwhile for their time spent with you, and include lots of valuable information and regular opportunities to get more content. Whether you offer a free newsletter, a calendar of events, columns from experts or book reviews, content and its structure becomes the backbone of your Web site.

■ **DESIGN:** With the content and structure in place, site design comes next. Whether you're using an outside designer or doing it

HOT LINK

RESEARCH WHAT MAKES AN EFFECTIVE WEB SITE. SOME GOOD RESOURCES ARE:

● **THE ONLINE WEB DESIGN TUTORIAL** AT WWW.VANDERBILT.EDU/CREATE/TECH. THE SITE PRACTICES WHAT IT PREACHES—IT IS CLEARLY DESIGNED AND OFFERS A COMPLETE AND EASY-TO-UNDERSTAND OVERVIEW OF WEB SITE DESIGN.

● **E-BUSINESS SUBTOPICS** AT WEBMONKEY (HTTP://HOTWIRED.LYCOS.COM/WEBMONKEY/E-BUSINESS) COMBINES THE KNOWLEDGE OF *WIRED* MAGAZINE AND THE LYCOS NETWORK TO ANSWER YOUR E-BUSINESS QUESTIONS.

yourself, concentrate on simplicity, readability and consistency. Before you start using HTML tags right and left, remember what you want to accomplish.

For example, if you have a pet products Web site, you recognize that many pet owners have both dogs and cats. You want them to be able to shop and order in the way that's most comfortable for them. Perhaps they want to get their pet food order out of the way first, then shop for toys and fashion accessories. Maybe they prefer to shop for their cats, then focus on shopping for their doggie goodies.

Cue them with graphics, colors and fonts that make sense to you. Should all cat-related text and icons items contain blue while dog items be red? Should all food text and graphics be green, toys red and accessories yellow? Choose a graphic/color/font scheme that makes sense to you. These subtle cues make all the difference in how visitors respond to your Web site. Keep surfing the Net to research what combinations of fonts, colors and graphics appeal to you, and incorporate pleasant and effective design elements into your site.

- **Navigation:** Make it easy and enjoyable for visitors to browse the site. Use no more than two or three links to major areas, never leave visitors at a dead end, and don't make them back up three or four links to get from one content area to another. Design pro grams such as Front Page Express make it easy to create links to other sites. For example, if you have a Web site for convention planners, make it easy for visitors to link to city sites where they can find information about theaters, river cruises, museums and the like so convention attendees can check out recreational activities on their own.

- **Credibility:** This is an issue that should not be lost in the bells and whistles of establishing a Web site. Your site should reach out to every visitor, telling her why she should buy your product or your service. It should look very professional and give potential customers the same feeling of confidence that a phone call or face-to-face visit with you would. Remind the visitors that you do not exist only in cyberspace. Your company's full contact information: contact name, company name, street address, city, state, telephone, fax and e-mail address should appear on your home page.

HANDY TOOLS

Your Web site announces your online presence to the world, so give it your best shot. Fortunately, there are loads of tools to help you improve your Web site's appearance.

For those of us who love the feel of a book, three good ones on building Web sites are *Creating Web Pages for Dummies* (John Wiley & Sons) by Bud Smith and Arthur Bebak; *Hotwired Style: Principles for Building Smart Web Sites* (Hardwired Books) by Jeffrey Veen; and *Entrepreneur* magazine's start-up guide No. 1819, *How to Start an e-Business* by Robert McGarvey and Melissa Campanelli. All three give hands-on advice and illustrations of Web site design, with helpful do's and don'ts.

DOLLAR STRETCHER

BANKS, CREDIT CARD ISSUERS, AIRLINES AND OFFICE SUPPLY STORES CUT DEALS WITH INTERNET-BASED PARTNERS, INCLUDING WEB DESIGNERS WHO OFFER VALUE-ADDED SERVICES TO THEIR SMALL-BUSINESS CUSTOMERS. BE ON THE ALERT FOR THESE DEALS.

If you master HTML and write the script yourself, more power to you. You can buy a copy of Microsoft FrontPage for $169 to create and maintain your own site.

There are also many hosting companies or Web site solution companies that offer combination Web hosting/Web site building packages. Most of them have tools that allow you to build a professional-looking Web site as part of an all-in-one package sold alongside their hosting services. Some of the leading companies offering these types of packages are Earthlink (www.earthlink.net), Interland (www.interland.com), Verio (www.verio.com), Affinity Internet (www.affinity.com), and Homestead Technologies (www.homestead.com). Prices for these standard packages—which also include other features such as e-mail—vary, running from $10 to $85 per month plus setup fees.

HOST WITH THE MOST

Congratulations. You have downloaded or purchased an HTML editor, used an online service or hired a designer. You have put

everything together and you actually have a Web site that runs beautifully on your computer. How does it all get on the Net? And, since you're not connected all the time, how will people find the site when you're offline?

You get online 24/7 by leasing space on someone else's server, or host service. A server is simply a computer that is permanently connected to the Internet. Companies that arrange for the storage and handling of Web sites for businesses are called Web Space Services (WSS) or Internet Service Providers (ISPs). There are also resellers who sell space on other companies' servers, usually at competitive rates. Some resellers add value with design, consulting or marketing services.

You connect to a host via the Net using your existing Internet access provider, and then upload your HTML files and graphics in the rented space. From there, anyone can visit your site, whether you're connected to the Net at that moment or not.

Choosing A Hosting Service

There are tons of Web site hosts, so many that you need a strategy to sort through all of them. Log on to Compare Web Hosts (www.comparewebhosts.com), where you can compare hosts based on price (most begin at $25 to $50 per month). Other variables include amount of disk space allocated to you, number of e-mail services offered, customer service support availability, database support and setup fees. For even more information, check out another site, CNet's guide to Internet services at www.cnet.com/internet/0-3761.html.

How much disk space do you need to store your Web site? Generally, 1MB can hold several hundred text pages, fewer pages when images are included. Web hosts typically offer between 10MB and 35MB of free storage. The better Web host contracts offer more than 100MB of disk space, and they should be adequate for most situations. If you're unsure how much disk space you need, check with your designer or computer consultant before you sign on a Web server's dotted line.

KA-CHING

The best part of e-commerce is that customers do the work while you make the sales. You've probably noticed that companies of all sizes, from SOHOs to the Fortune 500, use sticks and carrots to encourage Web usage vs. telephone support for all sorts of transactions. Every time you serve yourself on the Net, whether it's to purchase an airline ticket, a can of cat food, or 100 shares of stocks, you've saved the seller money on salaries and, ultimately, office space and phone charges. Nevertheless, business owners should consider carefully how many sales support services they want to handle themselves.

One option is to have your Web host handle your transactions. It can collect the orders, handle credit card transactions, send an automatic e-mail to customers thanking them for their orders, and forward the order to you for handling and shipping.

Another option is to buy an electronic shopping cart program so site visitors can complete the transaction online. A site using a shopping cart program would have these four components:

BRIGHT IDEA

ALTHOUGH PEOPLE HAVE GOTTEN INCREASINGLY COMFORTABLE WITH THE NET AS A SECURE PLACE FOR CREDIT CARD INFORMATION, A LITTLE REASSURANCE DOESN'T HURT. HAVE WHOMEVER SETS UP YOUR SHOPPING CART PROGRAM PROVIDE A MESSAGE TO CUSTOMERS DETAILING YOUR FIRM'S POLICY ON PROTECTING THEIR CREDIT CARD INFORMATION.

1. **CATALOG:** Customers can view products, get information and compare prices.
2. **SHOPPING CART:** The icon works like the real thing. It tracks all the items in the basket and can add or delete items as the customer goes along.
3. **CHECKOUT COUNTER:** The shopper reviews the items in her cart, makes changes and decides on shipping preferences, gift wrapping and the like.
4. **ORDER PROCESSING:** The program processes the credit card, verifies all information and sends everything to the database.

If all you need to do is to verify and accept credit card information for simple transactions such as conference registration or selling a single item, QuickBooks Pro ($300 from www.quicken.com) may work fine. QuickBooks lets you apply for merchant account services and process credit cards over the Internet simply and efficiently.

Final Check

By now you should be champing at the bit. You're ready to launch your online business. Here's a checklist to keep you on track:

- **KEEP YOUR E-COMMERCE STRATEGY** in focus.
- **ENSURE THAT YOUR WEB SITE LOADS QUICKLY** with at least a 56K modem connection.

The World Wide Wait

Have you tried to visit a Web site and waited...and waited until something appeared on your screen? Industry gurus say that people won't wait more than eight or 10 seconds for a site to load, but blame loading delays only partially on poor Web site design. Your customers' modem speed (or lack of it) can create the logjam as well.

While more and more people are connecting to the Internet via high-speed, or broadband, connections delivered via cable modem or DSL providers, many computer users still connect via dial-up access using a traditional analog modem. This modem converts digital signals from your computer into analog frequencies for outgoing data, and vice versa, at 56K or lower (56K is currently the standard).

When your customers dial to connect to the ISP, the modem contacts the phone line, which, in turn, contacts the ISP and, *voilà*, connected. As a result, make sure your Web site can be loaded in seconds with at least a 56K modem.

Slow modems and graphics overload aren't the only things that make Web sites run poorly. Browsers, software that enables Internet users to navigate the Web, differ in how the Web sites they access perform. Netscape handles Web pages one way, while accessing a site through an Internet Explorer browser makes some pages look another way.

Whenever you have the chance to use computers with different browsers, check your site. Note differences in appearance, ease of navigation and speed.

One more thing: If you're checking your site from different computers, you may encounter error messages about "scripts running," computer freezes and other glitches. Have your technowhiz fix them. Nothing destroys your credibility like computer mishaps.

- **PUT FULL CONTACT INFORMATION** on your home page.
- **MAKE SURE YOUR ONLINE MESSAGE** is clear.
- **KEEP GRAPHICS CLEAN** and eye-catching.
- **CHECK THAT YOUR WEB SITE IS FREE OF GLITCHES** and dead ends that frustrate visitors.
- **ENSURE YOUR SITE** meets its objectives.
- **ENABLE VISITORS TO GET INFORMATION** quickly and easily.
- **MAKE SURE YOUR WEB SITE MESHES** with the rest of your business.

Once your Web site is up and running, it's time to get to the really important jobs. The first is getting visitors to your site, followed by encouraging them to become paying customers. Last but not least, keep them coming back for more. To learn how to do all this and more, turn to Chapter 37, "Click This Way."

GLOSSARY

ACCESS LOG: a list of Web site visitors automatically generated by compiling cookies (pieces of data sent to a browser)

BROADBAND: in general, broadband is a high-speed data "pipe," which can carry multiple channels at once; many people connect to the Internet via high-speed, or broadband, connections delivered via cable modem or DSL providers (see below)

BROWSER: software used for navigating the Web

CABLE MODEM: modem that connects to your cable TV line to give you high-speed access to the Internet

DOMAIN NAME: the words or phrases a user types into their browser to go to a Web site

DSL (OR xDSL): DSL or xDSL refers to Digital Subscriber Line, which is a way of connecting to the Internet at high speeds over your copper telephone line

E-COMMERCE: the process of conducting business on the Internet

E-MAIL AUTOFORWARD: automatic forwarding of a customer's e-mail by the web server from one e-mail address to another

E-MAIL AUTORESPONDER: an automatic e-mail response generated by the Web server in response to a customer's e-mail inquiry

FULFILLMENT: shipping and handling of sales orders

HTML (HYPERTEXT MARKUP LANGUAGE): the formatting language used by software programmers to create Web documents

HTML TAGS: code added to documents to format the document and link Web sites correctly

Icon: a graphic image that allows users to click to the subject represented by that picture

ISP (Internet Service Provider): see Online service

Link: a programming command that allows users to jump from one Web page to another in one mouse click

Modem: hardware that connects computers over telephone lines

Online service: a company that offers Internet access

Script: hard copy of a Web site's contents that contains all text and graphics arrangement in sequential order, from the home page to the last page

Search engine: a navigational tool that lets Web users type in a word or phrase to get multiple listings of sites containing that word or phrase

Server: a host computer, see Web host

Shareware: software that can be tried for free before a user buys it

Shopping cart program: software that allows the processing of online sales transactions

Uptime: the amount of time a Web server's hosted sites are accessible to Web site visitors

URL (universal resource locator): the accepted convention for specifying Web addresses (domain names)

Web host: any computer that is dedicated (always connected) to the Internet and has access to the World Wide Web

WSS (Web Space Services): companies that arrange for storage and handling of Web sites

Click This Way

Using the Net to advertise and market your business

Your Web site is up and you have promoted it on everything from business cards to T-shirts. Your shopping cart program is primed for action. There's only one problem. Nobody shows up.

The Net is littered with tens of thousands of dead sites, abandoned because no one visited. You can always tell a dead site—it was last updated on its launch date. So how can you make yours successful?

Throw some money at it—judiciously. "It's a good idea to stick with low-cost, grass-roots techniques," says Jim Daniels, president of JDD Publishing in Smithfield, Rhode Island, who has written several books about Internet marketing and publishes the *BizWeb eGazette* newsletter, which has more than 150,000 subscribers worldwide and is accessible at www.bizweb2000.com/gazette.

Also, if you can afford one, hire a PR firm. In general, raising your firm's visibility through media exposure lets you talk about your Web site to a broad range of potential customers.

A Marketing Tool

Think of your Web site as a marketing tool like the others you use to promote your business. Because its return is hard to gauge, your job is to learn how to get the most from the Web. "Why would someone want to visit my site?" That's your key question. If your site talks only about your company and how great you are, chances are, no one will come back. Attracting visitors requires magnets: things that excite people and make them return for more.

Savvy marketers master permission marketing, which provides incentives for customers to learn more about your product or service. Let's say you run the Clicks and Bricks Bed and Breakfast in Vermont. Spring and fall are your off-seasons, and you'd like to reach out to former visitors and those who have sent e-mails inquiring about the Clicks and Bricks B&B.

Using the principles of permission marketing, you can:

- **USE YOUR DATABASE OF CUSTOMER** and prospect e-mails to build an audience for a promotional campaign.
- **RECOGNIZE THAT THOSE CONSUMERS** have indicated a willingness to talk to you. So find something to say to them. You could offer them a "three nights for the price of two" promotion or run a contest for a free two-night midweek stay. It's offers like these that

keep customers and prospects engaged.

- **ENCOURAGE A LEARNING RELATIONSHIP** with your customers. Send e-mails or print brochures about upcoming local events such the annual fuzzy worm festival, or offer two-for-one coupons for an upcoming art show. Remind them of Vermont's allure in the spring and autumn.
- **DEEPEN YOUR COMMUNICATION** as site visitors become customers and first-timers become return visitors. Send birthday or anniversary cards. Reward them with a glossy national B&B directory. Show them that you value their patronage.

Attracting Visitors To Your Site

As the number of Web sites has skyrocketed from more than 1 billion in 2000 to more than 3 billion in 2003, getting visitors to your site is a maddening challenge. Your strategies for doing so may include search engines, banner ads, affiliates and links to related sites. Let's consider them one at a time.

- **SEARCH ENGINES:** A search engine is a navigational tool that lets you type in a word or phrase and get a multipage list of Web sites containing that word or phrase. Research shows that almost 90 percent of Web users find Web sites through search engines.

  What's more, online search is a rapidly growing and profitable segment of the Internet and is expected to be a $47 billion industry worldwide by 2007, according to a recent survey from U.S Bancorp Piper Jaffray Inc., an investment research firm.

  While there are many search engines out there and they all differ in structure, search strategy and efficiency, the leading search engines are Yahoo! Search, Google, MSN Search, AOL Search and Ask Jeeves, according to a recent report from Internet research firm comScore Networks. For the best exposure, be sure your Web site is listed on these sites. To use search engines effectively to draw visitors to your site, the keywords you choose in your domain name, title tag, and the text of your main page can spell the difference in your search engine rankings. Keyword-rich domain names, title tags and main pages boost traffic. And when using keywords,

SMART TIP

USING SEARCH ENGINES IS A MATTER OF PERSONAL PREFERENCE. TRY SOME ENGINES LISTED IN THIS CHAPTER TO DISCOVER WHICH RETURN THE MOST "HITS," OR MATCHES, WITH YOUR KEYWORDS.

it's important to have them appear naturally.

The easiest way to get ranked on search engines is to submit your domain name to various search engines. Maximizing the number of times your URL comes up in a search result is an ongoing process. It takes patience to monitor the search engines by visiting them frequently and studying your log files to see which search engines send you the most traffic. If you need to make changes in your Web site, particularly your opening page, to move up in the search engine rankings, do so.

With so many search engines out there, you might also use a Web tool like the one at TrafficBoost.com to submit your Web site address to more than 500 of them for a modest fee for one-time submission, slightly more for an initial hit and three quarterly updates. Also check out SelfPromotion.com, a free resource for do-it-yourself Web promotion. Here you can find information and tips about search engine submission, along with automatic submission tools that help you submit your URL to all the major search engines. Once listed, try the tool at Top-10 Promotions (www.top-10.com) to check your site's rankings on the major search engines. Be flexible in your approach to search engines. If you get good results with AOL Search using one set of keywords and do well with Google using another set of keywords, that's fine.

Also keep in mind that the narrower the category, the better your chance of scoring hits; for example, "percussion instruments" and "ice skating dresses" are more specific than "office supplies" and "car rentals" and have a better chance of scoring hits.

■ **PAID SEARCH SERVICES:** Many companies are also using paid search services as a supplement to search engines. These services basically allow you to pay to have your Web site be part of the results of a user's query on a search engine site. There are three types of paid search services: paid submission, pay-for-inclusion and pay-for-placement.

In *paid submission*, you can submit your Web site for review by a search service for a preset fee with the expectation that the site will be accepted and included in that company's search engine—provided it meets the stated guidelines for submission. Yahoo! is the major search engine that accepts this type of submission. While paid submissions guarantee a timely review of the submitted site and notice of acceptance or rejection, you are not guaranteed inclusion or a particular placement order in the listings. Yahoo! charges $299 for this service.

In *pay-for-inclusion*, you can submit your Web site for guaranteed inclusion in a search engine's database of listings for a set period of time. Inktomi and AltaVista are the two major search engines that accept these types of listings. While pay-for-inclusion guarantees indexing of submitted pages or sites in a search database, you are not guaranteed that the pages will rank well for particular queries. Inktomi charges $39 per year per URL, and AltaVista charges $39 per URL for a six-month subscription.

In *pay-for-placement*, you can guarantee a ranking in a search listing for the terms of your choice. Also known as paid placement, paid listings or sponsored listings, this program guarantees placement in search results. The leaders in pay-for-placement are Overture Services Inc. (which was recently acquired by Yahoo!) and Google Technology Inc.

These programs allow you to bid on the terms you wish to appear for, and you then agree to pay a certain amount each time someone clicks on your listing. Costs for pay-for-placement start at around a nickel a click and go up considerably based on how high you want your site to appear—and competition for keywords has the biggest bearing on that. For example, a bid on "web hosting" will result in payment of a few bucks a click easily if you want to get on the first page of results. But if you are promoting say, lighthouse tours, you may be able to get on top paying just a dime a click.

SMART TIP

ANOTHER INNOVATIVE WAY TO GET VISITORS TO YOUR WEB SITE IS THROUGH ONLINE NEWSGROUPS, WHICH ARE BASICALLY ONLINE FORUMS FOR SHARING INFORMATION. EACH ONE IS AN AREA ON THE INTERNET THAT ALLOWS  USERS TO POST MESSAGES AND REPLY TO OTHER USERS. FIND A TARGETED NEWSGROUP THAT WOULD BE INTERESTED IN THE PRODUCT OR SERVICE YOU ARE SELLING ON YOUR WEB SITE, AND POST A MESSAGE THAT EXPLAINS YOUR OFFERINGS—YOU'LL BE SURPRISED AT THE RESPONSE YOU'LL GET. FOR A LIST OF NEWSGROUPS, VISIT GOOGLE GROUPS AT HTTP://GROUPS.GOOGLE.COM.

Google sells paid listings that appear above and to the side of its regular results. Unlike the pay-per-click search engines of Overture, Google's paid listings program operates on a "CPM" or "cost per impression" basis, which means you pay a small amount for each time your ad appears rather than for how often someone clicks on it.

Other paid search programs gaining popularity are from Findwhat.com and Sprinks (www.sprinks.com/index), a pay-per-click division of About Inc., a Primedia company.

■ **AFFILIATES:** Firms that sell products and services on their Web sites for commissions offer another way to draw site visitors. The Web is democratic; a SOHO can be an affiliate of a Fortune 500 firm, as can other corporate giants, midsize businesses and even charities.

Affiliates place merchant promotions on their Web sites to sell goods or services. They control the type of promotion, location on the site, and the length of time it runs. In return, the affiliate earns commission on click-throughs, leads or purchases made through the site. For example, your town's Big Bank is the affiliate looking for local merchants to advertise on its site. It has a restaurant, an office supply store, a realtor, a law firm and an accounting firm with ads or promotions on its site. Depending on what they negotiated with Big Bank, they'll receive commissions on sales that initiated from their Web site. Commissions vary from 2.5 to 15 percent at the low end and up to 50 percent at the high end.

HOT LINK

WANT TO KNOW MORE ABOUT SEARCH ENGINES? SEARCHENGINEWATCH.COM

CAN ANSWER YOUR QUESTIONS. IT COMPARES THE MAJOR SEARCH ENGINES AND TELLS YOU HOW TO GET LISTED. IT ALSO PROVIDES TIPS FOR SEARCHERS SO YOU CAN LEARN TO THINK LIKE YOUR CUSTOMERS AND MAKE IT EASIER FOR THEM TO FIND YOU. PLUS, YOU CAN GET A FREE NEWSLETTER.

You may want to consider joining an affiliate program network, which provide all the tools and services affiliates and merchants need to create, manage and optimize successful affiliate marketing programs. Sites that offer quality programs include LinkShare (www.linkshare.com) and Be Free (www.befree.com). Other top sites are Performics (www.performics.com) and Commission Junction (www.cj.com). If you are an affiliate, you can join these networks for free.

Another route is using your favorite search engines to find

e-Mail Etiquette

Writing e-mail may seem more casual and less formal than other types of communication, but when it comes to your business, take no chances. Online messages offer many opportunities for misunderstandings because there are no gestures, body language or facial expressions to give you cues as to meaning. Here are some tips:

● **TYPE IN UPPER AND LOWERCASE LETTERS.** All uppercase seems to be shouting and all lowercase seems childish.

● **CHECK YOUR SPELLING AND GRAMMAR.** The messages you send reflect on your business, and errors make you look sloppy. If your e-mail program doesn't offer spelling check, compose your messages in a word processing program that does. And remember, spelling check can't catch every mistake.

● **WRITE EVERY MESSAGE AS IF YOUR MOTHER, YOUR BEST FRIEND AND YOUR WORST ENEMY WILL READ IT.** Message forwarding is easy, so you can never know exactly where your e-mail will go after you press the send key.

● **USE A SIGNATURE FILE**—a few lines automatically inserted at the end of every message you send—to include your name along with your company's name, address and phone number. This saves you the trouble of typing it every time while also giving people an alternate way to contact you.

● **BE CONCISE.** Long messages take time to download, and busy recipients may find them easier to delete unread. Simple language will also help cut down on miscommunication.

● **WRITE CLEAR, DESCRIPTIVE SUBJECT LINES.** Help your readers see your point at a glance.

companies that have potential as affiliates. For example, if you sell ice skating dresses, you might want to affiliate with skating, dancewear and sports medicine partners.

Keeping Visitors At Your Site

A good Web site design and strategy for attracting visitors takes you three-quarters of the way to success. The final step is getting people to try your offerings and to come back for more, and the best way to do that is to treat each customer as unique. Fortunately, the

Web lends itself to the kind of personalization that's relatively easy and inexpensive for even the smallest business.

With a little effort, you can address each site visitor's needs effectively. Combined with offline strategic work such as hitting customers every other week with a free newsletter or offering them a two-for-one special if they haven't visited your site in two months, readily available e-commerce tools enable you to personalize as nothing else can.

The basis for customization is the cookie—not the kind you eat but a morsel of information that lets sites "know" where customers go. A cookie is a piece of data that's sent to the browser along with an HTML page when someone visits a site. The browser saves the cookie to the visitor's hard drive. When that customer revisits the site, the cookie goes back to the Web server along with his new request, enabling your site to "recognize" the return visitor.

Here are some ideas for marketing programs you can create from an analysis of stored cookies and e-mail:

- **WHEN A CUSTOMER ALWAYS REORDERS THE SAME ITEM,** make it easy for him to reorder by sending reminder e-mails.
- **SEND A POSTCARD TO CUSTOMERS WHO HAVEN'T BOUGHT** anything online in three months, offering a $10 or $20 reward for shopping online.
- **SEND AN E-MAIL WITH A NEW PROMOTION** a few weeks or months after a customer makes a purchase.
- **OFFER A CHANCE TO WIN SOMETHING** and make it easy to enter the contest for visitors who drop in at least once a week.

If personalization seems too complicated, you can still design your Web site to speak to different groups of people. Let's say you're a realtor wanting your site to meet several needs. Create a screen with button bars like this one:

- **IF YOU'RE A BUYER, CLICK HERE.**

- **IF YOU'RE THINKING OF LISTING YOUR HOUSE FOR SALE, CLICK HERE.**
- **IF YOU'RE A REALTOR FROM OUTSIDE THE AREA, CLICK HERE.**
- **IF YOU WANT TO JOIN OUR TEAM, CLICK HERE.**

This form of customization addresses the needs of different groups. You have made an effort to provide information tailored to each market segment. It doesn't cost a million dollars yet increases your credibility and efficiency.

Getting visitors to stick around long enough to explore your site is just as important as tempting them to visit in the first place. Here are some tips on capturing your visitors' attention.

- **MAKE CONNECTIONS.** If possible, hyperlink your e-mail address; this means visitors can simply click to open a blank message and send you a note.
- **HAVE FUN.** People who surf the Internet are looking for fun. You don't have to be wild and wacky (unless you want to). Just make sure you offer original content presented in an entertaining way.
- **DON'T OVERDOSE ON GRAPHICS.** Since not everyone has a high-speed modem, go easy on the art. If it takes too long to download, users will get antsy.
- **ADD VALUE.** Offering something useful that customers can do adds tremendous value to your site. For example, customers can track their own packages at the FedEx site, or concoct a recipe for a new drink at the Stolichnoya vodka site. While it doesn't have to be quite so elaborate, offering users the ability to download forms, play games or create something useful or fun will keep them coming back.
- **KEEP IT SIMPLE.** Don't build a site that's more than three or four levels deep. Internet users love to surf, but they get bored when they have to sift through loads of information to find what they're looking for.
- **PROVIDE A MAP.** Use icons and button bars to create clear navigational paths. A well-designed site should have a button at the bottom of each subpage that transports the visitor back to the site's homepage.
- **STAGE A CONTEST.** Nothing is more compelling than giving something away. Have the contestants fill out a registration form so you can find out who's coming to your site.
- **MAKE PAYMENT A SNAP.** If you're setting up an online storefront, give customers an easy way to pay you. Consider including an online order form, toll-free ordering number or fax line.

The Ad-Free Zone

When you design your Web site's marketing plan, remember the Internet is a community with its own set of rules that you as an entrepreneur must understand to be successful. The primary rule is: Don't send "spam," which is the Net word for unsolicited advertising e-mail, much like the "junk" mail you get in your postal mail box at your house.

Don't let the fear of spam keep you away from all types of e-mail advertising, however. Jason Catlett, president of Junkbusters Corp., which monitors junk e-mail, junk mail and junk telemarketing, says the key is to exercise "good behavior."

"The basic rules are: Don't spam and don't post commercial messages to newsgroups that have rules against these types of messages," Catlett explains. He says the best way to market on the Web is to get people to come to your Web site, instead of sending your message to them. Another option is to offer e-mail information, product information or newsletters to people who request them. This way, you avoid sending messages to people who aren't interested. Make sure you offer users an easy way off your mailing list. Sending spam has become illegal in some areas, so be sure you mind your manners.

The Internet Engineering Task Force is a volunteer organization that helps set Internet standards and guidelines. For more information, visit its Web site at www.ietf.org.

SMART TIP

IF YOU WANT TO GET NOTICED ONLINE, OFFER TO PROVIDE CONTENT TO OTHERS. ELECTRONIC NEWSLETTERS AND MAGAZINES ALWAYS NEED NEW INFORMATION. ONE OF THE BEST WAYS TO CREATE AN ONLINE PRESENCE IS TO E-MAIL SITES AND VOLUNTEER CONTENT ON A REGULAR BASIS.

GLOSSARY

AFFILIATE: a company that sells another company's products or services on its site for a commission

COOKIE: a piece of data given to your browser by a Web server when you visit a Web page; the browser stores the cookie in a file and sends a message back to the server each time you revisit that Web page

PAID SEARCH SERVICES: services that allow you to pay to have your Web site be part of the results of a user's query on a search engine site; there are three types: paid submission, pay-for-inclusion and pay-for-placement

SEARCH ENGINE: an Internet navigational tool that lets you type in a word or phrase and get a multipage list of Web sites containing that word or phrase

PART

8

By The
Books

CHAPTER 38

Bean-Counting
101

The basics of bookkeeping

By J. Tol Broome Jr., a freelance business writer and banker
with 22 years of experience in commercial lending

So you say you would rather wrestle an alligator with one hand tied behind your back than get bogged down in numbers? Well, you aren't alone. Many small-business owners would rather focus on making and selling their products than on keeping their books and records in order. However, bookkeeping is just as important as production and marketing. Many a great business idea has failed due to a poor bookkeeping system.

Simply put, a business's bookkeeping system tracks the money coming in vs. the money going out. And, ultimately, you won't be able to keep your doors open if you have more dollars going out than coming in.

Aside from every business owner's inherent desire to stay in business, there are two other key reasons to set up a good bookkeeping system:

1. **IT IS LEGALLY REQUIRED.**
2. **BOOKKEEPING RECORDS ARE AN EXCELLENT BUSINESS MANAGEMENT TOOL.**

Of course, staying out of jail is a good thing. And a good basic accounting system will provide useful financial information that will enable you to run your business proactively rather than reactively when it comes to important financial decisions.

THE BOOKKEEPING ADVANTAGE

As a new business owner, you are in an enviable position in setting up a bookkeeping system for your venture. You are not bound to the "we've always done it that way" mentality that bogs down many businesses. For your new endeavor, you have the advantage of being able to develop the bookkeeping system that is most compatible with your business type as well as your financial management skills.

While many businesses still operate using a manual (checkbook and receipts) bookkeeping system, it is not a good idea for a new business to use this type of system. It is far more efficient to go with an automated system, and there are now many bookkeeping software packages on the market that won't break your wallet.

For a financially complex business such as a manufacturing concern, you can buy industry-specific software, but there also are many generic programs available that would suffice for most new businesses (see "It All Adds Up," on page 639).

A good accounting system meets three criteria. First, it is accurate; the numbers must be right. Automation will help ensure accuracy, but it won't guarantee it. Bookkeeping numbers should be checked and rechecked to maintain accuracy.

Second, a good accounting system is relevant. The system provides information that is required and needed. The law requires that certain pieces of financial information be tracked for tax-reporting purposes. Obviously, these items (which comprise a basic income statement and balance sheet) must be measured and tracked. However, it's equally important to include information that you'll need to run your business successfully.

Third, a good accounting system is user-friendly. It should not require a CPA to operate and interpret it. Most of the Windows-based bookkeeping software packages are pretty user-friendly. They include tutorials and help screens that walk you through the programs. Find one with which you are comfortable, even if it doesn't have some of the bells and whistles of more complicated programs.

BASIC ACCOUNTING PRINCIPALS

Most businesses typically use one of two basic accounting methods in their bookkeeping systems: cash basis and accrual basis. While most businesses use the accrual basis, the most appropriate method for your company depends on your sales volume, whether or not you sell on credit and your business structure.

The cash method is the most simple in that the books are kept based on the actual flow of cash in and out of the business. Income is recorded when it is received, and expenses are reported when they are actually paid. The cash method is used by many sole proprietors and businesses with no inventory. From a tax standpoint, it is sometimes advantageous for a new business to use the cash method of accounting. That way, recording income can be put off until the next tax year, while expenses are counted right away.

BRIGHT IDEA

The Web site of the American Institute of Certified Public Accountants (www.aicpa.org) provides links to news updates, accounting-related software, state CPA societies and answers to frequently asked tax questions.

Make No Mistake

When setting up your bookkeeping system, keep the following four points in mind:

1. **COMPETENCY:** To run a small business effectively, you must become familiar with your bookkeeping system as well as the financial reports it will generate. Even if you hire an internal bookkeeper on Day One, it is critical that you understand the numbers. Don't make the mistake of focusing all your efforts on marketing and production/operations while leaving the financial facet in someone else's hands. Successful entrepreneurs are proficient in all aspects of their ventures, including the numbers. Most community colleges offer basic accounting and finance courses. If numbers aren't your thing, sign up for one. It will be well worth the time investment.

2. **COMPUTERIZATION:** Don't let your lack of computer skills keep you from automating your bookkeeping system. If you aren't computer-literate, community colleges also offer a host of classes that provide training both in general computer use as well as specific software programs (such as Microsoft Office or Lotus).

   You have to think long term here. Just because a manual system might suffice in the early stages of your operation doesn't mean that you should ignore automation. Think about what will be needed three to five years down the road. Converting from a manual to an automated system is no fun—you can avoid this costly time drain by going automated upfront.

3. **CONSISTENCY:** When deciding on a computer software package for your bookkeeping system, don't just consider the price. The important issues to consider when buying bookkeeping software are: a) the track record of the software manufacturer b) the track record of the software system itself (even Microsoft releases flops every now and then), and c) the amount of technical assistance provided by the manufacturer.

4. **COMPATIBILITY:** Before you make a final bookkeeping software decision, check to see if the system is compatible with the other software you plan to use in your venture. Imagine the frustration you would experience if the spreadsheets you create in Microsoft Excel, say, for payroll-tracking, cannot be exported into your bookkeeping system.

With the accrual method, income and expenses are recorded as they occur, regardless of whether or not cash has actually changed hands. An excellent example is a sale on credit. The sale is entered into the books when the invoice is generated rather than when the cash is collected. Likewise, an expense occurs when materials are ordered or when a workday has been logged in by an employee, not when the check is actually written. The downside of this method is that you pay income taxes on revenue before you've actually received it.

Should you use the cash or accrual method? The accrual method is required if your business's annual sales exceed $5 million and your venture is structured as a corporation. In addition, businesses with inventory must also use this method. It also is highly recommended for any business that sells on credit, as it more accurately matches income and expenses during a given time period.

The cash method may be appropriate for a small, cash-based business or a small service company. You should consult your accountant when deciding on an accounting method.

ACCOUNTING SYSTEM COMPONENTS

Every accounting system has key components. Even if you farm out all your bookkeeping to an outside accountant, you should understand the basic elements of an accounting system. While some may vary depending on the type of business, these components typically consist of the chart of accounts, general ledger, accounts receivable, inventory, fixed-asset accounting, accounts payable and payroll.

Chart Of Accounts

The first step in setting up an accounting system for your new business is deciding what you want to track. A chart of accounts is kept by every business to record and follow specific entries (see "Sample Chart Of Accounts," on page 628). Whether you decide to use a manual system or a software program, you can customize the chart of accounts to your business. Account numbers are used as an easy account identification system. For most businesses, a three-number system will suffice; however, a four-number system is sometimes used for more complex ventures.

The chart of accounts is the fuel for your accounting system.

Sample Chart Of Accounts

	Account #
BALANCE SHEET (1-500)	
Assets (1-300)	
Cash (1-50)	
Petty Cash on Hand	11
Cash in Bank—General Bank Account	21
Cash in Bank—Payroll Bank Account	31
Receivables From Others (51-100)	
Notes Receivable	51
Accounts Receivable—Customers	61
Accounts Receivable—Others	71
Inventories (101-150)	
Inventory—Finished Goods for Sale	101
Inventory—Work in Process	111
Inventory—Raw Materials	121
Prepaid Expenses (151-200)	
Prepaid Advertising	151
Prepaid Insurance	161
Prepaid Rent	181
Property and Equipment (201-250)	
Land	201
Buildings	211
Buildings—Allowance for Depreciation	212
Automobiles and Trucks	216
Automobiles and Trucks—Allowance for Depreciation	217
Furniture and Office Equipment	221
Furniture and Office Equipment—Allowance for Depreciation	222
Machinery	226
Machinery—Allowance for Depreciation	227
Leasehold Improvements	246
Leasehold Improvements—Allowance for Amortization	247
Miscellaneous Assets (251-300)	
Organization Expenses (Start-up Costs)	251
Franchise Rights	271
Liabilities (301-450)	
Notes and Amounts Payable to Others (301-350)	
Notes Payable—Short Term	301

Current Maturities of Long-Term Debt	302
Accounts Payable (Trade Bills Due)	311
Sales Tax Payable	321
FICA Tax Withheld	331
Federal Income Taxes Withheld	332
State Income Taxes Withheld	333

Expenses Owed to Others (351-400)

Accrued Wages	351
Accrued Interest	361
Accrued FUTA	371
Accrued State Unemployment Tax	372
Accrued Federal Income Taxes	391
Accrued State Income Taxes	392

Long-Term Obligations (401-450)

Notes Payable—Long Term	401
Mortgages Payable	411
Deferred Taxes	421

Stockholder's Equity (451-500)

Paid in Capital (Owner's Investment in Business)	451
Capital Stock (Stock Issued)	461
Owner Draws (Cash Taken Out by Owner Other Than Salary)	481
Retained Earnings (Cumulative Profits Not Expended)	491

INCOME STATEMENT (Accounts 501-999)	Account #
Sales and Other Income (501-550)	
Sales of Merchandise	501
Sales Returns and Allowances	502
Cash Discounts Allowed (To Customers)	503
Miscellaneous Income	541
Cost of Goods Sold (551-600)	
Cost of Merchandise Sold	551
Freight Expense	561
Business Operating Expenses (601-700)	
Wages	601
Supplies	611

Sample Chart Of Accounts

Rental of Equipment	621
Repairs to Equipment	631
Truck Maintenance	641
Selling Expenses (701-750)	
Advertising	701
Automobile Expenses—Sales Force	711
Commissions	721
Entertainment	731
Administrative Expenses (751-800)	
Salaries	751
Office Supplies	761
Postage	762
Telephone	763
Dues and Subscriptions	764
Insurance	771
Automobile Expenses	781
Professional Services (Attorney and CPA)	786
Bad Debts (Uncollectible	
Accounts Receivable)	791
Interest	796
Miscellaneous Expenses (801-850)	
Building Expenses (851-900)	
Rent	851
Building Repairs	861
Utilities	871
Depreciation (901-950)	
Depreciation—Buildings	911
Depreciation—Automobiles	916
Depreciation—Furniture and	
Office Equipment	921
Depreciation—Machinery	926
Depreciation—Leasehold Improvements	946
Taxes (951-999)	
FICA	951
FUTA	952
Real Estate Taxes	961
Federal Income Taxes	991
State Income Taxes	992

Source: American Institute of Certified Public Accountants

After the chart of accounts, you establish a general ledger system, which is the engine that actually runs your business's accounting system on a daily basis.

General Ledger

Every account that is on your chart of accounts will be included in your general ledger, which should be set up in the same order as the chart of accounts. While the general ledger does not include every single accounting entry in a given period, it does reflect a summary of all transactions made.

If your new business will be a small, cash-based business, you can set up much of your general ledger out of your checkbook. The checkbook includes several pieces of information vital to the general ledger—cumulative cash balance, date of the entry, amount of the entry and purpose of the entry. However, if you plan to sell and buy on account, as most businesses do, a checkbook alone will not suffice as a log for general ledger transactions. And even for a cash-based business, a checkbook cannot be your sole source for establishing a balance sheet.

An important component of any general ledger is source documents. Two examples of source documents are copies of invoices to customers and invites from suppliers. Source documents are critical in that they provide an audit trail in case you or someone else has to go back and study financial transactions made in your business.

For instance, a customer might claim that he never received an invoice from you. Your source document will prove otherwise. And your source documents are a required component for your accountant at tax time. Other examples of source documents include canceled checks, utility bills, payroll tax records and loan statements.

All general ledger entries are double entries. And that makes sense. For every financial transac-

tion in your business, the money (or commitment to pay) goes from one place to another. For instance, when you write your payroll checks, the money flows out of your payroll account (cash) into the hands of your employees (an expense). When you sell goods on account, you record a sale (income) but must have a journal entry to make sure you collect that account later (an account receivable). The

General Ledger Entries

While the bookkeeping process for your business can be rather intricate, single debit and credit entries are really quite basic. Remember that for every entry, there is an equal and offsetting co-entry. Also keep in mind that the different types of accounts have both debits and credits depending on whether the account is increased or decreased (see the chart on page 633). Here are five examples of equal and offsetting general ledger entries for a sock manufacturing business:

	DEBIT	CREDIT
1. PURCHASING A DELIVERY TRUCK		
Cash (Asset)		$20,000
Fixed Asset (Asset)	$20,000	
2. PURCHASING YARN ON ACCOUNT TO MAKE THE SOCKS		
Accounts Payable (Liability)		$25,000
Inventory (Asset)	$25,000	
3. SELLING A SOCK ORDER TO A CUSTOMER ON ACCOUNT		
Accounts Receivable (Asset)	$10,000	
Sales (Income)		$10,000
4. COLLECTING THE ACCOUNT RECEIVABLE FROM THE SAME CUSTOMER		
Accounts Receivable (Asset)		$10,000
Cash (Asset)	$10,000	
5. FUNDING PAYROLL AT THE END OF THE MONTH		
Payroll Expense (Expense)	$20,000	
Cash (Asset)		$20,000

system used in recording entries on a general ledger is called a system of debits and credits. In fact, if you can gain even a basic understanding of debits and credits, you will be well on your way to understanding your entire accounting system.

As outlined above, for every debit, there should be an equal and offsetting credit. It is when the debits and credits are not equal or do not offset each other that your books don't balance. A key advantage of any automated bookkeeping system is that it will police your debit-and-credit entries as they are made, making it far more difficult not to balance. It won't take many 3 a.m. error-finding sessions in a manual system to persuade you to automate your bookkeeping system!

All debits and credits either increase or decrease an account balance. These basic relationships are summarized in the chart below:

Account Type	Debit	Credit
Assets	Increases	Decreases
Liability	Decreases	Increases
Stockholder's Equity	Decreases	Increases
Income	Decreases	Increases
Expense	Increases	Decreases

In a general ledger, debits always go on the left and credits always go on the right. (For examples of general ledger debit-and-credit entries, see the chart on page 632).

While many double entries are made directly to the general ledger, you'll find its' necessary to maintain subledgers for a number of accounts in which there is regular activity. The information is then taken in a summary format from the subledgers and transferred to the general ledger. Subledgers showing cash receipts and cash disbursements are pretty easy to follow. However, some subledgers, such as accounts receivable, inventory, fixed assets, accounts payable and payroll can prove to be a challenge in their daily maintenance.

Accounts Receivable

If you plan to sell goods or services on account in your business, you will need a method of tracking who owes you how much and when it is due. This is where the accounts receivable subledger comes in. If you will be selling to a number of different customers, then an automated system is a must.

A good bookkeeping software system will allow you to set up subledgers for each customer. So when a sale is made on account, you can track it specifically to the customer. This is essential to ensure that billing and collection are done in a timely manner.

Inventory

Unless you are starting a service business, a good inventory-control feature will be an essential part of your bookkeeping system. If you are going to be manufacturing products, you will have to track raw materials, work-in-process and finished goods, and separate subledgers should be established for each of these inventory categories. Even if you are a wholesaler or a retailer, you will be selling many types of inventory and will need an effective system to track each item offered for sale.

Another key reason to track inventory very closely is the direct relationship to cost of goods sold. Since nearly all businesses that stock inventory are required to use the accrual method for accounting, good inventory records are a must for accurately tracking the material cost associated with each item sold.

From a management standpoint, tracking inventory is also important. An effective and up-to-date inventory-control system will provide you with the following critical information:

■ **WHICH ITEMS SELL WELL** and which items are slow moving
■ **WHEN TO ORDER MORE** raw materials or other items

Aging Of Accounts Receivable

REPORTING PERIOD From: _____ To: _____

Date	Invoice Number	Account	Account Number	Description	Amount 30 Days	Amount 60 Days	Amount 90+ Days	Total

- **WHERE THE INVENTORY IS STORED** when it comes time to ship
- **NUMBER OF DAYS** in the production process for each item
- **THE TYPICAL ORDER** of key customers
- **MINIMUM INVENTORY LEVEL** needed to meet daily orders

(For more information on inventory-control systems, see Part 4, Chapter 20.)

Fixed Assets

Fixed assets are items that are for long-term use, generally five years or more. They're not bought and sold in the normal course of business operation. Fixed assets include vehicles, land, buildings, leasehold improvements, machinery and equipment.

In an accrual system of accounting, fixed assets aren't fully expensed when they are purchased but rather they are expensed over a period of time that coincides with the useful life (the amount of time the asset is expected to last) of the item. This process is known as depreciation. Most businesses that own fixed assets keep subledgers for each asset category as well as for each depreciation schedule.

In most cases, depreciation is easy to compute. The cost of the asset is divided by its useful life. For instance, a $60,000 piece of equipment with a five-year useful life would be depreciated at a rate of $12,000 per year. This is known as straight-line depreciation.

There are other more complicated methods of fixed-asset depreciation that allow for accelerated depreciation on the front end, which is advantageous from a tax standpoint. You should seek the advice of your CPA before setting up depreciation schedules for fixed-asset purchases.

Accounts Payable

The accounts payable subledger is similar to that used to track accounts receivable. The difference is, accounts payable occur when

---

BEWARE!

ALL BUSINESSES ARE SUBJECT TO LAWS GOVERNING THE PAYMENT OF FEDERAL AND STATE WITHHOLDING TAXES. HERE ARE THREE RULES THAT MUST NEVER BE VIOLATED IN YOUR BUSINESS:

1. **MAKE SURE** YOU HAVE CURRENT WITHHOLDING TAX TABLES.
2. **ALWAYS MAKE** YOUR PAYROLL DEPOSITS ON TIME.
3. **STAY UP-TO-DATE** AND ACCURATE WITH PAYROLL RECORD-KEEPING REPORTING REQUIREMENTS.

Aging Of Accounts Payable

REPORTING PERIOD From: _____ To: _____

Date	Invoice Number	Account	Account Number	Description	Amount 30 Days	Amount 60 Days	Total

you purchase inventory or other assets on credit from a supplier.

It is important to track accounts payable in a timely manner to ensure that you know how much you owe each supplier and when payment is due. Many a good supplier relationship has been damaged due to a sloppy accounts payable system. Also, if your suppliers offer discounts for payment within 10 days of invoice, a good automated accounts payable system will alert you when to pay to maximize the discounts earned.

DOLLAR STRETCHER

MANAGING YOUR ACCOUNTS PAYABLE EFFECTIVELY CAN SIGNIFICANTLY ENHANCE YOUR CASH FLOW. FOLLOWING ARE THREE TIPS FOR YOUR ACCOUNTS PAYABLE SYSTEM THAT WILL IMPROVE YOUR BUSINESS'S CASH FLOW:

1. TAKE DISCOUNTS WHENEVER FEASIBLE. SAVING 1 OR 2 PERCENT ON AN ORDER CAN BE SIGNIFICANT.

2. IF DISCOUNTS AREN'T OFFERED, DON'T PAY EARLY. THERE'S NO NEED TO DRAIN YOUR CASH FLOW UNNECESSARILY.

3. KEEP YOUR SUPPLIERS INFORMED. IF YOU DO FALL BEHIND, KEEP YOUR LINES OF COMMUNICATION OPEN WITH YOUR SUPPLIERS. YOU CAN ILL AFFORD TO GET PUT ON C.O.D.

Payroll

Payroll accounting can be quite a challenge for the new business owner. There are many federal and state laws regulating what you have to track related to payroll (see Part 8, Chapter 41). Failure to do so could result in heavy fines—or worse.

Many business owners use outside payroll services. These companies guarantee compliance with all the applicable laws. This keeps the business owner out of trouble with the law and saves time that can be devoted to something else in the business. If you choose to do your own payroll, it's recommended that you purchase an automated payroll system. Even if the rest of your books are done manually, an automated payroll system will save you time and help considerably with compliance. There's not a lot of margin for error when you're dealing with the federal government!

COST ACCOUNTING

Cost accounting is the process of allocating all costs associated with generating a sale, both direct and indirect. Direct costs include materials, direct labor (the total wages paid to the workers who made

It All Adds Up

In the not too distant past, to set up an automated bookkeeping system you had to spend countless hours yourself or hire a programmer to customize an accounting system for your business. And since most new business owners did not have the time to do it themselves or the financial resources to hire a programmer, cumbersome manual systems were used, or the bookkeeping function was completely outsourced to an accountant or book-keeping service.

Fortunately, those days are over. In today's market, new business owners will find a number of very affordable and full-featured accounting software packages from which to choose. These popular accounting packages not only allow business owners to track and manage every aspect of their companies' finances, but they also reduce accounting expenses by saving accounting firms time and effort in producing companies' year-end tax return and/or financial statements.

Here are some of the most popular "canned" accounting software packages: Inuit's Quickbooks Pro, Peachtree's Complete Accounting, and Accpac's Simply Accounting. They range in price from $40 to $800. Regardless of which package you buy, it will be one of the most beneficial purchases you make in starting your small business.

the product), foreman/plant manager salaries and freight. Indirect costs include all other costs associated with keeping your doors open.

As profit margins have shrunk in many businesses, particularly manufacturing ventures, cost accounting has become an increasingly valuable tool. By knowing the total costs associated with the production of a product, you can determine which inventory items are the most profitable to make. This will enable you to focus your sales efforts on those inventory items rather than on products that offer little or no bottom-line enhancement.

To set up an effective cost accounting system, you should seek input from your CPA. Cost accounting can get fairly complicated, and the money you might spend for a CPA will be more than made up for in the expertise he or she will provide in customizing a cost accounting system for your business.

UNDER CONTROL

Do you know any business owners who have suffered significant losses due to employee theft or embezzlement? They probably did not have an effective internal-control system in place. Many successful ventures have been set back or even put out of business by an unscrupulous employee or financial service provider. And it is often someone whom the business owner least suspected of wrongdoing.

When setting up a bookkeeping system, you need to focus a good deal of effort on instituting a sound system of policies and procedures governing internal control. Here are 10 areas where you need internal control:

1. **YOU NEED A WRITTEN POLICY THAT CLEARLY SPELLS OUT YOUR INTERNAL-CONTROL SYSTEM.** Make sure all employees read this policy. Having a policy not only spells out the procedures to be followed, but it also lets your employees know you are serious about internal controls.

2. **ON A REGULAR BASIS, REVIEW THE INTERNAL-CONTROL POLICY TO ENSURE IT IS UP-TO-DATE.** When changes are made, hold meetings with employees to discuss the changes and to maintain a focus on this vital area.

3. **MAKE SURE ALL EMPLOYEES TAKE AT LEAST ONE WEEK'S VACATION EACH YEAR.** This is often the time during which embezzlement is discovered.

4. **CROSS-TRAIN OTHERS IN THE COMPANY TO HANDLE BOOKKEEPING.** If the person who is stealing from you is sick or on vacation, you'll have a hard time catching him if you let the work go unprocessed until his or her return.

5. **PERFORM BACKGROUND CHECKS BEFORE HIRING NEW EMPLOYEES.** This may sound obvious, but dishonest employees often are hired by unsuspecting employers who failed to check references before making the offer.

6. **USE DUAL CONTROL.** You're asking for trouble if you have the same person running the accounts payable system, making journal entries, printing and signing checks, and reconciling the checkbook.

7. **HAVE YOUR CPA OR OUTSIDE BOOKKEEPER PERFORM UNANNOUNCED SPOT AUDITS.** You may be uncomfortable performing these audits yourself, but if your policy calls for periodic

Petty Cash Journal

REPORTING PERIOD From: _____ To: _____ Balance: _____

Date	Voucher Number	Account	Account Number	Payee	Approved By	Total	Balance

Total Voucher Amount _____

Total Receipts _____

Cash On Hand _____

Overage/Shortage _____

Petty Cash Reimbursement _____

Balance Forward _____

Audited By: _____

Approved By: _____

audits, the CPA looks like the bad guy.

8. **BE CAREFUL WHO YOU HIRE AS AN OUTSIDE FINANCIAL SERVICES PROVIDER.** There are countless stories of entrepreneurs being ripped off by supposedly trusted professional service providers such as accountants and attorneys. Don't relinquish total control of your cash to an outside bookkeeper. And if he or she seems reluctant to share information with you when you ask for it, this could be a sign of deceptive financial advisory practices.

9. **BACK UP YOUR COMPUTER INFORMATION REGULARLY.** This is an important function for all aspects of your business. If you begin to suspect an employee of stealing, the ability to study past transactions will be vital in finding out if your suspicions are justified.

10. **IN THE EARLY STAGES OF YOUR BUSINESS, YOU MAY BE ABLE TO MONITOR MUCH OF THE CASH-CONTROL PROCEDURES YOURSELF.** However, as your business grows, you will be forced to delegate certain internal-control functions. When you do, make sure you choose qualified, well-trained employees who have proved to be trustworthy. And make sure your policy clearly stipulates the person who is authorized to perform internal control tasks such as processing invoices and signing checks.

FINANCIAL STATEMENTS

One of the primary benefits of a good bookkeeping system is the generation of timely and useful financial statements. Most automated software packages offer the capability of producing monthly financial statements. This information includes a balance sheet, an income statement, a reconciliation of net worth and a cash-flow statement. These monthly reports provide invaluable information on the historical measures you need to make the financial decisions that will positively impact your business tomorrow.

Refer to the next chapter for a look at these financial state-

SMART TIP

"THE CHECK IS IN THE MAIL." OR SO THEY SAY—BUT IS IT REALLY? IF YOU SWITCH TO ELECTRONIC BILLING AND PAYMENT, YOU'LL ALWAYS KNOW FOR SURE. ANOTHER ADVANTAGE IS A REDUCTION IN ERRORS. IF YOU WANT TO START E-BILLING, YOU'LL NEED SOFTWARE AND SOME TRAINING. OR YOU CAN FIND A SERVICE PROVIDER FOR A ONE-TIME SETUP FEE AND PER-TRANSACTION CHARGES.

For The Record

As you set up your bookkeeping system, you will need to establish procedures for keeping financial records. The IRS requires that you keep records on hand for certain specified periods of time. And with some financial records, it just makes good business sense to keep them so you can access them at a later date.

One key point here is to make sure these records are kept in a safe place. Whether you store them on-site or at a remote location (some business owners use self-storage units), make sure you use a fireproof cabinet or safe.

Another recommendation is to minimize paper buildup by storing as much as possible on computer disks or CD-ROMs, microfilm or digital CDs. Here is a list of what you need to save and for how long as recommended by the accounting firm PricewaterhouseCoopers:

RECORD TYPE	HOW LONG?
Income tax reports, protests, court briefs, appeal	Indefinitely
Annual financial statements	Indefinitely
Monthly financial statements	3 years
Books of account, such as the general ledger	Indefinitely
Subledgers	3 years
Canceled, payroll and dividend checks	6 years
Income tax payment checks	Indefinitely
Bank reconciliations, voided checks, check stubs and register tapes	6 years
Sales records such as invoices, monthly statements, remittance advisories, shipping papers, bills of lading and customers' purchase orders	6 years
Purchase records, including purchase orders and payment vouchers	6 years
Travel and entertainment records, including account books, diaries and expense statements and receipts	6 years
Documents substantiating fixed-asset additions, depreciation policies and salvage values assigned to assets	Indefinitely
Personnel and payroll records, such as payments and reports to taxing authorities, including federal income tax withholding, FICA contributions, unemployment taxes and workers' compensation insurance	6 years
Corporate documents, including certificates of incorporation, corporate charter, constitution and bylaws, deeds and easements, stock, stock transfer records, minutes of board of director meetings, retirement and pension records, labor contracts, and license, patent, trademark and registration applications	Indefinitely

ments in detail and how you can use them for effective short- and long-term financial planning.

GLOSSARY

ACCOUNTS PAYABLE: a company liability that represents amounts due for goods or services purchased on credit

ACCOUNTS RECEIVABLE: a company asset that represents amounts owed for goods or services sold on credit

ASSET: tangible or intangible object of value to its owner

CHART OF ACCOUNTS: the list of accounts that will be tracked within the general ledger

COST ACCOUNTING: the process of allocating all direct and indirect expenses associated with the production and/or sale of a product

CREDIT: the right-side entries in a double-entry accounting system

DEBIT: the left-side entries in a double-entry accounting system

DEPRECIATION: allocation of the cost resulting from the purchase of a fixed asset over the entire period of its use

DOUBLE-ENTRY ACCOUNTING: a system of accounting in which the total of all left-side entries is equal to and offset by the total of all right-side entries

EXPENSE: money spent for goods or services

FIXED ASSETS: assets that are not bought and sold in the normal course of business but that are purchased for long-term use in the production or sales process

GENERAL LEDGER: the main records of the assets, liabilities, owner's equity, income and expenses of an organization

INCOME: money received for goods or services produced or as a return on investment

INTERNAL CONTROL: a system that is designed to minimize the risk of financial loss due to incompetence or dishonesty of an employee or an outside bookkeeper

INVENTORY: the assets produced by a manufacturing business or the assets bought and sold for profit by a wholesaling or retailing business

LIABILITY: an obligation to another party

OWNER'S EQUITY: excess of total assets minus total liabilities

Making
A Statement

How to create financial statements

By J. Tol Broome Jr., a freelance business writer and banker
with 22 years of experience in commercial lending

In the last chapter, we explored the key facets of establishing a good bookkeeping system for your new business. And while a well-organized bookkeeping system is vital, even more critical is what you do with it to establish your methods for financial management and control.

Think of your new bookkeeping system as the body of a car. A car body can be engineered, painted and finished to look sleek and powerful. However, the car body won't get anywhere without an engine. Your financial management system is the engine that will make your car achieve peak performance.

You may be wondering what exactly is meant by the term "financial management." It is the process you use to put your numbers to work to make your business more successful. With a good financial management system, you will know not only how your business is doing financially, but why. And you will be able to use it to make decisions to improve the operation of your business.

Why is financial management important? Because a good financial management system enables you to accomplish important big-picture and daily financial objectives. A good financial management system helps you become a better macromanager by enabling you to:

- **MANAGE PROACTIVELY** rather than reactively
- **BORROW MONEY MORE EASILY;** not only can you plan ahead for financing needs, but sharing your budget with your banker will help in the loan approval process
- **PROVIDE FINANCIAL PLANNING** information for investors
- **MAKE YOUR OPERATION MORE PROFITABLE** and efficient
- **ACCESS A GREAT DECISION-MAKING TOOL** for key financial considerations

  Financial planning and control help you become a better micromanager by enabling you to:
- **AVOID INVESTING TOO MUCH** money in fixed assets
- **MAINTAIN SHORT-TERM WORKING-CAPITAL** needs to support accounts receivable and inventory more efficiently
- **SET SALES GOALS;** you need to be growth-oriented, not just an "order taker"
- **IMPROVE GROSS PROFIT MARGIN** by pricing your services more effectively or by reducing supplier prices, direct labor, etc. that affect costs of goods sold

- **OPERATE MORE EFFICIENTLY** by keeping selling and general and administrative expenses down more effectively
- **PERFORM TAX PLANNING**
- **PLAN AHEAD** for employee benefits
- **PERFORM SENSITIVITY ANALYSIS** with the different financial variables involved

CREATING FINANCIAL STATEMENTS

The first step in developing a financial management system is the creation of financial statements. To manage proactively, you should plan to generate financial statements on a monthly basis. Your financial statements should include an income statement, a balance sheet and a cash-flow statement (see pages 648, 651 and 656, respectively).

A good automated accounting software package will create the monthly financial statements for you. If your bookkeeping system is manual, you can use an internal or external bookkeeper to provide you with monthly financial statements.

Income Statement

Simply put, the income statement measures all your revenue sources vs. business expenses for a given time period. Let's consider an apparel manufacturer as an example in outlining the major components of the income statement:

- **SALES:** This is the gross revenues generated from the sale of clothing less returns (cancellations) and allowances (reduction in price for discounts taken by customers).

- **COST OF GOODS SOLD:** This is the direct cost associated with manufacturing the clothing. These costs include materials used, direct labor, plant manager salaries, freight and other costs associated with operating a plant (e.g., utilities, equipment repairs, etc.).

- **GROSS PROFIT:** The gross profit

BRIGHT IDEA

MANY BUSINESS OWNERS MAKE THE MISTAKE OF PREPARING FINANCIAL STATEMENTS ONLY AT YEAR-END WHEN THE IRS REQUIRES IT. THE CONSEQUENCE IS REACTIVE FINANCIAL PLANNING. IF YOU WANT TO BE A PROACTIVE FINANCIAL MANAGER, GENERATE MONTHLY FINANCIAL STATEMENTS AND USE THEM TO MAKE THE KEY FINANCIAL DECISIONS THAT AFFECT THE DAILY SUCCESS OF YOUR BUSINESS.

Income Statement

ABC Clothing Inc.

	Year 1	Year 2
Sales	$1,000,000	$1,500,000
Cost of Goods Sold	-750,000	-1,050,000
Gross Profit	250,000	450,000
Operating Expenses	-200,000	-275,000
Operating Profit	50,000	175,000
Other Income and Expenses	3,000	5,000
Net Profit Before Taxes	53,000	180,000
Income Taxes	-15,900	-54,000
Net Profit After Taxes	**$37,100**	**$126,000**

represents the amount of direct profit associated with the actual manufacturing of the clothing. It is calculated as sales less the cost of goods sold.

■ **OPERATING EXPENSES:** These are the selling, general and administrative expenses that are necessary to run the business. Examples include office salaries, insurance, advertising, sales commissions and rent. (See the "Schedule Of Operating Expenses" on page 649 for a more detailed list of operating expenses.)

■ **DEPRECIATION:** Depreciation expense is usually included in operating expenses and/or cost of goods sold, but it is worthy of special mention due to its unusual nature. Depreciation results when a company purchases a fixed asset and expenses it over the entire period of its planned use, not just in the year purchased. The IRS requires certain depreciation schedules to be followed for tax reasons. Depreciation is a noncash expense in that the cash flows out when the asset is purchased, but the cost is taken over a period of years depending on the type of asset.

Whether depreciation is included in cost of goods sold or in operating expenses depends on the type of asset being depreciated. Depreciation is listed with cost of goods sold if the expense associated with the fixed asset is used in the direct production of inventory. Examples include the purchase of production equipment and machinery and a building that houses a production plant.

Depreciation is listed with operating expenses if the cost is associated with fixed assets used for selling, general and administrative purposes. Examples include vehicles for salespeople or an office computer and phone system.

■ **OPERATING PROFIT:** This is the amount of profit earned during the normal course of operations. It is computed by subtracting

Schedule Of Operating Expenses

ABC Clothing Inc.

	Year 1	Year 2
Advertising	$5,000	$15,000
Auto Expenses	3,000	7,500
Bank Charges	750	1,200
Depreciation	30,000	30,000
Dues & Subscriptions	500	750
Employee Benefits	5,000	10,000
Insurance	6,000	10,000
Interest	17,800	15,000
Office Expenses	2,500	4,000
Officers' Salaries	40,000	60,000
Payroll Taxes	6,000	9,000
Professional Fees	4,000	7,500
Rent	24,000	24,000
Repairs & Maintenance	2,000	2,500
Salaries & Wages	40,000	60,000
Security	2,250	2,250
Supplies	2,000	3,000
Taxes & Licenses	1,000	1,500
Telephone	4,800	6,000
Utilities	2,400	2,400
Other	1,000	3,400
Total Operating Expenses	**$200,000**	**$275,000**

the operating expenses from the gross profit.

- **OTHER INCOME AND EXPENSES:** Other income and expenses represent those items that do not occur during the normal course of business operation. For instance, a clothing maker does not normally earn income from rental property or interest on investments, so these income sources are accounted for separately. Interest expense on debt is also included in this category. A net figure is computed by subtracting other expenses from other income.

- **NET PROFIT BEFORE TAXES:** This figure represents the amount of income earned by the business before paying taxes. The number is computed by adding other income (or subtracting if other expenses exceed other income) to the operating profit.

- **INCOME TAXES:** This is the total amount of state and federal income taxes paid.

- **NET PROFIT AFTER TAXES:** This is the "bottom line" earnings of the business. It is computed by subtracting taxes paid from net income before taxes.

Balance Sheet

The balance sheet provides a snapshot of the business's assets, liabilities and owner's equity for a given time. Again, using an apparel manufacturer as an example, here are the key components of the balance sheet:

- **CURRENT ASSETS:** These are the assets in a business that can be converted to cash in one year or less. They include cash, stocks and other liquid investments, accounts receivable, inventory and prepaid expenses. For a clothing manufacturer, the inventory

Balance Sheet

ABC Clothing Inc.

	Year 1	Year 2
Assets:		
Current Assets:		
Cash	$10,000	$20,000
Accounts Receivable	82,000	144,000
Inventory	185,000	230,000
Prepaid Expenses	5,000	5,000
Total Current Assets	282,000	399,000
Fixed Assets:		
Land	0	0
Buildings	0	0
Equipment	150,000	120,000
Accumulated Depreciation	-30,000	-30,000
Total Fixed Assets	120,000	90,000
Intangibles	0	0
Other Assets	10,000	11,000
Total Assets	**$412,000**	**$500,000**
Liabilities & Equity:		
Current Liabilities:		
Notes Payable—Short Term	60,000	42,400
Current Maturities of Long-Term Debt	30,000	30,000
Accounts Payable	82,000	86,000
Accrued Expenses	7,900	13,500
Taxes Payable	0	0
Stockholder Loans	0	0
Total Current Liabilities	179,900	171,900
Long-Term Debt	120,000	90,000
Total Liabilities	$299,900	$261,900
Stockholders' Equity:		
Common Stock	75,000	75,000
Paid-in-capital	0	0
Retained Earnings	37,100	163,100
Total Stockholders' Equity	112,100	238,100
Total Liabilities & Equity	**$412,000**	**$500,000**

would include raw materials (yarn, thread, etc.), work-in-progress (started but not finished), and finished goods (shirts and pants ready to sell to customers). Accounts receivable represent the amount of money owed to the business by customers who have purchased on credit.

■ **FIXED ASSETS:** These are the tangible assets of a business that will not be converted to cash within a year during the normal course of operation. Fixed assets are for long-term use and include land, buildings, leasehold improvements, equipment, machinery and vehicles.

■ **INTANGIBLE ASSETS:** These are assets that you cannot touch or see but that have value. Intangible assets include franchise rights, goodwill, noncompete agreements, patents and many other items.

■ **OTHER ASSETS:** There are many assets that can be classified as other assets, and most business balance sheets have an other-assets category as a "catch-all." Some of the most common other assets include cash value of life insurance, long-term investment property and compensation due from employees.

■ **CURRENT LIABILITIES:** These are the obligations of the business that are due within one year. Current liabilities include notes payable on lines of credit or other short-term loans, current maturities of long-term debt, accounts payable to trade creditors, accrued expenses and taxes (an accrual is an expense such as the payroll that is due to employees for hours worked but has not been paid), and amounts due to stockholders.

■ **LONG-TERM LIABILITIES:** These are the obligations of the business that are not due for at least one year. Long-term liabilities typically consist of all bank debt or stockholder loans payable outside of the following 12-month period.

■ **OWNER'S EQUITY:** This figure represents the total amount invested by the stockholders plus the accumulated profit of the business. Components include common stock, paid-in-capital (amounts invested not involving a stock purchase) and retained earnings (cumulative earnings since inception of the business less dividends paid to stockholders).

Cash-Flow Statement

The cash-flow statement is designed to convert the accrual basis of accounting used to prepare the income statement and balance sheet back to a cash basis. This may sound redundant, but it is necessary. The accrual basis of accounting generally is preferred for the income statement and balance sheet because it more accurately matches revenue sources to the expenses incurred generating those specific revenue sources. However, it also is important to analyze the actual level of cash flowing into and out of the business.

Like the income statement, the statement of cash-flow measures financial activity over a period of time. The cash-flow statement also tracks the effects of changes in balance sheet accounts.

The cash-flow statement is one of the most useful financial management tools you will have to run your business. The cash-flow statement is divided into four categories:

1. **NET CASH FROM OPERATING ACTIVITIES:** Operating activities are the daily internal activities of a business that either require cash or generate it. They include cash collections from customers; cash paid to suppliers and employees; cash paid for operating expenses, interest and taxes; and cash revenue from interest dividends.

2. **NET CASH FLOW FROM INVESTING ACTIVITIES:** Investing activities are discretionary investments made by management. These primarily consist of the purchase (or sale) of equipment.

3. **NET CASH FLOW FROM FINANCING ACTIVITIES:** Financing activities are those external sources and uses of cash that affect cash-flow. These include sales of common stock, changes in short- or long-term loans and dividends paid.

4. **NET CHANGE IN CASH AND MARKETABLE SECURITIES:** The results of the first three calculations are used to determine the total change in

DOLLAR STRETCHER

MANY SMALL-BUSINESS OWNERS FEEL FINANCIALLY ISOLATED WHEN THEY START THEIR VENTURE. THEY CAN'T AFFORD TO SEEK PAID PROFESSIONAL ADVICE AND OFTEN DON'T

 KNOW WHERE TO TURN FOR HELP IN PUTTING OUT FINANCIAL FIRES. HERE ARE THREE FREE RESOURCES THAT CAN PROVIDE INVALUABLE FINANCIAL GUIDANCE FOR NEW BUSINESS OWNERS:

1. **YOUR BANKER:** EVEN IF YOU AREN'T BORROWING MONEY TO START YOUR BUSINESS, GET TO KNOW A LOAN OFFICER WHERE YOU HAVE YOUR CHECKING ACCOUNT. MEET PERIODICALLY TO DISCUSS THE FINANCIAL DIRECTION OF YOUR VENTURE.

2. **OTHER BUSINESS OWNERS:** MAKE THE TIME TO NETWORK WITH OTHER SMALL-BUSINESS OWNERS, REGARDLESS OF WHETHER OR NOT THEY ARE IN THE SAME FIELD.

3. **SERVICE CORPS OF RETIRED EXECUTIVES (SCORE):** THIS NATIONAL ORGANIZATION IS A VOLUNTEER ENTITY SET UP FOR THE SOLE PURPOSE OF HELPING NEW BUSINESS OWNERS SUCCEED.

cash and marketable securities caused by fluctuations in operating, investing and financing cash flow. This number is then checked against the change in cash reflected on the balance sheet from period to period to verify that the calculation has been done correctly.

Balance Boosters

A common problem for small-business owners is the struggle to maintain adequate cash-flow levels. And increasing sales is not always the answer. Here are some tips that enhance your bank balance regardless of whether or not sales are on the rise:

- **PRACTICE GOOD INVENTORY MANAGEMENT.** Don't try to be all things to all people, particularly if you are a wholesaler or retailer. Keeping slow-moving inventory in stock "just in case" someone asks costs money.

- **CONCENTRATE ON HIGHER MARGIN ITEMS.** Focus your efforts on selling those items that generate the most profit rather than on the items that sell the fastest.

- **TAKE FULL ADVANTAGE OF TRADE TERMS.** Wait until the day a bill or an invoice is due to pay it. Your cash flow will be enhanced, and your valued supplier relationships will not be harmed because you will still be paying on time.

- **SHOP FOR LOWER PRICED SUPPLIERS.** Before you get started, check with a number of different suppliers to see which one offers the best price and terms.

- **CONTROL OPERATING EXPENSES BETTER.** Utilities expenses can be lowered by minimizing the use of electricity and by adjusting the thermostat upward or downward a few degrees during the summer and winter months. Insurance and telephone service providers should be comparison shopped on a regular basis. Keep a close eye on employee downtime and overtime. And shop for the best lease rates.

- **EXTEND BANK LOANS ON LONGER TERMS.** Many banks are more than willing to extend the term on a loan to businesses in search of cash-flow relief. For instance, by extending the term on a $20,000 loan (at 9 percent interest) from two years to three, a business realizes annual cash-flow enhancement of $3,336.

CASH-FLOW ANALYSIS

The cash flow statement enables you to track cash as it flows in and out of your business and reveals to you the causes of cash-flow shortfalls and surpluses. The operating activities are the daily occurrences that are essential to any business operation. If these are positive, it indicates to the owner that the business is self-sufficient in funding its daily operational cash flows internally. If the number is negative, then it indicates that outside funds were needed to sustain the operation of the business.

Investing activities generally use cash because most businesses are more likely to acquire new equipment and machinery than to sell old fixed assets. When a company does need cash to fund investing activities in a given year, it must come from an internal operating cash-flow surplus, financing activity increases or cash reserves built up in prior years.

Financing activities represent the external sources of funds available to the business. Financing activities typically will be a provider of funds when a company has shortfalls in operating or investing activities. The reverse is often true when operating activities are a source of excess cash flow, as the overflow often is used to reduce debt.

The increase/decrease in cash figure at the bottom of the cash-flow statement represents the net result of operating, investing and financing activities. If a business ever runs out of cash, it can't survive, so this is a key number.

Our hypothetical clothing business, ABC Clothing Inc., provides a good example. In Year 1, the growth in the business's accounts receivable and inventory required $115,000 in cash to fund operating activities. The purchase of $150,000 in equipment also drained cash-flow. ABC funded these needs with the sale of common stock of $75,000 and loans totaling $210,000. The outcome was that the company increased its cash resources by $10,000.

Year 2 was a different story. Because the company had a net income of $126,000; there was a good deal more cash ($58,600) flowing in from customers than flowing out to suppliers, employees, other operating expenses, interest and taxes. This enabled ABC to reduce its overall outside debt by $47,600 and increase its cash balance by $10,000.

When you start your business, you'll be able to use the cash-flow statement to analyze your sources and uses of cash not only from year to year, but also from month to month if you set up your accounting

Cash-Flow Statement

ABC Clothing Inc.

	Year 1	Year 2
Cash Flow From Operating Activities*:		
Cash received from customers	$918,000	$1,438,000
Interest received	3,000	5,000
Cash paid to suppliers for inventory	(853,000)	(1,091,000)
Cash paid to employees	(80,000)	(120,000)
Cash paid for other operating expenses	(69,300)	(104,400)
Interest paid	(17,800)	(15,000)
Taxes paid	(15,900)	(54,000)
Net cash provided (used) by operating activities	($115,000)	$58,600
Cash Flow From Investing Activities:		
Additions to property, plant and equipment	(150,000)	0
Increase/decrease in other assets	(10,000)	(1,000)
Other investing activities	0	0
Net cash provided (used) by investing activities	($160,000)	($1,000)
Cash Flow From Financing Activities:		
Sales of common stock	75,000	0
Increase (decrease) in short-term loans (includes current maturities of long-term debt)	90,000	(17,600)
Additions to long-term loans	120,000	0
Reductions of long-term loans	0	(30,000)
Dividends paid	0	0
Net cash provided (used) by financing activities	285,000	(47,600)
Increase (decrease) in cash	**$10,000**	**$10,000**

Cash-Flow Statement

* Calculations are as follows:

Cash received from customers =	Sales	- Increase in accounts receivable + Decrease in accounts receivable + Increase in deferred revenue - Decrease in deferred revenue
Cash paid to suppliers for inventory =	Cost of Goods Sold	+ Increase in inventory - Decrease in inventory - Increase in accounts payable + Decrease in accounts payable
Cash paid to employees =	Salary Expense	- Increase in accrued salaries payable + Decrease in accrued salaries payable
Cash paid for other operating expenses =	Other Operating Expenses	- Depreciation and amortization + Increase in prepaid expenses - Decrease in prepaid expenses - Increase in accrued operating expenses + Decrease in accrued operating expenses
Interest received =	Interest Revenue	- Increase in interest receivable + Decrease in interest receivable
Interest paid =	Interest Expenses	- Increase in accrued interest payable + Decrease in accrued interest payable
Taxes paid =	Tax Expenses	- Increase in deferred tax liability + Decrease in deferred tax liability - Decrease in deferred tax asset + Increase in deferred tax asset - Increase in accrued taxes payable + Decrease in accrued taxes payable - Decrease in prepaid tax + Increase in prepaid tax

system to produce monthly statements. You will find the cash-flow statement to be an invaluable tool in understanding the hows and whys of cash flowing into and out of your business.

As a new business owner, you will need accurate and timely financial information to help you manage your business effectively. Your financial statements will also be critical budgeting tools as you seek to achieve financial milestones in your business.

GLOSSARY

ACCRUED EXPENSES: expenses that have been accounted for on the income statement but that have not yet been paid

BALANCE SHEET: a "snapshot" of the assets, liabilities and owner's equity of a business for a given period

CASH-FLOW STATEMENT: the financial statement that reflects all inflows and outflows of cash resulting from operating, investing and financing activities during a specific time period

COMMON STOCK: shares of stock that make up the total ownership of a corporation

COST OF GOODS SOLD: the cost that a business incurs to produce a product for sale to its customers

CURRENT MATURITIES OF LONG-TERM DEBT: the portion of long-term debt that is due in one year or less

INCOME STATEMENT: a financial statement that charts revenues and expenses over a period of time

INTANGIBLE ASSET: an asset of a business such as patents, franchise rights and goodwill that does not physically exist but that has value to the business

LONG-TERM DEBT: the portion of external debt (usually from banks) that is due after one year

NOTES PAYABLE: short-term notes of less than one year either under lines of credit or with a stated repayment date

OPERATING EXPENSES: the selling and general and administrative expenses incurred by a business

PAID-IN-CAPITAL: the additional amount paid for common stock over and above the value upon issuance

RETAINED EARNINGS: the cumulative amount of after-tax earnings less dividends paid that the owner draws over the life of a business

SALES: the gross amount of revenue generated by a business

CHAPTER 40

Watch Your
Pennies

Effectively managing your finances

By J. Tol Broome Jr., a freelance business writer and banker
with 22 years of experience in commercial lending

N ow that you have the framework for establishing a bookkeeping system and for creating financial statements, what's next? In this chapter, we will explore how to analyze the data that results from an effective financial management and control system. Additionally, we'll consider the key elements of a good budgeting system. The financial analysis tools we will discuss are computing gross profit margin and markup, in addition to break-even, working capital and financial ratio analyses. In the section on budgeting, we will look at when, what and how to budget as well as how to perform a sensitivity analysis.

GROSS PROFIT MARGIN AND MARKUP

One of the most important financial concepts you will need to learn in running your new business is the computation of gross profit. And the tool that you use to maintain gross profit is markup.

The gross profit on a product sold is computed as:

Sales - Cost of Goods Sold = Gross Profit

To understand gross profit, it is important to know the distinction between variable and fixed costs. Variable costs are those that change based on the amount of product being made and are incurred as a direct result of producing the product. Variable costs include:

- **MATERIALS USED**
- **DIRECT LABOR**
- **PACKAGING**
- **FREIGHT**
- **PLANT SUPERVISOR SALARIES**
- **UTILITIES FOR A PLANT OR A WAREHOUSE**
- **DEPRECIATION EXPENSE** on production equipment and machinery

Fixed costs generally are more static in nature. They include:

- **OFFICE EXPENSES** such as supplies, utilities, a telephone for the office, etc.
- **SALARIES AND WAGES OF OFFICE STAFF,** salespeople and officers and owners
- **PAYROLL TAXES AND EMPLOYEE BENEFITS**

- **ADVERTISING, PROMOTIONAL AND OTHER SALES EXPENSES**
- **INSURANCE**
- **AUTO EXPENSES FOR SALESPEOPLE**
- **PROFESSIONAL FEES**
- **RENT**

Variable expenses are recorded as cost of goods sold. Fixed expenses are counted as operating expenses (sometimes called selling and general and administrative expenses).

Gross Profit Margin

While the gross profit is a dollar amount, the gross profit margin is expressed as a percentage. It's equally important to track since it allows you to keep an eye on profitability trends. This is critical, because many businesses have gotten into financial trouble with an increasing gross profit that coincided with a declining gross profit margin. The gross profit margin is computed as follows:

Gross Profit/Sales = Gross Profit Margin

There are two key ways for you to improve your gross profit margin. First, you can increase your prices. Second, you can decrease the costs to produce your goods. Of course, both are easier said than done.

An increase in prices can cause sales to drop. If sales drop too far, you may not generate enough gross profit dollars to cover operating expenses. Price increases require a very careful reading of inflation rates, competitive factors, and basic supply and demand for the product you are producing.

The second method of increasing gross profit margin is to lower the variable costs to produce your product. This can be accomplished by decreasing material costs or making the product more efficiently. Volume discounts are a good way to reduce material costs. The more material you buy from suppliers, the more likely they are to offer you discounts. Another way to reduce material costs is to find a less costly supplier. However, you might sacrifice quality if the goods purchased are not made as well.

SMART TIP

As you start your business, it will be important to track external financial trends to ensure you are headed in the right direction. It also will be critical to compare your company's performance to others in your industry. If you are a member of a trade association, the group should offer comparative industry data. Information may also be available from your CPA or banker.

Whether you are starting a manufacturing, wholesaling, retailing or service business, you should always be on the lookout for ways to deliver your product or service more efficiently. However, you also must balance efficiency and quality issues to ensure that they do not get out of balance.

Let's look at the gross profit of ABC Clothing Inc. (see page 648) as an example of the computation of gross profit margin. In Year 1, the sales were $1 million and the gross profit was $250,000, resulting in a gross profit margin of 25 percent ($250,000/$1 million). In Year 2, sales were $1.5 million and the gross profit was $450,000, resulting in a gross profit margin of 30 percent ($450,000/$1.5 million).

It is apparent that ABC Clothing earned not only more gross profit dollars in Year 2, but also a higher gross profit margin. The company either raised prices, lowered variable material costs from suppliers or found a way to produce its clothing more efficiently (which usually means fewer labor hours per product produced).

BRIGHT IDEA

WHEN YOU SET UP YOUR COMPUTER-IZED BOOKKEEPING SYSTEM TO CREATE AUTOMATIC MONTHLY FINANCIAL STATEMENTS, MAKE SURE YOU ALSO AUTOMATE YOUR BUSI-NESS'S FINANCIAL RATIOS. THERE'S NO SENSE IN HAVING TO COMPUTE THEM MANUALLY WHEN THE INFORMATION IS AVAILABLE OFF YOUR PC. REVIEWING FINANCIAL RATIOS MONTHLY WILL HELP YOU KEEP AN EYE ON YOUR BUSINESS'S FINANCIAL TRENDS.

Computing Markup

ABC Clothing did a better job in Year 2 of managing its markup on the clothing products that they manufactured. Many business owners often get confused when relating markup to gross profit margin. They are first cousins in that both computations deal with the same variables. The difference is that gross profit margin is figured as a percentage of the selling price, while markup is figured as a percentage of the seller's cost.

Markup is computed as follows:

(Selling Price - Cost to Produce)/Cost to Produce = Markup Percentage

Let's compute markup for ABC Clothing for Year 1:

($1 million - $750,000)/$750,000 = 33.3%

Now, let's compute markup for ABC Clothing for Year 2:

($1.5 million - $1.05 million)/$1.05 million = 42.9%

While computing markup for an entire year for a business is very simple, using this valuable markup tool daily to work up price quotes is more complicated. However, it is even more vital. Computing

Markup Computation For ABC Clothing Price Quote

	Hours/ Dozen	Cost/ Hour	Cost/ Dozen	No. Of Dozens	Total Cost
Labor	1.00	$7.00		100	$700.00
Supervision	0.05	$20.00		100	$100.00
Total Labor Cost					$800.00
Fabric			$35.00	100	$3,500.00
Sewing Thread			$2.50	100	$250.00
Buttons			$2.50	100	$250.00
Total Materials Cost			$40.00	100	$4,000.00
Total Labor & Materials Costs					$4,800.00
Desired Markup					0.429
Price Quote To Customer					**$6,859.20**

markup on last year's numbers helps you understand where you've been and gives you a benchmark for success. But computing markup on individual jobs will affect your business going forward and can often make the difference in running a profitable operation.

In bidding individual jobs, you must carefully estimate the variable costs associated with each job. And the calculation is different in that you typically seek a desired markup with a known cost to arrive at the price quote. Here is the computation to find a price quote using markup:

(Desired Markup x Total Variable Costs)

\+ Total Variable Costs = Price Quote

Let's again use ABC Clothing as an example. ABC has been asked to quote on a job to produce 100 dozen shirts. Based on prior experience, the owner estimates that the job will require 100 labor hours of direct labor and five hours of supervision from the plant manager. The total material costs based on quotes from suppliers (fabric, sewing thread, buttons, etc.) will be $40 per dozen. If ABC Clothing seeks a markup of 42.9 percent on all orders in Year 2, it would use a markup table (like the one above) to calculate the price quote.

What if you are a new business owner and don't have any experience to base an estimate on? Then you will need to research material costs

Price Quote Work Sheet For A Service Business

	Hours/ Unit	Cost/ Hour	Cost/ Unit	Number Of Units	Total Cost
Labor #1		$			$
Labor #2		$			$
Supervision		$			$
Total Labor Cost[1]					$
Other Variable Costs			$		$
Total Labor & Other Variable Costs[2]					$
Desired Markup[3]					%
Price Quote To Customer[4]					**$**

1. Depending on the type of service business, there may be many more labor contributions. All should be considered.
2. Derived by adding together Total Labor Costs & Other Variable Costs.
3. Stated as a percentage markup on the costs to provide the service. In most service businesses, this will range from 25% (0.25) to 100% (1.0).
4. Price Quote computed as follows:
   Total Labor Costs + Other Variable Costs + ([Total Labor Costs + Other Variable Costs] x Desired Markup)

by getting quotes from suppliers as well as study the labor rates in the area. You should also research industry manufacturing prices. Armed with this information, you will have a well-educated "guess" to base your job quote on.

How you use markup to set prices will depend on the type of business you are starting. If you are launching a manufacturing, whole-sale or retail operation, you will be able to compute markup using the aforementioned formulas to factor in all the variables in the cost of producing or generating the items you will be selling. Markup can also be used to bid one job or to set prices for an entire product line.

If you are starting a service business, however, markup is more difficult to calculate, particularly for new business owners. With most service businesses, the key variable cost associated with delivering the service to your customers will be you and your employees' time. In

Price Quote Work Sheet For A Nonservice Business

	Hours/ Unit	Cost/ Hour	Cost/ Unit	Number Of Units	Total Cost
Labor		$			$
Supervision		$			$
Total Labor Cost[1]					$
Materials Item #1			$		$
Materials Item #2			$		$
Materials Item #3			$		$
Total Materials Cost[2]			$		$
Other Variable Production Costs			$		$
Total Labor, Materials & Other Variable Production Costs[3]					$
Desired Markup[4]					%
Price Quote To Customer[5]					$

1. Depending on the type of company, there may be many more labor contributions. All should be considered.
2. Depending on the type of company, there may be many types of materials used to produce a product. All should be considered.
3. Derived by adding together Total Labor Costs, Total Materials Cost & Other Variable Production Costs.
4. Stated as a percentage markup on production costs. In some businesses, this may be as low as 5% (.05); in others it might be 100% (1.0) or higher.
5. Price Quote computed as follows:
   Total Labor Costs + Total Materials Costs + Other Variable Production Costs + ([Total Labor Costs + Total Materials Costs + Other Variable Production Costs] x Desired Markup)

computing proper markup for a service business, you must pay close attention to the time spent to provide the service to customers, as well as to market prices of the services provided. In starting a service business, you will need to research the going rate paid to employees and the market prices for the services you will be providing.

For instance, if you are starting a temporary help agency, you will need to know what rate is typically paid to employees in this industry as well as the market rate charged to your customers for temporary labor. This will enable you to compute the proper markup in setting your price to ensure that you will be profitable.

(See the "Markup Computation" chart on page 663 for how the price quote was calculated for ABC Clothing, then go to pages 664 and 665, for price-quote work sheets you can use in your own business.)

BREAK-EVEN ANALYSIS

One useful tool in tracking your business's cash flow will be the break-even analysis. It is a fairly simple calculation and can prove very helpful in deciding whether to make an equipment purchase or in knowing how close you are to your break-even level. Here are the variables needed to compute a break-even sales analysis:

- **GROSS PROFIT MARGIN**
- **OPERATING EXPENSES** (less depreciation)
- **TOTAL OF MONTHLY** debt payments for the year (annual debt service)

Since we are dealing with cash flow, and depreciation is a noncash expense, it is subtracted from the operating expenses. The break-even calculation for sales is:

(Operating Expenses + Annual Debt Service)/
Gross Profit Margin = Break-even Sales

Let's use ABC Clothing as an example and compute this company's break-even sales for years one and two:

	Year 1	Year 2
Gross Profit Margin	25.0%	30.0%
Operating Expenses (less depreciation)	$170,000	$245,000
Annual Current Maturities of Long-term Debt*	$30,000	$30,000

This represents the principal portion of annual debt service; the interest portion of annual debt service is already included in operating expenses.

Break-even Sales for Year 1: ($170,000 + $30,000)/.25 = $800,000
Break-even Sales for Year 2: ($245,000 + $30,000)/.30 = $916,667

It is apparent from these calculations that ABC Clothing was well ahead of break-even sales both in Year 1 ($1 million sales) and Year 2 ($1.5 million).

Break-even analysis also can be used to calculate break-even sales needed for the other variables in the equation. Let's say the owner of ABC Clothing was confident he or she could generate sales of $750,000, and the company's operating expenses are $170,000 with $30,000 in annual current maturities of long-term debt. The break-even gross margin needed would be calculated as follows:

$$(\$170,000 + \$30,000)/\$750,000 = 26.7\%$$

Now let's use ABC Clothing to determine the break-even operating expenses. If we know that the gross margin is 25 percent, the sales are $750,000 and the current maturities of long-term debt are $30,000, we can calculate the break-even operating expenses as follows:

$$(.25 \times \$750,000) - \$30,000 = \$157,500$$

BEWARE!

HERE ARE 10 SIGNS THAT YOU MIGHT BE EXPERIENCING EMBEZZLEMENT OR EMPLOYEE THEFT IN YOUR BUSINESS:

1. **UNWILLINGNESS** OF EMPLOYEES TO TAKE VACATION
2. **EMPLOYEES WHO** REFUSE TO DELEGATE CERTAIN TASKS
3. **A LACK OF** DUAL CONTROL FOR TASKS INVOLVING CASH
4. **LEDGERS AND SUBLEDGERS** THAT DON'T BALANCE
5. **FINANCIAL STATEMENTS** THAT DON'T BALANCE
6. **LACK OF** AUDIT TRAILS
7. **REGULAR COMPLAINTS** FROM CUSTOMERS THAT INVENTORY SHIPMENTS AREN'T COMPLETE
8. **UNWILLINGNESS** OF BOOKKEEPER OR ACCOUNTANT TO SHARE INFORMATION
9. **ERRATIC BEHAVIOR** BY AN EMPLOYEE
10. **UNEXPECTED** BOUNCING OF CHECKS

WORKING CAPITAL ANALYSIS

Working capital is one of the most difficult financial concepts for the small-business owner to understand. In fact, the term means a lot of different things to a lot of different people. By definition, working capital is the amount by which current assets exceed current liabilities. However, if you simply run this calculation each period to try to analyze working capital, you won't accomplish much in figuring out what your working capital needs are and how to meet them.

A more useful tool for determining your working capital needs is the operating cycle. The operating cycle analyzes the accounts receivable, inventory and accounts payable cycles in terms of days. In other words, accounts receivable are analyzed by the average number of days it takes to collect an account. Inventory is analyzed by the average number of days it takes to turn over the sale of a product (from the point it comes in your door to the point it is converted to cash or an account receivable). Accounts payable are analyzed by the average number of days it takes to pay a supplier invoice.

Operating Cycle*

ABC Clothing Inc.

	Year 1	Year 2
Accounts Receivable Days	30	35
Inventory Days	90	80
Operating Cycle	120	115
Accounts Payable Days	-32	-29
Days To Be Financed	88	86
Purchases	$935,000	$1,095,000
$ Per Day Accounts Receivable	$2,740	$4,110
$ Per Day Inventory	$2,055	$2,877
$ Per Day Accounts Payable	$2,562	$3,000

*Calculations are as follows:
Accounts Receivable Days = (Accounts Receivable x 365)/Sales
Inventory Days = (Inventory x 365)/Cost of Goods Sold
Accounts Payable Days = (Accounts Payable x 365)/Purchases
Purchases = Cost of Goods Sold + Ending Inventory - Beginning Inventory
$ Per Day Accounts Receivable = 1/365 x Sales
$ Per Day Inventory = 1/365 x Cost of Goods Sold
$ Per Day Accounts Payable = 1/365 x Purchases

Most businesses cannot finance the operating cycle (accounts receivable days + inventory days) with accounts payable financing alone. Consequently, working capital financing is needed. This shortfall is typically covered by the net profits generated internally or by externally borrowed funds or by a combination of the two.

Most businesses need short-term working capital at some point in their operations. For instance, retailers must find working capital to fund seasonal inventory buildup between September and November for Christmas sales. But even a business that is not seasonal occasionally experiences peak months when orders are unusually high. This creates a need for working capital to fund the resulting inventory

Operating Cycle* Work Sheet

	Year 1	Year 2
Accounts Receivable Days		
Inventory Days		
Operating Cycle		
Accounts Payable Days		
Days To Be Financed		
Purchases	$	$
$ Per Day Accounts Receivable	$	$
$ Per Day Inventory	$	$
$ Per Day Accounts Payable	$	$

*Calculations are as follows:

Accounts Receivable Days = (Accounts Receivable x 365)/Sales

Inventory Days = (Inventory x 365)/Cost of Goods Sold

Accounts Payable Days = (Accounts Payable x 365)/Purchases

Purchases = Cost of Goods Sold + Ending Inventory - Beginning Inventory

$ Per Day Accounts Receivable = 1/365 x Sales

$ Per Day Inventory = 1/365 x Cost of Goods Sold

$ Per Day Accounts Payable = 1/365 x Purchases

and accounts receivable buildup.

Some small businesses have enough cash reserves to fund seasonal working capital needs. However, this is very rare for a new business. If your new venture experiences a need for short-term working capital during its first few years of operation, you will have several potential sources of funding. The important thing is to plan ahead. If you get caught off-guard, you might miss out on the one big order that could put your business over the hump.

Here are the five most common sources of short-term working capital financing:

1. **EQUITY:** If your business is in its first year of operation and has not yet become profitable, then you might have to rely on equity funds for short-term working capital needs. These funds might be injected from your own personal resources or from a family member, a friend or a third-party investor.

2. **TRADE CREDITORS:** If you have a particularly good relationship established with your trade creditors, you might be able to solicit their help in providing short-term working capital. If you have paid on time in the past, a trade creditor may be willing to extend terms to enable you to meet a big order. For instance, if you receive a big order that you can fulfill, ship out and collect in 60 days, you could obtain 60-day terms from your supplier if 30-day terms are normally given. The trade creditor will want proof of the order and may want to file a lien on it as security, but if it enables you to proceed, that should not be a problem.

3. **FACTORING:** Factoring is another resource for short-term working capital financing. Once you have filled an order, a factoring company buys your account receivable and then handles the collection. This type of financing is more expensive than conventional bank financing but is often used by new businesses.

4. **LINE OF CREDIT:** Lines of credit are not often given by banks to new businesses. However, if your new business is well-capitalized by equity and you have good collateral, your business might qualify for one. A line of credit allows you to borrow funds for short-term needs when they arise. The funds are repaid once you collect the accounts receivable that resulted from the short-term sales peak. Lines of credit typically are made for one year at a time and are expected to be paid off for 30 to 60 consecutive days sometime during the year to ensure that the funds are used for short-term needs only.

5. **SHORT-TERM LOAN:** While your new business may not qualify for

a line of credit from a bank, you might have success in obtaining a one-time short-term loan (less than a year) to finance your temporary working capital needs. If you have established a good banking relationship with a banker, he or she might be willing to provide a short-term note for one order or for a seasonal inventory and/or accounts receivable buildup.

In addition to analyzing the average number of days it takes to make a product (inventory days) and collect on an account (accounts receivable days) vs. the number of days financed by accounts payable, the operating cycle analysis provides one other important analysis.

From the operating cycle, a computation can be made of the dollars required to support one day of accounts receivable and inventory and the dollars provided by a day of accounts payable. Let's consider ABC Clothing's operating cycle (see page 669). Had the company maintained accounts receivable at Year 1 levels in Year 2, it would have freed up $20,500 in cash flow ($4,110 x 5 days). Likewise, the 10-day improvement in inventory management in Year 2 enhanced cash flow by $28,770 ($2,877 x 10 days).

You can see that working capital has a direct impact on cash flow in a business. Since cash flow is the name of the game for all business owners, a good understanding of working capital is imperative to make any venture successful.

BUILDING A FINANCIAL BUDGET

For many small-business owners, the process of budgeting is limited to figuring out where to get the cash to meet next week's payroll. There are so many financial fires to put out in a given week that it's hard to find the time to do any short- or long-range financial planning. But failing to plan financially might mean that you are unknowingly planning to fail.

Business budgeting is one of the most powerful financial tools available to any small-business owner. Put simply, maintaining a good short- and long-range financial plan enables you to control your cash flow instead of having it control you.

The most effective financial budget includes both a short-range month-to-month plan for at least a calendar year and a quarter-to-quarter long-range plan you use for financial statement reporting. It should be prepared during the two months preceding the fiscal year-end to allow ample time for sufficient information-gathering.

The long-range plan should cover a period of at least three years (some go up to five years) on a quarterly basis, or even an annual basis. The long-term budget should be updated when the short-range plan is prepared.

While some owners prefer to leave the one-year budget unchanged for the year for which it provides projections, others adjust the budget during the year based on certain financial occurrences, such as an unplanned equipment purchase or a larger-than-expected upward sales trend. Using the budget as an ongoing planning tool during a given year certainly is recommended. However, here is a word to the wise: Financial budgeting is vital, but it is important to avoid getting so caught up in the budget process that you forget to keep doing business.

What Do You Budget?

Many financial budgets provide a plan only for the income statement; however, it is important to budget both the income statement and balance sheet. This enables you to consider potential cash-flow needs for your entire operation, not just as they pertain to income and expenses. For instance, if you had already been in business for a couple of years and were adding a new product line, you would need to consider the impact of inventory purchases on cash flow.

Budgeting only the income statement also doesn't allow a full analysis of potential capital expenditures on your financial picture. For instance, if you are planning to purchase real estate for your operation, you need to budget the effect the debt service will have on cash flow. In the future, a budget can also help you determine the potential effects of expanding your facilities and the resulting higher rent payments or debt service.

How Do You Budget?

In the start-up phase, you will have to make reasonable assumptions about your business in establishing your budget. You will need to ask questions such as:

- **How much can be sold** in year one?
- **How much will sales grow** in the following years?
- **How will the products** and/or services you are selling be priced?
- **How much will it cost** to produce your product? How much inventory will you need?

- **WHAT WILL YOUR OPERATING** expenses be?
- **HOW MANY EMPLOYEES WILL YOU NEED?** How much will you pay them? How much will you pay yourself? What benefits will you offer? What will your payroll and unemployment taxes be?

How Do You Rate?

Ratio analysis is a financial management tool that enables you to compare the trends in your financial performance as well as provides some measurements to compare your performance against others in your industry. Comparing ratios from year to year highlights areas in which you are performing well as well as areas that need tweaking. Most industry trade groups can provide you with industry averages for key ratios that will provide a benchmark against which you can compare your company.

Financial ratios can be divided into four subcategories: profitability, liquidity, activity and leverage. Here are 15 financial ratios that you can use to manage your new business. (See 674 for sample financial ratios for ABC Clothing.)

● **PROFITABILITY RATIOS**
Gross Profit/Sales = Gross Profit Margin
Operating Profit/Sales = Operating Profit Margin
Net Profit/Sales = Net Profit Margin
Net Profit/Owner's Equity = Return on Equity
Net Profit/Total Assets = Return on Assets

● **LIQUIDITY RATIOS**
Current Assets/Current Liabilities = Current Ratio
(Current Assets - Inventory)/Current Liabilities = Quick Ratio
Working Capital/Sales = Working Capital Ratio

● **ACTIVITY RATIOS**
(Accounts Receivable x 365)/Sales = Accounts Receivable Days
(Inventory x 365)/Cost of Goods Sold = Inventory Days
(Accounts Payable x 365)/Purchases = Accounts Payable Days
Sales/Total Assets = Sales to Assets

● **LEVERAGE RATIOS**
Total Liabilities/Owner's Equity = Debt to Equity
Total Liabilities/Total Assets = Debt Ratio
(Net Income + Depreciation)/Current Maturities of Long-Term Debt = Debt Coverage Ratio

■ **WHAT WILL THE INCOME TAX RATE BE?** Will your business be an S corporation or a C corporation?

■ **WHAT WILL YOUR FACILITIES NEEDS BE?** How much will it cost you in rent or debt service for these facilities?

■ **WHAT EQUIPMENT WILL BE NEEDED** to start the business? How much will it cost? Will there be additional equipment needs in subsequent years?

■ **WHAT PAYMENT TERMS WILL YOU OFFER** customers if you sell on credit? What payment terms will your suppliers give you?

■ **HOW MUCH WILL YOU NEED** to borrow?

■ **WHAT WILL THE COLLATERAL BE?** What will the interest rate be?

As for the actual preparation of the budget, you can create it man-

Comparative Financial Ratios

ABC Clothing Inc.

	Year 1	Year 2
Profitability Ratios:		
Gross Profit Margin	25.0%	30.0%
Operating Profit Margin	5.0%	11.7%
Net Profit Margin	3.7%	8.4%
Return on Equity	33.1%	52.9%
Return on Assets	9.0%	25.2%
Liquidity Ratios:		
Current	1.57	2.32
Quick	0.54	0.98
Working Capital to Sales	0.10	0.15
Activity Ratios:		
Accounts Receivable Days	30	35
Inventory Days	90	85
Accounts Payable Days	32	29
Sales to Assets	2.43	3.00
Leverage Ratios:		
Debt to Equity	2.68	1.10
Debt Ratio	0.73	0.52
Debt Coverage	2.24	5.20

ually or with the budgeting function that comes with most book-keeping software packages. You can also purchase separate budgeting software such as Quicken or Microsoft Money. Yes, this seems like a lot of information to forecast. But it's not as cumbersome as it looks. (See page 677 for a sample financial budget; you should find a similar format in any budgeting software.)

The first step is to set up a plan for the following year on a month-to-month basis. Starting with the first month, establish specific budgeted dollar levels for each category of the budget. The sales numbers will be critical since they will be used to compute gross profit margin and will help determine operating expenses, as well as the accounts receivable and inventory levels necessary to support the business. In determining how much of your product or service you can sell, study the market in which you will operate, your competition, potential demand that you might already have seen, and economic conditions. For cost of goods sold, you will need to calculate the actual costs associated with producing each item on a percentage basis.

For your operating expenses, consider items such as advertising, auto, depreciation, insurance, etc. Then factor in a tax rate based on actual business tax rates that you can obtain from your accountant.

On the balance sheet, break down inventory by category. For instance, a clothing manufacturer has raw materials, work-in-process and finished goods. For inventory, accounts receivable and accounts payable, you will figure the total amounts based on a projected number of days on hand. (See page 669 for the calculations needed to compute these three key numbers for your budget.)

Consider each specific item in fixed assets broken out for real estate, equipment, investments, etc. If your new business requires a franchise fee or copyrights or patents, this will be reflected as an intangible asset.

On the liability side, break down each bank loan separately. Do the same for the stockholder's equity—common stock, preferred stock, paid-in-capital, treasury stock and retained earnings.

Do this for each month for the first 12 months. Then prepare the quarter-to-quarter budgets for years two and three. For the first year's budget, you will want to consider seasonality factors. For example, most retailers experience heavy sales from October to December. If your business will be highly seasonal, you will have wide ranging changes in cash-flow needs. For this reason, you will want to consider seasonality in the budget rather than take your

675

annual projected year-one sales level and divide by 12.

As for the process, you will need to prepare the income statement budgets first, then balance sheet, then cash flow. You will need to know the net income figure before you can prepare a pro forma balance sheet because the profit number must be plugged into retained earnings. And for the cash-flow projection, you will need both

Smarter To Barter?

Remember how pioneers would trade a deer skin for a musket? Literally, by trading a buck, somebody would get a buck. It was called bartering. Today, the concept is back in a big way—especially online. The companies are everywhere on the Net: Exchange Anything.com, BarterItOnline.com, Barter.com, Mr.Swap.com...need we say more?

In the past decade, bartering has grown more than 300 percent. More than 1 million companies are bartering, and it's a $4 billion industry. It can also be an invaluable tool for a start-up company. Why?

It can be good for your business in good times, but it can be even better in bad, and, let's face facts, most start-ups have their share of down times. The main advantage to going the barter route is that if you have unwanted inventory, you can use it to trade rather than spend money you don't have, and pile more onto your already stretched-too-thin budget.

Here's how bartering works: Let's say a landscaper needs a root canal. The landscaper belongs to a bartering organization and learns that a local dentist is also part of the same organization. But it turns out the dentist doesn't need any landscaping done. OK, fine. So the landscaper instead does work for a small public relations firm and a restaurant management consultant. For that work, he has been banking "bartering dollars," enough to pay for other members' services, like a dentist, who will then use those bartering dollars to get something from another member. Meanwhile, to belong to a bartering organization, you're paying a monthly membership fee of $5 to $30.

Who determines what each service or product is worth? You pay the fair market value, which is determined by buyer and seller. But beware: There are some dishonest barters out there who will charge higher prices to members or not give a service or product that was part of a deal. You need to keep track of bartering purchases and provide clients with Form 1099-B, so you can file it on your taxes.

Financial Budget And Income Statement Work Sheet

	Month 1	Month 2	Month 3	Month 4	Month 5	Month 6	Month 7	Month 8	Month 9	Month 10	Month 11	Month 12	Total Year 1
Sales													
Cost of Goods Sold													
Gross Profit													
Operating Expenses:													
Advertising													
Auto Expenses													
Bank Charges													
Depreciation													
Dues & Subscriptions													
Employee Benefits													
Insurance													
Interest													
Office Expenses													
Officers' Salaries													
Payroll Taxes													
Professional Fees													
Rent													
Repairs & Maintenance													
Salaries & Wages													
Security													
Supplies													
Taxes & Licenses													
Telephone													
Utilities													
Other													
Total Operating Expenses													
Net Profit Before Taxes													
Income Taxes													
Net Profit After Taxes													

Balance Sheet Work Sheet

	Month 1	Month 2	Month 3	Month 4	Month 5	Month 6	Month 7	Month 8	Month 9	Month 10	Month 11	Month 12	Total Year 1
Assets:													
Cash													
Investments													
Accounts Receivable													
Inventory													
Prepaid Expenses													
Other Current Assets													
Land													
Buildings													
Equipment													
Less: Accumulated Depreciation													
Long-Term Investments													
Intangibles													
Other Assets													
Total Assets													
Liabilities & Equity:													
Notes Payable—Short Term													
Current Maturities of Long-Term Debt													
Accounts Payable													
Accrued Expenses													
Taxes Payable													
Stockholder Loans													
Other Current Liabilities													
Bonds Payable													
Long-Term Debt													
Common Stock													
Paid-in-capital													
Treasury Stock													
Retained Earnings													
Total Liabilities & Equity													

Cash-Flow Work Sheet

	Month 1	Month 2	Month 3	Month 4	Month 5	Month 6	Month 7	Month 8	Month 9	Month 10	Month 11	Month 12	Total Year 1
Cash Available:													
Net Income After Taxes													
Depreciation													
Amortization													
Decrease in A/R													
Decrease in Inventory													
Increase in Accounts Payable													
Increase in Notes Payable-ST													
Increase in Long-Term Debt													
Decrease in Other Assets													
Increase in Other Liabilities													
Total Cash Available													
Cash Disbursements:													
Owners' Draw/Dividends													
Increase in A/R													
Increase in Inventory													
Decrease in Accounts Payable													
Capital Expenditures													
Decrease in Notes Payable-ST													
Current Maturities of Long-Term Debt													
Increase in Other Assets													
Decrease in Other Liabilities													
Total Cash Disbursements													
Monthly Cash Flow													
Cumulative Cash Flow													

Where Credit Is Due

When you book a credit sale in your business, you must collect from the customer to realize your profit. Many a solid business has suffered a severe setback or even been put under by its failure to collect accounts receivable.

It is vital that you stay on top of your A/R if you sell on credit. Here are some tips that will help you maintain high-quality accounts receivable:

- **CHECK OUT REFERENCES UP FRONT.** Find out how your prospective customer has paid other suppliers before selling on credit. Ask for supplier and bank references and follow up on them.
- **SET CREDIT LIMITS, AND MONITOR THEM.** Establish credit limits for each customer. Set up a system to regularly compare balances owed and credit limits.
- **PROCESS INVOICES IMMEDIATELY.** Send out invoices as soon as goods are shipped. Falling behind on sending invoices will result in slower collection of accounts receivable, which costs you cash flow.
- **DON'T RESELL TO HABITUALLY SLOW-PAYING ACCOUNTS.** If you find that a certain customer stays way behind in payment to you, stop selling to that company. Habitual slow pay is a sign of financial instability, and you can ill afford to write off an account of any significant size during the early years of your business.

income statement and balance sheet numbers.

No matter whether you will budget manually or use software, it is advisable to seek input from your CPA in preparing your initial budget. His or her role will depend on the internal resources available to you and your background in finance. You may want to hire your CPA to prepare the financial plan for you, or you may simply involve him or her in an advisory role. Regardless of the level of involvement, your CPA's input will prove invaluable in providing an independent review of your short- and long-term financial plan.

In future years, your monthly financial statements and accountant-prepared year-end statements will be very useful in preparing a budget.

SENSITIVITY ANALYSIS

One other major benefit of maintaining a financial budget is the ability to perform a sensitivity analysis. Once you have a plan in place, you can make adjustments to it to consider the potential effects of certain variables on your operation. All you have to do is plug in the change and see how it affects your company's financial performance.

Here's how it works: Let's say you've budgeted a 10 percent sales growth for the coming year. You can easily adjust the sales growth number to 5 percent or 15 percent in the budget to see how it affects

Stocking Up

If your business will produce or sell inventory, your inventory management system will be crucial to your business' success. Keeping too much inventory on hand will cost you cash flow and will increase the risk of obsolescence. Conversely, an inventory level that is too lean can cost you sales.

Here are some suggestions to help you better manage your inventory:

- **PAY ATTENTION TO SEASONALITY.** Depending on the type of business you are starting, you may have certain inventory items that sell only during certain times of the year. Order early in anticipation of the peak season. Then make sure you sell the stock so that you don't get stuck holding on to it for a year.
- **RELY ON SUPPLIERS.** If you can find suppliers that are well-stocked and can ship quickly, you can essentially let them stock your inventory for you. "Just in time" inventory management can save valuable working capital that could be invested in other areas of your business.
- **STOCK WHAT SELLS.** This may seem obvious, but too many business owners try to be all things to all people when it comes to inventory management. When you see what sells, focus your purchasing efforts on those items.
- **MARK DOWN STALE ITEMS.** Once you're up and running, you will find that certain items sell better than others. Mark down the items that don't sell, and then don't replace them.
- **WATCH WASTE.** Keep a close eye on waste. If production mistakes aren't caught early, you can ruin a whole batch of inventory, which can be extremely costly.

your business's performance. You can perform a sensitivity analysis for any other financial variable as well. The most common items for which sensitivity analysis is done are:

- Sales
- Cost of goods sold and gross profit
- Operating expenses
- Interest rates
- Accounts receivable days
- Inventory days
- Accounts payable days on hand
- Major fixed asset purchases or reductions
- Acquisitions or closings

To be an effective and proactive business owner, you will need to learn to generate and understand the financial management tools discussed in this chapter. Even if you don't consider yourself a "numbers person," you will find that regular analysis of your financial data will be vital as you start and grow your business.

GLOSSARY

FINANCIAL BUDGET: a projection of future financial performance

GROSS PROFIT MARGIN: the percentage of gross profit realized on goods sold after subtracting cost of goods sold from sales

MARKUP: the percentage above the cost of producing a product that is charged to the customer

RATIO ANALYSIS: the use of certain financial ratios to compare the performance of a business with years past and with industry peers

SENSITIVITY ANALYSIS: the process of changing financial variables in a financial budget to determine their potential impact on the company's future performance

The Tax Man Cometh

What you need to know about taxes

By Joan Szabo, a freelance writer who has covered
tax issues for more than 15 years

W hen it comes to taxes, there's no way to get around the fact that you have to pay them regularly. Federal, state and local taxes combined can take a big chunk out of your company's money, leaving you with less cash to operate your business.

That's why it's important to stay abreast of your business's tax situation and work with a qualified accountant to understand all that's required of you by federal and state governments. The task is by no means simple. New business owners face a host of tax requirements and ever-changing rules.

If you miss deadlines or fail to comply with specific rules, you may be hit with large penalties, and, in the worst-case scenario, be forced to close up shop. You'll also want to pay close attention to tax planning, which will help you find legitimate ways to trim your overall tax liability. Your goal is to take the deductions to which you're entitled and to defer taxes as long as you possibly can.

While a knowledgeable accountant specializing in small-business tax issues will keep you out of potential tax quagmires, you'll be on more solid footing if you spend time acquiring your own working knowledge and understanding of the tax laws.

FIRST THINGS FIRST

One of the first steps you will take as a business owner is to obtain a taxpayer identification number so the IRS can process your returns. There are two types of identification numbers: a Social Security number and an Employer Identification Number (EIN).

The EIN is a nine-digit number the IRS issues. It is used to identify the tax accounts of corporations, partnerships and other entities. You need an EIN if you have employees, operate your business as a corporation or partnership, or have a Keogh plan. Be sure to include your taxpayer ID on all returns or other documents you send to the IRS.

You can apply for an EIN through the phone, fax or mail,

HOT LINK

GET THE SCOOP ON WAGE REPORTING FOR YOURSELF AND YOUR EMPLOYEES AT THE SOCIAL SECURITY WEB SITE: WWW.SSA.GOV.

depending on how soon you need to use the EIN. If you apply by mail, be sure to send in Form SS-4 (*Application for Employer Identification Number*) at least four or five weeks before you need the EIN to file a return or make a deposit. If you apply by phone (toll-free at 866-816-2065), the IRS will give you one immediately. Before you call, the IRS suggests you complete Form SS-4 so you have all relevant information available. The person making the call to the IRS must be authorized to sign the form.

INS AND OUTS OF PAYROLL TAXES

If you do any hiring, your employees must complete Form I-9 and Form W-4. Form I-9 provides verification that each new employee is legally eligible to work in the United States. This form can be obtained from Immigration and Naturalization Service (INS) offices; keep this form in your files in the event an IRS or INS inspector wants to see it. You also should complete a state withholding certificate (similar to the W-4) for your state.

Form W-4 indicates the employee's filing status and withholding allowances. These allowances are used to determine how much federal income tax to withhold from an employee's wages. The IRS can provide you with a tax table to determine the withholding amounts for your employees. To receive a copy of this table, call the IRS and ask for Circular E and the supplement to Circular E.

SMART TIP

CONSIDER USING A PAYROLL TAX SERVICE TO TAKE CARE OF ALL PAYROLL TAX REQUIRE-MENTS. THE FEES CHARGED BY SUCH SERVICES ARE RELATIVELY REASONABLE. IN ADDITION, THESE FIRMS SPECIALIZE IN THIS AREA AND KNOW THE INS AND OUTS OF ALL THE RULES AND REGULATIONS. WITH A SERVICE, YOU DON'T HAVE TO WORRY ABOUT MAKING MISTAKES OR BEING TARDY WITH PAYMENTS.

You must also withhold Social Security and Medicare taxes—these are known as FICA (Federal Insurance Contributions Act) taxes. The FICA tax actually consists of two taxes: a 6.2 percent Social Security tax and a 1.45 percent Medicare tax. To calculate the tax you need to withhold for each employee, multiply an employee's gross wages for a pay period by the tax rates. In addition, as an employer, you are required to pay a matching amount of FICA taxes on each of your employees.

Here's how it works: If an employee has gross wages of $1,000 every two weeks, you must withhold $62 ($1,000 x 0.062) in Social Security taxes and $14.50 ($1,000 x .0145) in Medicare taxes, or $76.50. As an employer, you owe a matching amount as well, so the total amount in FICA taxes to be paid is $153. The maximum amount of wages currently subject to Social Security tax is $87,000. There is no limit on the amount of wages subject to the Medicare tax.

The IRS requires any business paying more than $200,000 annually in payroll taxes or other federal taxes to pay them through the Electronic Federal Tax Payment System (EFTPS). If you pay under that amount, you can still deliver a check for payroll taxes owed with your deposit coupons to their bank (the same bank as the check is drawn on). The form to use is 8109 (*Federal Tax Deposit Coupon*). On each coupon show the deposit amount, the type of tax, the period for which you are making a deposit and your phone number. You typically pay these taxes monthly, depending on the size of your business. Approximately five to six weeks after you receive your EIN, the IRS will send you the coupon book.

In addition to making your monthly payroll deposits, you are required to file Form 941 (*Employer's Quarterly Federal Tax Return*). This is a form that provides the government with information on the federal income taxes you withheld from your employees' pay as well as the FICA taxes you withheld and paid. It also tells the government when the taxes were withheld so the IRS can determine if the federal tax deposit was made on time.

Another tax you have to pay is FUTA (Federal Unemployment Tax Act) taxes, which are used to compensate workers who lose their jobs. You report and pay

FUTA tax separately from FICA and withheld income taxes.

You pay FUTA tax on your payroll if during the current or prior calendar year you meet one of two tests: You paid total wages of $1,500 to your employees in any calendar quarter, or you have at least one employee working on any given day in each of 20 different calendar weeks.

The FUTA tax is figured on the first $7,000 in wages paid to each employee annually. The gross FUTA tax rate is 6.2 percent. However, you are given a credit of up to 5.4 percent for the state unemployment tax you pay, effectively reducing the tax rate. As an employer, you pay FUTA tax only from your own funds. Employees do not have this tax withheld from their pay. You generally deposit FUTA taxes quarterly. In addition, you must file an annual return for your FUTA taxes using Form 940 (*Employer's Annual Federal Unemployment Tax Return*), which must be filed by January 31 of the following year. Most small employers are eligible to use Form 940-EZ.

Federal payroll taxes are not your only concern. States and localities have their own taxes, which will most likely affect you. Most states (nine do not) have a personal income tax, which means you are also required to withhold this tax from your employee's wages. The same is true if you do business in a city or locality with an income tax.

When applying for an EIN from your state, which you will need to do business there, ask about the procedures and forms for withholding and depositing state income taxes. The place to start is with your state department of revenue.

At the end of the tax year, you must furnish copies of Form W-2 (*Wage and Tax Statement*) to each employee who worked for you during the year. Be sure to give the forms to your employees by January 31 of the year after the calendar year covered by the form. Form W-2 provides information on how much money each employee earned and the amount of federal, state and FICA taxes you withheld. You must send copies of W-2s to the Social Security Administration as well.

DECLARATION OF INDEPENDENTS

You may decide your business can't afford to hire too many full-time employees, and you'd like to use the services of an independent contractor. With an independent contractor, you don't have to withhold and pay the person's income, Social Security and Medicare taxes.

Tax Talk

Employee benefits such as health insurance and pension plan contributions provide attractive tax deductions. With a qualified pension plan, you not only receive a tax deduction for the contributions you make on behalf of your employees, but the money you contribute to your own retirement account is also deductible and is allowed to grow tax-deferred until withdrawn. (A qualified plan meets the requirements of the Employee Retirement Income Security Act [ERISA] and the Internal Revenue Code.)

There are a number of different plans available, ranging from a Savings Incentive Match Plan for Employees (SIMPLE) to a traditional 401(k) plan (see Part 4, Chapter 24). The pension design may be slightly different, but they all offer important tax benefits for business owners. So take the time to see which plan will work best for you.

As far as health insurance is concerned, if your business is incorporated and you work for it as an employee, you can deduct all costs for your own insurance as well as for the coverage for your employees. Effective for 2004 tax years and beyond, self-employed individuals can deduct 100 percent of the amount paid for health insurance for themselves and their families.

While independent contractors do translate to lower payroll costs, be advised that the IRS scrutinizes this whole area very carefully. The IRS wants to make sure that your workers are properly classified and paying the government the necessary income and payroll taxes that are due.

To stay out of hot water with the IRS, be sure the workers you classify as independent contractors meet the IRS definition of an independent contractor. The IRS has a 20-point test its auditors use to determine the proper classification. Here is a list of some of the major points:

- **WHO HAS CONTROL?** A worker is an employee if the person for whom he works has the right to direct and control him concerning when and where to do the work. The employer need not actually exercise control; it is sufficient that he has the right to do so.
- **RIGHT TO FIRE:** An employee can be fired by an employer. An independent contractor cannot be fired so long as he or she produces a result that meets the specifications of the contract.

- **TRAINING:** An employee may be trained to perform services in a particular manner. However, independent contractors ordinarily use their own methods and receive no training from the employer.
- **SET HOURS OF WORK:** Workers for whom you set specific hours of work are more likely to be employees. Independent contractors, on the other hand, usually establish their own work hours.

To stay on the right side of the IRS, it is best to document the relationship you have with any independent contractors in a written contract. This can be a simple agreement that spells out the duties of the independent contractor. The agreement should state that the independent contractor, not the employer, is responsible for withholding any necessary taxes. In addition, have the independent contractor submit invoices. Also, be sure you file Form 1099-MISC (*Miscellaneous Income*) at year-end. By law, you are required to file and give someone Form 1099 if you pay that person more than $600 a year. The form must be given to the independent contractor by January 31 of the following year. Form 1099 with its transmittal Form 1096 must be filed with the IRS by February 28 of the following year.

"Whether an individual is determined to be an independent contractor or an employee, it is required that you obtain their complete name, Social Security number and address before any money is paid. If this information is not obtained, you are required to withhold backup withholding taxes for federal income taxes," advises Jennifer Jones, a CPA in Fairfax, Virginia.

If the IRS finds you have misclassified an employee as an independent contractor, you will pay a percentage of income taxes that should have been withheld on the employee's wages and be liable for your share of the FICA and unemployment taxes, plus penalties and interest. Even worse, if the IRS determines your misclassification was "willful," you could owe the IRS the full amount of income tax that should have been withheld (with an adjustment if the employee has paid or pays part of the tax), the full amount of both the employer's and employee's share for FICA taxes (with possibly an offset if the employee paid self-employment taxes), interest and penalties.

Be advised that there is some relief being offered. If a business realizes it is in violation of the law regarding independent contractors, it can inform the IRS of the problem and then properly classify the workers without being hit with an IRS assessment for prior-year taxes.

SELECTING YOUR TAX YEAR

When you launch your business, you'll have to decide what tax year to use. The tax year is the annual accounting period used to keep your records and report your income and expenses. There are two accounting periods: a calendar year and a fiscal year.

A calendar year is 12 consecutive months starting January 1 and ending December 31. Most sole proprietors, partnerships, limited liability companies and S corporations use the calendar year as their tax year. If you operate a business as a sole proprietorship, the IRS says the tax year for your business is the same as your individual tax year.

A fiscal tax year is 12 consecutive months ending on the last day of any month other than December. For business owners who start a company during the year and have substantial expenses or losses, it may be smart to select a fiscal year that goes beyond the end of the first calendar year. This way, as much income as possible is offset by start-up expenses and losses.

FILING YOUR TAX RETURN

Your federal tax filing obligations and due dates generally are based on the legal structure you've selected for your business and whether you use a calendar or fiscal year.

■ **SOLE PROPRIETORSHIPS:** If you are a sole proprietor, every year you must file Schedule C (*Profit or Loss From Business*) with your Form 1040 (*U.S. Individual Income Tax Return*) to report your business's net profit and loss. You also must file Schedule SE (Self-Employment Tax) with your 1040. If you are a calendar-year taxpayer, your tax filing date is April 15. Fiscal-year taxpayers must file their returns no later than the 15th day of the fourth month after the end of their tax year. In addition to your annual tax return, many self-employed individuals such as sole proprietors and partners make quarterly estimated tax payments to cover their income and Social

BEWARE!

ONCE YOU HAVE SELECTED TO FILE ON EITHER A CALENDAR- OR FISCAL-YEAR BASIS, YOU HAVE TO GET PERMISSION FROM THE IRS TO CHANGE IT. TO DO SO, YOU MUST FILE FORM 1128, AND YOU MAY HAVE TO PAY A FEE.

Security tax liability. You must make estimated tax payments if you expect to owe at least $1,000 in federal tax for the year and your withholding will be less than the smaller of: 1) 90 percent of your current-year tax liability or 2) 100 percent of your previous year's tax liability if your adjusted gross income is $150,000 or less. The federal government allows you to pay estimated taxes in four equal amounts throughout the year on the 15th of April, June, September and January.

- **PARTNERSHIPS AND LIMITED LIABILITY COMPANIES (LLCs):** Companies set up with these structures must file Form 1065 (*U.S. Return of Partnership Income*) that reports income and loss to the IRS. The partnership must furnish copies of Schedule K-1 (*Partner's Share of Income, Credits, Deductions*), which is part of Form 1065, to the partners or LLC members by the filing date for Form 1065. The due dates are the same as those for sole proprietors.

- **CORPORATIONS:** If your business is structured as a regular corporation, you must file Form 1120 (*U.S. Corporation Income Tax Return*). For calendar-year taxpayers, the due date for the return is March 15. For fiscal-year corporations, the return must be filed by the 15th day of the third month after the end of your corporation's tax year.

- **S CORPORATIONS:** Owners of these companies must file Form 1120S (*U.S. Income Tax Return for an S Corporation*). Like partnerships, shareholders must receive a copy of Schedule K-1, which is part of Form 1120S. The due dates are the same as those for regular corporations.

SALES TAXES

Sales taxes vary by state and are imposed at the retail level. It's important to know the rules in the states and localities where you operate your business, because if you are a retailer, you must collect state sales tax on each sale you make.

While many states and localities exempt service businesses from sales taxes, some have recently begun to change their laws in this area and are applying the sales tax to some services. If you are a service business, contact your state revenue and/or local revenue offices for information on the laws in your area.

Before you open your doors, be sure to register to collect sales tax by applying for a sales permit for each separate place of business you have in the state. A license or permit is important because in some states it is a criminal offense to undertake sales without one. In addition, if you fail to collect sales tax, you can be held liable for the uncollected amount.

If you're an out-of-state retailer, such as a mail order seller, who ships and sells goods in another state, be careful. In the past, many retailers have not collected sales taxes on the sales of these goods. Be sure you or your accountant knows the state sales tax requirements where you do business. Just because you don't have a physical location in a state doesn't always mean you don't have to collect the sales tax.

Many states require business owners to make an advance deposit against future taxes. Some states will accept a surety bond from your insurance company in lieu of the deposit.

BRIGHT IDEA

THE IRS OFFERS STEP (SMALL BUSINESS TAX EDUCATION PROGRAM), A COOPERATIVE EFFORT WITH LOCAL ORGANIZA-TIONS TO PROVIDE BUSI-NESS TAX EDUCATION TO SMALL-BUSINESS OWN-ERS. INSTRUCTORS TEACH YOU THE TAX ADVANTAGES AND DISAD-VANTAGES OF THE VARIOUS FORMS OF BUSINESS ORGANIZATION, WHAT RECORDS TO KEEP AND HOW TO KEEP THEM, HOW TO PREPARE BUSINESS TAX RETURNS, HOW TO USE FEDERAL TAX DEPOSIT COUPONS AND MORE. THE COSTS FOR THE PROGRAM VARY—SOME ARE FREE. TO FIND OUT MORE, CALL (800) 829-1040 AND ASK FOR THE TAXPAYER EDUCATION COORDINATOR.

It's possible for retailers to defer paying sales taxes on merchandise they purchase from suppliers. Once the merchandise is sold, however, the taxes are due. The retailer adds the sales taxes (where applicable) to the purchase. To defer sales taxes, you need a reseller permit or certificate. For more details on obtaining a permit, contact your state tax department.

TAX-DEDUCTIBLE BUSINESS EXPENSES

According to the IRS, the operating costs of running your business are deductible if they are "ordinary and necessary." The IRS defines "ordinary" as expenses that are common and accepted in your field of business. "Necessary expenses" are those that are appropriate and helpful for your business. Following are some of the business expenses you may be able to deduct.

Equipment Purchases

Under the annual Section 179 expensing allowance, business owners can deduct the full cost of their equipment purchase rather than depreciating it over several years. Under prior law, the allowance was limited to $25,000.

But the Jobs and Growth Tax Relief Act of 2003 changed that by providing a temporary boost. In 2004 through 2005, the amount you can deduct quadruples to $100,000 Remember, the allowance is phased out on a dollar-for-dollar basis when qualifying assets costing over $400,000 are placed in service. For example, if a company buys $430,000 of equipment in 2004, its Section 179 allowance is cut back to $70,000.

The Job Creation and Worker Assistance Act of 2002 also provided entrepreneurs with a temporary depreciation bonus. The 2003 law expands on the 2002 law and allows small firms to deduct an additional first-year depreciation of 50 percent of the cost of most new equipment. The business owner must acquire the equipment after May 5, 2003, and before January 1, 2005, and place it in service before the January 1, 2005 date.

Business Expenses

Some common business expenses for which you can take a deduction include advertising expenses, employee benefit programs, insurance, legal and professional services, telephone and utilities costs, rent, office supplies, employee wages, membership dues to professional associations, and business publication subscriptions.

Auto Expenses

If you use your car for business purposes, the IRS allows you to either deduct your actual business-related expenses or claim the standard mileage rate, which is a specified amount of money you can deduct for each business mile you drive. The rate is generally adjusted each year by the IRS. To calculate your deduction, multiply your business miles by the standard mileage rate for the year.

If you use the standard mileage rate, the IRS says you must use it in the first year the car is available for use in your business. Later, you can use either the standard mileage rate or actual expenses method. However, if you use two or more cars for business at the same time, you cannot take the standard mileage rate for these cars. For tax purposes, be sure to keep a log of your business miles, as well

Start Me Up

The expenses you incur when launching a new business can run into a lot of money. But how do you treat them when it comes time to do your taxes? For the most part, it is not possible to claim these start-up expenses as business deductions.

But you can amortize start-up and organizational costs over a time frame of 60 months or more, as long as the expenses actually bring forth a real-live operational business. Amortization is a method of recovering (or deducting) certain capital costs over a fixed period of time.

If you spent time looking for a business but did not purchase one, however, the expenses you incurred during the search may be deductible and don't have to be spread out over five years.

The kind of costs you can amortize include advertising expenses and any wages you paid for training employees. In addition, you can amortize expenses associated with investigating the potential of starting the business, such as market or product research and site selection.

as the costs of business-related parking fees and tolls, because you can deduct these expenses.

With the actual cost method, the IRS allows you to deduct various expenses, including depreciation, gas, insurance, leasing fees, oil, repairs, tolls and parking fees. If you use this method, keep records of your car's costs during the year and multiply those expenses by the percentage of total car mileage driven for business purposes.

While using the standard mileage rate is easier for record-keeping, you may receive a larger deduction using the actual cost method. If you qualify to use both methods, the IRS recommends figuring your deduction both ways to see which gives you a larger deduction, as long as you have kept detailed records to substantiate the actual cost method.

Meal And Entertainment Expenses

To earn a deduction for business entertainment, it must be either directly related to your business or associated with it. To be deductible, meals and entertainment must be "ordinary and necessary" and not "lavish" or "extravagant." The deduction is limited to 50 percent of the cost of qualifying meals and entertainment.

To prove expenses are directly related to your business, you must show there was more than a general expectation of gaining some business benefit other than goodwill, that you conducted business during the entertainment, and active conduct of business was your main purpose.

To meet the "associated" with your business test, the entertainment must directly precede or come after a substantial business discussion. In addition, you must have had a clear business purpose when you took on the expense.

Be sure to maintain receipts for any entertainment or meal that cost $75 or more. Whatever the cost, you should record all your expenses in an account book. The information to record is the business reason for the expense, amount spent, dates, location, type of entertainment, and the name, title and occupation of the people you entertained.

Travel Expenses

You can deduct ordinary and necessary expenses you incur while traveling away from home on business. Your records should show the amount of each expense for items such as transportation, meals and

In The Red?

If you find after you've tallied up all your business deductions and subtracted them from your income that you're in the red for the year, don't despair. There's something called the net operating loss deduction that will help. It allows you to offset one year's losses against another year's income.

The IRS lets you carry this operating loss back two years and use it to offset the income of those previous two years. Doing so may result in a refund. If you still have some losses left after carrying them back, you can carry them forward for up to 20 years. If you don't want to use the two-year carryback period, you can elect to deduct the net operating loss over the next 20 years. However, once you make that election, you can't reverse it. Remember, if there is any unused loss after 20 years, you may no longer apply it to any income.

lodging. Be sure to record the date of departure and return for each trip, the number of days you spent on business, the name of the city, and the business reason for the travel or the business benefits you expect to achieve. Keep track of your cleaning and laundry expenses while traveling because these are deductible as is the cost of telephone, fax and modem usage.

Home Office

If you use a portion of your home exclusively and regularly for business, you may be able to claim the home office deduction on your annual tax return. This generally applies to sole proprietorships. To claim the deduction, the part of the home you use for your office must be your principal place of business, or you must use it to meet or deal with clients in the normal course of business. Keep in mind that you can't claim the deduction if you have an outside office as well.

Business owners who keep records, schedule appointments and perform other administrative or management activities from their home offices qualify for a deduction as long as they don't have any other fixed place of business where they do a large amount of administrative or management work. This holds true even if they don't see clients or customers in their home offices. The IRS scrutinizes this deduction very carefully, so be sure to follow the rules and keep good records. (For more on home offices, see Part 4, Chapter 18.)

DOLLAR STRETCHER

To help you wade through all the tax laws and regulations, the IRS offers these free publications: *Tax Guide for Small Business* (Publication No. 334), *Business Expenses* (Publication No. 535), *Travel, Entertainment, Gift and Car Expenses* (Publication No. 463), *Circular E, Employer's Tax Guide* (Publication No. 15), and *Employer's Supplemental Tax Guide* (Publication No. 15-A). To obtain copies of these publications, you can download them from the IRS Web site at www.irs.gov.

TAX PLANNING

As you operate your business, be on the lookout for ways to reduce your federal and state tax liability. Small-business owners typically have a lot of ups and downs from one year to the next. If you make a lot of money one year and have to pay taxes on all that profit, your business won't have the reserves needed to tide you over in some other year when business may not be as good.

That's why it's important to defer or reduce taxes whenever possible. This is a good way to cut business costs without affecting the quality of your product or service.

Throughout the year, periodically review your tax situation with the help of your accountant. If your income is increasing, look for deductions to help reduce your taxes. For example, if you are a cash-basis taxpayer, think about doing some needed business repairs or stocking up on office supplies and inventory before the end of the year. Cash-basis taxpayers can also defer income into the next year by waiting until the end of December to mail invoices.

For businesses using the accrual method, review your accounts receivable to see if anything is partially worthless. If it is, you can take a deduction for a portion of the amount of the uncollected debt. Check with your accountant to determine whether you meet IRS requirements to claim a bad-debt deduction.

Both cash and accrual taxpayers can make charitable donations before the end of the year and take deductions for them. Beware, if you donate $250 or more, a canceled check is no longer considered adequate documentation, so make sure the charity gives written substantiation of the contribution amount or a description of the property given.

HOT LINK

BELIEVE IT OR NOT, THE IRS DOES PUBLISH UNDERSTANDABLE BUSINESS TAX INFORMATION. VISIT THE SMALL BUSINESS CORNER ON ITS WEB SITE: WWW.IRS.GOV.

Tax planning is a year-long endeavor. Be sure you know what deductions are available to you, and keep good records to support them. This way, you can reap tax savings, which you can use to successfully operate and grow your business.

If At First You Don't Succeed...

Learning from your failures

W hat's the key to business success? Is it adequate capital? A good business plan? A slick advertising campaign? All these factors play crucial roles, of course, but surprisingly, many prosperous entrepreneurs say that previous business failures, more than anything else, helped them attain their current successes.

The old adage "Learn from your mistakes" may be a cliché, but thousands of successful business owners have done just that. Instead of letting business failure frustrate them, these entrepreneurs profited from the painful experience, garnering some valuable lessons they could not have learned any other way.

The following chapter will help give you a new perspective on the inevitable failures that accompany business ownership—from the customer who rejects your sales proposal to the bank that says no to your loan application. Read on...and learn how you, too, can profit from failure.

BUSINESS FAILURE

Behind every successful person lurk the remains of past failures. Consider the historic examples of Abraham Lincoln, who suffered defeat in four elections before being voted president; Babe Ruth, who struck out 1,330 times en route to hitting 714 homers, including a record 60 in the 1927 baseball season; and, more recently, Tom Monaghan, who failed in business twice before launching Domino's Pizza.

Failure hurts, traumatizes and can destroy, but it also challenges, motivates and humbles us, cutting through the illusion that success is easy. At a "failure conference" at the University of Michigan, Ann Arbor, several years ago, Warren Avis, founder of Avis Rent A Car, shared some of the business blunders that cost him bundles over the years.

"Failure has a tremendous impact from which you can derive strength if you analyze [the experience] and try to understand why you have failed," said Avis. "You cannot avoid failure, but you must quit feeling sorry for yourself and get up and try again."

As Avis' comments illustrate, there is a big difference between failure and being a failure. The true failure simply gives up; the savvy entrepreneur tries again, learns from his or her mistakes and ultimately succeeds.

Causes Of Failure

Experts and entrepreneurs have pinpointed several common causes of entrepreneurial failure:

- **UNSOUND IDEAS** (a toy that is dangerous to children or a service that the market does not need) are more than likely to fail early on. These examples illustrate the need for taking more time at the drawing board.
- **POOR PLANNING** (lack of capital or a poorly positioned product or service) can cripple or doom a viable concept early in the game, driving home the importance of a thoroughly researched and well-formulated business plan.
- **A PRODUCT WHOSE MARKET IS NOT READY FOR IT** or is already long gone (a great spacesuit or a better buggy whip) proves the importance of timing and placement.
- **IRONICALLY, SUCCESS CAN OFTEN LEAD TO FAILURE.** An entrepreneur who has never experienced failure may believe he or she is infallible, which can prevent him or her from planning for worst-case scenarios.
- **WHEN AN ENTREPRENEUR GETS PRODUCT ORDERS** that he or she lacks the money, manpower or production capacity to fill, success can also lead to failure. Many entrepreneurs don't realize that when your sales increase, you need more money—not less—to keep up with demand.
- **PERSONNEL DIFFICULTIES.** If partners or key employees disagree on the business's goals or the methods used to achieve them, power struggles may erupt that can destroy the business.
- **INADEQUATE CAPITALIZATION.** This is the most common cause of business failure, but, typically, it is precipitated by one of the causes above.

> **SMART TIP**
>
> FOR MAXIMUM BUSINESS SUCCESS, BE DISCIPLINED ABOUT RELAXING. IT SOUNDS CONTRADICTORY, BUT IT WORKS. SCHEDULE IN TIME FOR SLEEP, EXERCISE AND R&R. THEN, KEEP THOSE APPOINTMENTS AS DILIGENTLY AS YOU WOULD KEEP AN APPOINTMENT WITH AN IMPORTANT CUSTOMER. IF YOU GIVE 150 PERCENT TO YOUR BUSINESS AND HAVE NOTHING LEFT FOR YOURSELF, YOUR BUSINESS WILL SUFFER IN THE END.

Failing To Succeed

Many experts and entrepreneurs believe some degree of failure is essential to long-term success. "The more you fail, the more you succeed," contends Jack Matson, author of *Using Intelligent Fast Failure*.

To develop "intelligent failure"—the type that Matson says later forms building blocks to success—the first step is to get over the fear of failure. After all, you're constantly dealing with failure in everything you do. If one thing doesn't work, that means it has failed, so you simply try something else—both in your personal life and in your business.

Consider job seekers, for example, who schedule dozens of interviews knowing that most of them will result in rejection; inventors, who must often try hundreds of ideas to find one that works; and salespeople, who know the vast majority of cold calls will not lead to a sale. (In fact, every business begins with what could be termed a failure—an unmet need, a problem awaiting a solution.)

Look for the partial successes in any failure; these can become cornerstones for future efforts. Matson suggests a technique he calls "straffing" (Success Through Rapid Accelerated Failures). He encourages entrepreneurs to generate lots of different ideas simultaneously and try them out quickly to find out which ones work. "The usual approach is what I call 'slow, stupid failure,'" Matson explains. "You try your first idea and fail; try the second idea and fail; try the third idea and fail...and

Words From The Wise

Here's Avis Rent A Car founder Warren Avis' advice about failure, gained over years of business experience:

- **THERE'S NO SUCH THING** as the perfect deal; look for what is wrong with it.
- **DESPITE POPULAR OPINION** to the contrary, the first solution to a problem is usually not the best. Force yourself to list at least four other solutions; 80 percent of the time, one of them will be better than your original solution.
- **IF PROPERLY PUT TOGETHER**, groups make better decisions than individuals. Take advantage of the talents others possess, especially the oddball who sees things a bit differently.
- **EXPECT THE UNEXPECTED**—more often than not, it happens. Be prepared for the worst.
- **NEVER SAY NEVER.**

SMART TIP

ATTITUDE ADJUSTMENT IS KEY TO DEALING WITH STRESS. SURE, BAD THINGS HAPPEN, BUT OFTEN, THERE IS A DIFFERENCE BETWEEN REALITY AND YOUR PERCEPTION OF IT. PSYCHOLOGISTS CALL THE INTERNAL RESPONSE TO A PROBLEM "SELF-TALK," AND MANY SAY IT CAUSES MOST OF OUR STRESS. WHEN TENSION HITS, ASK YOURSELF "IS THIS REALLY A CRISIS, OR AM I MAKING A MOUNTAIN OUT OF A MOLEHILL?"

then give up." Instead, he proposes "fast, intelligent failure," in which you try out many ideas at the same time. This greatly accelerates the learning process and compresses failure time, allowing you to progress more rapidly toward a solution. Each idea will possess some positive elements that can be combined with the positive elements of other discarded ideas to form a new solution.

Creativity is crucial to the successful entrepreneur. Business owners need to develop new ways of looking at the same problems or situations. To illustrate this point, audiences at a University of Michigan failure conference were asked to build the tallest structure they could, using only notched ice cream sticks handed out by assistants. The results offered some insight into different ways of learning from failure creatively:

- **SOME PARTICIPANTS PERSISTED IN BUILDING THE SAME TYPE OF STRUCTURE DESPITE REPEATED COLLAPSES, WHILE OTHER PARTICIPANTS ALTERED THEIR DESIGNS, TRYING OUT DIFFERENT APPROACHES.** Typically, people who tried different options were able to build higher structures.

- **SOME PARTICIPANTS PEEKED AT WHAT THEIR NEIGHBORS WERE BUILDING AND BORROWED OR STOLE IDEAS.** This can be a great way to leapfrog technology. There's no sense in reinventing the wheel each time.

- **OTHER PEOPLE WORKED IN GROUPS TO POOL RESOURCES.** Groups can capitalize on each other's ideas and share in the success (or the blame if the venture is a flop).

Bouncing Back

It's got to be among the 10 most dreaded words in the English language. "No" means rejection, plain and simple. Whether it's the loss of an account, distribution or financing, it hurts.

But successful entrepreneurs quickly find ways to combat rejection. They look at it objectively and learn from it. Those who are able to overcome rejection tend to share certain traits: determination, open-mindedness and belief in themselves. Self-confidence keeps you bouncing back, no matter how much rejection comes your way.

One secret to handling rejection is so simple, many entrepreneurs never think of it: Just ask why. If you ask for an explanation of why your service isn't good enough, often rejection becomes a positive tool to help you open the next door.

BEWARE!

WANT TO KNOW WHAT WARNING SIGNS TO LOOK OUT FOR? MARK RICE, DEAN OF THE F.W. OLIN GRADUATE SCHOOL OF BUSINESS AT BABSON COLLEGE, SAYS MOST FAILURES STEM FROM ONE OF THREE CAUSES: FAILURE TO MARKET ADEQUATELY; LACK OF CAPITAL; OR INTERNAL PROBLEMS HIRING, RETAINING AND TRAINING GOOD PEOPLE. THE LAST TWO OFTEN STEM FROM TOO-RAPID GROWTH.

For example, a polite response that gets results could be something like "If you don't mind my asking, could you tell me why you're unable to distribute my product? If I knew the reason, maybe we could find a comfortable middle ground for both of us. I'd like to find a way to work with you." Customers love to be asked for help and to give advice, which helps build rapport and set the foundation for long-term relationships. And it's the long term that's important. Be patient; just because someone said no now doesn't mean they'll feel the same way six months down the road.

Businesses, like Rome, are not built in a day, but, as entrepreneurs who have weathered difficult times will attest, the end result is well worth the struggle.

Learning From Failure

The best way to protect yourself against business failure is by going back to the basics: a good business plan, a solid marketing plan, an experienced management team and adequate capitalization. Even with all those factors in place, however, there are inevitably surprises and errors along the way. The key is learning from those errors as you go along so that small failures

BEWARE!

HOW DO YOU KNOW IF PERSEVERANCE IS SMART—OR FOOLHARDY? THE KEY IS A HEALTHY ADAPTATION OF THE "IF AT FIRST YOU DON'T SUCCEED" ADAGE. YES, YOU SHOULD TRY AND TRY AGAIN—BUT YOU SHOULD TRY DIFFERENTLY OR TRY SOMETHING ELSE. IF YOU FIND YOURSELF REPEATING THE SAME MISTAKES OVER AND OVER AGAIN, IT'S TIME TO MOVE ON.

Stress Test

Problems and setbacks are made worse by stress. Yet since stress is an unavoidable part of owning your own business, you need to learn to deal with it. Here are some simple steps you can take to lessen your stress—and run a better business.

- **IDENTIFY THE "STRESS FACTORS" IN YOUR LIFE.** Be as specific as you can—not just "lack of time" or "Monday mornings"—but who or what bothers you and how much on a scale of, say, 1 to 10. Often, just the act of recognizing something as stressful releases a lot of tension.

- **MAKE A SCHEDULE, AND STICK TO IT.** Have you ever said "Just thinking about all the things I have to do makes me tired?" Stress builds when we keep reviewing what we have to do without doing it. Make lists of everything you need to start, finish, remember or worry about. Once you write it down, you can dump it from your mind.

- **DELEGATE.** You may not have employees yet, but why not call in a freelancer or a temp to help out, especially during crunch times? You can even ask a family member to help with paperwork, filing, mailing or other simple but time-consuming tasks.

- **CULTIVATE A RELAXING WORKPLACE.** Make sure you have adequate lighting, a comfortable desk and good ventilation. Work near a window, or make sure you get outside at least once a day, even if it's for just a five-minute walk down the block. Tidy up your office; this not only makes you feel less panicked psychologically, but it also helps by making it easier to find things.

- **SLEEP AND EAT RIGHT.** Make sure you get seven to eight hours' sleep per night. Eliminate fast-food meals from your diet. Drink coffee in moderation—two cups per day, max.

- **GET PHYSICAL.** Exercise is crucial in combating stress. Try doing workouts that are the opposite of your work. In other words, if you are around people all day, go for a solitary run. If you work isolated at home in a one-person office, take an aerobics class where you can enjoy socializing as well as stretching.

don't balloon into big ones.

To learn from experience, including past mistakes, we need accurate perceptions and honest self-appraisal. While denial may heal the wounds failure inflicts on our egos, the successful entrepreneur spends quite a lot of time analyzing his or her mistakes and finding innovative ways to profit from them.

Should failures, setbacks, mistakes or whatever you want to call them occur, the important thing to do is put them in the best possible perspective—and thereby learn the most useful lesson possible. Try not to look at failure from too negative a perspective, lest it become a life sentence...or, at least, a large and long-lasting rut.

Work to get out from under your failures and into your best frame of mind, to where problems yield solutions. At that point, even the very worst mistakes can be the best learning experiences. Always ask yourself "What is the lesson in this setback? What is the opportunity?" You can often assign several causes for any one failure, and you should be as clear in identifying them as you can. Observe, adjust and, when necessary, move on.

Moving on is key. Don't beat yourself up about setbacks or the past; use them to change the future. Failure is something entrepreneurs must have a high tolerance for since it is an almost inevitable step along the way to success.

There is also danger in failing to persevere despite momentarily daunting odds. Although perseverance must be based on a rational view of reality, that reality must be balanced with a courageous sense of vision. Even Alexander Graham Bell's telephone was rejected several times before it went on to revolutionize communication. The lesson to be learned here is the value of daring and persistence.

For those who listen, setbacks are good teachers. (Those who don't listen are doomed to repeat their mistakes rather than learning from them.) Besides honing business skills, setbacks can call forth an inner resiliency. Those who fail are more likely to see the big picture, take the lesson to be learned from

BEWARE!

IT'S HARD TO BE OBJECTIVE WHEN ANALYZING YOUR OWN MISTAKES. GET OUTSIDE HELP IF POSSIBLE. TRY SETTING UP AN INFORMAL "ADVISORY BOARD" INCLUDING YOUR LAWYER, ACCOUNTANT, BANKER AND COLLEAGUES. ASK THEM WHERE YOU WENT WRONG AND HOW YOU CAN MAKE IT RIGHT. THESE PEOPLE CAN ACT AS A SOUNDING BOARD, HELPING YOU MAKE SMARTER DECISIONS IN THE FUTURE.

the failure, and try to incorporate that lesson into their daily lives as well as their business lives. As a result, they are less likely to be disturbed by the daily pressures. They know not to sweat the small stuff but to concentrate on solving the big problems.

Do entrepreneurs learn more from setbacks than from successes? "Success is a reward for hard work—not a teacher," says one entrepreneur. "It is the hard lessons I've learned along the way that led to my success."

Business
Resources

ACCOUNTING AND TAXES

Associations

AMERICAN ACCOUNTING ASSOCIATION, 5717 Bessie Dr., Sarasota, FL 34233, (941) 921-7747, www.aaa-edu.org

AMERICAN INSTITUTE OF CERTIFIED PUBLIC ACCOUNTANTS, 1211 Ave. of the Americas, New York, NY 10036, (212) 596-6200, fax: (212) 596-6213, www.aicpa.org

ASSOCIATION OF CREDIT AND COLLECTION PROFESSIONALS, P.O. Box 390106, Minneapolis, MN 55439, (952) 926-6547, www.ica-credit.org

CCH INC., 4025 W. Peterson Ave., Chicago, IL 60646, (800) TELL-CCH, www.cch.com

FINANCIAL EXECUTIVES INSTITUTE, 200 Campus Dr., P.O. Box 674, Florham Park, NJ 07932, (973) 765-1000, fax: (973) 765-1018, www.fei.org

INDEPENDENT ACCOUNTANTS INTERNATIONAL, e-mail: info@accountants.org, www.accountants.org

INSTITUTE OF CERTIFIED MANAGEMENT ACCOUNTANTS, 10 Paragon Dr., Montvale, NJ 07645, (800) 638-4427 or (201) 573-9000, fax: (201) 573-0559, www.imanet.org

Books

ACCOUNTING AND RECORDKEEPING MADE EASY FOR THE SELF-EMPLOYED, Jack Fox, John Wiley & Sons, www.wiley.com

DAY-TO-DAY BUSINESS ACCOUNTING, Arlene K. Mose, John Jackson and Gary Downs, Prentice Hall

THE McGRAW-HILL 36-HOUR ACCOUNTING COURSE, Robert L. Dixon and Harold E. Arnett, McGraw-Hill Trade

SIMPLIFIED SMALL BUSINESS ACCOUNTING, Daniel Sitarz, Nova Publishing, 1103 West College St., Carbondale, IL 62901, (800) 462-6420, fax: (618) 457-2541, www.novapublishing.com

SMART TAX WRITE-OFFS: HUNDREDS OF TAX DEDUCTION IDEAS FOR HOME-BASED BUSINESSES, Independent Contractors, All Entrepreneurs, Norm Ray, Rayve Productions, P.O. Box 726, Windsor, CA 95492, (800) 852-4890

THE VEST POCKET CPA, Nicky A. Dauber, Joel G. Siegel and Jae K. Shim, Prentice Hall Press

Magazines And Publications

ACCOUNTING OFFICE MANAGEMENT & ADMINISTRATION REPORT, 29 W. 35th St., 5th Fl., New York, NY 10001, (212) 244-0360, www.ioma.com

ACCOUNTING PERIODS AND METHODS (IRS Publication #538), www.irs.gov

MANAGEMENT ACCOUNTING QUARTERLY, Institute of Management Accounting, 10 Paragon Dr., Montvale, NJ 07645, (800) 638-4427, ext. 265, fax: (201) 573-0559, e-mail: sfmag@imanet.org, www.mamag.com

STARTING A BUSINESS AND KEEPING RECORDS, (IRS Publication #583), www.irs.gov

THE TAX ADVISER, Harborside Financial Center, 201 Plaza 3, Jersey City, NJ 07311-3881, (888) 777-7077, fax: (201) 521-5447, www.aicpa.org/pubs/taxadv/index.htm

TAXES—THE TAX MAGAZINE, CCH Inc., 4025 W. Peterson Ave., Chicago, IL 60646, (800) TELL-CCH, www.cch.com

YOUR TAX QUESTIONS ANSWERED, E. Slott & Co. 100 Merrick Rd., #200 E., Rockville Centre, NY 11570, (516) 336-8282, fax: (516) 536-8852, www.irahelp.com

ADVERTISING AND MARKETING

Associations

AMERICAN ADVERTISING FEDERATION, 1101 Vermont Ave. NW, #500, Washington, DC 20005, (202) 898-0089, fax: (202) 898-0159, e-mail: aaf@aaf.org, www.aaf.org

AMERICAN MARKETING ASSOCIATION, 311 S. Wacker Dr., #5800, Chicago, IL 60606, (800) AMA-1150, (312) 542-9000, fax: (312) 542-9001, e-mail: info@ama.org, www.ama.org

ASSOCIATION OF NATIONAL ADVERTISERS, 708 Third Ave., New York, NY 10017-4270, (212) 697-5950, fax: (212) 661-8057, www.ana.net

DIRECT MARKETING ASSOCIATION, 1120 Ave. of the Americas, New York, NY 10036, (212) 768-7277, fax: (212) 302-6714, www.the-dma.org

MARKETING RESEARCH ASSOCIATION, 1344 Silas Deane Hwy., #306, P.O. Box 230, Rocky Hill, CT 06067-0230, (860) 257-4008, fax: (860) 257-3990, e-mail: email@mra-net.org, www.mra-net.org

OUTDOOR ADVERTISING ASSOCIATION OF AMERICA, 1850 M St. NW, #1040, Washington, DC 20036, (202) 833-5566, www.oaaa.org

RADIO ADVERTISING BUREAU, 1320 Greenway Dr., #500, Irving, TX 75038, (800) 232-3131, www.rab.com

Books

THE ADVERTISING HANDBOOK FOR SMALL BUSINESS: MAKE A BIG IMPACT WITH A SMALL BUDGET, Dell Dennison, Self-Counsel Press, www.self-counsel.com

ADVERTISING ON THE INTERNET, Robbin Zeff and Bradley Aronson, John Wiley & Sons, www.wiley.com

THE BUILDING BLOCKS OF BUSINESS WRITING, Jack Swenson, Crisp Publications, (800) 442-7477

THE COMPLETE IDIOT'S GUIDE TO MARKETING BASICS, Sarah White, Alpha Books

GETTING BUSINESS TO COME TO YOU: A COMPLETE DO-IT-YOURSELF GUIDE TO ATTRACTING ALL THE BUSINESS YOU CAN ENJOY, Paul and Sarah Edwards and Laura Clampitt Douglas, J.P. Tarcher

GUERRILLA ADVERTISING: Secrets for Making Big Profits From Your Small Business, Jay Conrad Levinson, Houghton Mifflin

GUERRILLA MARKETING FOR THE HOME-BASED BUSINESS, Jay Conrad Levinson and Seth Godin, Houghton Mifflin

HOW TO SAY IT: CHOICE WORDS, PHRASES, SENTENCES & PARAGRAPHS FOR EVERY SITUATION, Rosalie Maggio, Prentice Hall

SELLING THE INVISIBLE: A FIELD GUIDE TO MODERN MARKETING, Harry Beckwith, Warner Books

SIX STEPS TO FREE PUBLICITY: AND DOZENS OF OTHER WAYS TO WIN FREE MEDIA ATTENTION FOR YOUR BUSINESS, Marcia Yudkin, Plume

SUCCESSFUL SALES & MARKETING: SMART WAYS TO BOOST YOUR BOTTOM LINE, Entrepreneur Media Inc., (800) 421-2300, www.smallbizbooks.com

Magazines And Publications

ADCRAFTER, 3011 W. Grand Bl., #1715, Detroit, MI 48202, (313)872-7850, fax: (313) 872-7858, e-mail: adcraft@adcraft.com, www.adcraft.org

ADVERTISING AGE, 711 Third Ave., New York, NY 10017, (212) 210-0100, fax: (212) 210-0200, www.adage.com

ADVERTISING/COMMUNICATIONS TIMES, 123 Chestnut St., #202, Philadelphia, PA 19106, (215) 629-1666, fax: (215) 923-8358, e-mail: adcomtimes@aol.com, www.adcommtimes.com

ADWEEK, 770 Broadway, New York, NY 10003, (646) 654-5336, fax: (646) 654-5365, www.adweek.com

AMERICAN ADVERTISING, 1101 Vermont Ave. NW, #500, Washington, DC 20005, (202) 898-0089, fax: (202) 898-0159, e-mail: aaf@aaf.org, www.aaf.org

AMERICAN DEMOGRAPHICS, 11 Riverbend Dr. S., P.O. Box 4274, Stamford, CT 06907-0247, (203) 358-9900, www.demographics.com

B TO B, AD AGE, 360 Michigan Ave., Chicago, IL 60601, (312) 649-5200, www.netb2b.com

DIRECT MAGAZINE, 11 Riverbend Dr. S., Box 4949, Stamford, CT 06907-0265, (203) 358-9900, fax: (203) 358-5821, www.directmag.com

DIRECT MARKETING NEWS, 100 Avenue of the Americas, New York, NY 10013, (212) 925-7300, fax: (212) 925-8752, www.dmnews.com

JOURNAL OF MARKETING RESEARCH, American Marketing Association, 311 S. Wacker Dr., #5800, Chicago, IL 60606-5819, (800) AMA-1150, www.ama.org/pubs/jmr

MEDIA CENTRAL (publishes *American Demographics, Inside.com*), 11 Riverbend Dr. S., P.O. Box 4278, Stanford, CT 06907, (203) 358-9900, www.mediacentral.com

QUIRK'S MARKETING RESEARCH REVIEW, 8030 Cedar Ave. S., #229, Minneapolis, MN 55425, (612) 854-5101, www.quirks.com

TRADESHOW WEEK, 5700 Wilshire Blvd., #120, Los Angeles, CA 90036, (323)965-5300, fax: (323) 965-5330, www.tradeshowweek.com

CREDIT SERVICES

DUN & BRADSTREET (provides business credit-reporting services), (800) 234-3867, www.dnb.com

EQUIFAX (provides credit-reporting services), (800) 685-1111, www.equifax.com

EXPERIAN provides credit-reporting services), (800) 682-7654, www.experian.com

FIRST DATA MERCHANT SERVICES CORP. (provides credit-processing services), 6200 South Quebec St., Greenwood Village, CO 80111, (800) 735-3362, (303) 488-8000, www.firstdata.com

TELECHECK (provides check-guarantee services), 5251 Westheimer, Houston, TX 77056, (800) TELE-CHECK, www.telecheck.com

TRANSUNION (provides credit-reporting services), (800) 916-8800, www.transunion.com

CUSTOMER SERVICE

Books

DELIVERING KNOCK YOUR SOCKS OFF SERVICE, Kristen Anderson and Ron Zemke, Amacom

KNOCK YOUR SOCKS OFF ANSWERS: SOLVING CUSTOMER NIGHTMARES & SOOTHING NIGHTMARE CUSTOMERS, Kristen Anderson and Ron Zenke, Amacom

POSITIVELY OUTRAGEOUS SERVICE, T. Scott Gross, Warner Books

RAVING FANS: A REVOLUTIONARY APPROACH TO CUSTOMER SERVICE, Ken Blanchard and Sheldon Bowles, William Morrow & Co.

EQUIPMENT

Cellular Phones

MOTOROLA PERSONAL COMMUNICATIONS, 600 N. Hwy. 45, Libertyville, IL 60048, (800) 331-6456, www.motorola.com

OKI TELECOM, 70 Crestridge Dr., #150, Suwanee, GA 30024, (678) 482-9640, fax: (678) 482-9142, www.oki.com

PANASONIC TELECOMMUNICATIONS SYSTEMS CO., 2 Panasonic Wy., Secaucus, NJ 07094, (800) 414-4408, www.panasonic.com

UNIDEN AMERICA, 4700 Amon Carter Blvd., Ft. Worth, TX 76155, (800) 235-3874, www.uniden.com

Computers

APPLE COMPUTER, 1 Infinite Loop, Cupertino, CA 95014, (800) 767-2775, (408) 996-1010, www.apple.com

COMPAQ COMPUTER, P.O. Box 692000, Houston, TX 77269-2000, (800) 345-1518, (281) 370-0670, fax: (281) 514-1740, www.compaq.com

HEWLETT-PACKARD, 3000 Hanover St., Palo Alto, CA 94304, (800) 752-0900, (650) 857-1501, www.hp.com

IBM, 1133 Westchester Ave., White Plains, NY 10604, 888-IBM-5800, www.ibm.com

Copiers/Fax Machines

CANON USA, 1 Canon Plaza, Lake Success, NY 11042, (800) 652-2666, (516) 328-5000, www.usa.canon.com

SHARP ELECTRONICS, Sharp Plaza, Mahwah, NJ 07430, (800) 237-4277, www.sharp-usa.com

XEROX, 800 Long Ridge Rd., Stamford, CT 06902, (800) ASK-XEROX, www.xerox.com

Mailing Equipment

NEOPOST, 30955 Huntwood Ave., Hayward, CA 94544-7084, (800) 624-7892, fax: (510) 487-6746, www.neopost.com

Software

EUDORA (e-mail software), Qualcomm Inc., 5775 Morehouse Dr., San Diego, CA 92121, (800) 2-EUDORA, (858) 587-1121, fax: (858) 658-2100, e-mail: eudora-custserv@eudora.com, www.eudora.com

INTUIT (Quicken & Quickbooks), 2535 Garcia Ave., Mountain View, CA 94039-7850, (650) 944-6000, www.quicken.com

LOTUS (SmartSuite, Approach, 1-2-3 Organizer), IBM Corp., 1133 Westchester Ave., White Plains, NY 10604, (888) IBM-5800, www.lotus.com

MICROSOFT (Windows, Word, Excel, Microsoft Office, Access, Front Page Publisher), 1 Microsoft Wy., Redmond, WA 98052-6399, (800) 426-9400, (425) 882-8080, fax: (425) 936-7329, www.microsoft.com

SYMANTEC (Norton Utilities, Norton Antivirus), 20330 Stevens Creek Bl., Cupertino, CA 95014-2132, (408) 517-8000, www.symantec.com

FRANCHISE AND BUSINESS OPPORTUNITIES

Association

AMERICAN ASSOCIATION OF FRANCHISEES AND DEALERS, P.O. Box 81887, San Diego, CA 92138-1887, (800) 733-9858, fax: (619) 209-

3777, e-mail: benefits@aafd.org, www.aafd.org

Books

FRANCHISING AND LICENSING: TWO WAYS TO BUILD YOUR BUSINESS, Andrew J. Sherman, Amacom

HOME BUSINESSES YOU CAN BUY: THE DEFINITIVE GUIDE TO EXPLORING FRANCHISES, MULTI-LEVEL MARKETING AND BUSINESS OPPORTUNITIES, PLUS HOW TO AVOID SCAMS, Paul and Sarah Edwards and Walter Zooi, Putnam

220 BEST FRANCHISES TO BUY, Lynie Arden, Philip Lief Group, Broadway Books, www.randomhouse.com/broadwaybooks

GENERAL SMALL-BUSINESS RESOURCES

Associations

AMERICAN MANAGEMENT ASSOCIATION, 1601 Broadway, New York, NY 10019, (212) 586-8100, (800) 262-9699, fax: (212) 903-8168, www.amanet.org

CENTER FOR ENTREPRENEURIAL MANAGEMENT INC., 295 Greenwich St., #514, Penthouse, New York, NY 10007, (212) 925-7911, fax: (212) 925-7463, www.ceoclubs.org

THE EDWARD LOWE FOUNDATION, 58220 Decatur Rd., P.O. Box 8, Cassopolis, MI 49031, (800) 232-LOWE, (616) 445-4200, www.lowe.org

EQUIPMENT LEASING ASSOCIATION OF AMERICA, 4301 N. Fairfax Dr., #550, Arlington, VA 22203, (703) 527-8655, fax: (703) 522-7099, www.elaonline.com

EXECUTIVE SUITE ASSOCIATION (provides executive suite location assistance), 200 E. Campus View Bl., #200, Columbus, OH 43235, (614) 985-3633, fax: (614) 985-3601, e-mail: esacentral@aol.com, www.execsuites.org

INDEPENDENT INSURANCE AGENTS OF AMERICA, 127 S. Payton St., Alexandria, VA 22314, (800) 221-7917, fax: (703) 683-7556, e-mail: info@iiaa.org, www.independentagent.com

THE NATIONAL ASSOCIATION FOR THE SELF-EMPLOYED, P.O. Box 612067, DFW Airport, Dallas, TX 75261-2067, (800) 232-6273, fax: (800) 551-4446, www.nase.org

NATIONAL ASSOCIATION OF PROFESSIONAL EMPLOYEE ORGANIZATIONS,

901 N. Pitt St., #150, Alexandria, VA 22314, (703) 836-0466, fax: (703) 836-0976, e-mail: info@napeo.org, www.napeo.org

THE NATIONAL MANAGEMENT ASSOCIATION, 2210 Arbor Blvd., Dayton, OH 45439, (937) 294-0421, www.nma1.org

NATIONAL RESOURCE CENTER FOR CONSUMERS OF LEGAL SERVICES, 6596 Main St., Gloucester, VA 23061, (804) 693-9330, fax: (804) 693-7363, e-mail: info@nrccls.org, www.nrccls.org

SMALL BUSINESS SERVICE BUREAU, 544 Main St., Worcester, MA 01615-0014, (800) 343-0939, e-mail: membership@sbsb.com, www.sbsb.com

SOCIETY OF INDUSTRIAL AND OFFICE REALTORS, 700 11th St. NW, #510, Washington, DC 20001-4507, (202) 737-1150, fax: (202) 737-8796, www.sior.com

Books

THE BUYER'S GUIDE TO BUSINESS INSURANCE, Don Bury, Psi Research-Oasis Press

THE EMPLOYER'S LEGAL HANDBOOK, Fred Steingold, Nolo.com, 950 Parker St., Berkeley, CA 94710, (800) 728-3555, fax: (800) 645-0895, www.nolo.com

THE ENTREPRENEUR SMALL BUSINESS PROBLEM SOLVER: AN ENCYCLOPEDIC REFERENCE AND GUIDE, William Cohen, John Wiley & Sons, www.wiley.com

THE HOME OFFICE AND SMALL BUSINESS ANSWER BOOK: SOLUTIONS TO THE MOST FREQUENTLY ASKED QUESTIONS ABOUT STARTING AND RUNNING HOME OFFICES AND SMALL BUSINESSES, Janet Attard, Henry Holt

HOW TO MAKE MILLIONS WITH YOUR IDEAS: AN ENTREPRENEUR'S GUIDE, Dan S. Kennedy, Plume

INSURING THE BOTTOM LINE: HOW TO PROTECT YOUR COMPANY FROM LIABILITIES, CATASTROPHES AND OTHER BUSINESS RISKS, David Russell, Silver Lake Publishing

INTERVIEWING AND SELECTING HIGH PERFORMERS, Richard H. Beatty, John Wiley & Sons, www.wiley.com

THE PORTABLE MBA IN ENTREPRENEURSHIP, William D. Bygrave, John Wiley & Sons, www.wiley.com

SECRETS OF SELF-EMPLOYMENT: SURVIVING AND THRIVING ON THE UPS AND DOWNS OF BEING YOUR OWN BOSS, Paul and Sarah Edwards, Putnam

HIRING TOP PERFORMERS, Bob Adams and Peter Veruki, Adams Media, www.adamsmedia.com

VISIONARY BUSINESS: AN ENTREPRENEUR'S GUIDE TO SUCCESS, Marc Allen, New World Library

Magazines And Publications

BARRON'S, THE DOW JONES BUSINESS AND FINANCIAL WEEKLY, 200 Liberty St., New York, NY 10281, (800) 369-2834, fax: (609) 520-4731, www.barrons.com

THE BUSINESS OWNER, 16 Fox Ln., Locust Valley, NY 11560, (516) 671-8100, fax: (516) 671-8099

BUSINESSWEEK, 1221 Ave. of the Americas, 43rd Fl., New York, NY 10020, (800) 635-1200, www.businessweek.com

ENTREPRENEURIAL MANAGER'S NEWSLETTER, Center for Entrepreneurial Management, 295 Greenwich St., #514, New York, NY 10007, (212) 925-7911, www.ceoclubs.org

ENTREPRENEUR MAGAZINE, Entrepreneur Media Inc., 2445 McCabe Way, #400, Irvine, CA 92614, (949) 261-2325, www.entrepreneur.com

THE PRICING ADVISOR, 3277 Roswell Rd., #620, Atlanta, GA 30305, (770) 509-9933, fax: (770) 509-1963, e-mail: info@pricingsociety.com, www.pricing-advisor.com

THE WALL STREET JOURNAL, (800) 568-7625, www.wsj.com

HOMEBASED BUSINESS RESOURCES

Associations

AMERICAN ASSOCIATION OF HOME-BASED BUSINESSES, (888) 823-2366, e-mail: dsb@jbsba.com, www.jbsba.com

AMERICAN HOME BUSINESS ASSOCIATION, 17 Harkim Rd., Greenwich, CT 06831, (203) 531-8552, www.homebusiness.com

HOME BUSINESS INSTITUTE, P.O. Box 480215, Delray Beach, FL 33448, (888) DIAL-HBI, (561) 865-0865, www.hbiweb.com

MOTHER'S HOME BUSINESS NETWORK, P.O. Box 423, East Meadow, NY 11554, (516) 997-7394, fax: (516) 997-0839, www.homeworkingmom.com

NATIONAL ASSOCIATION OF HOME BASED BUSINESSES, 10451 Mill Run Cir., Owings Mills, MD 21117, (410) 363-3698, www.usahomebusiness.com

Books

THE HOME BASED BUSINESS OCCUPATIONAL HANDBOOK, National Association of Home Based Businesses, 10451 Mill Run Cir., Ownings

Mills, MD 21117, (410) 363-3698, www.usahomebusiness.com

THE HOME TEAM: HOW TO LIVE LOVE'S WORK AT HOME, Scott Gregory and Shirley Silvk Gregory, Panda Publishing, www.bookhome.com

THE PERFECT BUSINESS: HOW TO MAKE A MILLION FROM HOME WITH NO PAYROLL, NO EMPLOYEE HEADACHES, NO DEBTS AND NO SLEEPLESS NIGHTS!, Michael Leboeuf, Fireside

START AND RUN A PROFITABLE HOME-BASED BUSINESS, Edna Sheedy, Self-Counsel Press

WORKING FROM HOME: EVERYTHING YOU NEED TO KNOW ABOUT LIVING AND WORKING UNDER THE SAME ROOF, Paul and Sarah Edwards, Putnam

INVENTORS AND IDEA PROTECTION

Associations

AFFILIATED INVENTORS FOUNDATION INC., 1405 Potter Dr., #107, Colorado Springs, CO 80909, (800) 525-5885, www.affiliatedinventors. com

AMERICAN SOCIETY OF INVENTORS, P.O. Box 58426, Philadelphia, PA 19102, (215) 546-6601, www.americaninventor.org

INNOVATION ASSESSMENT CENTER, Washington State University, P.O. Box 644851, Pullman, WA 99164-4851, (509) 335-1576, fax: (509) 335-0949, www.cbe.wsu.edu/~entrep/iac

INVENTION SERVICES INTERNATIONAL (sponsors the Invention Convention Trade Show), (800) 458-5624, www.inventionconvention. com

THE INVENTORS ASSISTANCE LEAGUE INTERNATIONAL INC., 403 S. Central Ave., Glendale, CA 91204, (818) 246-6546, (877) IDEA-BIN, fax: (818) 244-1882, www.inventions.org

NATIONAL INVENTORS FOUNDATION, 403 S. Central Ave., Glendale, CA 91204, (818) 246-6546, (877) IDEA-BIN, www.inventions.org

Books

BRINGING YOUR PRODUCT TO MARKET, Entrepreneur Media Inc., (800) 421-2300, www.smallbizbooks.com

HOW TO LICENSE YOUR MILLION DOLLAR IDEA: EVERYTHING YOU NEED TO KNOW TO MAKE MONEY FROM YOUR NEW PRODUCT IDEA, Harvey Reese, John Wiley & Sons, www.wiley.com

THE INVENTOR'S NOTEBOOK, Fred E. Grissom, David Pressman,

Nolo.com, 950 Parker St., Berkeley, CA 94710, (800) 992-6656, (510) 549-1976

How to Register Your Own Trademark, Mark Warda, Sourcebooks Inc., 121 N. Washington St., Naperville, IL 60540, (800) 43-BRIGHT

ONLINE SERVICES AND THE INTERNET

Internet

Small Business Showcase, (800) 706-6225, (888) 354-3335, fax: (817) 428-4269, www.sbshow.com

24-7 Media, 1250 Broadway, 28th Fl., New York, NY 10010, (212) 231-7100, fax: (212) 760-1774, www.247media.com

Internet Resources

Accounting Software Directory, www.cpanews.com

Boardwatch Magazine (provides Internet service information and Internet service provider directories), Light Reading, 23 Leonard St., New York, NY, (212) 925-0020, www.boardwatch.com

The Dialog Corp., 11000 Regency Pkwy., #10, Cary, NC 27511, (919) 462-8600, www.dialog.com

Dow Jones Interactive Publishing, Dow Jones & Co., Customer Service, P.O. Box 300, Princeton, NJ 08543-0300, (800) 369-7466, www.dowjones.com

ICANN (Internet Corp. for Assigned Names & Numbers) (Web site domain name registration), 4676 Admiralty Wy., #330, Marina Del Rey, CA 90292, (310) 823-9358, fax: (310) 823-8649, e-mail: icann@ icann.org, www.icann.org

Marketing on the Internet, Jill H. Ellsworth and Matthew V. Ellsworth, John Wiley & Sons, www.wiley.com

Online Law: The SPA's Legal Guide to Doing Business on the Internet, Andrew R. Basile Jr. and Geoffrey Gilbert, Addison-Wesley

Rules of the Net: On-Line Operating Instructions for Human Beings, Gerald Van Der Leun and Thomas Mandel, Hyperion

Submit It! (free service that promotes your Web site to online directories and search engines), www.submit-it.com

U.S. Business Advisor (division of the Small Business Administration), www.business.gov

THE VIRTUAL OFFICE SURVIVAL HANDBOOK: WHAT TELECOMMUTERS AND ENTREPRENEURS NEED TO SUCCEED IN TODAY'S NONTRADITIONAL WORKPLACE, Alice Bredin, John Wiley & Sons, www.wiley.com

THE WHOLE INTERNET USER'S GUIDE AND CATALOG, O'Reilly & Associates, 101 Morris St., Sebastopol, CA 95472-3858, (800) 998-9938, fax: (707) 829-0104, www.oreilly.com

WORLD WIDE WEB MARKETING: INTEGRATING THE INTERNET INTO YOUR MARKETING STRATEGY, Jim Sterne, John Wiley & Sons, www.wiley.com

YOUR PERSONAL NET STUDY: YOUR COMPLETE GUIDE TO THE INTERNET & ONLINE SERVICES, Michael Wolff, Dell Publishing

Internet Service Providers

AT&T WORLDNET SERVICE, AT&T Customer Service, P.O. Box 563, Morrisville, NC 27560, (800) 967-5363, www.att.com

EARTHLINK, 1430 Peachtree St. NW, #400, Atlanta, GA 30309, (800) 395-8425, www.earthlink.net

Online Services

AMERICA ONLINE, 22000 AOL Wy., Dulles, VA 20166, (800) 827-6364, (703) 448-8700, www.aol.com

COMPUSERVE, 5000 Arlington Centre Blvd., Columbus, OH 43220, (800) 854-7595, www.compuserve.com

MICROSOFT NETWORK ONLINE SERVICE, Attn: MSN Customer Service, P.O. Box 42045, St. Petersburg, Fl 33742-2045, (800) 386-5550, (425) 635-7019, www.msn.com

NETSCAPE COMMUNICATIONS CORP., 501 E. Middlefield Rd., Mountain View, CA 94043, (800) 638-7483, (650) 254-1900, www.netscape.com

PRODIGY, 65 River Place Bl., Bldg. III, Austin, TX 78730, (800) 213-0992, www.prodigy.com

Web Browsers

MICROSOFT INTERNET EXPLORER, 1 Microsoft Wy., Redmond, WA 98052, (800) 386-5550, (425) 635-7019, www.microsoft.com

NETSCAPE COMMUNICATOR, Netscape Communications, 501 E. Middlefield Rd., Mountain View, CA 94043, (800) 638-7483, (650) 254-1900, fax: (650) 528-4124, www.netscape.com/company

Web Search Engines

ALTAVISTA, www.altavista.com
EXCITE, www.excite.com
GOOGLE, www.google.com
HOTBOT, www.hotbot.com
LYCOS, www.lycos.com
WEBCRAWLER, www.webcrawler.com
YAHOO!, www.yahoo.com

START-UP ASSISTANCE

Associations

AMERICAN BANKERS ASSOCIATION, 1120 Connecticut Ave. NW, Washington, DC 20037, (800) BANKERS, www.aba.com

AMERICAN LEAGUE OF FINANCIAL INSTITUTIONS, 900 19th St. NW, #400, Washington, DC 20006, (202) 628-5624, www.alfi.org

AMERICA'S COMMUNITY BANKERS, 900 19th St. NW, #400, Washington, DC 20006, (202) 857-3100, fax: (202) 296-8716, e-mail: info@acbankers.org, www.acbankers.org

ASSOCIATION OF SMALL BUSINESS DEVELOPMENT CENTERS, 8990 Burke Lake Rd., Burke, VA 22015, (703) 764-9850, fax: (703) 764-1234, e-mail: info@asbdc-us.org, www.asbdc-us.org

COMMERCIAL FINANCE ASSOCIATION, 225 W. 34th St., #1815, New York, NY 10122, (212) 594-3490, fax: (212) 564-6053, www.cfa.com

INDEPENDENT BANKERS ASSOCIATION OF AMERICA, 1 Thomas Cir. NW, #400, Washington, DC 20005, (202) 659-8111, fax: (202) 659-3604, e-mail: info@icba.org, www.ibaa.org

NATIONAL ASSOCIATION OF SMALL BUSINESS INVESTMENT COMPANIES, 666 11th St. NW, #750, Washington, DC 20001, (202) 628-5055, fax: (202) 628-5080, e-mail: nasbic@nasbic.org, www.nasbic.org

NATIONAL BUSINESS INCUBATION ASSOCIATION (provides incubator location assistance), 20 E. Circle Dr., #190, Athens, OH 45701-3751, (740) 593-4331, fax: (740) 593-1996, www.nbia.org

NATIONAL VENTURE CAPTIAL ASSOCIATION, 1655 N. Ft. Myer Dr., #850, Arlington, VA 22209, (703) 524-2549, fax: (703) 524-3940, www.nvca.org

SERVICE CORPS OF RETIRED EXECUTIVES (National Office), 409 Third St. SW, 6th Fl., Washington, DC 20024, (800) 634-0245, www.score.org

Books

BUSINESS PLAN EXAMPLE, American Institute of Small Business, 7515 Wayzata Blvd., Minneapolis, MN 55426, (800) 328-2906, fax: (612) 545-7020

CAPITAL RAISING REFERENCES FOR SMALL BUSINESSES, National Association of Small Business Investment Companies Direct, 666 11th St. NW, #750, Washington, DC 20001, (202) 628-5055, fax: (202) 628-5080, e-mail: nasbic@nasbic.org, www.nasbic.org

CREATING A SUCCESSFUL BUSINESS PLAN: A STEP-BY-STEP GUIDE TO WRITING A WINNING BUSINESS PLAN, Entrepreneur Media Inc., (800) 421-2300, www.smallbizbooks.com

EASY FINANCIALS FOR YOUR HOME-BASED BUSINESS: THE FRIENDLY GUIDE TO SUCCESSFUL MANAGEMENT SYSTEMS FOR BUSY HOME ENTREPRENEURS, Norm Ray, Rayve Productions, P.O. Box 726, Windsor, CA 95492, (800) 852-4890, fax: (707) 838-2220, e-mail: ravepro@aol.com, www.spannet.org/rayve

THE FAST FORWARD MBA IN FINANCE, John A. Tracy, John Wiley & Sons, www.wiley.com

FINANCING YOUR SMALL BUSINESS, Entrepreneur Media Inc., (800) 421-2300, www.smallbizbooks.com

GUERILLA FINANCING: ALTERNATIVE TECHNIQUES TO FINANCE ANY SMALL BUSINESS, Bruce Jon Blechman and Jay Conrad Levinson, Houghton Mifflin

UNDERSTANDING FINANCIAL STATEMENTS, Lyn M. Fraser, Prentice Hall

Magazines And Publications

BANKERS DIGEST, 9550 Forest Ln., #125, Dallas, TX 75243, (214) 221-4544, fax: (214) 221-4546, e-mail: Bankersd@Airmail.Net, www.bankersdigest.com

BUSINESS CREDIT, (800) 955-8815, (410) 740-5560, fax: (410) 740-5574, www.nacm.org/bcmag/bcm_index.html

CORPORATE FINANCING WEEK, 477 Madison Ave., New York, NY 10022, (212) 224-3800, fax: (212) 224-3491, www.corporatefinancingweek.com

CREDIT, AMERICAN FINANCIAL SERVICES ASSOCIATION, 919 18th St. NW, Washington, DC 20006, (202) 296-5544, fax: (202) 223-0321, www.americanfinsvcs.org

D&B REPORTS, 1 Diamond Hill Rd., Murray Hill, NJ 07974, (800) 234-3867, (908) 665-5000, fax: (908) 665-5803, www.dnb.com

TMA JOURNAL, 7315 Wisconsin Ave., #600, Bethesda, MD 20814, (301) 907-2862, fax: (301) 907-2864, www.afponline.org

Government Listings

GOVERNMENT AGENCIES

COPYRIGHT CLEARANCE CENTER, 222 Rosewood Dr., Danvers, MA 01923, (978) 750-8400, www.copyright.com

COPYRIGHT OFFICE, Library of Congress, 101 Independence Ave. SE, Washington, DC 20559-6000, (202) 707-3000, www.loc.gov/copyright

DEPARTMENT OF AGRICULTURE,1400 Independence Ave. SW, Washington, DC 20250, (202) 720-7420, www.usda.gov

DEPARTMENT OF COMMERCE, 1401 Constitution Ave. NW, Washington, DC 20230, (202) 482-2000, fax: (202) 482-5270, www.doc.gov

DEPARTMENT OF ENERGY, 1000 Independence Ave. SW, Washington, DC 20585, (800) 342-5363 or (202) 586-5000, www.doe.gov

DEPARTMENT OF INTERIOR, 1849 C St. NW, Washington, DC 20240, (202) 208-3100, www.doi.gov

DEPARTMENT OF LABOR, 200 Constitution Ave. NW, Rm. S-1004, Washington, DC 20210, (866) 487-2365 or (202) 219-6666, www.dol.gov

DEPARTMENT OF TREASURY, Main Treasury Bldg., 1500 Pennsylvania Ave. NW, Washington, DC 20220, (202) 622-1502, www.ustreas.gov

EXPORT-IMPORT BANK OF THE UNITED STATES, 11 Vermont Ave. NW, #911, Washington, DC 20571, (800) 565-3946, ext. 3908 or (202) 565-3940, www.exim.gov

FEDERAL COMMUNICATIONS COMMISSION, 445 12th St. SW,

20544, (885) 225-5322, www.ftc.gov

FEDERAL TRADE COMMISSION, 600 Pennsylvania Ave. NW, Washington, DC, 20580, (202) 326-2222, www.ftc.gov

INTERNATIONAL MAIL CALCULATOR, http://ircalc.usps.gov

IRS, 1111 Constitution Ave. NW, Washington, DC 20224, (202) 622-5000, www.irs.ustreas.gov

U.S. CONSUMER PRODUCT SAFETY COMMISSION, Office of Compliance, 4330 East-West Hwy., Bethesda, MD 20814, (301) 504-0990, www.cpsc.gov

U.S. FOOD AND DRUG ADMINISTRATION, 5600 Fishers Ln., Rockville, MD 20857, (888) 463-6332, www.fda.gov

U.S. PATENT & TRADEMARK OFFICE, Crystal Plaza 3, Rm. 2C02, Washington, DC 20231, (800) 786-9199, www.uspto.gov

U.S. PRINTING OFFICE, Superintendent of Documents, Washington, DC 20402, (202) 512-1800, www.access.gpo.gov

SECURITIES & EXCHANGE COMMISSION, 450 Fifth St. NW, Washington, DC 20549, (202) 942-8088, www.sec.gov

SMALL BUSINESS ADMINISTRATION, 409 Third St. SW, Washington, DC 20416, (800) 827-5722, www.sba.gov

SBA DISTRICT OFFICES

The SBA has several types of field offices. The district offices offer the fullest range of services. To access all district office Web sites, go to www.sba.gov/regions/states.html.

ALABAMA: 801 Tom Martin Dr., Birmingham, AL 35211, (205) 290-7101

ALASKA: 510 L St., #310, Anchorage, AK 99501, (907) 271-4022

ARIZONA: 2828 N. Central Ave., #800, Phoenix, AZ 85004-1093, (602) 745-7200

ARKANSAS: 2120 Riverfront Dr., #100, Little Rock, AR 72202, (501) 324-5871

CALIFORNIA: 2719 Air Fresno Dr., #200, Fresno, CA 93727-1547, (559) 487-5791

330 N. Brand Blvd., #1200, Glendale, CA 91203-2304, (818) 552-3210

550 W. C St., #550, San Diego, CA 92101, (619) 557-7250

455 Market St., 6th Fl., San Francisco, CA 94105-1988, (415)

744-6820

650 Capitol Mall, #7-500, Sacramento, CA 95814-2413, (916) 930-3700

200 W. Santa Ana Blvd., #700, Santa Ana, CA 92701-4134, (714) 550-7420

COLORADO: 721 19th St., #426, Denver, CO 80202-2517, (303) 844-2607

CONNECTICUT: 330 Main St., 2nd Fl., Hartford, CT 06106-1800, (860) 240-4700

DELAWARE: 824 N. Market St., #610, Wilmington, DE 19801-3011, (302) 573-6294

DISTRICT OF COLUMBIA: 1110 Vermont Ave. NW, #900, Washington, DC 20005, (202) 606-4000

FLORIDA: 100 S. Biscayne Blvd., 7th Fl., Miami, FL 33131-2011, (305) 536-5521

7825 Baymeadows Wy., #100-B, Jacksonville, FL 32256-7504, (904) 443-1900

GEORGIA: 233 Peachtree St. NE, #1900, Atlanta, GA 30303, (404) 331-0100

HAWAII: 300 Ala Moana Blvd., Rm. 2-235, Box 50207, Honolulu, HI 96850-4981, (808) 541-2990

IDAHO: 1020 Main St., #290, Boise, ID 83702-5745, (208) 334-1696

ILLINOIS: 500 W. Madison St., #1250, Chicago, IL 60661-2511, (312) 353-4528

511 W. Capitol Ave., #302, Springfield, IL 62704, (217) 492-4416

INDIANA: 429 N. Pennsylvania St., #100, Indianapolis, IN 46204-1873, (317) 226-7272

IOWA: Mail Code 0736, The Lattner Bldg., 215 Fourth Ave. SE, #200, Cedar Rapids, IA 52401-1806, (319) 362-6405

210 Walnut St., Rm. 749, Des Moines, IA 50309-2186, (515) 284-4422

KANSAS: 271 W. Third St. N., #2500, Wichita, KS 67202-1212, (316) 269-6616

KENTUCKY: 600 Dr. Martin Luther King Jr. Pl., #188, Louisville, KY 40202, (502) 582-5761

LOUISIANA: 365 Canal St., #2820, New Orleans, LA 70130, (504) 589-6685

MAINE: Edward S. Muskie Federal Bldg., 68 Sewall St., Rm. 512, Augusta, ME 04330, (207) 622-8274

MARYLAND: 10 S. Howard St., #6220, Baltimore, MD 21201-2525,

(410) 962-4392

MASSACHUSETTS: 10 Causeway St., Rm. 265, Boston, MA 02222-1093, (617) 565-5590

MICHIGAN: McNamara Bldg., 477 Michigan Ave., Rm. 515, Detroit, MI 48226, (313) 226-6075

MINNESOTA: Butler Square 210-C, 100 N. Sixth St., Minneapolis, MN 55403, (612) 370-2324

MISSISSIPPI: Am South Bank Plaza, 210 E. Capitol St., #900, Jackson, MS 39201, (601) 965-4378

MISSOURI: 323 W. Eighth St., #501, Kansas City, MO 64105, (816) 374-6708

815 Olive St., Rm. 242, St. Louis, MO 63101, (314) 539-6600

MONTANA: Federal Building, 10 W. 15th St., #1100, Helena, MT 59626, (800) 776-9144, ext. 2 or (406) 441-1081

NEBRASKA: 11145 Mill Valley Rd., Omaha, NE 68154, (402) 221-4691

NEVADA: 300 S. Las Vegas Blvd., #1100, Las Vegas, NV 89101, (702) 388-6611

NEW HAMPSHIRE: 143 N. Main St., #202, Concord, NH 03301-1248, (603) 225-1400

NEW JERSEY: 2 Gateway Center, 15th Fl., Newark, NJ 07102, (973) 645-2434

NEW MEXICO: 625 Silver Ave. SW, #320, Albuquerque, NM 87102, (505) 346-7909

NEW YORK: 111 W. Huron St., #1311, Buffalo, NY 14202, (716) 551-4301

26 Federal Plaza, #3100, New York, NY 10278, (212) 264-4354

401 S. Salina St., 5th Fl., Syracuse, NY 13202-2415, (315) 471-9393

NORTH CAROLINA: 6302 Fairview Rd., #300, Charlotte, NC 28210-2227, (704) 344-6563

NORTH DAKOTA: 657 Second Ave. N., Rm. 219, Fargo, ND 58108, (701) 239-5131

OHIO:1111 Superior Ave., #630, Cleveland, OH 44114-2507, (216) 522-4180

2 Nationwide Plaza, #1400, Columbus, OH 43215-2542, (614) 469-6860

OKLAHOMA: 210 Park Ave., #1300, Oklahoma City, OK 73102, (405) 231-5521

OREGON: 1515 SW Fifth Ave., #1050, Portland, OR 97201-5494, (503) 326-2682

PENNSYLVANIA: Robert N.C. Nix Federal Bldg., 900 Market St., 5th Fl., Philadelphia, PA 19107, (215) 580-2722

Federal Bldg., Rm. 1128, 1000 Liberty Ave., Pittsburgh, PA 15222-4004, (412) 395-6560

PUERTO RICO: Citibank Tower, 252 Ponce de Leon Blvd., #201, Hato Rey, PR 00918, (787) 766-5572

RHODE ISLAND: 380 Westminster St., 5th Fl., Providence, RI 02903, (401) 528-4561

SOUTH CAROLINA: 1835 Assembly St., Rm. 358, Columbia, SC 29201, (803) 765-5377

SOUTH DAKOTA: 110 S. Phillips Ave., #200, Sioux Falls, SD 57102-1109, (605) 330-4231

TENNESSEE: 50 Vantage Wy., #201, Nashville, TN 37228-1500, (615) 736-5881

TEXAS: 4300 Amon Carter Blvd., #114, Ft. Worth, TX 75155, (817) 885-5500

8701 S. Gessner Dr., #1200, Houston, TX 77074, (713) 773-6500

222 E. Van Buren St., Rm. 500, Harlingen, TX 78550-6855, (956) 427-8533

1205 Texas Ave., Rm. 408, Lubbock, TX 79401-2693, (806) 472-7462

Federal Bldg., 5th Fl., 727 E. Durango Blvd., Rm. A-527, San Antonio, TX 78206-1204, (210) 472-5900

UTAH: 125 S. State St., Rm. 2231, Salt Lake City, UT 84138-1195, (801) 524-3209

VERMONT: 87 State St., Rm. 205, Box 605, Montpelier, VT 05601, (802) 828-4422

VIRGINIA: Federal Bldg., 400 N. Eighth St., #1150, Richmond, VA 23240, (804) 771-2400

WASHINGTON: 1200 Sixth Ave., #1700, Seattle, WA 98101-1128, (206) 553-7310

Spokane Regional Business Center, 801 W. Riverside Ave., #200, Spokane, WA 99201, (509) 353-2800

WEST VIRGINIA: 320 West Pike St., #330, Clarksburg, WV 26301, (304) 623-5631

WISCONSIN: 740 Regent St., #100, Madison, WI 53715, (608) 441-5263

WYOMING: 100 E. B St., Rm. 4001, P.O Box 2839, Casper, WY 82602-2839, (307) 261-6500

SMALL BUSINESS DEVELOPMENT CENTERS

The following SBDCs can direct you to the SBDC in your region. You can access all SBDC Web sites at www.sba.gov/sbdc and then click on "Your Nearest SBDC."

ALABAMA: University of Alabama, Box 870223, Tuscaloosa, AL 35487, (205) 348-7443

ALASKA: University of Alaska, Anchorage, 430 W. Seventh Ave., #110, Anchorage, AK 99501, (907) 274-7232

ARIZONA: 2411 W. 14th St., #132, Tempe, AZ 85281, (480) 731-8720

ARKANSAS: University of Arkansas, Little Rock, 2801 S. University Ave., Little Rock, AR 72204, (501) 324-9043

CALIFORNIA: San Joaquin Delta College, 445 N. San Joaquin St., Stockton, CA 95202, (209) 943-5089

COLORADO: Colorado Business Assistance Center, 2413 Washington St., Denver, CO 80205, (303) 592-5920

CONNECTICUT: University of Connecticut, 2100 Hillside Rd., #1041, Storrs, CT 06269-1041, (860) 486-4135

DELAWARE: University of Delaware, 1 Innovation Wy., #301, Newark, DE 19711, (302) 831-1555

DISTRICT OF COLUMBIA: Howard University School of Business, 2600 Sixth St. NW, Rm. 128, Washington, DC 20059, (202) 806-1550

FLORIDA: 19 W. Garden St., #300, Pensacola, FL 32501, (850) 470-4980 or (850) 595-6060

GEORGIA: University of Georgia, Chicopee Complex, 1180 E. Broad St., Athens, GA 30602-5412, (706) 542-7436

GUAM: Pacific Islands, UOG Station, Mangilao, Guam 96923, (671) 735-2590

HAWAII: University of Hawaii, Hilo, 200 W. Kawili St., Hilo, HI 96720-4091, (800) 897-4456

IDAHO: Boise State University, 1910 University Dr., Boise, ID 83725-1655, (208) 426-1640

ILLINOIS: Greater North Pulaski, 4054 W. North Ave., Chicago, IL 60639, (800) 252-2923 or (773) 384-2262

INDIANA: 1 N. Capitol Ave., #900, Indianapolis, IN 46204, (317) 234-2082

Iowa: 137 Lynn Ave., #5, Ames, IA 50014, (515) 292-6351

Kansas: 137 Skirk Hall, 1501 S. Joplin St., Pittsburg, KS 66762, (620) 235-4920

Kentucky: 225 Gatton College of Business & Economics, Lexington, KY 40506-0034, (859) 257-7668

Louisiana: University of Louisiana at Monroe, Administration 2-57, Monroe, LA 71209-6435, (318) 342-5506

Maine: University of Southern Maine, 96 Falmouth St., P.O Box 9300, Portland, ME 04104-9300, (207) 780-4420

Maryland: 7100 E. Baltimore Ave., #402, College Park, MD 20740-3627, (301) 403-8300

Massachusetts: University of Massachusetts, 205 School of Management, P.O. Box 34935, Amherst, MA 01003, (413) 545-6301

Michigan: Grand Valley State University, Seidman School of Business, 510 W. Fulton St., Grand Rapids, MI 49504, (616) 336-7480

Minnesota: Department of Trade & Economic Development, 100 Metro Sq., 121 Seventh Pl., St. Paul, MN 55101-2146, (651) 296-5205

Mississippi: University of Mississippi, P.O. Box 1848, B 19 Jeanette Phillips Dr., University, MS 38677-1848, (662) 915-5001

Missouri: 1205 University Pl., #1800, Columbia, MO 65211, (573) 882-7096

Montana: 1424 Ninth Ave., Helena, MT 59620, (406) 444-4780

Nebraska: College of Business Administration, 60th & Dodge St., Rm. 407, Omaha, NE 68182-0248, (402) 554-2521

Nevada: University of Nevada at Reno, CBA, MS 32, Reno, NV 89557-0100, (702) 784-1717

New Hampshire: 670 N. Commercial St., 4th Fl., #25, Manchester, NH 03101, (603) 624-2000

New Jersey: 49 Bleeker St., Newark, NJ 07102-1913, (973) 353-1927

New Mexico: Santa Fe Community College, Lead Center, 6401 S. Richards Ave., Santa Fe, NM 87508, (800) 281-7232 or (505) 428-1362

New York: University at Albany, One Pinnacle Plaza, #218, Albany, NY 12203, (518) 453-9567

North Carolina: SB & TDC, 5 W. Hargett St., #600, Raleigh, NC 27601-1348, (800) 258-0862 or (919) 715-7272

North Dakota: University of North Dakota, 118 Gamble Hall, P.O Box 7308, Grand Forks, ND 58202, (800) 445-7232 or (701) 777-3700

OHIO: 37 N. High St., Columbus, OH 43215, (614) 221-1321 or (614) 225-6910

OKLAHOMA: Southeastern Oklahoma State University, 517 W. University Blvd., Durant, OK 74701, (580) 745-7577

OREGON: 44 W. Broadway, #501, Eugene, OR 97401-3021, (541) 726-2250

PENNSYLVANIA: University of Pennsylvania, Vance Hall-3733 Spruce St., 4th Fl., Philadelphia, PA 19104, (215) 898-1219

RHODE ISLAND: Bryant College, 1150 Douglas Pike, Smithfield, RI 02917, (401) 232-6111

SOUTH CAROLINA: University of South Carolina, The Darla Moore School of Business, Columbia, SC 29208, (803) 777-4907

SOUTH DAKOTA: University of South Dakota, School of Business, 414 E. Clark St., Vermillion, SD 57069-2390, (605) 677-5011

TENNESSEE: University of Memphis, South Campus, Bldg. 1, Box 526324, Memphis, TN 38152, (901) 678-2500 or (901) 678-2000

TEXAS: 2302 Fannin St., #200, Houston, TX 77002, (713) 752-8444

UTAH: 125 S. State St., Rm. 2231, Salt Lake City, UT 84111, (801) 957-3840

VERMONT: P.O. Box 188, Randolph Center, VT 05061-0188, (800) 464-7232 or (802) 728-9101

VIRGINIA: 116 E. Franklin St., #100, Richmond, VA 23219, (804) 783-9314

WASHINGTON: Washington State University, P.O. Box 644851, Pullman, WA 99164-4851, (509) 335-1576 or (509) 335-0949

WEST VIRGINIA: State Capitol Complex, Bldg, 6, Rm. 652, 1900 Kanawha Blvd. E., Charleston, WV 25305, (888) 982-7732 or (304) 558-2960

WISCONSIN: University of Wisconsin, Whitewater, 2000 Carlson Hall, Whitewater, WI 53190, (800) 621-7235 or (262) 472-3217

WYOMING: 111 W. Second St., #502, Casper, WY 82601, (307) 234-6683

STATE COMMERCE & ECONOMIC DEVELOPMENT DEPARTMENTS

ALABAMA: 401 Adams Ave., #670, Montgomery, AL 36130, (334) 242-0400, (800) 248-0033, www.ado.state.al.us

ALASKA: P.O. Box 110800, Juneau, AK 99811-0801, (907) 465-2500, www.dced.state.ak.us

ARIZONA: Executive Tower, #600, 1700 W. Washington, Phoenix, AZ 85007, (602) 771-1100, www.state.az.us

ARKANSAS: Advocacy & Business Services, 1 Capitol Mall, Little Rock, AR 72201, (501) 682-1060 or (501) 682-1121, www.1-800-arkansas.com

CALIFORNIA: Trade & Commerce Agency, Office of Secretary/ Legal, 1102 Q St., #6000, Sacramento, CA 95814, (916) 322-1394, www.commerce.ca.gov

COLORADO: 1625 Broadway, #1710, Denver, CO 80202, (303) 892-3864, www.state.co.us/oed/edc

CONNECTICUT: Economic Resource Center, 805 Brook St., Bldg. 4, Rocky Hill, CT 06067, (800) 392-2122 or (860) 571-7136, www.cerc.com

DELAWARE: Economic Development Office, 99 Kings Hwy., Dover, DE 19901, (302) 739-4271, www.state.de.us/dedo

DISTRICT OF COLUMBIA: 1350 Pennsylvania Ave. NW, #317, Washington, DC 20004, (202) 727-6365, www.dc.gov/agencies/ index.asp

FLORIDA: Enterprise Florida, 390 N. Orange Ave., #1300, Orlando, FL 32801, (407) 316-4600 or (407) 316-4700, www.eflorida.com

GEORGIA: Department of Community Affairs, 60 Executive Park S. NE, Atlanta, GA 30329-2231, (404) 679-4940, www.dca.state.ga.us

HAWAII: Business Action Center, 2nd Level, 1130 N. Nimitz Hwy., Rm. A-254, Honolulu, HI 96817, (808) 586-2545, www.hawaii.gov/dbedt

IDAHO: 700 W. State St., P.O. Box 83720, Boise, ID 83720-0093, (800) 842-5858 or (208) 334-2470, www.idoc.state.id.us

ILLINOIS: Dept. of Commerce & Community Affairs, Springfield-Bressmer Bldg., 3rd Fl., S-3, 620 E. Adams St., Springfield, IL 62701, (217) 524-6293 or (217) 524-1931, www.commerce.state.il.us

INDIANA: 1 N. Capitol Ave., #700, Indianapolis, IN 46204-2288, (317) 232-8800, www.state.in.us/doc

IOWA: 200 E. Grand Ave., Des Moines, IA 50309, (515) 242-4700 or (800) 532-1216, www.state.ia.us/ided

KANSAS: Dept. of Commerce & Housing, Business Development Division, 1000 SW Jackson St., #100, Topeka, KS 66612-1354, (785) 296-5298, www.kdoch.state.ks.us/ProgramApp/index_mm.jsp

KENTUCKY: Capitol Plaza Tower, 500 Mero St., Frankfort, KY

40601, (502) 564-7140, www.thinkkentucky.com

LOUISIANA: P.O. Box 94185, Baton Rouge, LA 70804-9185, (225) 342-3000, www.lded.state.la.us

MAINE: Dept. of Economic & Community Development, 59 Statehouse Station, Augusta, ME 04333-0059, (800) 872-3838 or (207) 624-9804, www.econdevmaine.com

MARYLAND: Division of Regional Development, 217 E. Redwood St., 10th Fl., Baltimore, MD 21202, (410) 762-3376, www.mdbusiness. state.md.us/business/offices.asp

MASSACHUSETTS: Office of Business Development, 10 Park Plaza, #3720, Boston, MA 02116, (617) 973-8686 or (617) 973-8600, www.state.ma.us/mobd

MICHIGAN: 300 N. Washington Sq., Lansing, MI 48913, (517) 373-9808, www.michigan.gov

MINNESOTA: Small Business Assistance Office, 121 7th Place E., #500, St. Paul, MN 55101, (800) 657-3858 or (651) 282-2103, www.dted.state.mn.us

MISSISSIPPI: Division of Existing Industry & Business, P.O. Box 849, Jackson, MS 39205-0849, (601) 359-3593, www.mississippi.org

MISSOURI: P.O. Box 118, 301 W. High St., Rm. 720, Jefferson City, MO 65101, (573) 751-2863, www.ded.mo.gov

MONTANA: 1424 Ninth Ave., Helena, MT 59601, (406) 444-3797, www.commerce.state.mt.us

NEBRASKA: 301 Centennial Mall S., P.O. Box 94666, Lincoln, NE 68509-4666, (800) 426-6505 or (402) 471-3111, www.neded.org

NEVADA: Dept. of Business & Industry, Center for Business Advocacy, 555 E. Washington Ave., #4900, Las Vegas, NV 89101, (702) 486-2750, www.dbi.state.nv.us

NEW HAMPSHIRE: Office of Business & Industrial Development, 172 Pembroke Rd., Concord, NH 03302-1856, (603) 271-2341, www.dred.state.nh.us

NEW JERSEY: PO. Box 820, 20 State St., Trenton, NJ 08625, (888) 239-1288 or (609) 292-2146, www.newjersey.gov/njbiz/y_smallbus_offsmbus.shtml

NEW MEXICO: P.O. Box 20003, 1100 St. Francis Dr., Santa Fe, NM 87504, (800) 374-3061 or (505) 827-0300, www.edd.state.nm.us

NEW YORK: Empire State Development, 30 S. Pearl St., Albany, NY 12245, (800) 782-8369, www.empire.state.ny.us

NORTH CAROLINA: SB & Technology Development Center, 5 W. Hargett St., #600, Raleigh, NC 27601-1348, (800) 258-0862 or

(919) 715-7272, www.sbtdc.org

NORTH DAKOTA: University of North Dakota, Center for Innovation, Rural Technology Incubator, P.O. Box 8372, 4300 Dartmouth Dr., Grand Forks, ND 58202, (701) 777-3132, www.innovators.net

OHIO: One-Stop Business Center, P.O. Box 1001, 77 S. High St., 28th Fl., Columbus, OH 43216-1001, (614) 644-4232, www.odod. state.oh.us/onestop

OKLAHOMA: Dept. of Commerce, OKC Metro, P.O. Box 26980, 900 N. Stiles Ave., Oklahoma City, OK 73126-0980, (800) 879-6552 or (405) 815-6552, www.odoc.state.ok.us

OREGON: 775 Summer St. NE, #200, Salem, OR 97301-1280, (503) 986-0123, (800) 233-3306, www.econ.state.or.us

PENNSYLVANIA: Small Business Resource Center, Commonwealth Keystone Bldg., 400 N St., 4th Fl., Harrisburg, PA 17120-0225, (717) 783-5700, www.inventpa.com

RHODE ISLAND: 1 W. Exchange St., Providence, RI 02903, (401) 222-2601, www.riedc.com

SOUTH CAROLINA: Enterprise Inc., P.O. Box 1149, Columbia, SC 29202, (803) 252-8806, www.myscgov.com

SOUTH DAKOTA: 711 E. Wells Ave., Pierre, SD 57501-3369, (800) 872-6190 or (605) 773-5032, www.sdgreatprofits.com

TENNESSEE: Small Business Service, William R. Snodgrass TN Tower, 312 8th Ave. N., 11th Fl., Nashville, TN 37243-0405, (615) 741-2626, www.state.tn.us/ecd/con_bsv.htm

TEXAS: Office of Small Business Assistance, P.O. Box 12728, 1700 N. Congress Ave., Austin, TX 78711-2728, (512) 936-0100, www.tded.state.tx.us/SmallBusiness

UTAH: 324 S. State St., #500, Salt Lake City, UT 84111, (801) 538-8700, www.dced.state.ut.us

VERMONT: National Life Bldg, Drawer 20, Montpelier, VT 05620-0501, (802) 828-3211, www.state.vt.us/dca (Commerce and Community Development Agency), www.thinkvermont.com (Economic Development Agency)

VIRGINIA: Dept. of Business Assistance Development Center Network, 707 E. Main St., #300, Richmond, VA 23219, (804) 371-8200, www.dba.state.va.us

P.O. Box 446, Richmond, VA 23218-0446, (804) 371-8200, www.dba.state.va.us/smdev

WASHINGTON: Community Trade & Economic Development, Business Assistance Division, 128 10th Ave. SW, 4th Fl., Olympia,

WA 98504, (360) 725-4100, www.cted.wa.gov

WEST VIRGINIA: Capitol Complex/Bldg. 6, 1900 Washington St. E., Rm. 553, Charleston, WV 25305-0311, (304) 558-2234, www.wvdo.org

WISCONSIN: 201 W. Washington Ave., Madison, WI 53717, (608) 266-1018, www.commerce.state.wi.us

WYOMING: Wyoming Business Council, 214 West 15th St., Cheyenne, WY 82001, (800) 262-3425 or (307) 777-2800, www. wyomingbusiness.org

Small-Business-
Friendly Banks

FOLLOWING IS A LISTING of the Small Business Administration's top small-business-friendly banks in each state.

Alabama

COMMUNITY BANK, Blountsville, AL, (205) 429-1000

FARMERS & MERCHANTS BANK, Piedmont, AL, (256) 447-9041

FIRST COMMUNITY BANK, Chatom, AL, (251)847-2214, www.fcb-al.com

FIRST NATIONAL BANK OF CENTRAL ALABAMA, Aliceville, AL, (205) 373-2922, www.fnbca.com

PEOPLES BANK OF NORTH ALABAMA, Cullman, AL, (256) 737-7000, www.bamabank.com

WEST ALABAMA BANK & TRUST, Reform, AL, (205) 375-6261, www.wabt.com

Alaska

WELLS FARGO BANK ALASKA, N.A., Anchorage, AK, (907) 522-8888, www.wellsfargo.com

Arizona

COMMUNITY BANK OF ARIZONA, Wickenburg, AZ, (928) 684-7884

FRONTIER STATE BANK, Show Low, AZ, (928) 537-2933

MOHAVE STATE BANK, Lake Havasu City, AZ, (928)855-0000, www.mohavestbank.com

SUNSTATE BANK, Casa Grande, AZ, (520)836-4666, www.

sunstatebank.com

Arkansas

BANK OF POCAHONTAS, Pocahontas, AR, (870) 892-5286, www.bankopoc.com

BANK OF SALEM, Salem, AR, (870) 895-2591

BANK OF YELLVILLE, Yellville, AR, (870) 449-4231, www.bankofyellville.com

COMMERCIAL BANK, Monticello, AR, (870) 367-6221

DE WITT BANK & TRUST, De Witt, AR, (870) 946-8089

DIAMOND STATE BANK, Murfreesboro, AR, (870) 285-2172

FIRST NATIONAL BANK OF EASTERN ARKANSAS, Forrest City, AR, (870) 633-3112, www.fnbea.com

FIRST NATIONAL BANK OF PHILLIPS COUNTY, Helena, AR, (870) 816-1100

FIRST NATIONAL BANK OF SHARP COUNTY, Ash Flat, AR, (870) 994-2311, www.fnbsharpcounty.com

FIRST STATE BANK, Huntsville, AR, (479) 738-2147

FIRST STATE BANK, Plainview, AR, (479) 272-4221, www.fsbmybank.com

SOUTHERN STATE BANK, Malvern, AR, (501) 332-2462, www.southernstatebank.com

UNION BANK OF MENA, Mena, AR, (479) 394-2211, www.unionbankofmena.com

California

BANK OF THE SIERRA, Porterville, CA, (559) 782-4900, www.bankofthesierra.com

CALIFORNIA CENTER BANK, Los Angeles, CA, (213) 386-2222, www.centerbank.com

CITIZENS' BUSINESS BANK, Burbank, CA, (818)843-0707, www.cbbank.com

COMMUNITY COMMERCE BANK, Los Angeles, CA, (323) 268-6100, www.ccombank.com

COMMUNITY NATIONAL BANK, Fallbrook, CA, (760) 723-8811, www.comnb.com

FIRST NATIONAL BANK OF NORTH COUNTY, Carlsbad, CA, (760) 434-6171

PLUMAS BANK, Quincy, CA, (530) 283-6800, www.plumasbank.com

SAEHAN BANK, Los Angeles, CA, (213) 389-5550, www.saehanbank.com

UNITED PACIFIC BANK, City of Industry, CA, (626) 965-6230

VALENCIA BANK & TRUST, Santa Clarita, CA, (661) 287-9900, www.valenciabank.com

VALLEY INDEPENDENT BANK, El Centro, CA, (760) 337-3200, www.vibank.com

WILSHIRE STATE BANK, Los Angeles, CA, (213) 387-3200, www.wilshirebank.com

Colorado

BANK OF GRAND JUNCTION, Grand Junction, CO, (970) 241-9000, www.bogj.com

CENTENNIAL BANK, Pueblo, CO, (719) 543-0763, www.colorados bank.com

CITIZENS STATE BANK OF OURAY, Ouray, CO, (970) 325-4478, www.ouraynet.com/banking

FARMERS STATE BANK OF CALHAN, Calhan, CO, (719) 347-2727, www.farmers-statebank.com

FIRST COMMUNITY INDUSTRIAL BANK, Denver, CO, (303) 399-3400

FIRST NATIONAL BANK IN TRINIDAD, Trinidad, CO, (719) 846-9881

FIRST NATIONAL BANK OF DURANGO, Durango, CO, (970) 247-3020, www.fnbdurango.com

FIRST NATIONAL BANK OF LAS ANIMAS, Las Animas, CO, (719) 456-1512

PARK STATE BANK AND TRUST, Woodland Park, CO, (719) 687-9234

PINE RIVER VALLEY BANK, Bayfield, CO, (970) 884-9583, www.pinerivervalleybank.com

WELD COUNTY BANK, Evans, CO, (970) 506-1000, www. weldcountybank.com

Connecticut

CITIZENS NATIONAL BANK, Putnam, CT, (860) 928-7921, www.cnbct.com

CORNERSTONE BANK, Stamford, CT, (203) 356-0111, www. cornerstonebank.com

VALLEY BANK, Bristol, CT, (860) 582-8868

Delaware

BANK OF DELMARVA N.A., Seaford, DE, (302) 629-2700, www.bankofdelmarva.com

CITIBANK DELAWARE, New Castle, DE, (302) 323-3900, www.

citicorp.com

COUNTY BANK, Rehoboth Beach, DE, (302) 226-9800

District of Columbia

UNITED BANK, Washington, DC, (703) 502-7100, www.united bank-va.com

Florida

APALACHICOLA STATE BANK, Apalachicola, FL, (850) 653-8805

COLUMBIA COUNTY BANK, Lake City, FL, (386) 752-5646, www.ccbanc.com

COMMUNITY BANK OF FLORIDA, Homestead, FL, (305) 246-2211, www.communitybankfl.com

DESTIN BANK, Destin, FL, (850)837-8100, www.destinbank.com

DRUMMOND COMMUNITY BANK, Chiefland, FL, (352) 493-2277, www.drummondcommunitybank.com

FARMERS & MERCHANTS BANK, Monticello, FL, (850) 997-2591, www.fmbbank.com

FIRST NATIONAL BANK OF ALACHUA, Alachua, FL, (904) 462-1041, www.fnba.net

FIRST NATIONAL BANK OF WAUCHULA, Wauchula, FL, (863) 773-4136

HEMISPHERE NATIONAL BANK, Miami, FL, (305) 341-5300, www.hnbfl.com

PERKINS STATE BANK, Williston, FL, (352) 528-3101, www. perkinsstatebank.com

Georgia

ALTAMAHA BANK & TRUST, Uvalda, GA, (912) 594-6525

BANK OF DUDLEY, Dudley, GA, (478) 676-3196, www.bankof dudley.com

CAPITOL CITY BANK & TRUST, Atlanta, GA, (404) 752-6067, www.capitolcitybank-atl.com

COMMUNITY NATIONAL BANK, Ashburn, GA, (229) 567-9686

FARMERS & MERCHANTS BANK, Lakeland, GA, (229) 482-3585, www.fmbnk.com

FARMERS & MERCHANTS BANK, Statesboro, GA, (912) 489-2600, www.fmbnk.com

FIRST BANK OF COASTAL GEORGIA, Pembroke, GA, (912) 653-4396, www.firstbankofcg.com

FIRST NATIONAL BANK AND TRUST, Louisville, GA, (478) 625-2000, www.fnb-trust.com

FIRST STATE BANK, Stockbridge, GA, (770) 474-7293, www.firststate online.com

MCINTOSH STATE BANK, Jackson, GA, (770) 775-8300, www.mcintosh bancshares.com

PATTERSON BANK, Patterson, GA, (912) 647-5332, www.patterson bank.com

PLANTERS FIRST BANK, Cordele, GA, (229) 273-2416

STATE BANK OF COCHRAN, Cochran, GA, (478) 934-4501

Hawaii

CITY BANK, Honolulu, HI, (808) 535-2909, www.citybankhawaii.com

Idaho

D.L. EVANS BANK, Burley, ID, (208) 678-9076, www.dlevans.com

PEND OREILLE BANK, Sandpoint, ID, (208) 265-2232, www.po bank.com

Illinois

AMERICAN NATIONAL BANK OF DEKALB COUNTY, Sycamore, IL, (815) 895-9121, www.myhomevalley.com

ANNA NATIONAL BANK, Anna, IL, (618) 833-8506, www. annanational.com

BANK OF PONTIAC, Pontiac, IL, (815) 842-1069, www.bank ofpontiac.com

FIRST NATIONAL BANK IN AMBOY, Amboy, IL, (815) 857-3625, www.fnbamboy.com

FIRST NATIONAL BANK IN TOLEDO, Toledo, IL, (217) 849-2701, www.firstneighbor.com

FIRST TRUST BANK OF ILLINOIS, Kankakee, IL, (815) 929-4000, www.firsttrustbankil.com

GERMANTOWN TRUST & SAVINGS BANK, Breese, IL, (618) 526-4202

NATIONAL BANK OF PETERSBURG, Petersburg, IL, (217) 632-3241

PEOTONE BANK AND TRUST, Peotone, IL, (708) 258-3231, www.peotonebank.com

TRUSTBANK, Olney, IL, (618) 395-4311, www.trustbank.net

Indiana

CAMPBELL & FETTER BANK, Kendallville, IN, (260) 343-3300

CITIZENS FIRST STATE BANK, Hartford City, IN, (765) 348-2350

COMMUNITY FIRST BANK, Corydon, IN, (812) 738-1751

COMMUNITY STATE BANK, Avilla, IN, (260) 897-3361

DEMOTTE STATE BANK, De Motte, IN, (219) 987-4141, www.netdsb.com

FARMERS & MERCHANTS BANK, Boswell, IN, (765) 869-5513

FIRST NATIONAL BANK OF MONTEREY, Monterey, IN, (574) 542-2121

FOWLER STATE BANK, Fowler, IN, (765) 884-1200

HEARTLAND COMMUNITY BANK, Franklin, IN, (317) 738-3915, www.hcb-in.com

HOMETOWN NATIONAL BANK, New Albany, IN, (812) 949-2265, www.hometownnationalbank.com

JACKSON COUNTY BANK, Seymour, IN, (812) 522-3607, www.jcbank.com

MARKLE BANK, MARKLE, IN, (260) 375-4550, www.marklebank.com

SCOTT COUNTY STATE BANK, Scottsburg, IN, (812) 752-4501

STATE BANK OF OXFORD, Oxford, IN, (765) 385-2213, www.statebankoxford.com

Iowa

AMERICAN STATE BANK, Osceola, IA, (641) 342-2175, www.americanstatebank.com

BANK IOWA, Oskaloosa, IA, (641) 673-7400, www.bankoskaloosa.com

BANK IOWA, Red Oak, IA, (712) 623-6960, www.bankredoak.com

BLUE GRASS SAVINGS BANK, Blue Grass, IA, (563) 381-1732

COMMUNITY STATE BANK, Indianola, IA, (515) 961-5880, www.csbindianola.com

CRESCO UNION SAVINGS BANK, Cresco, IA, (563) 547-2040, www.cusb.com

DECORAH BANK & TRUST, Decorah, IA, (563) 382-9661, www.securitybank-decorah.com

FARMERS STATE BANK, Jesup, IA, (319) 827-1050, www.fsb1879.com

FREEDOM SECURITY BANK, Coralville, IA, (319) 688-9005

HERITAGE BANK, Holstein, IA, (712) 368-4316, www.heritageiowa.com

HOUGHTON STATE BANK, Red Oak, IA, (712) 623-4823

HUMBOLDT TRUST & SAVINGS BANK, Humboldt, IA, (515) 332-1451, www.bankhumboldt.com

LEE COUNTY BANK & TRUST CO., Fort Madison, IA, (319) 372-2243, www.lcbtrust.com

LIBERTYVILLE SAVINGS BANK, Fairfield, IA, (641) 693-3141, www.libertyvillesavingsbank.com

LINCOLN SAVINGS BANK, Reinbeck, IA, (319) 345-6441, www.lincolnsavingsbank.com

MAQUOKETA STATE BANK, Maquoketa, IA, (563) 652-2491, www.maquoketasb.com

NORTHWOODS STATE BANK, Northwood, IA, (641) 324-1023, www.nsbbank.com

PILOT GROVE SAVINGS BANK, Pilot Grove, IA, (319) 469-3951, www.pilotgrovesavingsbank.com

SHELBY COUNTY STATE BANK, Harlan, IA, (712) 755-5112, www.scsbnet.com

Kansas

CITIZENS STATE BANK, Gridley, KS, (620) 836-2888

COMMUNITY NATIONAL BANK, Chanute, KS, (620) 431-2265

FIRST NATIONAL BANK, Independence, KS, (620) 331-7733

FARMERS STATE BANK OF MCPHERSON, McPherson, KS, (620) 241-3090

FIRST NATIONAL BANK OF WAMEGO, Wamego, KS, (785) 456-2221, www.fnbofwamego.com

FIRST NATIONAL BANK, Palco, KS, (785) 737-2311, www.bankhays.com

FIRST NATIONAL BANK OF GIRARD, Girard, KS, (620) 724-6111

FIRST NATIONAL BANK OF SOUTHERN KANSAS, Mount Hope, KS, (316) 661-2471

FIRST OPTION BANK, Osawatomie, KS, (913) 755-3811

FIRST STATE BANK, Norton, KS, (785) 877-3341, www.firststatebank.com

GARDNER NATIONAL BANK, Gardner, KS, (913) 856-7199, www.gardnernational.com

LABETTE COUNTY STATE BANK, Altamont, KS, (620) 784-5311

MORRILL STATE BANK & TRUST CO., Sabetha, KS, (785) 284-3433

THE PEOPLES BANK, Pratt, KS, (620) 672-5611, www.thepeoplesbank.net

PEOPLES BANK & TRUST, McPherson, KS, (620) 241-2100, www.peoplesbankonline.com

ROSE HILL BANK, Rose Hill, KS, (316) 776-2131, www.rosehillbank.com

STATE BANK, Winfield, KS, (620) 221-3040, www.thestatebankonline.com

STOCKGROWERS STATE BANK, Ashland, KS, (620) 635-4032,

www.stockgrowersbank.com

UNION STATE BANK, Everest, KS, (785) 548-7521

Kentucky

BANK OF COLUMBIA, Columbia, KY, (270) 384-6433, www.bankcolumbia.com

BANK OF THE BLUEGRASS & TRUST CO., Lexington, KY, (859) 233-4500, www.bankofthebluegrass.com

CITIZENS BANK, McKee, KY, (606) 287-8390

EDMONTON STATE BANK, Glasgow, KY, (270) 659-0171

THE FARMERS BANK, Hardinsburg, KY, (270) 756-2166, www.thefarmersbank-ky.com

FARMERS DEPOSIT BANK, Eminence, KY, (502) 845-5639, www.farmersdepositbank.com

FIRST NATIONAL BANK OF CENTRAL CITY, Central City, KY, (270) 754-3300, www.fnbcc.net

OHIO VALLEY NATIONAL BANK, Henderson, KY, (270) 831-1500, www.ovbank.com

PEOPLES BANK & TRUST CO. OF HAZARD, Hazard, KY, (606) 436-2161

PEOPLES BANK OF FLEMING COUNTY, Flemingsburg, KY, (606) 845-2461, www.pbfco.com

SOUTH CENTRAL BANK, Glasgow, KY, (270) 651-7466, www.southcentralbank.biz

Louisiana

AMERICAN BANK, Welsh, LA, (337) 734-2226

CITY SAVINGS BANK AND TRUST CO., DeRidder, LA, (337) 463-8661

COMMUNITY BANK, Mansfield, LA, (318) 872-3831

EVANGELINE BANK AND TRUST CO., Ville Platt, LA, (337) 363-5541, www.therealbank.com

FIRST LOUISIANA NATIONAL BANK, Breaux Bridge, LA, (337) 332-5960

GULF COAST BANK, Abbeville, LA, (337) 893-7733, www.gcbank.com

HANCOCK BANK OF LOUISIANA, Baton Rouge, LA, (225) 346-6380, www.hancockbank.com

JEFF DAVIS BANK & TRUST, Jennings, LA, (337) 824-3424, www.jdbank.com

LIBERTY BANK AND TRUST, New Orleans, LA, (504) 240-5100, www.libertybank.net

RESOURCE BANK, Mandeville, LA, (985) 674-1455, www.resourcebk.com

Maine

FIRST CITIZENS BANK, Presque Isle, ME, (207) 768-3222, www.fcbmaine.com

UNION TRUST CO., Ellsworth, ME, (207) 667-2504, www.uniontrust.com

Maryland

BANK OF THE EASTERN SHORE, Cambridge, MD, (410) 228-5800, www.bankofes.com

FARMERS & MECHANICS BANK, Frederick, MD, (301) 644-4400, www.fmbancorp.com

FIRST UNITED BANK AND TRUST CO., Oakland, MD, (888) 692-2654

HEBRON SAVINGS BANK, Hebron, MD, (410) 749-1185, www.hebronsavingsbank.com

HORIZON BANK & TRUST CO., Braintree, MA, (781) 794-9992, www.bankhorizon.com

PATAPSCO BANK, Dundalk, MD, (410) 285-1010, www.patapscobank.com

PENINSULA BANK, Princess Anne, MD, (410) 651-2404, www.peninsulabankmd.com

PEOPLES BANK OF KENT COUNTY, Chestertown, MD, (410) 778-3500, www.pbkc.com

ST. MICHAELS BANK, St. Michaels, MD, (410) 745-5091, www.stmichaelsbankmd.com

TALBOT BANK OF EASTON, Easton, MD, (410) 822-1400, www.talbot-bank.com

Massachusetts

BANK OF WESTERN MASSACHUSETTS, Springfield, MA, (413) 781-2265, www.bankwmass.com

ENTERPRISE BANK & TRUST CO., Lowell, MA, (978) 459-9000, www.ebtc.com

PARK WEST BANK & TRUST CO., West Springfield, MA, (413) 747-1400, www.westbankonline.com

Michigan

1ST BANK, West Branch, MI, (989) 345-7900

ALDEN STATE BANK, Alden, MI, (231) 331-4481, www.torchlake.com/aldenbank

CHEMICAL BANK WEST, Cadillac, MI, (231) 775-6151, www.

chemicalbankmi.com

COMMUNITY STATE BANK, St. Charles, MI, (989) 865-9945, www.gotocsb.com

FIRST BANK, Mount Pleasant, MI, (989) 773-2335

HILLSDALE COUNTY NATIONAL BANK, Hillsdale, MI, (517) 439-4300, www.countynationalbank.com

MACATAWA BANK, Zeeland, MI, (616) 748-9491, www.macatawabank.com

MICHIGAN HERITAGE BANK, Farmington, MI, (248) 538-2545, www.miheritage.com

OXFORD BANK, Oxford, MI, (248) 628-2533, www.oxfordbank.com

STATE BANK OF ESCANABA, Escanaba, MI, (906) 786-1331

WEST SHORE BANK, Scottville, MI, (231) 757-4751, www.westshorebank.com

Minnesota

BOUNDARY WATERS COMMUNITY BANK, Ely, MN, (218) 365-6181, www.bwcb.com

FIRST INTEGRITY BANK, National Association, Staples, MN, (218) 894-1522, www.firstintegrity.org

FIRST NATIONAL BANK, Bagley, MN, (218) 694-6233, www.fnbbagley.com

FIRST STATE BANK ALEXANDRIA-CARLOS, Alexandria, MN, (320) 763-7700

GRAND MARAIS STATE BANK, Grand Marais, MN, (218) 387-2441, www.grandmaraisstatebank.com

HERITAGE BANK N.A., Willmar, MN, (320) 235-5722, www.heritagebankna.com

HOME STATE BANK, Kandiyohi, MN, (320) 382-6111, www.hsbofmn.com

KASSON STATE BANK, Kasson, MN, (507) 634-7022

LAKES STATE BANK, Pequot Lakes, MN, (218) 538-4473, www.lakesstatebank.com

LANDMARK COMMUNITY BANK, Isanti, MN, (763) 444-5528

PEOPLES NATIONAL BANK OF MORA, Mora, MN, (320) 679-3100, www.pnbmora.com

UNITED COMMUNITY BANK, Perham, MN, (218) 346-5700

UNIVERSITY BANK, St. Paul, MN, (651) 265-5600, www.universitybank.com

WOODLAND BANK, Remer, MN, (218) 566-2355, www.

woodlandbank.com

Mississippi

BANK OF HOLLY SPRINGS, Holly Springs, MS, (662) 252-2511, www.bankofhollysprings.com

BANK OF NEW ALBANY, New Albany, MS, (662) 534-9511

FIRST NATIONAL BANK OF SOUTHERN MISSISSIPPI, Hattiesburg, MS, (601) 268-8998, www.thefirstbank.com

FIRST NATIONAL BANK OF PONTOTOC, Pontotoc, MS, (662) 489-1631

FIRST STATE BANK, Waynesboro, MS, (601) 735-3124, www.firststatebnk.com

HANCOCK BANK, Purvis, MS, (601) 794-8026, www.hancockbank.com

MECHANICS BANK, Water Valley, MS, (662) 473-2261

MERCHANTS & MARINE BANK, Pascagoula, MS,(228) 934-1323, www.mandmbank.com

OMNI BANK, Mantee, MS, (662) 456-5341

PIKE COUNTY NATIONAL BANK, McComb, MS, (601) 684-7575

Missouri

BANK OF BLOOMSDALE, Bloomsdale, MO, (573) 483-2514

CENTURY BANK OF THE OZARKS, Gainesville, MO, (417) 679-3321, www.cbozarks.com

CITIZENS UNION STATE BANK AND TRUST, Clinton, MO, (660) 885-2241, www.citizensunionstatebank.com

COMMUNITY STATE BANK, Bowling Green, MO, (573) 324-2233, www.c-s-b.com

FIRST COMMUNITY BANK, Knob Noster, MO, (660) 563-3011, www.first-community-bank.com

FIRST COMMUNITY BANK, Poplar Bluff, MO, (573) 778-0101, www.1stcombank.com

FIRST MISSOURI STATE BANK, Poplar Bluff, MO, (573) 785-6800, www.firstmissouristatebank.net

FIRST NATIONAL BANK, Mountain View, MO, (417) 934-2033, www.fnb-fnb.com

FIRST STATE BANK, Purdy, MO, (417) 442-3247, www.fsb-purdy.com

KEARNEY TRUST CO., Kearney, MO, (816) 628-6666, www.kearneytrust.com

O'BANNON BANK, Buffalo, MO, (417) 345-6207, www.

obannonbank.com

PEOPLES BANK, Cuba, MO, (573) 885-2511, www.peoplesbk.com

SECURITY BANK OF SOUTHWEST MISSOURI, Cassville, MO, (417) 847-4794

SOUTHWEST MISSOURI BANK, Carthage, MO, (417) 358-9331, www.smbonline.com

Montana

CITIZENS STATE BANK, Hamilton, MT, (406) 363-3551, www.citizensstbank.com

FIRST BOULDER VALLEY BANK, Boulder, MT, (406) 225-3351

FIRST CITIZENS BANK OF BUTTE, Butte, MT, (406) 494-4400

FIRST STATE BANK, Thompson Falls, MT, (406) 827-3565, www.fsbtf.com

INDEPENDENCE BANK, Havre, MT, (800) 823-2274

ROCKY MOUNTAIN BANK, Billings, MT, (406) 656-3140, www.rmbank.com

RUBY VALLEY NATIONAL BANK, Twin Bridges, MT, (406) 684-5678

UNITED STATES NATIONAL BANK, Red Lodge, MT, (406) 446-1422

Nebraska

AMERICAN EXCHANGE BANK, Elmwood, NE, (402) 994-2175, www.aebank.com

CENTENNIAL BANK, Omaha, NE, (402) 891-0003

COMMERCIAL STATE BANK, Wausa, NE, (402) 586-2266, www.wausabank.com

COMMUNITY BANK, Alma, NE, (308) 928-2929

DAKOTA COUNTY STATE BANK, South Sioux City, NE, (402) 494-4215, www.dcsb.com

FARMERS STATE BANK, Bennet, NE, (402) 782-3500

FIRST NATIONAL BANK IN ORD, Ord, NE, (308) 728-3201

GOTHENBURG STATE BANK & TRUST CO., Gothenburg, NE, (308) 537-7181

MIDWEST BANK, Pierce, NE, (402) 329-6221, www.midwestbanks.com

PINNACLE BANK, Beatrice, NE, (402) 228-3333

PLATTE VALLEY NATIONAL BANK, Scottsbluff, NE, (308) 632-7004, www.pvnbank.com

Nevada

FIRST NATIONAL BANK, Ely, NV, (775) 289-4441

GREAT BASIN BANK OF NEVADA, Elko, NV, (775) 753-3800, www.greatbasinbank.com

NEVADA BANK & TRUST CO., Caliente, NV, (775) 726-3135, www.nevadabankandtrust.com

New Hampshire

FIRST COLEBROOK BANK, Colebrook, NH, (603) 237-5551, www.firstcolebrookbank.com

VILLAGE BANK & TRUST CO., Gilford, NH, (603) 528-3000, www.villagebanknh.com

New Jersey

1ST CONSTITUTION BANK, Cranbury, NJ, (609) 655-4500, www.1stconstitution.com

BANK OF GLOUCESTER COUNTY, Woodbury, NJ, (856) 845-0700, www.hometownbankers.com

COMMERCE BANK SHORE NA, Forked River, NJ, (609) 693-1111, www.commerceonline.com

LAKELAND BANK, Newfoundland, NJ, (973) 697-2040, www.msnb.com

MINOTOLA NATIONAL BANK, Vineland, NJ, (856) 696-8100, www.minotola.com

NEWFIELD NATIONAL BANK, Newfield, NJ, (856) 692-3440, www.newfieldbank.com

PANASIA BANK N.A., Fort Lee, NJ, (201) 947-6666, www.panasiabank.com

SKYLANDS COMMUNITY BANK, Hackettstown, NJ, (908) 850-9010, www.skylandscombank.com

UNION CENTER NATIONAL BANK, Morristown, NJ, (973) 267-5588, www.ucnb.com

WOODSTOWN NATIONAL BANK, Woodstown, NJ, (856) 769-3300, www.woodstownbank.com

New Mexico

CITIZENS BANK OF CLOVIS, Clovis, NM, (505) 769-1911, www.citizensbankofclovis.com

FIRST NATIONAL BANK IN LAS VEGAS, Las Vegas, NM, (505) 425-7584

PEOPLES BANK, Taos, NM, (505) 758-4500, www.bankingunusual.com

PORTALES NATIONAL BANK, Portales, NM, (505) 356-5090, www.portalesnb.com

VALLEY BANK OF COMMERCE, Roswell, NM, (505) 623-2265

New York

ADIRONDACK BANK N.A., Saranac Lake, NY, (518) 891-2323, www.adirondackbank.com

BANK OF CASTILE, Castile, NY, (585) 493-2576, www.bankofcastile.com

BATH NATIONAL BANK, Bath, NY, (607) 776-3381, www.bathnational.com

CATTARAUGUS COUNTY BANK, Little Valley, NY, (716) 938-9128, www.ccblv.com

ELLENVILLE NATIONAL BANK, Ellenville, NY, (845) 647-4300, www.enbebank.com

FIRST NATIONAL BANK OF GROTON, Groton, NY, (607) 898-5871

NATIONAL BANK OF GENEVA, Geneva, NY, (315) 789-2300, www.nbgeneva.com

SAVANNAH BANK NATIONAL N.A., Savannah, NY, (315) 365-2896

SOLVAY BANK, Solvay, NY, (315) 468-1661, www.solvaybank.com

STEUBEN TRUST CO., Hornell, NY, (607) 324-5010, www.steubentrust.com

North Carolina

AMERICAN COMMUNITY BANK, Monroe, NC, (704) 225-8444, www.americancommunitybank.com

CATAWBA VALLEY BANK, Hickory, NC, (828) 431-2300, www.catawbavalleybank.com

FARMERS & MERCHANTS BANK, Granite Quarry, NC, (704) 279-7291, www.fmbnc.com

FIRST CITIZENS BANK & TRUST, Raleigh, NC, (919) 716-7226, www.firstcitizens.com

FOUR OAKS BANK & TRUST CO., Four Oaks, NC, (919) 963-2177, www.fouroaksbank.com

LUMBEE GUARANTY BANK, Pembroke, NC, (910) 521-9707

NORTHWESTERN NATIONAL BANK, Wilkesboro, NC, (336) 903-0600

SURREY BANK & TRUST, Mount Airy, NC, (336) 719-2310

YADKIN VALLEY BANK & TRUST CO., Elkin, NC, (336) 526-6301, www.yadkinvalleybank.com

North Dakota

AMERICAN STATE BANK AND TRUST CO., Williston, ND, (701) 774-4104, www.asbt.com

CHOICE FINANCIAL GROUP, Langdon, ND, (701) 256-2265

CHOICE FINANCIAL GROUP, Walhalla, ND, (701) 549-3761

DAKOTA BANK, Valley City, ND, (701) 845-2712

FIRST INTERNATIONAL BANK AND TRUST CO., Watford City, ND, (701) 842-2381, www.fibtlink.com

FIRST STATE BANK OF MUNICH, Munich, ND, (701) 682-5331, www.zzcountry.com/get/munich/bizweb.asp

FIRST UNITED BANK, Park River, ND, (701) 284-7810, www.firstunitedonline.com

NATIONAL BANK OF HARVEY, Harvey, ND, (701) 324-4611

STATE BANK OF BOTTINEAU, Bottineau, ND, (701) 228-3621

STUTSMAN COUNTY STATE BANK, Jamestown, ND, (701) 253-5600, www.stutsmanbank.com

Ohio

1ST NATIONAL COMMUNITY BANK, East Liverpool, OH, (330) 385-9200, www.1stncb.com

COMMUNITY FIRST BANK & TRUST CO., Celina, OH, (419) 586-5624, www.comfirst.com

FARMERS STATE BANK, New Madison, OH, (937) 996-1071, www.farmersstatebank.com

FIRST NATIONAL BANK, Shelby, OH, (419) 342-4010, www.shelbyfnb.com

HICKSVILLE BANK, Hicksville, OH, (419) 542-7726, www.thehicksvillebank.com

MERCHANTS NATIONAL BANK, Hillsboro, OH, (937) 393-1993

NORTH VALLEY BANK, Zanesville, OH, (740) 450-2265, www.nvboh.com

SAVINGS BANK, Circleville, OH, (740) 474-3191

SUTTON BANK, Attica, OH, (419) 426-3641, www.suttonbank.com

UNION BANK CO., Columbus Grove, OH, (419) 659-2141, www.theubank.com

VINTON COUNTY NATIONAL BANK, McArthur, OH, (740) 596-2525, www.vintoncountybank.com

Oklahoma

AMERICAN EXCHANGE BANK, Henryetta, OK, (918) 652-3321

BANK OF CHEROKEE CITY, Hulbert, OK, (918) 772-2572

BANK OF UNION, Union City, OK, (405) 483-5308

CHICKASHA BANK & TRUST CO., Chickasha, OK, (405) 222-0550, www.chickashabank.com

COMMUNITY STATE BANK, Poteau, OK, (918) 647-8101

FIRST AMERICAN BANK & TRUST CO., Purcell, OK, (405) 527-7888, www.bankfab.com

FIRSTBANK, Antlers, OK, (580) 298-3368

FIRST BANK & TRUST CO., Broken Bow, OK, (580) 584-9123

FIRST NATIONAL BANK & TRUST CO., Chickasha, OK, (405) 224-2200, www.fnbchickasha.com

FIRST NATIONAL BANK & TRUST CO., Miami, OK, (918) 542-3371, www.fnbmiami.com

FIRST NATIONAL BANK & TRUST CO., Weatherford, OK, (580) 772-5574, www.fnbwford.com

FIRST STATE BANK, Pond Creek, OK, (580) 532-6611

FIRST STATE BANK, Tahlequah, OK, (918) 456-6108

PAULS VALLEY NATIONAL BANK, Pauls Valley, OK, (405) 238-9321, www.pvnational.com

PEOPLE'S NATIONAL BANK OF CHECOTAH, Checotah, OK, (918) 473-2296

Oregon

COLUMBIA RIVER BANKING CO., The Dalles, OR, (541) 298-6649, www.columbiariverbank.com

COMMUNITY BANK, Joseph, OR, (541) 432-9050, www.community banknet.com

UMPQUA BANK, Coos Bay, OR, (541) 267-5356, www.ump quabank.com

UMPQUA BANK, Corvallis, OR, (541) 752-0474, www.umpqua bank.com

UMPQUA BANK, Newport, OR, (541) 265-7000, www.umpqua bank.com

UMPQUA BANK, Springfield, OR, (541) 726-6100, www.ump quabank.com

WEST COAST BANK, Lake Oswego, OR, (503) 624-5864, www.wcb.com

Pennsylvania

COMMUNITY BANKS, Millersburg, PA, (717) 692-4781, www.

communitybanks.com

COMMUNITY BANK & TRUST CO., Clarks Summit, PA, (570) 586-6876, www.combk.com

COUNTY NATIONAL BANK, Clearfield, PA, (814) 765-9621, www.bankcnb.com

CSB BANK, Curwensville, PA, (814) 236-2550, www.csb-bank.com

ELDERTON STATE BANK, Elderton, PA, (724) 354-2111

FIRST NATIONAL COMMUNITY BANK, Dunmore, PA, (570) 348-4817

HAMLIN BANK & TRUST CO., Smethport, PA, (814) 887-5555

HONESDALE NATIONAL BANK, Honesdale, PA, (570) 253-3355, www.hnbbank.com

JERSEY SHORE STATE BANK, Jersey Shore, PA, (570) 398-2213, www.jssb.com

LUZERNE NATIONAL BANK, Luzerne, PA, (570) 288-4511, www.luzernenational.com

MERCER COUNTY STATE BANK, Sandy Lake, PA, (724) 376-7015, www.mcsbank.com

NEW TRIPOLI NATIONAL BANK, New Tripoli, PA, (610) 298-8811

OLD FORGE BANK, Old Forge, PA. (570) 457-8345, www.oldforgebankpa.com

PFC BANK, Ford City, PA, (724) 763-1221

RHODE ISLAND, Washington Trust Co., Westerly, RI, (401) 351-6240, www.washtrust.com

South Carolina

ANDERSON BROTHERS BANK, Mullins, SC, (843) 464-6271

ARTHUR STATE BANK, Union, SC, (864) 427-1213, www.affiliatedbanks.com

BANK OF GREELEYVILLE, Greeleyville, SC, (843) 426-2161, www.bog1.com

BANK OF YORK, York, SC, (803) 684-2265, www.bankofyork.com

CAPITALBANK, Greenwood, SC, (864) 941-8200, www.capitalbanksc.com

CONWAY NATIONAL BANK, Conway, SC, (843) 248-5721

ENTERPRISE BANK OF SC, Ehrhardt, SC, (803) 267-4351

PALMETTO STATE BANK, Hampton, SC, (803) 943-2671

South Dakota

CAMPBELL COUNTY BANK, Herreid, SD, (605) 437-2294, www.campbellcountybank.com

FARMERS & MERCHANTS STATE BANK, Iroquois, SD, (605) 546-2544

FIRST FIDELITY BANK, Burke, SD, (605) 775-2641

FIRST STATE BANK OF ROSCOE, Roscoe, SD, (605) 287-4451

FIRST STATE BANK OF WARNER, Warner, SD, (605) 225-9605

FULTON STATE BANK, Fulton, SD, (605) 996-5731

GREAT PLAINS BANK, Eureka, SD, (605) 284-2633

MERCHANTS STATE BANK, Freeman, SD, (605) 925-4222

PEOPLES STATE BANK, De Smet, SD, (605)854-3321

SECURITY STATE BANK, Tyndall, SD, (605) 589-3313

Tennessee

AMERICAN CITY BANK, Tullahoma, TN. (931) 455-0026, www.americancitybank.com

CITIZENS BANK, Carthage, TN, (615) 256-2912, www.citizens bank.net

CITIZENS BANK OF EAST TENNESSEE, Rogersville, TN, (423) 272-2200

CITIZENS COMMUNITY BANK., Winchester, TN, (931) 967-3342

COMMERCIAL BANK & TRUST CO., Paris, TN, (731) 642-3341, www.cbtcnet.com

COMMUNITY SOUTH BANK, Parsons, TN, (731) 847-6316, www.communitysouth.com

FIRST NATIONAL BANK OF MANCHESTER, Manchester, TN, (931) 728-3518, www.fnbmanchester.com

FIRST BANK OF TENNESSEE, Spring City, TN, (423) 365-8400

FIRST VOLUNTEER BANK OF TENNESSEE, Chattanooga, TN, (423) 265-5001

PEOPLES BANK, Clifton, TN, (931) 676-3311, www.pbbanking.com

TRADERS NATIONAL BANK, Tullahoma, TN, (931) 455-3426, www.tradersbank.com

Texas

COMMUNITY NATIONAL BANK, Hondo, TX, (830) 741-3066

ENNIS STATE BANK, Ennis, TX, (972) 875-9676, www. ennisstatebank.com

FIRST NATIONAL BANK, Borger, TX, (806) 273-2865, www. fnbborger.com

FIRST NATIONAL BANK, George West, TX, (361) 449-1571, www.fnbgw.com

FIRST NATIONAL BANK, Hughes Springs, TX, (903) 639-2521

FIRST NATIONAL BANK, Newton, TX, (409) 379-8587

FIRST NATIONAL BANK OF ALBANY BRECKENRIDGE, Albany, TX, (915) 762-2221

LEGEND BANK, Bowie, TX, (940) 872-5400, www.legend-bank.com

PEOPLES NATIONAL BANK, Paris, TX, (903) 785-1099, www.pnbparis.com

PEOPLES STATE BANK, Clyde, TX, (915) 893-4211

SECURITY STATE BANK, McCamey, TX, (915) 652-8661, www.ssbank.com

STATE BANK, De Kalb, TX, (903) 667-2553

STATE NATIONAL BANK OF TEXAS, Iowa Park, TX, (940) 592-4131

TEXAS BANK, Henderson, TX, (903) 657-1466, www.texasbnk.com

Utah

FIRST NATIONAL BANK, Morgan, UT, (801)876-3442, www.morgan1st.com

GUNNISON VALLEY BANK, Gunnison, UT, (435) 528-7221

SUNFIRST BANK, St. George, UT, (435) 673-9610, www.sunfirstbank.com

TRANSPORTATION ALLIANCE BANK, Ogden, UT, (801) 624-4800, www.tabbank.com

VILLAGE BANK, St. George, UT, (435) 674-5200, www.thevillagebank.com

VOLVO COMMERCIAL CREDIT CORP. UTAH, Salt Lake City, UT, (801) 266-8522, www.acceltrans.com

Vermont

COMMUNITY NATIONAL BANK, Derby, VT, (802) 334-7915, www.communitynationalbank.com

PEOPLES TRUST CO. OF ST. ALBANS, St. Albans, VT, (802) 524-3773

Virginia

BANK OF CHARLOTTE COUNTY, Phenix, VA, (434) 542-5111, www.bankofcharlotte.com

BANK OF MARION, Marion, VA, (276) 783-3116

BB&T, Gloucester, VA, (804) 693-0628, www.bbandt.com

BENCHMARK COMMUNITY BANK, Kenbridge, VA, (434) 676-8444, www.bcbonline.com

GRAYSON NATIONAL BANK, Independence, VA, (276) 773-2861

HIGHLANDS UNION BANK, Abingdon, VA, (276) 628 9181, www.hubank.com

NEW PEOPLES BANK, Honaker, VA, (276) 873-6288, www. newpeoplesbank.com

PEOPLES COMMUNITY BANK, Montross, VA, (804) 493-8031

POWELL VALLEY NATIONAL BANK, Jonesville, VA, (276) 346-1414, www.powellvalleybank.com

VIRGINIA BANK & TRUST CO., Danville, VA, (434) 793-6411

Washington

AMERICANWEST BANK, Spokane, WA, (509) 467-9084

COMMUNITY FIRST BANK, Kennewick, WA, (509) 783-3435, www.community1st.com

FIRST HERITAGE BANK, Snohomish, WA, (360) 568-0536

PRIME PACIFIC BANK, Lynnwood, WA, (425) 712-9898

SECURITY STATE BANK, Centralia, WA, (360) 736-2861, www. ssbwa.com

WHIDBEY ISLAND BANK, Oak Harbor, WA, (360) 675-5968, www.wibank.com

YAKIMA NATIONAL BANK N.A., Yakima, WA, (509) 577-9000

West Virginia

BANK OF GASSAWAY, Gassaway, WV, (304) 364-5138

CALHOUN BANK, Grantsville, WV, (304) 354-6116, www.calhoun banks.com

CLAY COUNTY BANK, Clay, WV, (304) 587-4221, www. claycountybank.com

COMMUNITY BANK OF PARKERSBURG, Parkersburg, WV, (304) 485-7991, www.communitybankpkbg.com

PENDLETON COUNTY BANK, Franklin, WV, (304) 358-2311, www.yourbank.com

POCA VALLEY BANK, Walton, WV, (304) 577-6611, www.poca valleybank.com

TRADERS BANK, Spencer, WV, (304) 927-3340, www.traders banking.com

Wisconsin

CHIPPEWA VALLEY BANK, Winter, WI, (715) 266-3501, www. chippewavalleybank.com

COMMUNITY BANK, Superior, WI, (715) 392-8241

COMMUNITY BANK OF CENTRAL WISCONSIN, Colby, WI, (715) 223-3998, www.commbnk.com

COMMUNITY FIRST BANK, Boscobel, WI, (608) 375-4117, www.cfbank.com

FARMERS STATE BANK OF WAUPACA, Waupaca, WI, (715) 258-1400, www.fsbwaupaca.com

FIDELITY NATIONAL BANK, Medford, WI, (715) 748-5333, www.fidelitybnk.com

FORTRESS BANK OF WESTBY, Westby, WI, (608) 634-3787, www.fortressbanks.com

JOHNSON BANK, Hayward, WI, (715) 634-7550, www.johnsonbank.com

LAONA STATE BANK, Laona, WI, (715) 674-2911

MID AMERICA BANK, Footville, WI, (608) 876-6121, www.bankmidamerica.com

NORTHERN STATE BANK, Ashland, WI, (715) 682-2772, www.nsbashland.com

REEDSBURG BANK, Reedsburg, WI, (608) 524-8251, www.reedsburgbank.com

ROYAL BANK, Elroy, WI, (608) 462-8163, www.royalbank-usa.com

STERLING BANK, Barron, WI, (715) 537-3141, www.sterlingbank.ws

Wyoming

BANK OF COMMERCE, Rawlins, WY, (307) 324-2265, www.bocrawlins.com

BANK OF STAR VALLEY, Afton, WY, (307) 885-0000

CONVERSE COUNTY BANK, Douglas, WY, (307) 358-5300

FIRST NATIONAL BANK OF BUFFALO, Buffalo, WY, (307) 684-2555, www.fnb buffalo.com

HILLTOP NATIONAL BANK, Casper, WY, (307) 265-2740, www.hnbwyo.com

Index

S

Introduction

So you have made the decision to start your own business. Congratulations! You are joining the ranks of entrepreneurs and business leaders who are the reason our great country has been able to flourish as a business giant among the countries of the world. While all business owners certainly suffer setbacks as they drive their businesses toward success, on September 11, 2001, the business world, and the rest of the world, was turned upside down for a while.

Terrorists may have destroyed the Twin Towers in New York City and parts of the Pentagon near Washington, DC, but Americans—both business leaders and ordinary citizens—have responded with a renewed sense of purpose. A purpose that will ultimately depend on business leaders to become a beacon of hope in a sometimes dark and gloomy world.

As America began almost immediately to rebuild, business owners were responding and answering the call. They kept the economy moving forward at a time when our nation was relying on them to do so. And they did it successfully. You can, too!

You can join the ranks of American business owners and leaders who have been making this country a shining example to the rest of the world. But as with any successful journey, it begins with a plan. A carefully crafted plan. A *business plan*!

Each chapter in this book is devoted to analyzing, explaining, and, wherever and whenever possible, making entertaining, an important concept relating to business plans. The chapter topics range from why you even need a plan to what to do with it when you're finished. You'll learn techniques for figuring your break-even ratio and tips for approaching potential investors. You'll hear stories about the business plans of famous entrepreneurs and even learn about a few entrepreneurs who admit that they don't write plans—willingly, at least.

Along the way, you'll find sprinkled definitions of important terms, contact information for useful resources, warnings of especially common or serious mistakes, and pointers to steer you in the right direction. When you've finished reading the book, you'll be prepared to write a sound, comprehensive, convincing plan for almost any business, whether it's a brand-new start-up or an existing company. More important, however, you'll be the owner of a thoroughly prepared mind and need just the slightest nod from good fortune to proceed.

Following is a chapter-by-chapter summary of the book. The chapters are intended to be read in sequence, with exercises, worksheets, and samples to be studied, completed, and examined along the way. If after finishing you need more help with a particular section, the chapters can be reviewed as self-contained tutorials on their particular topics.

Chapter 1: Business Plan Basics

This chapter shows that there are many compelling answers to the question, Why write a business plan? It explores the basic definition of a business plan and when and why to write one. It provides detailed information on sources of capital and techniques for using your plan to raise money. It also describes using a plan as a tool for marketing your company to prospective partners, suppliers, customers, and even employees.

Chapter 2: Money Hunt

Writing a business plan is an activity closely tied to the idea of raising money for a start-up business. This chapter examines sources of funding and explains how business plans can be used to help entrepreneurs obtain financing from the most commonly used sources.

Chapter 3: The Big Picture

One of the most important purposes of a business plan is to evaluate a business proposition's chances for success. This chapter shows how to use a plan to see if a new venture is likely to achieve the desired results.

Chapter 4: Set Your Course

No two plans are the same, but they all follow similar routes to creation. This chapter tells how to navigate the major steps, including determining your personal goals and objectives and how they figure in planning. It also provides a first, brief look at the major plan elements: Executive Summary, Management, Product or Service, Marketing, Operations, and Financial Data, along with brief explanations of each.

Chapter 5: Match Game

You're unique and, in all likelihood, so is your plan. Plans differ among industries, for one thing, and they also have different purposes. You want to pick the general type of plan that fits your needs and your company. This chapter explains how to do that, as well as presents descriptions of the major types of plans, such as working plans, miniplans, and presentations.

Chapter 6: Sum It Up

The executive summary is the most important part of your plan. This chapter tells you why, and details exactly what should go into a well-conceived summary.

Chapter 7: Team Work

The section of your business plan where you describe your management team is likely to be one of the first readers turn to. You'll need to explain what each member of your team does, how you plan to grow it if necessary, and who your advisors are. This chapter explains the techniques and underlying import of all these tasks of the management section.

Chapter 8: Announcing...

Most entrepreneurs really enjoy describing the product or services that is their business's reason for being. This chapter tells how to channel that enthusiasm into answering the questions investors and other plan readers most often ask.

Chapter 9: Field Notes

Every business plan has to make the industry in which it will operate crystal clear. In this section you'll also describe the state of your industry using market research, trend analysis, and competitive factors to explain why you picked this industry; whether it's growing or shrinking; and what makes you better.

Chapter 10: Marketing Smarts

No matter how great your product or services are, if you don't know how to persuade someone to buy them, and show that you know it in your business plan, your plan will get short shrift. This primer in marketing strategy will tell how to employ the four Ps of traditional marketing as well as prepare a follow-up marketing plan for the next generation of products.

Chapter 11: The Works

Operations is another area few entrepreneurs have trouble mustering enthusiasm for. As usual, however, the entrepreneurial enthusiasm has to be directed at the right targets if the plan is to achieve maximum impact on its readers. This chapter tells how to write operations sections for manufacturers, service firms, and retailers, with special considerations for each.

Chapter 12: State Your Case

The most intimidating part of a business plan for many entrepreneurs is the required financial statements, including historical and projected balance sheets, income statements, and cash flow statements. This chapter dispels fears by clearly presenting explanations of the major financial statements and analytical ratios, along with instructions on how to prepare them and common pitfalls.

Chapter 13: Extra, Extra

Many plans have important information that doesn't fit into the major sections. This chapter tells you what to consider for a plan's appendix, including employee resumes, product samples, press clippings, and the like.

Chapter 14: Looking Good

Good presentation can make a good plan even better. You need to pick the proper stationery, printing, and design for your plan. You need to make sure that you use charts, graphs, and tables when appropriate, without overdoing it. This chapter provides straightforward tips for doing that, along with hints on multimedia presentations and other elements of a plan package such as cover sheets and cover letters.

Chapter 15: Help Line

There is as much information and assistance available on business plan writing as any entrepreneur could hope for. This chapter describes some of it, including software for writing business plans, books and how-to manuals, Web sites, trade groups and associations, business plan consultants, and even business plan competitions.

Chapter 16: The Internet and Your Planning Efforts

The Internet has leveled the playing field for business owners in the new millennium. In the old days, it was difficult or even impossible to find business information that would help your business succeed. Not any longer, because the Internet has become a wealth of information that is there for the picking. Learn how you can take advantage of the Internet to help your business succeed.

Appendices: Sample Business Plans

Here you will find sample business plans for five very different types of businesses. Everything from A to Z can be found in these plans, which can be used in part or in whole as models for your own business plan.

The Government Listings appendix provides contact information for Small Business Development Centers, Small Business Administration district offices, and state economic development departments across the country.

Scattered throughout the book you'll find various tip boxes. Each will provide useful information of a different type.

PLAN OF ACTION
Here we direct you to sources for more information and guidance.

PLAN PITFALL
This box warns you of common errors made by plan writers.

FACT OR FICTION?
Get straight answers to common business plan questions.

PLAN POINTER
This box offers advice on ways to improve your plan.

BUZZWORD
This box offers brief definitions of terms you'll run into in the process of writing your plan.

Available at all fine bookstores and online booksellers.
www.entrepreneurpress.com.